Contents

KT-524-666

INTRODUCTION   4

What to see	6	Things not to miss	8
When to go	6	Itineraries	16

BASICS   18

Getting there	19	Media	27
Arrival	21	Money	28
Getting around	23	Travel essentials	28
Festivals and public holidays	26		

THE GUIDE   36

1 The Centro Storico	36	8 The Celian Hill and San Giovanni	128
2 Campo de' Fiori and the Ghetto	51	9 The Aventine Hill and south	138
3 Piazza Venezia and the Capitoline Hill	62	10 Trastevere and the Janiculum Hill	157
4 Ancient Rome	74	11 Villa Borghese and north	167
5 The Tridente and Trevi	91	12 The Vatican	185
6 The Quirinale and Via Veneto	103	13 Day-trips from Rome	210
7 The Esquiline, Monti and Termini	112		

LISTINGS   225

14 Accommodation	225	19 Gay and lesbian Rome	281
15 Eating	239	20 Shops and markets	284
16 Drinking	263	21 Sports and outdoor activities	297
17 Clubs and live music	271	22 Kids' Rome	302
18 Culture and entertainment	276		

CONTEXTS   307

History	308	Books and films	332
Architecture	319	Language	338
Writing on Rome	322		

SMALL PRINT & INDEX   343

OPPOSITE FONTANA DELLE NAIADI, PIAZZA DELLA REPUBBLICA **PREVIOUS PAGE** SPANISH STEPS

Introduction to

Rome

When most people think of Rome they imagine sights and monuments: the Colosseum, Forum, the Vatican and St Peter's – giant, see-before-you-die sights that are reason enough for a visit. And it's true that there is perhaps no more monumental city in the world than Rome; yet the city is so much more than the sum of these parts. There's an unpretentiousness to it and its inhabitants that belies the historical significance, and marks it out from its rivals further north. It's almost as if Rome doesn't have to try too hard, aware that it is simply the most fascinating city in Italy – and arguably the world.

Packed with the relics of well over two thousand years of inhabitation, you could spend a month in Rome and still only scratch the surface. There are the city's celebrated **ancient** features, but Rome boasts an almost uninterrupted historical sequence of spectacular monuments – from early Christian basilicas, Romanesque churches and Renaissance palaces, right up to the fountains and churches of the Baroque period, which perhaps more than any other era has determined the look of the city today. The modern epoch has left its mark too, with the ponderous **neoclassical architecture** of the post-Unification period and the self-aggrandizing edifices of the **Mussolini** years. All these various eras crowd in on one another to an almost overwhelming degree: there are medieval churches atop ancient basilicas above Roman palaces; houses and apartment blocks incorporate fragments of eroded Roman columns, carvings and inscriptions; roads and piazzas follow the lines of ancient amphitheatres and stadiums.

Culturally Rome is relatively provincial, and its **food**, while delicious, is earthy rather than refined. But its atmosphere is like no other city – a busy capital, yet an appealingly relaxed place, with a centre that has been relatively little affected by chains and multinationals. The city does have a **modern edge**, and the opening of prestige new buildings and a general updating of the city centre have given a sense that Rome has at last joined Europe's mainstream. Whether its character will change remains to be seen.

ABOVE PIAZZA SAN PIETRO

What to see

Rome's city centre is divided neatly into distinct blocks. The warren of streets that makes up the **Centro Storico** occupies the hook of land on the east bank of the River Tiber. From here Rome's central core spreads out: east across Via del Corso to the major shopping streets and alleys around the Spanish Steps – the **Tridente**; southeast across Corso Vittorio to **Campo de' Fiori** and around; to the major sites of the **ancient city** to the south; and to the huge expanse of the **Villa Borghese** park to the north. The west bank of the river, distanced from the main hum of the rest of the city, is home to the **Vatican and Saint Peter's**, and, to the south, **Trastevere** – even in ancient times a distinct entity from the city proper.

But where should you start in any tour of Rome? There are the obvious key sights, and you should try to see these if you can. But if you're here for only a day or two it would be a pity not to spend time just exploring the **Centro Storico**, whose churches, palaces and back alleys are a fascinating glimpse into the city's history. Central Rome is full of reminders of the glories of the **ancient** city: most obviously the **Colosseum**, and **Forum** and **Palatine**, but also the **Capitoline Museums** and the museums of the **Museo Nazionale Romano** (in Palazzo Massimo and Altemps) and of course the **Pantheon**, perhaps the most intact structure of the period. **Baroque Rome** is everywhere you look, in piazzas, church facades, street furniture and fountains, and most notably in **St Peter's Basilica**, one of the grandest Baroque creations in Christendom. Rome is also a city of great **art collections**, many of them the property of illustrious Roman families and still housed and displayed in their palaces, such as the **Galleria Doria-Pamphilj**; others are now property of the state and housed in appropriately grand buildings and palaces like the **Palazzo Barberini** and **Galleria Borghese**.

To see most of the city centre, the best way to get around is to walk. The same goes for the ancient sites, and the Vatican and Trastevere – although you might want to jump on a bus to cross the river. Keep public transport for the longer hops, down to **Testaccio** or **Via Appia Antica**, and, of course, for trips out of the city – to the excavations at **Ostia** and **Tivoli**, or one of the nearby **beaches**.

When to go

Rome is a year-round city, and you can really visit at any **time of year**. If you can though, avoid visiting in July and August, when the weather is hot and sticky, and those Romans who don't make their living exclusively from the tourist industry have left town; many businesses close in August. The weather is more comfortable in May, June and September, when days will be warm but not unbearably so; April, outside Easter, and October, are quieter and the weather can still be clement. The winter months can also be nice, with many of the city's more popular sights relatively uncrowded: there may be rain but temperatures are usually mild.

CLOCKWISE FROM TOP LEFT VILLA BORGHESE; SAN GIOVANNI IN LATERANO; CAFÉ DI MARZIO; SANTA MARIA IN TRASTEVERE

20

things not to miss

It's not possible to see everything that Rome has to offer in one visit – and we don't suggest you try. What follows, in no particular order, is a selective taste of the city's highlights; from outstanding art collections and historic architecture to picturesque parks. Each highlight has a page reference to take you straight into the Guide, where you can find out more. Coloured numbers refer to chapters in the Guide section.

1 THE PANTHEON
Page 39
By far the most intact of Rome's ancient monuments, and still sporting its second-largest dome.

2 PIZZA
Page 248
There's nothing quite like thin, crispy-based Roman pizza, fresh from a wood-burning oven.

3 MUSEO NAZIONALE ROMANO
Pages 48 & 124
Palazzo Altemps and Palazzo Massimo make up the greatest part of the Museo Nazionale Romano, and between them hold some of the city's finest ancient finds.

4 GALLERIA BORGHESE

Page 168
A fantastic array of Bernini sculptures together with superb collections of Renaissance paintings in a beautifully restored seventeenth-century villa.

5 GELATO

Page 244
The traditional – and best – way to finish off an evening out.

6 ROMAN FORUM AND PALATINE

Pages 79 & 85
The heart of the ancient world is almost unrecognizable today, but no less evocative for that.

7 VATICAN MUSEUMS

Page 195
The world's largest museum complex, jam-packed with treasures that include iconic parts of the building itself, like the Sistine Chapel and Raphael Rooms.

8 TREVI FOUNTAIN

Page 100
Stumbling upon the Trevi Fountain by accident is one of the greatest of all Rome experiences.

7

8

9

10

KEATS

11

9 BASILICA OF SAN CLEMENTE
Page 132
The epitome of Rome: an ancient temple under an ancient basilica topped by an ancient church.

10 KEATS-SHELLEY HOUSE
Page 94
The artist's garret where John Keats died has been admirably preserved as a shrine to the poet and his Romantic chums.

11 PIAZZA NAVONA
Page 42
If Rome has a centre, this is probably it.

12 OSTIA ANTICA
Page 214
One of the best-preserved of all Italy's ancient Roman sites, and within easy reach of the capital.

13 ARA PACIS
Page 99
This ancient hunk of stone from the Augustan era gives perhaps the greatest glimpse of the Roman Imperial family.

14 FOOTBALL
Page 298
If you can, catch a local Roma-Lazio derby at the Stadio Olimpico.

13

14

15 CAMPO DE'FIORI
Page 52

The morning market here is one of Rome's oldest, while in the evening the square's bars and restaurants form one of the city centre's main nightlife hubs.

16 CAPITOLINE MUSEUMS
Page 67

In a city of great museums these two buildings, crammed full of Roman statuary and Renaissance paintings, are among the top-drawer attractions.

17 VILLA BORGHESE
Page 168

The city centre's largest open space has plenty to occupy you – superb galleries, a zoo and boating lake.

18 COLOSSEUM
Page 87

The most photographed of Rome's monuments, and no wonder. In terms of size and ingenuity, it's hard to beat.

19 ST PETER'S BASILICA
Page 190

Not the most beautiful church you'll ever visit, but in terms of grandeur and significance, it may be the most impressive.

20 MODERN ROME
Pages 179 & 180

Check out the best of the city's contemporary architecture at MAXXI and the Auditorium – two cutting-edge cultural hubs.

Itineraries

There's no greater pleasure than wandering around Rome with no particular destination in mind, but if time is tight you might want to follow one of our itineraries to pursue a special interest or to make sure you squeeze everything in. Follow our suggestions to the letter or just dip in and out, the choice is yours.

DAY ONE

Capitoline Hill Rome began here, and the two museums that flank the elegant square are among the city's key sights. **See p.66**

Roman Forum Some of the most ruined ruins you'll see, but also the most atmospheric. **See p.79**

Colosseum The most recognizable and perhaps the greatest ancient Roman monument of them all. **See p.87**

Lunch The *Enoteca Provincia Romana*, opposite the Vittoriano, makes a perfect and delicious lunch stop on your way from the Colosseum to the Trevi Fountain. **See p.250**

Trevi Fountain No trip to the city could be complete without a visit here. **See p.100**

Ara Pacis Enclosed in an impressive purpose-built structure, this amazing frieze displays the imperial family during the time of Augustus. **See p.99**

Galleria Borghese The Bernini sculptures here are the pure essence of Rome. **See p.168**

Dinner A meal in lively Trastevere is a must – and you can't go wrong at *Le Mani in Pasta*. **See p.260**

DAY TWO

St Peter's Basilica It would be a pity to leave Rome without seeing perhaps the city's greatest Baroque attraction. **See p.190**

Vatican Museums So much more than the Sistine Chapel – this staggering complex of museums is not to be missed. **See p.195**

Lunch *Dal Toscano*, a long-established Tuscan restaurant close by the Vatican walls, is a good place to recover from museum fatigue. **See p.262**

Piazza di Spagna The Spanish Steps, Keats-Shelley House and the square itself are among the city's most compelling attractions. **See p.94**

Piazza Navona One of the Centro Storico's loveliest open spaces, and close to the church of San Luigi dei Francesi and Palazzo Altemps. **See p.42**

The Pantheon Rome's most intact ancient sight, and near one of the city's great churches, Santa Maria sopra Minerva. **See p.39**

The Ghetto Stroll through the old Jewish Quarter, an ancient part of the city centre. **See p.59**

Dinner *Piperno* is the best of the Ghetto's restaurants, with fantastic Roman food served in lovely surroundings. **See p.249**

FOODIE ROME

Dagnino We love the coffee and pastries at this Sicilian stalwart, which is among the city's best places to start the day. **See p.255**

Testaccio The morning market here may have moved to sterile new premises, but the food stalls at its core remain one of the city's best traditional sources of fresh meat and produce. **See p.143**

Eataly Just in case the Testaccio market didn't have what you were looking for, this Ostiense newcomer may be the answer, a glorious multi-storey homage to the best Italian edible goodies. **See p.291**

Citta del Gusto Down in the depths of Trastevere, this is home to the country's foremost food organization; it runs cookery and wine-tasting sessions and courses, plus it has a shop, wine bar and restaurant. **See p.258**

Roscioli Foodie heaven, arguably where you'll find the best *carbonara* in town, alongside fresh bread from their bakery across the road. **See p.291**

Antica Caciara Trasteverina Fortified by lunch, cross the river to peek in at one of the city's oldest and best cheese shops. **See p.289**

Pastificio San Lorenzo Experience great classic Roman cooking in a contemporary environment for your evening meal. **See p.256**

Gelateria Corona Finish the day in Italian style, at this fabulous family-owned *gelateria* serving great combinations of ice cream and sorbets made in the traditional way. **See p.244**

HIDDEN ROME

Museo Storico della Liberazione Just around the corner from the basilica of San Giovanni, this is one of the city's most moving attractions, housed in the former HQ of the Gestapo during the Nazi occupation. **See p.135**

The Pulsating Lung Right in the heart of tourist Rome, yet most people walk right past this small, eccentric gallery of art and inventions. **See p.77**

Galleria Colonna One of the city's finest family palace collections of art, yet only open Saturday mornings so relatively unknown. **See p.101**

Rooms of St Ignatius Just next to the entrance to the much-visited Gesù church, few visitors also take in the intriguing rooms of St Ignatius, with their amazing false perspective by Borromini. **See p.58**

Museo Criminologico For those fascinated by the Mafia and Italian organized crime, this is an intriguing if somewhat gruesome glimpse of that world. **See p.56**

Museo Storico dell'Arte Sanitaria Ancient medical museums assert a strange fascination, and this one, tucked away at the back of the modern hospital of Santo Spirito, is no exception. **See p.187**

Priorato di Malta You need an appointment to visit the gardens and Piranesi church of the secretive home of the Knights of Malta, but it's worth making the effort – or just peek, as most do, through the keyhole for its famous view of the dome of St Peter. **See p.142**

ROMA PORTA S.PAOLO

ROMA PORTA S.PAOLO

PORTA SAN PAOLO STATION

Basics

19 Getting there

21 Arrival

23 Getting around

26 Festivals and public holidays

27 Media

28 Money

28 Travel essentials

Getting there

There are lots of flights from the UK to Rome these days, and the lowest-priced air tickets are generally cheaper than those for the long train or bus journey. From the US and Canada there are direct flights to Rome, although you could also consider flying via London or another European gateway and picking up a cheap onward flight from there. There are no direct flights to Italy from Australia, New Zealand or South Africa, but plenty of airlines fly to Rome via Asian or European cities, again including London.

It's easy to find flights online, and most websites offering cheap flights give plenty of hotel and other options too. Nonetheless, a plethora of operators sell **short-break deals** to Rome, and you might want to consider those specialists which offer small-group tours focusing on art, gastronomy or archaeological sights (see p.21).

Flights from the UK and Ireland

There are plenty of direct flights from the **UK** and **Ireland** to Rome. Of the scheduled airlines, British Airways and Alitalia between them fly several times a day from London Heathrow. Of the low-cost carriers, easyJet fly from London Gatwick and Bristol to Fiumicino; Ryanair fly from London Stansted, Dublin, East Midlands, Manchester and Glasgow to Ciampino; Monarch from London Luton, Birmingham and Leeds/Bradford to Fiumicino; Norwegian from London Gatwick, Liverpool and Manchester to Fiumicino; and Jet2 from Leeds/ Bradford, Manchester, Newcastle and Glasgow to Fiumicino. From Ireland, Ryanair fly from Dublin to Ciampino, while Aer Lingus has twice-daily nonstop flights from Dublin to Rome Fiumicino. It is possible to find deals from Ireland if you book early, but prices are usually significantly higher and unless you're in a hurry it can sometimes make more sense to pick up an inexpensive flight to London or Birmingham and get a connecting flight from there. Alternatively, you could fly from Ireland to Brussels with Ryanair, who operate a cheap service from Brussels Charleroi to Rome.

Fares depend more than ever on how far in advance you book, the time of year and nowadays what days of the week you want to travel (and indeed what time of day). Travelling between June and August, when the weather is best, will cost

more than in the depths of winter (excluding Christmas and New Year). As always the cheapest tickets come with restrictions: any changes incur additional fees, and tickets are rarely valid for longer than a month. Book far enough in advance with one of the low-cost airlines and you can pick up a ticket for around £100 return plus taxes and hold baggage, even in summer; book anything less than three weeks in advance and this could as much as triple. Scheduled airline fares, booked within a month of travel, will cost £120–200 during winter, spring and autumn, and £250–350 in summer. Check directly online with the airlines, as well as Ⓦ Skyscanner, Ⓦ Kayak, and other online search engines.

Flights from the US and Canada

Alitalia fly the widest choice of direct routes between **the US** and Rome, with daily nonstop flights from New York, Newark, Chicago, Boston, Los Angeles and Miami. Of the American carriers that operate nonstop services, Delta fly from New York, Chicago and Atlanta; US Airways fly from Charlotte; Continental fly from Newark and Washington DC; American from New York and Chicago; and United from Washington DC. In addition, many European carriers fly (via their hubs) to Italy from all major US and Canadian cities: for example British Airways fly via London, Lufthansa via Frankfurt and KLM via Amsterdam. Non-stop scheduled fares don't vary as much as you might think, and you'll often be basing your choice on routes, timings and ticket restrictions and even the airline's reputation for comfort and service. It's a long flight, around nine hours from New York, Boston and the eastern Canadian cities, twelve hours from Chicago and fifteen hours from Los Angeles, so it's as well to be fairly comfortable and arrive at a reasonably sociable hour.

The cheapest **round-trip fares** to Rome, travelling midweek in low season, start at around US$600 from New York, rising to US$750 in spring and fall and US$1000 during the summer. Add another US$100–200 for flights from other US destinations Note that these prices do not include taxes.

Air Canada, Alitalia and Lufthansa operate nonstop flights **from Toronto and Montreal** to Rome; fares are around Can$600 in low season, and around Can$1000 in summer, not including taxes.

Flights from Australia, New Zealand and South Africa

There are no nonstop flights to Italy **from Australia**. Round-trip fares to Rome from the main cities go

> **A BETTER KIND OF TRAVEL**
>
> At Rough Guides we are passionately committed to travel. We believe it helps us understand the world we live in and the people we share it with – and of course tourism is vital to many developing economies. But the scale of modern tourism has also damaged some places irreparably, and climate change is accelerated by most forms of transport, especially flying. All Rough Guides' flights are carbon-offset, and every year we donate money to a variety of environmental charities.

for Aus$1200–1500 in low season, and around Aus$2000 in high season. You are likely to get most flexibility by travelling with Malaysia Airlines, Emirates, British Airways or Qantas, which offer a range of discounted Italian tour packages and air passes. **From New Zealand** there are also no nonstop flights to Rome and it's pretty much the same choice of operators, with round-trip fares costing from around NZ$2000 during low season to around NZ$3000 in high season. Finally, there are no direct flights **from South Africa** to Rome, and most flights make one European stop using one of the big carriers – Lufthansa, KLM, Olympic and South African Airways all offer decent deals. Reckon on paying around ZAR5000 return from Johannesburg, around ZAR7000–8000 from Cape Town or Durban.

Trains

Travelling **by train** to Rome won't save much money, but it can be an enjoyable and leisurely (as well as environmentally friendly) way of getting there, and you can stop off in other parts of Europe on the way. The choice of **routes** and fares is complex, but most trains from the UK pass through Paris and head down through France to northern Italy and then on to Rome. Advance booking is essential and can often save you quite a lot of money; there are discounts for under-26s and special offers are common. The journey takes around 21 hours and the best way to do it is to leave London on the lunchtime Eurostar train, which arrives in Paris later that afternoon, and then leave Paris on the early evening train, travelling overnight to Rome. A return **fare** from London to Rome can be found for a total of £230–350 for the two legs (London–Paris from £69 return, Paris–Rome for £170–280 return), depending on whether you travel in a six-berth couchette or a two-berth sleeper. The train has a decently priced restaurant car and is a wonderfully comfortable way to travel to Rome – see the rail-planning site Ⓦ seat61.com for all the options,

or Ⓦ raileurope.co.uk – though bear in mind that there's usually more availability, and tickets are often cheaper, if you book direct with the national train operators.

Package tours and specialist operators

There's no shortage of operators organizing **packages to Rome**, many of which offer specialist tours. For an ordinary city break, you can reckon on spending £600–800 for two staying for three nights in a three- to four-star hotel between April and October, including flights, though special offers can sometimes cut prices drastically, especially for late bookings. **Specialist tours** with guest lecturers tend to cost around £1500 for a week. Travelling from the US, you can expect to pay from around US$1500 for a week in a three-star hotel, which may not include flights, although tours limited to Rome can be hard to find – most take in Tuscany, or focus on the three cities of Rome, Florence and Venice. We've listed some of the better specialist operators below.

AIRLINES

Aer Lingus Ⓦ aerlingus.com.
Air Canada Ⓦ aircanada.com.
Air New Zealand Ⓦ airnewzealand.com.
Alitalia Ⓦ alitalia.com.
American Ⓦ aa.com.
British Airways Ⓦ ba.com.
Continental Airlines Ⓦ continental.com.
Delta Air Lines Ⓦ delta.com.
easyJet Ⓦ easyjet.com.
Emirates Ⓦ emirates.com.
Jet2 Ⓦ jet2.com.
KLM (Royal Dutch Airlines) Ⓦ klm.com.
Lufthansa Ⓦ lufthansa.com.
Malaysia Airlines Ⓦ malaysiaairlines.com.
Monarch Ⓦ monarch.co.uk.
Norwegian Airlines Ⓦ norwegian.com.
Olympic Air Ⓦ olympicair.com.
Qantas Ⓦ qantas.com.au.

Ryanair W ryanair.com.
South African Airways W flysaa.com.
United Airlines W united.com.
US Airways W usairways.com.

RAIL CONTACTS

European Rail UK T 020 7619 1083, W europeanrail.com.
Eurostar UK T 0843 218 6186, W eurostar.com.
Man in Seat Sixty-One W seat61.com.
Rail Europe UK T 0844 848 4078, US T 1800 622 8600, Canada T 1800 361 7245, W raileurope.co.uk.

TRAVEL AGENTS

North South Travel UK T 01245 608 291, W northsouthtravel .co.uk. Friendly, competitive travel agency, offering discounted fares worldwide. Profits are used to support projects in the developing world, especially the promotion of sustainable tourism.
STA Travel UK T 0333 321 0099, US T 1-800 781 4040, Australia T 134 782, New Zealand T 0800 474 400, South Africa T 0861 781 781; W statravel.co.uk. Worldwide specialists in independent travel; also student IDs, travel insurance, car rental, rail passes and more. Good discounts for students and under-26s.
Trailfinders UK T 020 7368 1200, Ireland T 021 464 8800, Australia T 1300 780 212; W trailfinders.com. One of the best-informed and most efficient agents for independent travellers.
Travel CUTS Canada T 1800 667 2887, US T 1-800 592 2887; W travelcuts.com. Canadian youth and student travel firm.
USIT Ireland T 01 602 1906, Northern Ireland T 028 9032 7111; W usit.ie. Ireland's main student and youth travel specialists.

TOUR OPERATORS

ACE Study Tours UK T 01223 835 055, W acestudytours.co.uk.
Central Holidays US T 1800 935 5000, W centralholidays.com.
CIT Australia T 02 9267 1255, W cit.com.au.
Citalia UK T 0870 909 7555, W citalia.co.uk.
Europe Through the Back Door US T 425 771 8303, W ricksteves.com.
Explore Holidays Australia T 02 9857 6200 or T 1300 731 000, W exploreholidays.com.au.
Martin Randall Travel UK T 020 8742 3355, W martinrandall.com.

Arrival

Reaching the centre of Rome is pretty straightforward for air and rail travellers. You'll most likely end up at Termini station, very close to the top attractions and the bulk of accommodation. If you take a taxi or bus to the centre, remember that Rome's traffic can add significantly to your journey time (though not your fare, as rates from the airports are fixed).

By air

Rome has two **airports**: Leonardo da Vinci, better known as Fiumicino, which handles the majority of scheduled flights, and Ciampino, where you may arrive if you're travelling with one of the low-cost airlines or on a charter flight.

Fiumicino airport

Fiumicino, or FCO (W adr.it; enquiries T 06 65951) is Rome's largest airport, about 30km southwest of the city centre, near the coast. There are four terminals, T1, T2, T3 and the new T5, and although they are all pretty close to each other it pays to know which one you are going to. The airport is connected to the centre of Rome by a direct train, the **Leonardo Express**, which takes thirty minutes to get to Termini and costs €14 from a *tabacchi* (or €15 from the official ticket office); services begin at 6.38am and then leave every thirty minutes until 11.38pm. Alternatively, there are slower trains every fifteen minutes to Ostiense and Tiburtina stations, both on the edge of the city centre; tickets cost €8. Both stations are stops on Rome's metro (€1.50; see box, p.23), or you can catch city bus #175 from Ostiense, or #492 or #649 from Tiburtina, to the centre of town (again €1.50). **Trains to Fiumicino** leave Termini at 22 and 52 minutes past each hour, from platform 24 on the far right-hand side of the station.

Several **bus services** link the airport with Termini. The least frequent service is the one run by COTRAL, which has around six services a day from 1.15am to 3.30pm (7pm at weekends) to Termini's Piazza dei Cinquecento (€4.50 or €7 on board; W cotralspa.it). The others are operated by SIT, which runs every thirty minutes from 7am to 11.45pm to Via Marsala 5 (€6 one way; W sitbusshuttle.it), and Terravision, which also runs every thirty minutes to Termini but costs less (€4 one-way, €8 return; W terravision.eu). All buses take about 45 minutes. Note that some bus services depart from the west side of Termini.

Taxis from Fiumicino to the city centre cost a flat-rate (*tariffa fissa*) €48 for up to four people including one bag each and the journey time to the city centre is about 30–40 minutes.

Ciampino airport

The city's second airport, **Ciampino**, or CIA (T 06 65951, W adr.it) is also pretty close to the city, only 15km southeast, but it's much smaller than Fiumicino and there are still no direct rail connections between the airport and city centre. Terravision (W terravision.eu) and SIT bus (W sitbusshuttle.it) run **shuttle bus** services to Termini, which leave roughly every thirty minutes and cost €4 one-way from Ciampino (€6 to go back, €8 return). They pull up on Via Marsala, right by the station (journey time around 40min). Otherwise ATRAL buses (Ⓦatral-lazio.com) run to Via Giolitti, on the south side of Termini, every fifty minutes or so (€3.90). If you don't want to get off at Termini, and are staying near a metro stop on the A line (near the Spanish Steps or Via Veneto areas, for example), you could take an ATRAL bus (€1.20) from the airport to Anagnina metro station at the end of metro line A; buses run every 40min and take 20–30min between Ciampino and Anagnina; from Anagnina you can take the metro to your destination (€1.50).

Taxis cost a flat €30 and the journey time to the city centre is 30–40 minutes. However, be warned that many drivers don't like taking people into the city centre from Ciampino, especially for this fixed rate, and it can sometimes be hard to persuade someone to take you; stand your ground if no one seems to want to put their hand up, and don't pay more than €30 plus tip.

By train

Travelling **by train** from most places in Italy, or indeed Europe, you arrive at the central **Termini station**, the meeting point of the two metro lines and many bus routes. There are **left-luggage** facilities here, by platform 24 (open daily 6am–midnight; €4 per piece for the first 5hr, then 60c per hr). Other services in the vast complex include a tourist information office and the usual car rental outlets on the Via Giolitti side, a fitness centre, two post offices and lots and lots of shops, including a good bookshop, wine shop, and a supermarket and a branch of the COIN department store.

Among other train stations in Rome, newly renovated **Tiburtina** is a stop for some north–south intercity trains, and certain parts of Lazio and elsewhere, as are Trastevere, San Pietro, Ostiense and Tuscolana; if you're staying near any of these and travelling out of town it's always worth checking if you can pick up a train there and avoid Termini altogether. Selected routes **around Lazio**

are also handled by Termini's Regionali platforms (near the Fiumicino platform, a further 5min walk beyond the end of the regular platforms). The Roma-Nord line (*trenino*) station on Piazzale Flaminio runs to Viterbo and stations in between, and the Roma Lido/Porta San Paolo station next to Piramide Metro station serves stations down to Ostia Lido (including Ostia Antica).

By bus

Arriving **by bus** can leave you in any one of a number of places around the city. The main station for buses from outside the Rome region is **Tiburtina**, also the city's second train station. Others include Ponte Mammolo (trains from Tivoli and Subiaco); Lepanto (Cerveteri, Civitavecchia, Bracciano area); EUR Fermi (Nettuno, Anzio, southern Lazio coast); Anagnina (Castelli Romani); and Saxa Rubra (Viterbo and around). All of these stations are on a metro line, except Saxa Rubra, which is on the Roma-Nord line and connected by trains every fifteen minutes with the station at Piazzale Flaminio, on metro line A.

By car

Coming into the city **by car** can be quite confusing and isn't really advisable unless you're used to driving in Italy and know where you are going to park (see p.26). If you're on the A1 highway coming from the north take the exit "Roma Nord"; from the south, follow exit "Roma Est". Both lead you to the **Grande Raccordo Anulare** (GRA), which circles the city and is connected with all of the major arteries into the city centre – the Via Cassia from the north, Via Salaria from the northeast, Via Tiburtina or Via Nomentana from the east, Via Appia Nuova and the Pontina from the south, Via Prenestina and Via Casilina or Via Cristoforo Colombo from the southeast and Via Aurelia or Via Flaminia from the northwest.

From Ciampino, either follow Via Appia Nuova into the centre or join the GRA at junction 23 and follow the signs to the centre. **From Fiumicino**, just follow the A12 motorway into the city centre; it

---

TRAIN ENQUIRIES

For general enquiries contact **Trenitalia** (Ⓦtrenitalia.it, ☎892 021 or ☎06 6847 5475). For enquiries about schedules and prices, call ☎1998 892021 (24hrs a day). There are train information offices at Termini on the first concourse (daily 7am–9pm) and on the left side of the second concourse (daily 6am–midnight).

crosses the river just north of EUR, from where it's a short drive north up Via Cristoforo Colombo to the city walls and, beyond, to the Baths of Caracalla.

Getting around

As in most Italian cities, the best way to get around Rome is to walk – you'll see more and will better appreciate the city. Rome wasn't built for motor traffic, and it shows in the congestion, the pollution and the bad tempers of its drivers. However, it's a big city and has good public transport on the whole – a largely efficient blend of buses, a few trams and a two-line metro – which you'll almost certainly need to use at some point if you want to see anything outside the immediate centre.

ATAC (*Azienda Tramvie ed Autobus del Comune di Roma*) runs the city's **bus, tram and metro service** and on the whole is pretty efficient; its website – ⓦ atac.roma.it – has plenty of **information** in English and an excellent route planner; and there's an enquiries line (Mon–Sat 8am–8pm; ☎ 06 57003), but it's Italian-only. There's also a sporadically open information booth in front of Termini on Piazza dei Cinquecento as well as basic transport information displayed outside, though while the works on metro line C are going on you may struggle to find much on-the-ground help around here.

By bus and tram

The city's **bus and tram** service is on the whole pretty good – cheap, reliable and as quick as the clogged streets of the city centre allow. Remember to board through the rear doors and punch your ticket as you enter. There is also a small network of **electric minibuses** that negotiate the narrow backstreets of the old centre. Around midnight a network of **nightbuses** clicks into service, accessing most parts of the city up to about 5am; it's worth keeping spare tickets handy as it can be difficult to buy one in the early hours. Nightbuses are easily identified by the letter N above the "bus notturno" schedule.

By metro

Rome's **metro** runs from 5.30am to 11.30pm daily, except on Saturdays, when it closes at 12.30am. The metro consists of two lines – **A (red) and B (blue)**– and they're working on line C, which is due to be finished by 2015 (though its city-centre stations, at Chiesa Nuova and Piazza Venezia, have been cancelled). The metro is mainly focused on ferrying commuters out to the suburbs, rather than transporting tourists around the city centre, but it can be useful for quick hops across the centre: Termini is the hub of both lines, and useful stations include ones at the Colosseum, Piazza Barberini, Piazza del Popolo (the stop is called Flaminio), Piazza di Spagna and Ottaviano (for the Vatican).

The system also incorporates the major **overground trains** that head out to the suburbs – the Roma-Lido line, which connects the city to Ostia, and the Roma Laziale and Roma-Nord lines, which run respectively east and north of the city centre.

By taxi

The easiest way to get a **taxi** is to find the nearest taxi stand (*fermata dei taxi*) – central ones are listed below. Alternatively, you can call a taxi (☎ 06 3570, 06 4994, 06 4157, 06 6645, 06 88177 or 06 5551), but these usually cost more, €3.50 for the call plus

---

TICKETS AND PASSES

Flat-fare tickets cost €1.50 each and are good for any number of bus or tram rides and one metro ride within 100 minutes of validating them. You need to punch your ticket before you ride on the metro and as you get on a bus or tram; otherwise you can be fined. **Tickets** are available from tobacconists, or *tabacchi*, newsstands, some coffee bars and ticket machines located in all metro stations and at major bus stops. You can also get a **day pass** (BIG), valid on all city transport until midnight of the day purchased, for €6, a **three-day pass** (BTI) for €16.50 or a **seven-day pass** (CIS) for €24. A **monthly pass** costs €35, and must be bought by the fifth day of each calendar month. Public transport is free with the **Roma Pass** (see p.34). BIRG tickets (**regional transport passes**) for COTRAL and ATAC services are well worth buying if you are going out of Rome for the day (see box, p.26). Finally, it's worth knowing that there are hefty spot **fines** of up to €100 for **fare-dodging**, and pleading a foreigner's ignorance will get you nowhere.

USEFUL TRANSPORT ROUTES

BUSES

#23 Piazzale Clodio–Piazza Risorgimento–Ponte Vittorio Emanuele–Ponte Garibaldi–Via Marmorata–Piazzale Ostiense–Centrale Montemartini–Basilica di S. Paolo.

#30 Express (Mon–Sat only) Piazzale Clodio–Piazza Mazzini–Piazza Cavour–Corso Rinascimento–Largo Argentina–Piazza Venezia–Lungotevere Aventino–Via Marmorata–Piramide–Via C. Colombo–EUR.

#40 Express Termini–Via Nazionale–Piazza Venezia–Largo Argentina–Piazza Pia.

#60 Express Via Nomentana–Porta Pia–Via XX Settembre–Piazza della Repubblica–Via Nazionale–Piazza Venezia–Imperial Forums–Colosseum–Circus Maximus–Piramide.

#62 Piazza Bologna–Via Nomentana–Porta Pia–Piazza Barberini–Piazza San Silvestro–Via del Corso–Piazza Venezia–Corso V. Emanuele–Borgo Angelico– Piazza Pia.

#64 Termini–Piazza della Repubblica–Via Nazionale–Piazza Venezia–Largo Argentina–Corso V. Emanuele–Stazione S. Pietro.

#75 Via Poerio (Monteverde)–Via Induno–Porta Portese–Testaccio–Piramide–Circus Maximus–Colosseum–Via Cavour–Termini–Piazza Indipendenza.

#175 Termini–Piazza Barberini–Via del Corso–Piazza Venezia–Colosseum–Circus Maximus–Aventine–Stazione Ostiense.

#271 S. Paolo–Via Ostiense–Piramide–Viale Aventino–Circus Maximus–Colosseum–Piazza Venezia–Ponte Sisto–Castel Sant'Angelo–Via Vitelleschi–Piazza Risorgimento–Ottaviano–Foro Italico.

#492 Stazione Tiburtina–Piazzale Verano–Termini–Piazza Barberini–Via del Corso–Piazza Venezia–Largo Argentina–Corso del Rinascimento–Piazza Cavour–Piazza Risorgimento–Cipro (Vatican Museums).

#590 Same route as metro line A but with access for disabled; runs every ninety minutes.

#660 Largo Colli Albani–Via Appia Nuova–Via Appia Antica.

#714 Termini–Santa Maria Maggiore–Via Merulana–San Giovanni in Laterano–Terme di Caracalla–EUR.

#910 Termini–Piazza della Repubblica–Via Pinciana (Villa Borghese)–Piazza Euclide–Palazzetto dello Sport–Piazza Mancini.

MINIBUSES

These **small buses** negotiate circular routes through the narrow streets of Rome's centre.

#116 Porta Pinciana–Via Veneto–Via del Tritone–Piazza di Spagna–Piazza San Silvestro–Corso Rinascimento–Campo de' Fiori–Piazza Farnese–Lungotevere Sangallo–Terminal Gianicolo.

#117 San Giovanni in Laterano–Piazza Celimontana–Via dei Due Macelli–Via del Babuino–Piazza del Popolo–Via del Corso–Piazza Venezia–Via Nazionale–Via dei Serpenti–Colosseum–Via Labicana.

#119 Piazza del Popolo–Via del Corso–Piazza Venezia–Largo Argentina–Via del Tritone–Piazza Barberini–Via Veneto–Porta Pinciana–Piazza Barberini–Piazza di Spagna–Via del Babuino–Piazza del Popolo.

TRAMS

#2 Piazzale Flaminio–Via Flaminia–Viale Tiziano–MAXXI–Piazza Mancini.

#3 Stazione Trastevere–Via Marmorata–Piramide–Circus Maximus–Colosseum–San Giovanni–San Lorenzo–Via Nomentana–Parioli–Viale Belle Arti.

#8 Casaletto–Stazione Trastevere–Piazza Mastai–Viale Trastevere–Largo Argentina–Piazza Venezia.

#14 Termini–Piazza Vittorio Emanuele–Porta Maggiore–Via Prenestina (Pigneto).

#19 Porta Maggiore–San Lorenzo–Piazzale Verano–Viale Regina Margherita–Viale Belle Arti–Via Flaminia–Ottaviano–Piazza Risorgimento.

NIGHTBUSES

#N1 Same route as metro line A.

#N2 Same route as metro line B.

#N7 Piazzale Clodio–Piazzale Flaminio–Piazza Cavour–Largo Argentina–Piazza Venezia–Via Nazionale–Termini.

#N8 Viale Trastevere–Piazza Venezia–Via Nazionale–Termini.

#N10 Piazzale Ostiense–Lungotevere De' Cenci–Via Crescenzio–Viale Belle Arte–Viale Regina Margherita–Via Labicana.

---

the meter starts ticking the moment the taxi is dispatched to collect you. **Meters** start at €3 (€4.50 on Sundays and €6.50 between 10pm and 6am), plus a charge of about €1 per item of luggage; the meter clicks up at the rate of €1 or so every kilometre. A journey from one side of the city centre to the other should cost around €10, or around €15 on Sunday or at night. Pick-ups from Termini station incur a supplement of €2. Most taxis are white, and all carry a **rate card** in English giving the current tariff, and the extra charges for luggage, late-night, Sundays and holidays and airport journeys.

The most centrally located **taxi ranks** are at Corso Rinascimento (Piazza Navona); Largo Argentina; Piazza Barberini; Santa Maria Maggiore; Piazza Belli (Trastevere); Piazza dei Cinquecento (Termini); Piazza del Popolo; Piazza San Silvestro; Piazza di Spagna; Piazza Venezia and Via Veneto (Porta Pinciana).

By bike and scooter

Renting a **bike, moped** or **scooter** can be a more efficient way of nipping around Rome's clogged streets than driving, and there are plenty of places offering this facility, although you'll need to have a full driving licence. Rates are around €3–4 an hour/€10 a day for bikes, and about €30 a day for mopeds, €40–50 a day for scooters. Some of the more central rental places are listed on p.26; you can also rent bikes on the Via Appia Antica (see p.150).

There's also a sporadic bike-sharing programme, **Roma-Bike**, where you pick up and drop off bicycles at any of 20 designated points around the centre. You can buy a prepaid card at metro stops

---

TOURS

A number of companies run **organized trips** around the city centre, though these are for the most part quite pricey; for general orientation and a glance at the main sights, the ATAC-run #110 open-top bus (see below) is better value. The following offer the best of the more in-depth tours:

Context Travel Via Baccina 40 ☎ 06 9762 5204, ⓦ contexttravel.com. Context do excellent small-group walking tours (maximum 6 people) of sights and neighbourhoods, led by engaging experts, on subjects ranging from architecture to gastronomic Rome – and of course they do all the major sights too. Perhaps the best choice in the city if you want something both in-depth and personal. Tours from €65 per person.

Enjoy Rome Via Marghera 8a (Mon–Fri 9am–5.30pm, Sat 8.30am–2pm); ☎ 06 445 1843, ⓦ enjoyrome.com. Walking tours of the city given by native English speakers in groups of no more than 25 people. Standard 3hr tours of places such as the Vatican, Ancient Rome and Trastevere cost €30; tours of the Via Appia, and special themes like Caravaggio's or Bernini's Rome cost around €50.

Il Sogno Viale Regina Margherita 192 ☎ 06 8530 1758, ⓦ romeguide.it. This long-established cooperative runs a range of tours of individual sights and is perhaps the best option for a guided tour of a specific place.

Through Eternity ☎ 06 700 9336, ⓦ througheternity.com. Everything from straightforward visits to the Vatican and Capitoline Museums for €44 to themed tours like Rome at Twilight (€32).

Vastours Via Piemonte 32 ☎ 06 481 4246, ⓦ vastours.com. This nationwide company operates a wide range of 3hr excursions by coach with English-speaking guides, for €35–50. They also do decent trips to Ostia Antica and Tivoli for around €60 per person, as well as papal audiences (€35).

BUS AND BOAT TOURS

Three main **tourist buses** circle Rome and its major sights. They're in competition with each other, but you can get combined tickets for two of them.

Archeobus ☎ 800 281 281, ⓦ trambusopen.com. The Archeobus is another hop-on-hop-off service that links some of the most compelling ancient sights, and is much the best way of seeing some of the monuments on and around Via Appia Antica. It starts at Piazza dei Cinquecento outside Termini, and heads down to the southern edge of the city via Piazza Venezia, Piazza Bocca della Verità, Circo Massimo, Terme di Caracalla and the Porta San Sebastiano. On Via Appia, there are stops at Domine Quo Vadis, the catacombs of San Callisto and San Sebastiano, Cecilia Metella and Circus of Maxentius. Buses run daily every thirty minutes between 9am and 4.30pm. Tickets cost €12 and are valid for 48 hours; integrated tickets are available, including the #110 bus (see below), and family tickets cost €40. They can be bought on board, at Piazza dei Cinquecento or online, and, like the #110 bus, discounts are available on entrance fees at a number of attractions on presentation of your ticket.

Batelli di Roma ⓦ battellidiroma.com. Boat trips up the Tiber from the Ponte Sant'Angelo to Isola Tiberina give you the chance to experience Rome from the water. Trips run every hour between 10am and 6.30pm and last 1hr 10min; tickets cost €15 per person.

Bus #110 ☎ 800 281 281, ⓦ trambusopen.com. Good for general orientation and a quick glance at the sights, this ATAC-run open-top bus has a guided commentary. It leaves from Piazza dei Cinquecento outside Termini station and stops at all the major sights, including the Colosseum, Piazza Venezia, St Peter's, the Trevi Fountain and the Villa Borghese. The whole round trip takes two hours, and in summer departures are every fifteen minutes from 8.30am until 8.30pm daily, including holidays and Sundays. Tickets cost €20 and are valid for 48 hours, allowing you to get on wherever you like and hop on and off throughout the day. Family tickets are available for €50; combined tickets for the #110 and Archeobus (see above) cost €25 and are valid for 72 hours. Tickets can be bought on board, before you get on at Piazza dei Cinquecento or online; discounts are available on entrance fees at a number of attractions on presentation of your ticket.

Roma Cristiana ☎ 06 6989 6334, ⓦ operaromanapellegrinaggi .org. The Vatican's tourist bus service with commentary links Rome's major basilicas and other Christian sites, starting in front of Termini on Piazza dei Cinquecento, and also at St Peter's. Services run daily every thirty minutes between 8.40am and 7pm, and tickets cost €13, or €18 for 24 hours; they can be bought on board, at Piazza dei Cinquecento or at the PIT kiosks on Piazza Pio XII, next to St Peter's Square, and San Giovanni in Laterano.

TRAVEL AROUND LAZIO

The **Lazio transport system** is divided into zones which spread concentrically out from the city. If you're considering travelling outside Rome, it's possible to buy **season tickets** – either by the day or week – to travel within them. The **BIRG** (Biglietto Integrato Regionale Giornaliero) is valid all day for unlimited travel on the state railway, COTRAL buses and the Rome metro, but not trains to the airport. Prices range from €3.30 to €14, depending on the zone. A €9.30 ticket, covering four zones, for example, ferries you between Rome and Viterbo. You can also buy weekly passes – the **CIRS** (Carta Integrata Regionale Settimanale) – which cost from €13.50 to €61.50, depending on the number of zones (up to 7 including the city centre). Vendors – train and bus ticket offices, newspaper stands and tobacconists – can advise you on which zones you need to include, or see Ⓦ atac.roma.it.

Termini, Spagna, Ottaviano or any of the end-of-the-line stops for €10 – it's €5 for the card, and €5 to get you started; after that it costs €0.50 an hour (☎06 57003, Ⓦ roma-n-bike.com).

BIKE RENTAL OUTLETS

Barberini Via della Purificazione 84 ☎06 488 5485, Ⓦ rentscooter.it. Rents bicycles, mopeds and scooters. Bikes cost €10 per day, mopeds and scooters from €30. Daily 9am–7pm.

Bici e Baci Via del Viminale 5 ☎06 482 8443; Via Cavour 302 ☎06 9453 9240; Ⓦ bicibaci.com. Bicycles for €4 an hour, €11 a day; mopeds from €6 an hour, €19 a day; scooters €10 an hour, €40 a day. Check out, too, the basement scooter museum at their Via Cavour location. Daily 8am–7pm.

Collalti Via del Pellegrino 80a–82 ☎06 6880 1084. Bike rental and repairs by the hour or day. Bikes cost €3.50 an hour, €12 a day, €16 from Sat–Mon. Mon–Sat 9am–7pm; closed 1–3.30pm.

OnRoad Via Cavour 80 ☎06 481 5669; Corso Vittorio Emanuele II 204 ☎06 6880 1966; Ⓦ scooterhire.it. Mopeds and scooters from €35 a day. Daily 9am–7pm.

Treno e Scooter Rent Piazza dei Cinquecento, Termini ☎06 4890 5823, Ⓦ trenoescooter.com. On the right as you come out of the station. Bikes for hire for €10 a day; mopeds and scooters from €34 a day. Daily 9am–2pm & 4–7pm.

By car

Driving in central Rome can be a nightmare, and is something to be avoided at all costs. In any case much of the centro storico is within the **ZTL** (*zona di traffico limitato*), in which traffic is restricted during the day; if you are driving to a hotel in the centre, check if they are in the ZTL and if they can get you permission to enter. Only residents are allowed to **park** for free in central Rome, so you will always need to pay. You can park on the street for around €1.20 an hour (8am–8pm) – places will be usually designated by blue lines – and there are coin-operated pay-and-display parking meters. There are **garages** in Villa Borghese (around €2.20/hr); in front of Termini station (€2/hr); at

Terminal Gianicolo (€2.10/hr), which is a short walk to the Vatican; and next to each of the end-of-the-line metro stations, from where it's easy to get into the city centre.

In the event of a **breakdown**, call ☎116, or consult the Yellow Pages (*Pagine Gialle*) under "Autoriparazioni" for specialized repair shops.

If you are **renting a car**, all the usual suspects have desks at Fiumicino, Ciampino, Termini and elsewhere in the city, including the area on and around Via Veneto; the major operators are listed below.

CAR RENTAL OUTLETS

Avis Ⓦ avis.com.
Europcar Ⓦ europcar.com.
Hertz Ⓦ hertz.com.
Maggiore Ⓦ maggiore.it.
Sixt Ⓦ sixt.com.

Festivals and public holidays

Rome puts on a decent array of festivals and events throughout the year; see the calendar below. On public holidays (denoted by PH), many sights and shops are closed, as well as some bars and restaurants.

January–April

New Year's Day Jan 1 PH

Epiphany (*La Befana*) Jan 6. See p.306. PH

Carnevale Mid-Feb. For ten days Roman kids dress up and are paraded round the city by their proud parents, and clubs put on themed nights. Look out for the carnival delicacies sold throughout the city: *frappe* (deep-fried pastry strips) and *castagnole* (bite-sized pastries). Piazza Navona hosts good *Commedia dell'Arte* performances and Piazza del Popolo puts on a horse show.

Rome Marathon Mid-March. See p.299.

Easter During Holy Week, Catholics from across the world descend on Rome to witness the pope's address. On Good Friday, a solemn procession makes its way from the Colosseum to the Capitoline Hill, while on Easter Sunday the main event is the pope's blessing in St Peter's Square.

Pasquetta Easter Monday. Many Romans head out of town, traditionally for a picnic in the countryside. PH

Settimana della Cultura Ⓦ beniculturali.it. For one week in April, you can enter all state-owned museums free of charge.

Festa della Primavera. In late April, the Spanish Steps are lined with pots of azaleas.

Natale di Roma April 21. A spectacular fireworks display set off from the Campidoglio and a weekend costume parade mark Rome's birthday.

Liberation Day April 25. PH

May–August

Labour Day May 1. "Primo Maggio" is celebrated with a free rock concert in Piazza San Giovanni. PH

Mille Miglia Ⓦ 1000miglia.eu. Mid-May. Many antique cars roll through the city as part of a Brescia-Rome-Brescia tour.

Giro d'Italia Early to late May. One of cycling's three Grand Tours, this three-week road race around Italy finishes in Rome.

Festa delle Letterature Late May to June. International literature festival. See p.277.

Festival Piazza di Siena Ⓦ piazzadisiena.com. Late May. This swanky show-jumping event takes place in Villa Borghese.

Day of the Republic June 2. The day is marked with a military parade along Via dei Fori Imperiali, and the gardens of the Quirinale Palace are open to the public (expect long queues). PH

Estate Romana June–Sept. Rome's summer arts festival, with events throughout the city, including open-air cinema and al fresco bars and restaurants by the river, in particular on Isola Tiberina. See p.273.

Villa Celimontana June–Sept. Summer open-air jazz festival. See p.273.

Concerti del Tempietto Ⓦ tempietto.org. June–Oct. Classical concerts with dramatic backdrops, such as the ancient Roman Teatro di Marcello and the Art Nouveau Casina delle Civette at Villa Torlonia.

Roma Incontra il Mondo Ⓦ villaada.org. Mid-June to mid-Aug. An eclectic programme of pop, rock and indie concerts takes place in Rome's largest park, Villa Ada. Tickets €8–22.

Teatro dell'Opera Ⓦ operaroma.it. Late June to mid-Aug. The prestigious Teatro dell'Opera's summer season takes place in the spectacularly floodlit setting of the Baths of Caracalla.

Festa di Noantri Mid-July. Two weeks of street performances and events in Trastevere culminate in a huge fireworks display.

Festa delle Catene Aug 1. The chains of St Peter are displayed during a special Mass in the church of San Pietro in Vincoli.

Festa della Madonna della Neve Aug 5. The miracle of a summer snowfall (see p.118) is remembered in the Basilica of Santa Maria Maggiore with a shower of white petals in front of the main altar.

Ferragosto Aug 15. Original "holiday of Augustus", later the Feast of the Assumption; Rome empties as locals in search of cooling breezes head for the sea and mountains. PH

September–December

RomaEuropa Festival Late Sept to Dec. Big international contemporary arts festival, with performances at some of the larger city centre venues. See p.277.

Taste of Roma Ⓦ tasteofroma.it. Sept. Rome's big food festival, held at the Auditorium Parco della Musica, is worth planning a trip around, with demonstrations from top Italian chefs, lots of food stalls and general yumminess.

Rome International Film Festival Late Oct/Nov. See p.277.

Ognissanti All Souls' Day Nov 1. Romans visit family graves in the Verano cemetery in San Lorenzo. PH

Rome Jazz Festival Late Oct/Nov. Two-week festival that showcases the best of Italian jazz and experimental music, and attracts big names from around the world. See p.273.

Immacolata Concezione Dec 8. In honour of the Immaculate Conception of the Blessed Virgin Mary, a religious ceremony takes place in the Piazza di Spagna, often attended by the pope. PH

Christmas (Natale) Dec 25. PH

Santo Stefano (St Stephen) Dec 26. PH

Media

The city's free daily (Italian-language) newspapers – *City* and *Metro* – are available in bars and cafés all over town, and provide weather reports, what's on info and useful phone numbers. If you want to get into a bit more depth or to practise your Italian, you might want to dip into one of the Italian dailies – though be advised that however good your Italian is, most of the country's national newspapers offer a pretty turgid read.

Of the big **national newspapers**, the posh paper is the right-of-centre *Corriere della Sera*, to which *La Repubblica* is the left-of-centre alternative – both have Rome news supplements daily. The **Rome papers** are the popular *Il Messaggero*, the right-leaning *Il Tempo* and the Vatican daily *L'Osservatore Romano*, which also prints an English edition once a week. You'll notice that the sports coverage in all these papers is relatively thin. If you want in-depth football reporting you need to try one of three national **sports dailies** – either the pink *Gazzetta dello Sport*, the Rome-based *Corriere dello Sport* or *Tuttosport*.

For **what's-on and listings information**, the twice-monthly English expat magazine, *Wanted in Rome* (€1; Ⓦ wantedinrome.com) is a useful source of information, especially if you're looking for an apartment or work, and is available at central newsstands. For those with a bit of Italian, the daily arts pages of *Il Messaggero* list movies, plays and major musical events, and Thursday's *La Repubblica* includes the "Trova Roma" supplement, another handy guide to current offerings.. Finally, **English-language newspapers**, such as *The International Herald Tribune* and *The Financial Times*, are available the same day of publication, usually after lunch, at newsstands all over town.

Money

Italy's currency is the euro (€), split into 100 cents. There are seven euro notes – in denominations of 500, 200, 100, 50, 20, 10 and 5 euros, each a different colour and size – and eight different coin denominations, with 2 and 1 euros, then 50, 20, 10, 5, 2 and 1 cents. For the latest rates exchange check ⓦoanda.com or ⓦxe.com.

If you're travelling from the UK it's a good idea to have some euros on you when you arrive; otherwise to get euros just use your **debit or credit card** in the local ATM machines (*Bancomats*); there's usually a charge but it's no more expensive than getting money any other way. As you might expect, credit **and debit** cards are widely accepted in hotels and most shops, though some of the smaller restaurants are cash-only, so check first. **Travellers' cheques** (available through American Express, Thomas Cook and Visa) are becoming increasingly rare, but if you do use them, buying online in advance usually works out cheapest. It's advisable to buy euro travellers' cheques rather than dollars or pounds sterling since you won't have to pay commission when you cash them.

Banking hours are normally Monday to Friday mornings from 8.30am until 1.30pm, and for an hour in the afternoon (usually between 2.30 & 4pm). Outside banking hours, the larger hotels will change money, and there are plenty of exchange bureaux – normally open evenings and weekends. Try American Express at Piazza di Spagna 38 (☎06 67641; Mon–Fri

9am–5.30pm, Sat 9am–12.30pm) or Western Union, which is available at lots of banks and locations throughout the city. Post offices will exchange American Express travellers' cheques and cash commission-free. The last resort should be any of the many *Ufficio Cambio* kiosks, almost always offering the worst rates (despite "no commission" signs).

LOST OR STOLEN CREDIT CARDS AND TRAVELLERS' CHEQUES

CREDIT CARDS
American Express ☎ 800 914 912 or ☎ 06 72282.
MasterCard ☎ 800 870 866.
Visa ☎ 800 819 014.

TRAVELLERS' CHEQUES
American Express ☎ 800 914 912.
Visa ☎ 800 874 155.

Travel essentials

Climate

Visiting Rome at any time of year is a pleasure, although some months are of course better than others as regards **climate**. If you can, avoid visiting in July and August, when the weather is prone to being hot, sticky and humid. Temperatures are usually more comfortable in May, June and September, when most days will be warm but not unbearably so, and it's almost always less humid, and April and October are usually good weather-wise, warm enough if prone to the odd shower. The winter months can be pleasant, and temperatures are usually mild but you will almost certainly have some rain, especially in November and December. Recently Rome experienced snow in February, but it was the first proper snowfall in 24 years.

Crime and personal safety

Rome is a pretty safe city by any standards, but particularly when compared to its counterparts in

AVERAGE MONTHLY TEMPERATURES AND RAINFALL												
	Jan	Feb	Mar	Apr	May	Jun	Jul	Aug	Sep	Oct	Nov	Dec
TEMPERATURE												
max/min (°C)	12/3	13/4	15/5	18/8	23/11	27/15	30/17	30/18	27/15	22/11	16/7	13/4
max/min (°F)	53/37	55/38	59/41	65/46	73/52	81/58	87/63	87/64	80/59	71/51	61/44	55/39
RAINFALL												
mm		103	98	68	65	48	34	23	33	68	94	130	111

the US and UK. The main thing is to make sure you're not too obvious a target for petty criminals by taking some **common-sense precautions**. Most of the crime you're likely to come across will be **bag-snatching**, where gangs of either street kids or *scippatori* ("snatchers") operate. *Scippatori* work on foot or on scooters, disappearing before you've had time to react; the kids are more likely to crowd you in a group, trying to work their way into your bags or pockets while you're trying to shoo them away. As well as handbags, they whip wallets, slash the side of a purse, tear off visible jewellery and, if they're really adroit, unstrap watches. You can minimize the risk of this happening by being discreet: don't flash anything of value, keep a firm hand on your camera, and carry shoulderbags, as Italian women do, slung across your body. It's also worth being vigilant when withdrawing money from ATMs. Be aware of anyone standing too close or trying to distract you – they may be trying to read your PIN or clone your card using a "skimmer" machine. Contact your bank or credit card provider immediately if you suspect you're a victim of **card fraud**.

There are not really any parts of town you should avoid, and although some of the areas around **Termini** can be a bit rough, the neighbourhood is changing and in any case it's more seedy than dangerous. Deserted stretches around **Ostiense or Testaccio** are probably worth avoiding at night, but again this is just to be on the safe side rather than because of any track record of violent crime in these areas.

If the worst happens, you may be forced to have some dealings with **the police**. In Italy this is principally divided between the **Vigili Urbani**, mainly concerned with directing traffic and issuing parking fines; the **Polizia Statale**, the main crime-fighting force; and the **Carabinieri**, with their military-style uniforms and white shoulder belts, who also deal with general crime, public order and drug control. The Polizia enjoy a fierce rivalry with the Carabinieri and are the ones you'll perhaps have most chance of coming into contact with, since thefts should be reported to them. Rome's main *questura* or **police station** is at Piazza del Collegio Romano 3, just behind the Palazzo Doria Pamphilj (☎ 06 4686).

Note that all foreigners in Italy are required by law to carry **ID** with them at all times, so it's worth making a photocopy of your passport or other ID just in case.

Electricity

The **electricity supply** is 220V, though anything requiring 240V will work. Most plugs have three round pins, though you'll find the older two-pin plug in some places; an adapter is very useful.

Entry requirements

British, Irish and other EU citizens can enter Italy and stay as long as they like on production of a valid **passport**. Citizens of the United States, Canada, Australia and New Zealand need only a valid passport, too, but are limited to stays of three months. South Africans require a Schengen visa, which entitles you to travel through many of the countries in the Eurozone. All other nationals should consult the Italian embassy in their own country about visa requirements. Legally, you're required to **register with the police** within three days of entering Italy, though if you're staying at a hotel this will be done for you.

FOREIGN EMBASSIES IN ROME

Australia Via Bosio 5 ☎ 06 852 721, ⓦ italy.embassy.gov.au /rome/home.html.
Britain Via XX Settembre 80a ☎ 06 4220 0001, ⓦ ukinitaly.fco .gov.uk/en.
Canada Via Zara 30 ☎ 06 85444 3937, ⓦ canadainternational .gc.ca/italy-italie.
Ireland Piazza Campitelli 3 ☎ 06 697 9121, ⓦ www .embassyofireland.it.
New Zealand Via Clitunno 44 ☎ 06 853 7501, ⓦ nzembassy.com /italy.
US Via Veneto 121 ☎ 06 46741, ⓦ italy.usembassy.gov.

Health

As a member of the European Union, Italy has **free reciprocal health agreements** with other member states. EU citizens are entitled to free treatment within Italy's public health-care system on production of a **European Health Insurance Card** (EHIC), which you can obtain by picking up a form at the post office, calling ☎ 0845 606 2030 or applying

---

EMERGENCIES

For help in an emergency, call one of the following national telephone numbers:
Police or any emergency service, including ambulance (*Soccorso Pubblico di Emergenza*) ☎ 113.
Carabinieri ☎ 112.
Ambulance (*Ambulanza*) ☎ 118.
Fire (*Vigili del Fuoco*) ☎ 115.
Road assistance (*Soccorso Stradale*) ☎ 116.

24-HOUR PHARMACIES

Farmacia del Senato Corso
Rinascimento 50 ☏ 06 6880 3835.
Farmacia della Stazione Piazza dei
Cinquecento 49 ☏ 06 488 0019.
Internazionale Piazza Barberini 49
☏ 06 487 1195.
Piram Via Nazionale 228 ☏ 06 488 0754.

online at ⓦ ehic.org.uk. Allow up to 21 days for delivery. The EHIC is free of charge and is valid for at least three years, and it basically entitles you to the same treatment as an insured person in Italy. The Australian Medicare system also has a reciprocal healthcare arrangement with Italy.

Vaccinations are not required, and Rome doesn't present any more health worries than anywhere else in Europe; the worst that's likely to happen to you is suffering from the extreme heat in summer or an upset stomach. The **water** that you'll see flowing from public fountains all over town is perfectly safe to drink, except where there are *acqua non potabile* signs. It's worth taking **insect repellent**, too, as the countryside around Rome is rather prone to mosquitoes.

Staff in **pharmacies** (*farmacia*) are well qualified to give you advice on minor ailments and to dispense prescriptions. If you need treatment, go to a **doctor** (*medico*); try AlphaMed at Via Zanardelli 36 (☏ 06 6830 9493; Mon–Fri 9am–8pm; ⓦ alphamedclinic.com), a central medical practice with English-speaking doctors, or Tobias Wallbrecher at Via Domenico Silveri 30 (☏ 06 638 0569; Mon–Fri 9am–1pm & 4–7pm; ⓦ twallsancosma.familydoctors.net), an English-speaking family doctor close to the Vatican. If you need to see a **dentist**, try English-speaking Absolute Dentistry at Via G. Pisanelli 1/3 (☏ 06 3600 3837, ⓦ absolutedentistry.it), which has a 24-hour emergency service. (☏ 339 250 701), or Arrigo Peri, Via Mecenate 77 (☏ 06 488 1614).

If you are seriously ill or involved in an accident, go straight to the **Pronto Soccorso** (Accident and Emergency) of the nearest **hospital**, or phone ☏ 113 and ask for *ospedale* or *ambulanza*. The most central hospitals are Fatebenefratelli on the Isola Tiberina (☏ 06 683 7299), San Giovanni at Via A. Aradam 8 (☏ 06 49971) and Santo Spirito, near the Vatican at Lungotevere in Sassia 1 (☏ 06 68351).

Insurance

Even though EU healthcare privileges apply in Italy, you'd do well to take out an **insurance policy** before travelling to cover against theft, loss, illness or injury. A typical policy usually provides cover for the loss of baggage, tickets and – up to a certain limit – cash or cheques, as well as cancellation or curtailment of your journey. Most policies exclude so-called **dangerous sports** unless an extra premium is paid: in Italy this can mean scuba-diving, windsurfing and trekking. Many policies can be chopped and changed to exclude coverage you don't need – for example, sickness and accident benefits can often be excluded or included at will.

If you do take **medical cover**, ascertain whether benefits will be paid as treatment proceeds or only after your return home, and whether there is a **24-hour medical emergency number**. When securing **baggage cover**, make sure the per-article limit will cover your most valuable possession. If you need to **make a claim**, you should keep receipts for medicines and medical treatment, and if you have anything stolen, you must obtain an official statement from the police (see p.29).

Internet

Internet cafés are not as ubiquitous as they once were but you should never be stuck for a place to get online (reckon on paying around €3 an hour). Note that by law, internet cafés are required to check your ID, so be sure to carry this with you.

ROUGH GUIDES TRAVEL INSURANCE

Rough Guides has teamed up with WorldNomads.com to offer great **travel insurance** deals. Policies are available to residents of over 150 countries, with cover for a wide range of adventure sports, 24-hour emergency assistance, high levels of medical and evacuation cover and a stream of travel safety information. Roughguides.com users can take advantage of their policies online 24/7, from anywhere in the world – even if you're already travelling. And since plans often change when you're on the road, you can extend your policy and even claim online. Roughguides.com users who buy travel insurance with WorldNomads.com can also leave a positive footprint and donate to a community development project. For more information go to ⓦ roughguides.com/shop.

ROME ONLINE

comune.roma.it The Italian-language website of Rome's city council has some information in English, and is particularly useful if you're spending longer in the city.

enjoyrome.com Site of the helpful tourist organization, with information on accommodation and tours.

inromenow.com Fairly up-to-date and very wide-ranging guide to the city.

parlafood.com Not just a great online guide to the best of Rome's food and drink, but a dynamic and delectable culinary website and blog, and a smartphone App, by one of the contributors to this guide.

rome.angloinfo.com Good current information directed at expats and English-speakers living in the city.

romefile.com Lots of information for both English-speaking visitors and expats.

romeguide.it Site of the "Il Sogno" cooperative, which aims to place young people in tourist industry jobs in Rome. A useful resource on sights and good for up-to-date information on concerts and events too.

tripbod.com Plan your trip to Rome with a local and get advice while you're here.

There are also lots of **wi-fi hotspots** around the city centre, including many of the main piazzas; see romawireless.com for details.

Bibli Via dei Fienaroli 28. Mon 5.30pm–midnight, Tues–Sun 11am–midnight. €3.50 an hour; free wi-fi too.

Il Mastello Via San Francesco a Ripa 62. Daily 7am–10.30pm.

Internet Café Via dei Marrucini 12. Mon–Fri 9.30am–1am, Sat 10am–1am, Sun 2pm–midnight.

Yex Piazza Sant'Andrea delle Valle 1. Daily 10am–10pm.

Laundries

You can usually get your **laundry** done in your hotel, but if you can't a laundry (*lavanderia*) is probably just a short walk from the hotel. One of the best places, if only because you can check your email while your undies are drying, is Il Mastello (see above). Others include Onda Blu at Via Principe Amedeo 70 near Termini (daily 8am–10pm), which also has internet facilities and branches all over town (☎ 800 861 346, ondablu.com), and Wash and Dry at Via Avignonesi 17 and Via della Pelliccia 35 (both daily 8am–10pm) as well as other branches around town (☎ 800 231 172, washedry .it). All offer a wash including soap and tumble-drying for around €10 for a 6kg (15lb) load.

Lost property

For **property lost** on a train call ☎ 06 4730 6682 (daily 7am–11pm); on a bus ☎ 06 581 6040 (Mon & Fri 8.30am–1pm, Tues–Thurs 2.30–6pm); on the metro ☎ 06 487 4309 or ☎ 06 6769 3214 (Mon, Tues Wed & Fri 8.30am–5pm).

Mail

General information on Italian **postal services** is available on ☎ 803 160 or at poste.it. Rome's main

post office (*ufficio postale*) is on Piazza San Silvestro (Mon–Fri 8.20am–7pm, Sat 8am–12.35pm); other post offices can be found at Via Arenula 4, Via della Scrofa 61, Corso V. Emanuele II 330 and at Termini station, where there are offices on each side of the station. Hours vary, but tend to be Monday to Friday 8.30am to 2pm, Saturday 8.30am to 1pm.

Stamps (*francobolli*) are sold in *tabacchi* too, as well as in some gift shops; they will often also weigh your letter. The Italian postal system is one of the slowest in Europe, and if your letter is urgent make sure you send it "*posta prioritaria*", which has varying rates according to weight and destination. If you don't trust the Italian post, you can use the **Vatican postal system** which is quicker and loses less, and you get the benefit of an exotic postmark. However, not unreasonably, you have to use Vatican stamps and post your items from the Vatican itself. For this there are post offices and boxes in Piazza San Pietro and in the Vatican Museums.

Maps

For **walking around the city** you should find the maps in this book more than adequate for your needs. If you require something more detailed, then the best choice is perhaps is the 1:12,500 *TCI* map (€7.90), which includes good coverage of the outskirts and suburban neighbourhoods. For public transport, **metro maps** are posted up in every station, and we've included one at the end of this book. Additionally, *Lozzi* publishes a map of Rome and of Lazio (€7), available from newsstands and bookshops.

Opening hours

The city's **opening hours** are becoming more flexible, but much of Rome still follows a traditional

CHIUSO PER RESTAURO

Although the situation is much better than it used to be in Rome, you may find buildings of all kinds **closed for restoration** (*chiuso per restauro*), and it's usually pretty uncertain when they might reopen. The most notable casualty at the time of writing was the Domus Aurea, which has been closed for the best part of a decade, and there is some work scheduled on the Trevi Fountain and Colosseum for 2014. Opening times also change all the time, so ask at one of the tourist information kiosks for an update. If there's something you really want to see and you don't know when you might be back in Rome, it might be worth trying to persuade a workman or priest/curator to show you around.

Italian routine. Most **shops and businesses** in Italy open Monday to Saturday from around 8am until 1pm, and from about 4pm until 7 or 8pm, although many shops close on Saturday afternoons and Monday mornings; a few of the more international businesses follow a nine-to-five schedule. Traditionally, everything except bars and restaurants closes on Sunday, though there's usually a *pasticceria* (pastry shop) open in the mornings and in general Sunday opening is becoming more common.

Most **museums and galleries** are closed on Mondays. Opening hours for state-run museums are generally 9am to 7pm, Tuesday to Saturday, and 9am to 1pm on Sunday. Most other museums roughly follow this pattern, too, although they are more likely to close for a couple of hours in the afternoon, and have shorter opening hours in winter. Many large museums also run late-night openings in summer (till 10pm or later Tues–Sat, or 8pm on Sun). The opening times of **ancient sites** are more flexible: most sites open every day, often including Sunday, from 9am until late evening – frequently specified as one hour before sunset, and thus changing according to the time of year. Some archaeological sites – eg the Colosseum – instituted **summer night visits** in 2013 which are ideal for avoiding both heat and crowds.

Most major **churches** open in the early morning, at around 7 or 8am, and close around noon or 1pm, opening up again at 4pm and closing at 6 or 7pm; hours may be shorter during the winter months. At any time of year some of the less-visited churches will open only for early-morning and evening services, and some are closed at all times except Sundays and on religious holidays; if you're determined to take a look, you may have to ask around for the key, or make an appointment with the custodian.

Rome is very used to tourists, but the rules for visiting churches are much as they are all over Italy. **Dress modestly**, which usually means no shorts (not even Bermuda-length ones) and covered shoulders, and trying to avoid wandering around during a service.

The other factors to be aware of are **public holidays** (see p.26) and the fact that in **August**, particularly during the weeks either side of Ferragosto (Aug 15), most of Rome flees to the coast, many shops, bars and restaurants close and the only people around are other tourists.

Phones

You can use your **mobile phone** – or *telefonino* – in Italy, and indeed you will hardly see an Italian without his or her mobile clasped to the ear. You are likely to be charged extra for incoming calls when abroad. If you want to retrieve messages while you're away, you might have to ask your provider for a new access code. You could also save money by purchasing an Italian **SIM card** when you arrive, which is really very simple. Pay as you Go cards on the WIND, TIM or Vodafone networks cost around €10 from any phone store plus €10 to top up, and they take up to 24 hours to be activated. You will have an Italian number of course, but all your calls and texts will be much cheaper while you're here and will more than cover the extra cost of the card.

INTERNATIONAL CALLS

CALLING HOME FROM ITALY

Australia + 61 + city code.
Ireland + 353 + city code.
New Zealand + 64 + city code.
UK and Northern Ireland + 44 + city code.
US and Canada + 1 + area code.
South Africa + 27 + city code.

CALLING ITALY FROM ABROAD

To **call Italy from abroad**, dial the access code (❶00 from the UK, Ireland and New Zealand, ❶011 from the US and Canada, ❶0011 from Australia), followed by 39, then the area code (❶06 for Rome).

Be sure to take your passport to the shop, however, as you'll need this to register the SIM. For further information about using your phone abroad, contact your network or check out ⓦtelecomsadvice.org.uk.

Public telephones, run by Telecom Italia, come in various forms, but they usually have clear instructions in English. Coin-operated machines are increasingly hard to find and you will probably have to buy a **telephone card** (*carta* or *scheda telefonica*), available from *tabacchi* and newsstands in denominations of €5 and €10. You always need to dial ⓣ06, the code for Rome, regardless of whether you are in the city, unless you are phoning a mobile number.

Numbers beginning ⓣ800 are free, ⓣ170 will get you through to an **English-speaking operator**, ⓣ176 to **international directory enquiries**. Any numbers that start with the number 3 will be a **mobile phone** and consequently more expensive to call. Italian phone tariffs are expensive, especially if you're calling long-distance or internationally, and even Rome residents use **phone calling cards** if they're calling long-distance. You can buy these easily from *tabacchi* for upwards of €5.

Common cards include the Columbus for calls to Western Europe and North America, the standard Scheda Telefonica Internazionale for the rest of the world and the Europa Card for calls to Europe, the US and Canada only. To use one of these cards, you dial a central number and then enter a pin code given on the reverse of the card, before dialling the number you want to reach. Finally, you can make **international reverse charge or collect calls** (*chiamata con addebito destinatario*) by dialling ⓣ170 and following the recorded instructions.

Smoking

Smoking is banned in all public indoor spaces in Italy, including restaurants, bars and clubs. Some establishments have separate smoking rooms, though this is rare.

Time

Rome is **one hour ahead of GMT**, six hours ahead of Eastern Standard Time and nine hours ahead of Pacific Standard Time.

Toilets

There are **public lavatories** on Piazza Zanardelli, just north of Piazza Navona, and on Piazza di Spagna, but these are something of a rarity in Rome. The only others are on Via dei Fori Imperiali, near the entrance to the Forum; in St Peter's Square, just to the left of the entrance to the basilica; in Piazza Vittorio Emanuele; and in Termini station and some city-centre metro stations. And, of course, the facilities in *McDonalds* and in the lobbies of five-star hotels are always worth trying if you're desperate.

Tourist information

There are official **tourist information booths** at Fiumicino in Terminal 2 (daily 9am–6.30pm) and in the Arrivals hall at Ciampino Airport (same hours), and inside Termini at Via Giolitti 34 (daily 8am–8.30pm. You'll also find **green information kiosks** or **PIT** (daily 9am–6pm) in key locations around the city centre (see p.34) that are useful for free maps, directions (the staff usually speak English) and details about nearby sights – though they can be pretty clueless if you want anything less obvious. The Rome **tourist office website** ⓦturismoroma.it can help make up some of the slack, and has plenty of information in English. The council-run **tourist information line** ⓣ06 0608 is open daily 9am–9pm (calls charged at local rates),

---

STUDYING IN ROME: ACADEMIES AND LIBRARIES

The **American Academy** is at Via Angelo Masina 5, 00153 Rome (ⓣ06 58461, ⓦaarome.org); the **British School at Rome** is at Via Gramsci 61, 00197 Rome (ⓣ06 326 4939, ⓦbsr.ac.uk). The best **library** is the one at the American church of **Santa Susanna**, Via XX Settembre 14 (ⓣ06 482 7510), which costs around €18 a year, and also has a good notice board for finding work, accommodation and so on (temporarily closed for renovation but usually Tues 10am–1pm, Wed 3–6pm, Fri 1–4pm, Sat & Sun 10am–12.30pm). Reference libraries include those of the **American Studies Center**, Via M. Caetani 32 (ⓣ06 6880 1613) and the British School at Rome (see above; Mon–Thurs 9am–1pm & 2–6.30pm, Fri 9am–1pm & 2–5pm), although it can be hard to get access unless you're a scholar. The **British Council**, Via delle Quattro Fontane 20 (Mon–Tues & Thurs–Fri 10am–1pm, Wed 2–5pm, closed Aug & Christmas; ⓣ06 478 141), has a small video library.

and the website Ⓦ060608.it is another useful resource. You could also try the privately run **Enjoy Rome**, Via Marghera 8a (Mon–Fri 9am–5.30pm, Sat 8.30am–2pm; ☎06 445 1843, Ⓦenjoyrome.com), whose friendly, English-speaking staff hand out lots of free information; they also operate a free room-finding service, organize tours and run a shuttle service to Fiumicino and Ciampino.

INFORMATION KIOSKS

Castel Sant'Angelo Piazza Pia.
Piazza Navona Piazza delle Cinque Lune.
Santa Maria Maggiore Via dell'Olmata.
Trastevere Piazza Sonnino.
Trevi Fountain Via Minghetti.
Via Nazionale Palazzo delle Esposizioni.

Tourist passes and discounts

There is no museum pass that will get you into all the main attractions in Rome. However, some sights are grouped together to make it easier and cheaper to visit them. The Forum, Palatine and Colosseum can be visited on a **combined ticket**, and Rome's ancient sculpture and other artefacts have been gathered together in the **Museo Nazionale Romano**, which operates on four main sites: Palazzo Massimo, the Terme di Diocleziano, Aula Ottagona, and the Palazzo Altemps; you can buy a ticket from each location that permits entry to all the others for just €7 and is valid for three days. There's also a combined ticket for the Baths of Caracalla, Tomb of Cecilia Metella and Villa dei Quintilii. Finally there's the **Roma Pass**, available from all museums in the circuit and tourist information kiosks (☎06 0608, Ⓦromapass.it), which costs €34 and is valid for three days. It entitles you to travel free on buses, trams and the metro, gives

free admission to two of some 45 museums or sights of your choice (the vast majority of places participate) and reduced entry to others – and, perhaps most importantly, the opportunity to avoid the queues at big sights (quite a lifesaver at the Colosseum).

The Vatican's **Omnia Pass** gives free access to the Vatican Museums, Mamertine Prison, the Colosseum, Forum and Palatine, and a choice of the same museums and transport included in the Roma pass, plus a free trip on the Roma Cristiana bus tour of the city, and priority access everywhere. However, it's expensive (€90; valid for 3 days) so you're paying a lot to jump the queues, and for the Vatican you can do this simply by booking online for €20.

Some sights and museums also give **discounts** or even free admission to **students and EU citizens under 18 or over 65** – but you need to make sure you have the relevant ID with you. Many theatres and cinemas will also offer discounts, as will the #110 tour bus and the Archeobus (15 percent and 20 percent respectively; see box, p.25).

Travellers with disabilities

Rome can be quite a challenge for those with **disabilities**: there are lots of steps, pavements are uneven and Italy as a whole is just not as accessible as a lot of northern Europe and North America. Only two stops on **metro line** A are accessible for disabled persons (Cipro and Valle Aurelia), but bus #591 does the same route and can accommodate those with disabilities. On line B, Circo Massimo, Colosseo and Cavour do not have accessibility, but bus #75 stops at those sights and new buses on this route can accommodate those with disabilities

---

ROME'S SPECIAL CHURCHES

In the course of visiting and reading about Rome you may come across the concept of the city's four **patriarchal basilicas**: St Peter's, San Giovanni in Laterano, San Paolo fuori le Mura and Santa Maria Maggiore. These are the four most important churches in Rome, and therefore of the Catholic Church, and they symbolically represent the various parts of the world where the Catholic faith has reached. Apart from Santa Maria Maggiore, each one is technically part of the Vatican state (ie not Italian territory), and each has a **Holy Door** that is only opened – by the pope – every 25 years. San Giovanni in Laterano used to be the home of the pope and the Vatican, and is still technically the cathedral of Rome. Over the centuries pilgrims have always made a point of visiting these churches, plus the three other so-called "**pilgrimage**" **churches** – San Lorenzo fuori le Mura (occasionally included as a patriarchal basilica), Santa Croce in Gerusalemme and the Santuario Madonna del Divino Amore outside the city. It's a tradition that continues to this day, though Christian visitor numbers are these days swelled several-fold by tourists and other visitors.

(although you may have to wait for a few of the older buses to go by). The buses on routes #81, #85, #90, #170, #490 and #H have also recently been furnished with **elevator platforms**.

There's a useful local organization devoted to promoting **accessible tourism**, Handy Turismo, Via dell'Acquedotto Paolo 73 (Mon–Fri 9am–5pm; ☎06 3507 5707, ⓦhandyturismo.it): see also ⓦaccessibleitaly.com for information on accessibility and tours.

Worship

Churches and other institutions in Rome have historically given assistance to pilgrims from all over the world, and those that focused on pilgrims from particular destinations have over the years become the national churches of that country. Though they remain part of the Vatican just like any other church, they regularly observe Mass in the language of their mother country.

INTERNATIONAL CHURCHES

England (Anglican) All Saints ⓦ allsaintsrome.org.
England (Catholic) Venerable English College ⓦ vecrome.org.
France San Luigi dei Francesi ⓦ saintlouis-rome.net.
Germany Santa Maria dell'Anima ⓦ www.santa-maria-anima.it.
Scotland St Andrews ⓦ presbyterianchurchrome.org.
Spain Santa Maria di Monserrato.
USA (Catholic) Santa Susanna ⓦ www.santasusanna.org.
USA (Episcopalian) San Paolo entro le Mura ⓦ stpaulsrome.it.

PIAZZA SAN LORENZO IN LUCINA

The Centro Storico

The real heart of Rome is the Centro Storico or "historic centre", which makes up the greater part of the roughly triangular knob of land that bulges into a bend in the Tiber. In the days of Ancient Rome, when it was known as the Campus Martius, this low-lying area lay outside the city centre and was mostly given over to barracks and sporting arenas. Later, it became the heart of the Renaissance city, and nowadays it's here that most people find the Rome they have been looking for – a city of small, crumbling piazzas, Renaissance churches and fountains, blind alleys and streets humming with scooters. Whichever direction you wander in, there's something to see; indeed, it's part of the appeal in this area that even the most aimless ambling leads you past effortlessly beautiful and historic spots.

Galleria Doria Pamphilj

Via del Corso 305 • Daily 9am–7pm • €11, including audioguide in English • ☎ 06 679 7323, Ⓦ www.doriapamphilj.it • Bus #40, #62 or #64 from Termini to Piazza Venezia

1

Walking north from Piazza Venezia, the first building on the left of Via del Corso, the **Palazzo Doria Pamphilj**, is among the city's finest Rococo palaces, with a facade added in 1734 to a building that was the product of years of construction and remodelling dating back to Roman times, when a storehouse stood on this site. The Doria Pamphilj family were (and are) one of Rome's most illustrious – they still own the building and live in part of it. They were also prodigious collectors of art, in particular **Prince Camillo Pamphilj**, who was the first member of the family to live here in the mid-seventeenth century. As a result, the **Galleria Doria Pamphilj** is one of Rome's best late-Renaissance art collections.

The private apartments

The first part of the gallery is made up of a series of **private apartments**, furnished in the style of the original palace, through which you're taken on the audiotour by the urbane Jonathan Pamphilj. These include the large and elegant **reception hall** of the original palace, crammed with landscape paintings by the seventeenth-century French artist, Dughet, off which there is a room where the Pamphilj pope, Innocent X, used to receive guests, complete with a portrait of the great man and a couple of side salons filled with busts and portraits of the rest of the family. There's also a **ballroom** with a corner terrace from which the band played and a small private chapel, which contains the apparently incorruptible body of the Roman martyr St Theodora, swathed in robes, and the relics of St Justin under the altar. Be sure to peek in at the former **bedroom** of Filippo Andrea and his English wife Mary Talbot, the last Pamphiljs to live in this part of the palace, whose nearby **sitting room** especially, with its overflowing bookcases, gives the apartments a relatively homely feel amid all the grandeur. It was Filippo, incidentally, who installed the luscious Bath of Diana on the ground floor, with its Pompeii-style frescoes and inviting circular steps.

The picture gallery

The **picture gallery** extends around a lush courtyard, the paintings mounted in the style of the time, crammed in frame-to-frame, floor-to-ceiling. The information is better than it once was, but many paintings are not labelled, making the audio tour more or less essential. On the first corner, there's a badly cracked bust of Innocent X by **Bernini**, which the sculptor apparently replaced in a week with the more famous version down the hall, in a room off to the left, where he appears to have captured the pope about to erupt into laughter. In the same room, Velázquez's famous painting of the same man is quite different, depicting a rather irritable character regarding the viewer with impatience. "It's too real!", its subject is supposed to have exclaimed when he saw it.

The rest of the collection is just as rich in interest, and there are many works worth lingering over. These include perhaps Rome's best concentration of **Dutch and Flemish paintings**, among them a rare Italian work by Brueghel the Elder, showing a naval battle being fought outside Naples, complete with Vesuvius, Castel Nuovo and other familiar landmarks; a highly realistic portrait of two old men by Quentin **Metsys**; and a Hans Memling *Deposition*. There's another Metsys painting – the fabulously grotesque *Moneylenders and their Clients* – close by Annibale **Carracci's** wonderfully bucolic *Flight into Egypt*, one of a set of lunettes displayed here which was completed by his pupil Albani. Nearby, there's a bust of Camillo's wife, Olimpia Aldobrandini Pamphilj, a formidable woman by all accounts and very much a collector in her own right. In the so-called Aldobrandini room, among some beautifully displayed classical statuary, busts, sarcophagi and figurines, are three paintings by **Caravaggio**. These include a tender *Repentant Magdalene* and a marvellous *Rest on the Flight into Egypt* – a truly lyrical work that shows an angel playing violin to Joseph and Mary, and so real it's

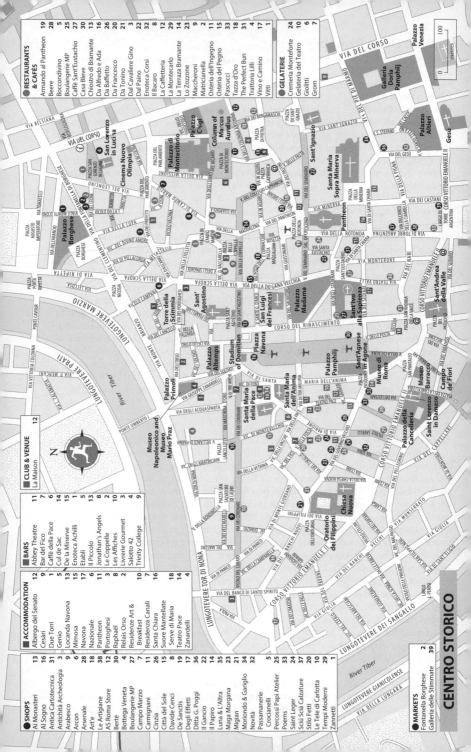

actually possible to play the piece of score Joseph is holding. All in all, the gallery is a fantastic collection of work, displayed in a wonderfully appropriate setting.

Sant'Ignazio

Piazza di Sant'Ignazio • Daily 7.30am–7pm, Sun from 9am • ☎ 06 679 4406, ⓦ chiesasantignazio.it

Via del Caravita, the next left off Via del Corso after the Doria Pamphilj palace, leads into the Centro Storico proper and Piazza di Sant'Ignazio, a lovely little square laid out like a theatre set and dominated by the facade of the Jesuit church of **Sant'Ignazio**. The saint isn't actually buried here; appropriately, for the founder of the Jesuit order, he's in the main Jesuit church, the Gesù, a little way south (see p.57). But it's a spacious structure, worth visiting for a marvellous **Baroque ceiling**, by Andrea Pozzo, showing the entry of St Ignatius into paradise – a spectacular work, employing sledgehammer trompe-l'oeil effects, notably in the mock cupola painted into the dome of the crossing. Stand on the disc in the centre of the nave, the focal point for the ingenious rendering of perspective: figures in various states of action and repose, conversation and silence, fix you with stares from their classical pediments.

Piazza di Pietra

On the northern side of Piazza di Sant'Ignazio lies **Piazza di Pietra**, a pleasant triangular open space dominated by the giant Corinthian columns of an ancient Roman temple, still supporting their frilled peristyle and incorporated in true Roman style into the building behind, now Rome's stock exchange. The temple was built by Antoninus Pius in 145 AD in memory of his father, Hadrian.

Pantheon

Piazza della Rotonda • Mon Sat 8.30am–7.30pm, Sun 9am–6pm, public hols 9am–1pm • Free

A short walk from Via del Corso, **Piazza della Rotonda** is one of the city's most picturesque squares, and perhaps suffering because of it, invariably thronged as it is with sight-weary tourists, hawkers and street musicians, besieging the café tables that fringe the edge. The waters of the fountain in the middle, an eighteenth-century construction topped by yet another obelisk, are a soothing influence, but the main focus of interest is the **Pantheon**, which forms the square's southern edge, easily the most complete ancient Roman structure in the city, and, along with the Colosseum, visually the most impressive.

Though originally a temple that formed part of Marcus Agrippa's redesign of the Campus Martius in around 27 BC – hence the inscription – it's since been proved that the building was entirely rebuilt by the **Emperor Hadrian** and finished around 125 AD. It remains a formidable architectural achievement, although like the city's other Roman monuments, it would have been much more sumptuous in its day. Consecrated as a Christian site in 609 AD, it was dedicated to **Santa Maria ai Martiri** in an allusion to the Christian bones that were found here; a thousand years later, the bronze roof was stripped from the ceiling of the portico by Pope Urban VIII, to be melted down for the baldacchino in St Peter's and the cannons of the Castel Sant'Angelo. Interestingly, some of the "stolen" bronze later found its way back here when, after Unification, the cannons were in turn melted down to provide materials for the tombs of two Italian kings, which are housed in the right and left chapels.

Inside, you get the best impression of the **engineering expertise** of Hadrian: the diameter is precisely equal to its height (43m), the hole in the centre of the dome – from which shafts of sunlight descend to illuminate the musty interior – a full 9m across. Most impressively, there are no visible arches or vaults to hold the whole thing up; instead, they're sunk into the concrete of the walls of the building. Again, it would

1

CLERICAL FASHIONS

Opposite the church of Santa Maria sopra Minerva, Via dei Cestari and Via di Santa Chiara host Rome's **clerical fashion district**, long-time home to a number of shops selling liturgical garments to priests, monks and nuns. Oddly enough, anyone is welcome to browse and even buy: should you be interested, a full set of cardinal's outfits, including a change of cassocks, a skullcap and something for special occasions, will set you back about €1500. Perhaps the most famous store of all is Gammarelli, Via di Santa Chiara 34 (☎06 6880 1314, ⓦgammarelli.com, Mon–Sat 9am–1pm, Mon–Fri also 2–6pm) in business since 1798. This is the official supplier to the pope, and it's this historic shop that's charged with delivering three sizes of white (or, strictly, ivory) garments to the Vatican during papal elections to ensure that, whoever is elected, there will be something ready in the new pope's size.

---

have been richly decorated, the coffered ceiling heavily stuccoed and the niches filled with the statues of gods.

Now, apart from the sheer size of the Pantheon, the main point of interest is the **tomb of Raphael**, between the second and third chapel on the left, with an inscription by the humanist cardinal Pietro Bembo: "Living, great Nature feared he might outvie Her works, and dying, fears herself may die." The same kind of sentiments might well have been reserved for the Pantheon itself.

Santa Maria sopra Minerva

Piazza della Minerva 42 · Mon–Fri 7am–7pm, Sat & Sun 8am–12.30pm & 3–7pm · ⓦ www.basilicaminerva.it

Just behind the Pantheon, the church of **Santa Maria sopra Minerva**, modelled on the church of Santa Maria Novella in Florence, is Rome's only **Gothic church**, and worth a look just for that, though its soaring lines have since been overburdened by marble and frescoes. Built in the late thirteenth century on the ruins of a temple to Minerva, it is also one of the city's art-treasure churches, crammed with the tombs and self-indulgences of wealthy Roman families. Of these, the **Carafa Chapel**, in the south transept, is the best known, holding Filippino Lippi's late-fifteenth-century fresco of the Assumption, a bright, effervescent piece of work. Below, one painting shows a hopeful Carafa (the religious zealot who became Pope Paul IV) being presented to the Virgin Mary by Thomas Aquinas; another depicts Aquinas confounding a group of heretics in the sight of two beautiful young boys. The children, visible in the foreground on the right, are the future Medici popes **Leo X** and **Clement VII**; the equestrian statue of Marcus Aurelius, destined for the Capitoline Hill, is just visible in the background. The lives of Leo and Clement come full circle in the church, where they are both buried, and remembered by two very grand tombs on either side of the high altar – Leo on the left, Clement on the right, and both of them proof, if any were needed, that beautiful boys don't always grow up to be beautiful men.

You should look, too, at *Christ Bearing the Cross*, on the left-hand side of the altar, a serene work that **Michelangelo** completed for the church in 1521, and underneath, the tomb of St Catherine of Siena, who died in a convent here in 1380. The room where she died is viewable through the sacristy, though you may need to ask someone to open it for you. You can leave the church by the passage to the left of the altar, taking in the **tomb of Fra Angelico**, who also died here in 1455, just in front of a chapel that contains a very soothing *Madonna and Child* by Benozzo Gozzoli, from 1449. You emerge on Via Sant'Ignazio, just around the corner from the church of the same name (see p.39).

Elephant Statue

Immediately outside the church of Santa Maria sopra Minerva, Bernini's diminutive **Elephant Statue** is one of Rome's most delightful small statues – and the celebrated

Baroque artist's most endearing piece of work, if not his most characteristic. It shows a cheery elephant trumpeting under the weight of the obelisk he carries on his back – a reference to Pope Alexander VII's reign and supposed to illustrate the fact that strength should support wisdom.

Sant'Ivo alla Sapienza

Corso del Rinascimento 40 · Sept–June Sun 9am–12.30pm · ☎ 06 0608, ⓦ sivoallasapienza.eu · Bus #62 or #64 from Termini

Between the Pantheon and Piazza Navona, accessible from Corso del Rinascimento, the rather blank facade of the **Palazzo della Sapienza** used to be the site of Rome's university (which retains the palace's name) and cradles an elegant Borromini-designed courtyard and the church of **Sant'Ivo alla Sapienza** – from the outside at least, one of Rome's most impressive churches, with a playful facade also designed by Borromini. Though originally built for the most famous Barberini pope, Urban VIII, the building actually spans the reign of three pontiffs. Both of the two small towers are topped with the weird, blancmange-like groupings that are the symbol of the Chigi family (representing the hills of Monti Paschi), and the central cupola spirals helter-skelter-fashion to its zenith, crowned with flames that are supposed to represent the sting of the Barberini bee, their family symbol. Inside, it's comparatively featureless but very cleverly designed – impressively light and spacious given the small space the church is squeezed into, rising to a tall parabolic cupola.

Palazzo Madama

Corso del Rinascimento 11 · Guided tours (Italian only) Sept–July first Sat of the month 10am–6pm, every 20min; 40min · Free; you must be at Piazza Madama 11 from 8.30am onwards to book a tour for later that day · ☎ 06 6706 2177, ⓦ www.senato.it · Bus #62 or #64 from Termini

Just north of Sant'Ivo, there's a constant police presence around the seventeenth-century **Palazzo Madama**, which owes its name to the "madame" Margaret of Parma, the illegitimate daughter of Charles V, who lived here in the sixteenth century, before its fancy Baroque facade was added. Nowadays, it holds the chamber and many of the offices of the Italian upper house or Senate – a rather ageist institution whose 315 representatives have to be at least 40 years old and elected every five years only by Italians over 25. **Tours**, conducted in Italian, take in the main debating chamber and various public spaces and form a good complement to tours of the lower house of the Italian parliament, located in the Palazzo di Montecitorio (see p.49).

San Luigi dei Francesi

Piazza San Luigi dei Francesi 5 · Daily 10am–12.30pm & 3–7pm, Thurs 10am–12.30pm only · ⓦ saintlouis-rome.net

At the bottom end of **Via della Scrofa**, the French national church of **San Luigi dei Francesi** is worth a look, mainly for the works by **Caravaggio** that have hung here since they were painted in the last years of the sixteenth century. In the last chapel on the left are three paintings: *The Calling of St Matthew*, in which Christ points to Matthew, who is illuminated by a shaft of sunlight; Matthew visited by an angel as he writes the Gospel; and the saint's martyrdom. Caravaggio's first public commission, these paintings were rejected at first, partly on grounds of indecorum, and it took considerable reworking by the artist before they were finally accepted. These days they are considered to be among the artist's greatest-ever works, especially *The Calling of St Matthew*, which manifests the simple, taut drama, as well as the low-life subject matter, that Caravaggio became so well known for.

1

Sant'Agostino

Piazza Sant'Agostino • Daily 7.45am–noon & 4–7.30pm

Just north of Piazza Navona, off to the left of Via della Scrofa, the Renaissance facade of the church of **Sant'Agostino** takes up one side of a drab piazza of the same name. It's not much to look at from the outside, but a handful of art treasures might draw you in: this was the church of Rome's creative community in the sixteenth century, and as such drew wealthy patrons and well-connected artists. Just inside the door, the serene statue of the *Madonna del Parto*, by **Sansovino**, is traditionally invoked during pregnancy, and is accordingly surrounded by photos of newborn babes and their blissful parents.

Further into the church, take a look at **Raphael**'s vibrant fresco of Isaiah, on the third pillar on the left, beneath which is another work by **Sansovino**, a craggy *St Anne, Virgin and Child*. But the biggest crowds gather around the first chapel on the left, where the *Madonna di Loreto*, painted in 1605 by **Caravaggio**, is a characteristic work of what was at the time almost revolutionary realism, showing two peasants praying at the feet of a sensuous Madonna and Child, their dirty feet and scruffy clothes contrasting with the pale, delicate feet and skin of Mary.

Torre della Scimmia

Just beyond Sant'Agostino, on Via dei Portoghesi, take a look at the **Torre della Scimmia** – literally the "Tower of the Monkey" – which grows almost organically out of a fork in the road above an ivy-covered *palazzo*. The story goes that in the seventeenth century, a pet monkey kidnapped a child and carried it to the top of the tower; the father of the child called upon the Virgin for help, and the monkey promptly clambered down, delivering the child to safety. By way of thanks, the man erected a shrine to the Virgin, which you can still see at the top of the tower, accompanied by a glowing lamp that is to this day kept constantly burning.

Piazza Navona and around

Bus #62 or #64 from Termini

The western half of the Centro Storico focuses on **Piazza Navona**, Rome's most famous square, and the surrounding area. This pedestrianized oval, as picturesque as any piazza in Italy, is lined with cafés and restaurants and often thronged with tourists, street artists and pigeons. The best time to come is at night, when the inevitably tourist-geared flavour of the place is at its most vibrant, with crowds hanging out around the **fountains** or people-watching while nursing a pricey drink at a table outside one of the **bars**, or watching the **buskers** and **street artists** entertain the throng. Piazza Navona takes its name from the Greek word for "struggle", *agone* – due to the games that were traditionally held here – and its shape from the first-century AD Stadium of Domitian, the principal venue of the athletic events and later chariot races that took place in the **Campus Martius** (see p.36). Until the mid-fifteenth century, the ruins of the arena were still here, overgrown and disused, but the square was given a facelift in the mid-seventeenth century by the Pamphilj Pope Innocent X, who built most of the grandiose palaces that surround it.

Palazzo Pamphilj

Closed to the public

Built by Pamphilj Pope Innocent X, the largest of the grandiose palaces, the **Palazzo Pamphilj**, fills much of the southwestern side of Piazza Navona. It's now home to the Brazilian embassy and is not open to the general public – which is a shame, given the fact that one of its state rooms has a lavish frescoed ceiling by Pietro da Cortona,

CLOCKWISE FROM TOP LEFT CHURCH OF SANTA MARIA SOPRA MINERVA (P.40); ANTIQUE SHOPS, VIA DEI CORONARI (P.47); STREET ENTERTAINERS, PIAZZA NAVONA (P.48); PALAZZO ALTEMPS (P.48) >

depicting the adventures of Aeneas, which you can glimpse at night if the lights are on in the embassy.

Sant'Agnese in Agone

Tues–Sat 9.30am–12.30pm & 3.30–7pm, Sun 10am–1pm & 4–8pm • ⓦ santagneseinagone.org

Pop Innocent X commissioned the church of **Sant'Agnese in Agone** next door to the Palazzo Pamphilj, initially from Carlo Rainaldi and later from Carlo Borromini, who took over after Rainaldi was sacked for being too slow. The story goes that the 13-year-old St Agnes was stripped naked before the crowds in the stadium as punishment for refusing to marry, whereupon she miraculously grew hair to cover herself. She was later martyred by a sword blow to her throat; nowadays she is the patron saint of young girls. The saint is depicted (fully clothed) being consumed by flames in the right-hand chapel; her skull is encased in a reliquary in a chapel at the back of the church, which, typically squeezed into the tightest of spaces by Borromini, is supposedly built on the spot where it all happened.

The fountains

Opposite the church of Sant'Agnese in Agone, the **Fontana dei Quattro Fiumi** (Fountain of the Four Rivers), one of three that punctuate the square, is a masterpiece of 1651, by Bernini, Borromini's arch-rival. Each figure represents one of what were considered at the time to be the four great rivers of the world – the Nile, Danube, Ganges and Plate – though only the horse, symbolizing the Danube, was actually carved by Bernini himself. It's said that all the figures are shielding their eyes in horror from Borromini's church facade (Bernini was an arrogant man who never had time for the work of the less successful Borromini), but the fountain had actually been completed before the facade was begun.

The grand complexity of rock is topped with an **Egyptian obelisk**, brought here by Pope Innocent X from the Circus of Maxentius. Bernini also had a hand in the fountain at the southern end of the square, the so-called Fontana del Moro, designing the central figure of the Moor in what is another fantastically playful piece of work, surrounded by toothsome dolphins and other marine figures. The fountain at the opposite end of the square, the Fontana del Nettuno, is equally fanciful, depicting Neptune struggling with a sea monster, surrounded by briny creatures in a riot of fishing nets, nymphets, beards, breasts, scales and suckers.

Piazza Pasquino

Just south of Piazza Navona, immediately behind Palazzo Braschi, the battered torso of **Pasquino** is easy to miss, even in the small triangular space of **Piazza Pasquino**, in the corner of which it still stands. Pasquino is perhaps the best known of Rome's "talking statues" of the Middle Ages and Renaissance times, to which anonymous comments on the affairs of the day would be attached – comments that had a serious as well as a humorous intent (see p.66). Pasquino gave us the word "pasquinade", meaning a satire or lampoon of a public figure, though whether the comments and photocopied poems that grace the statue these days live up to it or not is debatable.

Museo di Roma

Piazza San Pantaleo 10 • Tues–Sun 10am–8pm • €10, €12.50 with Museo Barracco • ☎ 06 0608, ⓦ museodiroma.it

Backing onto Piazza Navona, the eighteenth-century Palazzo Braschi is the home of the **Museo di Roma** which has a permanent collection relating to the history of the city from the Middle Ages to the present day. It's a large museum which is really only sporadically interesting. Indeed, the building – particularly the magnificent **Sala Nobile** where you go in, the main staircase and one or two of the renovated rooms, not least the exotically painted Sala Cinese and Sala Egiziana – is probably the main event. But there's interest in some of the **paintings**, too, which show the city during different eras – St Peter's Square before Bernini's colonnade was built; jousting in Piazza Navona and the Cortile Belvedere in the Vatican; big gatherings and processions in the Campidoglio and Piazza del Popolo – and frescoes from demolished palaces provide decent enough highlights. There are also portraits and busts of the most eminent Roman families, most of whom produced a pope at one time or another – not only the Braschi, but also the Corsini, Chigi and Odelaschi. These names resonate around historic parts of the city today, and their faces gaze out of the rooms here with deadly and penetrating self-importance.

Sant'Andrea della Valle

Piazza Sant'Andrea della Valle · Daily 7.30am–noon & 4.30–7.30pm, Sun till 12.45pm & 7.45pm · ☏ 06 686 133, ⓦ www.sant-andrea
-roma.it · Bus #62 or #64 from Termini

Dominating the busy stretch of Corso Vittorio Emanuele II just beyond Largo Argentina, the church of **Sant'Andrea della Valle** has the distinction of sporting the city's second-tallest dome (after St Peter's), built by Carlo Maderno, and of being the location for the first scene of the opera *Tosca* by Puccini. Inside, it's one of the most Baroque of Rome's churches, a high, barn-like building whose dome is decorated with paintings of the Glory of Paradise by Giovanni Lanfranco. The marvellous set of frescoes in the apse illustrating the life of St Andrew are by Lanfranco's contemporary, Domenichino, and centre on the monumental scene of the saint's crucifixion on the characteristic transverse cross. In a side chapel on the right, you may recognize some good-looking copies of not only Michelangelo's *Pietà* (the original is in St Peter's), but also of his figures of Leah and Rachel from the tomb of his patron, Julius II, in the church of San Pietro in Vincoli (see p.113).

Museo Barracco

Corso Vittorio Emanuele II 166a · June–Sept Tues–Sun 1–7pm, Oct–May Tues–Sun 10am–4pm · €6.50, €12.50 with Museo di Roma ·
☏ 06 0608, ⓦ museobarracco.it · Bus #62 or #64 from Termini

Set back slightly from busy Corso Vittorio Emanuele II, the so-called **Piccola Farnesina** palace was built by Antonio Sangallo the Younger. The palace itself actually never had anything to do with the Farnese family, and took the name "little Farnese" because of the lilies on the outside of the building, which were confused with the Farnese heraldic lilies. It's home to the **Museo Barracco** on the first and second floors, a small but extremely fine-quality collection of ancient sculpture that was donated to the city in 1902 by one Baron Barracco. There are ancient Egyptian pieces, including two sphinxes from the reigns of Hatshepsut and Rameses II, an austere head of an Egyptian priest, a bust of a young Rameses II and statues and reliefs of the god Bes from various eras.

Look out for ceramics and statuary from the Greek classical period – essentially the fourth and fifth centuries BC and Roman copies of the same period – which include a lovely, almost complete figurine of Hercules, a larger figure of an athlete copied from an original by Polyclitus, a highly realistic dog washing herself from the fourth century BC and a complete and very beautiful votive relief dedicated to Apollo. A small room at the front of the building contains later Roman pieces, most notably a small figure of Neptune from the first century BC and an odd, almost Giacometti-like column-sculpture of a hermaphrodite, along with beautifully realistic portrait busts of both anonymous and public figures like Sophocles and Euripides. The charming busts of two young Roman boys opposite date from the first century AD.

Palazzo della Cancelleria

Piazza della Cancelleria 1

Walking west along Corso Vittorio Emanuele II from the Museo Barracco, you come to the grand **Palazzo della Cancelleria**, the seat of the papal government that once ran the city; Bramante is thought to have had a hand in its design, and this gorgeous edifice exudes a cool poise quite at odds with the rather grimy nature of its location. You can't get in to see the interior, but you can stroll into the marvellously proportioned, multi-tiered courtyard, which is a treat enough in itself.

San Lorenzo in Damaso
Piazza della Cancelleria 1 · Daily 7.30am–12.30pm & 4.30–8pm

Just off Corso Vittorio Emanuele II, the church of **San Lorenzo in Damaso** forms part of the Palazzo della Cancelleria complex and is one of the oldest churches in Rome. It was rebuilt with the palace at the start of the sixteenth century and has since been greatly restored, the last time at the end of the nineteenth century. There is a painting by Federico Zuccaro over the altar (though it's hard to see behind the massive canopy), *The Coronation of the Virgin*, and a twelfth-century icon of the Virgin Mary in the chapel to the left of here.

Via del Governo Vecchio

In the heart of the old city, **Via del Governo Vecchio** leads west from Piazza Pasquino through one of Rome's liveliest quarters. The street was named for the Palazzo Nardini at no. 39, which was once the seat of the governors of Rome. It's currently being restored, but normally you can wander in to look at its elegant courtyard. However, this part of Rome is best known for its cool independent shops and boutiques and its vigorous restaurants and bars that fill the narrow streets with a buzzing nightlife.

Piazza dell'Orologio

On the west side of Via del Governo Vecchio, the delightful small square of **Piazza dell'Orologio** is so called because of the quaint clocktower that is its main feature. The clock is part of the **Oratorio dei Filippini**, designed by Carlo Borromini, which backs onto the Chiesa Nuova (see below) and is part of the same complex: the followers of San Filippo Neri (founder of the Chiesa Nuova) attended musical gatherings here as part of their worship, hence the musical term "oratorio". Nowadays it's given over to a library of nineteenth-century literature and hosts temporary exhibitions – take the time to sneak in and rest for five minutes in its elegant orange-tree-shaded courtyard. Just off the square, there's a scatter of antique and bric-a-brac shops which signal that you're just around the corner from Rome's antiques quarter, Via dei Coronari (see p.47).

Chiesa Nuova

Piazza della Chiese Nuova · Mon–Sat 7.30am–noon & 4.30–7.30pm, Sun 8am–1pm & 4.30–8pm; San Filippo Neri's rooms tour Tues, Thurs & Sat 10am; 30min · Free; book tours in advance by email stating language and preferred day and time · ✉ mauriziobotta @hotmail.com, 🌐 vallicella.org

The church of Santa Maria in Vallicella – or the **Chiesa Nuova**, as it's more often known – backs onto Via del Governo Vecchio and is another highly ornate Baroque church, which is strange, because its founder, **San Filippo Neri**, didn't want it decorated at all. Neri was an ascetic man, who tended the poor and sick in the streets around here for most of his life and commissioned this place of worship on the site of an earlier structure, Santa Maria in Vallicella, which had been donated to him and his followers by Pope Gregory XIII in 1577. Neri died in 1595, and this large church, as well as being his last resting place (he lies in the chapel to the left of the apse), is his principal memorial. Inside, three paintings by Rubens hang at the high altar, centring on the *Virgin with Angels*. Pietro da Cortona's ceiling paintings, meanwhile, show the Ascension of the Virgin in the apse, and, above the nave, the construction of the church and Neri's famous "**vision of fire**" of 1544, when a globe of fire entered his mouth and dilated his heart – a physical event which apparently affected his health thereafter. Finally, you can also visit San Filippo Neri's rooms in the church on **guided tours**, which include his bedroom and private chapel.

Via dei Coronari

Carlo Maderno lived across the road from the Chiesa Nuova at Via Banchi Nuovi 4, and there's a plaque marking the house. Turn left from here and head north, and you find yourself at the end of narrow **Via dei Coronari**, which leads back through the Centro Storico to the top end of Piazza Navona. This is the fulcrum of Rome's antiques trade, and, although the prices are as high as you might expect in such a location, there are a huge number of shops (the street consists of virtually nothing else), selling a tremendous variety of stuff, and a browse along here makes for one of the city's most absorbing bits of sightseeing.

Santa Maria dell'Anima

Via Santa Maria dell' Anima 64 • Daily 9am–12.45pm & 3–7pm • ☎ 06 6828 1802, Ⓦ www.santa-maria-anima.it

A few steps right off Via dei Coronari is Via Santa Maria dell'Anima, where the church of **Santa Maria dell'Anima** takes its name from the statue of the Virgin on its facade, between two pleading souls in purgatory. It's another darkly cosy Roman church, wide and squat and crammed into an impossibly small space. Nowadays, it's the German national church in Rome, and a richly decorated affair, almost square in shape, with a protruding main sanctuary flanked by Renaissance tombs. The one on the right, a beautiful, rather sad concoction, is that of the last non-Italian pope before John Paul II, the Dutchman Hadrian VI, who died in 1523, while at the far end, above the altar, you can just about make out a dark and glowing *Virgin with Saints* by Giulio Romano.

Santa Maria della Pace and the Chiostro del Bramante

Piazza Santa Maria della Pace • Church Mon, Wed & Sat 9am–noon, but often erratic; cloister daily 10am–11pm • ☎ 06 6880 9035, Ⓦ chiostrodelbramante.it

Just south of Via dei Coronari, the church of **Santa Maria della Pace** dates originally from the late fifteenth century but has a facade and portico that were added a couple of hundred years later by Pietro da Cortona. It's often closed when it shouldn't be, but if you're lucky enough to find it open, you can see Raphael's frescoes of various sibyls above the Chigi chapel (first on the right), executed in the early sixteenth century. But perhaps the most impressive part of the church is the attached **Chiostro del Bramante**, finished in 1504, a beautifully proportioned, two-tiered cloister that is given over to high-quality temporary art exhibitions and is at least the one part of the building you can be sure of seeing. It also has a good café and bookshop that you don't need an entrance ticket to visit (see p.243) and also rents rooms (p.228).

Stadium of Domitian

At the far end of Via dei Coronari, just off the north side of Piazza Navona below the level of the street, there are some visible remains of the **Stadium of Domitian**, which used to occupy the whole of the piazza and which can help you to learn a little more about the stadium and its relationship with present-day Piazza Navona. Sadly, the ruins have been inaccessible for some time, but you can get a reasonable view of them from the street, or from Piazza Navona 49, where there's a balcony built into the lobby.

1

Palazzo Altemps

Piazza Sant' Apollinare 46 • Tues–Sun 9am–7pm • €10 (includes Palazzo Massimo, Terme di Diocleziano & Crypta Balbi); valid for 3 days • ☎ 06 3996 7700, Ⓦ archeoroma.beniculturali.it

Just across the street from the north end of Piazza Navona, Piazza Sant'Apollinare is the home of the beautifully restored **Palazzo Altemps**. Begun in 1477 and completed just under a hundred years later, it now houses a branch of the **Museo Nazionale** Romano, a relatively new addition to the sights around Piazza Navona. The cream of the Museo Nazionale's collections of Roman statuary is here, and is well worth a visit. Divided between two storeys of the palace, in rooms which open off an elegant courtyard, most of what is on display derives from the collection of the seventeenth-century Roman cardinal, Ludovico Ludovisi. It's a mix of pieces he purchased to adorn his villa on the Quirinale Hill and found in the grounds of the villa itself, which occupied the site of a former residence of Julius Caesar.

The ground floor

First up, at the far end of the courtyard's loggia, is a statue of the emperor Antoninus Pius, who ruled from 138 to 161 AD, and, around the corner, a couple of marvellous heads of Zeus and Pluto, a large **bronze bust** of Marcus Aurelius, a bust of Julia, the disgraced daughter of Emperor Augustus, and a grave-looking likeness of the philosopher Demosthenes, from the second century AD. Further rooms hold more riches: there are two almost identical statues of Apollo the Lyrist, a magnificent statue of Athena taming a serpent, pieced together from fragments found near the church of Santa Maria sopra Minerva, an Aphrodite from an original by Praxiteles, a frieze from a third-century sarcophagus showing the labours of Hercules and, in the far corner of the courtyard, a shameless Dionysos with a satyr and panther, found on the Quirinale Hill.

The first floor

Upstairs, you get a slightly better sense of the original sumptuousness of the building – some of the frescoes remain, and the north loggia retains its original late-sixteenth-century decoration, simulating a vine-laden pergola, heavy with fruit, leaves and gambolling cherubs and now home to a series of busts of Roman emperors. The objects on display are if anything even finer than those downstairs. The **Painted Views room**, so called for the bucolic scenes on its walls, has a fine statue of Hermes, restored in the seventeenth century in an oratorical pose according to the fashion of the time. The **Cupboard Room**, next door, with its fresco of a display of wedding gifts against a floral background, has a wonderful statue of a warrior at rest called the *Ludovisi Ares*, which may represent Achilles and was restored by Bernini in 1622, and, most engagingly, a charmingly sensitive portrayal of Orestes and Electra, from the first century AD by a sculptor called Menelaus – his name is carved at the base of one of the figures.

Beyond are even more treasures, and it is hard to know where to look first. One room retains a frieze telling the story of **Moses** as a cartoon strip, with each scene displayed by nude figures as if on an unfurled tapestry. In the room itself is a colossal head of **Hera**, now thought to be a head of **Antonia** (Mark Antony's daughter and mother of Caligula and Claudius), and – what some consider the highlight of the entire collection – the famous Ludovisi Throne: an original fifth-century BC Greek work embellished with a delicate relief portraying the birth of Aphrodite. She is shown being hauled from the sea, where she was formed from Uranus's genitals, while on each side reliefs show a flute player and a woman sprinkling incense over a flame – rituals associated with the worship of Aphrodite.

Further on, there is a depiction of **Aphrodite** after a bath, a first-century AD boy strangling a goose and a relief of **Dionysos** in the former cardinal's bedroom – a bold, almost modern profile of a face in red marble. Beyond the bedroom is the **Fireplace Salon**, whose huge hearthside is embellished with caryatids and ibex – the symbol of the Altemps family – and holds the **Suicide of Galatian**, apparently commissioned by

Julius Caesar to adorn his Quirinale estate. At the other end of the room, an incredible sarcophagus depicts a battle between the Romans and barbarians in graphic, almost visceral sculptural detail, while in the small room next door there are some quieter, more erotic pieces – a lovely Pan and Daphne, a satyr and nymph and the muses Calliope and Urania. Once you've made it to here, you'll be ready for a quick peek at the **Altemps chapel**, off the opposite end of the fireplace room, and a skim back through your favourite pieces, before leaving what is one of Rome's best collections of classical art.

Palazzo Primoli

Bus #40 from Piazza Venezia and Termini

Around the corner from Palazzo Altemps, at the end of Via Zanardelli, the sixteenth-century **Palazzo Primoli** was the home of a descendant of Napoleon, Joseph Primoli. Newly restored, it houses two minor museums that may command your attention on the way to the Vatican, just across the Tiber from here.

Museo Mario Praz

Via Giuseppe Zanardelli 1 · Tues–Sun hourly tours 9am–2pm & 2.30–6.30pm; 45min · Free · ☎ 06 686 1089, ⓦ museopraz
.beniculturali.it

The first of Palazzo Primoli's two museums, the **Museo Mario Praz**, on the top floor, was the home of one Mario Praz, a teacher of English literature, art historian and writer who lived here for fifteen or so years until his death in 1982. It is kept pretty much as the elegant and cultured Praz left it, its nine rooms stacked to the gills with books, magazines, paintings and ornate furniture. Praz lived in a larger apartment in the Palazzo Ricci on Via Giulia before moving here and amassed heaps of stuff – a period described in his signature book, *La Casa della Vita*. Tours of the apartment give you a glimpse of the vanished way of life of a connoisseur.

Museo Napoleonico

Piazza di Ponte Umberto 1 · Tues–Sat 10am–6pm · €8 · ☎ 06 6880 6286, ⓦ museonapoleonico.it

Situated on the ground floor of the Palazzo Primoli, facing the river, the **Museo Napoleonico** is reasonably interesting even if you're not an enthusiast for the great Frenchman and his dynasty, which had a considerable influence on nineteenth-century Italy. Rome was home for the Bonapartes in the 1820s, after Pauline married Camillo Borghese; Napoleon's mother, Letizia, also lived nearby (on Via del Corso) – and this is a rather weighty assortment of their personal effects. There's a letter from Napoleon himself from his exile in St Helena, a room devoted to Pauline Borghese, another to Caroline Bonaparte (who married the French ruler of Naples at the time, Joachim Murat), busts and paintings (including a stirring depiction of Napoleon in battle), portraits of Napoleon's nieces, Carlotta and Zenaide, hung amongst a number of Carlotta's own quite adept paintings – and even a Napoleonic bike. You can even find a plaster cast of Pauline Borghese's right breast, done in situ by Canova, for his famous statue in the Galleria Borghese.

Palazzo di Montecitorio

Piazza di Montecitorio · First Sun of every month 10am–6pm; hourly guided tours; 45min; Italian only · Free · ☎ 06 67601, ⓦ www
.camera.it · Bus #175 from Termini

A couple of minutes' walk east from the Torre della Scimmia, the obelisk in the centre of **Piazza di Montecitorio** was brought to Rome by Augustus to celebrate his victory over Cleopatra and set up in the Campus Martius, where it formed the gnomon of a giant sundial. The square takes its name from the bulky **Palazzo di Montecitorio** on its northern side, a Bernini creation from 1650 and home since 1871 to the lower house of the Italian parliament. You can only visit by guided tour, but for those who know Rome well, and have even the slightest interest in Italy's notoriously shaky parliamentary system, a visit can be very worthwhile.

The building is in fact two knocked into one: the original, Bernini-designed structure, and another incorporating the main Hall of Deputies. The main building is full of grand reception rooms around a large courtyard, of which the **Sala della Lupa**, used for press conferences and presidential meetings with foreign dignitaries, is so called for its frescoes glorifying Rome as the country's capital, and the she-wolf that stands centre stage – a Mussolini addition. On the other side of the courtyard, the first-floor **Sala della Regina** is a massive room lined with tapestries that contains the entrance to the presidential part of the Hall of Deputies next door. The Hall itself is an impressive nineteenth-century space with seats for 635 deputies arranged in a semicircle under an Art Nouveau skylight; above the Speaker's platform, a bronze representing the spirit of Italy, flanked by regal military groupings, does a great job of enhancing the solemnity the chamber tries hard to exude.

Piazza Colonna

Bus #175 from Termini

Next door to Piazza Montecitorio, and about halfway down Via del Corso, **Piazza Colonna** is flanked on its north side by the late-sixteenth-century **Palazzo Chigi**, the official residence of the prime minister and as such not open to the public. The **Column of Marcus Aurelius**, which gives Piazza Colonna its name, was erected between 180 and 190 AD to commemorate military victories in northern Europe, and, like the column of Trajan which inspired it, is decorated with reliefs depicting scenes from the campaigns. The statue of St Paul on top was added by Sixtus V, made from bronze from the ancient doors of the church of Sant'Agnese fuori le Mura (see p.83). The square used to be the site of the city's principal coffee-roasters' market, so was always a busy spot, and it still has an elegant backdrop in the Palazzo Wedekind, home to the offices of Rome's *Il Tempo* newspaper, whose dozen or so Ionic columns, originally Roman, support a gracious balustraded terrace.

San Lorenzo in Lucina

Piazza San Lorenzo in Lucina · Daily 8am–noon & 5–8pm; underground tours first Sat of every month 5pm · €2 · ⓦ www .sanlorenzoinlucina.it · Bus #175 from Termini

Just off Via del Corso, the triangular square of **Piazza di San Lorenzo in Lucina** is a pleasant space, a little bit undiscovered by tourists compared to its counterparts of Navona and Rotonda; spread with café tables, it makes a nice place to stop for a coffee or a bite to eat. On one side, the church of **San Lorenzo in Lucina**, with its manifestly ancient campanile and columned portico, stands out among the largely undistinguished buildings around; it originally dates from the fifth century but was rebuilt in the twelfth. Inside, like so many Roman churches, it doesn't look or feel nearly so old (in fact, much of it dates from the seventeenth century), but there are several features of interest, not least a section of the griddle on which St Lawrence was roasted (see p.127), in the first chapel on the right – though this is almost impossible to see. A little further down, on the same side, the tomb of the French painter Nicolas Poussin is a delicate nineteenth-century marble affair by his compatriot Chateaubriand; Poussin spent much of his life in Rome and died here in 1665. Beyond, take a look also at Bernini's bust of the moustachioed doctor of Innocent X, Fonseca, in the next chapel but one, and the *Crucifixion* by Guido Reni, in the apse. There are also excavations under the church which you can visit, including parts of the original basilica along with Roman frescoes and insulae from the second and third centuries AD.

MARKET AT CAMPO DE' FIORI

Campo de' Fiori and the Ghetto

This chapter is really Rome's old centre part two, covering the area which lies between Corso Vittorio Emanuele II and the Tiber. As in the Centro Storico proper, cramped streets open out onto small squares flanked by churches, although it's more of a working quarter – less monumental, with more functional buildings and shops, and a main square, Campo de' Fiori, where the fruit and veg stalls and rough-and-ready bars form a marked contrast to the pavement artists and sleek cafés of Piazza Navona. To the east, it merges into the atmospheric streets and scrabbly Roman ruins of the old Jewish Ghetto, a small but thriving neighbourhood that nuzzles close to the city's giant central synagogue, and leads to Isola Tiberina, while just north of here lies the major traffic intersection and ancient Roman site of Largo di Torre Argentina.

Campo de' Fiori

Market Mon–Sat 8am–1pm; cleanup is about 2–5pm, when the square is least appealing • Bus #62 or #64 from Termini, or #116 minibus

Just to the south of Corso Vittorio Emanuele II, a network of streets centres on the long oblong of **Campo de' Fiori** – in many ways, Rome's most appealing square. Home to a lively fruit and vegetable market, it's surrounded by restaurants and cafés and is busy pretty much all day, although its function as heart of the area's nightlife, and the consequent glut of bars and outdoor drinkers, has taken away much of its unique appeal, in the evenings at least.

No one really knows how the square came by its name, which means "field of flowers". One theory holds that it was derived from the Roman Campus Martius which used to cover most of this part of town. Another claims it is after Flora, the mistress of Pompey, whose theatre used to stand on what is now the northeast corner of the square – a huge complex by all accounts, which stretched right over to Largo Argentina, and where Julius Caesar was famously stabbed on the Ides of March, 44 BC. You can still see the foundations in the basement of the *Da Pancrazio* restaurant, on the tiny Piazza del Biscione, and the semicircular Via de' Grotta Pinta retains the rounded shape of the theatre. Later, Campo de' Fiori was an important point on papal processions between the Vatican and the major basilicas of Rome (notably San Giovanni in Laterano) and a site of public executions. The most notorious killing here is commemorated by the statue of Giordano Bruno, in the middle of the square. Bruno was a late-sixteenth-century freethinker who followed the teachings of Copernicus and was denounced to the Inquisition; his trial lasted for years under a succession of different popes, and finally, when he refused to renounce his philosophical beliefs, he was burnt at the stake.

Palazzo Farnese

Piazza Farnese • Tours Mon, Wed & Fri in French or Italian 3pm, 4pm & 5pm, English Wed 5pm; 45min • €5; book at least 1 week in advance and bring your passport when you visit • ☎ 349 368 3013, ⓦ inventerrome.com • Bus #62 or #64 from Termini, or #116 minibus

Just south of Campo de' Fiori, Piazza Farnese is a quite different square, with great fountains spurting out of carved lilies – the Farnese emblem – into marble tubs brought from the Baths of Caracalla, and the sober bulk of the **Palazzo Farnese** itself. Commissioned in 1514 by Alessandro Farnese – later Pope Paul III – from Antonio di Sangallo the Younger, the building was worked on after the architect's death by Michelangelo, who added the top tier of windows and cornice. It now houses the French embassy, and access needs to be organized well in advance, but even from the outside, it's a tremendously elegant and powerful building – indeed, of all the fabulous locations that Rome's embassies enjoy, this has to be the best, and is certainly worth visiting if you can – the Farnese were great enthusiasts and collectors, and classical statues litter the hallways and salons of the palace.

First floor

On the first floor or *piano nobile*, the **Salone d'Ercole** has a copy of the so-called Farnese Hercules (the original of which used to stand here but is now in Naples), surrounded by busts of Roman emperors in a room decorated with the feats of Hercules by Federico Zuccari. Zuccari also had a hand in the room next door, the **Sala dei Fausti Farnesiani** or "Room of the Farnese Deeds", which is decorated with frescoes by Franceco Salinati illustrating the great acts of the family – though this is sadly not always open for tours, as it's used for official functions.

Carracci Gallery

Carracci Gallery is currently closed for restoration, due to reopen mid to late-2014; in the meantime, another room in the palace (the Camerino) displays Carracci's earlier works.

The real treasure is at the back of the building – the Bolognese painter Annibale Carracci's *Loves of the Gods*, finished in 1603 and sitting in the **Carracci Gallery**. It's a work of such magnificent vitality, with complex and dramatically arranged figures, great swathes of naked flesh and vivid colours, that it is often seen as the first great work of the Baroque era. Commissioned by Odoardo Farnese, the main painting, centring on the marriage of Bacchus and Ariadne, which is supposed to represent the binding of the Aldobrandini and Farnese families, leaps out of its frame in an erotic hotchpotch of cavorting, a fantastic, fleshy spectacle of virtuoso technique and perfect anatomy, surrounded by similarly fervent works illustrating various classical themes. Between and below them, nude figures peer out – amazing exercises in perspective that seem almost to be alongside you in the room. Carracci did the main plan and the central painting himself, but left the rest to his brother and cousin, **Agostino** and **Ludovico**, and assistants like **Guido Reni** and **Guercino**, who went on to become some of the most sought-after artists of the seventeenth century. It's a great piece of work, perhaps only eclipsed in Rome by the Sistine Chapel itself, and it's sad to note that Carracci, disillusioned by the work and bitter about the relative pittance that he was paid for it, didn't paint much afterwards and died penniless a few years later.

The **Camerino**, a small room open to the public for the first time while renovations take place in the Carracci Gallery, displays the artist's work after his arrival to Rome in 1595; these frescoes enabled him to receive the commission for the larger gallery.

Galleria Spada

Piazza di Capo di Ferro 3 · Tues–Sun 8.30am–7.30pm · €5 · Guided tour every 45min, 30min · ☎ 06 683 2409, Ⓦ galleriaborghese.it · Bus #62 or #64 from Termini, or minibus #116

If you can't get in to the Palazzo Farnese, you'll have to make do with the Palazzo Spada, a couple of blocks east down Via Capo di Ferro. The **Galleria Spada** is inside – walk right through the courtyard to the back of the building. Although its four rooms, decorated in the manner of a Roman noble family, aren't spectacularly interesting unless you're a connoisseur of seventeenth- and eighteenth-century Italian painting, it does show what a collector's eye Cardinal Bernardino Spada, in particular, had. Highlights include two portraits of Spada by **Reni** and **Guercino**, alongside a *St Jerome*, also by Reni; *Cleopatra*, by **Lavinia Fontana**, who outranked both her father and husband as a sixteenth-century artist; works by Italian-influenced Dutch artists like **Jan van Scorel**; and, among bits and pieces of Roman statuary, a seated philosopher. The building itself is great: its facade is frilled with stucco adornments and, left off the small courtyard, there's a crafty trompe l'oeil by **Borromini** – a tunnel whose actual length is multiplied about four times through the architect's tricks with perspective.

Ponte Sisto

Immediately behind the Palazzo Spada lies the river and a pedestrian bridge across to Trastevere, the **Ponte Sisto**. Built by Pope Sixtus IV in 1479 on the site of a ruined structure, it was the first bridge to be built across the Tiber since Roman times. It is a relatively narrow structure, and the inscriptions on each side of the entrance recall Sixtus IV's achievements, although they do not record the fact that the money to build it came from Cardinal Juan de Torquemada – uncle of the notoriously grisly tyrant of the Inquisition. One thing you can't see from the bridge itself is a large round hole in the middle, which functioned as an overflow in times of flood.

Via Giulia

Bus #62 or #64 from Termini, or #116 minibus

Via Giulia runs parallel to the Tiber from the Ponte Sisto, and was laid out by Julius II to connect the bridge with the Vatican. The street was conceived as the centre of papal Rome, and Julius commissioned Bramante to line it with imposing palaces. Bramante

CAMPO DE' FIORI AND THE GHETTO

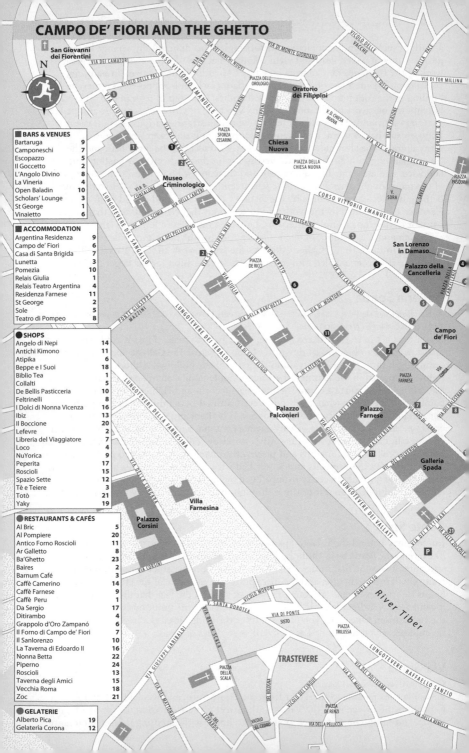

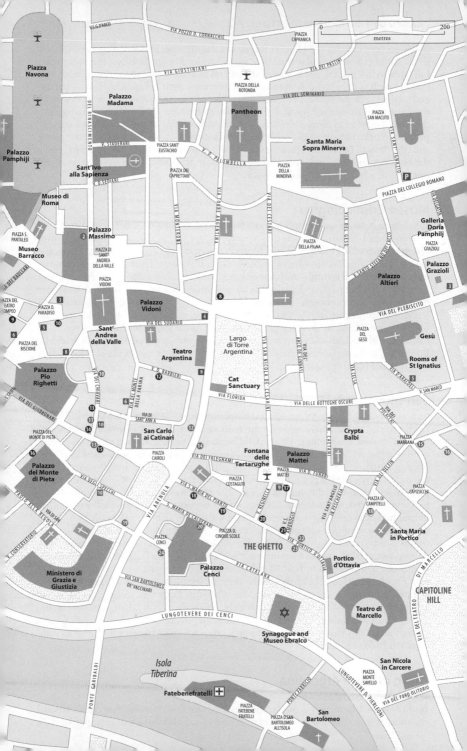

didn't get very far with the plan, as Julius was shortly after succeeded by Leo X, but the street soon became a popular residence for wealthier Roman families. It is still packed full with stylish **palazzi** and **antiques shops** and as such makes for a nice wander, with features such as the playful **Fontana del Mascherone**, right behind the Farnese palace and topped with the Farnese emblem, to tickle your interest along the way. Just beyond the fountain, behind the high wall of the Palazzo Farnese, the ivy-draped arch across the street connects to more French diplomatic offices, the remnant of a Renaissance plan to link the Farnese palace with the **Villa Farnesina** across the river. Further along still, the **Palazzo Falconieri**, recognizable by the quizzical falcons crowning each end of the building and now the home of the Hungarian Academy, was largely the work of Borromini, who enlarged it in 1646–49.

Museo Criminologico

Via del Gonfalone 29 • Tues–Sat 9am–1pm, Tues & Thurs also 2.30–6.30pm • €2 • ☎ 06 6889 9941 or ☎ 06 6889 9942, ⓦ www .museocriminologico.it • Bus #62 or #64 from Termini, or #116 minibus

On the corner of Via Gonfalone, the **Museo Criminologico** offers a small but intriguing look at crime in general and Italy's underworld in particular. There are some gruesome early **instruments of torture** – manacles, lashes, head braces – a display on the unfortunate Beatrice Cenci (see p.60) and a selection of guillotines, nooses and various articles worn by the condemned, although inevitably the most interesting stuff – if you can read Italian – is that most pertinent to the world of Italian crime: the Mafia, the Brigate Rosse and Italian prison life. All in all, it is a perfect antidote to the more effete Renaissance splendours of Via Giulia and around, although it's worth knowing that Italy's Anti-Mafia Bureau has its headquarters at nearby Via Giulia 52, which explains the usually fairly robust police presence outside.

San Giovanni dei Fiorentini

Piazza dell 'Oro 1 • Daily 7.30am–noon & 5–7pm • ⓦ sangiovannideifiorentini.net • Bus #62 or #64 from Termini, or #116 minibus

At the far end of Via Giulia, right by the river, the church of **San Giovanni dei Fiorentini** is set on its own small square, Piazza dell'Oro, and is the burial place of the seventeenth-century architect **Borromini**. Its eighteenth-century facade is as monumental as any of Rome's churches, but inside it is a relatively plain affair, originally built by Sansovino on the orders of the Medici pope, Leo X, who wanted to see an expression of Florentine pride in what was then the heart of Rome. The church was finished in the early 1600s by **Carlo Maderno**, who added the dome, and is buried here, along with Borromini, who helped him after finishing work on the nearby Palazzo Falconieri. Beneath here, Raggi's flamboyant seventeenth-century altarpiece depicts the Baptism of Christ, and in the nearby south transept, Salvatore Rosa's *Martyrdom of Saints Cosmas and Damian* – the patrons of the Medici – has a fleeing male nude figure in the foreground that Rosa challenged Michelangelo to beat: "Let Michelangelo come and see if he can paint a better nude than this!" The chapel to the right of the high altar has a faded fresco by **Filippino Lippi** that is said to have miraculous powers. Look out, too, for the naive statue of a young John the Baptist in the south aisle, above the sacristy door, next to which there's a bust of another Florentine pope, Clement XII, carved by Bernini. San Giovanni extends a special welcome to pets, and you'll often see churchgoers wandering in with dogs, cat baskets and the like.

Largo di Torre Argentina

Bus #40, #62, #64 and several others from Termini

Largo di Torre Argentina is a good-sized square, frantic with traffic that circles around the ruins of four (Republican-era) temples and the channel of an ancient public lavatory. It's more a place to catch a bus or tram than to linger deliberately, and in any case, the temples are closed to the public for most of the year (but for the occasional guided tour – details are sometimes posted at the site), but to be honest they don't add a lot to what you can see from the road, and the main attraction here is the square's thriving colony of cats.

Cat Sanctuary

Largo di Torre Argentina · Daily noon–6pm · Free · ☎ 06 4542 5240, ⓦ romancats.com

You can visit the **cat sanctuary** down the steps on the southwestern corner of Largo di Torre Argentina, and, if you wish, donate money or buy a catty gift from their small shop, or even "adopt" a cat for a monthly fee. Around two hundred and fifty cats live in the excavations here, most of them domestic creatures dumped by their owners, and the people who look after them are all volunteers and receive no support from the city. In fact, the helpers here care for all of the city centre's four thousand or so stray cats, whose colonies spread from the Forum to the ruins at Piazza Vittorio Emanuele.

Teatro Argentina

Largo di Torre Argentina 52 · ☎ 06 06 08, ⓦ teatrodiroma.net

On the western side of Largo di Torre Argentina, the **Teatro Argentina** was the venue for the first performance of Rossini's *Barber of Seville*, in 1816. It was not a success: Rossini was apparently booed into taking refuge in a nearby pastry shop. The theatre was built in 1731, almost entirely of wood, according to legend over the spot in Pompey's theatre (see p.300) where Julius Caesar was assassinated. Today, it is one of the city's most important theatres, with the occasional production in English and some concerts. Its small **museum** can be visited by appointment, with displays on the history of the district, objects from the original building and displays relating to historic productions.

Palazzo Altieri

Piazza del Gesù 49 · Not open to the public

Via del Plebiscito, a dark, rather gloomy thoroughfare, links Largo Argentina with Piazza Venezia, 500m or so away. Halfway down on the left, flanking the north side of Piazza del Gesù, the grey decaying bulk of the **Palazzo Altieri** was a monster of a project in its time that – a contemporary satire posted on the Pasquino statue quipped – looked set to consume Rome by its very size. The Altieri pope, Clement X, had the palace built around the house of an old woman who refused to make way for it: the two spyhole windows that were left can still be seen above the ground-floor windows, three windows to the right of the main entrance. Unfortunately, you can't visit the palace, which is now used as offices.

Palazzo Grazioli

Via del Plebiscito 102

Beyond Palazzo Altieri, set back from the road on the left, **Palazzo Grazioli** is both Via del Plebiscito's best guarded and most notorious building in modern times, due to its function as the Rome residence of three-times former prime minister Silvio Berlusconi, who announced his resignation here in November 2011.

Gesù

Via degli Astalli 16 · Daily 7am–12.30pm & 4–7.30pm · ⓦ chiesadelgesu.org · Bus #62 or #64 from Termini

Lording it over Piazza del Gesù (said to be the windiest in Rome) is the church of the **Gesù**, the first **Jesuit church** to be built in Rome, and an appropriately dramatic symbol

2

ALDO MORO

Via Michelangelo Caetani is the site of a memorial to the former Italian prime minister **Aldo Moro**, whose body was left here in the boot of a car on the morning of May 9, 1978, 54 days after his kidnap by the **Brigate Rosse**, or "Red Brigades". It was a carefully chosen spot, not only for the impudence it showed on the part of the terrorists in that it was right in the centre of Rome, but also for its position midway between the headquarters of the Communist and Christian Democrat parties. A plaque (and sometimes a wreath) marks the spot, and tells part of the story of how Moro, a reform-minded Christian Democrat, was the first right-wing politician to attempt to build an alliance with the then popular Italian Communists. Whether it was really left-wing terrorists who kidnapped him, darker, right-wing forces allied to the establishment, or perhaps a combination of the two, there's no doubt that Moro's attempt to alleviate the Right's postwar monopoly of power found very little favour with others in power at the time – though that didn't make his death any less of a shock.

During the **"Mani pulite"** years that followed, corruption in both politics and business was supposed to have been exposed and eliminated, but arguably little changed: the prime minister who took over after Moro's death was none other than the elder statesman of Italian politics **Giulio Andreotti**, whose alleged involvement with the Mafia saw him twice tried – and acquitted – for collusion, most recently in 2003. Political cynicism resurfaced in the 1990s and is still much in evidence today; as such, the tragedy of Moro's death still carries a lot of resonance for Romans.

---

of the Counter Reformation. High and wide, with a single-aisled nave and short transepts edging out under a huge dome, it was ideal for the large, fervent congregations the movement wanted to draw; indeed, it has since served as the model for Jesuit churches everywhere and is still well patronized. The facade is by **Giacomo della Porta**, the interior the work of **Vignola**, and the glitzy tomb of the order's founder who also commissioned this church, St Ignatius, in the north transept, is topped by a huge globe of lapis lazuli – the largest piece in existence. Opposite, the tomb of sixteenth-century Jesuit missionary **St Francis Xavier**, decorated with a painting by **Carlo Maratta** showing his death on a Chinese island, holds a reliquary containing the saint's severed arm; the rest of his (incorruptible) body remains a focus of pilgrimage in Goa, India. Otherwise, it's the staggering richness of the church's gold interior that you remember, especially the paintings by the Genoese painter **Baciccia** in the dome and the nave, particularly the *Triumph of the Name of Jesus*, an ingenious trompe l'oeil which oozes out of its frame in a tangle of writhing bodies, flowing drapery and stucco angels stuck like limpets.

Rooms of St Ignatius

Via degli Astalli 16 • Mon–Sat 4–6pm, Sun 10am–noon • Free • ⓦ ignatianspirituality.com/7187/the-rooms-of-st-ignatius

Next door to the Gesù church, the **Rooms of St Ignatius** occupy part of the first floor of the Jesuit headquarters. St Ignatius lived here from 1544 until his death in 1556, and there are just three simple chambers, where the saint and founder of the Jesuit order studied, worshipped and received visitors. One was his private chapel, and the other two hold artefacts from his life – his shoes, vest and cloak, the robe he was buried in, his writing desks and original documents, and a bronze bust of the great man based on his death mask. But the true draw here is the **decorative corridor** just outside. Designed by **Andrea Pozzo** in 1680, it's a superb exercise in perspective, an illusion of a grand hall in what is a relatively small space. Stand on the rose in the centre and the room's architectural fancies, putti, garlands and scallop shells are precise and true; walk up and down and the ceiling beams bend, the figures stretch and the scrollwork buckles – giving the bizarre feeling of a room shifting before your eyes. It's a feast of technical trickery and grandiose brushwork – all in weird contrast to the basketball courts that occupy the quadrangle down below.

Crypta Balbi

Via delle Botteghe Oscure 31 · Tues–Sun 9am–7.45pm; obligatory tours hourly; 30min · €7, also includes Palazzo Altemps, Palazzo Massimo, Terme di Diocleziano & Aula Ottagona; valid 3 days · ☎ 06 3996 7700, ⓦ archeoroma.beniculturali.it

Crypta Balbi, on the corner of Via Michelangelo Caetani and Via delle Botteghe Oscure, is the site of a Roman theatre, the remains of which later became incorporated into a number of medieval houses. There's a ground-floor exhibition which takes you through the evolution of the site in painstaking (and sometimes excruciating) detail, with lots of English explanation, along with bits of pottery, capitals and marble plaques. More interesting is a **tour** down into the site proper, where excavations are ongoing; try to glean what you can from the various arches, theatre segments, latrines, column bases and supporting walls that make up the cellar of the current building. The real interest is in the close dissection of one city block over two thousand years – an exercise that could presumably be equally well applied to almost any city corner in Rome.

2

The Ghetto

Bus #40 from Termini

Across Via Arenula from the Campo de' Fiori area, the contrast with stately Via Giulia can be felt immediately, where the crumbling area of the **Ghetto**, and its narrow, confusing switchback streets and alleys (round which you can take tours; see p.60), makes for one of Rome's most atmospheric neighbourhoods – and one of its most resurgent, with lots of kosher cafés and restaurants serving some of the city's best traditional Roman cuisine and a host of other Jewish-related shops (see box below).

Via Portico d'Ottavia

The main artery of the Jewish area is **Via Portico d'Ottavia**, a short pedestrian street which leads southeast from Via Arenula to the **Portico d'Ottavia**, a not terribly well-preserved second-century BC gate, rebuilt by Augustus and dedicated to his sister in 23 BC, and then rebuilt again by Septimius Severus in 203 AD.

Teatro di Marcello

Between Via Portico d'Ottavia and Via del Teatro di Marcello · Daily 9am–7pm, winter till 6pm · ⓦ tempietto.it

The Portico d'Ottavia is next door to the **Teatro di Marcello**, and together they form a site of mild interest and a short cut through to **Via del Teatro di Marcello** and the **Capitoline Hill**. The theatre has served many purposes over the years: begun by Julius

---

THE JEWS OF ROME

Rome's **Jewish population** stretches as far back as the second century BC, and, as the empire expanded into the Middle East, their numbers eventually swelled to around forty thousand, but they were never an especially persecuted group until 1555, when Pope Paul IV issued a series of punitive laws that forced them into what was then one of the city's most squalid districts, right by the river and prone to flooding from the Tiber. A wall was built around the area, and all Jews, in a chilling omen of things to come, were made to wear yellow caps and shawls when they left the district; they were also only allowed to practise two professions: buying and selling clothes and money-lending. Later, after Unification, the **ghetto** was opened up, but during the 1930s, under Mussolini's racial legislation, they were still barred from certain professions and prohibited from marrying non-Jews. The **Nazi occupation** in 1943 brought inevitable deportations, but the majority of Rome's Jewish population survived and currently numbers roughly fourteen thousand (around half Italy's total); although only a fraction of that number actually live in the Ghetto, it is an ethnically thriving district, with new kosher restaurants, shops and other businesses opening all the time. Ironically, too, it has become one of the most sought-after – and expensive – parts of the city centre in which to live. Who would have thought it, back in 1555?

Caesar and finished by Augustus, it was pillaged in the fourth century and not properly restored until the Middle Ages, after which it became a formidable fortified palace for a succession of different rulers, including the Orsini family. It has been recently restored and provides a grand backdrop for classical concerts in the summer (see p.273).

Piazza Mattei and the Palazzo Mattei

On the north side of Via Portico d'Ottavia, narrow Via della Reginella leads to **Piazza Mattei**, whose **Fontana delle Tartarughe**, or "Turtle Fountain", is a delightful late-sixteenth-century creation, perhaps restored by Bernini, who apparently added the tortoises. The **Palazzo Mattei**, designed by Carlo Maderno, flanks one side of the square, and stretches down Via dei Funari ("Ropemakers' Street") to the corner of Via Michelangelo Caetani. The palace is now partly occupied by the Centro degli Studi Americani, but it's possible to wander into the courtyard, whose antique friezes and statues still give some sense of the power and grandeur of this once-great Roman family, former patrons of a young Caravaggio, who lived here for a short time.

Santa Maria in Portico

Piazza di Campitelli 9 • Daily 7am–12.30pm & 3.30–7pm • ⓦ santamariainportico.it

Santa Maria in Portico (or Santa Maria in Campitelli), opposite the Irish Embassy on Piazza di Campitelli, is a heavy, ornate church built by **Carlo Rainaldi** in 1667 to house an ancient enamel image of the **Virgin Mary**, deemed to have miraculous powers following respite from a plague. The image was originally housed in another church on Via Portico d'Ottavia but was moved here by Pope Alexander VII so as to be in more appropriately splendid surroundings. Everything in the church focuses on this small framed picture, encased in an incredibly ornate golden altarpiece, which fills the entire space between the clustered columns of the apse. It's actually quite hard to see, but **votive images** all around the church give you a close-up look. There's not much else in the church, although the paintings, including a dramatic *Virgin with Saints* by Luca Giordano, in the second chapel on the right, represent Baroque at its most rampant, while opposite, a chapel contains the body of **St John Leonardi**, who was made the patron saint of pharmacists by Benedict XVI in 2006, and who wrote a history of the church's revered icon in the early seventeenth century.

Palazzo Cenci

Piazza delle Cinque Scole

Just south of Via Portico d'Ottavia, **Piazza delle Cinque Scole**, named for the five religious schools that once stood here, is overlooked by one side of the **Palazzo Cenci**, which huddles into the dark streets here. It's a reminder of the untimely death of one **Beatrice Cenci**, who was executed, with her stepmother, on the Ponte Sant'Angelo in 1599 for the murder of her incestuous father – a story immortalized in verse by Shelley and in paint by an unknown artist whose portrait of the unfortunate Beatrice still hangs in the Palazzo Barberini.

Synagogue and Museo Ebraica

Lungotevere Cenci X • **Museum** Mid-June to mid-Sept Mon–Thurs & Sun 10am–4.15pm, Fri 9am–1.15pm; mid-Sept to mid-June daily 10am–6.15pm, Fri till 3.15pm; closed Sat & Jewish hols • €10 • **Guided Ghetto tours** Regularly throughout the day; 50min • €8 • **Regular synagogue tours** Regularly throughout the day; 20min • Free • ☎ 06 6840 0661, ⓦ museoebraico.roma.it

At the far end of Via Portico d' Ottavia is the area's principal Jewish sight: the huge **synagogue**, built in 1904 and dominating the streets around and indeed the river beyond with its bulk. Carabinieri stand guard 24 hours a day outside, ever since a PLO attack on the building in 1982 killed a 2-year-old boy (Stefano Gay Taché) and injured many others; a free-standing plaque marks the spot.

The **Museo Ebraica**, in the bowels of the building, spreads through several rooms and covering several major themes – in Italian, Hebrew and English – including **Jewish** ritual (Italian Jews are neither purely Sephardic nor Ashkenazi), the **history** of the Jews in Rome and the Ghetto in particular, and of course the **war years**, when around two thousand citizens were deported from the area (most didn't return). There are also bits and pieces from the previous synagogue on display, a variety of ritual cloths and textiles and wartime posters and propaganda. You have to take a **tour** to see the "**tempio maggiore**" or synagogue upstairs – actually one of sixteen in Rome, but definitely the grandest, built in orthodox style with seating for men downstairs and women in the side galleries. The impressive interior rises to a high, rainbow-hued dome, and the tours give good background on the building and the Jewish community in general.

Isola Tiberina
Almost opposite the synagogue, the **Ponte Fabricio** crosses the Tiber to **Isola Tiberina**. Built in 62 BC, it's the only classical bridge to remain intact without help from the restorers (the Ponte Cestio, on the other side of the island, was partially rebuilt in the last century). The **island** itself offers a calm respite from the city centre proper, and is mostly given over to Rome's oldest **hospital**, the **Fatebenefratelli**, founded in 1548 – appropriately, it would seem, as the island was originally home to a third-century BC temple of Aesclepius, the Roman god of healing. Beyond Isola Tiberina, you can see the remains of the **Ponte Rotto** (Broken Bridge) on the river, all that remains of the first stone bridge to span the Tiber. Built between 179 and 142 BC, it collapsed at the end of the sixteenth century.

San Bartolomeo
Piazza di San Bartolomeo all'Isola • Mon–Sat 9am–1pm & 3.30–5.30pm, Sun 9am–1pm & 6.30–8pm • W sanbartolomeo.org

Opposite the Fatebenefratelli's entrance, the church of **San Bartolomeo** stands on the original site of the temple of Aesclepius, and is worth a peep inside for its ancient columns, probably rescued from the temple, and an ancient wellhead on the altar steps, carved with figures relating to the founding of the church, including St Bartholomew himself. The saint also features in the painting above the altar, hands tied above his head, on the point of being skinned alive – his famous and gruesome mode of martyrdom.

Piazza Venezia and the Capitoline Hill

For many people, the modern centre of Rome is Piazza Venezia – not so much a square as a road junction, and a busy one at that, but a good place to start your wanderings, midway between the Renaissance centre and most of the city's ancient ruins. Flanked on all sides by imposing buildings, the piazza is a dignified focal point, and a spot you'll find yourself returning to time and again. The great white bulk of the Vittorio Emanuele monument also makes it Rome's best landmarked open space by some way. The Vittoriano, as it's known, is one of the key sights in the city, both for its views and for the alternative route it gives to the Piazza del Campidoglio and the unmissable museums on the Capitoline Hill, the first-settled and most central of Rome's seven hills.

Piazza Venezia and around

Many transport routes converge on Piazza Venezia, but buses #40, #62 and #64 are a quick way to get here from Termini; tram #8 connects Piazza Venezia with Trastevere

There's not much need to hang about on **Piazza Venezia** itself: it's more a place to catch a bus or pick up a taxi than soak up the atmosphere. A legacy of nineteenth-century Rome, it looked quite different a couple of hundred years ago, when it was the domain of the Venetian pope, Paul II, whose **Palazzo Venezia** dominated this part of the city, its gardens reaching around its south side, where the Vittoriano now stands.

Palazzo Venezia

Via del Plebiscito 118 • Tues–Sun 8.30am–7.30pm • €5 • ☎ 06 32810, ⓦ galleriaborghese.it

Taking up the western side of Piazza Venezia is the first large Renaissance palace in the city, **Palazzo Venezia**, built in the mid-fifteenth century and for several centuries the embassy of the Venetian Republic. Famously, **Mussolini** moved in here while in power, occupying the vast Sala del Mappamondo (unfortunately only viewable if you're attending an exhibition) and making his declamatory speeches to the huge crowds below from the small balcony facing onto the piazza proper. In those days, the palace lights would be left on to give the impression of constant activity in what was the centre of the Fascist government and war effort. Now, it's a more peripheral building, a venue for good temporary exhibitions and home, on the first floor, to a Renaissance art museum.

Museo Nazionale di Palazzo Venezia

The arts and crafts in the Museo Nazionale di **Palazzo Venezia** are made up of the magpie-ish collection of Pope Paul II. The paintings include a large number of fifteenth-century devotional works from central and northern Italy.

Among numerous Crucifixions and Madonnas, look out for an arresting double portrait of two young men by **Giorgione** in the first room; a late-sixteenth-century *Deposition of Christ* by **Borgianni** in room 6, in which Christ is viewed from the feet up by way of clever use of perspective (a copy, basically, of Mantegna's painting of the same subject); and, in a small anteroom, **Algardi**'s 1650 bust of a severe-looking Innocent X (worth seeing, if only for comparison with Bernini's more celebrated depiction in the Galleria Doria Pamphilj; see p.37). There are also a number of polychromatic wooden **statues**, notably two figures from a Magi group from Le Marche and a lovely *Madonna and Child* from Lazio, both thirteenth-century. The ceiling paintings in room 7 are by **Vasari**, and depict Ceres, the Roman goddess of agriculture and the various months and seasons; they were in fact designed for another building and moved here in the late nineteenth century.

Beyond here, a corridor lined with ceramics skirts the courtyard to link with the *palazzetto* next door, where you can find a couple of rooms of beautifully displayed **bronzes** – a wide array of figures, animals and copies of ancient sculptures by **Bernini** and **Giambologna**, among others. Around the corner are more sculptural pieces, including a tortured head of Seneca, by **Guido Reni**, and **Algardi**'s representation of San Filippo Neri with an angel, a study of St Theresa for Bernini's statue in the church of Santa Maria Vittoria, and some designs for the Trevi Fountain by **Pietro Bracci**; finally, there are some rooms full of weapons and ceramic jars from an ancient monastic pharmacy. Walk out to the palace's upper loggia for a view over the palm-filled courtyard – the loggia is crammed full of ancient sculptural fragments, and the **gardens** are some of the prettiest in Rome.

San Marco

Piazza di San Marco 52 • Tues–Sat 9am–12.30pm & 4–6pm, Sun 9am–1pm & 4–8pm • ⓦ sanmarcoevangelista.it

Adjacent to the Palazzo Venezia, on its southern side, the church of **San Marco**, accessible from Piazza San Marco, is one of the oldest basilicas in Rome. This dark,

3

cosy church was founded in 336 AD on the spot where the apostle is supposed to have lived while in the city. It was rebuilt in 833 and added to by various Renaissance and eighteenth-century popes – Paul II restored it and added the graceful portico and gilded ceiling. It has a beautiful Cosmati-work floor, and an apse **mosaic** which dates from the ninth century and shows Pope Gregory IV offering his church to Christ, above a gracious semicircle of sheep that bear more than a passing resemblance to

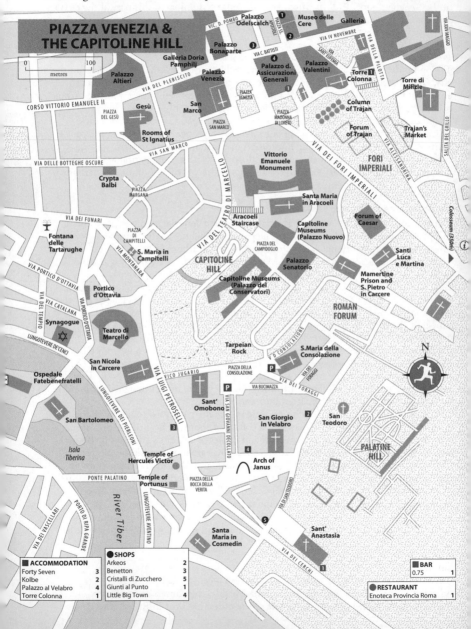

PIAZZA VENEZIA & THE CAPITOLINE HILL

◼ ACCOMMODATION	
Forty Seven	3
Kolbe	2
Palazzo al Velabro	4
Torre Colonna	1

● SHOPS	
Arkeos	2
Benetton	3
Cristalli di Zucchero	5
Giunti al Punto	1
Little Big Town	4

◼ BAR	
0.75	1

● RESTAURANT	
Enoteca Provincia Roma	1

llamas. Back outside, tucked away in the corner, the statue of the busty harridan is "**Madam Lucretia**", actually an ancient depiction of Isis. Like Pasquino a few hundred metres away, she is one of Rome's so-called talking statues (see box, p.66), commenting in a satirical fashion on the affairs of the day.

Palazzo Bonaparte

On the northern side of Piazza Venezia, the canyon of Via del Corso, Rome's main street, begins its journey to the other side of the city centre at the Piazza del Popolo, its opening stretch flanked by the nineteenth-century **Palazzo Bonaparte** on the left, with its green-shuttered balcony. It was from here that Napoleon's mother Letizia Bonaparte, who lived here after he was deposed until her death in 1836, used to keep an eye on the comings and goings outside, though nowadays it's privately owned and the shutters are usually closed.

Palazzo Valentini

Via IV November 119a • Daily except Tues 9.30am–5.30pm • €10, booking and tours obligatory • ☎ 06 32810, ⓦ palazzovalentini.it

Just off Piazza Venezia, the solid, late-sixteenth-century **Palazzo Valentini** is the home of Rome's regional government and as such is a busy place, full of scurrying office workers and folk trying to find their way to appointments. But it's also the location of some recent archaeological **excavations** which uncovered ancient Roman baths and a residential complex, and these have in part been opened up to the public. **Tours** are high-tech affairs, breathlessly narrated and deliberately dramatic, but they succeed pretty well in bringing the excavations to life, with glass floors and catwalks taking you through the site and technology that recreates the rooms as they might have looked in ancient times. In the baths complex, there are patches of marble and opus sectile floor, fragments of statuary, columns and other artefacts that were found down here, along with part of a neighbouring house – equally fine, and with stretches of mosaic flooring in between medieval foundations. It's not just an exercise in Roman archaeology either: some of the pieces – various ceramics, and even the remains of somebody's dinner – date back to the original sixteenth-century palace, when the site was used as a dumping ground for rubbish.

Vittoriano

Piazza Venezia 3 • Daily 9.30am–6pm; lifts daily 9.30am–6.30pm, Fri–Sun till 7.30pm • €7 • ☎ 06 699 1718

The other buildings on Piazza Venezia pale into insignificance beside the marble monstrosity rearing up across the street from San Marco – the Vittorio Emanuele Monument or **Vittoriano**, erected at the end of the nineteenth century as the "Altar of the Nation" to commemorate Italian Unification. It has been variously likened to a typewriter (because of its shape), and, by American GIs, to a wedding cake (the white marble used will never mellow with age). King Vittorio Emanuele II, by all accounts a modest man, probably wouldn't have thought much of it. Indeed, the only person who seems to have benefited from the building is the prime minister at the time who was a deputy for Brescia, from where (perhaps not entirely coincidentally) the marble was supplied.

There are things to see inside the monument (see below) but it's the **outside** of the structure that should command most of your attention, and it's great to clamber up and down the sweeping terraces and flights of steps which once upon a time you could only gaze at from the street. The structure is full of the weighty **symbolism** that was typical of the period. The figures either side of the entrance represent the two seas that surround Italy – the Tyrrhenian (on the right) and the Adriatic (on the left). At the top of the first lot of stairs is the Tomb of the Unknown Soldier, flanked by eternal flames and a permanent guard of honour, behind which a huge 1920s bas-relief represents the nation, focused on a figure of Minerva – for Rome – in the centre.

Up another flight of stairs sits the figure of Vittorio Emanuele II on horseback, at 10m x 12m one of the **world's largest statues** (his moustache alone is 3m long, and apparently twenty people once had lunch in the horse's belly), on a plinth friezed with figures representing the major cities of the Italian Republic. Above here, the huge, sweeping **gallery** stretches the width of the monument, with figures symbolizing the regions of Italy, while behind, glass lifts whisk you to the top of the monument for amazing views from between the massive *quadriglie*, or chariots, on each side. The whole thing is undeniably impressive, if only for the sheer audaciousness of its conception. Wherever you stand, though, the **views** of the city are the thing, perhaps because it's the one place in Rome from which you can't see the Vittoriano. There's a café around the back, from where you can take a very useful short cut through to Piazza del Campidoglio behind (see p.67).

The Vittoriano's museums

Daily 9.30am–6pm • Free

Inside the Vittoriano, the engaging **Museo di Risorgimento** follows the long corridor that runs around the back of the building, full of busts, weaponry and mementoes of the Unification struggle and beyond. There's also a gallery of flags from various Italian regiments, which gives onto the **Tomb of the Unknown Soldier** itself, along with the story of the transportation and ceremonial interment of the body in 1921. Finally, temporary art and other exhibitions are held in the echoing chambers of the so-called **Complesso del Vittoriano**, which makes up the southeastern wing of the monument, accessible from Via di San Pietro in Carcere.

Capitoline Hill

The real pity about the Vittoriano is that it obscures views of the **Capitoline Hill** behind – once, in the days of imperial Rome, the spiritual and political centre of the Roman Empire. The upside of this is that it gives a perfect route to the Capitoline, via the café right behind the Vittoriano and a passageway that delivers you right by the back entrance of Santa Maria in Aracoeli (see p.67), and just above the Piazza del Campidoglio.

The Capitoline's name derives from its position as the *caput mundi*, or **head of the world**", and its influence and importance resonate to this day, not least in language – "capitol" and "capital" originated here, as did "money", which comes from the temple to Juno Moneta that once stood on the hill and housed the Roman mint. The Capitoline also played a significant role in medieval and Renaissance times: the flamboyant fourteenth-century dictator, **Cola di Rienzo**, stood here in triumph in 1347 and was murdered here by an angry mob seven years later – a humble nineteenth-century statue marks the spot where he is said to have died. **Michelangelo** gave the hill's Piazza del

---

ROME'S TALKING STATUES

As the home of the papacy, Rome has long been a political city, and its people have always enjoyed commenting on and arguing about the important issues of the day. In Renaissance times, the antics of the Church, in particular the pope and the powerful Roman families who vied to fill the post, were the subject of intense curiosity and scrutiny. A number of "**talking statues**" – usually ancient, unidentified pieces, among them Madam Lucretia outside the basilica of San Marco; Pasquino just off Piazza Navona; the "baboon" on Via del Babuino; the "facchino", or porter, on Via Lata, just off Via del Corso; and Marforio, now in the courtyard of the Palazzo Nuovo – were a focus for this. They were hung with witty rhymes and notes commenting on the hubris and foolishness of the movers and shakers of the papal city, a kind of gossip column-cum-parliamentary sketch where people would gather to talk and laugh at their political masters.

Campidoglio its present form, redesigning it as a symbol of Rome's regeneration after the city was sacked by the troops of Holy Roman Emperor Charles V in 1527. These days, the Capitoline forms a tight, self-contained group of essential attractions, with the focus on its pair of **museums** and the **church** of Santa Maria in Aracoeli.

Santa Maria in Aracoeli

Piazza del Campidoglio 4 • Daily 9am–12.30pm & 2.30–5.30pm • Access via Aracoeli Staircase, or avoid the steps by going via Piazza del Campidoglio or the back of the Vittoriano

The church of **Santa Maria in Aracoeli** crowns the highest point on the Capitoline Hill and is built on the site of a temple to Jupiter where, according to legend, the Tiburtine Sibyl foretold the birth of Christ. The flight of steps that lead up here, the **Aracoeli Staircase**, was erected by Cola di Rienzo in 1348 and is one of the city's steepest climbs. The church, one of Rome's most ancient basilicas, is worth the climb. Inside, in the first chapel on the right, there are some fine, humane **frescoes** by Pinturicchio recording the life of San Bernardino, with realistic tableaux of landscapes and bustling town scenes. There are also some older, more recently uncovered fragments of fresco by Pietro Cavallini further down the same aisle, most notably a beautiful *Madonna and Child* – which is in keeping with the church's best-known feature, the so-called **Bambino**, a small statue of the child Christ that was carved from the wood of a Gethsemane olive tree. Said to have healing powers, the statue was traditionally called out to the sickbeds of the ill and dying all over the city, its coach commanding instant right of way through the heavy Rome traffic. The Bambino was stolen in 1994, however, and a copy now stands in its place, in a small chapel to the left of the high altar.

Piazza del Campidoglio and the Capitoline Museums

Both museums are on Piazza del Campidoglio • Tues–Sun 9am–8pm • €13, joint ticket with Centrale Montemartini (see p.145) €15; audioguide €5 • ☏ 06 0608, ⓦ museicapitolini.org • Bus #H from Termini

Next door to the Aracoeli Staircase, the **Cordonata** is an elegant, smoothly rising ramp, and as such a much gentler climb. Topped with Roman statues of Castor and Pollux, it leads to **Piazza del Campidoglio**, one of Rome's most perfectly proportioned squares, designed by Michelangelo in the last years of his life for Pope Paul III, who was determined to hammer Rome back into shape for a visit by the Holy Roman Emperor, Charles V. In fact, Michelangelo died before his plan was completed (the square wasn't finished until the late seventeenth century), but his designs were faithfully executed, balancing the piazza, redesigning the facade of what is now Palazzo dei Conservatori and projecting an identical building across the way, known as Palazzo Nuovo. These buildings, which have been completely renovated in recent years, are home to the **Capitoline Museums** and feature some of the city's most important ancient sculpture.

Both are angled slightly to focus on **Palazzo Senatorio**, Rome's town hall, with its double staircase and fountain, flanked by statues representing the Tiber and the Nile. In the centre of the square, Michelangelo placed an equestrian statue of Emperor Marcus Aurelius, which had previously stood unharmed for years outside San Giovanni in Laterano; early Christians had refrained from melting it down because they believed it to be of the Emperor Constantine (the first Roman ruler to acknowledge and follow Christianity). The original is now beautifully displayed in the new wing of the Palazzo dei Conservatori, and a copy has taken its place at the centre of the piazza.

If you see no other museums of ancient sculpture in Rome, try at least to see the Capitoline Museums, perhaps the most venerable of all the city's collections. They're divided into two parts, one devoted only to **sculpture**, the other more extensive and wide-ranging with a gallery of **paintings** as well. You should, if possible, see both areas of the museum rather than choosing one, and tickets remain valid all day, so you can easily take a break for a stroll around the other Capitoline sights in between.

Palazzo dei Conservatori

The **Palazzo dei Conservatori** which occupies the right-hand side of the Piazza del Campidoglio is perhaps the natural place to start a tour of the Capitoline Museums, home as it is to the ticket office and the larger, more varied collection, with ancient sculpture on the first floor and in the new wing at the back, and paintings on the second floor. It has undergone quite a transformation in recent years with the incorporation of the Palazzo Caffarelli-Clementino into the museum, with its new wing housing some large ancient statuary and the newly discovered foundations of the Capitoline's original temple of Jupiter.

Ground and first floors

Some of the museum's ancient sculpture is littered around the ground-floor **courtyard** by the entrance – most impressively the feet, hand and other fragments of a gigantic statue, believed to be of the Emperor Constantine, and one of the most popular images of Rome. Upstairs, the first room you enter is the massive **Sala degli Orazi e Curiazi**, where the curators of the collections used to meet, appropriately decorated with giant late-sixteenth-century frescoes showing legendary tales from the early days of the city – the *Discovery of the She-wolf*, at the western end, faces the *Rape of the Sabine Women* at the opposite end, while presiding over all are colossal statues of Pope Urban VIII and his successor Innocent X, by Bernini and Algardi respectively. Appropriately, it was the venue for the signing of the Treaty of Rome in 1957, and for the presentation of the EU's ill-fated draft constitution nearly fifty years later.

The rooms that follow have more friezes and murals showing events from Roman history, notably the **Sala dei Capitani**, which celebrates various generals with statues in Roman military dress, among them Marco Antonio Colonna, who famously defeated the Turks at Lepanto in 1571, and Carlo Barberini (brother of pope Urban VIII), by Bernini and Algardi. The corner room beyond contains the so-called *Spinario*, a Roman statue of a boy picking a thorn out of his foot, and a striking bronze head, known as Brutus, from the fourth century BC. The sacred symbol of Rome, the Etruscan bronze she-wolf nursing **Romulus and Remus**, the mythic founders of the city, gets a room to itself next door; the twins themselves are not Etruscan but were added by Pollaiuolo in the late fifteenth century while, on the walls, the Fasti are an amazing record of magistrates and other political figures from the height of the Augustan age, rescued from the Forum.

The next-door room is given over to two bronze Roman geese and a bust of Michelangelo, which Daniele da Volterra based on the artist's death mask, while further on there are more **Roman bronzes** – eagles this time – in a room with a Roman sculpture of the breast-laden Diana of Ephesus. Retrace your steps slightly for the **Sala di Annibale**, covered in wonderfully vivid fifteenth-century paintings recording Rome's wars with Carthage, and so named for a rendering of Hannibal seated impressively on an elephant, before moving on to the airy new wing, where the original statue of Marcus Aurelius, formerly in the square outside, takes centre stage. Alongside it stand a giant bronze statue of Constantine (or at least its head, hand and orb), a rippling bronze of Hercules, found near the Circus of Maxentius, plus a full-size statue of Helena, the mother of Constantine, reclining gracefully. Behind are part of the foundations and a retaining wall from the Capitoline's original temple of Jupiter, discovered when the work for the new wing was undertaken.

There are some great exhibits around the main hall here: some remnants from the **Iron Age** on the Capitoline, statuary rescued from ancient gardens on the Esquiline Hill, including a statue of the Emperor Commodus – the son of the decidedly more heroic Marcus Aurelius – as Hercules, the milk-white Esquiline Venus and plenty more besides. When museum fatigue sets in, you can climb up to the second-floor **café**, whose terrace commands one of the best views in Rome.

3

Second floor

The second-floor picture gallery (*pinacoteca*) holds **Renaissance painting** from the fourteenth to the late-seventeenth century, with labels in Italian and English. The collection fills nine rooms, and **highlights** include a couple of portraits by Van Dyck and a penetrating *Portrait of a Crossbowman* by Lorenzo Lotto; a pair of paintings from 1590 by Tintoretto – a *Baptism of Christ* and a *Flagellation*; some nice small-scale work by Annibale Carracci; and a very fine early work by Ludovico Carracci, *Head of a Boy*. There are also several sugary pieces by Guido Reni, done at the end of his life, including St Sebastian. In one of two large galleries, there's a vast picture by Guercino depicting the *Burial of Santa Petronilla* (an early Roman martyr who was the supposed daughter of St Peter), which used to hang in St Peter's and arrived here via the Quirinale palace and the Louvre. It is displayed alongside several other works by the same artist, notably a lovely, contemplative Persian Sibyl and a wonderful picture of Cleopatra cowed before a young and victorious Octavius (later Augustus), and two paintings by Caravaggio, one a replica of the young John the Baptist which hangs in the Galleria Doria Pamphilj, the other a famous canvas known as *The Fortune-Teller* – an early work that's an adept study in deception. The large room at the back holds paintings from the Sacchetti collection, which includes a number of works by Pietro da Cortona, among them portraits of his patron Marchese Matteo Sacchetti and the steely Pope Urban VIII, as well as his lively depiction of the *Rape of the Sabine Women* – credited with kick-starting the Baroque age in 1630.

Palazzo Nuovo

Palazzo Nuovo, across the square from the Palazzo dei Conservatori, is also accessible by way of an underground **walkway** that takes in yet more sculpture, the remains of a Roman temple and a terrace which has probably the best, and certainly the most close-up, views of the Roman Forum just below. The Palazzo Nuovo is the more manageable of the two Capitoline Museums, its first floor concentrating some of the best of the city's Roman sculpture into half a dozen or so rooms and a long gallery crammed with elegant statuary.

There's the remarkable, controlled statue of the *Dying Gaul*, a Roman copy of a Greek original; a naturalistic *Boy with Goose* – another copy; an original, grappling Eros and Psyche; a *Satyr Resting*, after a piece by Praxiteles, that was the inspiration for Nathaniel Hawthorne's book *The Marble Faun*; and the red marble *Laughing Silenus*, another Roman copy of a Hellenistic original. In the main **Salone**, statues of an old and a young centaur face each other, and a naturalistic hunter holds up a rabbit he has just killed. Walk through from here to the **Sala degli Imperatori**, with its busts of Roman emperors and other famous names, including a young Augustus and a cruel Caracalla, and the **Sala dei Filosofi**, with portrait busts of lots of well-known ancient thinkers such as Socrates and Pythagoras, as well as political wheeler-dealers like Cicero. Also, don't miss the *Capitoline Venus* – a coy, delicate piece, again based on a work by Praxiteles, housed in a room on its own. Finally, the **palace courtyard** is dominated by the large **Fountain of Marforio**, a bearded figure who was known as one of Rome's "talking statues" (see box, p.66), renowned in Renaissance times for speaking out in satirical verse against the authorities.

Tarpeian Rock

After seeing the Capitoline Museums, take a walk around behind the Palazzo Senatorio for another great view down over the Forum, with the Colosseum in the background. There's a copy of the statue of Romulus and Remus suckling the she-wolf here, while on the right, Via di Monte Tarpeio follows the brink of the old **Tarpeian Rock** – named after Tarpeia, who betrayed the city to the Sabines – from which traitors were thrown in ancient times.

Mamertine Prison

Clivo Argentario 1 • Daily 9am–7.30pm • €5 including headsets tour • ☎ 06 8881 6186, ⓦ operaromanapellegrinaggi.org

Steps lead down from the Piazza del Campidoglio to the edge of the Forum (though you can no longer enter here) and **San Pietro in Carcere**, a low-vaulted church that lies above the ancient **Mamertine Prison**. Spies, vanquished soldiers and other enemies of the state, including St Peter and St Paul, were incarcerated here during Roman times. The church and prison, together with some recent excavations of stretches of city wall, are now part of a multimedia-assisted **tour**, taking in the murky depths of the jail, in which you can see the column to which St Peter was chained, along with the spring the saint is said to have used to baptize his guards and other prisoners. There's a make-do altar and a cross – upside-down, because this was how Peter was (at his own request) crucified. At the top of the staircase, hollowed out of the honeycomb of stone, is an imprint claimed to be of St Peter's head as he tumbled down the stairs (though when the prison was in use, the only access was through a hole in the ceiling, which is still there). Other parts of the tours take in further excavations and a film on the life and times of the saint, finishing with a brief bit of evangelizing in the church above.

3

Santi Luca e Martina

Via della Curia 2 • Sat 9am–8pm, Oct–April till 6pm • ⓦ www.accademiasanluca.it/chiesa

Opposite San Pietro in Carcere, the church of **Santi Luca e Martina** is two churches in one, an elegant building that has been here since the eighth century, when it was dedicated to the little-known Christian martyr Martina, who preached on this site back in the third century AD. Later, it was given by Sixtus V to the artists' group, Accademia San Luca, who dedicated it to St Luke, the patron saint of painters, as well, and had it rebuilt in the mid-seventeenth century by Pietro da Cortona, who in turn is buried in the church in a tomb of his own design. These days, the upper church is dedicated to Santa Martina, with a statue of the saint on the altar, and the lower to St Luke, with an altar by Pietro da Cortona and two works by Alessandro Algardi: a newly restored bas-relief of the *Deposition of Christ* and a terracotta Pietà.

San Nicola in Carcere

Via del Teatro di Marcello 46 • Daily 4–7pm, closed Aug • Excavations €3 • Bus #H from Termini

Immediately south of the Capitoline Hill, a little way down Via del Teatro di Marcello, the church of **San Nicola in Carcere** was built in the eighth century on the site of three Republican temples. It was later dedicated to St Nicholas, the patron saint of seafarers – this used to be the riverfront, and was the site of a lively fish market. The church is nice enough, but the real interest is in the **ancient remnants** it incorporates. The nave is formed by a wonderful mixture of ancient columns, both Ionic and Corinthian, while down below, informal guided tours of the excavations show how the church is supported by the central Temple of Juno and the columns of two temples either side. You can walk down the narrow Roman street that ran between the temples, squeezing between the massive blocks of the central temple and the column bases of the Temple of Janus that hold up one side of the church – columns that are clearly visible on the outside, too.

Santa Maria della Consolazione

Piazza della Consolazione 94 • Daily 6am–noon & 3.30–6.30pm • Bus #H from Termini

Just off Via del Teatro di Marcello, on the eastern side of the Capitoline Hill, the church of **Santa Maria della Consolazione** was originally the chapel of a hospital that used to exist just behind. Inside, the Mattei chapel, immediately to the right of the entrance, has a wonderful series of **frescoes** by Zuccari depicting scenes from the life of Christ, including a naturalistic and dynamic flagellation scene on the left.

San Teodoro

Via di San Teodoro 7 • Mon–Fri 9.30am–12.30pm • Bus #H from Termini

A few steps from the church of Santa Maria della Consolazione, between the Capitoline and Palatine hills, the round church of **San Teodoro** is Rome's Greek national church; it's an ancient structure, though one that has been somewhat smoothed over inside by the paint and plaster of later years. St Theodore was martyred on this spot in the fourth century AD, and the church originally dates from the sixth century. The apse **mosaics** are contemporary with the original church, and show Christ with saints, including a bearded Theodore, next to St Peter on the right.

Sant' Anastasia

Via di San Teodoro 1 • 24hr • Bus #170 from Termini

Tucked right up against the Palatine Hill, just off the Circo Massimo, the basilica of **Sant' Anastasia** is a very ancient church, founded by a Roman noblewoman (called Anastasia) in the fourth century and later dedicated to the saint of the same name. It's a great example of how Roman churches can be very old but have been so refurbished over the years that they feel anything but. It apparently has extensive remains of a Roman house below its floor, but these are normally closed to the public, and in fact the church was itself closed until relatively recently due to the instability of its foundations. However, since 2001, it has been a designated centre of "**Perpetual Adoration**", which means it's open all the time, with someone always present at prayer.

Temples of Portunus and Hercules Victor

Piazza della Bocca della Verità • No inside access

Down towards the Tiber, Via di Teatro di Marcello becomes Via Luigi Petroselli and meets the riverside highway at **Piazza della Bocca della Verità**, also known as the Forum Boarium due to its function as a cattle market in ancient times. This marketplace contains two of the city's better-preserved Roman temples, the **Temple of Portunus** and the **Temple of Hercules Victor** – the latter long known as the Temple of Vesta because, like all vestal temples, it is circular. Both date from the end of the second century BC, and although you can't get inside, they're fine examples of Republican-era places of worship; the Temple of Hercules Victor is, for what it's worth, the oldest surviving marble structure in Rome.

Santa Maria in Cosmedin

Piazza della Bocca della Verità 18 • Daily 9.30am–5.50pm • Crypt chapel €1 • Bus #170 from Termini

Most people don't bother to enter the church of **Santa Maria in Cosmedin**, which is a shame, because it's one of Rome's most beautiful and typical medieval basilicas, with a thirteenth-century baldacchino over a pink ancient Roman bathtub that serves as the altar and a colourful and ingenious Cosmati mosaic floor. You can visit a small crypt chapel built by Pope Hadrian I in the eighth century and supported by a pillar literally hammered into the floor, and the sacristy acts as a rather dowdy gift shop and displays one of the church's greatest treasures – an eighth-century mosaic of the *Adoration of the Magi*. However, the church's fame rests on the so-called **Bocca della Verità** ("Mouth of Truth") in the portico outside, an ancient Roman drain cover in the shape of an enormous face that in medieval times would apparently swallow the hand of anyone who hadn't told the truth. It was particularly popular with husbands anxious to test the faithfulness of their wives; now it is one of the city's biggest tour-bus attractions, and there are queues most of the day of people having their photograph taken with their hand inside – Roman tourism at its most banal.

San Giorgio in Velabro and around

Via del Velabro 19 • Daily 9am–7pm • ☎ 06 6979 7536, ⓦ sangiorgioinvelabro.org • Bus #170 from Termini

On its northern side, Piazza della Bocca della Verità peters out peacefully at the stolid **Arch of Janus**, perhaps Rome's most weathered triumphal arch, beyond which the campanile of the church of **San Giorgio in Velabro** is a stunted echo of that of Santa Maria across the way. Inside is one of the city's barest and most beautiful old basilicas, an ancient-columned nave lit by bare stone windows carved with an intricate design. Only the late-twelfth-century fresco in the apse, the work of Pietro Cavallini, lightens the melancholy mood, showing Christ and the Virgin, and various saints, including St George on the left, to whom the church is dedicated – and whose cranial bones lie in the reliquary under the high altar canopy, placed here in 749 AD shortly after the original basilica was built.

Immediately to the left of the church, the building incorporates a small arch, erected by the Forum Boarium market traders in honour of Septimius Severus and his family – whose portraits you can see on the inside (although it's often fenced off these days), apart from that of his son Geta which, like the version on Septimius Severus's arch in the main forum, was erased after his assassination by his brother Caracalla. Opposite the church, behind an iron gate, you can see the arches of the **Cloaca Maxima**, the ancient city's main sewer, which emerges on the Tiber just to the left of the nearby Ponte Palatino.

Ponte Palatino

The busy **Ponte Palatino**, which connects the Capitoline side of the river to Trastevere on the opposite bank, is sometimes known as the "English Bridge" for the way the traffic flows across on it on the left (facilitating U-turns from the right to left bank of the river). Look closely at the right bank of the river from the bridge itself and you should be able to spot the giant arch placed there to take the outflow of the ancient Cloaca Maxima sewer, now overgrown with trees and bushes.

3

LOOKING TOWARDS THE TEMPLE OF SATURN IN THE ROMAN FOR

Ancient Rome

There are remnants of Rome's ancient glories all over the city, but the most concentrated and central grouping is in the area stretching southeast from the Capitoline Hill, which we've called ancient Rome. Mussolini ploughed Via dei Fori Imperiali through here in the 1930s with the idea of turning it into a massive archaeological park, and to an extent that's exactly what it is; you can easily spend a day or more lazily picking your way through the rubble of what was once the heart of the ancient world. An obvious place to start is the Forum, immediately below the Capitoline Hill, before heading up the greener heights of the Palatine Hill or continuing on to the Colosseum. Try also to see Trajan's Markets, across the street, and if you're really keen, the giant ruins of the Baths of Caracalla, covered in Chapter 9.

VISITING ANCIENT ROME

The information listed here covers the Forum, Palatine Hill and the Colosseum.

Arrival Buses #40, #62 and #64 run from Termini to Piazza Venezia; buses #75 and #175 travel from Termini down to the end of Via Cavour, opposite the entrance to the Forum and not far from the Colosseum.

Opening hours The Forum (which includes the Palatine Hill) and Colosseum are open at the following times: Daily: Mid-Feb to mid-March 8.30am–4pm; mid- to end March 8.30am–4.30pm; April–Aug 8.30am–6.15pm; Sept 8.30am–6pm; Oct 8.30am–5.30pm; Nov to mid-Feb 8.30am–3.30pm.

Admission Combined tickets for the Colosseum and the Forum (including the Palatine Hill) cost €12; valid for 2 days. EU citizens aged 18–24 €7.50; under-18s and over-65s free.

Access The main entrance to the Forum is halfway down Via dei Fori Imperiali, and you can reach the Palatine Hill from an entrance within the Forum. There is a second entrance to the Palatine Hill near the Colosseum on Via San Gregorio. Both entrances also serve as exits. There are also two exits from the Forum, one behind the Arch of Septimius Severus, near the Capitoline Hill (p.66), and the other behind the Arch of Titus near the Colosseum.

Queues These can be a problem, particularly at the Colosseum, and while they do move quickly, during summer they're rarely less than 100m long and are often besieged by touts. The best bet is to buy your combined ticket at either entrance to the Forum early in the morning when things are usually quiet or book tickets in advance at ⓦ ticketclic.it. Alternatively, buy an Archeocard or RomaPass (see p.34), which allow you to use a different queue.

Tours There are guided tours (included in the ticket prices) of the Colosseum all day every day (roughly every 30min from 9.15am; 30min), and of the Forum daily at 1pm; there are also regular tours of the underground and other closed-off areas (1hr 10 min; €9). Tours can be booked at the ticket offices on arrival, or in advance on ☏ 06 3996 7700 (Mon–Sat 9am–6pm, Sat till 2pm) and online at ⓦ tickitaly.com. Audioguides for both the Forum and the Colosseum cost €6 each. It's now also possible to visit the Colosseum at night on guided tours; try ⓦ viator.com or ⓦ darkrome.com.

Further information The visitor centre (daily 9.30am–6.30pm), just beyond Via Cavour on Via dei Fori Imperiali, has information on ancient sights, as well as a bookshop, toilets and a café. For practical details, go to ⓦ archeoroma.beniculturali.it or ☏ 060608.it, or call ☏ 06 06 08. See also ⓦ cvrlab.org, which has digital reconstructions of key buildings.

Via dei Fori Imperiali

Closed to traffic every Sun

From Piazza Venezia, **Via dei Fori Imperiali**, a soulless boulevard imposed on the area by Mussolini in 1932, cuts southeast through the heart of Rome's ancient sites. Before then, this was a warren of medieval streets that wound around the ruins of the ancient city centre, but, as with the Via della Conciliazione up to St Peter's, Il Duce preferred to build something to his own glory rather than preserve that of another era. A long-standing plan (previously championed by Mussolini) to make the entire ancient part of the city into a huge **archaeological park** stretching right down to the catacombs on the Via Appia Antica is still mooted, but although excavations have been undertaken in recent years, they are continuing slowly. It's a dilemma for the city planners: Via dei Fori Imperiali is a major **traffic artery**, a function which must be preserved. One way around this would be to dig a tunnel under the road – an expensive option, but one that is apparently being considered. For the moment, if you want a tranquil stroll between the major sights, you'll have to settle for coming on a Sunday, when a long stretch from Piazza Venezia to Via Appia Antica is closed to traffic, and pedestrians take to the streets to stroll past the ruins of the ancient city.

Imperial Forums

Limited access · Free · ⓦ capitolium.org

By the time the Imperial era arrived, the original Forum (see p.79) was no longer large enough to serve the demands of the empire, and the city's public institutions began to spread with the construction of a series of **Imperial Forums**. Julius Caesar began the expansion in around 50 BC with a new Senate building and several basilicas and temples

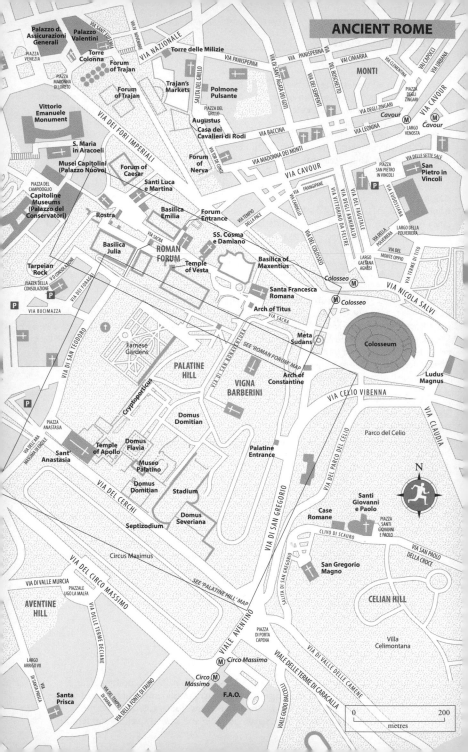

ANCIENT ROME

Palazzo d. Assicurazioni Generali
Palazzo Valentini
Torre Colonna
Forum of Trajan
Forum of Trajan
Torre delle Milizie
Trajan's Markets
Polmone Pulsante
MONTI
Vittorio Emanuele Monument
Augustus
Casa dei Cavalieri di Rodi
Cavour
Cavour
S. Maria in Aracoeli
Forum of Nerva
Musei Capitolini (Palazzo Nuovo)
Forum of Caesar
San Pietro in Vincoli
Capitoline Museums (Palazzo dei Conservatori)
Santi Luca e Martina
Rostra
Basilica Emilia
Forum Entrance
Basilica Julia
SS. Cosma e Damiano
ROMAN FORUM
Tarpeian Rock
Temple of Vesta
Basilica of Maxentius
Colosseo
Santa Francesca Romana
Arch of Titus
Colosseo
Farnese Gardens
Meta Sudans
SEE 'ROMAN FORUM' MAP
Colosseum
PALATINE HILL
VIGNA BARBERINI
Arch of Constantine
Ludus Magnus
Cryptoporticus
Domus Domitian
Palatine Entrance
Parco del Celio
Temple of Apollo
Domus Flavia
Sant' Anastasia
Museo Palatino
Domus Domitian
Stadium
Santi Giovanni e Paolo
Case Romane
Domus Severiana
Septizodium
Circus Maximus
San Gregorio Magno
SEE 'PALATINE HILL' MAP
CELIAN HILL
AVENTINE HILL
Villa Celimontana
Circo Massimo
Circo Massimo
Santa Prisca
F.A.O.

N

0   200
metres

that together formed the **Forum of Caesar**. After his assassination, his nephew and successor Augustus added his own forum and so did the later Flavian emperors – Vespasian, Nerva and Trajan, who also built the neighbouring Trajan's Markets. Archaeologists have excavated a fair segment of the forums over the last decades, but access to most of the area still isn't possible, and in any case you can't help but feel that most of the interesting stuff still lies under the unyielding tarmac of the Via dei Fori Imperiali.

Trajan's Column
Forum of Trajan

Built at the very pinnacle of Roman power and prestige, **Trajan's Column**, at the start of Via dei Fori Imperiali, was erected to celebrate the emperor's victories in Dacia (modern Romania) in 113 AD. About 30m high, the column is covered from top to bottom with **reliefs** commemorating the highlights of the campaign with some 2500 figures carved on a series of marble drums. The **carving** on the base shows the trophies brought back and bears an inscription saying that the column was dedicated to Trajan by the Senate and People of Rome. The **statue** on the top is of St Peter, placed here by Pope Sixtus V in the late sixteenth century, and made from the bronze doors of Sant'Agnese fuori le Mura on Via Nomentana (see p.183).

Basilica Ulpia and the Forum of Trajan
Via dei Fori Imperiali

Trajan's Column once stood in front of the **Basilica Ulpia**, an immense structure, 176m long by 59m wide, which was devoted to the administration of justice. The basilica had five aisles and a huge apse at either end, but although the central nave is discernible from the large paved area behind the Column, the remains are really very scant. The same applies to the adjacent **Forum of Trajan**, once an elaborate complex of monuments, apartments and shops that is today recalled by a flotilla of battered stone columns marooned in a sunken area beside the road – and in front of the semicircular Trajan's Markets (see p.78).

Forum of Augustus
Via dei Fori Imperiali

On Via dei Fori Imperiali, the Forum of Trajan backs onto the **Forum of Augustus**, whose shattered remains date from 42 BC – the walkway linking the main boulevard with Via Alessandrina marks the boundary between the two. Amongst a sea of broken columns, the most conspicuous remains are the monumental staircase, elevated platform and four marble columns of what was once the Temple of Mars the Avenger, put up by **Augustus** in memory of his uncle and adoptive father, Julius Caesar, after the last of his assassins had committed suicide following their defeat in battle. The temple is backed by a large wall of grey stone erected to prevent fire from spreading into the forums from the densely inhabited neighbourhood of Suburra up on the Esquiline Hill. The distinctive brick house round the corner to the left of the wall is the **Casa dei Cavalieri di Rodi**, a fifteenth-century structure that now houses the Order of the

---

THE PULSATING LUNG

If you're happy to give the Imperial Forums a miss, you can follow an interesting route from the Markets of Trajan to close by the main entrance to the original Forum (basically to the bottom end of Via Cavour) by following the **Salita del Grillo** from the southwestern end of Via Panisperna. This takes in the workshop of octogenarian local artist Saverio Ungheri – the **Polmone Pulsante** on the left at Salita del Grillo 21 (daily 4–8pm) – a peculiar place, full of his paintings and odd installations, including the eponymous "pulsating lung" and a pulsating crown – all of which Sr Ungheri is usually on hand to explain. Not what you expect in the heart of tourist Rome, and all the better for it.

Knights of St John – hence the red flag with a cross that's usually flown from its arcaded gallery.

Forum of Nerva
Via dei Fori Imperiali

To the immediate east of the Forum of Augustus lie the scant ruins of the **Forum of Nerva**, which is also known as the "transitional forum" for its role in connecting the Forum of Augustus with the original forum – Nerva's construction ran north–south under what is now Via dei Fori Imperiali. It was built by the crazed and cruel Emperor Domitian, but only finished after his murder by his successor, the elderly Emperor Nerva, who completed the temple of Minerva and naturally dedicated the complex to himself; two columns supporting a gateway set in a stretch of wall close to the foot of Via Cavour are pretty much all that is left.

Forum of Caesar
Via dei Fori Imperiali

The ruinous **Forum of Caesar**, the first of the Imperial Forums to be built, occupies a sunken plot of ground on the south side of Via dei Fori Imperiali. The main survivors are the three columns and mini-pediment of the temple of Venus Genetrix, the Roman goddess of motherhood and mother of Aeneas, from whom Caesar claimed descent – a claim which enraged Roman republicans.

4 Trajan's Markets
Via IV November 94 · Tues–Sun 9am–7pm, last admission 6pm · €11; audio guide €3.50 · ☎ 06 0608, ⓦ mercatiditraiano.it

Built into the side of the Quirinal Hill – and reached via a flight of steps from beside Trajan's Column – **Trajan's Markets** are perhaps the most exciting city-centre Roman ruins to be recently excavated and opened to the public. The site encompasses a perfectly preserved crescent of shops and arcades that don't leave as much to the imagination as many parts of the ancient city. The **great hall** in which you enter is an impressive two-storeyed space, flanked by rooms that house displays on each of the Imperial Forums. Exhibits include a large marble head of Constantine, a torso of a warrior and a cupid frieze from the temple of Venus Genetrix in the Forum of Caesar (see above). Interestingly, the marble head was discovered in an old sewer and may have been thrown there during a pagan revolt against Constantine that swept Rome in 326 AD. You can descend from the hall to the shop-lined **Via Biberatica**, which winds around the bottom of the arcade and the side of the hall, before clambering up the stairs to look at the fragments of masonry and statuary in the museum. From the belvedere at this level, there is also an enjoyable view of the Forum of Trajan down below.

Torre delle Milizie
No admission

It's worth taking a look at the **Torre delle Milizie**, behind the markets, which is fondly imagined to be the brick tower from which Nero watched Rome burn, although it's actually a twelfth-century fortification left over from days when Rome was divided into warring factions within the city walls. The top was destroyed by a blast of lightning in the fifteenth century and acquired its lean from an earthquake in 1348.

Santi Cosma e Damiano
Via dei Fori Imperiali 1 · Daily 9am–1pm & 3–6pm · Free, but €1 donation for presepio

The proud circular structure standing just to the left of the entrance to the Roman Forum is the church of **Santi Cosma e Damiano**, which is entered via a lovely Renaissance cloister. Inside, the truncated nave almost certainly started out as a

THE DECLINE AND FALL OF THE FORUM

In 667 AD, **Constans II**, ruler of the Eastern empire, paid a state visit to Rome. He came to the Forum, and, seeing all the temples and basilicas held together with bronze and iron cramps, decided that they would serve better in his war against Islam and ordered all the metal to be transported back home and forged into spear-points, arrowheads and armour. It took just twelve days to dismantle the metal props, but the result was a disaster: everything was captured en route to Constantinople by Saracen raiders, and the columns and arches supporting all the buildings in the Forum fell down with the next earth tremor. By the early ninth century, hardly anything remained standing, leaving it ripe for the looters of later years – one reason why so little is left today.

Roman library and the original vestibule was created from the so-called Temple of Romulus, which you can look down into but can't enter from the church (it's reached from inside the Forum). The exquisite mosaics in the apse show the naturalistically depicted figures of the two saints (and brothers) being presented to Christ by St Peter and St Paul, flanked by St Felix on the left and St Theodore on the right. You can also visit the Neapolitan **presepio** or "**Christmas crib**", displayed in a room in a corner of the cloister, a detailed piece of work with literally dozens of figures spread amongst the ruins of ancient Rome.

Roman Forum

The original **Roman Forum** was the centre of Republican-era Rome. Even in ancient times, Rome was a very large city, in many places stretching out as far as the Aurelian Wall (see p.147) in a sprawl of apartment blocks (*insulae*). The Forum was home to its political and religious institutions, its shops and market stalls, and a meeting-place for all – which it remained until the Imperial era, when Rome's increased importance as a world power led to the building of the Imperial Forums nearby (see p.75). The original Forum never really recovered from its downgrading, and it's odd to think that during the time when the empire was at its height, neglect had already set in. A **fire** in the third century AD destroyed many of the buildings, and although the damage was repaired, Rome was by this time in a general state of decay, the coming of Christianity only serving to accelerate the process, particularly for its pagan temples and institutions. After the fall of the city to barbarian invaders, the whole area was left in ruin, its relics quarried for the construction of other parts of Rome during both medieval and Renaissance times; the odd church or tower was built in situ out of the more viable piles. **Excavation** of the site didn't start until the beginning of the nineteenth century, and has continued pretty much without stopping: you'll notice a fair part of the site, especially up on the Palatine Hill, closed off for further digs, a process that will no doubt take many more decades.

These days, the Forum is not surprisingly one of the city's **top attractions**, but it can also be a bit disappointing, since you need a good imagination and some grasp of history to really appreciate the place. But these five or so acres were once the heart of the Mediterranean world, and are a very real testament to a power that held a large chunk of the earth in its thrall for close on five centuries, and whose influence reverberates right up to the present day – in language, in architecture, in political terms and systems, even in the romance that time has lent to its ruins. Our **suggested route** around the Forum begins with the **western section** and continues east from the **Temple of Vesta**.

Via Sacra

Just down the slope from the site entrance, take some time to get orientated. You can sit down on one of the miscellaneous hunks of stone that lie next to the near side of the **Via Sacra**, which dog-legs its way through the core of the Forum, from below the

4

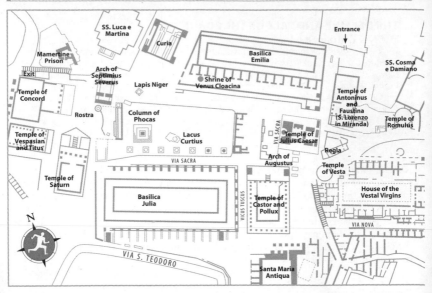

4

Capitoline Hill in the west (where you can exit for the Capitoline Museums; see p.67) to the far eastern extent of the site and the Arch of Titus (where there's another handy exit for the Colosseum; see p.87). This was the best-known street of ancient Rome, along which victorious emperors and generals would ride in procession to give thanks at the Capitoline's Temple of Jupiter. It's possible, however, that the modern street isn't the original Via Sacra, and was in fact only given the name in the 1550s, when the Holy Roman Emperor, Charles V, visited Pope Paul III and the only triumphal arch they could find to march under was the Arch of Septimius Severus (see p.84).

Regia

The shallow steps across the Via Sacra (near the entrance) are part of the **Regia**, or House of the Kings, an extremely ancient – and ruined – group of foundations that probably date from the reign of the second king of Rome, Numa, who ruled from 715 to 673 BC. There was a shrine of Mars here, housing the shields and spears of the god of war, which generals embarking on a campaign rattled before setting off. If the shields and spears rattled of their own accord, it was a bad omen, requiring purification and repentance rites. The Regia later became the residence of Julius Caesar, who moved in here in 45 BC – an imperious act which contributed to his downfall.

Temple of Antoninus and Faustina

Across from the Regia, the **Temple of Antoninus and Faustina** is the best-preserved temple in the Forum, mainly because it was converted into the church of **San Lorenzo in Miranda** during the seventh century. The six huge Corinthian columns across its front are still connected by an inscribed lintel, dedicating the temple by order of the Senate to the god Antoninus and the goddess Faustina, the parents of Marcus Aurelius – Roman emperors were always considered to be deities. Above the inscription was the roof architrave, along whose sides part of the original frieze of griffins, candelabra and acanthus scrolls can be seen. Otherwise, the brick stairs leading up to the floor of the temple are a modern reconstruction, while the Baroque facade of the church dates from 1602.

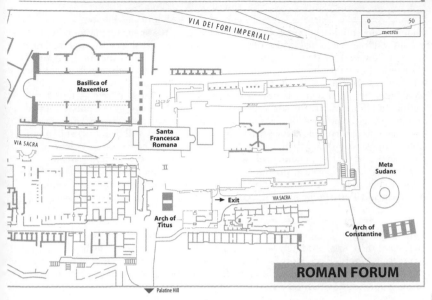

VIA DEI FORI IMPERIALI

0   50
metres

Basilica of
Maxentius

Santa
Francesca
Romana

VIA SACRA

II

Meta
Sudans

→ Exit   VIA SACRA

Arch of
Titus

Arch of
Constantine

ROMAN FORUM

Palatine Hill

4

Temple of Julius Caesar

Next to the Regia, the assorted piles of rubble that have been immersed in preservative cement are the remains of the **Temple of Julius Caesar**, a grand edifice erected two years after Julius Caesar's assassination, as part of his posthumous deification. The little green roof on the edge of the rubble covers the round brick stump where Caesar was cremated, and around which the temple was built. You may hear tour guides declaiming Mark Antony's "Friends, Romans, countrymen" speech from here; bear in mind that not only was the speech made up by Shakespeare, but also that Mark Antony only read Caesar's will, and that he would have done it from the Rostra (see p.84).

Basilica Emilia

The football pitch of broken columns beginning opposite the Temple of Julius Caesar – and cutting off the Via Sacra – marks the site of the **Basilica Emilia**, built in the second century BC to house law courts, and, in the little booths and boutiques flanking its south side, moneychangers. Also on the basilica's south side, a modern plaque signs the circular stone foundation of the **shrine of Venus Cloacina**, whose waters were used for ritual purification. The shrine was built where the Cloaca Maxima canal entered the Forum before slicing down to the River Tiber, thereby draining the Forum, which was originally marshland.

Curia

The large cube-shaped building at the west end of the Basilica Emilia is the **Curia**, built on the orders of Julius Caesar as part of his programme for expanding the Forum – it connects with the Forum of Caesar outside – although what you see today is a third-century AD reconstruction built during the era of the Emperor Diocletian. The Senate met here during the Republican period, and augurs would come to announce the wishes of the gods. For centuries, the Curia served as a church, only reverting to its original form in the 1930s, when it was restored, and its bronze doors – which had been removed in the seventeenth century to San Giovanni in Laterano, where they remain – were replaced with reproductions.

Inside, three wide stairs rise left and right, on which about three hundred senators on folding chairs could be accommodated. In the centre is the **speaker's platform**, with a porphyry statue of a togaed figure. Otherwise, apart from the floor, elegantly patterned in red, yellow, green and white marble, there's not much left of its ancient decor, only the grey and white marble facing each side of the speaker's platform, which would once have covered the entire hall. The ceiling is a modern replacement, and in Roman times would have been gilded. The large marble reliefs here, the **Plutei of Trajan** – found outside and brought here for safekeeping – show Trajan in the midst of public-spirited acts, forgiving the public debt owed by citizens to the state (porters carry large register books and place them before the seated emperor, where they will be burnt) and, on the right, giving a woman a sack of money, a representation of the emperor's welfare plan for widows and orphans. Look closely at the reliefs, and you can see how parts of the Forum would have looked at the time: in one, a fig tree, the columns and arches of the Basilica Julia, the facade of the Temple of Saturn, a triumphal arch and the Temple of Vespasian and Titus; in the other, the columns and eaves of the Temple of Castor and Pollux and the Arch of Augustus.

Lapis Niger

In front of the Curia, seemingly wreathed in permanent scaffolding, the black paving of the **Lapis Niger** ("Black Stone") marks the traditional site of the tomb of Romulus, the steps beneath (usually closed) leading down to a monument that was considered sacred ground during classical times.

Temple of Castor and Pollux

Close to the Temple of Julius Caesar lies the **Temple of Castor and Pollux**, effectively a large pile of rubble topped by three graceful Corinthian columns. The temple was dedicated in 484 BC to the divine twins, or Dioscuri, the offspring of Jupiter by Leda, who appeared miraculously to ensure victory for the Romans in a key battle. The story goes that a group of Roman citizens were gathered around a water fountain on this spot fretting about the war, when Castor and Pollux appeared and reassured them that the battle was won – hence the temple, and their adoption as the special protectors of Rome.

Basilica Julia

Next door to the Temple of Castor and Pollux are the long, shallow steps of the **Basilica Julia**, built by Julius Caesar in the 50s BC after he returned from the Gallic Wars. All that remain are a few column bases and one nearly complete column, and you can't climb the stairs – although you can still see the occasional gameboard scratched in the marble steps where idlers in the Forum played their pebble-toss games.

Lacus Curtius and Column of Phocas

Opposite the Basilica Julia, guardrails lead into a kind of alcove in the pavement, which overloks the site of the **Lacus Curtius** – the spot where, according to legend, a chasm opened in the city's earliest days and the soothsayers determined that it would be closed only when Rome had sacrificed its most valuable possession into it. Marcus Curtius, a Roman soldier who declared that Rome's most valuable possession was a loyal citizen, hurled himself and his horse into the void, and it duly shut. Close by, the so-called **Column of Phocas** is a commemorative column that has managed to retain its dedicatory inscription.

Temples of Saturn, Vespasian and Titus, and Concord

The short slope at the west end of the Via Sacra brings you to the **Temple of Saturn**, the oldest temple in the Forum, dating originally from 497 BC, although the base and eight columns you see today are the result of a series of restorations carried out between

42 BC and 380 AD. The temple was also the Roman treasury and mint. To the right of the temple, three columns still stand from the **Temple of Vespasian and Titus** of the 80s AD. Still further to the right, behind the Arch of Septimius Severus, the large pile of brick and cement rubble is all that remains of the **Temple of Concord**, dedicated by Tiberius in 10 AD.

Arch of Septimius Severus

In front of the Temple of Concord stands the conspicuous **Arch of Septimius Severus**, which was constructed in the early third century AD by his sons Caracalla and Geta to mark their father's victories in what is now Iran. The friezes on it recall Severus and in particular Caracalla, who ruled Rome with undisciplined terror for seven years. There's a space where Geta was commemorated – Caracalla, who had inherited the empire jointly, had him executed in 213 AD, and his name expediently removed from the arch altogether.

Rostra

To the left of the arch of Septimius Severus, the low brown wall of the **Rostra** faces the wide-open scatter of paving, dumped stones and beached columns that makes up the central portion of the Forum, which in its heyday would have been crowded with politicians, tribunes and traders. The Rostra was the place where important speeches were made, and it was probably from here that Mark Antony spoke about Caesar after his death.

Temple of Vesta and the House of the Vestal Virgins

Behind the Regia, the **Temple of Vesta** burnt down on several occasions, but three columns have survived, perched on top of a curving brick wall. Behind, immediately to the east, lies the **House of the Vestal Virgins**, a second-century AD reconstruction of a building originally built by Nero. Vesta was the Roman goddess of the hearth and home, and her cult was an important one in ancient Rome. Her temple was in charge of the so-called **Vestal Virgins**, who had the responsibility of keeping the sacred flame of Vesta alight and were obliged to remain chaste for the thirty years that they served (they usually started at around age 10). If the flame should go out, the woman responsible was scourged; if she should lose her chastity, she was buried alive (her male partner-in-crime was flogged to death in front of the Curia). Because of the importance of their office, they were accorded special privileges: a choice section in the Colosseum was reserved for them; only they and the empress could ride in a wheeled vehicle within the confines of the city; and they had the right to pardon any criminal who managed to get close enough to one of them to beseech their mercy. A vestal virgin could resign her post if she wished, but she had the benefit of residing in a very comfortable palace: four floors of rooms around a central courtyard. The rooms are mainly ruins now, though they're fairly recognizable, and you can get a good sense of the shape of the place from the remains of the courtyard, still with its pool in the centre and fringed by a few statues of the women themselves.

Temple of Romulus

Opposite the House of the Vestal Virgins, the curved facade of the **Temple of Romulus** (the son of the Emperor Maxentius, not the founder of Rome), dating from 309 AD, has been sanctified and for centuries served as the vestibule for the church of Santi Cosma e Damiano behind (see p.78).

Basilica of Maxentius

Just past the Temple of Romulus along the Via Sacra, take the short path on the left up to the towering **Basilica of Maxentius**, sometimes called the Basilica of Constantine, which is, in terms of size and ingenuity, probably the Forum's most impressive remains.

Begun by Maxentius, the structure was continued by his co-emperor and rival, Constantine, after he had defeated him at the Battle of Ponte Milvio in 312 AD. By the time the basilica was built, Roman architects and engineers were expert at building with poured cement. It's said that Michelangelo studied the hexagonal coffered arches here when grappling with the dome of St Peter's, and apparently Renaissance architects frequently used its apse and arches as a model. Incidentally, the church you can see through the metal fence is that of Santa Francesca Romana – very much worth a look, but only accessible from outside the Forum, near the Colosseum.

Arch of Titus

The Via Sacra climbs east up to the **Arch of Titus**, which stands commandingly on a low arm of the Palatine Hill, looking one way down the remainder of the Via Sacra to the Colosseum, and back over the Forum proper. The arch was built by Titus's brother, Domitian, after the emperor's death in 81 AD, to commemorate his victories in Judaea in 70 AD and his triumphal return from that campaign. It sets in stone the inauguration of the Vespasian dynasty and Rome's return to peace and stability following the disruption that ensued after Nero's death. The arch is a **much-restored structure**, and you can see, in reliefs on the inside, scenes of Titus riding in a chariot with Nike, goddess of Victory, being escorted by representatives of the Senate and plebs, and, on the opposite side, spoils being removed from the Temple in Jerusalem.

Palatine Hill

Turning right at the Arch of Titus takes you up to the main entrance of the **Palatine Hill**, supposedly where the city of Rome was founded by Romulus and Remus, and home to some of its most important classical remains. In a way, it's a more pleasant site to tour than the Forum – larger, greener and more of a park, plus it's a pleasant place to relax after the crowds of the ruins below. In the days of the Republic, the Palatine was the most desirable address in Rome (the word "palace" is derived from it), and the big names continued to colonize it during the Imperial era, trying to outdo each other with ever larger and more magnificent dwellings. The only fly in the ointment is the lack of signage, and you have to keep your eyes peeled to follow any half-decent itinerary.

4

Cryptoporticus

Strolling up the main path from the Palatine entrance, fork right across the waste ground to reach the **Cryptoporticus**, a long underground corridor built by Nero to link the Domus Tiberiana (see p.86) with the Forum. Several of the early emperors were particularly keen on these passageways, and it was in one of them that the Emperor Caligula was stabbed to death away from the protective eyes of his German bodyguards. At 130m long, Nero's Cryptoporticus is the only one of these passageways open to the public, and at the far end the roof is decorated with casts of a few of the stucco panels that once ran its whole length.

House of Livia

At the end of the Cryptoporticus, climb up to the **House of Livia** – originally believed to have been the residence of Livia, the wife of Augustus, but now identified as simply another part of the neighbouring House of Augustus (see p.86). It has been recently restored, with a courtyard and inner rooms decorated with frescoes and trompe l'oeil in vivid colours.

Farnese Gardens and Domus Tiberiana

Climb up the steps near the House of Livia and you're in the bottom corner of the **Farnese Gardens**, one of the first botanical gardens in Europe, laid out by Cardinal Alessandro Farnese in the mid-sixteenth century and now – in part at least – a tidily planted, shady retreat from the exposed heat of the ruins. The Farnese gardens surround the recently excavated foundations of the **Domus Tiberiana**, a once lavish palace begun by Nero, embellished by Tiberius and extended by Hadrian a century or so later. The gardens culminate in a handsome terrace, from where there are wide views over the Forum.

House of Augustus
Just steps away from the House of Livia, the **House of Augustus** has been the subject of intense archaeological investigation and speculation. Augustus seems to have acquired this site in about 20 BC and spent the next thirty years building his **palace** here, expanding and amending it as circumstances changed. Now that the outside and interior walls have been excavated, the complicated layout of the rooms is visible, but although wall paintings, marble pavements and stuccoed vaults have been discovered, these are often covered to protect them from the elements.

Domus Flavia
The **Domus Flavia**, the work of the Emperor Domitian, occupies most of the central part of the Palatine site and was once its most splendid residence. It's now almost completely ruined, but the original peristyle (columned porch) is easy enough to identify, with its fountain and hexagonal brick arrangement in the centre.

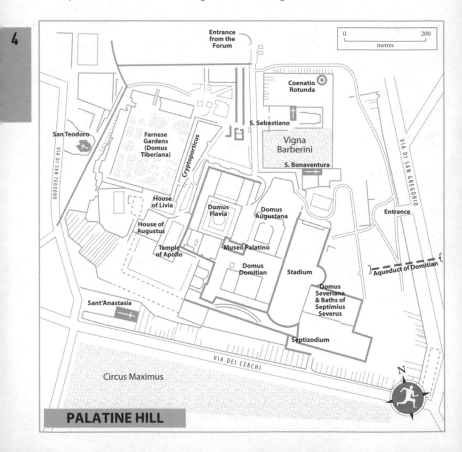

Museo Palatino
Daily 9am–6pm • Free

The large grey building behind the Domus Flavia houses the **Museo Palatino**, which contains an assortment of statues, pottery and architectural fragments that have been excavated on the Palatine during the last 150 years. The ground floor has finds from the early years of Rome and the original Iron Age village that pre-dated it. The upper floor leaps ahead to the Imperial age, and highlights include three beautifully preserved black marble herms, statues of women that supposedly filled the niches in Augustus's Temple of Apollo; a piece of terracotta frieze from the same temple showing Apollo and Hercules in dispute (a reference, perhaps, to Augustus's rivalry with Mark Antony, who frequently identified himself with Hercules); and busts of various emperors: two of Nero, one old, one young, Hadrian, Antoninus Pius and a very young Marcus Aurelius. There are nice details, too: notably, a fragment of a relief showing Apollo playing the lyre; and the bottom of a relief of a togaed figure carrying a brace of ducks – supposedly the personification of winter – from the fourth century AD.

Domus Domitian and Domus Augustana
East of the Museo Palatino lie the scattered ruins of the gargantuan **Domus Domitian**, built between 81 and 96 AD, and the smaller **Domus Augustana** which was not the home of Augustus as its name suggests, but the private house of any emperor (or "Augustus"). In both cases, the ruins are hard to decipher with the exception of the **Stadium**, a semi-circular, sunken garden and part-time hippodrome that was part of the Domus Domitian. The Stadium is in an excellent state of preservation and you can walk down the steps for a closer look.

Domus Severiana and the Septizodium
The far side of the Stadium is overlooked by the substantial remains of the **Domus Severiana**, which was built at the behest of the Emperor Septimius Severus towards the end of the second century AD – as were the adjoining **Baths of Septimius Severus** and, further to the south, the **Septizodium**. Little retains of the last two structures, but, from the site of the Septizodium (a large decorative facade built to impress visitors as they arrived in Rome), there are grand views over to the Aventine Hill.

Vigna Barberini and Coenatio Rotunda
Near the main entrance to the Palatine, a sign directs you through a tunnel to the green spaces of the **Vigna Barberini** which was once an imperial vineyard. Further on, right on the corner of the Palatine and overlooking the Colosseum, you can see the base of the 4m–thick pillar at the heart of the so-called **Coenatio Rotunda**, or Nero's rotating dining hall, which was part of the Domus Aurea (see p.116) and was said by Suetonius to "perpetually revolve, both day and night, in the manner of the celestial bodies". He went on, "the ceilings, inlaid with ivory, scattered flowers while a device of pipes sprinkled sweet oil upon the guests."

Colosseum
The **Colosseum** is Rome's most awe-inspiring ancient monument, and one which, unlike the Forum, needs little historical knowledge or imagination to deduce its function. This enormous structure was so solidly built, that despite the depredations of nearly two thousand years – earthquakes, fires, riots, wars and, not least, plundering for its seemingly inexhaustible supply of ready-cut travertine blocks – it still stands relatively intact, a readily recognizable symbol not just of the city of Rome, but of the entire ancient world. Inevitably, it's not nearly as grand as it once was – sections are missing, it's badly cracked and there are gaping holes where metal brackets once linked the great blocks together. The basic structure of the place is easy to see, however, and

4

has served as a model for **stadiums** around the world ever since: until Sydney 2000, it appeared on all winners' medals in the Olympics, and it still graces the Italian 5c coin. You'll not be alone in appreciating it, and during summer the combination of people and scaffolding can make a visit more like touring a modern building-site than an ancient monument. But come early morning before the tour buses have arrived or late in the evening, go up a level to get a real sense of the size of the building, and the arena can seem more like the marvel it really is.

Once inside the arena, steep **stairways** lead up to the **lower level**, which you are free to wander; here also, in the connecting corridor, is a space for temporary exhibitions on all things Roman, a display of fragments of masonry and a decent bookshop. More stairs lead to the **upper level**, which again you are free to explore, although even here you are still only about halfway up the original structure – and all the higher parts of the stadium are closed. From both levels, you can gaze down into the innards of the arena and observe its maze of brick walls, which can be seen at close quarters on a **guided tour** (booked in advance or on arrival; see p.75).

Beginnings

A **lake** once lay where the Colosseum stands today, drained by a small stream that wove between the Palatine and Celian hills before emptying into the Tiber. Things changed after the great **fire** of 64 AD, when Nero set about building his outrageous palace, the Domus Aurea (see p.116). The lake became part of the palace gardens, an imperial plaything where mock nautical battles could be enacted, and behind it, fronting the vestibule of the palace, **Nero** erected a huge statue of himself as a sun god: it was so big that 24 elephants were needed to put the base in place. Four years later, Nero was dead, and, after a trio of quick-fire emperors, **Vespasian** seized power and soon set a new course. To prove that the wayward days of Nero were over and the city was being given back to the people, Vespasian drained the lake and began the construction of the Flavian Amphitheatre, as it was originally known, in 70 AD. Incredibly, given the size of the project, the Colosseum was inaugurated by Vespasian's son Titus just eight years later, an event celebrated by a hundred days of continuous **games**; it was finally completed by **Domitian**, Titus's brother and the third of the Flavian emperors.

Construction and organization

Prior to Vespasian, gladiatorial and other bloody games had been conducted in a makeshift stadium in the Roman Forum, near the Curia. The stands were temporary and constructed of wood, and had to be erected and taken down every time there were games. It is said that seventy thousand Hebrew slaves did the heavy work at the Colosseum. Fifty thousand cartloads of pre-cut travertine stone were hauled from the quarries at Tivoli, a distance of 27km. In the depths of what must have been the muddy bottom of the lake, a **labyrinth** was laid out, walling in passages for the contestants and creating areas for assembling and storing sets, scenery and other requirements for gladiatorial contests. The overall structure was tastefully designed, with close attention paid to decoration. On the outside, the arena's three **arcades** rose in strict classical fashion to a flat surface at the top punctuated only by windows, where there was a series of supports for **masts** that protruded at the upper limit. These masts, 240 in total, were used to extend a canvas awning over the spectators inside the arena.

Inside, beyond the corridors that led up to the **seats**, lavishly decorated with painted stucco, there was room for a total of around sixty thousand people seated and ten thousand or so standing; the design was such that all seventy thousand could enter and be seated in a matter of minutes. **Seating** was allocated according to social status, with the emperor and his attendants naturally occupying the best seats in the house, and the social class of the spectators diminishing further up the stands. There were no ticket sales as we conceive of them; rather, tickets were distributed through – and according to the social status of – Roman heads of households. These "**tickets**" were in fact wooden tags, with the entrance, row, aisle and seat number carved on them. Inside the amphitheatre, the **labyrinth** below was covered over with a wooden floor, punctuated at various places for trapdoors and lifts to raise and lower the animals that were to take part in the games. The **floor** was covered with canvas to make it waterproof, and the canvas was covered with several centimetres of sand to absorb blood; in fact, our word "arena" is derived from the Latin word for sand. There was also a busy sideline in sponges soaked in the blood of the newly departed – the blood was said to cure epilepsy.

Around the Colosseum

Once you've seen the Colosseum, it's worth having a wander around outside, not just to be photographed with the hordes of roaming gladiators but to have a closer look at some of the various ancient ruins that lie nearby, the largest of which is the impressive **Arch of Constantine**; make the short walk, too, to the somewhat hidden church of **Santa Francesca Romana** for an alternative view of the Forum and the saint's body, among other miraculous relics.

Arch of Constantine

The huge **Arch of Constantine** was placed here in the early decades of the fourth century AD, after Constantine had consolidated his power as sole emperor. The deterioration of

---

BEASTLY HAPPENINGS AT THE COLOSSEUM

The Romans flocked to the Colosseum for many things, but **gladiatorial contests** were the big attraction. Gladiatorial **combat** as a Roman tradition was a direct import from the Etruscans, who thought it seemly to sacrifice a few prisoners of war or slaves at the funeral games of an important person. By the second century BC, such contents had become so institutionalized in Rome that a **gladiatorial school**, or Ludus Magnus (see p.90), was installed in the city – a rather grim affair, consisting of a barracks for gladiators and a ring in which they could practise with blunt weapons, under supervision.

Gladiatorial combat was probably the greatest and cruellest of all **bloodsports**. At the start of the games, the gladiators would enter through the monumental door at the eastern end of the arena. They would make a procession around the ring and halt in front of the emperor's box, where they would make their famous **greeting**, "Hail Caesar, we who are about to die salute you." Gladiators were divided into several **classes**, each performing different types of combat. There was the heavily armed "Samnite", named after the type of arms the Romans had captured on the defeat of that tribe in 310 BC, equipped with heavy armour, an oblong bronze shield, a visored helmet with crest and plumes and a sword (*gladius*). Usually a Samnite would be pitted against a combatant without armour, equipped only with a cast net and a trident, whose main protection was that he was unencumbered and therefore could be fleet of foot. He had, however, only one cast of his net in which to entangle the Samnite and kill him with his trident. Neither man was allowed to flee from the arena, and, once captured or disarmed, the roaring mob would be asked whether the loser should be killed or allowed to live. If he had put up a good fight he would usually be spared; if he had not fought as valiantly as he should, he would be **slaughtered** on the spot. The early Christian church waged a long and often unpopular campaign against gladiatorial combat, and in the end they carried the day: in 404 AD, a monk named **Telemachus** tried to separate two fighting gladiators, and the crowd stoned him to death, prompting the Emperor Honorius to abolish gladiatorial fighting altogether.

The other activities conducted in the Colosseum involved **animals**. In the hundred-day games that inaugurated the Colosseum, something like nine thousand beasts were massacred – roughly twelve killings a minute – and during the 450 years of activity here several breeds of African elephant and lion were rendered extinct. There were also gladiatorial games which involved "**hunting**" wild animals, and sometimes creatures would be pitted against each other – bears would be tied to bulls and have to fight to the finish, lions would take on tigers, dogs would be set against wolves and so on. The last games involving animals were conducted in the year 523 AD, after which the Colosseum gradually fell into disuse and disrepair.

4

the arts during the later stages of the Roman Empire meant there were hardly any **sculptors** around who could produce original work, and most of the sculptural decoration on the arch had to be removed from other monuments. The builders were probably quite ignorant of the significance of the pieces they borrowed: the round medallions are taken from a temple dedicated to the Emperor Hadrian's lover, Antinous, and show Antinous and Hadrian engaged in the hunt. The other pieces, removed from the Forum of Trajan, show Dacian prisoners captured in Trajan's war there. The large **inscription** in the centre was made for the arch and dedicates it to Constantine for his wisdom – presumably in making Christianity the official religion of the empire, although no one really knows what this refers to.

Meta Sudans

Between the Arch of Constantine and the Colosseum, at a pivotal point in the Via Sacra, stood a monumental fountain or **Meta Sudans**, the outline of which can still be seen today in the form of a series of recently excavated low brick walls. A "meta" was the marker in the centre of a racecourse, and was usually an obelisk or some other large, easily visible object. In this case, it was a conical fountain that was probably dedicated to Apollo, and produced a slow supply of water that resembled sweat, hence its name – the "**Sweating Meta**".

Ludus Magnus

Tunnels not open to the public

On the far side of the Colosseum, the sunken brick ruins at the foot of Via di San Giovanni in Laterano are what's left of the **Ludus Magnus**, the main training school for gladiators. The complex included a small arena built by Domitian that was surrounded by gladiators' barracks, connected to the Colosseum by tunnels – some of which still exist but are sadly not open to public view.

Santa Francesca Romana

Piazza di Santa Francesca Romana 4 • Daily 9.30am–12.30pm & 3.30–7pm • ☎ 06 679 5528

Standing on the edge of the Forum, but reached by way of a narrow side-road from the Colosseum, the church of **Santa Francesca Romana** is sometimes known as **Santa Maria Nova** after the church of Santa Maria Antique, which it replaced as a place of worship in the tenth century. The church is dedicated to a fifteenth-century Trastevere noblewoman and later nun who did good works for the poor and experienced a vision of her guardian angel that lasted several years – quite long enough to get her beatified. The church is a fascinating building on many levels. Highlights include a series of beautiful twelfth-century mosaics in the apse, above a venerated depiction of the Madonna and Child from the same era and the elaborate tomb of Pope Gregory XI, who brought the papacy back to Rome from Avignon in the late fourteenth century. Close by – to the right of the high altar in the transept – protective grilles have been bolted over two **flagstones** brought here from the Via Sacra. Legend asserts that the dips on the flagstones bear the imprint of the knees of St Peter, who knelt in prayer to ask God to punish Simon the Sorcerer, who was busy flying through the air; God obliged, and Simon crash-landed. Not far from here, steps lead down into the crypt, where the skeletal body of St Francesca lies prone, clothed, holding a prayer book and surrounded by votive photos.

THE BARCACCIA FOUNTAIN AND SPANISH STEPS

The Tridente and Trevi

The northern part of Rome's city centre is sometimes known as the Tridente,
due to the trident shape of the roads leading down from the apex of Piazza
del Popolo – Via del Corso in the centre, Via di Ripetta on the left and Via del
Babuino on the right. It comprises some of the busiest streets in the city, with
a host of shopping and sights along Via del Corso and up towards Piazza di
Spagna, while to the south, the area around the Trevi Fountain is similarly
– and unsurprisingly – thronged. That said, the fountain itself is well worth
seeing, however obvious a sight it may seem, and the knot of streets around
holds a few worthwhile stops, as well as being a logical prelude to seeing the
sights of the Quirinale immediately above (see p.103).

5

Via del Corso

Buses #62, #63 & #81, and minibuses #117 & #119, among others, run along the bottom end of Via del Corso – the top end, above Largo Goldoni, is closed to traffic much of the time

The central prong of the Tridente, **Via del Corso** is Rome's main thoroughfare, linking Piazza Venezia at its southern end with Piazza del Popolo to the north. You can follow it all the way up, dipping into the Centro Storico as and when you feel like it. The streets on this side of the centre focus on the ancient Roman dome of the **Pantheon** (see p.39) and further north on the offices of the **Italian parliament** and prime minister (see p.49), while on the opposite side it gives onto the swish shopping thoroughfares that lead up to Piazza di Spagna.

Named after the races that used to take place along here during Renaissance times, the street has had its fair share of famous residents during the years: Goethe lived at no. 18 for two years, close to the Piazza del Popolo end (see below); the Shelleys – Percy and Mary – lived for several years in the Palazzo Vesporio, at Via del Corso 375 (now a bank), during which time they lost their son William to a fever (see p.144). Since the middle of the last century, it has become Rome's principal **shopping** street, home to mid-range boutiques and chain stores that make it a busy stretch during the day, full of hurrying pedestrians and crammed buses, but a relatively dead one come the evening. The good news is that the top end, beyond Largo Goldoni, where the bulk of the shops are, is pedestrianized, making shopping and strolling much easier and more enjoyable.

Santi Ambrogio e Carlo

Via del Corso 437 • Daily 7am–12.30pm & 4.30–6.30pm • ⓦ www.sancarlo.pcn.net

The largest if not the most essential sight on the Corso, the church of **Santi Ambrogio e Carlo** – or "San Carlo al Corso", as it's more often known – is the Milanese church in Rome, dedicated to its most famous bishop (Ambrose, who died in 397 AD) and Carlo Borromeo, who was a humble and reforming archbishop of Milan around 1200 years later. The dome is one of the largest in the city and crowns a vast and highly decorative seventeenth-century church; the chapel at the back is home to a reliquary containing the heart of Carlo Borromeo.

Casa di Goethe

Via del Corso 18 • Tues–Sun 10am–6pm • €5 • ⓣ 06 3265 0412, ⓦ casadigoethe.it

A short way down Via del Corso from Piazza del Popolo, on the left at no. 18, the **Casa di Goethe** is a genuinely engaging small museum. There seem to be houses all over Italy that Goethe stayed in, but he did spend over two years in this one, and wrote much of his classic travelogue *Italian Journey* here – indeed, each room is decorated with a quote from the book. Goethe had long dreamed of travelling to Italy, inspired by a journey his father made years earlier, and he came here – incognito, as Filippo Miller – in 1786, after touring the north of the country. His routine here was a **bohemian** one, associating with expat artists and writers, far removed from his life in Germany, where he was a celebrated writer. The house has been restored as a modern exhibition space and holds books, letters, prints and drawings, plus a reconstruction of his study in Vienna. Among the objects on display are Piranesi prints of public spaces in Rome, watercolours by Goethe himself and drawings by the German artist **Tischbein**, with whom he shared the house, including a lovely one of Goethe leaning out of the window over Via del Corso and a more formal painting of him reclining in the foreground of an idealized Roman *campagna* landscape.

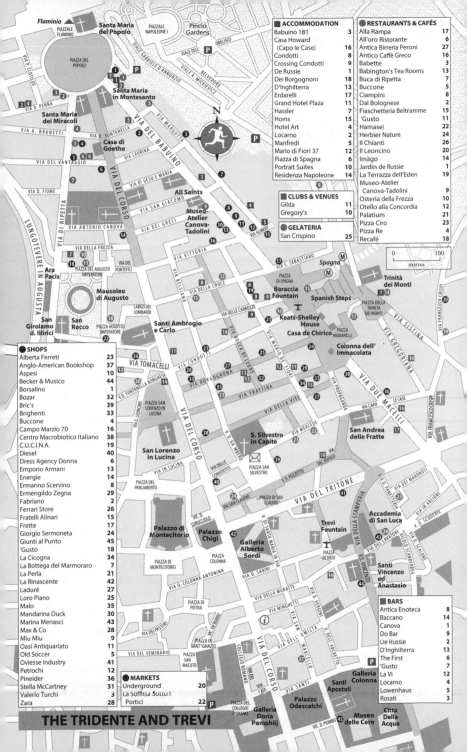

THE TRIDENTE AND TREVI

■ ACCOMMODATION
Babuino 181	3
Casa Howard (Capo le Case)	16
Condotti	8
Crossing Condotti	9
De Russie	1
Dei Borgognoni	18
D'Inghilterra	13
Erdarelli	17
Grand Hotel Plaza	11
Hassler	7
Homs	15
Hotel Art	4
Locarno	2
Manfredi	5
Mario di Fiori 37	12
Piazza di Spagna	6
Portrait Suites	10
Residenza Napoleone	14

● RESTAURANTS & CAFÉS
Alla Rampa	17
All'oro Ristorante	6
Antica Birreria Peroni	27
Antico Caffè Greco	16
Babette	3
Babington's Tea Rooms	13
Buca di Ripetta	7
Buccone	5
Ciampini	8
Dal Bolognese	2
Fiaschetteria Beltramme	15
'Gusto	11
Hamasei	22
Herbier Nature	24
Il Chianti	26
Il Leoncino	20
Imàgo	1
Jardin de Russie	1
La Terrazza dell'Eden	19
Museo-Atelier Canova-Tadolini	9
Osteria della Frezza	10
Otello alla Concordia	12
Palatium	21
Pizza Ciro	23
Pizza Re	4
Recafé	18

■ CLUBS & VENUES
Gilda	11
Gregory's	10

● GELATERIA
San Crispino	25

● SHOPS
Alberta Ferreti	23
Anglo-American Bookshop	37
Aspesi	10
Becker & Musico	44
Borsalino	1
Bozar	32
Bric's	39
Brighenti	33
Buccone	4
Campo Marzio 70	16
Centro Macrobiotico Italiano	38
C.U.C.I.N.A.	19
Diesel	40
Dress Agency Donna	6
Emporio Armani	13
Energie	14
Ermanno Scervino	8
Ermenegildo Zegna	29
Fabriano	2
Ferrari Store	26
Fratelli Alinari	15
Frette	17
Giorgio Sermoneta	24
Giunti al Punto	45
'Gusto	18
La Cicogna	34
La Bottega del Marmoraro	7
La Perla	21
La Rinascente	42
Laduré	27
Loro Piano	25
Malo	35
Mandarina Duck	30
Marina Menasci	43
Max & Co	28
Miu Miu	9
Oasi Antiquariato	11
Old Soccer	5
Oviesse Industry	41
Petrochi	12
Pineider	36
Stella McCartney	31
Valerio Turchi	3
Zara	28

● MARKETS
Underground	20
La Soffitta Sotto I Portici	22

■ BARS
Antica Enoteca	8
Baccano	14
Canova	1
Do Bar	9
De Russie	2
D'Inghilterra	13
The First	6
'Gusto	7
La Vi	12
Locarno	4
Lowenhaus	5
Rosati	3

0   100
metres

5

Piazza di Spagna

Metro stop Spagna, line A

The area around **Piazza di Spagna** is travellers' Rome. Historically, it was the artistic quarter of the capital, and wealthy young men and women on eighteenth- and nineteenth-century grand tours would come here in search of the colourful and exotic. **Keats** and **Giorgio de Chirico** are just two of the many artists and writers who have lived on Piazza di Spagna; **Goethe** had lodgings along Via del Corso; and places such as *Caffè Greco* (see p.250) and *Babington's Tea Rooms* (see p.250) were the meeting-places of a local artistic and expat community for almost two centuries. Today, these institutions have been supplemented by latter-day traps for the tourist dollar, local residents are more likely to be investment bankers than artists or poets and Via Condotti and the surrounding streets are these days strictly international designer territory, with some of Rome's fanciest stores. But the air of a Rome being discovered – even colonized – by foreigners persists, even if most of those hanging out on the Spanish Steps are flying-visit teenagers.

Piazza di Spagna itself underlines the area's international credentials, taking its name from the Spanish embassy which has stood here since the seventeenth century – though, oddly enough, part of the square was once known as Piazza di Francia for the French church of **Trinità dei Monti** at the top of the Spanish Steps (see p.96). It's a long, thin straggle of a square, almost entirely enclosed by buildings, and centring on the distinctive, boat-shaped **Fontana della Barcaccia**, the last work of Pietro Bernini, father of the more famous Gianlorenzo. It apparently commemorates the great flood of Christmas Day 1598, when a barge from the Tiber was washed up on the slopes of Pincio Hill, close by. The square itself is fringed by high-end clothes and jewellery shops and is normally thronged with tourists, but, for all that, it's one of the city's most appealing open spaces.

The large **Colonna dell'Immacolata** at the southern end commemorates Pius IX's official announcement, in 1854, of the dogma of the Immaculate Conception, while, close by, hackles were raised when McDonald's unveiled plans to open a branch on the square in the early 1980s. Its presence here is proof that the American multinational won what turned out to be quite a battle. But it's to the city's credit that this is one of the most discreet examples you'll encounter, tucked into one end of the piazza, with thematically appropriate interior decor.

Keats-Shelley House

Piazza di Spagna 26 • Mon–Sat 10am–1pm & 2–6pm • €5 • ☎ 06 678 4235, ⓦ keats-shelley-house.org • To rent the building's third-floor apartment, contact Landmark Trust ☎ 01628 825925, ⓦ landmarktrust.org.uk

Facing directly onto Piazza di Spagna, opposite the Barcaccia fountain, the house where the poet John Keats (see p.144) died in 1821 now serves as the **Keats-Shelley House**, an archive of English-language literary and historical works and a museum of manuscripts and literary mementoes relating to the Keats circle of the early nineteenth century – namely Keats himself, Percy and Mary Shelley and Byron (who at one time lived across the square). Its four rooms contain manuscripts, letters and the like, and various personal effects of Keats, Shelley, Byron and associates, including an ancient silver scallop shell reliquary containing locks of Keats's, Shelley's, Milton's and Elizabeth Barrett Browning's hair – once owned by Pope Pius V – and an alabaster urn with Shelley's jawbone. Keats's death mask, stored in the corner room in which he died from tuberculosis, captures a resigned grimace, while the books that line the walls form the museum's library, which is devoted to the period and its literature.

Keats didn't really enjoy his time in Rome, referring to it as his "**posthumous life**": he came here only under pressure from doctors and friends when it was arguably already too late. He was also tormented by his love for **Fanny Brawne**, whom he had left behind in London, and he spent months in pain before he finally died, at the age of just 25,

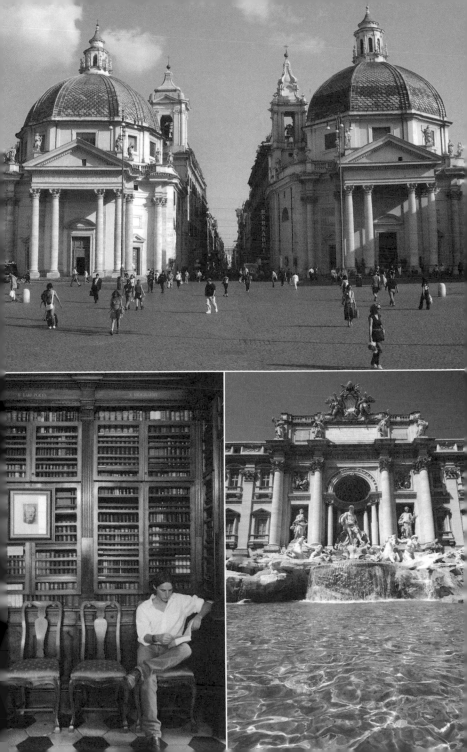

5

confined to the house with his artist friend Joseph Severn, to whom he remarked that he could already feel "the flowers growing over him". If you really want to get into the Romantic poet experience, there's an apartment on the third floor available to rent through the UK-based Landmark Trust.

Casa de Chirico

Piazza di Spagna 31 · Tues–Sat & the first Sun of every month 10am–noon, closed Aug; obligatory tours hourly, book in advance · €7 · ☎ 06 679 6546, ⓦ fondazionedechirico.org

Almost next door to the Keats-Shelley House, the fourth-floor **Casa de Chirico** was the home of the Greek-Italian metaphysical artist Giorgio de Chirico for thirty years, until his death in 1978, and is now a small, evocative museum. His wife, **Isa**, lived on here until 1990, when she too died, after which the apartment was donated to the city. It's kept pretty much as she left it, and it gives a fantastic glimpse into how De Chirico lived, as well as having a great many of his paintings on display.

There are works from his **classic period** in the entrance hall and first living area, including portraits of himself, often dressed up, and others of his wife, who modelled for him until he died. The chair in which he used to watch TV (only with the sound turned down, apparently) sits by the door, while the next-door living room is filled with paintings from his last few years, all harking back to his **proto-surrealist heyday**. Upstairs, in keeping with the untouched nature of the house, De Chirico's cell-like bedroom is left with his books and rather uncomfortable-looking single bed, while, across the hall, the video player in Isa's bedroom is marked with stickers placed there to remind her how it worked. At the end of the corridor, De Chirico's **studio**, lit by a skylight in the terrace above, holds his brushes and canvases, more books and records, a portrait of his mother and a photo of his brother, Andrea, also a writer and artist.

Spanish Steps

If you don't think you can make it to the top of the steps on foot, you can use a lift in the entrance of the Spagna metro station, down Vicolo del Bottino

The **Spanish Steps** (or Scalinata di Spagna) sweep down in a cascade of balustrades and balconies beside Giorgio de Chirico's house, the hangout, during the nineteenth century, of young hopefuls waiting to be chosen as artists' models. The scene has not changed much; it is still a venue for international posing and fast pick-ups late into the summer nights. It was, in fact, a largely **French initiative** to build them – before their construction, the French church of Trinità dei Monti was accessible only by way of a rough path up the steep slope. After a few decades of haggling over the plans, the steps were finally laid in 1725, and now form one of the city's most distinctive attractions, built to a design, by one **Francesco de Sanctis**, that is deliberately showy, perfect for strollers to glide up and down while chatting and looking each other up and down. The steps also contain a religious message – the three flights and three landings are an allusion to the Holy Trinity.

Trinità dei Monti

Piazza della Trinità dei Monti · Daily 9am–noon & 4–6pm

At the top of the Spanish Steps is the **Trinità dei Monti**, a largely sixteenth-century church designed by **Carlo Maderno** and paid for by the French king. Its rose-coloured Baroque facade overlooks the rest of Rome from its hilltop site, and it's worth clambering up here just for the views. The church also has a couple of impressive works by Daniele da Volterra, notably a soft, beautifully composed fresco of the *Assumption* in the third chapel on the right, whose array of finely realized figures includes a portrait of his teacher Michelangelo (he's the greybeard on the far right), while a *Deposition*, across the nave in the second chapel on the left, has another ingenious arrangement, with

Christ hauled down from the cross as his mother and other figures grieve below. The French seventeenth-century artist Poussin considered this work, which was probably painted from a series of cartoons by Michelangelo, as the world's third-greatest painting (Raphael's *Transfiguration* was, he thought, the best).

Villa Medici

Viale della Trinità dei Monti 1 · Guided tours of the gardens daily: April, May, Sept & Oct 11am, noon (in English), 2pm, 3pm & 4.30pm; June–Aug 11am, noon (in English), 3pm, 4.30pm & 6pm; Nov–March 11am, noon (in English), 2.30pm & 4pm · €9, Wed €11 (additionally includes the villa); 1hr · ☎ 06 67611, ⓦ villamedici.it

Walking north from the top of the Spanish Steps, you reach the sixteenth-century **Villa Medici**. This was where **Galileo** was imprisoned in the 1630s by the Vatican's Holy Office for heretically claiming that the earth was not the centre of the universe but instead revolved around the sun. He was forced to recant his theory and say seven penitential psalms a week for his trouble. Nowadays, the villa is home to the French Academy, and although it's often open for exhibitions and concerts, for much of the year the only parts that are open to the public are its formal **gardens**, and then only on guided tours. As well as the gardens themselves, these take in the little **Studiolo** on the far side, decorated by Jacopo Zucchi in the mid-sixteenth century with frescoes of lush vegetation, birds and depictions of the villa itself, and the **Gipsoteca** just beyond, full of casts of classical sculpture, while the views of the city from the villa's terrace are among the best in Rome. During the summer, you can also sometimes visit a selection of historic rooms inside the villa – the bedroom of Ferdinando de' Medici and a handful of other frescoed chambers – though tours are again compulsory and mainly in Italian and French. Finally, there's a very comfy **café**, with lots of sofas from which to enjoy the views.

Via del Babuino

Leading north from Piazza di Spagna to Piazza del Popolo, **Via del Babuino** and the narrow **Via Margutta**, where the film-maker Federico Fellini once lived, set the tone for the area, which in the 1960s was the core of a thriving art community and home to the city's best galleries and a fair number of its artists. High rents forced out all but the most successful, and the neighbourhood now supports a prosperous trade in antiques and designer fashions. Via del Babuino – literally "Street of the Baboon" – gets its name from the statue of **Silenus** (Fontana del Babuino) which reclines about halfway down on the left. In ancient times, the wall behind was a focus for satirical graffiti, although it is now coated with graffiti-proof paint. A little further down on the left, the church of **All Saints** is the official Anglican church of Rome, its solid steeple and brick construction, erected in the late nineteenth century, serving as a further reminder of the English connections in this part of town.

Museo-Atelier Canova-Tadolini

Via del Babuino 150a · Daily 8am–midnight · ☎ 06 3211 0702, ⓦ canovatadolini.com

Right by the statue of Silenus, the **Museo-Atelier Canova-Tadolini** is really a café-restaurant (see p.250), but a highly original one, littered as it is with the sculptural work of four generations of the Tadolini family. The nineteenth-century sculptor Canova donated the building to Adam Tadolini, his most promising student, in 1818, and the family occupied the building for the next 150 years.

Piazza del Popolo

Minibuses #117 & #119 both stop on Piazza del Popolo, and you can also reach it on metro line A to Flaminio, just outside the city gate

At the far end of Via del Babuino, the oval-shaped expanse of **Piazza del Popolo** is a dignified meeting of roads laid out in 1538 by Pope Paul III (Alessandro Farnese) to

5

make an impressive entrance to the city; it owes its present symmetry to Valadier, who added the central fountain in 1814. The monumental **Porta del Popolo** went up in 1655, the work of Bernini, whose patron Alexander VII's Chigi family symbol – the heap of hills surmounted by a star – can clearly be seen above the main gateway. During summer, the steps around the obelisk and fountain, and the cafés on either side of the square, are popular hangouts. But the piazza's real attraction is the unbroken view it gives all the way back down Via del Corso, between the perfectly paired churches of **Santa Maria dei Miracoli** and **Santa Maria in Montesanto**, to the central columns of the Vittorio Emanuele Monument. If you get to choose your first view of the centre of Rome, make it this one.

Santa Maria del Popolo

Piazza del Popolo 12 • Mon–Sat 7am–12.30pm & 4–7pm, Sun 7.30am–1pm & 4.30–7.15pm • ☎ 06 361 0836, ⓦ www
.santamariadelpopolo.it

On the far side of Piazza del Popolo, hard against the city walls, **Santa Maria del Popolo** holds some of the best Renaissance art of any Roman church, with works by Raphael, Bramante, Pinturicchio, Sansovino and Caravaggio. It was originally erected here in 1099, over the burial place of Nero, in order to sanctify what was believed to be an evil place (the emperor's ghost had "appeared" here several times), but took its present form in the fifteenth century. Inside, there are frescoes by Pinturicchio in the first chapel of the south aisle, including a lovely *Adoration of Christ*, full of tiny details receding into the distance. Pinturicchio also did some work in the next chapel but one – the altarpiece *Madonna and Child and Saints* – and in the Bramante-designed apse, which in turn boasts two fine tombs by Andrea Sansovino.

The **Chigi chapel**, the second from the entrance in the northern aisle, was designed by **Raphael** for Agostino Chigi in 1516 (he lies in the tomb on the right, his brother Sigismondo on the left), although most of the work was actually undertaken by other artists and not finished until the seventeenth century. The odd pyramid-shaped memorials on either side have come in for lots of recent speculation, due to Dan Brown's fictional conspiracy theories – in *Angels & Demons*, its statues helped lead to the secretive Illuminati. Michelangelo's protégé, Sebastiano del Piombo, was responsible for the altarpiece; and two of the sculptures in the corner niches, of Daniel with the lions, on the left as you enter, and Habakkuk, diagonally opposite, are by Bernini.

However, it's two pictures by **Caravaggio**, in the left-hand Cerasi chapel of the north transept, that attract the most attention. These are typically dramatic works: one, the *Conversion of St Paul*, shows Paul and horse bathed in a beatific radiance, while the other, the *Crucifixion of St Peter*, has Peter as an aged but strong figure, dominated by the musclebound figures hoisting him up. Like his paintings in the churches of San Luigi dei Francesi and Sant'Agostino (see p.41 & p.42), both works were considered extremely risqué in their time, their heavy chiaroscuro and deliberate realism too much for the Church authorities; one contemporary critic referred to the *Conversion of St Paul*, a painting dominated by the exquisitely lit horse's hindquarters, as "an accident in a blacksmith's shop". In the middle, Carracci's boldly coloured altarpiece, with its golds and pinks, offers a massive contrast.

Piazza del Augusto Imperatore

Leading from Piazza del Popolo to **Piazza del Augusto Imperatore**, Via di Ripetta was laid out by Pope Leo X to provide a straight route out of the city centre from the old river port area here. Piazza del Augusto Imperatore itself is an odd square, made up of largely Mussolini-era buildings surrounding a peaceful ring of cypresses, circled by paths and flowering shrubs – what's left, basically, of the massive **Mausoleum di Augustus**, the burial place of the emperor and his family. Augustus died in 14 AD, giving way to his son Tiberius, who ruled until 37 AD (the last 10 years from the island of Capri), when his nephew's son Caligula took over and effectively signalled the end of the Augustan age, and the order, prosperity and expansion that defined it. As Augustus himself had it, according to Suetonius: "I found Rome built simply out of bricks: I left her clad in marble." The mausoleum has been transformed into many buildings over the years, including a medieval fortress, and is currently under long-term **restoration**, at the end of which you'll hopefully be able to get in to see the passageways and central crypt, where the ashes of the members of the Augustan dynasty were kept.

Ara Pacis

Lungotevere in Augusta, at Via Tomacelli · Tues–Sun 9am–7pm · €8.50, audioguide €4 · ☎ 06 0608, Ⓦ arapacis.it · Bus #628 from Piazza Venezia; from Termini, metro line A to Spagna or Flaminio and a short walk

On the far side of Piazza del Augusto Imperatore, the **Ara Pacis** or "Altar of Augustan Peace" is now enclosed in a controversial purpose-built structure designed by the New York-based architect **Richard Meier**, its angular lines and sheer white surfaces dominating the river side of the square. A marble block enclosed by sculpted walls, the altar was built in 13 BC, probably to celebrate Augustus's victory over Spain and Gaul and the peace it heralded. Much of it had been dug up piecemeal over the years, but the bulk was uncovered in the middle of the last century, in the heart of the Campus Martius, a few hundred yards south, where it had originally stood. Putting it back together was no easy task: excavation involved digging down to a depth of 10m and freezing the water table, after which many other parts had to be retrieved from museums the world over, or plaster copies made.

The result, on the surrounding walls especially, is a superb example of **imperial Roman sculpture**, particularly in the victory procession itself, on the mausoleum side of the altar. This is a picture of a family at the height of its power, with little inkling of the scandal and tragedy that would afflict it in years to come. The first part is almost completely gone, but the head of Augustus is complete, as are the figures that follow: the priests with their skullcap headgear, then, behind the figure carrying an axe, Augustus's great general, Marcus Agrippa, hooded, clutching a rolled piece of parchment, with his son Gaius pulling on his toga. Then, respectively, come Augustus's wife Livia, followed by her son (and Augustus's eventual successor) Tiberius and niece Antonia, the latter caught simply and realistically turning to her husband, Drusus, while holding the hand of her son Germanicus. Of the various other children clutching the togas of the elders, the last is said to be the young Claudius, while the old man towards the end may be Maecenas, Augustus's most trusted adviser during his heyday. On the front of the altar is a frieze of Aeneas making a sacrifice, while on the back is a well-preserved representation of Mother Earth bestowing peace and prosperity on Rome, holding two babies in her arms – said by some to be Lucius and Gaius, Augustus's grandchildren and his planned successors. On the river side, the veiled figure is believed to be their mother, Julia, Augustus's daughter, with Lucius in front of her. Julia later married her stepbrother Tiberius and was constantly disgraced for her promiscuity about Rome, and both children died young, before they could take on the responsibility that Augustus had planned for them.

Via Sistina

Leading south from the top of the Spanish Steps to Piazza Barberini, **Via Sistina** was the first of Pope Sixtus V's planning improvements to sixteenth-century Rome, a dead-straight street designed to connect Santa Maria Maggiore to Trinità dei Monti, which it almost still does, under a variety of names, and in the other direction to Piazza del Popolo, which it never quite managed. Nowadays, it's the quickest way of getting to the Via Veneto and Quirinale areas from the Spanish Steps.

5

Sant'Andrea delle Fratte

Via Sant'Andrea delle Fratte 1 • Daily 6.30am–12.30pm & 4.30–7.30pm • ⓦ santandreadellefratte.it

A hundred metres or so southwest of Via Sistina, **Sant'Andrea delle Fratte** is tucked into a tight spot – like so many churches by **Borromini**, who designed the characteristic campanile. This is another church in which the great men of the Baroque era came together: inside, the apse is flanked by two histrionic angels designed by Bernini, originally intended for the Ponte Sant'Angelo, the bridge which connects the Centro Storico and Prati. To the left of the north door, a plaque remembers **Angelica Kauffmann**, an accomplished late-eighteenth-century Swiss painter and great friend of the English artist Joshua Reynolds, who lived in Rome and was a good friend of Goethe (see p.92), while the door in the opposite aisle gives way to a very pleasant tree-filled cloister.

San Silvestro in Capite

Piazza San Silvestro 17a • Daily 9am–1pm & 4–7pm • ⓦ sansilvestroincapite.com

On the eastern side of Via del Corso, Piazza San Silvestro was, until recently, a busy bus terminus but is now a quieter pedestrian square, complete with benches. Nonetheless, nowhere illustrates better how history sits cheek-by-jowl with the modern world in Rome than the church of **San Silvestro in Capite**. The peaceful, plant-filled terracotta courtyard that you walk through to get in feels a million miles away from the fume-drenched traffic of the Corso outside. Inside, the blackened skull of John the Baptist that gives the church the second half of its name is displayed in a small chapel that doubles as a side entrance. The church itself was at one point the centre of the Franciscan movement in Rome, home to Margherita Colonna who espoused the then left-field beliefs of St Francis and whipped up a storm in the Catholic hierarchy. These days, its interior is classic over-stuffed Roman Baroque, although the dark, ancient feel suits its long and illustrious history well.

Galleria Alberto Sordi

Piazza Colonna • Daily 10am–10pm • ☎ 06 6919 0769, ⓦ galleriaalbertosordi.it

Just south of Pizza San Silvestro, across Via del Tritone, the classic Y-shaped nineteenth-century shopping arcade of **Galleria Alberto Sordi** has recently reopened after years of neglect. Renamed after an Italian film star (actors used to hang out here seeking work), it's as spruce and sleek as it was in its heyday, and provides a welcome escape from this ultra-busy part of central Rome, especially on a hot day.

Trevi Fountain

Piazza di Trevi • bus #175 from Termini

The tight web of narrow, apparently aimless streets south of Via del Tritone open out on one of Rome's more surprising sights – the **Trevi Fountain**, or Fontana di Trevi, a huge, very Baroque gush of water over statues and rocks built onto the backside of a Renaissance palace; it's fed by one of Rome's most celebrated water sources, the **Acqua Vergine**, which also surfaces at the Barcaccia Fountain in Piazza di Spagna. The original Trevi Fountain, designed by Alberti, was around the corner in Via dei Crociferi, but Urban VIII decided to upgrade it in line with his other grandiose schemes of the time and employed Bernini, among others, to design an alternative. Work didn't begin until 1732, when **Niccolò Salvi** won a competition held by Clement XII to design the fountain, and even then it took thirty years to finish the project. Salvi died in the process, his lungs shot due to the time he spent in the dank waterworks of the fountain. The Trevi Fountain is now, of course, the place you come to chuck in a coin if you want to guarantee your return to Rome, though you might remember Anita Ekberg throwing herself into it in *La Dolce Vita* (there are police here to discourage you from doing the same thing). Recently restored, it's one of the city's most vigorous outdoor spots to hang out.

Accademia di San Luca

Piazza dell'Accademia di San Luca 77 · Mon–Sat 10am–7pm · Free · ☎ 06 679 8850, Ⓦ www.accademiasanluca.it

A short walk from the Trevi Fountain, following Via della Stamperia towards Via del Tritone, the **Accademia di San Luca** is first and foremost Rome's school of art; it has a small collection of art and hosts regular exhibitions. The building itself is worth visiting, in any case, for its **Borromini ramp**, which spirals up from the main lobby instead of a staircase, but it's also worth a peep at the collection in the third-floor gallery, which includes a handful of sculptures by Canova, including a bust of Clement XIII and a rare self-portrait, some pieces by the 19th-century Danish sculptor Bertel Thorvaldsen, architectural drawings and a host of portraits of prominent academicians over the years, from Algardi and Bernini to Vanvitelli.

Santi Vincenzo ed Anastasio

Vicolo dei Modelli 73 · Daily 7.30am–noon & 4–7pm · ☎ 06 678 3098

Directly opposite the Trevi Fountain, the grubby little church of **Santi Vincenzo ed Anastasio** is the parish church of the Quirinale Palace, and, bizarrely, holds in marble urns the hearts and viscera of the 22 popes who used the palace as a papal residence. Two tablets – one either side of the high altar – record each of the popes whose bits and pieces lie downstairs, from Sixtus V, who died in 1590, to Leo XIII, who passed away in 1903.

Città dell'Acqua

Vicolo del Puttarello 25 · Wed Fri 11am–5.30pm, Sat & Sun 11am–7pm · €3 · ☎ 339 778 6192

Just around the corner from the Trevi Fountain, a small art-house cinema stands above a couple of recently opened ancient Roman excavations. The so-called **Città dell'Acqua** holds a couple of ancient Roman structures: one a palace of some kind, the other a building which was at some point converted into a series of cisterns, which still hold water today. Walkways weave about amongst the ruins and take in a few finds from the site, but there's not a great deal to see.

Galleria Colonna

Via della Pilotta 17 · Sat 9am–1.15pm, closed Aug; terrace café March–Oct · €12; guided tours in English free (11.45am) · Gardens not open to the public · ☎ 06 678 4350, Ⓦ galleriacolonna.it · Bus #62 or #63 from Termini to Piazza Venezia.

A short stroll south from the Trevi Fountain brings you to the **Galleria Colonna**, part of the Palazzo Colonna complex, whose gardens stretch up the hill from here, linked to the palace by bridges over the narrow street. The gallery is outranked by many of Rome's other palatial collections, but it's worth visiting, not only for its small yet high-quality collection of art, but also for the glimpse it gives you of the home of one of Rome's most powerful Renaissance families, a little bit more of which is open to public now than was previously.

The so-called **Battle Column** room has two lascivious paintings of Venus and Cupid facing each other across the room – one by Bronzino on the far side, the other by Ghirlandaio – that were once considered so risqué that clothes were painted on in 1840 (they were removed during a restoration a few years ago). There are more fleshy creations by Ghirlandaio in the same room, while the ceiling paintings in the adjacent chandelier-decked **Great Hall** glorify the deeds of Marcantonio Colonna, notably his

5

great victory against the Turks at the Battle of Lepanto. Of the paintings, the highlight is maybe the gallery's collection of landscapes by Dughet (Poussin's brother-in-law), housed in the next room, frescoed with more scenes of the Battle of Lepanto, while other rooms remember the Colonna pope, Martin V, not least the frescoes in the **Room of the Apotheosis** which show him being received into heaven, and Pisanello's pious portrait of him in the next room. Other paintings which stand out here include Annibale Carracci's early and unusually spontaneous *Bean Eater* (though its attribution to him has since been questioned), a *Portrait of a Venetian Gentleman*, caught in a supremely confident pose by Veronese, *Narcissus* and a portrait of an old man by Tintoretto and Bronzino's lovely *Madonna with Saints Elizabeth and John*.

Santi Apostoli

Piazza dei Santi Apostoli 51 · Daily 7am–noon & 4–7pm · ☎ 06 699 571, ⓦ www.santiapostoli.eu

The back of Palazzo Colonna is taken up by the large church of **Santi Apostoli**, dedicated to the apostles Philip and James, a sixth-century basilica whose ancient origins are hard to detect now, encased as it is in an eighteenth-century shell and Napoleonic facade, and completely done up with Baroque finery inside. It, too, was part of the Colonna estate and is a Franciscan church, thanks to the family's early embrace of the movement, its wide, airy interior still looked after by the friars, who pad silently around while you take in its clash of Byzantine, Renaissance and Baroque architectural styles. The ceiling paintings are by the Genoese painter Baciccia, more famous for his work in the Gesù (see p.57), and the north aisle contains the nineteenth-century Italian sculptor Canova's first work in Rome, the very grand tomb of Clement XIV above the door to the sacristy. But the church's statue-encrusted portico is perhaps its most impressive feature, commissioned by Pope Julius II, who lived in the palace next door. It overlooks the equally grandiose **Palazzo Odescalchi** opposite, which was renovated by Bernini in the 1660s but is currently not open to the public.

Museo delle Cere

Piazza dei Santi Apostoli 68 · Daily 9am–9pm · €9 · ☎ 06 679 6482, ⓦ museodellecere.com

A short walk from Piazza Venezia, the **Museo delle Cere** is a quirky first-floor museum of waxworks that hosts a diverse array of characters from history and Italian culture: not essential viewing by any means, but certainly different from anything else you'll see in Rome. It starts with a room devoted to the **Fascist Council** of 1943, with Mussolini at its head, gloomily – and fairly spookily – giving up on the war. Off to the right are various titans of the war and postwar era: Hitler and Himmler; the **Yalta conference** threesome of Churchill, Stalin and Roosevelt; and Mao and Khrushchev. Things lighten up a bit in other rooms, with **footballers** Totti – captain of AS Roma – and Nesta, the former Lazio captain, **Pavarotti** and the gravel-voiced Italian rock balladeer **Zucchero**. Deeper into the museum, you're treated to various ancient musicians and artists, the usual chamber of horrors suspects – murderers, electric chairs and the like – and even some wax dinosaurs, although by far the most frightening exhibit shows a fairy-tale prince about to waken the sleeping princess; look at her long enough, and you'll see that she's actually breathing.

SAN CARLO ALLE QUATTRO FONTANE

The Quirinale and Via Veneto

Up above the historic centre, and across Via Nazionale from the Esquiline Hill and Monti, the Quirinale is perhaps the most appealing of the hills that rise up on the eastern side of the centre of Rome, and the first to be properly developed, when, in the seventeenth century, those who could afford it moved up here from the city centre. Nowadays, the district holds some of the city's most compelling sights, namely the Palazzo del Quirinale (though this is only open on Sundays); the Palazzo Barberini, home of some Rome's best art; and a couple of its most ingenious Baroque churches. Via Veneto, too, is worth the stroll up from Piazza Barberini – once the capital's most celebrated urban thoroughfare and still sporting the odd hint of Sixties glamour, as well as some distinguished architecture.

Piazza Barberini

At the bottom of the Quirinal Hill, the junction of Via Sistina and the shopping street of Via del Tritone centres on the busy intersection of **Piazza Barberini**, which itself focuses on Bernini's **Fontana del Tritone** – a sea-god gushing a high jet of water from a conch shell in the centre of the square. The recently restored fountain lends a unity to the square in more ways than one: traditionally, this quarter of the city was associated with the Barberini, a family who were the greatest patrons of Bernini, and the sculptor's works in their honour are thick on the ground around here. He finished the Tritone fountain in 1644, before designing the **Fontana delle Api**, otherwise known as the "Fountain of the Bees", which you can see at the bottom end of Via Veneto. Unlike the Tritone fountain, you could walk right past this without noticing it – a smaller, quirkier work, its broad scallop shell studded with the bees that were the symbol of the Barberini.

Galleria Nazionale d'Arte Antica

Via delle Quattro Fontane 13 • Tues–Sun 9am–7pm • €7, €9 including Palazzo Corsini, valid 3 days; audioguides €2.50 • Apartment tours can be booked in advance on ☎ 06 481 4591, ☎ 06 32810, 🌐 galleriaborghese.it • Metro line A from Termini to Barberini; from Piazza Venezia, take bus #62, #175, #160 or #492

On the southeast side of Piazza Barberini, the **Palazzo Barberini** is home to a series of apartments that were once occupied by the Barberini family and, more importantly, that nowadays house the **Galleria Nazionale d'Arte Antica**, a rich patchwork of mainly Italian art from the early Renaissance to late Baroque period that is now better displayed than ever in a set of recently renovated galleries. Perhaps the most impressive feature of the gallery is the building itself, worked on at different times by the most favoured architects of the day – Bernini, Borromini, Maderno – and the epitome of Baroque grandeur. In an impressive show of balanced commissioning, there are **two main staircases**, one by Bernini and a second by his rival Borromini, and the two couldn't be more different – the former an ordered rectangle of ascending grandeur, the latter a more playful and more organic spiral staircase. But the palace's first-floor **Gran Salone** is its artistic highspot, with a ceiling frescoed by Pietro da Cortona that is one of the best examples of exuberant Baroque trompe l'oeil you'll ever see, a manic rendering of the *Triumph of Divine Providence* that almost crawls down the walls to meet you. Note the bees – the Barberini family symbol – flying towards the figure of Providence.

Ground floor

The collection is divided into three sections, the first of which, on the ground floor, covers the **early Renaissance period**, with a couple of *Pietàs* by Giacomo Francia, one of which, with St Paul, is one of the most overlooked works in the collection. Look out also for Piero di Cosimo's *St Mary Magdalene*, with lovely colour and detail, along with numerous Madonnas, including Fra' Filippo Lippi's warmly maternal *Madonna and Child*, painted in 1437 and introducing background details, notably architecture, into Italian religious painting for the first time.

First floor

The second section, on the first floor, is perhaps the core of the collection, with works taking you through the **Renaissance** and **Baroque eras**, and finishing up with the Salone di Cortona, magnificently empty but for a couple of seats from which to admire the ceiling. The first room – 12 – holds Raphael's beguiling *La Fornarina*, a painting of a Trasteveran baker's daughter thought to have been the artist's mistress (Raphael's name appears clearly on the woman's bracelet), although some experts claim the painting to be the work of a pupil. Later rooms have two works by Tintoretto – *Christ and the Woman taken in Adultery* and *St Jerome* – as well as Titian's lively *Venus and*

Adonis and Lotto's *Mystical Marriage of St Catherine*, while a further gallery brings together the collection's impressive array of **portraiture**: Bronzino's rendering of the marvellously erect Stefano Colonna, and a portrait of Henry VIII by Hans Holbein which feels almost as well known – probably because the painter produced so many of the monarch. Painted on the day of his marriage to his fourth wife, Anne of Cleves, he's depicted as a rather irritable but beautifully dressed middle-aged man – a stark

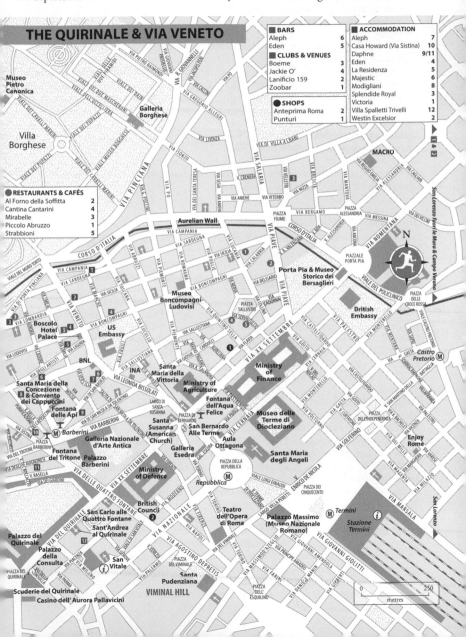

THE QUIRINALE & VIA VENETO

■ BARS	
Aleph	6
Eden	5

■ CLUBS & VENUES	
Boeme	3
Jackie O'	4
Lanificio 159	1
Zoobar	1

● SHOPS	
Anteprima Roma	2
Punturi	1

■ ACCOMMODATION	
Aleph	7
Casa Howard (Via Sistina)	10
Daphne	9/11
Eden	4
La Residenza	5
Majestic	6
Modigliani	8
Splendide Royal	3
Victoria	1
Villa Spalletti Trivelli	12
Westin Excelsior	2

● RESTAURANTS & CAFÉS	
Al Forno della Soffitta	2
Cantina Cantarini	4
Mirabelle	3
Piccolo Abruzzo	1
Strabbioni	5

contrast to the rather ascetic figure of Erasmus of Rotterdam by Quentin Matsys, which sometimes hangs nearby. Next door are two unusually small paintings by El Greco, the *Baptism of Christ* and *Adoration of the Shepherds*, and then, further on, a couple of rooms of work by Caravaggio – notably *Judith and Holofernes* – and his followers, for example the seventeenth-century Neapolitan Ribera's controlled study of *St Gregory the Great* and Simon Vouet's *Fortune Tellers*, whose duplicitous peasants are reminiscent of Caravaggio's own in the Capitoline Museums (see p.70).

6

Top floor

Finally, the new galleries on the top floor finish off the collection by taking you from the **late Baroque era**, starting with works by more Neapolitan Baroque painters and their acolytes, most significantly Luca Giordano, whose marvellously realistic *Portrait of a Master Builder* could almost have been painted yesterday, and the Calabrian Matia Preti, whose dark, dramatic canvases again owe a huge debt to Caravaggio. Next door, Bernini's portrait of Urban VIII, the Barberini pope, has been rightfully reinstated in the pontiff's own palace. The final rooms cover the late seventeenth and eighteenth centuries, and as such are perhaps less interesting but for a few exceptions, among them a number of cityscapes of Rome by Gaspar van Wittel and classic Venetian scenes by Guardi and Canaletto, along with Neapolitan paintings by Solimena and Francesco de Mura and a handful of paintings from France, including a rustic pair depicting *Morning* and *Evening* by François Boucher.

Santa Maria della Concezione

Via Veneto 27 • Daily 7.45am–noon & 3.45–7.30pm • ☎ 06 487 1185 • Metro line A from Termini to Barberini; from Piazza Venezia, take bus #62, #175, #160 or #492

A little way up Via Veneto from Piazza Barberini, on the right, the Capuchin church of **Santa Maria della Concezione** was one of many sponsored creations of the Barberini family in the area (founded in 1626), although it's not a particularly significant building in itself, and its only real treasure is Guido Reni's androgynous *St Michael Trampling on the Devil*, in the first chapel on the right. The Devil in the picture is said to be a portrait of Innocent X, whom the artist despised, and who was apparently a sworn enemy of the Barberini family. Take a look at the tomb slab of the founder of the church, Antonio Barberini, in front of the altar, which has an inscription – "Here lies dust, ashes, nothing" – that is quite at odds with the worldly, wealthy impression you get of the Barberini elsewhere in the city.

Convento dei Cappuccini

Daily 9am–7pm • €6 (including museum), audioguide €4 • ☎ 06 8880 3695, ⓦ cappucciniviaveneto.it

The main reason people come to Santa Maria della Concezione is to see the **Convento dei Cappuccini**, to the right of the church, which is famously home to the **bones** of four thousand monks who died between 1528 and 1870, set into the walls of a series of six chapels – a monument to "Our Sister of Bodily Death", in the words of St Francis, that was erected in 1793. Some bones and skulls are simply piled up, but others appear in abstract or Christian patterns or as fully clothed skeletons, their faces peering out of their cowls in twisted expressions of agony. The effect lies somewhere between chilling and ludicrous, and makes for one of the more macabre and bizarre sights of Rome. As for the **Cappuchin order**, they are the most **ascetic** and extreme interpretation of the Franciscan order, dressed in roped habits and traditionally dedicated to a life of poverty. There's an attached **museum** with lots of good background on them (much of it in English), including a couple of short films, devotional items and paintings (including a *St Francis* attributed to Caravaggio) and a display on the charismatic Father Mariano of Turin, perhaps the most famous Cappuchin friar of modern times, who had his own TV show until his death in 1972 and now rests here.

> ## VIA RASELLA
>
> More or less opposite Palazzo Barberini, **Via Rasella** was the scene of an ambush of a Nazi military patrol in 1944 that led to one of the worst Italian wartime atrocities – the reprisal massacre of 335 innocent Romans at the Ardeatine Caves outside the city walls. A **memorial** now stands on the site of the executions, near the Via Appia Antica (see p.151), and the event is commemorated there every March 24 with a solemn ceremony; it's also documented in the Richard Burton movie *Massacre in Rome* (see p.335). Oddly enough, Mussolini had a flat on Via Rasella when he first came to Rome, in which he apparently entertained a string of mistresses.

6

Via Veneto and around

Via Vittorio Veneto, usually referred to as **Via Veneto**, bends north from Piazza Barberini up to the southern edge of the Villa Borghese, and is a cool, materialistic antidote to the murky atmosphere of the nearby Capuchin grotto. The pricey bars and restaurants lining the street were once the haunt of Rome's beautiful people, made famous by Fellini's *La Dolce Vita*, but they left a long time ago, and Via Veneto is these days, to some extent, living off **past glories**, if the *Dolce Vita*-era photos adorning the outside of *Harry's Bar*, *Café de Paris* and its other iconic establishments are anything to go by. The street has a full complement of all the posh hotel names you could possibly think of: the *Excelsior*, *Majestic*, the *Imperial* – they're all here, some more upmarket than others, though nearly all are chains.

Boscolo Hotel Palace

Via Veneto 70

Via Veneto is home to some of the city's best and most imposing Modernist and Fascist-era buildings and is worth a wander for just that. The **Boscolo Hotel Palace** is the work of the Fascists' favourite architect, Marcello Piacentini. Its solid travertine elegance, punctuated by Art Deco lamps supported by sleek nymphets, is reminiscent of a bygone age – a feel that is emphasized in the bar inside, frescoed with scenes of the wealthy and beautiful people of 1920s Rome.

Ministry for Economic Development

Via Veneto 33

Not far from the *Grand Hotel Palace*, the **Ministry for Economic Development** is a more brutal Fascist-era edifice, built of giant tufa blocks that set off well the bronze door panels of the main entrance, depicting musclebound scenes of industry, agriculture, commerce, transport and the like. If the doors are open, try to get a peek in the lobby, whose staircase and stained glass might well be the model for the all-powerful Ministry in Terry Gilliam's film *Brazil*.

Via Bissolati

The giant **INA Building**, at Via Leonida Bissolati 23, was built in the 1920s, and the friezes of ships on either side of its main door are indicative of its original – and current – function. Across the road, the brick and travertine **BNL Building** is another Piacentini creation, and anchors the corner well, a dignified presence compared to the seemingly besieged **US embassy** on the opposite corner.

Museo Boncompagni-Ludovisi

Via Boncompagni 18 · Tues–Sun 8.30am–7pm · Free · ☎ 06 4282 4074, ⓦ www.museoboncompagni.beniculturali.it

A five-minute walk east from Via Veneto, the **Museo Boncompagni-Ludovisi** is a small cultural highlight of the neighbourhood, an adjunct to the Modern Art Museum in Villa Borghese (see p.175), with displays of decorative arts and fashion through the ages. Housed in a mid-nineteenth-century *palazzo*, it has a small collection of furniture, porcelain and paintings, but its main focus is **Italian fashion**, with an array of nineteenth- and twentieth-century cocktail and evening dresses, among other items.

San Carlo alle Quattro Fontane

Via del Quirinale 23 • Mon–Fri 10am–1pm & 3–6pm, Sat 10am–1pm, Sun noon–1pm • ☎ 06 488 3261, ⓦ sancarlino.eu • Bus #40, #64, #170 or #H from either Piazza Venezia or Termini to Via Nazionale and a short walk

Via delle Quattro Fontane takes a route right over the Quirinal Hill from Piazza Barberini, and its crossroads with Via XX Settembre is the seventeenth-century landmark church of **San Carlo alle Quattro Fontane**. This was Borromini's first real design commission, and in it he displays all the ingenuity he later became known for, elegantly cramming the church into a tiny and awkwardly shaped site that apparently covers roughly the same surface area as one of the main columns inside St Peter's. Tucked in beside the church, the cloister is squeezed into a tight but elegant oblong, topped with a charming balustrade.

Outside the church are the **four fountains** that give the street and church their name, each cut into a niche in a corner of the crossroads that marks the highest point on the Quirinal Hill. They were put here in 1593 and represent the Tiber and Aniene rivers and Strength and Fidelity, and they make a fine (if busy) spot to look back down towards the Trinità dei Monti obelisk in one direction and the Santa Maria Maggiore obelisk in the other – all part of Sixtus V's grand city plan.

Giardino di Sant'Andrea al Quirinale

Via del Quirinale 27 • Daily 7am–sunset • Free

The small shaded public gardens between the churches of San Carlo alle Quattro Fontane and Sant'Andrea al Quirinale, the **Giardino di Sant'Andrea al Quirinale**, make a good place for a sit down and a picnic lunch; they also provide a direct route down to Via Nazionale and the Esquiline area beyond.

Sant'Andrea al Quirinale

Via del Quirinale 29 • Closed until summer 2014 for restoration; usual opening hours Mon–Sat 8.30am–noon & 3.30–7pm, Sun 9am–noon & 4–7pm • Sacristy €1 • ☎ 06 474 4872, ⓦ gesuitialquirinale.it • Bus #40, #64, #170 or #H from either Piazza Venezia or Termini to Via Nazionale and a short walk

A few steps southwest of the church of San Carlo alle Quattro Fontane, flanked on the left by gardens (see above), the domed church of **Sant'Andrea al Quirinale** is a flamboyant building that Bernini planned in a flat oval shape to fit into its wide but shallow site. Like San Carlo, it's unusual and ingenious inside, and was apparently the church that Bernini himself was most pleased with, its wide, elliptical nave cleverly made into a grand space despite its relatively small size. Once you've taken this in, you can visit the **sacristy** – whose frescoes are similarly artful, with cherubs pulling aside painted drapery to let in light from mock windows – and the upstairs rooms of one St Stanislaus Kostka, where the Polish saint lived (and died) in 1568. The rooms have changed quite a lot since then, with paintings by the Jesuit artist Andrea Pozzo illustrating the life of the saint and a chapel focused on a disturbingly lifelike painted statue of Stanislaus lying on his deathbed. At press time, the church was undergoing restorations and closed to the public.

Palazzo del Quirinale

Piazza del Quirinale • Sun 8.30am–noon • €5 • ☎ 06 46991, ⓦ quirinale.it • Bus #40, #64, #170 or #H from either Piazza Venezia or Termini to Via Nazionale and a short walk; or walk direct from Piazza Venezia (10min)

Opposite the church of Sant'Andrea al Quirinale is the featureless wall – the so-called *manica lunga* or "long sleeve" – of the **Palazzo del Quirinale**, a sixteenth-century structure that was the official summer residence of the popes until Unification, when it became the **royal palace**. Its entrance fronts onto the Piazza del Quirinale (see below), and it's now the home of Italy's president (a largely ceremonial role). It's worth braving the security for a glimpse of the style in which popes, despots, kings and now presidents like to live, with a fine set of state rooms and some very accomplished works of art – though note the limited opening hours.

Salone dei Corazzieri and Cappella Paolina

The first and perhaps most impressive of the works here is Melozzo da Forlí's fifteenth-century fresco of Christ, on the staircase off the courtyard, a fragment of a work that was painted for the apse of Santi Apostoli – the rest is in the Vatican (see p.208). Once inside, the spectacular first room, the **Salone dei Corazzieri**, was partly decorated by Carlo Maderno and essentially intended to glorify the life of Paul V, with frescoes interspersing the life of Moses with scenes showing the pope greeting various foreign emissaries and ambassadors. In case you were in any doubt of Paul V's achievements, Maderno throws in monochrome representations of some of his big building projects, including the Acqua Paola at one end of the room and St Peter's and the Quirinale itself at the other end. You can't always enter Maderno's **Cappella Paolina**, through the next door, but it's no great loss: its dimensions are precisely the same as the Sistine Chapel but it couldn't be more different, studded with a tasteless decorative ceiling, its walls covered in colourless nineteenth-century representations of the Apostles.

Salone del Balcone and beyond

More grand rooms follow: the **Salone del Balcone** was where Pius IX gave his blessing on his election as pope; the next room contains a copy of Raphael's *John the Baptist* by Giulio Romano; the three rooms beyond used to be one enormously long space but were remodelled during Napoleon's occupation of the place. Even now, they cut quite a dash, frescoed under the direction of Pietro da Cortona in 1656 to a commission by Pope Alexander VII, with big biblical events depicted in accomplished and naturalistic style by a variety of artists, culminating in a dazzling *Adoration of the Shepherds* by Carlo Maratta. The final rooms are largely decorated in the style of the Savoy kings, who took over the palace in the nineteenth century, but the last room you see, the **Salone delle Feste** – originally the Sala Regia, where Paul V received foreign dignitaries – still packs quite a punch, its ceiling massively higher than the others at 16m, and decorated with Agostino Tassi's pseudo-oriental perspectives.

Piazza del Quirinale

If the Palazzo Quirinale is closed, you can make do with appreciating its exceptional setting in the **Piazza del Quirinale**, from which views stretch right across the centre of Rome. The main feature of the piazza is the huge statue of the Dioscuri, the name given to Castor and Pollux. These are massive 5m-high Roman copies of classical **Greek statues**, showing the two godlike twins, the sons of Jupiter, who according to legend won victory for the Romans in an important battle (see p.82). The statues originally stood at the entrance to the Baths of Constantine, the ruins of which lay nearby, and were brought here by Pope Sixtus V in the early sixteenth century to embellish the square – part of the pope's attempts to dignify and beautify the city with many large, vista-laden squares and long, straight avenues. Nowadays, it forms an odd concoction with the obelisk, originally from the Mausoleum of Augustus, which tops the arrangement, and the vast shallow bowl in front, which was apparently once resident at the Roman Forum – all in all, a classic example of how Rome has recycled most of its classical debris.

Scuderie del Quirinale

Via XXIV Maggio 16 · Opening times vary but usually daily 10am–8pm, with extended hours at weekends · Exhibition admission usually around €10, or €18 including Palazzo dello Esposizioni · ☎ 06 3996 7500, ⓦ scuderiequirinale.it

The eighteenth-century **Scuderie del Quirinale** faces the Palazzo del Quirinale from across the square, completing the triangle of buildings that make up the piazza. Originally the papal stables, it has been imaginatively restored as display space for some of the major travelling exhibitions that come to the city. It has an excellent art bookshop on the ground floor, and the equestrian spiral staircase that winds up to the main exhibition rooms is impressive. There's also a decent **restaurant and café**, and the modern glass staircase added to the side of the building offers by far the best view over Rome from the Quirinale.

Casino dell'Aurora Pallavicini

Via XXIV Maggio 43 · First of every month 10am–noon & 3–5pm · Free · ☎ 06 8346 7000, ⓦ casinoaurorapallavicini.it · Private visits only available for groups of 20+ and booked at least 15–18 days in advance

Opposite the Scuderie del Quirinale, the **Palazzo Pallavicini-Rospigliosi** was originally commissioned by Cardinal Scipione Borghese in 1603, on the site of the Baths of Constantine, specifically to be near the papal action at the Palazzo del Quirinale. There's a decent collection of Baroque painting in the gallery inside, but this can only be visited in large groups and by appointment; the only part you can turn up unannounced to see is the **Casino dell'Aurora Pallavicini**, and this only once a month. The Casino is attached to the gardens on the left, where you can admire the Roman sarcophagi that frieze the facade, which is wonderfully well preserved and full of tangled figures and exotic animals. It's a theme that is continued inside, with depictions of Roman triumphs at each end. However, the main focus is Guido Reni's ceiling fresco, *Aurora Scattering Flowers before the Sun* – a typically accomplished and smooth work, but somehow lacking in drama. In each corner, the poised and bucolic scenes of each season provide a nice counterpoint.

Via XX Settembre

Bus #40, #64, #170 or #H from either Piazza Venezia or Termini to Via Nazionale and a short walk

Via XX Settembre spears out towards the **Aurelian Wall** – the city walls – from Via del Quirinale – not Rome's most appealing thoroughfare by any means, flanked by the deliberately faceless bureaucracies of the national government, erected after Unification in anticipation of Rome's ascension as a new world capital. It was, however, the route by which Italian troops entered the city on September 20, 1870, after the French troops defending the city had withdrawn, and the place where they breached the wall is marked with a column.

Santa Susanna

Via XX Settembre 15 · Currently closed for restoration but usually daily 9am–noon & 4–7pm · ☎ 06 4201 4554, ⓦ www.santasusanna.org

The headquarters of **American Catholics in Rome**, halfway up Via XX Settembre and just north of Piazza della Repubblica, the church of **Santa Susanna** is one of an elegant cluster of facades, and it's a prominent landmark, although behind its well-proportioned Carlo Maderno frontage it's not an especially notable building in itself, except for some bright and soothing frescoes.

Fontana dell'Acqua Felice

Via XX Settembre

Santa Susanna looks across the busy junction to the **Fontana dell'Acqua Felice**, which is playfully fronted by four basking lions, and focuses on a massive, bearded figure of Moses in the central one of three arches. Marking the end of the Acqua Felice aqueduct, the fountain forms part of Pope Sixtus V's late-sixteenth-century attempts to spruce up the city centre with large-scale public works.

San Bernardo alle Terme

Via Torino 94 • Daily 6.30am–noon & 4–7pm • ☎ 06 488 2122

Opposite Santa Susanna and the Fontana dell'Acqua Felice, the church of **San Bernardo alle Terme** is so named (from *terme* – baths or springs) for the fact that it was once part of the vast complex of Diocletian's baths, and with its coffered ceiling and roof light, it's like a mini-pantheon inside – although it is, of course, highly restored.

Santa Maria della Vittoria

Via XX Settembre 17 • Daily 8.30am–noon & 3.30–6pm, Sun only 3.30–6pm

Immediately opposite the Acqua Felice fountain, the church of **Santa Maria della Vittoria** was, like Santa Susanna, built by Carlo Maderno. Its interior is one of the most elaborate examples of Baroque decoration in Rome: almost shockingly excessive to modern eyes, its ceiling and walls are pitted with carvings, and statues are crammed into remote corners as in an over-stuffed attic. The church's best-known feature, Bernini's carving of the *Ecstasy of St Teresa*, the centrepiece of the sepulchral **chapel of Cardinal Cornaro**, continues the histrionics. A deliberately melodramatic work, it features a theatrically posed **St Teresa of Avila** against a backdrop of theatre-boxes on each side of the chapel, from which the Cornaro cardinals murmur and nudge each other, as they watch the spectacle. St Teresa is one of the Catholic Church's most enduring mystics, and Bernini records the moment when, in 1537, she had a vision of an angel piercing her heart with a dart. It is a very Baroque piece of work in the most populist sense: not only is the event quite literally staged, but St Teresa's ecstasy verges on the worldly as she lies back in groaning submission beneath a mass of dishevelled garments and drapery.

British Embassy

Via XX Settembre 80a • Visits by appointment only on ☎ 06 4220 0001 or ✉ infoRome@fco.gov.uk

At the northeast end of Via XX Settembre, the **British Embassy** building cuts quite a dash behind its high security-controlled gates and fences, a striking modern statement amid the neighbourhood's heavy nineteenth-century *palazzi*. The previous building had been blown to pieces in 1946 by **terrorists**, and the diplomats were forced to camp out for a couple of decades in Villa Wolkonsky, in the south of the city near San Giovanni, until Sir Basil Spence designed and built this purpose-built affair, which opened in 1971. Set on **stilts** above a courtyard and pool, it's both a practical and aesthetic statement – clearly very secure, although the stilts were in fact deployed so as not to obscure the view of the gardens at ground level. As a positive statement of Britain's contemporary role in the world, it doesn't get much better than this.

Porta Pia

Marking the northern end of Via XX Settembre, the **Porta Pia** was one of the last works of Michelangelo, erected under Pope Pius IV in 1561, and one of the major remaining gates in the third-century AD Aurelian Wall – constructed by the emperor of the same name in 275 AD to protect the city from attack. The gate in fact doesn't bear much relation to Michelangelo's much fancier original design, and was finished after his death. These days, it's most famous as the spot at which Italian troops first entered Rome on September 20, 1870.

Museo Storico dei Bersaglieri

Porta Pia • Temporarily closed but usually open Mon–Thurs 9am–4.30pm, Fri 9am–1pm • ☎ 06 486 723

The Porta Pia houses the small **Museo Storico dei Bersaglieri**, dedicated to a crack body of troops founded in 1836 (they're the ones with the large floppy feathers in their hats) and with displays on the founder, Alessandro La Marmora, along with sections on the Unification struggle, World War II and other conflicts.

SANTA PRASSEDE

The Esquiline, Monti and Termini

Immediately north of the Colosseum, the Esquiline is the highest and largest of the city's seven hills, an area of vineyards and olive groves that was one of the most fashionable residential quarters of ancient Rome. These days, as the location of Termini station and the bulk of Rome's budget hotels, it's a part of town that most travellers to Rome encounter at some point. Via Cavour is a busy artery and hosts key sights like the Santa Maria Maggiore basilica; the Piazza Vittorio area has a long-running market and the bulk of the city centre's Chinese population. To the west, between Via Cavour and the shopping street of Via Nazionale, Monti is one of the city centre's most appealing neighbourhoods, home to both grocery stores and restorers' workshops as well as buzzy bars and restaurants.

Parco di Colle Oppio

Daily 7am–sunset

Almost opposite the Colosseum, and perhaps the easiest way to get from Rome's tourist centre into the heart of the Esquiline, the **Parco di Colle Oppio**, built on the Oppian Hill, one of the peaks of the ancient Roman Esquiline, is a fairly undistinguished open space and a slightly unsavoury spot after dark, but by day it's worth a wander, dotted as it is with remnants of the various Roman structures that once stood here: piles of rubble, the imposing fenced-off remains of **Trajan's Baths**, a public baths built in 109 AD that's still being excavated. The round brick stumps you can see are well-heads that led down into the Esquiline's other big ancient Roman sight, Nero's **Domus Aurea** or "Golden House" which lies underneath the baths complex.

Via Cavour

Via Cavour is one of Rome's busiest thoroughfares, slashed through the Monti neighbourhood in the 1890s to connect the station district to the river – although the last part, to connect it to the Tiber, was never completed. It's not an interesting street by any standards, but those to either side give some hint of the neighbourhood it destroyed, whether it's the peaceful thoroughfares on its southern side, around San Pietro in Vincoli and down towards the **Colosseum**, or the narrow switchbacks of the Monti district proper off its northern edge.

Monti

Metro line B to Cavour from Termini; from Piazza Venezia, take bus #117

Between Via Cavour and Via Nazionale, and up as far as the church of Santa Maria Maggiore, is the small area that has come to be known as **Monti**, an atmospheric quarter focusing on Via dei Serpenti and Via del Boschetto, and the narrow streets between them, including Via Panisperna, which you can follow all the way up to the basilica.

Piazza Madonna dei Monti

Monti's social centre – if it has one – is probably **Piazza Madonna dei Monti**, a small, vibrant open space at the end of Via dei Serpenti and Via del Boschetto. The architect **Giacomo della Porta** contributed the fountain in the centre, where, legend has it, heathen girls and boys were once brought to be baptized into the Catholic Church. It makes a nice spot for a drink or something to eat, whether you're exploring the neighbourhood or not; indeed, it has the advantage of being just five minutes' walk from the Colosseum and is quite a spot at night when it's crammed with people hanging out and drinking.

Madonna dei Monti

Via della Madonna dei Monti 41 · Daily 7am–noon & 5–7.30pm · ☎ 06 485 531, ⓦ santamariaaimonti.it

The large building next to the Piazza Madonna dei Monti, at the bottom of Via dei Serpenti, is the church of the **Madonna dei Monti**, built on the site of a convent, where a miraculous image of the Virgin was found and whose high dome and generous proportions make it well worth a peep. It was built in 1580 and is the work of Giacomo della Porta, designer of the fountain in the piazza.

San Pietro in Vincoli

Piazza di San Pietro in Vincoli 4a · Daily 8am–12.30pm & 3–7pm · ☎ 06 9784 4952 · Bus #70 from Piazza Venezia; from Termini, take metro line B to Cavour

At the bottom end of Via Cavour, steps lead from the street's southern side up to the tranquil piazza in front of the recently restored church of **San Pietro in Vincoli**, one of Rome's most delightfully plain places of worship, built to house an important relic, the

THE ESQUILINE, MONTI & TERMINI

PIAZZA SALLUSTIO

V. LOMBARDIA

V. BONCOMPAGNI

VIA SERVIO TULLIO

VIA PIAVE

1

British Embassy

V. GAETA

US Embassy

VIA VITTORIO VENETO

VIA BONCOMPAGNI

VIA LIGURIA

VIA PIEMONTE

VIA LIGULLO

VIA QUINTINO SELLA

VIA GOITO

VIA XX SETTEMBRE

VIA PALESTRO

VIA CERNAIA

VIA MONTEBELLO

1

VIA LEONIDA BISSOLATI

VIA SALLUSTIANA

VIA GOITO

VIA CARDUCCI

VIA AURELIANA

VIA FLAVIA

VIA GIOSUE

VIA SALUSTIANA

VIA CALANDRA

VIA SALLUSTIANA

VIA MASSIMO

Santa Maria della Vittoria

Ministry of Agriculture

Ministry of Finance

V. CASTELFIDARDO

1

V. CASTELFIDARDO

2

Convento dei Cappuccini

VIA DI SAN BASILIO

VIA LEONIDA BISSOLATI

LARGO DI SANTA SUSANNA

VIA BALZIMINO

Ministry of Finance

VIA GAETA

VIA VOLTURNO

VIA CURTATONE

VIA GAETA

VIA MAGENTA

Fontana delle Api

VIA DI SAN NICOLA DA TOLENTINO

Santa Susanna

PIAZZA DI BERNARDO

Fontanna dell' Aqua Felice

Museo delle Terme di Diocleziano

VIA CERNAIA

VIA SOLFERINO

M Barberini

V. BARBERINI

San Bernardo alle Terme

2

Aula Ottagona

10

Fontana del Tritone

Galleria Nazionale d'Arte Antica

VIA NICOLA DA TOLENTINO

4 **3**

VIA MARSALA

2

Palazzo Barberini

VIA DEL GIARDINI

VIA DELLE QUATTRO FONTANE

VIA XX SETTEMBRE

VALENZA

VIA TORINO

VIA CADORNA

PIAZZA DELLA REPUBBLICA

Santa Maria degli Angeli

P

Villa Aldobrandini

VIA DEL GIARDINI

Ministry of Defence

VIA MOSCA

VIALE LUIGI EINAUDI

V. ENRICO DE NICOLA

PIAZZA DEI CINQUECENTO

British Council

12

V. TEME DI DIOCLEZIANO

VILLA PORTEI LARGO

Statue of Pope John Paul II

M **14**

Repubblica

San Carlo alle Quattro Fontane

15

16

VIA NAZIONALE

Palazzo Massimo

M

Termini

Termini Station

Sant'Andrea al Quirinale

VIA PIACENZA

St Paul's within the Walls

VIA NAPOLI

17

Palazzo delle Esposizioni

5

VIA AGOSTINO DEPRETIS

VIA DEL VIMINALE

VIA TORINO

18

VIA MASSIMO D'AZEGLIO

VIA GIOVANNI AMENDOLA

VIA GIOVANNI GIOLITTI

i

VIA PIACENZA

VIA MILANO

VIA GENOVA

PIAZZA DEL VIMINALE

19

VIA PRINCIPE AMEDEO

VIA DANIELE MANIN

VIA FILIPPO TURATI

VIA PARMA

6

VIA PALERMO

20

VIA FARINI

VIA GIOBERTI

Villa Aldobrandini

VIA NAZIONALE

9

10

V. FRASCHE

Santa Pudenziana

VIA URBANA

PIAZZA DELL' ESQUILINO

Santa Maria Maggiore

VIA CARLO CATTANEO

PIAZZA MANFREL FANTI

VIA MAZZARINO

San Lorenzo In Panisperna

11

VIA CESARE BALBO

VIA SANTA MARIA MAGGIORE

VIA PAOLINA

PIAZZA DI SANTA MARIA MAGGIORE

i

VIA CARLO ALBERTO

VIA MILANO

VIA PANISPERNA

VIA URBANA

VIA CAVOUR

VIA DI SAN VITO

VIMINALE HILL

7

VIA PANISPERNA

VIA BALOCO

VIA CIMARRA

15 16

17

8 **7**

V. CLEMENTINA

MONTI

23

VIA SFORZA

4

Santa Prassede

VIA DI SAN MARTINO AI MONTI

VIA MERULANA

24

VIA DELL'OLMATA

18

VIA NAPOLEONE III

P. PELLEGRINO ROSSI

VIA DEI SERPENTI

8

M Cavour

VIA URBANA

PIAZZA DEGLI ZINGARI

20 25

PIAZZA MADONNA DEI MONTI

VIA LEONINA

12

VIA GIOVANNI LANZA

PIAZZA DI SAN MARTINO AI MONTI

VIA G. LANZA

V. DELLO STATUTO

10 Auditori of Maece

VIA BACCINA

26

Madonna dei Monti

VIA CAVOUR

VIA IN SELCI

11

San Martino Al Monti

LARGO LEOPARDI

11

VIA DELLA MADONNA DEI MONTI

13

27

23 22 21

15

VIA DEL COLOSSEO

28

VIA FRANGIPANE

PIAZZALE DI SAN PIETRO IN VINCOLI

VIA DELLE SETTE SALE

VIALE DEL MONTE OPPIO

ESQUILINE HILL

VIA MERULANA

VIA CABURRO

Domus Aurea

V. DELLE CARINE

VIA DELLE TERME DI TRAIANO

VIA ANGELO CARLO ROMA

i

CLIVIO DI ACILIO

V. MONTE OPPIO

VIA GUICCIARDINI

M Colosseo

PIAZZA DEL COLOSSEO

Parco di Colle Oppio

VIA RUGGERO BONGHI

Arch of Titus

Colosseum

VIALE DOMUS AUREA

VIA LABICANA

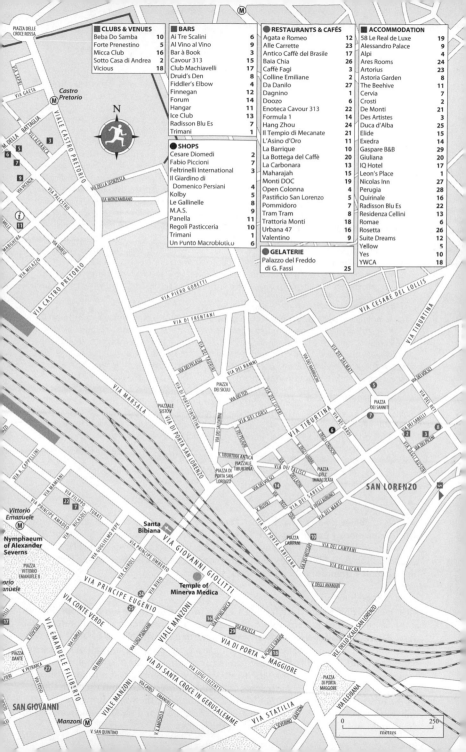

CLUBS & VENUES
Beba Do Samba	10
Forte Prenestino	5
Micca Club	16
Sotto Casa di Andrea	2
Vicious	18

BARS
Ai Tre Scalini	6
Al Vino al Vino	9
Bar à Book	3
Cavour 313	15
Club Machiavelli	17
Druid's Den	8
Fiddler's Elbow	4
Finnegan	12
Forum	14
Hangar	11
Ice Club	13
Radisson Blu Es	7
Trimani	1

SHOPS
Cesare Diomedi	2
Fabio Piccioni	7
Feltrinelli International	3
Il Giardino di Domenico Persiani	4
Kolby	8
Le Gallinelle	5
M.A.S.	9
Panella	11
Regoli Pasticceria	10
Trimani	1
Un Punto Macrobiotico	6

RESTAURANTS & CAFÉS
Agata e Romeo	12
Alle Carrette	23
Antico Caffè del Brasile	17
Baia Chia	26
Caffè Fagi	3
Colline Emiliane	2
Da Danilo	27
Dagnino	1
Doozo	6
Enoteca Cavour 313	22
Formula 1	14
Hang Zhou	24
Il Tempio di Mecanate	21
L'Asino d'Oro	11
La Barrique	10
La Bottega del Caffè	20
La Carbonara	13
Maharajah	15
Monti DOC	19
Open Colonna	4
Pastificio San Lorenzo	5
Pommidoro	7
Tram Tram	8
Trattoria Monti	18
Urbana 47	16
Valentino	9

GELATERIE
Palazzo del Freddo di G. Fassi	25

ACCOMMODATION
58 Le Real de Luxe	19
Alessandro Palace	9
Alpi	4
Ares Rooms	24
Artorius	23
Astoria Garden	8
The Beehive	11
Cervia	7
Crosti	2
De Monti	21
Des Artistes	3
Duca d'Alba	25
Elide	15
Exedra	14
Gaspare B&B	29
Giuliana	20
IQ Hotel	17
Leon's Place	1
Nicolas Inn	27
Perugia	28
Quirinale	16
Radisson Blu Es	22
Residenza Cellini	13
Romae	6
Rosetta	26
Suite Dreams	12
Yellow	5
Yes	10
YWCA	18

7

DOMUS AUREA

It's been more or less permanently closed since 2006, and following a wall collapse in 2010 is unlikely to be open any time soon, but the **Domus Aurea** is nonetheless potentially the city's most intriguing and magnificent ancient building. The "house" was a vast undertaking built on the summit of the Oppian Hill, in Parco di Colle Oppio, and into its sides after a fire of 64 AD (allegedly started by Nero) devastated this part of Rome. It was not intended to be a residence at all; rather, it was a series of banqueting rooms, nymphaeums, small baths, terraces and gardens, facing what at the time was a small lake fed by the underground springs and streams that drained from the surrounding hills.

Rome was used to Nero's excesses, but it had never seen anything like the Golden House before. The facade was supposed to have been coated in solid gold, there was hot and cold running water in the baths, one of the dining rooms was rigged up to shower flower petals and natural scent on guests and the grounds – which covered over two square kilometres – held vineyards and game. Nero didn't get to enjoy his palace for long – he died a couple of years after it was finished, and Vespasian tore a lot of the exposed facade down in disgust, draining its lake and building the Colosseum on top. Later, Trajan built his baths on top of the rest of the complex, and it was pretty much forgotten until its **wall paintings** were discovered by Renaissance artists, including Raphael. When these artists first visited these rooms, they had to descend ladders into what they first believed was some kind of mystical cave, or **grotto**; their attempts to imitate what they found here gave us the word "grotesque".

THE ROOMS

The temperature inside always hovers at around 10°C and this, combined with the almost 100 percent humidity, makes it necessary to wear a sweater or jacket even in the middle of the Roman summer. The house can at first be confusing – Trajan's attempts to obliterate the palace with his baths complex mean that the baths' foundations merge into parts of the palace, and vice versa. There are various covered fountains, service corridors, terraces and, most spectacularly, the **Octagonal Room**, domed, with a hole in the middle, which is supposed to have rotated as the day progressed to emulate the passage of the sun. Most of the rooms are decorated in the so-called Third Pompeiian style, with garlands of flowers, fruit, vines and foliage, interspersed with mythical animals and fanciful depictions of people looking back through windows at the viewer. Perhaps the best-preserved frescoes are in the **Room of Achilles on Skyros**, and illustrate Homer's story of Achilles being sent to the island of Skyros disguised as a woman to prevent him from being drawn into the Trojan War. In one fresco, Achilles is in drag at the Skyros court; another shows him putting his feminine clothes aside and picking up a shield, brought to him by Ulysses (in the crested helmet) to catch him out and make him betray his disguise.

two sets of chains (*vincoli*) that held St Peter when he was in Jerusalem and in Rome, which miraculously joined together. During the papacy of Sixtus IV, it was the cardinal seat of the pope's nephew, Giuliano della Rovere, who became Pope Julius II, of Sistine Chapel ceiling fame. The chains of St Peter can still be seen in the *confessio* beneath the high altar, in a beautiful gold and rock crystal reliquary.

Tomb of Pope Julius

Most people come to the church of San Pietro in Vincoli for the **tomb of Pope Julius II** at the far end of the southern aisle, which occupied **Michelangelo** on and off for much of his career. Michelangelo reluctantly gave it up to paint the Sistine Chapel, and was never able to return to it for very long, being always at the beck and call of successive popes, who understandably had little interest in promoting the glory of one of their predecessors. No one knows how the tomb would have looked had it been finished – it's generally assumed that **Moses** would have been on one end and the risen **Christ** on the other, with a statue of **Julius** himself surmounting the whole thing – and the only statues Michelangelo completed are the *Moses*, *Leah* and *Rachel*, which are still in the church, and two *Dying Slaves*, now in the Louvre.

Moses, pictured as descended from Sinai to find the Israelites worshipping the golden calf, and flanked by the gentle figures of Leah and Rachel, is one of the artist's most captivating works and the rest of the composition – completed by later artists – seems dull and static by comparison. Because of a medieval mistranslation of Scripture, Moses is depicted with **satyr's horns** instead of the "radiance of the Lord" that Exodus tells us shone around his head. Nonetheless, this powerful statue is so lifelike that Michelangelo is alleged to have struck its knee with his hammer and shouted, "Speak, damn you!" The rest of the group was finished by Michelangelo's **pupils**, while the statue of Julius II at the top, by Maso del Bosco, modelled on an Etruscan coffin lid, sadly fails to evoke the character of this apparently active, courageous and violent man – who was in fact laid to rest in St Peter's.

North aisle and apse
There's not much else to see in the church, and during the summer months it can be a bit of a scrum to see the tomb. But it's nice to wander around the building's less congested areas. In the north aisle, there's a seventh-century **mosaic** of St Sebastian, and to the right of the door is the tomb of the Pollaiuolo brothers, Antonio and Piero, the fifteenth-century Tuscan **sculptors** who were responsible for Sixtus IV's elaborate tomb in St Peter's (see p.194). The **frescoes** in the apse are pretty fabulous, too, three late sixteenth-century works by Giacomo Coppi that tell the story of Peter's chains.

San Lorenzo in Panisperna
Via Panisperna 90 • Fri 9am–noon

Walking north through Monti towards Santa Maria Maggiore, it's worth making a brief stop at the church of **San Lorenzo in Panisperna**, originally built on the site of the saint's martyrdom and traditionally the place where monks distributed bread and ham ("*pane e perna*") to the poor – hence the name of the street. Outside, the modern statue is of St Bridget of Sweden, who, in the fourteenth century, founded an order of nuns back in her home country and begged here on behalf of the poor, after she came to Rome. There's not much to see inside the church (note the limited opening hours), apart from the **chapel** where she was buried before being shipped back to Sweden, but it has a nice **courtyard**, along with a large fresco of the martyrdom of St Lawrence in the apse, painted by Pasquale Cati, one of Michelangelo's lesser-known pupils. Another chapel holds the grill on which it's claimed the saint was martyred.

Santa Pudenziana
Via Urbana 160 • Daily 8.30am–noon & 3–6pm, Sun from 9am • ☎ 06 481 4622, 🖰 www.oratoriosantapudenziana.it

Just off Via Cavour, the church of **Santa Pudenziana**, down below street level, has extremely ancient origins. It was dedicated to St Praedes's supposed sister and was for many years believed to have been built on the site where St Peter lived and worshipped, though this has since been entirely discredited, and it's now thought to have simply been the site of a **Roman bathhouse**. The two relics the church used to house – the chair that St Peter used as his throne and the table at which he said Mass – have both long gone, to the Vatican and the Lateran, respectively. But the church still has one feature of ancient origin, the superb fifth-century **apse mosaics** – some "of the oldest Christian figurative mosaics in Rome, though they've been tampered with and restored over the years. They're still fluid and beautiful works, centring on a golden enthroned Christ surrounded by the Apostles – not quite all of them, you'll notice, due to the fact that the mosaic was reduced in size when the church was restored in the sixteenth century, and they cut off one from either side. Nonetheless, the mosaic is marvellous, not least for the graphic arrangement of the Apostles that remain, and the expressiveness of their features, each one of which is purposefully different from the next.

7

Santa Maria Maggiore

Via Liberiana 27 • Daily 7am–7pm • ☎ 06 6988 6802, ⓦ www.vatican.va/various/basiliche/sm_maggiore/index_en.html • A short walk
from Termini, bus #70 from Piazza Venezia

Via Cavour opens out at Piazza dell'Esquilino, behind the basilica of **Santa Maria
Maggiore**, which is built on the highest peak of the Esquiline Hill. This is one of
Rome's four great **basilicas**, second only in the pecking order to St Peter's itself, and
it has one of the city's best-preserved Byzantine interiors – a fact belied by its dull
eighteenth-century exterior. Unlike the other great places of pilgrimage in Rome, it
was not built on any special Constantinian site, but instead went up during the fifth
century after the Council of Ephesus recognized the **cult of the Virgin**, and churches
venerating Our Lady began to spring up all over the Christian world. According to
legend, the Virgin Mary appeared to Pope Liberius in a dream on the night of August
4, 352 AD, telling him to build a church on the Esquiline Hill, on a spot where he
would find a patch of newly fallen **snow** the next morning. The snow would outline
exactly the plan of the church that should be built there in her honour – which, of
course, is exactly what happened, and the first church here was called Santa Maria della
Neve ("of the snow").

The present structure dates from about 420 AD and was completed during the reign
of Sixtus III, who was pope between 432 and 440 AD. Santa Maria Maggiore is noted
for two special **ceremonies**. One, on August 5, celebrates the miraculous snowfall: at
midday Mass, white rose petals are showered on the congregation from the ceiling, and
at night, the fire department operates an artificial snow machine in the piazza in front
and showers the area in snow that, naturally, melts immediately. The other takes place
on Christmas morning, when the reliquary containing the basilica's most prized
possession, part of the crib of Christ, is processed around the church and then
displayed on the high altar.

The basilica

The **basilica** was encased in its eighteenth-century shell during the papacy of
Benedict XIV, although the campanile, the highest in Rome, is older than this –
built in 1377 under Pope Gregory XI. Inside, however, the original building
survives intact, its broad nave fringed on both sides with strikingly well-kept
mosaics (binoculars help), most of which date from the time of Pope Sixtus III and
recount, in comic-strip form, incidents from the Old Testament. The ceiling, which
shows the arms of the Spanish Borgia popes, Calixtus III and Alexander VI, was
gilded in 1493 with gold sent by Queen Isabella as part payment of a loan from
Innocent VIII to finance the voyage of Columbus to the New World. The large
chapel in the right transept holds the elaborate tomb of Sixtus V.

Sistine Chapel

On the right, another and less famous **Sistine Chapel** is decorated with marble taken
from the Roman Septizodium (see p.87), and with frescoes and reliefs portraying
events from Sixtus V's reign. In the middle, a bronze baldacchino carried by four angels
covers another small chapel. The chapel also contains the tomb of another zealous and
reforming pope, Pius V, whose statue faces that of Sixtus; he's probably best known for
excommunicating Queen Elizabeth I of England, in 1570.

Pauline Chapel

Outside the Sistine Chapel is the modest tomb slab of the Bernini family, including
Gian Lorenzo himself, to the right by the sanctuary steps, while opposite, the
sumptuous **Pauline Chapel** is home to the tombs of the Borghese pope, Paul V, on the
left, and his immediate predecessor Clement VIII, opposite. The floor is decorated
with the Borghese arms, an eagle and dragon, and the magnificently gilded ceiling
shows glimpses of heaven. The altar, of lapis lazuli and agate, holds a Madonna and

---

SIXTUS V

Although he reigned only five years, from 1585 to 1590, **Sixtus V**'s papacy was one of Rome's most memorable. He laid out several new **streets**, notably the long, straight thoroughfare that runs from the top of Trinità dei Monti to Santa Maria Maggiore (at various points Via Sistina, Via delle Quattro Fontane and Via de Pretis); he erected many of the present **obelisks** that dot the city, including those in Piazza San Pietro and Piazza San Giovanni; and he launched an attack on **bandits** in the surrounding countryside and **criminal gangs** in the city. As a priest at the time remarked: "I am in Rome after an absence of ten years, and do not recognize it, so new does all appear to me to be: monuments, streets, piazzas, fountains, aqueducts, obelisks and other wonders, all the works of Sixtus V."

Sixtus was, like Julius II, a man of action and a Franciscan friar. He was perhaps most famously responsible for the execution of Beatrice Cenci (see p.60), although his reign was also notorious for his stripping the Roman Forum of its marbles and the Colosseum of its stone for St Peter's. He also demolished the Septizodium, at the southeast end of the Palatine Hill, marble from which decorated his tomb..

7

Child dating from the twelfth or thirteenth century. Between the two chapels, the **confessio** contains a kneeling statue of the dogmatic Pope Pius IX, the longest-serving pope in history, and the last one to hold real power – he was kicked out with Italian Unification in 1870, after 31 years. The reliquary here is said to have fragments of the crib of Christ inside, in rock crystal and silver, while the high altar, above it, houses the relics of St Matthew, among other Christian martyrs. But it's the **mosaics** of the arch that really dazzle, a vivid representation of scenes from the life of Christ – the *Annunciation*, the *Adoration of the Magi* (in which Christ is depicted not as a child, unusually, but as a king himself) plus the *Massacre of the Innocents* on the left and the *Presentation in the Temple* and *Herod Receiving the Magi* on the right. The central apse mosaics are later, but are no less impressive, commissioned by the late-thirteenth-century pope, Nicholas IV, and showing the *Coronation of the Virgin*, with angels, saints and the pope himself.

Museum
Daily 9am–6.30pm • €3

There's a **museum** underneath the basilica which sports what even by Roman standards is a wide variety of relics – architectural drawings of the basilica, a hair of the Virgin and the arms of saints Luke and Matthew, as well as the usual liturgical garments. The standout exhibit, though, is the collection of carved figures from a nativity scene, or **presepio**, by Arnolfo di Cambio – originally created in 1291 to decorate a chapel to hold the basilica's holy crib relics.

The loggia and apostolic palace
Daily 9am–6.30pm • €3 (including tour)

The **Loggia della Belvedere**, above the main entrance, has some magnificent mosaics showing Christ among various saints, sitting above four scenes that tell the story of the miracle of the snow: the one on the far left shows Mary appearing to Pope Liberius, the one on the far right shows the miraculous snowfall. **Tours** also take in the apostolic palace above the basilica, including the "Room of the Popes" off the loggia, which was the work of Paul V, and as a result has his insignia on every door to prove it and a fabulous wooden ceiling decorated with his Borghese coat of arms. The room is so-called for its portraits of popes associated with Santa Maria Maggiore, but more interesting are the various devotional items you can see, including a copy of a letter by the hand of St Peter that John Paul II had made for the basilica – though it's Bernini's splendid **spiral staircase** next door that really steals the show.

Domus Romana
Daily 9am–6.30pm • €5 (including tour)

As if Santa Maria Maggiore's Christian relics weren't enough, excavations under the basilica have also uncovered a large first-century AD Roman villa, the **Domus Romana**, and there are regular **tours** taking in the most accessible parts, which have some fragments of Roman mosaics and frescoes, including some stunning geometric work and the remains of an ancient pictorial calendar, as well as the walls and roof tiles from the original fourth-century basilica.

Santa Prassede
Via di Santa Prassede 9a • Daily 7am–noon & 4–6.30pm • €1 to light the mosaics • ☎ 06 488 2456

Across the road from Santa Maria Maggiore, the ninth-century church of **Santa Prassede** occupies an ancient site where it's claimed St Praedes harboured Christians on the run from persecution. She apparently collected the blood and remains of the martyrs and placed them in a well where she herself was later buried; a red marble disc in the floor of the nave marks the spot. In the southern aisle, the chapel of St Zeno was built by Pope Paschal I as a **mausoleum** for his mother, Theodora, and is decorated with marvellous ninth-century mosaics that make it glitter like a jewel-encrusted box. Theodora is depicted on the left-hand arch. The chapel also contains a fragment of a column that Christ was supposedly tied to when he was scourged. In the apse are more ninth-century mosaics, showing Christ between saints Peter, Pudentiana and Zeno (on the right) and saints Paul, Praxedes and Paschal I (on the left). Note that Paschal's halo (like Theodora's) is in a rectangular form, indicating that he was alive when the mosaics were placed here.

San Martino ai Monti
Viale del Monte Oppio 28 • Daily 8am–noon & 4–7pm • ☎ 06 478 4701

Two minutes from Santa Prassede, the church of **San Martino ai Monti** backs onto the square of the same name and is another place of worship that dates back to the earliest days of Christianity. It was dedicated to saints Sylvester and Martin in the sixth century and incorporates an ancient Roman structure, but it was almost entirely rebuilt in the 1650s and sports a ceiling that shows the arms of the Medicis, specifically the family's last pope, Leo XI, who ruled briefly in 1605. A series of frescoes lining the aisles depict scenes of the Roman countryside and the interiors of the old Roman basilicas of St Peter and San Giovanni before they were gussied up in their present Baroque splendour – St Peter's is at the far end of the north aisle, San Giovanni in the same aisle near the door.

Piazza Vittorio Emanuele II and around
Metro line A to Vittorio or a short walk from Termini; bus #70 from Piazza Venezia

Two minutes' walk southeast from Santa Maria Maggiore, **Piazza Vittorio Emanuele II** was the centre of a district which became known as the "*quartiere piemontese*" when the government located many of its major ministries here after Unification. The arcades of the square, certainly, recall central Turin, as do the solid palatial buildings that surround it. It used to host a daily market, but this moved a few years ago to new premises between train tracks into Termini, between Via Ricasoli and Via Lamarmora, where there are two covered halls, one selling clothes, the other food (Mon–Sat 7am–2pm). The area around is to some extent central Rome's **immigrant quarter**, with a heavy concentration of African and Middle Eastern, Indian and especially Chinese shops and restaurants. Parts of the area between the train tracks and the square, and indeed to some extent around the square itself, are almost Rome's **Chinatown**, with a bustling concentration of Chinese jewellery stores, hairdressers and food shops.

CLOCKWISE FROM TOP LEFT SANTA MARIA MAGGIORE (P.118); TRE SCALINI BAR (P.268); MOSAIC, PALAZZO MASSIMO (P.124); COUPLE ON SCOOTER, VIA CAVOUR (P.113) >

Piazza Vittorio itself retains a shabby, down-at-heel grandeur: in summer, it's a focus for outdoor **film showings**, which means during the day, it's full of people taking the weight off and staring at giant empty screens. There's also a children's playground, and in the northeastern corner of the piazza, an 18m-high pile of Roman bricks is all that is left of a monumental public fountain known as the **Nymphaeum of Alexander Severus** (emperor from 222 to 235 AD) – a distribution point for water arriving in the city by a branch of the Acqua Claudia aqueduct and now home to a prosperous colony of cats. Have a look, too, at the **Porta Magica**, a doorway basically, the only remnant of the seventeenth-century Villa Palombara, flanked by two mysterious, bearded, almost Buddha-like figures and inscriptions which some claim refer to the ancient art of alchemy.

Museo Nazionale di Arte Orientale
Via Merulana 248 • Tues, Wed & Fri 9am–2pm, Thurs, Sat & Sun 9am–7.30pm • €6 • ☎ 06 4697 4832, ⓦ museorientale.beniculturali.it

It's a short walk south from San Martino ai Monti to busy Largo Brancaccio, where the imposing Palazzo Brancaccio houses the **Museo Nazionale di Arte Orientale** – a first-rate collection of oriental art (the best in Italy) that has recently been restored. Beginning with Marco Polo in the thirteenth century, the Italians have always had connections with the East, and the quality of this collection of Islamic, Chinese, Indian and Southeast Asian art reflects this fact – not to mention making a refreshing break from the multiple ages of Western art you are exposed to in Rome. There are finds dating back to 1500 BC from a necropolis in Pakistan; architectural fragments, artworks and jewellery from Tibet, Nepal and Pakistan; a solid collection from China, with predictable Buddhas and vases alongside curiosities such as Han dynasty figures and a large Wei dynasty Buddha with two bodhisattvas; and coins from twelfth-century Iran and northwest India.

Auditorium of Maecenas
Largo Leopardi 2 • Opening hours vary • €3

Outside the Oriental Art museum, Largo Leopardi is home to the remains of the so-called **Auditorium of Maecenas**, the sole remnant of a villa that was home to the trusted friend and adviser of Augustus; the rest was swept up and incorporated into Nero's Domus Aurea (see p.116) long after Maecenas's death. Inside, it's basically a large room with some seating arranged around an apse at one end, which is decorated with some badly damaged paintings. It is possible to visit, during the summer months at least, but opening times are very erratic.

Santa Bibiana
Via Giolitti 154 • Daily 7.30–9.45am & 5.30–7.30pm • ☎ 06 466 1021, ⓦ santabibiana.com

A couple of blocks northeast of Piazza Vittorio Emanuele II, right up against the train tracks, the church of **Santa Bibiana** is an inauspicious location for Bernini's first church in Rome. A rebuilding of a much older church, it incorporates a number of ancient columns, including the one at which the fifth-century martyr is supposed to have been tortured. The **statue** of the saint, however, in a niche on the high altar, is pure, theatrical Bernini, completed in 1626, and gives a hint of what was to come in his later work, most notably in the church of Santa Maria della Vittoria, just the other side of Termini station (see p.126).

Temple of Minerva Medica
Viale Manzoni 64 • Usually not open to the public • ⓦ iltempiodiminerva.com

Just down the train tracks from the church of Santa Bibiana, the **Temple of Minerva Medica** is the substantial ruin of a late Imperial nymphaeum, an impressive, ten-sided construction which traditionally signals your arrival in Rome by train. It's generally closed for visits, but you can appreciate its size and structure well enough from the outside – although it's admittedly not in the loveliest of locations.

Via Nazionale

Buses #64, #170 and #H among others run both ways along Via Nazionale to Piazza della Repubblica

Following the dip between the Viminal and Quirinal hills, **Via Nazionale** connects Piazza Venezia and the centre of town with the area around Termini station and the eastern districts beyond. A focus for much development after Unification, its heavy, overbearing buildings were constructed to give Rome some semblance of modern sophistication when it became capital of the new country, but most are now occupied by hotels and mainstream shops and boutiques. At its bottom end, at the junction of Via XXIV Maggio, the palm-filled gardens of the **Villa Aldobrandini** are a pleasant respite from the traffic, high above the street and reached from the entrance on Via Mazzarino.

Palazzo delle Esposizioni

Via Nazionale 194 · Tues–Thurs & Sun 10am–8pm, Fri & Sat 10am–10.30pm, limited opening hours in Aug; bookshop & café same hours · Admission varies, but usually €10–12.50 · ☏ 06 3996 7500, ⓦ palazzoesposizioni.it

About halfway up Via Nazionale, the imposing **Palazzo delle Esposizioni** was designed in 1883 by Pio Piacentini (father of the more famous Marcello, favourite architect of Mussolini), and was until relatively recently a bit of a white elephant, boarded-up and sad. But it reopened with much fanfare in 2008 after a five-year revamp and now hosts regular large-scale exhibitions and cultural events. It also houses a cinema, an excellent art and design bookshop and café in its basement, and up the steps on the left side of the building are lifts to the fancy *Open Colonna* restaurant (see p.256).

St Paul's within the Walls

Via Napoli 58, at Via Nazionale · Daily 9am–4.30pm · ☏ 06 488 3339, ⓦ stpaulsrome.it

The American Episcopal church of **St Paul's within the Walls** was the first Protestant church to be built inside the walls of the city after the Unification of Italy in 1870 and is a peaceful and spiritual haven after the humdrum bustle of Via Nazionale. Dating from 1879, it was built in a neo-Gothic style by the British architect G.E. Street and is worth a quick peek inside for its works by **English artists**. The leaf-pattern ceramic tiles that line the walls of each side of the nave were designed by William Morris, and the apse mosaics, by the Pre-Raphaelite artist Edward Burne-Jones, depict one of the church's founders, the American financier J.P. Morgan as St Paul, alongside his family, Garibaldi, General Ulysses Grant and Abraham Lincoln. The 1913 mosaics on the western wall are by George Breck, who was director of the American Academy at the time.

Piazza della Repubblica and around

Buses #64, #170 and #H among others run both ways along Via Nazionale to Piazza della Repubblica

At the top of Via Nazionale, **Piazza della Repubblica** (formerly Piazza Esedra) is typical of Rome's nineteenth-century regeneration, a stern and dignified semicircle of buildings that used to be rather dilapidated but is now – with the help of the stylish *Hotel Exedra* – once again resurgent. The arcades make a fine place to stroll, despite the traffic, which roars ceaselessly around the Fontana delle Naiadi's languishing nymphs and sea monsters.

Santa Maria degli Angeli

Piazza della Repubblica/Via Cernaia 9 · Daily 7am–6.30pm, Sun till 7.30pm · ⓦ www.santamariadegliangeliroma.it

Piazza della Repubblica follows the semicircular outline of part of the Baths of Diocletian, built in 300 AD, the remains of which lie across the piazza and are partially contained in the church of **Santa Maria degli Angeli**. This is not Rome's most welcoming church by any means, but does give the best impression of the size and grandeur of Diocletian's bath complex, or at least of the tepidarium, whose structure it utilizes. It's a huge, open building, with an interior standardized by Vanvitelli into a rich eighteenth-century confection after a couple of centuries of piecemeal adaptation (started by an aged Michelangelo). The pink **granite pillars**, at 3m in diameter the largest in Rome, are original, and the main transept formed the main hall of the baths; only the crescent shape of the facade remains from the original caldarium (it had previously been hidden by a newer facing). The **meridian** that strikes diagonally across the floor in the south transept, flanked by representations of the twelve signs of the zodiac, was until 1846 the regulator of time for Romans (now a cannon shot fired daily at noon from the Janiculum Hill). Take the back exit through the sacristy and you'll find a small exhibition on the history of the baths and church.

Aula Ottagona

Via Giuseppe Romita 8 • Closed indefinitely for restoration

Just beyond the church of Santa Maria degli Angeli is another remnant of the baths, the **Aula Ottagona** (Octagonal Hall), formerly a planetarium and now part of the Museo delle Terme di Diocleziano (see below). The large domed room contains marble statues taken from the baths of Caracalla and Diocletian, and two remarkable statues of a boxer and athlete from the Quirinal Hill. Excavations underground – accessible by stairs – show the furnaces for heating water for the baths and the foundations of another building from the time of Diocletian.

Museo delle Terme di Diocleziano

Via Enrico di Nicola 79 • Tues–Sun 9am–7.45pm • €7 including Palazzo Altemps, Palazzo Massimo & Crypta Balbi; valid 3 days • ☎ 06 3996 7700, ⓦ archeoroma.beniculturali.it

The buildings that surround Santa Maria degli Angeli are (along with the church) also recycled parts of Diocletian's Baths – the complex was enormous, originally measuring 376m by 361m – and include the round church of San Bernardo alle Terme, off Via XX Settembre, and the round building in the other direction, at the corner of Via Viminale and Via delle Terme di Diocleziano. The rest of the baths – the huge halls and courtyards on the side towards Termini – have been renovated and, together with the Carthusian monastery attached to the church, now hold what is probably the least interesting part of the Museo Nazionale Romano, the **Museo delle Terme di Diocleziano** – the better sections are across the street in Palazzo Massimo (see below) and in Palazzo Altemps (see p.48).

Fronted by a **fragrant garden**, open to all, which centres on a large krater fountain with little cupids holding up its rim, the museum's most evocative part is the large **cloister** of the church whose sides are crammed with statuary, funerary monuments and sarcophagi and fragments from all over Rome. There's a lot to pick through, around three hundred bits and pieces in all, but standouts include the animal heads, found in the Forum of Trajan, a fine headless seated statue of Hercules from the second century AD and a nice, if again damaged, statue of a husband and wife. There's also an upstairs gallery that wraps around the cloister and includes finds dating back to the seventh century BC, and a downstairs section with more items – busts, terracotta statues, armour and weapons found in Roman tombs – all effectively, if rather academically, presented, but hardly compulsory viewing.

Palazzo Massimo

Largo di Villa Peretti 1 • Tues–Sun 9am–7.45pm • €7 including Palazzo Altemps, Museo delle Terme di Diocleziano & Crypta Balbi; valid 3 days • ☎ 06 3996 7700, ⓦ archeoroma.beniculturali.it

Across from Santa Maria degli Angeli, the snazzily restored **Palazzo Massimo**, is home to one of the two principal parts of the **Museo Nazionale Romano** (the other is in the Palazzo Altemps; see p.48) – a superb collection of Greek and Roman **antiquities**, second only to the Vatican's, which has been entirely reorganized and features many pieces that have remained undisplayed for decades.

Basement

The basement has displays of exquisite gold **jewellery** from the second century AD – necklaces, rings, brooches, all in immaculate condition – and some fine gold imperial hairnets. There's also – startlingly – the mummified remains of an eight-year-old girl, along with a fantastic **coin collection**, from the first bronze coinage of the fourth century BC to the surprisingly sophisticated coins of the Republic and imperial times, right up to the lira and concluding with a display devoted to the euro. It's all shown in glass cases equipped with magnifying glasses on runners, controlled by the buttons mounted on the front of each case.

Ground floor

The ground floor of the museum is devoted to statues from the **early empire**, including a gallery on the right with an unparalleled selection of unidentified busts found all over Rome. Their lack of clear identity is no barrier to appreciating them; they are amazing pieces of portraiture, and as vivid a representation of patrician Roman life as you'll find. Look out for the so-called *Statue of the Tivoli General*, the face of an old man mounted on the body of a youthful athlete – sometimes believed to be a portrait of L. Munatius Plancus, the military officer who named Octavian "Augustus" (literally "Reverend") and so officially started the cult of the emperor. At the far end of the courtyard are more busts, this time identifiable as members of the **imperial family**: a bronze of Germanicus, a marvellous small bust of Caligula, several representations of Livia, Tiberius, Antonia and Drusus and a lifesize statue of Augustus, piously dressed as the high priest of Rome with his toga covering his head. There are also some amazing Greek sculptures on the far side of the courtyard, including bronzes of a Hellenistic prince holding a spear, from the second century BC, and a wounded pugilist at rest from a century earlier.

First floor

The museum really gets going on the first-floor gallery, with later Roman sculpture, in particular groupings of the various **imperial dynasties** in roughly chronological order set around the courtyard, starting with the Flavian emperors, deliberately realistic and unidealized. The craggy determination of Vespasian and the pinched nobility of Nerva are in complete contrast to the next room, where Trajan appears next to his wife Plotina as Hercules, next to a bust of his cousin Hadrian, who is in turn next to his lover Antinous. These were some of the most successful years of the empire, and they continued with the Antonine emperors in the next room, which features Antonius Pius in a heroic nude pose and in several busts, flanked by likenesses of his daughter Faustina Minor. Faustina was the wife of Antonius's successor, Marcus Aurelius, who appears in the corridor outside. Also here is Commodus, the last and perhaps least successful of the Antonine emperors. Further on, past a room full of sarcophagi, including one showing the Muses conversing with philosophers, are the Severans, with the fierce-looking Caracalla gazing across past his father Septimius Severus to his brother Geta, whom he later murdered.

Just beyond the Severan emperors, a hyper-realistic **sarcophagus** from 190 AD shows Roman victories over barbarians. Next door, at the back of the courtyard, there is an amazing sleeping hermaphrodite, an almost totally complete Dionysus that was fished out of the Tiber and bronzework from two imperial galleys found in southern Lazio, at Nemi, dating from the time of Caligula. A balustrade is studded with figures, each one different with a face on each side, handles are decorated with the faces of panthers, wolves and lions and rudders come in the shape of forearms. On the other side of the courtyard are more astonishing pieces, this time from various imperial villas outside Rome, many of them copies of **Greek originals**, including figures of Apollo and Dionysus, an Amazon and a barbarian, full of movement and vigour, as well as more dynastic busts discovered at Hadrian's villa in Tivoli and a beautiful statue of a young girl holding a tray from Augustus's villa at Anzio.

Second floor

The second floor takes in some of the finest **Roman frescoes and mosaics** ever found, and it divides into three main parts. First there is a stunning set of **frescoes** from the

Villa di Livia, depicting an orchard dense with fruit and flowers and patrolled by partridges, doves and other birds. On the same side of the courtyard are floor **mosaics** showing naturalistic scenes – sea creatures, people boating – from the so-called Villa di Baccano on Via Cassia, a sumptuous mansion probably owned by the imperial Severan family. Four mosaic panels taken from a bedroom, featuring four chariot drivers and their horses, are so finely crafted that from a distance they look as if they've been painted, while in the adjoining room is a very rare example of *opus sectile*, a mosaic technique imported from the eastern provinces in the first century AD. Inlaid pieces of marble, mother-of-pearl, glass and hard stone are used instead of tesserae, the parts cut so as to enhance detail and give perspective depth.

More **mosaics** decorate the corridor outside, with floors showing Nile scenes, complete with crocodiles and hippos, while others come from Anzio, including one showing a reclining Hercules holding a cup and club while a wild boar emerges from a nearby cave. The final section displays **wall paintings** rescued from what was believed to be the riverside villa of Augustus's daughter Julia and his trusted general Agrippa, built for their wedding. The villa wasn't lived in for long – Agrippa died of a fever nine years after their marriage – but the decoration was sumptuous in the extreme, including a room painted with garlands and an Egyptian-style frieze, and two bedrooms painted deep red and covered with different figures.

Termini

Across the street from the Palazzo Massimo is the low white facade of **Termini** station (so named for its proximity to the Baths of Diocletian, nothing to do with being the terminus of Rome's rail lines) and the vast, bus-crammed hubbub that is **Piazza dei Cinquecento** in front, still beset with the works to build the city's third metro line. The station is a great building from any angle, an ambitious piece of modern architectural design that was completed in 1950 and still entirely dominates the streets around with its low, self-consciously futuristic lines – it's nicknamed "the dinosaur" for its curved front canopy. A recent **renovation** upgraded the building in general and converted much of its vast footprint to retail and restaurant space; it has a good bookshop, a department store, a couple of supermarkets open long hours, lots of other shops and even an exhibition space – plus the usual information and car-rental outlets on the Via Giovanni Giolitti side.

There are even a few stretches of Rome's original city wall, the **Servian Wall**, down in the busy basement, as indeed there is up above, among the bus and taxi stands on Piazza dei Cinquecento. Here, you might want to take a look at the 5m cloaked **statue of Pope John Paul II** by Olivier Rainaldi, unveiled in May 2011 to some dismay from the public and disappointment in the Vatican – indeed, a poll conducted by *La Repubblica* concluded that almost ninety percent of those asked disliked Rainaldi's effort. There's no doubting its presence, although it's hard to disagree with some Romans, who feel that the enormous bald figure bears more than a passing resemblance to Benito Mussolini.

San Lorenzo

Just east of Termini, and accessible on foot under the train tracks from Via Giovanni Giolitti, the neighbourhood of **San Lorenzo** spreads from the tracks to the main campus of Rome's university, at the far end of Via Tiburtina. Sheltering behind a short stretch of the **Aurelian Wall**, it's an originally working-class district, latterly popular with students, that retains something of the air of a local neighbourhood, quite different from the rest of the city centre. Via Tiburtina provides its main spine; it is flanked by a couple of small parks and playgrounds, off which are streets that are home to some good and often inexpensive local **restaurants** (see p.255).

Campo Verano
Piazzale Verano 1 • Daily 7am–6pm

At the far end of Via Tiburtina, facing a square flanked by monumental masons and flower-sellers, the **Campo Verano** cemetery has been the largest **Catholic burial-place** in Rome since 1830. It's worth a visit for the grandiose tombs, such as the she-wolf-topped stone of the poet, journalist and activist **Goffredo Mameli**, just inside, on the left. A contemporary of Garibaldi, he wrote the lyrics to the Italian National Anthem, *Il Canto degli Italiani*, in 1847, and fought on the side of Unification forces, receiving the bayonet wound that killed him in 1849, at the age of just 22. Otherwise, just wander – you're sure to come across something (or someone) interesting.

San Lorenzo fuori le Mura
Piazzale del Verano 3 • Daily 8am–noon & 4–6.30pm • Bus #492 from Piazza Venezia, bus #310 from Termini

The San Lorenzo area takes its name from the church of **San Lorenzo fuori le Mura** (literally "outside the walls") on Via Tiburtina, right by the Verano cemetery, one of the seven great **pilgrimage churches** of Rome. It is a beautiful, plain basilica, in many ways the city's most atmospheric, and, because of its relatively out-of-the-way location, one of the most spiritual in feel, fronted by a columned portico decorated with twelfth-century frescoes and with a lovely twelfth-century cloister to its side. The original church was built by Constantine on the site of **St Lawrence**'s burial place, not his martyrdom, which was apparently on the site of the church of San Lorenzo in Panisperna (see p.117). The saint was reputedly burnt to death on a gridiron, halfway through his ordeal uttering the immortal words, "Turn me, I am done on this side."

Inside the church
San Lorenzo is actually a combination of three churches – one a sixth-century reconstruction of Constantine's church by **Pope Pelagius II**, which now forms the chancel, another a fifth-century church from the time of **Sixtus III**, with a basilica from the thirteenth century by **Honorius II** joining the two. Because of its proximity to Rome's railyards, the church was bombed heavily during World War II, but it has been rebuilt with sensitivity, and remains much as it was originally. Inside, there are features from all periods: there's a fantastic ancient **Roman sarcophagus** by the main door; the **tomb** of one Cardinal Fieschi; a **Cosmati floor**, perhaps the city's most impressive; a thirteenth-century **pulpit**; and a **paschal candlestick** with a twisted stem.

The **baldacchino** in the choir is dated 1147 and sits on its own colourful Cosmati floor, beyond which a thirteenth-century bishop's throne is perfectly placed to see the sixth-century mosaic on the inside of the triumphal arch – a depiction of pope Pelagius II, St Stephen and St Lawrence offering his church to Christ (the underneath of the arch is decorated with fruit and flowers). Beneath here, in the *confessio* under the raised choir, lie the bodies of the two saints and more **mosaics**, nineteenth-century this time, adorning the tomb of Pope Pius IX. The body of the last papal ruler of Rome was carried here under cover of darkness in 1881, in a procession that was disrupted by a gang of Italian nationalists who attempted to throw his corpse into the river. Turn your back on the tomb, and you'll see the stone on which St Lawrence's body is said to have been laid after his death, preserved behind glass. Finally, upstairs again, through the sacristy, is the church's small Romanesque **cloister**, one of Rome's simplest and most peaceful, with a well-tended garden and fishpond in the middle and a fragment of a bomb remembering the bombardment of the church in World War II.

7

SAN CLEMENTE

The Celian Hill and San Giovanni

The area immediately behind the Colosseum, the Celian Hill is the most southerly of Rome's seven hills and one of its most peaceful, with few major roads and the park of Villa Celimontana at its heart. The area immediately east of here is known as San Giovanni, after the basilica complex that lies at the end of the long narrow thoroughfare of Via San Giovanni in Laterano, which was, before the creation of the separate Vatican city state, the headquarters of the Catholic Church. It's a mixed area, mainly residential, but it has some compelling sights in the basilica of San Giovanni itself, the church of Santa Croce in Gerusalemme beyond and the amazing triple-layered church of San Clemente – all in all a worthy add-on to a morning spent at the Colosseum.

Santo Stefano Rotondo

Via Santo Stefano Rotondo 7 · Tues–Sun 9.30am–12.30pm & 3–6pm · ⓦ www.santo-stefano-rotondo.it

Ten minutes' walk from the Colosseum down Via Claudia, and not on the Celian Hill proper, the round church of **Santo Stefano Rotondo** is a truly ancient structure, built in the 460s AD and consecrated by Pope Simplicius to commemorate Christianity's first martyr, St Stephen. Recently open again after a lengthy restoration, its four chapels form the shape of a cross in a circle, atmospherically lit by the 22 windows of the clerestory. The interior is a magnificent and moody circular space, made up of two concentric rings, but the feature that will really stick in your mind is the series of stomach-turning frescoes on the walls of the outer ring, showing various saints being martyred in different ways: impalings, drawings and quarterings, disembowelments, boilings in oil, hangings, beheadings – according to Charles Dickens, who visited in 1845, "such a panorama of horror and butchery no man could imagine in his sleep, though he were to eat a whole pig raw, for supper".

Santa Maria in Domnica

Piazza Navicella 10 · Daily 8.30am–12.30pm & 4.30–7pm

Across Via Claudia from the church of Santo Stefano Rotondo, Piazza della Navicella was named after the "navicella" or Roman stone boat that sits outside the church of **Santa Maria in Domnica**. This is a bare and beautiful sixth-century church, with a sixteenth-century ceiling showing more boats – in particular Noah's Ark – and the arms of the Medici, though its most significant features by far are its apse mosaics. Above the apse, a ninth-century mosaic of Christ has some wonderfully individualized apostles and angels, while in the apse itself another mosaic shows Pachal I, who restored the church, kneeling at the feet of the Virgin.

Villa Celimontana

The **Villa Celimontana** park can be accessed via Piazza della Navicella, next door to the church of Santa Maria in Domnica, or from Piazza Giovanni e Paolo (see below). These shady public gardens were built on the site of an ancient zoo that was home to some of the animals that were to die in the nearby arena. Nowadays they make a nice spot for a picnic, with lots of leafy walkways and grassy slopes, and you could do worse than take a stroll through before moving on to the other sights of the Celian Hill. There are also pony rides, worth considering if you're with kids, as well as a small playground, and outdoor jazz concerts on summer evenings (see p.273).

Santi Giovanni e Paolo

Piazza dei Santi Giovanni e Paolo 13 · Daily 8.30am–noon & 3.30–6.30pm

Right outside one entrance to the Villa Celimontana park, at the Celian Hill's summit, the church of **Santi Giovanni e Paolo**, marked by its colourful campanile, is set in a peaceful **piazza** that makes it a popular location for weddings – despite the adolescent autograph hunters who occasionally throng outside the TV studios opposite. Originally founded by a Roman senator called Pammachius, the church acts as an unofficial memorial to conscientious objection, dedicated to two dignitaries who were beheaded here in 361 AD after refusing military service. The remnants of what is believed to be their house are now open to the public in the **Case Romane** (see below). Inside the church's dark interior, thronged with chandeliers, a railed-off tablet in mid-nave marks the shrine where the saints were martyred and buried, while outside in the far corner of the square, beneath the campanile, you can see the arches of part of a **temple of Claudius**, the remains of which extend far down the hill towards the Colosseum.

Case Romane

Clivo di Scauro • Daily except Tues & Wed 10am–1pm & 3–6pm • €6 • ☎ 06 7045 4544, Ⓦ caseromane.it

The so-called **Case Romane** are around the corner from – but actually situated underneath – Santi Giovanni e Paolo, on Clivo di Scauro, where the buttresses of the church arch over the street. They were believed to be the relatively lavish residence of Giovanni and Paolo – the two prominent citizens who were martyred during the fourth century AD and commemorated in the church (see above). The twenty or so rooms are in fact more likely to be a series of dwellings, separated by a narrow lane, rather than a single residence. Patchily frescoed with pagan and Christian subjects, most of the chambers are dark, poky affairs; you'll need some imagination to see the palatially appointed living quarters they must have been. However, there are standouts, including the **Casa dei Genii**, frescoed with winged youths and cupids, and the **courtyard** or nymphaeum, which has a marvellous fresco of a goddess being waited on, sandwiched between cupids in boats, fishing and loading supplies. The **antiquarium**, too, beautifully pulls together finds from the site, among them a *Christ with Saints* fresco, and ceramics, amphorae and fascinating small domestic artefacts: an intact imperial-age spoon, a bronze reel, bone sewing needles and almost perfect oil lamps.

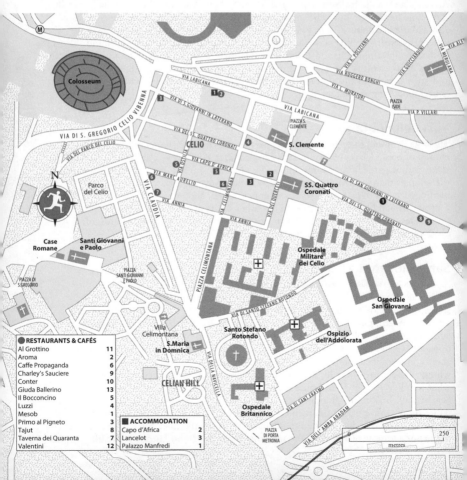

● RESTAURANTS & CAFÉS	
Al Grottino	11
Aroma	2
Caffe Propaganda	6
Charley's Sauciere	9
Conter	10
Giuda Ballerino	13
Il Bocconcino	5
Luzzi	4
Mesob	1
Primo al Pigneto	3
Tajut	8
Taverna dei Quaranta	7
Valentini	12

■ ACCOMMODATION	
Capo d'Africa	2
Lancelot	3
Palazzo Manfredi	1

San Gregorio Magno

Piazza di San Gregorio 1 • Daily 7.30am–12.30pm & 3–7pm; ring the bell marked "portineria" to gain admission

The road descends from the church and the Case Romane under a succession of brick arches to the originally medieval church of **San Gregorio Magno** on the left, in a commanding position above the traffic drone of the road below, looking across to the lollipop pines of the Palatine Hill opposite. St Gregory the Great founded a monastery on the site, and was a monk before becoming pope in 590 AD. Stabilizing Rome after the fall of the empire, he effectively established the powerful papal role that would endure for the best part of the following 1500 years; he also dispatched St Augustine in the early seventh century to convert England to Christianity.

Today's rather ordinary Baroque **interior** doesn't really do justice to the historical importance of the church, but the lovely **Cosmati floor** remains intact, and the chapel of the saint at the end of the south aisle has a beautifully carved bath showing scenes from St Gregory's life along with his marble throne, a beaten-up specimen that actually pre-dates the saint by five hundred years.

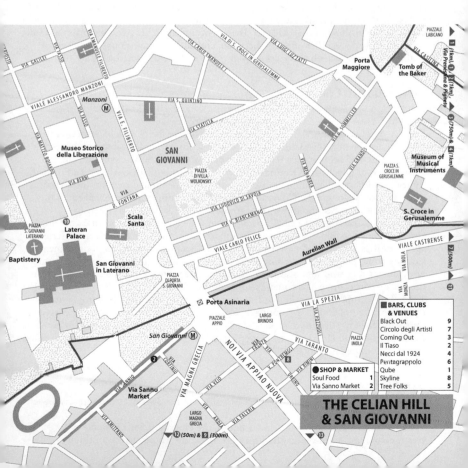

BARS, CLUBS & VENUES	
Black Out	9
Circolo degli Artisti	7
Coming Out	3
Il Tiaso	2
Necci dal 1924	4
Pentagrappolo	6
Qube	1
Skyline	8
Tree Folks	5

SHOP & MARKET	
Soul Food	1
Via Sanno Market	2

THE CELIAN HILL & SAN GIOVANNI

Chapels of Santa Barbara, Santa Silvia and Sant'Andrea

Piazza di San Gregorio 2 • Tues, Thurs, Sat & Sun 9.30am–12.30pm • ☎ 06 7049 4966 to book an obligatory guided tour

Just to the left of the church entrance, where the original monastery stood, there are three chapels surrounded by cypress trees. The central one, **Sant'Andrea**, contains two large frescoes depicting the martyrdom of the saint, one, by Domenichino, a busy, vibrant piece showing a greybearded Andrew at the mercy of brutal soldiers, and a second by Guido Reni showing *St Andrew with Sts Peter and Paul*. Either side of Sant'Andrea, the chapels of **Santa Barbara** and **Santa Silvia** are filled with more frescoes, the former in particular covered with scenes of Gregory the Great, and containing the table at which St Gregory apparently fed twelve paupers daily with his own hands for years.

Missionario della Carità

Piazza di San Gregorio 2 • Daily except Thurs 8–11.30am & 4.30–6.30pm • Free

Across the garden from the church of Sant'Andrea is the Rome headquarters of the organization founded by a person many would like to be made a latter-day saint, Mother Theresa of Calcutta (whose bust stands in front of San Gregorio Magno, a gift from the Indian government). A whitewashed and peaceful haven located in the former chickenhouses of the San Gregorio monastery since the 1970s, the **Missionario della Carità** houses around thirty women. They're a busy group, among other things looking after the hostel for the needy next door to the main church. But there are usually novices to show you the simple chapel in which they gather every morning at 5am, and of course the small room that Mother Theresa occupied on her frequent visits to Rome, with its tiny bed and other effects – her plate and cutlery, prayerbooks and items of clothing, along with a reliquary containing a piece of tissue stained with her blood.

Santi Quattro Coronati

Piazza dei Santi Quattro Coronati 20 • Daily 6.15am–8pm; Cloister and San Silvestro chapel Mon–Sat 9.30am–noon & 4.30–6pm, Sun 9–10.40am & 4–5.45pm • Church free; San Silvestro chapel €1 • ⓦ santiquattrocoronati.org

Between San Giovanni in Laterano and the Colosseum, the church of **Santi Quattro Coronati**, up the steps off Via dei Santi Quattro Coronati, is dedicated to four soldier martyrs who died because they refused to worship a statue of Aesclepius during the persecutions of Diocletian. Originally built in 1110 by Pope Paschal II, it's a fortified, somewhat dishevelled building whose interior feels quiet and ancient, a world away from the crowds around the Colosseum below. The atmosphere is intensified by the pretty **cloister**, accessed through a door in the north aisle, which is elegantly proportioned and contains a small, neat garden. The church itself has an extra-wide apse and some very old frescoes on the south and west walls, as well as a giant series of apse paintings showing the martyrdom of the soldiers and a *matroneum*, or women's gallery – something rarely seen nowadays. A convent of Augustinian nuns lives here now, and it's they who administer entrance to the **San Silvestro chapel**, accessible from the second courtyard, which contains some of the oldest frescoes in Rome, painted in 1248. They comprise a beautifully preserved comic strip that tells the story of how the fourth-century pope cured the Emperor Constantine of leprosy (he's the one covered in spots) and then baptized him. A pox-free Constantine is also shown giving his crown to the pope in a symbolic transfer of power, and all of it takes place beneath an enthroned Christ surrounded by saints.

San Clemente

Via Labicana 95 • Church daily 9am–7pm • Free • Lower church and Mithraic temple Mon–Sat 9am–12.30pm & 3–6pm, Sun noon–6pm • €5 • ⓦ basilicasanclemente.com

Halfway down Via San Giovanni in Laterano, the church of **San Clemente** is a cream-coloured twelfth-century basilica that brilliantly encapsulates continuity of history in the city – it is in fact a conglomeration of three places of worship from three very different eras in the history of Rome. Pope St Clement I, to whom the church is dedicated, was the third pope after St Peter (and is said to have been ordained by him), reigning from 90 AD until 99 AD, when he was exiled and martyred in the Crimea. His relics are kept in this church, and they have been venerated here from the very earliest times.

The basilica

The ground-floor church is a superb example of a medieval **basilica**: its facade and courtyard face east in the archaic fashion, and there are some fine, warm mosaics in the apse. The choir is partitioned off with beautiful white marble slabs bearing the earliest papal insignia in the city, the monogram of Pope John II, who reigned from 533 to 535 AD. The gilded ceiling bears the arms of Pope Clement XI, from the early years of the eighteenth century, during whose papacy the church was remodelled. Perhaps the highlights of the main church, though, are the fifteenth-century **frescoes** in the chapel of St Catherine by Masolino, whose soft yet vivid colours show scenes from the life of St Catherine on the left: at the top, the saint – in the blue dress – attempts (in vain) to convert the Emperor Maxentius to Christianity, and in fact succeeds in converting his wife (in green), for which the wife is beheaded. In the centre St Catherine is shown being pulled apart by two wheels – hence the famous firework – until an angel intervenes and she too is beheaded (a scene shown in the far-right panel). The central fresco shows the crucifixion, with a grief-stricken Mary Magdalen clinging to the cross while Christ's mother Mary is distraught in the foreground.

The lower church and Mithraic temple

Downstairs there's the nave of an **earlier church**, dating back to 392 AD, with a frescoed narthex depicting, among other things, the *Miracle of San Clemente* and the transferral of his body from St Peter's to San Clemente.

At the western end of this church, steps lead down to the labyrinthine third level, which contains a dank **Mithraic temple** of the late second century, alongside several rooms of a Roman house built after the fire of 64 AD. In the temple is a statue of Mithras slaying the bull and the seats upon which the worshippers sat during their ceremonies. The underground river that formerly fed the lake in front of the Domus Aurea can be heard rushing to its destination in the Tiber, behind the Circo Massimo, a reminder that Rome is built on very shaky foundations indeed. Next door to the Roman house, across a narrow alleyway, are the ground-floor rooms of a **first-century imperial building**, all of which can be explored by the spooky light of fluorescent tubes set in the ceiling and along the mossy brick walls.

San Giovanni in Laterano

Piazza di San Giovanni in Laterano 4 • Daily 7am–6.30pm • ☎ 06 6988 6392 for guided tours, ⓦ vatican.va/various/basiliche /san_giovanni/index_it.htm

The basilica of **San Giovanni in Laterano** is officially Rome's cathedral and the seat of the pope as bishop of Rome, and was for centuries the main papal residence. However, when the papacy returned from Avignon at the end of the fourteenth century, the Lateran palaces were in ruins and uninhabitable, and the pope moved across town to the Vatican, where he has remained ever since. The Lateran Treaty of 1929 accorded this and the other patriarchal basilicas extraterritorial status.

There has been a church on this site since the fourth century, the first established by Constantine, and the present building, reworked by Borromini in the mid-seventeenth century, evokes – like San Clemente or Santo Stefano – Rome's staggering wealth of history with a host of features from different periods: the statue of Constantine in the porch was found on the Quirinal Hill, while the doors of the church itself were taken from the Curia, or Senate House, of the Roman Forum. The obelisk that stands on the north side of the church is the oldest (and largest) in Rome, dating from the fifteenth century BC and brought here from Thebes by Constantine, originally for the Circus Maximus, but raised here by Sixtus V.

The basilica

The interior of San Giovanni has been extensively reworked over the centuries. Much of what you see today dates from the seventeenth century, when the Aldobrandini pope, Clement VIII, had the church remodelled for Holy Year. The **gilded ceiling** of the nave has as its centrepiece the papal arms of Pope Pius VI, from the late 1700s, while the ceiling in the crossing bears, on the left, the Aldobrandini family insignia, and on the right the tomb of Pope Innocent III, who died in 1216 and was buried here in the late 1800s at the behest of Pope Leo XIII, when he had this wing of the crossing remodelled. Leo XIII himself, who died in 1903, is buried opposite.

The first pillar on the left of the right-hand aisle shows a fragment of **Giotto**'s fresco of Boniface VIII, proclaiming the first Holy Year in 1300, a gentle work with gorgeous colours that is at odds with the immensity and grandeur of the rest of the building. On the next pillar along, a more recent monument commemorates Sylvester I – "the magician pope", bishop of Rome during much of Constantine's reign – and incorporates part of his original tomb, said to sweat and rattle his bones when a pope is about to die.

As for the **nave** itself, it's lined with eighteenth-century statues of the apostles in flashy and dramatic Rococo style, each one of which gives a clue as to their identity or manner of death: St Matthew, the tax collector, is shown with coins falling out of a sack; St Bartholomew holds a knife and his own skin (he was flayed alive); St Thomas holds a set square (he's the patron saint of architects) and St Simon a saw (he was, apparently, sawn to death). At the head of the nave, the heads of St Peter and St Paul, the church's prize relics, are kept secure behind the papal altar. The mosaics in the apse are undeniably impressive, but fake – they were added in the later nineteenth century to replace the lost originals – but the **baldacchino** just in front is most definitely genuine. It's a splash of Gothic grandeur made by the Tuscan sculptor Giovanni di Stefano in the fourteenth century that shelters the glassed-over bronze tomb of Martin V, the Colonna pope who was responsible for returning the papacy to Rome from Avignon in 1419.

The cloisters

Daily 9am–6pm • €5

Outside the church, the **cloisters**, accessed via a door by the north transept, are one of the most pleasing parts of the complex, decorated with early thirteenth-century Cosmati work and with fragments of the original basilica. Rooms off to the side form a small museum, displaying the papal throne of Pius V and various papal artefacts (including the vestments of Boniface VIII).

The Lateran Palace and Museo Storico Vaticano

Daily visits on the hour 9am–noon • €5

Adjoining the basilica is the **Lateran Palace**, home of the popes in the Middle Ages and also formally part of Vatican territory. Part of the palace is given over to the **Museo Storico Vaticano**, accessible from the portico of the basilica. Sixtus V destroyed the original building, which had fallen into disrepair, in the late 1500s, and raised the current structure in its place, and it retains most of the frescoes and other decoration from that time. One room in the Museo Storico Vaticano, the so-called **Sala degli Imperatori**, is named for its frescoes of Christian-era Roman emperors, but most importantly is home to the Lateran Treaty, which ceded control of Rome and the papal territories to the Italian state and was signed at the large writing desk next door on

February 11, 1929, in the well-named **Sala della Conciliazione**. This room is decorated with frescoes of those popes Sixtus V considered worthy of inclusion alongside the bust of himself, including St Peter, above the desk, and on the left St Sylvester, who famously baptized Constantine. Around the main courtyard beyond are portraits of all the popes from the sixteenth century to the present day, along with ceremonial garb worn by the soldiers, courtiers and other officials of the Vatican through the centuries.

The Baptistery

Daily 7am–12.30pm & 4–7.30pm · Free

Next door to the Lateran Palace, the **Baptistery** has been carefully restored, along with the side of the church itself, after a car bombing in 1993. It is the oldest surviving baptistery in the Christian world, an octagonal structure built during the fifth century that has been the model for many such buildings since. Oddly, it doesn't really feel its age, although the mosaics in the chapel on the far side and the bronze doors to the chapel on the right, brought here from the **Baths of Caracalla**, quickly remind you where you are.

Scala Santa

April–Sept Mon–Sat 6am–noon & 3.30–6.45pm, Sun 7am–12.30pm & 3.30–7pm; Oct–March Mon–Sat 6am–noon & 3–6.15pm, Sun 7am–12.30pm & 3.30–6.30pm · Free

Across Piazza di Porta San Giovanni from the San Giovanni basilica, the **Scala Santa** is claimed to be the staircase from Pontius Pilate's house down which Christ walked after his trial. It was said to have been brought to Rome by St Helena and was placed here by Pope Sixtus V, who also moved the chapel here – it was formerly the pope's private place of worship. The 28 steps are protected by boards, and the only way you're allowed to climb them is on your knees, which pilgrims do regularly – although there are staircases either side for the less penitent. At the top, the **Sancta Sanctorum**, or chapel of San Lorenzo, holds an ancient (sixth- or seventh-century) painting of Christ that is attributed to an angel, hence its name – *acheiropoeton*, or "not done by human hands". You can't enter the chapel, and, fittingly perhaps, you can only really get a view of it, with its beautiful thirteenth-century mosaic floor, by kneeling and peering through the grilles.

Museo Storico della Liberazione

Via Tasso 145 · Wed, Sat & Sun 9.30am–12.30pm, Tues, Thurs & Fri 9.30am–12.30pm & 3.30–7.30pm; closed Mon · Free · ☎ 06 700 3866, Ⓦ viatasso.eu

Five minutes' walk from the San Giovanni basilica, the **Museo Storico della Liberazione** occupies three floors of the building in which Nazi prisoners were held and interrogated during the wartime Occupation. It's a moving place and deliberately low-key – the original cells have been left as they were, with their windows bricked up by the SS, while the two isolation cells are marked with the desperate notes and messages from the people held here. The other cells focus on different themes of the Occupation: one is dedicated to the 335 victims of the Fosse Ardeatine massacre (see p. 151), another to prisoners who died at Forte Bravetta on the outskirts of the city. You can also see the former kitchen that was the cell of Colonel Giuseppe Montezemolo, who led the resistance and was executed at Ardeatine, complete with scraps of his clothing and other personal effects. The top floor has German propaganda notices, pages from clandestine newspapers and anti-German media, as well as photos, lists of names and notices given to families during the deportation of the Jews from the Ghetto. Twenty minutes after receiving these they had to be ready to leave; most of them never returned.

Via Sannio

Across the far side of the square in front of San Giovanni in Laterano, the **Porta Asinaria**, one of the city's grander gateways, marks the Aurelian Wall (see p.147). If you're here in the morning, you could visit the market (Mon–Sat until about 1.30pm) on **Via Sannio** just beyond, with numerous stalls shadowing the wall touting cheap bags, jewellery, clothes and underwear, and then continue on for five minutes to **Piazzale Metronio**, from where you can follow the line of the **Aurelian Wall** as far as **Porta San Sebastiano** and the Aurelian Wall museum (see p.147) – a twenty-minute walk in total.

Santa Croce in Gerusalemme

Piazza di Santa Croce in Gerusalemme · Daily 7am–12.45pm & 3.30–7.30pm · ⓦ santacroceroma.it

Five minutes' walk from the San Giovanni basilica, by way of Viale Carlo Felice, the ancient church of **Santa Croce in Gerusalemme** is one of the seven pilgrimage churches of Rome, believed to stand on the site of the palace of Constantine's mother St Helena, and the home to the relics of the True Cross she brought back from Jerusalem. Parts of it date from the fourth century AD, although the beautiful Renaissance apse frescoes by Antoniazzo Romano are late fifteenth-century, and show the discovery of the fragments, under a seated Christ – a marvellously Technicolor, naturalistic scene showing trees and mountains and the saint at the centre, with the True Cross and a kneeling cardinal. Steps behind lead down to the original level of Helena's house – now a chapel dedicated to the saint and decorated with marvellous Renaissance mosaics and with a statue of St Helena in a niche, beneath which messages are left. The tiles on the stairs down are an inscription relating to the True Cross discovery and were done at the same time as the apse frescoes.

The Relics Chapel

The **relics** St Helena kept so carefully are stored in a Mussolini-era **chapel** up some steps at the end of the left aisle, incorporating three pieces of the Cross itself, a nail and a couple of thorns, though most spectacular perhaps is a piece of the supposed signage from the Cross, showing the name of Jesus of Nazareth, found behind a (marked) brick in the vestibule outside. Off to the right there's a copy of another, equally famous, relic, the **Shroud of Turin**. Take time to ponder the chapel at the bottom of the staircase too – a rather sad shrine to a local girl Antonietta Meo, who died in 1937 at the age of 6 having written 162 letters to God. Some of these are on display, along with some toys, clothes and other effects. She is the youngest person ever to have been canonized by the Catholic Church.

Vegetable Garden

ⓣ 06 701 4769, extension 103, or ⓔ assamcroce@email.it

There's a lovely **vegetable garden** adjoining the church, which is looked after by monks, with a gate designed by the Greek-Italian artist Jannis Kounellis in 2007. You need to make an appointment if you want to look around, or you can just peek through the gate.

National Museum of Musical Instruments

Piazza di Santa Croce in Gerusalemme 9a · Tues–Sun 9am–6pm · €4 · ⓣ 06 701 4796, ⓦ galleriaborghese.it/nuove/estrumentiinfo.htm

The first floor of the palace next door to Santa Croce is the home of the **National Museum of Musical Instruments**, an interesting display of Italian and European instruments that has surprisingly good background information and labelling, much of which is in English. There are early Roman and Etruscan pieces, lots of stringed instruments and others divided into mechanical instruments, instruments used by travelling musicians, church instruments and early pianofortes. Not what you came to Rome for, perhaps, but worth a look if you're in this part of town.

Porta Maggiore

Just to the north of the church of Santa Croce in Gerusalemme, towards the train tracks, the **Porta Maggiore** is probably the most impressive of all the city gates, built in the first century AD to carry water into Rome from the aqueducts outside, and incorporated into the Aurelian Wall. The **aqueducts** that converge here are the **Acqua Claudia**, which dates from 45 AD, and the **Acqua Marcia**, from 200 BC. The Roman engineers built one on top of the other to channel the water of the Acqua Claudia into the city in a way that did not interfere with the pre-existing Aqua Marcia – a feat recounted in the monumental tablet over the central arches. The famous **Tomb of the Baker**, in white travertine, just outside the gate, is a monument from about 30 AD. The baker in question was a public contractor who made a fortune selling bread to the imperial government. The round holes in the tomb represent the openings of the baker's ovens – a style that strangely enough was picked up in the Mussolini era and can be seen time and again in Fascist architecture.

Pigneto

A ten-minute walk from the Porta Maggiore, **Pigneto** was originally a working-class district of apartment blocks, low-rise villas and cottages that grew up around the rail lines in the nineteenth century. It has always been slightly different – it was a favourite haunt of **Pasolini**, who shot some of his movies here – and is these days one of Rome's most up-and-coming neighbourhoods. The area hasn't been entirely gentrified, though, and retains a slight edge – although the completion of the Line C metro station that's being built on Via del Pigneto will surely hasten its regeneration.

The pedestrianized strip of **Via del Pigneto** hosts a small **market** each morning (and a flea market on the last Sunday of every month), and it and the surrounding streets are home to an increasing selection of decent restaurants, cafés and bars (see p.257). Most are new, but *Necci dal 1924*, at Via Fanfulla da Lodi 68, with its pleasant garden, was a great favourite of Pasolini's and still serves good food and drink all day.

8

PYRAMID OF CAIUS CESTIUS

The Aventine Hill and south

The area south of the Forum and Palatine holds some of the city's most compelling sights, from the relatively central Baths of Caracalla – one of the city's grandest ruins, and the venue of inspirational summer opera performances – to the catacombs on ancient Via Appia, with plenty worth seeing in between. Close by the Baths, you can scale the Aventine Hill, these days one of the city centre's most upscale residential areas, the other side of which is Testaccio, a semi-gentrified working-class enclave that is known for its daily market and hard-core Roman restaurants. It's also one of Rome's nightlife hubs, and this has spilled over into nearby Ostiense, whose regeneration has been partially helped along by the conversion of the Centrale Montemartini electricity plant into a gallery of ancient sculpture.

Circus Maximus

The southern side of the Palatine Hill drops down to the **Circus Maximus**, a long green expanse bordered by heavily trafficked roads that was the ancient city's main venue for chariot races. At one time this arena had a capacity of up to 400,000 spectators, and if it were still intact it would no doubt match the Colosseum for grandeur. As it is, a litter of stones at the Viale Aventino end is all that remains, together with a little medieval tower built by the Frangipani family at the southern end and, behind a chain-link fence traced out in marble blocks, the outline of the Septizodium, an imperial structure designed to show off the glories of the city and its empire to those arriving on the Via Appia. The huge **obelisk** that now stands in front of the church of San Giovanni in Laterano (see p.133) – at 385 tonnes and over 30m high the largest in the world – was once the central marker of the arena, and it's known that the obelisk now in Piazza del Popolo stood here too. The last race was held at the Circus Maximus in 549 AD, but it still retains something of its original purpose as an occasional venue for festivals, concerts and large gatherings (three million people crowded in here when AS Roma won the Scudetto in 2001).

Santa Sabina

Piazza Pietro d'Illiria 1 · Daily 6.30am–12.45pm & 3–6pm

On the opposite side of the Circus Maximus to the Palatine Hill, the Aventine is the most southerly of Rome's seven hills, a leafy, residential neighbourhood that's home to the lovely church of **Santa Sabina**, the principal church of the Dominicans in Rome. It's a strong contender for the city's most beautiful basilica, a high and wide structure, with a nave and portico that were restored back to their fifth-century appearance in the 1930s. In the portico, look at the main doors at the far end, which are contemporary with the church and boast eighteen panels carved with Christian scenes, forming an illustrated Bible that includes (top left) one of the oldest representations of the Crucifixion in existence. Inside, the windows above the arches of the nave are among the most beautiful features of the church, each one different, letting in light by way of lacy patterns carved into the stone. The mosaic inscription on the wall above the doors heralds the achievements of Celestino I, flanked by two female figures representing converted Jews and pagans. Immediately below, in the corner, a smooth piece of black marble, pitted with holes, was apparently thrown by the Devil at St Dominic himself while at prayer, shattering the marble pavement but miraculously not harming the saint.

It's claimed that the orange trees in the garden behind the church (which you have to ask to see) are descendants of those planted by St Dominic himself. Whatever the truth of this, the views from the gardens are splendid – right across the Tiber to the centre of Rome and St Peter's – and beyond here you can also be taken up to see the room where the saint stayed: it's now a small, heavily decorated chapel, but the timbered far end hints at a more spartan authenticity. The cloister, accessible by way of a door off the portico, has been under restoration for some time. Take the time to wander into the public gardens next door to the church, which are a favourite with mothers and babies, and give wonderful views across the river towards the Vatican.

Sant'Alessio

Piazza Sant'Alessio 23 · Daily 8am–noon & 3–7pm

A short walk beyond Santa Sabina on the right, the church of **Sant'Alessio** was originally a Romanesque structure but mostly dates from the eighteenth century now, apart from a nice mosaic floor and two tiny mosaic-covered columns in the apse. A popular medieval saint, Alessio is said to have left his betrothed on their wedding night and travelled for years as a beggar, eventually returning to his father's house incognito and living there as a servant until he died – hence the wooden staircase in the left aisle,

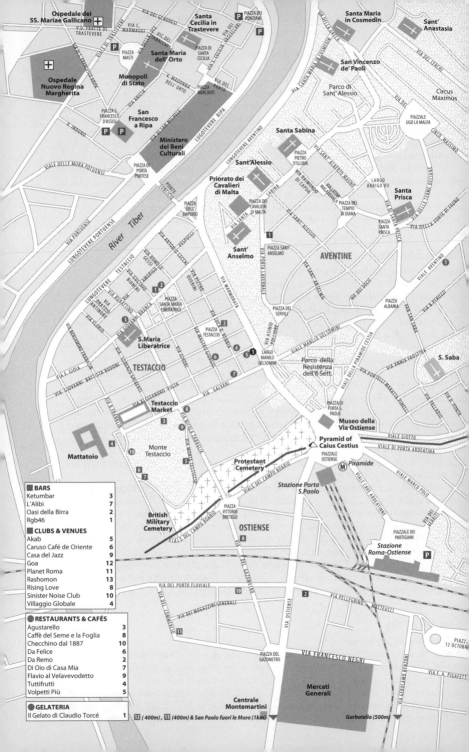

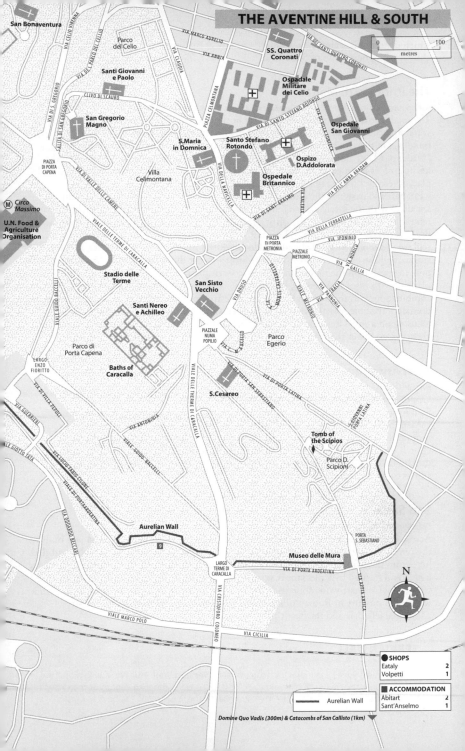

9

which denotes his secret "below stairs" existence. Again, there are nice gardens by the church with good views of St Peter's.

The Priorato di Malta

Piazza dei Cavalieri di Malta 4 ● 06 577 9193 · Closed to the public; tours bookable on ● 06 6758 1234

The road across the Aventine widens out at the Piazza dei Cavalieri di Malta, where you'll find the **Priorato dei Cavalieri di Malta** on the right, a priory that is one of several buildings in the city belonging to the Knights of Malta – now known simply as the "Order of Malta", which has a celebrated view of the dome of St Peter's through the keyhole of its main gate. The little piazza has marble triumphal insignia designed and placed here by Piranesi to celebrate the Knights' dramatic history.

Piranesi also designed the church of Santa Maria del Priorato inside, which you can see along with the lovely gardens, if you organize your visit in advance. The church was rebuilt by Piranesi in 1765, the only structure the famous engraver built. Its elaborate decor is typical of Roman churches, but it differentiates itself with its monochromatic sculptural simplicity. Virtually all the decoration is in grey stone or marble, or covered in stucco, and the effect is impressively uniform – a fact that Piranesi, caught in thoughtful pose in a statue on the right, is no doubt contemplating. The gardens are quite formally planted, with roses and topiary, but lush too, with palms and subtropical plants that in combination with the high walls and entry restrictions give the feel of a secret, cloistered domain – in short, exactly what a city garden should be. They're beautifully tended, focusing on a small fountain and cage of doves in the centre, though to be honest the views are no better than the ones from the public gardens next to Santa Sabina.

Sant'Anselmo

Piazza dei Cavalieri di Malta 5 · Daily 10am–noon & 4–7pm · ● 06 57911, ⓦ www.santanselmo.net

Opposite the Priorato di Malta, spare five minutes or so for the church of **Sant'Anselmo**, a Benedictine complex containing a church and college, with pleasant gardens and a shop selling all manner of produce, Benedictine and otherwise: limoncello, *grappa*, *amaro*, as well as chocolate, beer, books, CDs and toiletries. The church is a plain basilica built in the last decade of the nineteenth century – not of much interest in itself, but known for its Gregorian chant and reasonably regular concerts, usually held on Sunday evenings.

San Saba

Piazza Bernini 20 · Daily 8am–noon & 4–7pm

Across busy Piazza Albania from the Aventine Hill, the church of **San Saba** was built in the tenth century over a seventh-century structure constructed by monks who had fled here from the Middle East to escape the Arab advance. Topped with a fifteenth-century loggia and fronted by a pleasant if scruffy walled garden, it's worth visiting for its wonderful Cosmati-work door and floor, and an interior that feels very ancient, with a wonderful mixture of Roman pillars and thirteenth-century frescoes in a short additional left aisle and the beautifully proportioned apse.

SERVIAN WALL

Follow Via Sant'Anselmo through the leafy residential streets of the Aventine down to Piazza Albania, where there's a rare stretch of the so-called **Servian Wall** – the first wall to properly enclose Rome, built in the fourth century BC and named after the sixth-century Roman king Servius Tullius, who first planned it. Other stretches of the Servian Wall can be seen outside and in the basement at Termini.

The Baths of Caracalla

Viale delle Terme di Caracalla 52 • Mon 9am–2pm, Tues–Sun 9am–1hr before sunset • €7, including the Tomb of Cecilia Metella and the Villa dei Quintilii • ☎ 06 3996 7700

Southeast of the Aventine, the **Baths of Caracalla** give a far better sense of the monumental scale of Roman architecture than most of the extant ruins in the city – so much so that Shelley was moved to write his Romantic play *Prometheus Unbound* here in 1819. The baths are no more than a giant shell now, but the walls still rise to very nearly their original height. There are many fragments of mosaics – none spectacular, but quite a few bright and well preserved – and it's easy to discern a floor plan. Set in extensive walled gardens, the baths were built around the long spine of the central hall, or frigidarium, at each end of which are vast courtyards – *palestrae* – which were used for sports before bathing. Off to the left of the frigidarium was the tepidarium, and beyond this the domed chamber of the circular caldarium, which is easier to see outside the baths themselves. On the other side of the frigidarium was the *natatio* or swimming pool, a huge open space which would have been accessed by way of the *apodyteria*, or changing rooms, on either side – you can get the best sense of this by following the signed route from the entrance.

As for Caracalla, he was one of Rome's most brutal and shortest-lived rulers, and it's no wonder there's nothing else in the city built by him. The baths are the summer venue of the **Teatro dell'Opera** (one of Mussolini's better ideas), and attending an opera performance here is a thrilling way to see the baths at their most atmospheric (see p.278).

Santi Nereo ed Achilleo

Via delle Terme di Caracalla 28 • Daily 7.30am–noon & 4.30–7.30pm • ⓦ vallicella.org

Just outside the Baths of Caracalla, the church of **Santi Nereo ed Achilleo** makes for a peaceful spot after the crowds at the baths, and is of interest for the ninth-century mosaic on the arch above its apse, which depicts Christ and three prostrate apostles, between a scene of the *Annunciation* on the left and a *Virgin and Child* on the right. The beautiful Cosmati work on the marble choir screen and the altar itself is also worth a look, as is the ornate throne sitting on two lions in the apse, said to have been preached from by Gregory the Great (see p.314) – a fact emphasized by the apse fresco showing St Gregory preaching to various cardinals. This is full of charming detail: you'll notice one of the cardinals – second from the right – has trouble hearing, while others confer as to what the great pope might be saying.

Back outside the church, on the far side of the Piazzale Numa Pompilio roundabout, Via di Porta San Sebastiano leads onto the Via Appia Antica which heads towards the catacombs and other archeological delights, a few kilometres south (see p.49).

Testaccio

Bus #170 or 175 from Termini or Piazza Venezia, or metro line B

On the far side of the Aventine Hill, across Via Marmorata, the working-class neighbourhood of **Testaccio** groups around a couple of main squares – Piazza Testaccio and Piazza di Santa Maria Liberatrice. For many years this tight-knit community was synonymous with the slaughterhouse that sprawls down to the Tiber just beyond, and for its daily **food market** on Piazza Testaccio But the slaughterhouse closed long ago and although the market is still going strong, in the last couple of decades it has become more gentrified, with the result that the neighbourhood is a curious mixture of the old and the new: traditional trattorias celebrate their use of offal alongside veggie restaurants and cool cafés, and there's a busy gay and alternative club scene that exists cheek-by-jowl with the car-repair shops gouged into Monte Testaccio. The market is still thriving, but it's recently moved from its old home to a purpose-built new complex opposite the Mattatoio on Via Galvani, and its shiny new stalls are no doubt an improvement. But Piazza Testaccio can't help but feel a little forlorn without it, and the fact that the restaurants around the new market include a sushi bar and a place with all-you-can-eat ribs specials makes you think that maybe the neighbourhood has lost a little of its unique charm.

MACRO Testaccio

Piazza Orazio Giustiniani 4 • Tues–Sun 4pm–midnight • exhibitions €6 • ☎ 06 6710 70400

The slaughterhouse, or **Mattatoio**, was once the area's main employer and is now a huge, partly derelict complex. Much of it is disused today, though it does house the centro sociale "Villaggio Globale", a space used for concerts and offbeat events in summer, stabling for the city's horse-and-carriage drivers and a branch of the Museum of Contemporary Art of Rome, **MACRO Testaccio**, just inside the main gate, where a couple of large pavilions stage adventurous temporary exhibitions (for MACRO's main branch, see p.182).

Monte Testaccio

Entrance at Via Nicola Zabaglia 24; visits occasionally possible on request • ☎ 06 0608

Bang in the middle of Testaccio, a 50m mound of historic landfill known as **Monte Testaccio** gives the area its name. The ancient Romans broke terracotta amphorae up into small shards and laid them down in an orderly manner over several centuries, sprinkling quicklime on them to dissolve the residual wine or oil. It's estimated that there are around 53 million amphorae here and it makes for an odd sight, the ceramic curls clearly visible through the tufts of grass that crown its higher reaches, the bottom layers hollowed out by the workshops of car and bike mechanics – and, now, clubs and bars.

Protestant Cemetery

Via Caio Cestio 6 • Mon–Sat 9am–5pm, Sun 9am–1pm • Donation expected • ☎ 06 574 1900, ⓦ cemeteryrome.it • Metro B to Piramide

On the far side of Monte Testaccio, off Via Marmorata, the **Protestant Cemetery** isn't in fact a Protestant cemetery at all, but is reserved for non-Roman Catholics of all nationalities, so you'll also find famous Italian atheists, Christians of the Orthodox persuasion and the odd Jew or Muslim buried here. It is nonetheless one of the shrines to the English in Rome, and a fitting conclusion to a visit to the Keats-Shelley Memorial House on Piazza di Spagna (see p.94).

Most visitors come to see the grave of **Keats**, who lies next to his friend, the painter **Joseph Severn**, in the furthest corner of the less crowded, older part of the cemetery (turn left from the entrance), his stone inscribed as he wished with the words "here lies one whose name was writ in water". Severn died much later than Keats but asked to be laid here nonetheless, together with his brushes and palette. Just behind Severn and Keats lies Severn's 1-year-old son; behind, a plaque on the wall remembers the Swedish doctor and writer Axel Munthe, his wife Hilda and their two sons. As for **Shelley**, his ashes were brought here at Mary Shelley's request and interred, after much obstruction by the papal authorities, in the newer part of the cemetery, at the top against the back wall – the Shelleys had visited several years earlier, the poet praising it as "the most beautiful and solemn cemetery I ever beheld". It had been intended that Shelley should rest with his young son, William, who died while they were in Rome and was also buried here, but his remains couldn't be found (although his small grave is nearby). Mary Shelley was so broken-hearted by the deaths of her son and husband that it was twenty years before she could bring herself to visit their graves.

Shelley's great friend, the writer and adventurer **Edward Trelawny**, lies next to him, while in front of Shelley's grave is a slab marking the final resting-spot of the American Beat poet **Gregory Corso**, who died in 2001 but was buried here, at his request, next to his hero Shelley. To the right, a headless torso marked simply "Belinda" marks the grave of Belinda Lee – a little-known Hollywood starlet, who died in her mid-twenties in a car crash in Hollywood in 1961, just as her career was beginning to take off – and after a scandalous affair with one of the Orsini princes, hence her burial here. Among other famous internees, the political writer and activist Antonio Gramsci lies on the far right-hand side of the cemetery in the middle, and the Italian novelist Carlo Emilio Gadda is nearby. If you're at all interested in star-spotting you should either borrow or buy the **booklet** available at the entrance.

British War Cemetery

Via Nicola Zabaglia · Daily 8am–3pm, though only open when gardener is present due to vandalism, which means that it may close for 30min around lunchtime · Metro B to Piramide

Between Monte Testaccio and the Aurelian Wall, the **British War Cemetery** is the less famous counterpart to the Protestant Cemetery across the road, but it's no less contemplative a spot, the final resting-place of the four hundred or so young men from Britain and parts of the Commonwealth who were killed in action during 1943 and 1944 in the battle to liberate Italy and ultimately Rome. It's a beautifully kept and peaceful place, planted with lawns and framed by the arches of the old Roman wall behind, birdsong easily drowning out the hum of traffic on nearby Via Ostiense.

Museo della Via Ostiense

Piazza di Porta San Paolo 3 · Tues & Thurs 9am–4.30pm, Wed, Fri, Sat & first & third Sun of each month 9.30am–1.30pm · Free · ☏ 06 5728 4435 · Metro B to Piramide

Right by the pyramid, the **Museo della Via Ostiense**, housed in the old Porta San Paolo, is a museum devoted to the road that spears off on the far side of the intersection, originally built to join Rome to Ostia and its port. There's not a huge amount of interest here but if you have half an hour to kill on your way to catch a train to Ostia Antica from the Porta San Paolo station opposite, the model of Ostia is worth studying, as is that of the old port of Trajan. There are sepulchral monuments and other items that used to line the old road, and you can stand on top of the gate to contemplate the traffic chaos outside.

Pyramid of Caius Cestius

Piazzale Ostiense · Open to the public on 2nd & 4th Sat of each month · Cats can be visited any afternoon 2–4pm · Metro B to Piramide

Overlooking the cemetery, the most distinctive landmark in this part of town is the **Pyramid of Caius Cestius**, who died in 12 BC. Cestius had spent some time in Egypt, and part of his will decreed that all his slaves should be freed. The white pyramid you see today was thrown up by them in only 330 days of what must have been joyful building. You can visit the cats who live here, and the volunteers who care for them, in the afternoon.

Ostiense

The Porta San Paolo basically overlooks a major traffic junction from which Via Ostiense spears off west, the ancient link between Rome and its port of Ostia. The **Ostiense** neighbourhood is no great shakes in itself, but it's one of the city's most up-and-coming areas, home to those who can no longer afford to live in already-gentrified Testaccio.

Centrale Montemartini

Via Ostiense 106 · Tues–Sun 9am–7pm · €6.50, €15 for joint ticket with Capitoline Museums · ☏ 06 0608 · ⓦ centralemontemartini.org · Ten minutes' walk from Piramide metro station, or bus #271 from Piazza Venezia (Mon–Fri)

The former electricity generating plant of **Centrale Montemartini** was perhaps the first thing to put Ostiense on the map. It was originally requisitioned to display the cream

9

of the Capitoline Museums' sculpture while the main buildings were being renovated, but was so popular that it became the Capitoline's permanent outpost. The huge rooms of the power station are ideally suited to showing off ancient sculpture, although checking out the massive turbines and furnaces has a fascination of its own.

The size of the building is the thing, most obviously in the **Machine Hall**, where there's the head, feet and an arm from a colossal statue, once 8m high, found in Largo di Torre Argentina. Elsewhere in the chamber are various heads, some of emperors (Claudius, Tiberius, Domitian), a large Roman Athena and a fine statue of a Roman soldier from the Esquiline Hill, tucked away in a corner. In the adjacent **Furnace Hall**, the most obvious features are the furnace itself at the far end and a fragmented mosaic of hunting scenes that occupies half the floor – deer and boar, and figures on horseback or crouching to trap their prey in nets. Among the sculptures on display is an amazing third-century BC statue of a girl seated on a stool with legs crossed, a statue of the Muse Polymnia, leaning on a rock and staring thoughtfully into the distance, and a wonderful pair of magistrates, one old, one young, but both holding the handkerchief they would use to herald the start of competitions and circuses.

Garbatella

On the left of Via Ostiense is the vast derelict expanse of the Mercati Generali, beyond which **Garbatella** is one of the city's more interesting nineteenth-century residential developments, planned as new housing for the growing city in the 1920s. Originally known as the Borgata Giardino, it was – and to some extent still is – a solid, left-leaning, working-class district. An odd mixture of undistinguished postwar apartment blocks and low-rise cottages set in leafy gardens that evoke a peaceful, suburban feel, it makes quite a change from the industrial grittiness that pervades so much of this part of the city. If Garbatella has a centre, it's Piazza Damiano Sauli, whose shabby civic buildings centre on a trio of brick arches, through which you can walk to wander the area's shady lanes. It's becoming rather gentrified, as you might expect, but the district as a whole remains fairly close to its old roots, with a solid base of support for AS Roma and some decent, long-established restaurants that are alone worth the metro ride.

San Paolo fuori le Mura

Via Ostiense 186 · Daily 7am–7pm · Free · ⓦ abbaziasanpaolo.net · Metro line B to San Paolo and walk two minutes to the eastern entrance, or buses #23 and 271 from Piazza Venezia (Mon–Fri) stop outside the west entrance

Some 2km south of the Porta San Paolo, the basilica of **San Paolo fuori le Mura** or "St Paul's outside the Walls" is one of the four patriarchal basilicas of Rome (and thus not technically Italian territory), occupying the supposed site of St Paul's tomb, where he was laid to rest after being beheaded at Tre Fontane (see p.156). St Paul is joint patron saint of Rome, with St Peter. Of the four basilicas, this has probably fared the least well over the years. It was apparently once the grandest, connected to the Aurelian Wall by a colonnade over a kilometre in length, made up of eight hundred marble columns, but a ninth-century sacking by the Saracens and a devastating fire in 1823 (a couple of cack-handed roofers spilt burning tar, almost entirely destroying the church) means that the building you see now is largely a nineteenth-century reconstruction.

The interior

The church is a very successful – if somewhat clinical – rehash of the former building. Perhaps even more than St Peter's, it impresses with sheer size and grandeur, and whether you enter by way of the cloisters or the west door, it's impossible not to be awed by the space of the building inside, its crowds of columns topped by round-arched arcading, and the **medallions** of all the popes fringing the nave and transepts above, starting with St Peter to the right of the apse and ending with Benedict XVI at the top of the south aisle.

Of all the basilicas of Rome, this gives you the feel of what an ancient Roman basilica must have been like: the huge, barn-like structure, with its clerestory windows and roof beams supported by enormous columns, has a powerful and authentic sense of occasion.

Some parts of the building did survive the fire. In the south transept, the paschal candlestick at the head of the nave, behind two large statues of St Peter (on the left) and St Paul (on the right) is a remarkable piece of **Romanesque carving**, supported by half-human beasts and rising through entwined tendrils and strangely human limbs and bodies to scenes from Christ's life, the figures crowding in together as if for a photocall; it's inscribed by its makers, Nicola d'Angelo and Pietro Vassalletto. The bronze, eleventh-century doors at the end of the south aisle were also rescued from the old basilica, as was the thirteenth-century tabernacle by Arnolfo di Cambio, under which a slab from the time of Constantine, inscribed "Paolo Apostolo Mart", is supposed to lie – although it's hard to get a look at this. The arch across the apse is original, too, embellished with **mosaics** (donated by the Byzantine Empress Galla Placidia in the fifth century) that show angels, saints Peter and Paul, the symbols of the Gospels and Christ giving a blessing. The mosaics in the apse date from 1220 and show Luke, Paul, Peter and Andrew and the kneeling figure of Honorius III kissing the feet of Christ.

The cloister, chapel and pinacoteca

The cloister, through the shop, is probably Rome's finest piece of Cosmati work, its spiralling, mosaic-encrusted columns enclosing a peaceful rose garden. Just off here, the **Relics Chapel** houses a dustily kept set of artefacts, and the Pinacoteca shows engravings depicting San Paolo before and after the fire.

Aurelian Wall

From Piazza di Porta San Paolo, you can make a long detour back into the city centre following the **Aurelian Wall**, built by the Emperor Aurelian (and his successor Probus) in 275 AD to enclose Rome's seven hills and protect the city from invasion. The Aurelian Wall surrounds the city and, if you really are an enthusiast, you can walk its seventeen-kilometre circumference in an eight-hour day with a pause for lunch. However, for a taster, one of the best-preserved stretches runs between Porta San Paolo and Porta San Sebastiano, following Via di Porta Ardeatina: cross the road from Piramide metro station, turn right and follow the walls, keeping them always on your left.

Museo delle Mura

Via di Porta San Sebastiano 18 · Tues–Sun 9am–2pm · €5 · ☎ 06 0608, ⓦ museodellemuraroma.it · Bus #118

It is about two kilometres around the Aurelian Wall from Porta San Paolo to Porta San Sebastiano, built in the fifth century, where the **Museo delle Mura** occupies a couple of floors of the gate. It's the best place to get a sense of the wall's history, with displays of Aurelian's original plans and lots of photos of the past and present walls that are helpful in showing what is original and what medieval additions and how different structures have been incorporated into the walls over the years. The museum tells you more about the walls and the various gates than you really need to know, but you can climb up to the top of the gate for great views over the Roman countryside beyond, and walk a few hundred metres along the walls themselves – towards the east – before having to return to the museum.

Tomb of the Scipios

Via di Porta Latina 10 · Tues–Sun 9am–2pm · The site is normally locked but the key is available from the Museo delle Mura · €5 · Bus #118

Leading from the Baths of Caracalla to the Porta San Sebastiano, the Via Porta San Sebastiano, like the Via Appia further south, would once have been lined with the

9

tombs of rich families, and you can see one of these, a short walk from the Museo delle Mura – the **Tomb of the Scipios**. The Scipios were one of the great Republican dynasties, generals in the Punic Wars against Carthage, and this family tomb was discovered in 1780 and its Etruscan-style sarcophagus transported to the Vatican, where it is on display. There is a little more to see here than there used to be, and more information too, since a renovation and reopening a couple of years ago secured the site from landslides and improved access. But the excavations are still more or less a scatter of ruins of what would have been a large building full of niches, apses and most intriguingly tunnels to house the dead.

Via Appia Antica

Starting at the Porta San Sebastiano on the edge of the city centre, the **Via Appia Antica** (or "Appian Way") is the most famous of the consular roads that used to strike out in different directions from the ancient city. This road, built by the censor Appius Claudius in 312 BC, is the only Roman landmark mentioned in the Bible. During classical times it was the most important of all the Roman trade routes, the so-called "Queen of Roads", carrying supplies right down through Campania to the port of Brindisi, some 500km southeast. It's no longer the main route south out of the city – that's Via Appia Nuova from nearby Porta San Giovanni – but it was an important part of early Christian Rome, its verges lined with numerous pagan and Christian sites.

The best-known Christian sites in Via Appia Antica are the underground burial cemeteries or **catacombs** of the first Christians. Laws in ancient Rome forbade burial within the city walls, and most Romans were cremated. There are catacombs in other parts of the city – those attached to the church of Sant'Agnese on Via Nomentana (see p.184) are some of the best – but this is by far the largest concentration of underground Christian burial sites in the city. There are five complexes in all, dating from the first century to the fourth century, almost entirely emptied of bodies now but still decorated with the primitive signs and frescoes that were the hallmark of the then burgeoning Christian movement. Despite much speculation, no one really knows why the Christians decided to bury their dead in these tunnels: the rock here, **tufa**, is soft and easy to hollow out, but the digging involved must still have been phenomenal, and there is no real reason to suppose that the burial places had to be secret – they continued to bury their dead like this long after Christianity became the established religion. Whatever the reasons, they make intriguing viewing now. The three principal complexes are within walking distance of each other, though it's not really worth trying to see them all – the layers of shelves and drawers lose their fascination after a while. If you only go for one, you'd do best to focus on **San Sebastiano** or maybe **San Callisto** and explore the other attractions nearby.

VISITING VIA APPIA ANTICA

GETTING THERE

Archeobus If you want to see a lot of the area, including the Villa dei Quintilii and Parco degli Acquedotti, Archoebus (ⓦ trambusopen.com/en/archeobus.cfm) is a good choice, though the service only runs Fri–Sun. Buses run from Termini, the Colosseum and Baths of Caracalla every thirty minutes 9am–12.30pm and 1.30–4.30pm; tickets cost €12 for 48hr (family of four €40), and you can hop on and off as you wish; if you did the route in one go without getting off it would take 90mins. Archeobus tickets combined with a #110 Openbus ticket cost €25.

Buses The best bet if you're concentrating on Via Appia Antica proper – that is just the catacombs and the attractions close by – is to save your money and take the public buses that run south along Via Appia Antica and conveniently stop at or near most of the main attractions. Bus #118 runs from Piazzale Ostiense almost as far as San Sebastiano; you can also take bus #218 from San Giovanni in Laterano, which goes down Via Ardeatina, or bus #660, which runs from Colli Albani metro station to just beyond the Tomb of Cecilia Metella. A good thing to do is to get off the bus at the Appia Antica information office.

CLOCKWISE FROM TOP LEFT SHELLEY'S GRAVE STONE (P.144); BATHS OF CARACALLA (P.143); CENTRALE MONTEMARTINI (P.145) >

On foot From Porta San Sebastiano you can take in everything on foot; it takes about fifteen minutes to reach Domine Quo Vadis, 10 minutes from there to San Callisto, and from there another 10 minutes to San Sebastiano, and 5 minutes to the Fosse Ardeatino or Domitilla.

By bike Consider also getting yourself to the Parco Appia Antica information office (see below) where you can rent a bike (€3 an hour or €15 a day) – perhaps the best way of all to get around. You can cycle (or walk) from Quo Vadis to San Sebastiano, via San Callisto, without touching the road, which can be busy, and beyond San Sebastiano it's quiet and relatively traffic-free.

TOURIST INFORMATION

Parco Regionale dell'Appia Antica The information office for the area – which is actually classified as a national park – is at Via Appia Antica 58, on the right before you get to Domine Quo Vadis (April–Oct Mon–Sat 9.30am–1pm & 2–5.30pm, Sun 9.30am–6.30pm (5.30pm in Aug); Nov–March Mon–Sat 9.30am–1pm & 2–5pm, Sun 9.30am–5pm; ☎ 06 513 5316, ⓦ parcoappiaantica.it); you can pick up a good map and other information on the various Appia Antica sights and rent bikes here. Their website has lots of good information in English, including recommended walking tours and places to go horseriding in the area.

EATING

It's nice to take a picnic if you're making a day of it but there are also restaurants: *L'Archeologica*, just past the church at Via Appia Antica 125 (closed Tues), and *Cecilia Metella*, right opposite at Via Appia Antica 139 (closed Mon); neither is especially cheap but both have nice gardens for alfresco eating in summer.

Domine Quo Vadis

Via Appia Antica 51 • Daily 8am–6.30pm

About 500m from Porta San Sebastiano, where the road forks, the church of **Domine Quo Vadis** is the first obvious sight, and signals the start of the catacomb stretch of road. Legend has this as the place where St Peter saw Christ while fleeing from certain death in Rome and asked, "Where goest thou, Lord?", to which Christ replied that he was going to be crucified once more, leading Peter to turn around and accept his fate. The small church is ordinary enough inside, except for its replica of a piece of marble that is said to be marked with the footprints of Christ (the original is in the church of San Sebastiano; see p.151).

Catacombs of San Callisto

Via Appia Antica 110–126 • Daily except Wed 9am–noon & 2–5pm • Tours last 45min • €8 • ☎ 06 513 0151, ⓦ catacombe.roma.it

Opposite the church of Domine Quo Vadis, a tree-lined road leads across the fields a kilometre or so to the **Catacombs of San Callisto** – also accessible from Via Appia itself and from Via Ardeatina. They're the largest of Rome's catacombs, and the regular tours in English are usually run by priests, taking in a bit of preliminary explanation before heading into the high-vaulted passages, which stretch for some twenty miles and held around half a million bodies. The catacombs were founded in the second century AD, and many of the early popes are buried here in the papal crypt, including Callisto himself. St Callisto was in fact the guardian of the cemetery before he became pope; he was later killed in a riot and buried here in 222 AD, along with Sixtus II and seven other early popes. The numerous passages and burial vaults are as atmospheric as you would expect and also feature some well-preserved seventh- and eighth-century **frescoes**, and the **crypt of Santa Cecilia**, who was buried here after her martyrdom, before being shifted to the church dedicated to her in Trastevere (see p.164) – a copy of Carlo Maderno's famous statue marks the spot.

Catacombs of Santa Domitilla

Via delle Sette Chiese 282 • Daily except Tues 9am–noon & 2–5pm • €8 • ☎ 06 511 0342, ⓦ domitilla.info

In the opposite direction from the San Callisto exit, up Via delle Sette Chiese on the left, the **Catacombs of Santa Domitilla** are quieter than those of San Callisto. The catacombs stretch from underneath a renovated fourth-century basilica that was erected to the martyrs Achilleus and Nereus, who were killed and eventually buried here during the reign of Diocletian. They were Roman citizens who were killed for their Christian beliefs, and Domitilla was a Roman noblewoman who donated the land the catacombs occupy. The network is the largest of Rome's 62 catacombs, stretching for around 17km in all and thought to contain around 150,000 tombs. Tours last 45 minutes or so and wind about a small section beneath the church, taking in several late-fourth-century BC frescoes and the usual wall etchings and niches.

Mausoleo delle Fosse Ardeatine

Via Ardeatina 174 • Mon–Fri 8.15am–3.15pm, Sat & Sun 8.15am–4.45pm • Free

Near the alternative entrance to the San Callisto catacombs, the **Mausoleo delle Fosse Ardeatine** remembers the massacre of over three hundred civilians during the Nazi occupation of Rome, after the resistance had ambushed and killed 32 soldiers on Via Rasella in the centre of the city (an event remembered in the 1973 film *Massacre in Rome*). The Nazis killed ten civilians for every dead German, burying the bodies here and then exploding mines to cover up their crime. The bodies were dug up after the war and reinterred in the mausoleum. Chapels have been installed in the so-called **Grotta dell'Eccidio**, where the bodies were found, all of which have been interred in a nearby area under serried rows of stone slabs, each with a name and photo apart from the odd '*ignoto*' (or unknown). Just above here a path leads to a small museum with newspaper cuttings telling the story of the event, and various other artefacts relating to the Nazi occupation, resistance and eventual liberation.

Catacombs of San Sebastiano

Via Appia Antica 136 • Daily except Sun 10am–5pm • €8 • ☎ 06 785 0350, ⓦ catacombe.org

The **Catacombs of San Sebastiano**, on the right side of Via Appia Antica, are situated beneath a much-renovated basilica that was originally built by Constantine on the spot where the bodies of the apostles Peter and Paul are said to have been laid for a time. In the church, the first chapel on the left holds a statue of Sebastian as he lay dying, built above his original tomb, while opposite is the original slab of marble imprinted with the feet of Christ that you may have seen in the church of Domine Quo Vadis.

Downstairs, half-hour tours wind around the catacombs, dark corridors showing signs of early Christian worship – paintings of doves and fish, a contemporary carved oil lamp and inscriptions dating the tombs themselves. The most striking features, however, are not Christian at all, but three **pagan tombs** (one painted, two stuccoed), discovered when archeologists were burrowing beneath the floor of the basilica upstairs. Just above here, Constantine is said to have raised his chapel to Peter and Paul, and although St Peter was later removed to the Vatican, and St Paul to San Paolo fuori le Mura, the graffiti above record the fact that this was indeed, albeit temporarily, where the two apostles rested.

Villa and Circus of Maxentius

Via Appia Antica 153 • Tues–Sun 10am–4pm • €5 • ⓦ villadimassenzio.it

A couple of hundred metres further on from the San Sebastiano catacombs, the group of brick ruins trailing off into the fields to the left are the remains of the **Villa and Circus of Maxentius**, a large complex built by the emperor in the early fourth century AD before his defeat by Constantine. It's a clear, long oval of grass, similar to the Circus Maximus (see p.139) back in town, but slightly better preserved and in a rather more bucolic location – making it a fantastic place for a picnic, lolling around in the grass or perching on the ruins. Clambering about in the remains, you can make out the twelve starting gates to the circus, or racetrack, the enormous towers that contained the mechanism for lifting the gates at the beginning of the races and the remains of a basilica. Other structures that surround it include, closer to the road, the ruins of what was once a magnificent mausoleum of an unknown person or persons, the so-called **Tomb of Romulus**, in the middle of a huge quadrangle of walls.

Tomb of Cecilia Metella

Via Appia Antica 161 • Tues–Sun 9am–1hr before sunset • €7, including Terme di Caracalla and Villa dei Quintilii

Further along the Via Appia is the circular **Tomb of Cecilia Metella** from the Augustan period, converted into a castle in the fourteenth century. It's believed to be the tomb of

9

the daughter of one Quintus Metellus Creticus, who was a consul around 70 BC, and who married the son of Marcus Crassus, who – with Julius Caesar and Pompey – was one of a short-lived 'first triumvirate' of rulers of the late Roman Republic. The building itself is a huge brick-built drum, little more than a large pigeon coop these days, although various fragments and finds are littered around the adjacent later courtyards, and down below you can see what's left of a lava flow from thousands of years earlier.

Capo di Bove

Via Appia Antica 222 • Daily 10am–4pm • Free

About 500m beyond Cecilia Metella, the **Capo di Bove** consists of the remains of an ancient Roman baths complex that was part of the estate of Herodes Atticus, one-time tutor of Marcus Aurelius, who owned a lot of land locally. You can make out most of the rooms of the baths, as well as a few fragments of mosaic floors, while a small building beyond the site displays photos of the Via Appia and has further information on the complex.

Casale Rotondo

Beyond Cecilia Metella the Via Appia Antica hits proper countryside, and the road heads straight south: some stretches are still made up of the original Roman slabs, its verges littered with ancient rubble, including tombs, shrines, gateposts and watchtowers, most of them excavated during the nineteenth century. There's no bus out here (although the Archeobus comes part of the way), but it's by far the most atmospheric stretch of the ancient Via Appia, and a lovely walk or cycle through open countryside and past multiple gated villas. Where else can you enjoy a picnic on the ancient stones of a Roman funerary memorial? Follow the road as far as the circular tomb of the **Casale Rotondo** – the largest of Via Appia's monuments, dating from the last decades of the first century BC – beyond which you can either continue, or follow the main road left towards the Appia Nuova and the main entrance of the Villa dei Quintilii.

Villa dei Quintilii

Via Appia Nuova 1092 • Tues–Sun 9am–1hr before sunset • €7, including the Tomb of Cecilia Metella and Baths of Caracalla • ☏ 06 3996 7700 • Metro A to Colli Albani and then bus #664

The **Villa dei Quintilii** crowns the crest of a hill not far from the main road out to Ciampino. It's one of the largest and most complete suburban villas close to Rome, and dates from the mid-second century AD. As you might expect from the position of the place, the Quintilii were an influential Roman family; two brothers were consuls under Commodus, and subsequently executed by him in 182 AD.

The main building has a one-room **museum** with finds from the villa and surrounding area: a large statue of Zeus and three heads of Hermes, a lovely head of a woman and another of a man from the residential section of the villa, a fragment of a relief of *Mithras slaying the Bull* from the villa's baths, and three almost perfect wall designs of male nude figures in *opus sectile*. The villa itself is up a track on the mound of the hill, enjoying panoramic views of the Roman countryside on all sides. On the northern side, the **baths complex** rears up, with steps leading down to its well-preserved caldarium, in which a rectangular pool is overlooked by massive windows designed to keep the temperature inside comfortably warm. A few rooms over, the frigidarium is perhaps the best-preserved room in the complex, with considerable traces of its mosaic floor and two columns at the far end. Retracing your steps, you can also walk the corridors of the residential part of the villa, though sadly many of the rooms and steps are closed off, while on the far side of the complex you wander into what must have been a hugely impressive main reception hall, whose large windows would have made the most of the countryside views.

Parco degli Acquedotti

A few minutes from the Villa dei Quintilii on the Archeobus, or a few minutes' walk from Subaugusta metro station, the **Parco degli Acquedotti** is a lovely spot, where two aqueducts snake between the pines of suburban Rome. Of the pair, the **Acqua Claudia** is unusually intact, its arches leading off south into the far distance. Looking north, along its more ruinous stretches, you can see central Rome, marked by the dome of St Peter's. The other, more sunken aqueduct is the **Acqua Felice**, which is supplemented by a modern pipe. Eleven major aqueducts supplied ancient Rome with water, built between the fourth century BC and third century AD. At its height the population of the city was around a million, and between them the aqueducts ensured that each member of the Roman populace had access to around 75 litres a day – more, in fact, than the people of many modern countries use. Designed to allow water to flow freely towards the city, they mostly consisted of tunnels bored underground, and it was only when they got closer to the city that the water would run along a conduit raised on arches, to help the water pressure when it got to the city itself. They're still an impressive sight, and make a nice place for a picnic.

Cinecittà

Via Tuscolana 1055 • Wed–Mon 9.30am–6.30pm; Tours in English at 11:30am & 4pm • €20 • ☎ 06 722 931, ⓦ cinecittastudios.it •
Metro A to Cinecittà, the stop is right outside the studio entrance.

Still the largest film-making complex in Europe and one of the biggest in the world, **Cinecittà**, set in its own oasis of umbrella pines on the southeastern edge of the city, is steeped in history and legend. Built in the 1930s and opened by Mussolini in 1937, its first few years were given over to propaganda movies glorifying the Fascist regime. But after World War II, its reputation for quality and low costs plus its accessible location brought some of the big Hollywood producers here to make historical epics like *Ben Hur* and *Cleopatra* (the latter one of the most expensive films ever made at the time), as well as more low-key classics such as the *Pink Panther*.

Of course all the great Italian directors used Cinecittà, too: **Fellini** made nearly all of his movies here, and Vittorio di Sica, **Franco Zeffirelli**, **Luchino Visconti**, Pasolini and many others were regular visitors during their 1960s and 1970s heyday; it was also the creative home of **Sergio Leone**'s spaghetti westerns. And the studio still thrives, perhaps more than ever, after a major corporate takeover and a serious upgrade of its facilities in the 1990s. **Bernardo Bertolucci** made much of his *Last Emperor* here in 1987, and more recently **Martin Scorsese** used its giant sound stages to recreate the streets of New York for *Gangs of New York*; HBO also came here – where else? – to film their BBC-aired epic, *Rome*, in 2005, and although part of the complex was damaged by a serious fire in 2007 it finally caught up with its counterparts in the US and opened to the public for tours in 2012.

Studio tours

A visit to Cinecittà is as laid-back as the big Hollywood studio tours are structured. "Cinecittà Shows Off" traces the studios' history, with technology, props and costumes, and although you'll enjoy it all the more if you have some knowledge of

---

CINECITTÀ NEIGHBOURHOOD

You can explore the **Cinecittà neighbourhood** outside the studios, where, naturally there is a cinema, although it almost always shows films dubbed in Italian. If you're hungry, and are after richer pickings than are available at the studios, then you're in luck, because one of Rome's best restaurants is nearby: *Giuda Ballerino Osteria and Ristorante* at Largo Appio Claudio 344–348, ⓦ giudaballerino.com (see p.257).

9

Italian film, you don't have to be that much of a movie buff to enjoy the Liz and Dick *Cleopatra* garb. Other costume highlights include La Gradisca's red coat worn in Fellini's *Amarcord* and Cameron Diaz's dress from *Gangs of New York*. There are also **guided tours** of the sets, which vary depending on whether any filming is in progress but usually include sets from *Rome* and *Gangs of New York*. When you're done, you can take the weight off at one of two bars in the grounds – one of them an Art Deco place so simple in appearance it appears to be little changed since Cinecittà was built.

EUR

Bus #714 from Termini or metro line B

From Piazza di Porta San Paolo and the Piramide metro station, Via Ostiense leads south to join up with Via Cristoforo Colombo, which in turn runs down to **EUR** (pronounced "eh-oor") – the acronym for the district built for the "Esposizione Universale Roma" in 1942. Laid out to the designs of Marcello Piacentini for Mussolini, it was not finished until well after the war, and is not so much a neighbourhood as a statement in stone, a slightly soulless grid of square buildings, long vistas and wide processional boulevards linked tenuously to the rest of Rome by metro but light years away from the city in feel. The great flaw in EUR is that it's not really built for people: the streets are designed for easy traffic flow and the shops and cafés are easily outnumbered by offices, although the columned buildings provide shade in numerous arcades. Of the main structures, it's the prewar, Fascist-style constructions that are of most interest; the postwar development of the area threw up bland office blocks for the most part. Come here for its numerous museums, or if you have a yen for modern city architecture and planning. **Piazza Marconi** is the nominal centre of EUR, where the wide, classically inspired boulevards intersect to swerve around a friezed obelisk in the centre, and all EUR's museums are within easy reach of here.

Palazzo della Civiltà del Lavoro

A few minutes' walk from Piazza Marconi, in the northwest corner of EUR, the **Palazzo della Civiltà del Lavoro** is a visual highlight – Mussolini-inspired architecture at its most assured, and chauvinistic: the inscription around the top reads "One Nation, of Poets, Artists, Heroes, Saints, Thinkers, Scientists, Navigators and Travellers". With a heroic statue on each corner, it's a successful and imposing structure, and far and away the best piece of architecture in EUR. Some have called it the "square Colosseum", which sums up its mixture of modern and classical styles perfectly. It's been empty for several years now, but the Italian fashion house Fendi recently bought the lease and will move into the building in 2015.

Museo Nazionale delle Arti e delle Tradizioni Popolari

Piazza Marconi 8 • Tues–Sun 9am–8pm • €4 • ☎ 06 592 6148, ⓦ www.popolari.arti.beniculturali.it

The **Museo Nazionale delle Arti e delle Tradizioni Popolari** is a run-through of applied arts, costumes and religious artefacts from the Italian regions. It's hardly essential unless you have a specific interest, but it's exhaustive and gives a great insight into the diverse and intensely regional nature of Italy, not to mention how close the country is to its roots and traditions – an odd juxtaposition in the heart of EUR. Everything is labelled in Italian, so you might want to bring a dictionary.

Museo Nazionale Preistorico ed Etnografico Luigi Pigorini

Piazza Marconi 14 • Mon–Sat 9am–6pm, Sun 9am–1.30pm • €6 • ☎ 06 549 521, ⓦ pigorini.beniculturali.it

Really, the **Museo Nazionale Preistorico ed Etnografico Luigi Pigorini** is Rome's natural history and ethnographic museum rolled into one, and it does a pretty good job, arranged in manageable and easily comprehensible order. Its prehistoric section is mind-numbingly exhaustive, but the ethnographic collection does something to relieve things, with artefacts from South America, the Pacific and Africa.

Museo dell'Alto Medioevo

Viale Lincoln 3 • Tues, Fri & Sat 9am–2pm, Wed, Thurs Sun 9am–1pm • €2 • ☎ 06 5422 8199, Ⓦ archeoroma.beniculturali.it/en
/museums/national-museum-early-middle-ages

Housed in the same building as the Pigorini museum, further down the colonnade, the **Museo dell'Alto Medioevo** concentrates on artefacts from the fifth to the tenth centuries – local finds mainly, including some beautiful jewellery from the seventh century and a delicate fifth-century gold fibula found on the Palatine Hill.

Museo della Civiltà Romana

Piazza Agnelli 10 • Tues–Sat 9am–2pm, Sun 9am–1.30pm • €8.50, or €10.50 including Planetario e Museo Astronomico • ☎ 06 0608,
Ⓦ museocivfltaromana.it

Of all the museums, the most interesting is the **Museo della Civiltà Romana**. It's a very large building, and amid the reconstructed statuary, tablets and inscriptions, the ordinary stuff impresses most – small bronze lamps, medical instruments, carved zodiac

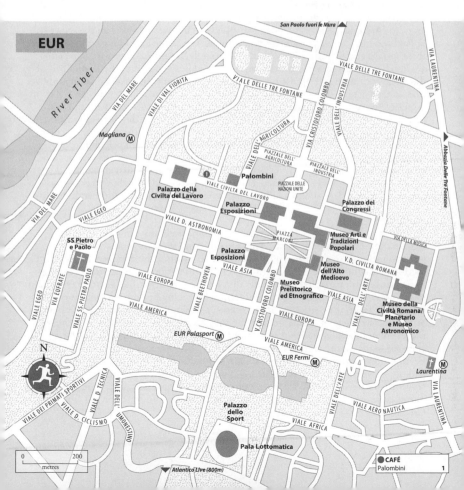

9

charts, musical instruments and the like. Among many reconstructions, the long corridor housing large casts of the reliefs from Trajan's Column is instructive, to say the least. The pièce de résistance is a room-filling model of Rome during the time of Constantine to a 1:250 scale that you can look down on from above – perfect for setting the rest of the city in context.

Planetario e Museo Astronomico

Piazza Agnelli 10 • July & Aug Tues–Fri 8.30–11.30pm, Sat & Sun 4.30–7pm & 8.30–11.30pm; Sept–June Tues–Fri 9am–2pm, Sat & Sun 9am–7pm • €8.50, or €10.50 including the Museo della Civiltà Romana • ☎ 06 0608, ⓦ planetarioroma.it

Part of the same complex as the Museo della Civiltà Romana, the **Planetario e Museo Astronomico** has a small exhibition of astronomy and the planets as well as regular programmes in its domed planetarium. However, they're in Italian only, and frankly not the most spectacular planetarium shows you'll see.

Abbazia delle Tre Fontane

Viale Acqua Salvie 1 • **Grounds** daily 6am–9pm • **Churches** daily 8am–1pm & 3–6pm • ☎ 06 540 1655, ⓦ abbaziatrefontane.it • Bus #761 from the Basilica di San Paolo goes right past, or it's a 10min walk from Laurentina metro station (line B)

The perfect antidote to the brutalist experiment of EUR is just a ten-minute walk away, the **Abbazia delle Tre Fontane**, a complex of churches founded on the spot where St Paul was martyred – it's said that when the saint was beheaded his head bounced and three springs erupted where it touched the ground. In those days this was a malarial area, and it was all but abandoned during the Middle Ages, but in the second half of the nineteenth century Trappist monks drained the swamp and planted eucalyptus trees in the vicinity; they still distil a eucalyptus-based chest remedy here, as well as an exquisite liqueur, chocolate bars, wine, toiletries and all manner of other monastic products – all sold at the small shop and bar by the entrance. The three churches were rebuilt in the sixteenth century and restored by the Trappists. They're not particularly outstanding buildings, appealing more for their peaceful location, which is relatively undisturbed by visitors, than any architectural distinction. Also, on the way out, the gatehouse contains ceiling frescoes from the thirteenth century that show the possessions of the abbey at the time. They're in a pretty bad state, but you can make out a few heads of Christ and a kind of picture map of Italy in the thirteenth century.

The churches

The first and largest of the Tre Fontane **churches**, originally built in 625 and rebuilt and finally restored by the Trappists, is **Santi Vincenzo e Anastasio**, its gloomy atmosphere exacerbated by the fact that most of the windows are of a thick marble that admits little light – although the stained-glass ones, dating from the Renaissance with papal heraldry from that period, are beautiful. The three fountains in the floor, supposedly formed by the saint's bouncing head, have long since run dry. To the right, the church of **Santa Maria Scala Coeli** owes its name to a vision St Bernard had here in which he saw the soul he was praying for ascend to heaven; the Cosmatesque altar where this is supposed to have happened is down the cramped stairs, in the crypt, where St Paul was allegedly kept prior to his beheading. Beyond, the church of the **Martirio di San Paolo** lies at the end of a tree-lined path and holds the pillar to which St Paul was tied in the right transept and a couple of very well-preserved mosaic pavements from Ostia Antica. Try to be here, if you can, in the early morning or evening, when the monks come in to sing Mass in Gregorian chant – a moving experience.

Trastevere and the Janiculum Hill

Sheltered under the Janiculum Hill, Trastevere was the artisan area of the city in classical times, neatly placed for the trade that came upriver from Ostia and was unloaded nearby. Located across the river and outside the city walls (the name means literally "across the Tiber"), its separation lent the neighbourhood a strong identity that lasted well into the twentieth century. Although these influences are long gone, it's still one of the city's nicest neighbourhoods for a stroll, with some very worthwhile sights, notably the Villa Farnesina and the churches of Santa Maria and Santa Cecilia. Its narrow streets and closeted squares are peaceful in the morning, but lively come the evening, as dozens of trattorias set out tables along the cobblestone streets – and they're still buzzing late at night, when its bars and clubs take over.

10

GETTING THERE	TRASTEVERE
By tram/bus The easiest way to reach Trastevere from the Centro Storico and other parts of the city centre is on tram	#8 from Piazza Venezia; from Termini take bus #714.

Piazza Belli and Viale Trastevere

Right by the river, the traffic junction of **Piazza Belli** marks the beginning of **Viale di Trastevere**, which cuts the district in two, between the more discovered and touristy part to the west (covered immediately below) and the quieter and more undisturbed streets to the east (see p.164). The brick building with the crenellations and tower on Piazza Belli is known as the **Casa di Dante**, although it's doubtful that the poet ever stayed here, while the top-hatted **statue** opposite is of the Roman poet Giuseppe Gioacchino Belli – "the poet of the people of Rome", according to the inscription – who in the nineteenth century produced thousands of sonnets recording life in the city in dialect and waged a long campaign against the reactionary Pope Gregory XVI. After the pope's demise, Belli quipped "I really liked Pope Gregory, because it gave me so much pleasure to speak ill of him".

San Crisogono

Piazza Sonnino 44 • Daily 7.30–11.30am & 4–7pm • Crypt €3

Next door to Piazza Belli is Piazza Sonnino, where the church of **San Crisogono** is a large, typically Roman basilica, with a nave lined with ancient columns and one of the city's finest Cosmati floors. The church itself is relatively featureless, apart from a beautiful thirteenth-century apse mosaic showing the church's name saint and St James; it's the remains of the earlier buildings below that mark the church out – two buildings really, an early Christian structure from the third century AD and a later fifth-century basilica whose substantial remnants cover almost the entire footprint of the main church. There are some very worn frescoes – St Chrysogonus himself in the centre of the apse, and a saint healing a sick man (covered in spots) in the north aisle, as well as various bits of Roman stonework, including a couple of impressively carved sarcophagi.

Santa Maria in Trastevere

Piazza di Santa Maria in Trastevere • Daily 7am–9pm • Free

The heart of Trastevere is the nearby Piazza di Santa Maria in Trastevere, which is named after the church of **Santa Maria in Trastevere** in its northwest corner, built on a site where a fountain of oil is said to have sprung on the day of Christ's birth, and held to be the first Christian place of worship in Rome. The greater part of the structure now dates from 1140, after a rebuilding by Innocent II, a pope from Trastevere. These days many people come here for the church's mosaics, which are among the city's most impressive: those on the cornice were completed a century or so after the rebuilding and show the Madonna surrounded by ten female figures with lamps – once thought to represent the Wise and Foolish Virgins. Inside, there's a nineteenth-century copy of a Cosmatesque pavement of spirals and circles, and more twelfth-century mosaics in the apse, Byzantine-inspired works which depict a solemn yet sensitive parade of saints thronged around Christ and Mary, while underneath a series of panels shows scenes from the life of the Virgin by the painter Pietro Cavallini. Beneath the high altar on the right, an inscription – "FONS OLEI" – marks the spot where the oil is supposed to have sprung up, to the right of which there is a chapel crowned with the crest of the British monarchy – placed here by Henry, Cardinal of York, when he and his family, the Stuarts, lived in exile in Rome.

Museo di Roma in Trastevere

Piazza Sant'Egidio 1 • Tues–Sun 10am–8pm • €7.50 • ☎ 06 581 6563, ⓦ museodiromaintrastevere.it

The long triangle of Piazza Sant'Egidio, in the heart of Trastevere, is home to the **Museo di Roma in Trastevere**, a small but well-chosen collection of artefacts illustrating Roman folklore. The displays include paintings of an older, more rural Rome and life-sized tableaux showing scenes of nineteenth-century Roman life – an *osteria*, a pharmacy, a saltarello dance and the like. The museum also has a lively programme of temporary exhibitions with photos and paintings of Rome and its inhabitants to the fore.

10

Piazza Trilussa

Facing the pedestrian Ponte Sisto (see p.53), **Piazza Trilussa** is a busy open space that focuses on the steps up to its grand 1613 fountain, where the waters of the Acqua Paola emerge. On the other side, the upper torso of the poet Trilussa, after whom the square is named, casually leans on a marble plinth as if declaiming his poems – one of which is printed beneath him. Trilussa is actually the pen-name (and an anagram) of Carlo Alberto Salustri, who, like the nineteenth-century Roman poet Belli (see p.158), wrote in dialect – often for humorous effect.

Palazzo Corsini

Galleria Nazionale d'Arte Antica in Palazzo Corsini • Via della Lungara 10 • Tues–Sun 8.30am–7.30pm • €5, €9 including Palazzo Barberini • ☎ 06 6880 2323, ⓦ galleriacorsini.beniculturali.it

On the edge of Trastevere proper, the **Palazzo Corsini** – sister gallery to the Palazzzo Barberini (see p.104) – was built for Cardinal Riario in the fifteenth century, and totally renovated between 1732 and 1736 by Ferdinando Fuga for the cardinal and art collector Neri Maria Corsini. Corsini collected most of the paintings on display here now, a relatively small collection that only takes up a few rooms on the first floor of the giant palace, which dwarfs everything in the immediate vicinity. It was a fitting final home for **Queen Christina of Sweden**, who renounced Protestantism and with it the Swedish throne in 1655, bringing her library and fortune to Rome, to the delight of the Chigi pope, Alexander VII. She lived first in Palazzo Farnese (see p.52) and then here for a number of years, dying in the palace in 1689. She is one of only five women to be buried in St Peter's, notwithstanding her rejection of Catholic convention: she often turned out in men's clothes, removed the strategically placed fig leaves on the statues in her palace and made no attempt to hide her bisexuality, at one stage having affairs with a nun and a cardinal at the same time, and giving the English ambassador at the time a real surprise by introducing her latest female companion as her 'bedfellow'.

The gallery

It's not hard to imagine the queen roaming the lofty rooms and draughty corridors of the palace – such is its haunting grandeur – and her bedchamber features among the rooms open to the public. Among the **art**, Room 1 boasts some fairly harmless landscapes by Dughet and Grimaldi, followed in Room 2 by more heavyweight works like the Neapolitan Salvator Rosa's large and graphic vision of Prometheus having his entrails ripped out. Room 3 – the Cardinal Gallery – has a real mixture: canvases by Lanfranco and Annibale Carracci, Preti's *Martyrdom of St Bartholomew*, Van Dyck's sensitive *Madonna delle Paglia*, a copy of Raphael's famous portrait of Julius II, Titian's portrait of Philip II and – on a more low-key note – a tavern scene by David Teniers.

In the next room the focus is on the curious **Corsini Throne**, thought to be a Roman copy of an Etruscan throne from the second or first century BC. Hewn out of marble, its back is carved with warriors in armour and helmets, below which wild boar the size of horses are pursued by hunters. The base is decorated with scenes of a sacrifice, notably the minotaur devouring a human being – only discernible by the kicking legs

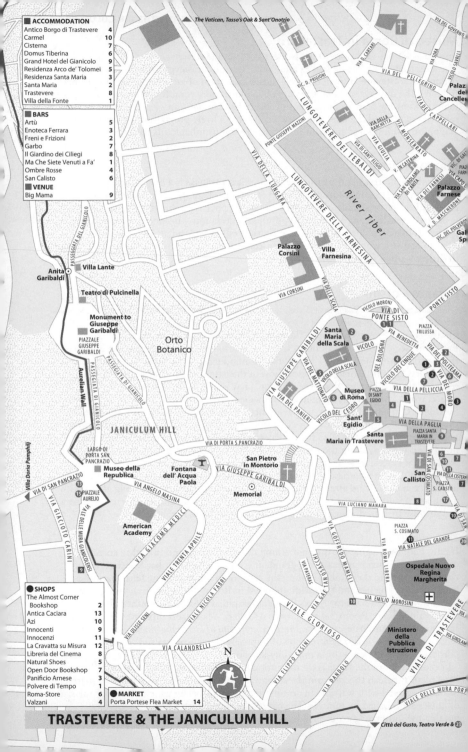

ACCOMMODATION

Antico Borgo di Trastevere	4
Carmel	10
Cisterna	7
Domus Tiberina	6
Grand Hotel del Gianicolo	5
Residenza Arco de' Tolomei	5
Residenza Santa Maria	3
Santa Maria	2
Trastevere	8
Villa della Fonte	1

BARS

Artù	5
Enoteca Ferrara	3
Freni e Frizioni	2
Garbo	7
Il Giardino dei Ciliegi	8
Ma Che Siete Venuti a Fa'	1
Ombre Rosse	4
San Calisto	6

VENUE

Big Mama	9

SHOPS

The Almost Corner Bookshop	2
Antica Caciara	13
Azi	10
Innocenti	9
Innocenzi	11
La Cravatta su Misura	12
Libreria del Cinema	8
Natural Shoes	5
Open Door Bookshop	7
Panificio Arnese	3
Polvere di Tempo	1
Roma-Store	6
Valzani	4

MARKET

Porta Portese Flea Market	14

TRASTEVERE & THE JANICULUM HILL

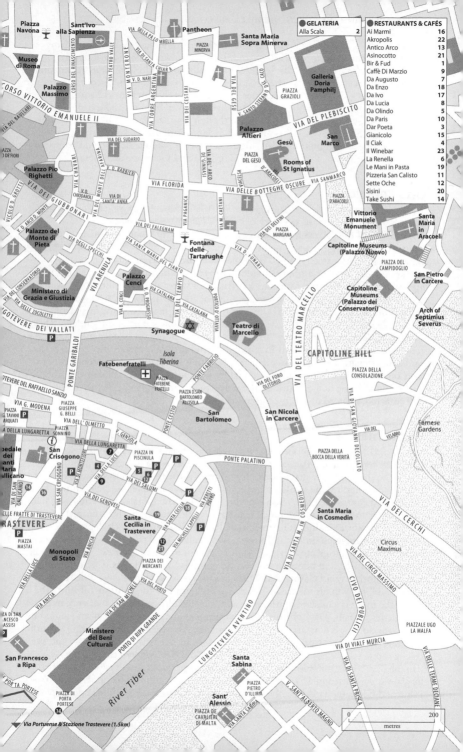

Piazza Navona
Sant'Ivo alla Sapienza
Pantheon
Santa Maria Sopra Minerva
PIAZZA MINERVA

Museo di Roma
PIAZZA GRAZIOLI
Galleria Doria Pamphilj

Palazzo Massimo

CORSO VITTORIO EMANUELE II

VIA DEL PLEBISCITO

Palazzo Altieri
San Marco

Gesù
Rooms of St Ignatius

Palazzo Pio Righetti

PIAZZA DEL GESÙ

VIA DELLE BOTTEGHE OSCURE

PIAZZA D'ARACOELI

Palazzo del Monte di Pieta

VIA FLORIDA

PIAZZA MARGANA

Fontana delle Tartarughe

Vittorio Emanuele Monument

Santa Maria in Aracoeli

Capitoline Museums (Palazzo Nuovo)

Ministero di Grazia e Giustizia

Palazzo Cenci

PIAZZA DEL CAMPIDOGLIO

San Pietro in Carcere

Capitoline Museums (Palazzo dei Conservatori)

Arch of Septimius Severus

LUNGOTEVERE DEI VALLATI

Synagogue

Teatro di Marcello

CAPITOLINE HILL

Fatebenefratelli

Isola Tiberina

PIAZZA DELLA CONSOLAZIONE

PIAZZA FATEBENE FRATELLI

LUNGOTEVERE DEL RAFFAELLO SANZIO

PIAZZA D'SAN BARTOLOMEO ALL'ISOLA

San Bartolomeo

San Nicola in Carcere

Farnese Gardens

VIA G. MODENA

PIAZZA GIUSEPPE G. BELLI

VIA DEL VELABRO

San Crisogono

VIA DELLA LUNGARETTA

PIAZZA IN PISCINULA

PONTE PALATINO

PIAZZA DELLA BOCCA DELLA VERITÀ

VIA DEI CERCHI

TRASTEVERE

PIAZZA MASTAI

Monopoli di Stato

Santa Cecilia in Trastevere

Santa Maria in Cosmedin

Circus Maximus

PIAZZA DEI MERCANTI

VIA DEL CIRCO MASSIMO

Ministero del Beni Culturali

PIAZZALE UGO LA MALFA

PORTO DI RIPA GRANDE

San Francesco a Ripa

Santa Sabina

PIAZZA DI PORTA PORTESE

River Tiber

Sant' Alessio

PIAZZA PIETRO D'ILLIRIA

LUNGOTEVERE AVENTINO

Via Portuense & Stazione Trastevere (1.5km)

PIAZZA DE CAVALIERI DI MALTA

GELATERIA	
Alla Scala	2

RESTAURANTS & CAFÉS	
Ai Marmi	16
Akropolis	22
Antico Arco	13
Asinocotto	21
Bir & Fud	1
Caffè Di Marzio	9
Da Augusto	7
Da Enzo	18
Da Ivo	17
Da Lucia	8
Da Olindo	5
Da Paris	10
Dar Poeta	3
Gianicolo	15
Il Ciak	4
Il Winebar	23
La Renella	6
Le Mani in Pasta	19
Pizzeria San Calisto	11
Sette Oche	12
Sisini	20
Take Sushi	14

0   200
metres

10

that protrude from the feasting beast. The throne is overlooked by two penetrating paintings by Rubens – *Testa del'Uomo* and *Testa del Vecchio* – alongside a famous portrayal of *Salome with the Head of John the Baptist* by Guido Reni. **Queen Christina's bedchamber**, next door, where she died in 1689, is decorated with frescoes by an unknown artist – cupids and grotesques with scenes of the miracles of Moses – and on the wall is a portrait of the queen as Diana by Justus van Egmont and a depiction of the Pantheon by Charles-Louis Clérisseau, though it's a rather fanciful interpretation, squeezing the Pyramid of Cestius and Arch of Janus into the background. Two rooms further on are Caravaggio's youthful, highly stylized *St John the Baptist*, and paintings by more Neapolitans – in this case Luca Giordano and Giuseppe de Ribera.

Orto Botanico

Largo Cristina di Svezia 24 • Entry at the top of Via Corsini; no entry from the Palazzo Corsini • April to mid–Oct daily 9am–6.30pm; mid–Oct to March daily 9am–5.30pm • €8 • ☎ 06 4991 7108, ⓦ ortobotanicoitalia.it/lazio/romalasapienzam

The grounds of the Palazzo Corsini are the site of the **Orto Botanico**, which, after Padua's botanical garden, is the most important in Italy – and a good example of eighteenth-century garden design. It's a pleasantly neglected expanse these days, a low-key bucolic retreat clasping the side of the Janiculum Hill. You can clamber up to high stands of bamboo and ferns cut by rivulets of water and stroll through a wood of century-old oaks, cedars and conifers. A grove of acclimatized palm trees stands in front of the so-called Fountain of the Tritons, a rather grand name for the relatively small-scale fountain that forms the centrepiece of the lower part of the gardens. There's a herbal garden with medicinal plants, greenhouses holding succulents and cacti and a collection of orchids that bloom in springtime and early summer. A nice touch is the garden of aromatic herbs put together for the blind; the plants can be identified by their smell or touch, and are accompanied by signs in Braille. The garden also has the distinction of being home to one of the oldest plane trees in Rome, between 350 and 400 years old, situated by the monumental staircase.

Villa Farnesina

Via della Lungara 230 • Mon–Sat 9am–2pm & second Sun of the month 9am–5pm • €6 • ☎ 06 6802 7268, ⓦ villafarnesina.it

Across the road from the Palazzo Corsini, the **Villa Farnesina** is perhaps more interesting than its larger neighbour. Built during the early sixteenth century by Baldassare Peruzzi for the banker Agostino Chigi, it is a unique building, known for its frescoes and contributed to by some of the masters of the Renaissance. Chigi situated his villa here to be close to the papal court and away from his business cronies.

Beyond the entrance, in the first room, is Raphael's **Galatea**, which depicts the eponymous sea nymph on her dolphin-drawn, scallop-shell chariot. Kenneth Clark called the fresco "the greatest evocation of paganism of the Renaissance" and it seems that Raphael fitted it in between his Vatican commissions for Julius II, but the painter and art historian Vasari claims that Michelangelo, passing by one day while Raphael was canoodling with his mistress, "La Fornarina", finished the painting for him. The rest of the room is a mixed bag thematically with bucolic country scenes and, in one of the lunettes, a giant, monochrome head, which was once said to have been painted by Michelangelo, but is now attributed to the architect of the building, Peruzzi. The other lunettes feature scenes from Ovid's *Metamorphoses* by Sebastiano del Piombo and the ceiling shows Chigi's horoscope constellations, again frescoed by Peruzzi.

In the next room, the Raphael-designed painting of **Cupid and Psyche** in a glassed-in loggia was completed in 1517 by the artist's assistants, Giulio Romano, Francesco Penni and Giovanni da Udine. Here again, Vasari claims Raphael didn't complete the

work because of his infatuation with his mistress, whose father's bakery was situated nearby, but more likely he was simply so overloaded with commissions that he couldn't possibly finish them all. Whoever was responsible, it's mightily impressive, a flowing, animated work bursting with muscular men and bare-bosomed women. Actually it would have made even more of an impact if completed as planned because the blue would have been much brighter – what you see is just the preparatory colour.

Upstairs, the **Sala delle Prospettive** features trompe-l'oeil balconies giving views onto contemporary Rome – one of the earliest examples of the technique. This room leads through to Chigi's **bedroom**, decorated with Sodoma's extremely bold and colourful scenes from the life of Alexander the Great and his wife Roxane.

10

Santa Cecilia in Trastevere

Piazza di Santa Cecilia, off Piazza dei Mercanti • Church & crypt daily 9.30am–12.30pm & 4–6pm; singing gallery daily 10am–12.30pm • Church free; crypt €3; singing gallery €3 • ☎ 06 4549 2739, ⓦ benedettinesantacecilia.it

In the midst of the quieter, eastern half of Trastevere, the church of **Santa Cecilia in Trastevere** is a cream–painted, rather sterile church – apart from a pretty front courtyard – whose antiseptic eighteenth-century appearance belies its historical associations. A church was originally built here over the site of the second-century home of **St Cecilia**, whose husband Valerian was executed for refusing to worship Roman gods and who herself was subsequently persecuted for her Christian beliefs. The story has it that Cecilia was locked in the caldarium (hot room) of her own baths for several days but refused to die, singing her way through the ordeal (Cecilia is the patron saint of music). Her head was finally half hacked off with an axe, though it took several blows before she finally expired.

Below the high altar, under a Gothic baldacchino, Stefano Maderno's limp, almost modern **statue** of the saint shows her incorruptible body as it was found when exhumed in 1599, with three deep cuts in her neck – a fragile, intensely human piece of work that has helped make Cecilia one of the most revered Roman saints. Behind all this presides an apse **mosaic** from the ninth century showing Paschal I, who founded the current church, being presented to Christ by St Cecilia flanked by various saints. The excavations of the baths and the rest of the Roman house are on view in the **crypt** below – a series of dank rooms with some fragments of mosaic and a gaudily decorated chapel at the far end – but more alluring by far is the **singing gallery** above the nave of the church, where Pietro Cavallini's late-thirteenth-century **fresco of the Last Judgement** is all that remains of the decoration that once covered the entire church. It's a powerful painting, an amazingly fluid, naturalistic piece of work for the time, with each of the Apostles, ranked six each side of Christ, captured as an individual portrait, while Christ sits in quiet, meditative majesty in the centre, flanked by angels.

San Francesco a Ripa

Piazza di San Francesco d'Assisi • Daily 8am–1pm & 2–7pm • Free • ☎ 06 581 9020, ⓦ sanfrancescoaripa.com

Not far from Santa Cecilia, the church of **San Francesco a Ripa** is best known for its association with St Francis, who once stayed here. You can see the actual room he slept in, which is now a shrine displaying the rock he used as a pillow, on a free guided tour – just ring the bell for the attendant; the shrine is beyond the sacristy and up some steep stairs. The church is also the burial place of the twentieth-century Italian artist Giorgio de Chirico (see p.96), who lived in Rome until his death in the 1970s and is buried behind the first chapel on the left, in a simple white room named after the painter. But perhaps the most visually memorable item in the church is the writhing, orgasmic statue of a minor saint, the *Blessed Ludovica Albertoni*, that Bernini sculpted towards the end of his career; it's located in the top chapel on the left. As a work of Baroque sauciness, it bears comparison with his more famous *Ecstasy of St Teresa* in the church of Santa Maria in Vittoria; indeed it's perhaps even more shameless in its depiction of an earthly realized divine ecstasy – the woman is actually kneading her breasts.

Porta Portese

Via Portuense • Sun 7am–1pm

Trastevere at its traditional if somewhat disreputable best can be witnessed on Sunday mornings, when the **Porta Portese flea market** stretches from the Piazza di Porta Portese down Via Portuense to Trastevere train station in a congested medley of antiques, old motor spares, cheap clothing, trendy clothing, household goods, bric-a-brac and assorted junk. Haggling is the rule, and keep a good hold of your wallet or purse. The market starts around 7am, and you should come early if you want to buy or even move around – most of the bargains, not to mention the "back of the lorry" goods, have gone by 10am, by which time the crush of people can be intense. It's pretty much all over by lunchtime.

Janiculum Hill

The **Janiculum Hill** may not be one of the original seven hills of Rome, but it is the one with the best and most accessible views of the city centre. It also has several **monuments** honouring those Italians who fought with Garibaldi here in 1849: the enemy were the French, who were attempting to put Pius IX back in control of the papal states after he had been ignominiously driven out by his rebellious subjects. It takes about fifteen minutes to walk to the top of the hill from Trastevere, and there are several possible routes, but perhaps the most enjoyable is to follow Vicolo del Cedro and then take the steps up to Via Garibaldi at a point near San Pietro in Montorio. Alternatively, you can avoid the steps by sticking to Via Garibaldi, which also begins in the Trastevere. Failing that, bus #115 crosses the hill from Viale Trastevere to the Gianicolo terminal on the Vatican side.

San Pietro in Montorio

Piazza di San Pietro in Montorio 2 • **Church** Mon–Fri 8.30am–noon & 3–4pm, Sat & Sun 8.30am–noon • **Tempietto** Tues–Sat 9.30am–12.30pm & 2–4.30pm • Free • ☎ 06 581 3940, ⊕ sanpietroinmontorio.it

Now part of a complex that includes the Spanish Academy and Spanish ambassador's residence, the church of **San Pietro in Montorio** was built on a site once believed to have been the place of the saint's crucifixion. The compact interior is particularly intimate – it's a favourite for weddings – and features some first-rate paintings, among them, on the right-hand side at the start of the nave, Sebastiano del Piombo's vivid and muscular *Flagellation*. Also, don't miss Bramante's little **Tempietto** in the courtyard to the right of the church's front door; it's one of the seminal works of the Renaissance, built on what was supposed to have been the precise spot of St Peter's martyrdom. The small circular building is like a classical temple in miniature, perfectly proportioned and neatly executed.

Fontana dell'Acqua Paola

Just above the church of San Pietro di Montorio, the **Fontana dell'Acqua Paola**, constructed for Paul V in 1612 with marble from the Roman Forum, gushes water at a bend in the road. It's a recently restored and very grandiose affair whose ancient water supply is provided by Lake Bracciano, way to the north of Rome, and in turn goes on to feed the fountain down below on Piazza Trilussa.

Passeggiata del Gianicolo

Just beyond the Fontana dell'Acqua Paola, turn right down leafy **Passeggiata del Gianicolo**, which threads its way along the ridge at the top of the Janiculum Hill to

10

Piazzale Giuseppe Garibaldi, where there's an equestrian monument to Garibaldi – an ostentatious work from 1895. There are panoramic views of the city from the terrace in front of the statue and just below is the spot from which a cannon is fired at noon each day for Romans to check their watches, leaving a whiff of powder in the air and setting all the car alarms off. Just beyond the *piazzale* is a **statue of Anita Garibaldi**, a fiery, melodramatic work (she cradles a baby in one arm, brandishes a pistol with the other and is galloping full speed on a horse) that recalls the important part she played in the 1849 battle and also marks her grave – she died later in the campaign. Immediately opposite this statue, the Renaissance **Villa Lante** is a jewel of a place that is now the home of the Finnish Academy in Rome and gives a panoramic view of the city, although you can only visit on official business or for an exhibition or performance. From here it takes about twenty minutes to walk down to the Vatican (see Chapter 12). Follow some steps off to the right and, next to a small amphitheatre, you'll find **Tasso's Oak**, the gnarled old oak tree where the sixteenth-century Italian poet Torquato Tasso, friend of Mannerist sculptor Benvenuto Cellini and author of *La Gerusalemme Deliverata* (*Jerusalem Delivered*), is said to have whiled away his last days.

Sant'Onofrio

Piazza Sant' Onofrio 2 • Daily 7.30am–1pm • ☎ 06 686 4498

At the bottom of the hill, next to the Jesuit children's hospital, the church of **Sant'Onofrio** sits on the road's bend, with an L-shaped portico and one of the city's most delightful small cloisters to the right. Tasso moved into the church in the last weeks of his life and died while living here; if you're lucky and it's open you can visit the poet's cell, which holds some manuscripts, his chair, his death mask and personal effects.

Museo della Republica Romana e della Memoria Garibaldina

Largo di Porta San Pancrazio • Tues–Fri 10am–2pm, Sat & Sun 10am–6pm • €6.50 • ☎ 06 0608, ⓦ museodellarepubblicaromana.it

An arm of the Passeggiata del Gianicolo leads back from the Piazzale Garibaldi to the **Porta San Pancrazio**, a city gate built during the reign of Urban VIII, destroyed by the French in 1849, and rebuilt by Pope Pius IX five years later. It has recently been restored yet again and now houses the modest **Museo della Republica Romana e della Memoria Garibaldina**, which has a series of exhibitions on Garibaldi's efforts to hold the French army at bay here on the Janiculum in 1849. To either side of the Porta are the heavily restored, brown–brick remains of the city walls begun by Aurelian in the third century AD. On the west side of the Porta is **Piazzale Aurelio**, the start of the old Roman Via Aurelia, and close by are the numerous buildings of the American Academy in Rome. By the time you get up here you might also be ready for a drink, in which case the American Academy's local bar, *Gianicolo* (see p.259), right on the square, is the perfect spot for a drink and a bite to eat.

Villa Doria Pamphilj

Via Aurelia Antica • Daily dawn–dusk • Free • ☎ 06 0608, ⓦ villapamphili.it

Just beyond the Porta, down Via di San Pancrazio, is the rather grand entrance to the grounds of the **Villa Doria Pamphilj**, the largest and most recent of Rome's parks, laid out in the mid-seventeenth century for Prince Camillo Pamphilj and acquired for the city in the 1970s. The stately white Baroque villa is not open to the public, but the sprawling greenery that surrounds it is an enchanting mix of formal parterres and shady lawns and glades, dotted with fountains and statues, and wilder, more bucolic tracts. From the main gate, a path leads downhill and round to the right for around 250m, emerging at the villa. From here, follow the path southwest past the house for around 500m to reach the tree-fringed lake, fed at its northern end by a once-grand cascade of tiny waterfalls and grottoes, and inhabited by scores of turtles that bask photogenically on its banks. It all makes for a delightful wander (beware, signposting is minimal), though it's best to bring a picnic as there's no café.

MAXXI

Villa Borghese and north

Some of the area immediately north of Rome's city centre is taken up by its most central park, the Villa Borghese, which serves as valuable outdoor space for both Romans and tourists, as well as hosting some of the city's best museums. The neighbourhoods beyond, Flaminio and the other residential districts of north central Rome, were until recently not of much interest in themselves, except perhaps for the Foro Italico across the river – worth visiting to watch football and see Mussolini's sports centre. But the Auditorium complex and brand-new MAXXI have inspired fresh interest in the area. To the east, beyond the upscale Parioli neighbourhood and vast Villa Ada park, Via Nomentana and the neighbourhoods either side are worth the journey for the Villa Torlonia park and two of Rome's most ancient and sensual churches.

Villa Borghese

The area outside the Aurelian walls, to the north and northeast of the city, was once a district of market gardens, olive groves and patrician villas, trailing off into open country. During the Renaissance, these vast tracts of land were appropriated as summer estates by the city's wealthy, particularly those affiliated in some way to the papal court. One of the most notable estates, the **Villa Borghese**, was the summer playground of the Borghese family and is now a public park, home to the city's most significant concentration of museums, including the Galleria Borghese, which houses the resplendent art collection of the aristocratic family – a Roman must-see in anyone's book – and the Villa Giulia, built by Pope Julius III for his summer repose and now the National Etruscan Museum. The park was bought by the city at the beginning of the twentieth century and is a huge area, and its woods, lake and grass, crisscrossed by roads, are as near as you can get to peace in the city centre. There are any number of attractions for those who want to do more than just stroll or sunbathe: a boating lake (€3 per person for 20min), a zoo – renamed the "Bioparco" in an attempt to rebrand a previously poor image (see p.303) – a cinema for children and some of the city's finest museums.

11

ARRIVAL AND DEPARTURE
VILLA BORGHESE

By tram Tram #3 runs right around the city centre to the Galleria Nazionale d'Arte Moderna on the northern side of the park, passing the Bioparco and zoological museum on the way.
By bus Bus #217 runs from Termini to the top end of Via

Pinciana, close to the Galleria Borghese; bus #63 runs from close by Piazza Venezia to the same place.
On foot Alternatively, you can just stroll up from the Spanish Steps to the Pincio Gardens where you can pick up your own transport for getting around the park.

GETTING AROUND

Vehicle rentals You can rent bikes, go-karts, rollerblades, golf buggies, segways or a *risciò* (a sort of pedal-driven chariot with a small electric motor) from various places in the park, and all make getting around much easier. Most options are available from two places in the Pincio Gardens (one on the corner of Viale di Villa Medici and Viale Orologio, and a second by the water clock); outside the Casa del Cinema; and outside the zoo. Segways are available from a

booth on the Piazza del Popolo side of the Pincio Gardens, golf buggies a short walk away at Piazzale delle Canestre.
Vehicle prices Bikes cost from €4/hr, €9/3hr, €12/day; mountain bikes from €5/hr, €12/3hr, €15/day; tandems from €8/hr, €20/3hr, €25/day; go-karts from €5/hr; rollerblades from €5/hr; 2-person *risciò* from €12/hr, 4-person from €20/hr; segways from €10/30min, €15/hr, €60/day; golf buggies from €10/30mins; €15/hr.

Pincio Gardens

On the edge of the Villa Borghese, overlooking Piazza del Popolo, the **Pincio Gardens** were laid out by Valadier in the early nineteenth century. Fringed with dilapidated busts of classical and Italian heroes, they give fine views over the roofs, domes and TV antennae of central Rome, right across to St Peter's and the Janiculum Hill. The benches are pleasantly shaded and a good place to take some weight off your feet. The nineteenth-century water clock at the back is a quirky attraction, and there's a carousel, a decent café-restaurant (see p.254), and a couple of places to hire bikes (see above).

Galleria Borghese

Piazzale del Museo Borghese · Tues–Sun 8.30am–7.30pm · €11 · Pre-booked visits obligatory at ☎ 06 32810 or online at ⓦ galleriaborghese.it or ⓦ tosc.it

The Casino Borghese, on the far eastern side of the park, is the first place you should make for. Built in the early seventeenth century, it was turned over to the state when the gardens became city property in 1902 as the **Galleria Borghese**. Indeed, reopened several years ago after a lengthy restoration, the Galleria Borghese has taken its place as one of Rome's great treasure houses and should not be missed.

Some history

When Camillo Borghese was elected pope and took the papal name Paul V in 1605, he elevated his favourite nephew, **Scipione Caffarelli Borghese**, to the cardinalate and put him in charge of diplomatic, ceremonial and cultural matters at the papal court. Scipione possessed an infallible instinct for recognizing artistic quality, and, driven by ruthless passion, used fair means or foul to acquire prized works of art. He was also shrewd enough to patronize outstanding talents such as Gian Lorenzo Bernini, Caravaggio, Domenichino, Guido Reni and Peter Paul Rubens. To house the works of these artists, as well as his collection of antique sculpture and other pieces, he built the Casino, or summerhouse, predictably sparing no expense. The palace, which was built in the early 1600s, is a celebration of the ancient splendour of the Roman Empire: over the years its art collection has been added to, and its rooms redecorated – most notably during the last quarter of the eighteenth century, when the ceilings were redone to match the artworks in each room. The recent **restoration** of the sumptuous interior seemed to go on forever, but now the gallery's Roman-era mosaics, rich stucco decorations and trompe-l'oeil ceilings provide the perfect surroundings in which to enjoy the artworks that Cardinal Scipione Borghese collected so voraciously.

The porch and entrance hall

Entrance is through a porch, which displays classical sculpture, notably several large statues of Dacian prisoners from the time of the Emperor Trajan. Inside, the entrance hall has a splendid **ceiling** by Marino Rossi, painted in 1775–78, depicting the foundation and early history of Rome – Jupiter is in the centre, surrounded by various moral and spiritual attributes and historical and mythological characters such as Romulus, Remus and the she-wolf. On the floor, a series of Roman mosaics from about 320 AD depict gladiators fighting and killing various animals and each other – a circle with a line drawn through it next to the name indicates the deceased, and blood gushes gruesomely from the pierced throats and hearts of the animals. Among a number of notable statues, there's a *Bacchus* from the second century AD, a *Fighting Satyr* and, on the wall facing the entrance door, a melodramatic piece in marble of Marcus Curtius flinging himself into the chasm (see p.82) – his horse is a Roman sculpture and the figure is by Bernini's father. There are also colossal heads of the emperors Hadrian and Antoninus Pius on the right, and a female head of the Antonine period, with a lotus flower to represent Isis, on the left.

The ground floor

The ground floor beyond the entrance hall contains sculpture, a mixture of ancient Roman items and seventeenth-century works, roughly linked together with late-eighteenth-century ceiling paintings showing scenes from the Trojan War. The first room off the entrance hall, whose paintings depict the Judgement of Paris, has as its centrepiece Canova's famous **statue of Pauline Borghese** posed as Venus (see box, p.172), with flimsy drapery that leaves little to the imagination.

Room of the Sun

The second ground-floor room, the **Room of the Sun**, has a marvellous statue of *David* by Bernini, finished in 1624, when the sculptor was just 25. The face is a self-portrait, said to have been carved with the help of a mirror held for him by Scipione Borghese himself, and its expression of grim determination is perfect. There's more work by Bernini in the next room, where his statue of *Apollo and Daphne* is a dramatic, poised work that captures the split second when Daphne is transformed into a laurel tree, with her fingers becoming leaves and her legs tree trunks. Mocked by Apollo, Cupid had taken revenge by firing a golden arrow which infected the god with immediate and ardent love, and shooting Daphne with a leaden one designed to hasten the rejection of amorous advances. Daphne, the daughter of a river god, called on her father to help

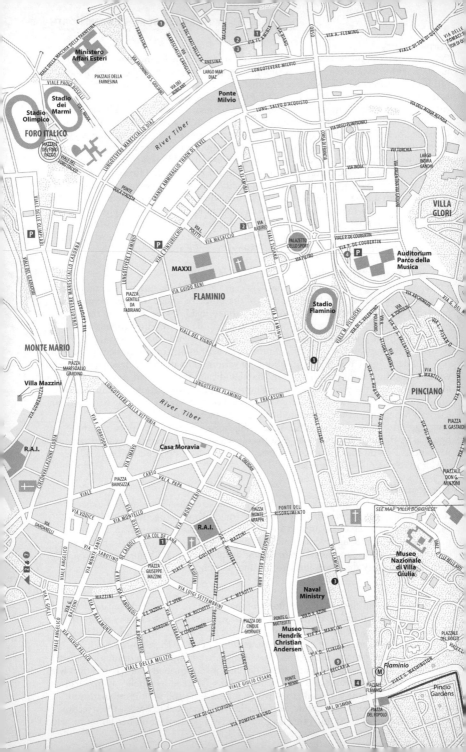

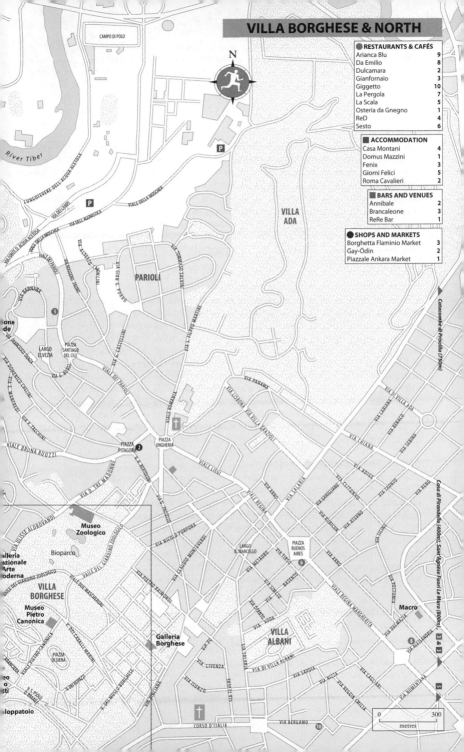

VILLA BORGHESE & NORTH

● RESTAURANTS & CAFÉS
Arianca Blu	9
Da Emilio	8
Dulcamara	2
Gianfornaio	3
Giggetto	10
La Pergola	7
La Scala	5
Osteria da Gnegno	1
ReD	4
Sesto	6

■ ACCOMMODATION
Casa Montani	4
Domus Mazzini	1
Fenix	3
Giorni Felici	5
Roma Cavalieri	2

■ BARS AND VENUES
Annibale	2
Brancaleone	3
ReRe Bar	1

● SHOPS AND MARKETS
Borghetta Flaminio Market	3
Gay-Odin	2
Piazzale Ankara Market	1

her avoid being trapped by Apollo, who was in hot pursuit; her father changed her into a laurel tree just as Apollo took her into his arms – a desperately sad piece of drama to which Bernini's statue does full justice. This statue also caused a great scandal when it was unveiled. The poet and playwright, Maffeo Barberini, who later became Pope Urban VIII, wrote a couplet in Latin, which is inscribed on the base, claiming that all who pursue fleshly lusts are doomed to end up holding only ashes and dust.

Room of the Emperors

Next door, the walls of the large **Room of the Emperors** are flanked by red porphyry seventeenth- and eighteenth-century busts of Roman emperors, facing another Bernini sculpture, the *Rape of Proserpine*, dating from 1622, a coolly virtuosic work that shows the story of the carrying off to the underworld of the beautiful goddess Proserpine, daughter of Ceres, goddess of the fertility of the earth. The brutal Pluto grasps the girl in his arms, his fingers digging into the flesh of her thigh as she fights off his advances, while the three-headed form of Cerberus snaps at their feet.

In the small room next door, there's a marvellous **statue of a sleeping hermaphrodite**, from the first century AD, and a large porphyry Roman bathtub whose feline feet are almost modern in style.

Aeneas Room

it's back to the Berninis in the following **Aeneas Room**, where a larger-than-life statue of Aeneas carrying his father, Anchises, out of the burning city of Troy, was sculpted by both father Pietro and his then 15-year-old son Gian Lorenzo in 1613. The statue portrays a crucial event in Roman myth when, after the defeat of the Trojans, Aeneas escaped with his family and embarked on the long voyage that ended up on the shores of what became Latium, his descendants eventually founding the city of Rome. The old man carries the statues representing their family household gods; the small boy carrying a flaming pot with what became the Vestal Fire is Aeneas's son Ascanius. Also here, in the far corner, is a late, in fact unfinished, work by Bernini, *Truth Revealed in Time*, done near the end of his career when he had been accused of faulty architectural work in part of St Peter's. Truth, with a sappy look on her face, clutches the sun, representing time, to her breast.

Egyptian Room and the Room of Silenus

The **Egyptian Room**, beyond, contains artefacts, friezes and paintings with an Egyptian theme, Roman floor mosaics and a statue of a satyr on a dolphin dating from the first century AD. Further on, the **Room of Silenus** contains a variety of paintings by Cardinal Scipione Borghese's protégé Caravaggio, including the *Madonna of the Grooms* from 1605 on the right wall, a painting that at the time was considered to have depicted Christ far too realistically to hang in a central Rome church; the cardinal happily bought it for his collection. Take note also of Caravaggio's self-portrait as Bacchus as you enter, gazing lasciviously at the coy boy with the basket of fruit opposite. St Jerome on the far wall is captured writing at a

PAULINE BORGHESE

Pauline Borghese, the sister of Napoleon and married (reluctantly) to the reigning Prince Borghese, was a shocking woman in her day, with grand habits. There are tales of jewels and clothes, of the Negro who used to carry her from her bath, of the servants she used as footstools and, of course, of her long line of lovers. The statue of her in the Villa Borghese was considered outrageous by everyone but herself: when asked how she could have posed almost naked, she simply replied, "Oh, there was a stove in the studio." The couch on which she reposes originally had a kind of clockwork mechanism inside, which allowed the statue to rotate while the viewer remained stationary.

table illuminated only by a source of light that streams in from the upper left of the picture. Previously thought to have been painted at the end of his life, *David Holding the Head of Goliath* on the right wall was in fact sent by Caravaggio to Scipione Borghese from exile in the hills south of Rome, where he had fled in 1606 to escape capital punishment for killing a man in a duel. The head of Goliath, portrayed in the last agonies of death, is believed to be a self-portrait, and the painting was designed to curry favour with the all-powerful cardinal and gain Caravaggio a pardon. The cardinal managed to get him off, but the artist died of malaria after landing in Italy at Porto Ercole, north of Rome, in 1610.

The first floor

Upstairs – reachable by a spiral staircase out of the **Room of the Emperors** – houses one of the richest small collections of paintings in the world. Turn left for a room with several important works by Raphael, his teacher Perugino and other masters of the Umbrian School from the late fifteenth and early sixteenth centuries, not least Raphael's *Deposition* over the fireplace, produced in 1507 for a noble of Perugia in memory of her son, and pillaged from Perugia cathedral by associates of Cardinal Scipione. Look also for the *Lady with a Unicorn* and *Portrait of a Man*, by Perugino, and, over the door, a copy of the artist's portrait of a tired-out Julius II, painted in the last year of the pope's life, 1513. The room also contains a beautiful, sensitive *Virgin with Child* by Giuliano Romano, while, nearby, Andrea del Sarto tackles the same subject with slightly more gusto. The next room contains more early-sixteenth-century

11

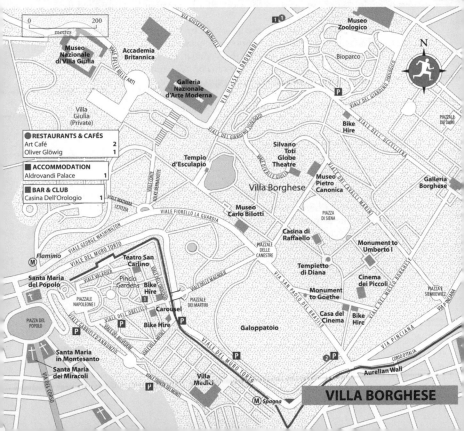

paintings, prominent among which are Cranach's *Venus and Cupid with a Honeycomb*, from 1531, and Brescianino's *Venus and Two Cupids*, from about 1520 – both remarkable at the time for their departure from classical models in their treatment of their subjects. The Cranach Venus, dressed in a diaphanous robe, shows Cupid and his honeycomb, demonstrating the dangers of carnal love. Opposite, they are complemented perfectly by Correggio's saucy *Danae*.

Retracing your steps, look out for two early-sixteenth-century copies of Leonardo's *Leda and the Swan* (the original has been lost), Lorenzo Lotto's touching *Portrait of a Man*, a soulful study that hints at grief over a wife lost in childbirth, symbolized by the tiny skull and rose petals under the subject's right hand, and, in the large **Gallery of Lanfranco** at the back of the building, a series of self-portraits done by Bernini at various stages of his long life. Next to these are a lifelike bust of Cardinal Scipione executed by Bernini in 1632, accurately portraying him as a worldly connoisseur of fine art and fine living, and a smaller bust of Pope Paul V, also by Bernini. Next door's *Young Man and Faun* is the sculptor's earliest-known work, from 1615.

Beyond here a small room has Dosso Dossi's *SS Cosma e Damiano* and Jacopo Bassano's lively and naturalistic *Last Supper*, while further on there are two paintings by Domenichino: the *Cumaean Sibyl* and a large *Diana*, the latter showing the goddess and her attendants celebrating and doing a bit of target practice – one of them has just shot a pheasant through the head and everybody else is jumping with enthusiasm; in the foreground a young nymph, lasciviously bathing, looks out with a lustful expression. Scipione was so keen on the work that he apparently imprisoned the artist until he agreed to sell it.

Next, the **Room of Psyche** has, along with works by Bellini and the other Venetians of the early 1500s, Titian's *Sacred and Profane Love*, painted in 1514 when he was about 25 years old, to celebrate the marriage of the Venetian noble Nicolò Aurelio (whose coat of arms is on the sarcophagus). It shows his bride, Laura Bagarotto, dressed in white representing Sacred Love, and Venus, representing Profane Love, carrying a lamp symbolizing the eternal Love of God. The bride cradles a bowl of jewels that refer to the fleeting happiness of life on earth.

Museo Carlo Bilotti

Viale Fiorello la Guardia • June–Sept Tues–Fri 1–7pm, Sat & Sun 10am–7pm; Oct–May Tues–Fri 10am–4pm, Sat & Sun 10am–7pm • €8 • ☎ 06 0608, ⓦ www.museocarlobilotti.it

Housed in the orangery of the Villa Borghese, the **Museo Carlo Bilotti** is, like the Galleria Borghese, made up of a family bequest, this time of Carlo Bilotti – a perfume and cosmetics baron who, until his death in 2006, collected art and hobnobbed with the brightest and best in the international art world. Portraits of him by Larry Rivers, and of his wife and daughter by Andy Warhol, open the exhibition and add to the slightly self-congratulatory air of the place. However, the paintings are beautifully displayed, and act as a nice adjunct to the Modern Art Museum ten minutes' walk away.

Most of the 22 works exhibited here are by the great modern Italian painter **Giorgio de Chirico**. It's a small but varied collection, and you get a good sense of de Chirico's versatility, from the Impressionistic *Nude Woman from Behind* to his almost perversely traditional *Self-Portrait with the Head of Minerva* and the pastiche Canaletto scene that hangs next to it. The weird stuff with which he made his name is here too, including *Metaphysics with Biscuits* and *Melancholy of a Street*, and plays on the *Archeologists* theme you might have seen in the Modern Art Museum, although these are 1960s copies of canvases he produced during his earlier "metaphysical" period. If you're a fan, head to the Casa de Chirico (see p.96), a kilometre or so southwest of here near the Spanish Steps.

Museo Pietro Canonica

Viale Pietro Canonica 2 · June–Sept Tues–Sun 1–7pm, Oct–May Tues–Sun 10am–4pm · €5 · ☎ 06 0608, ⓦ museocanonica.it

Across the road from the large oval of the Piazza di Siena, the **Museo Pietro Canonica** occupies the house and studio of the nineteenth-century Italian sculptor. Canonica was an establishment artist and as such not only did the city bequeath him this impressive, castellated bolt-hole to live in, but the museum devoted to him is virtually a roll-call of European historical names. Canonica seemingly knew everyone and sculpted everybody, and one room alone contains busts of a king of England (Edward VII), the man who took Turkey to independence (Mustafa Kemal Atatürk), numerous Italian royals and nineteenth-century dignitaries, and Pope Benedict XV (a supplement to the artist's memorial to him in St Peter's). Other rooms document nineteenth-century world history – Simón Bolívar astride a stallion (1954), Atatürk again, this time leading the Turkish charge, and an equestrian statue of King Faisal of Iraq (1933) – to name only the most prominent examples of an epic collection.

The museum also includes **Canonica's studio** on the ground floor, still with his tools and the piece he was working on when he died in 1959, along with a couple of portraits of the great man and some of his own botched attempts at landscapes – which show that he was probably right to stick to sculpture. Upstairs are the **apartments** Canonica occupied with his wife, who continued to live here until she died in 1987. The rooms are left much as they were then, with original furniture, the living room with a piano and a musical score on it (Canonica was also an accomplished musician and composer) and family photographs. Oddly, there is only one that shows Canonica himself, a holiday snap taken in the mountains, on the right side of the dining room.

11

Silvano Toti Globe Theatre

Largo Aqua Felix · ☎ 06 0608, ⓦ globetheatreroma.com

Next door to the Pietro Canonica museum, Rome's very own **Globe Theatre** is a strange sight, a typically flamboyant cultural initiative of former Rome mayor Walter Veltroni, built in just four months in 2003. Like its more famous counterpart in London, it's a copy of the sixteenth-century London original and is built entirely of wood (though the roof is not thatched) with a capacity of around 1250, a third of which is standing, facing a rectangular, canopied stage. It stages performances of Shakespeare's plays – in Italian – throughout the summer every evening about 9pm.

Galleria Nazionale d'Arte Moderna

Viale delle Belli Arti 131 · Tues–Sun 8.30am–7.30pm · €8 · ☎ 06 3229 8221, ⓦ gnam.arti.beniculturali.it

Two of the Villa Borghese's most important museums are situated on the northwestern side of the park, along the Viale delle Belle Arti, in the so-called "Academy Ghetto" – the Romanian, British, Dutch, Danish, Egyptian and other cultural academies are all situated here. The **Galleria Nazionale d'Arte Moderna** is probably the least obviously appealing building here, a huge Neoclassical construction housing a wide selection of nineteenth- and twentieth-century Italian (and a few foreign) names. However, the museum's compact and surprisingly engaging collection is beautifully displayed – and can make a refreshing change after several days of having the senses bombarded with Etruscan, Roman and Renaissance art. There is also a reasonably priced café, the *Caffè delle Arti*, out the back door at Via Gramsci 73, which is part of the gallery complex and is the best place to grab something to eat and drink if you're wilting.

The ground floor

The ground floor is given over to **nineteenth-century works**, with the left side focusing on pieces from 1800 to 1885, and covering all the major artistic movements of the nineteenth century, with **neo-classicism** represented by a giant statue of Hercules by

Canova in the central room. Another room displays mostly landscapes and cityscapes, and there are examples of **realism**, early impressionism and sentimental drama in works by the likes of Domenico Morelli and Vincenzo Gemito. The right side takes up where the left leaves off, in 1885, with the major **Impressionists and post-Impressionists** – Cézanne, Van Gogh, along with impressive early figurative works by Italian artists such as Umberto Boccione and Giacomo Balla. There is a room of mighty battle scenes promoting the glory and sacrifice of the Italian Unification, including Fattori's *Battle of Custoza*, and impressionistic and "Belle Epoque" portraits by – among others – Giuseppe de Nittis and Morelli's pupil Antonio Mancini. But what the gallery does best is to display the transition from **traditional painting to modernism**, with works like Boccione's *Portrait of Maestro Busoni* and Balla's series, *The Sick People*, *The Madman* and *The Beggar*, hung next to abstract canvases by the same artists, done just a decade or so later. There's also a lovely self-portrait of a doubtful Giorgio de Chirico alongside more mystical paintings by the artist, as well as those of his contemporaries Gino Severini and Giorgio Morandi. Look out, too, for the very effective reverse juxtaposition of Renato Gattuso's rather traditional battle scene from 1955 and the futurist Gerardo Dottori's series of fascist panels from 1935, paeans to the brutal modern world of weapons and machinery revered by the Futurists. A final room concentrates entirely on **abstract art**, not just by Italian painters but also by Mondrian, Miró and others.

The upper level

The upper floor of the museum displays work from 1926 onwards – drawings and paintings by Pirandello, Giacometti figures, and work by non-Italian pioneers like Jackson Pollock, Henry Moore, Rome's own ex-pat American painter Cy Twombly and Karel Appel, along with a lot of indifferent **contemporary** and **pop art** and a corridor of **kinetic sculptures**. Oddly perhaps the most enjoyable part of the museum is also the hardest to find – the mezzanine, which is a separate space devoted to a selection of key **modern Italian artists**, among them de Chirico, the sculptor Renate Gattuso and the fabulously talented Giacomo Balla, who came full circle towards the end of his life to give up the abstractions of Futurism for figurative painting once more.

Museo Nazionale Etrusco di Villa Giulia

Piazzale di Villa Giulia 9 • Tues–Sun 8.30am–7.30pm • €8 • ☎ 06 322 6751, ⓦ villagiulia.beniculturali.it

Right on the western edge of the Villa Borghese, Villa Giulia, five minutes' walk away from Via Flaminia, is a harmonious collection of courtyards, loggias, gardens and temples put together in a playful Mannerist style for Pope Julius III in the mid-sixteenth century, and arguably a more essential stop than the Modern Art Museum. It's home to the **Museo Nazionale Etrusco di Villa Giulia**, which, along with the Etruscan collection in the Vatican, is the world's primary collection of Etruscan treasures, and a good introduction – or conclusion – to the Etruscan sites in Lazio, which between them contributed most of the artefacts on display here. It's not an especially large museum, and it's worth taking the trouble to see the whole collection.

The east wing – ground floor

The entrance room of the east wing houses two pieces of **Etruscan sculpture**, one showing a man astride a seahorse, a recurring theme in ancient Mediterranean art, and an oddly amateurish centaur – basically a man pasted to the hindquarters of a horse – both from Vulci and dating from the sixth century BC. The next rooms contain bronze objects from the seventh and sixth centuries BC – **urns** used to contain the ashes of cremated persons, among which a beautiful bronze example, in the shape of a finely detailed dwelling hut, stands out – and a number of terracotta votive offerings of anatomical parts of the human body, their detail alluding to the Etruscans' accomplishments in medicine. A gold dental bridge shows their skill at dentistry too.

THE ETRUSCANS

The **Etruscans** remain something of a historical mystery. We know that they lived in central Italy – in Etruria – from around 900 BC until their incorporation into the Roman world in 88 BC. However, whether they were native to the region, or whether they had originally migrated here from overseas, specifically from **Asia Minor**, remains a matter of debate. The Romans borrowed heavily from their civilization, and thus in many ways the influence of the Etruscans is still felt today: our **alphabet**, for example, is based on the Etruscan system, and bishops' crooks and the "fasces" symbol (a bundle of rods with an axe that is found, among other places, behind the Speaker's rostrum in the US House of Representatives) are just two other Etruscan symbols that endure. The Etruscans were also masters of working in terracotta, gold and bronze, and accomplished carvers in stone, and it is these skills – together with their obvious sensuality and the ease with which they appeared to enjoy life – that make a visit to the **Villa Giulia** so beguiling.

The next room displays items found in **Veii** – among them Hercules and Apollo disputing over the sacred hind which Apollo had shot and Hercules claimed. Next door, in the octagonal room, the remarkable **Sarcophagus of the Married Couple** (dating from the sixth century BC, and actually containing the ashes of the deceased rather than the bodies), is from Cerveteri, and is one of the most famous pieces in the museum – a touchingly lifelike portrayal of a husband and wife lying on a couch. He has his right arm around her; she is offering him something from her right hand, probably an egg – a recurring theme in Etruscan art. Their clothes are modelled down to the finest detail, including the laces and soles of their shoes, and the pleats of the linen and lacy pillowcases. In case you're wondering, the holes in the backs of their heads, and at other spots, are ventilation holes to prevent the terracotta from exploding when the hollow piece was fired. Beyond are more finds from Cerveteri: hundreds of vases, pots, drinking vessels and other items, and, among a number of busts and images, clearly portraits of real people, a depiction of a man, complete with cauliflower right ear and a finely stitched cut to the right of his mouth – clearly a tough customer.

The east wing – first floor

Upstairs, in the balcony over the married couple sarcophagus, there are displays on the **Etruscan language**, and the *cistae* recovered from tombs around Praeneste – drum-like objects, engraved and adorned with figures, that were supposed to hold everything the body needed after death – including a special area devoted to the beautiful and justifiably famous Ficorini Cista, made by an Etruscan craftsman named Novios Plautios for a lady named Dindia Malconia and probably a wedding present. In the same room, marvellously intricate pieces of **gold jewellery** have been worked into tiny horses, birds, camels and other animals. Further on you'll find mostly bronzes, mirrors, candelabra, religious statues and tools used in everyday life. Notice, particularly, the elongated statues of priests and priestesses, some of whom hold eels in their hands and are engaged in some kind of rite. There is also a realistic bronze statuette of a ploughman at work, plodding along behind his oxen. After this hall you are at the bottom of the "U" curve that forms the building's outline, and holds an enormous collection of jewellery – all of it fascinating.

Branching off are items and reconstructions from the enormous temple excavated at **Pyrgi**, Cerveteri's seaport, in the 1960s, including replicas of gold foil plates thought at one time to offer a Rosetta Stone-like key to the Etruscan language; the plates are Etruscan, Punic and Greek, and represent some of the oldest pre-Roman inscriptions ever found. The rooms to the west of here hold items from the very earliest Etruscan collections, together with the story of how everything was brought together, a model of the villa and original architectural drawings by, among others, Michelangelo.

The atrium
In the atrium, two storeys high, are finds from the **temples** at Sassi Caduti and the Sanctuary of Apollo in Civita Castellana – Etruscan artistry at its best, with gaudily coloured terracotta figures that leer, run, jump and climb; a beautiful, lifelike torso of Apollo, dating from around the start of the fourth century BC; and a bust of Juno which has the air of a dignified matron, the flower pattern on her dress still visible, as are her earrings, necklace and crown.

The west wing – ground floor
The ground floor of the west wing displays more artefacts with obvious connections to the Etruscans, including North African ostrich eggs, an Etruscan symbol of resurrection and rebirth, and mirrors, some of which have mythological events etched on their backs. The next series of galleries has items from Lake Nemi and the Alban Hills in **southern Lazio**, with an oak log that was used as a coffin and cases of terracotta votive offerings – anatomical parts, babies in swaddling clothes and models of temples and houses. There are also more *cistae*, gold breastplates and belt buckles, bronze pots with griffins' heads looking in to see what's cooking and a wonderful bronze throne with elaborately worked scenes of hunting, military parades and horse racing.

The west wing – first floor
Through a gallery containing several hundred examples of Etruscan **pottery**, terracotta and bronze items, including charcoal braziers and pieces of armour, and, remarkably, a trumpet that has not sounded for two thousand years, leads you to the steps to the upper floor of the west wing, which is devoted to the Faliscians, a people from northeast Lazio who spoke a dialect of Latin but were culturally Etruscans. This part of the museum was reorganized relatively recently and is clearly labelled in English, with good information in each room from the excavations at Narce, Falerii Nuovi, Civita Castellana and other sites in the Faliscian area. The displays include a drinking horn in the shape of a dog's head that is so lifelike you almost expect it to bark; a *holmos*, or small table, to which the maker attached 24 little pendants; and a bronze disc breastplate from the seventh century BC decorated with a weird, almost modern abstract pattern of galloping creatures.

Museo Hendrik Christian Andersen

Via PS Mancini 20 • Tues–Sun 9.30am–7.30pm • Free • ☎ 06 321 9089, ✆ museoandersen.beniculturali.it • Tram #2 from Piazzale Flaminio

Around ten minutes' walk north from Piazzale Flaminio, the **Museo Hendrik Christian Andersen** is a delightful small collection – and one of the best of Rome's lesser-known free attractions. Affiliated to the Modern Art Museum, it's devoted to the work of the eponymous Norwegian–American sculptor and painter, who was a friend and contemporary of Henry James and lived in Rome for almost half his long life, producing the giant Neoclassical pieces in grand and heroic poses now in his old studio; it's hard to imagine a room more crammed full of elegantly shaped buttocks and penises. Don't miss the cast for his tomb in the Protestant Cemetery (see p.144), where he is buried with other members of his family.

Andersen wasn't just a sculptor: in the gallery next door are his 1912 plans for a utopian world city, a planned centre of civilization on so epic a scale that not surprisingly it was never built, although Mussolini later got behind it and it's conceivable that his EUR (see p.154) was based at least in part on Andersen's ideas. Upstairs, where the artist lived, is more restrained, now given over to his modest paintings of landscapes around Lazio and Campania, as well as a handful of family holiday snaps and scribbled postcards – personal insights into Andersen's full and creative life in Italy.

MAXXI

Via Guido Reni 4a • Tues–Fri & Sun 11am–7pm, Sat 11am–10pm • €11; audioguide €5 • ☎ 06 3996 7350, ⓦ fondazionemaxxi.it •
Tram #2 from Piazzale Flaminio

A ten-minute tram ride north of Piazza del Popolo, **MAXXI** is a new museum of twenty-first-century art and architecture. Opened to much fanfare in mid-2010, in a landmark building by the Anglo-Iraqi architect Zaha Hadid, it makes a great modern accompaniment to Renzo Piano's nearby Auditorium complex. Built around a former military barracks, it's mainly a venue for temporary exhibitions, but small permanent collections are being assembled from scratch: late-twentieth-century Italian works of art and the archives of influential Italian architects like Pier Luigi Nervi. The building, a simultaneously jagged and curvy concrete spaceship that looks like it's just landed in this otherwise rather ordinary part of the city, is worth a visit in its own right, with a towering lobby encompassing the inevitable café and bookshop, and bright, curvaceous galleries leading one into the other, connected by walkways that flow through the complex like passages in some giant termite mound. There's usually one major exhibition on, with other supporting installations, often including a snapshot of the permanent collection. There's also a larger bookshop and a larger café/restaurant in the converted buildings across the way.

Foro Italico

Bus #30 from Piazza Venezia to Clodio, then bus #69; or bus #32 from Ottaviano metro station (Line A)

It's just ten minutes' walk from Ponte Milvio – past the huge Italian Foreign Ministry building – to the **Foro Italico** sports centre, one of the few parts of Rome to survive intact pretty much the way Mussolini planned it. This is still used as a sports centre, but it's worth visiting as much for its period feel and architecture as anything else. Its centrepiece is the Ponte Duca d'Aosta, which connects the Foro Italico to the town side of the river, and is headed by a white marble obelisk capped with a gold pyramid that is engraved MUSSOLINI DUX in beautiful 1930s calligraphy. The marble finials at the side of each end of the bridge show soldiers in various heroic acts, loading machine guns and cannons, charging into the face of enemy fire, carrying the wounded and so forth, each bearing the face of Mussolini himself – a very eerie sight indeed.

Beyond the bridge, an avenue patched with more mosaics revering "Il Duce" leads up to a fountain surrounded by images of muscle-bound figures revelling in sporting activities. Either side of the fountain are the two main **stadiums**: the larger of the two, the Stadio Olimpico on the left, was used for the Olympic Games in 1960 and is still the venue for Rome's two football teams on alternate Sundays (see p.298). The smaller Stadio dei Marmi ("stadium of marbles") is ringed by sixty great male statues, groins modestly hidden by fig leaves, in a variety of elegantly macho poses – each representing both a sport and a province of Italy. It's a typically Fascist monument in many ways, but a rather ironic choice for what was a notoriously homophobic government.

CASA MORAVIA

It's rarely open, and you have to book in advance, but if you can time it right try to get to the **Casa Museo Alberto Moravia**, Lungotevere Vittoria 1 (☎06 0608, ⓦfondoalbertomoravia.it, ⓦmuseiincomuneroma.it; bus #224 or #280 from Lepanto on metro line A), which is open on the first Saturday of each month (except Aug) for guided tours at 10am and 11am; booking is obligatory, on ☎339 274 5206 or at ✉romantours@gmail.com. Moravia moved to this apartment in 1963, after he had split from his wife, the writer Elsa Morante. He was a very Roman writer, living all his life in the city, and the apartment is left just as it was when he died in 1990, with a retro kitchen, large Tiber-facing terrace and book-lined study, all decorated with paintings by various twentieth-century Italian artists.

Monte Mario

Bus #30 from Piazza Venezia to Clodio, then bus #69; or bus #32 from Ottaviano metro station (Line A)

Rome's highest hill at 139m, **Monte Mario** lies a mile or so north of the Vatican, easily visible by the telegraph masts that top its summit, as well as the dome of the city's former planetarium. Unsurprisingly the views from the top are among the city's best, and you can follow a path up from Via Gomenizza, on the far side of Piazzale Maresciallo Giardino, which you can reach by taking bus #32 from Ottaviano metro station.

There are actually two paths to choose from. The shorter of the two, at Via Gomenizza 81, leads to Villa Mazzanti, where there's an **information office** for the Monte Mario park (Mon–Fri 9am–3pm, Sat & Sun 10am–5pm). The other, less official-looking gate is 50m to the right of this, and from here a paved path zigzags up to the top in about thirty minutes and is wheelchair-feasible, if not exactly -friendly, all the way. There's a belvedere about two-thirds of the way up, just before the path flattens out, which gives panoramic views of the city, after which you leave the path and turn sharp right onto a road for 400m, past the observatory, to *Lo Zodiaco*, a café and restaurant right by the telegraph mast, with fine views over northern Rome and back to the centre. Here you can grab a coffee and a snack or get a full meal in the restaurant, which isn't badly priced considering the location, and there are telescopes for viewing plus various games for kids. From the front of the restaurant a narrower path – the well-named Via degli Inamorati – leads more steeply downhill, eventually joining up with the main path, just below the belvedere, from where it's maybe fifteen minutes' walk back to the bottom.

Ponte Milvio

Bus #30 from Piazza Venezia to Clodio, then bus #69; or tram #2 from Piazzale Flaminio

Immediately north of Flaminio, the Tiber sweeps around in a wide hook-shaped bend that is crossed by the **Ponte Milvio**, the old, originally Roman, footbridge where the Emperor Constantine defeated Maxentius in 312 AD. It provides wonderful views of the meandering Tiber, with the city springing up green on the hills to both sides and the silty river running fast below, but the main thing you'll notice about the bridge is its collection of **padlocks**, placed here by lovers who then throw the keys into the river – an enactment of a ritual popularized by Federico Moccia's best-selling novel, *Ho Voglia di Te* (*I Want You*), published in 2006. The lampposts the padlocks were attached to eventually started to collapse beneath the weight, which was when the council installed the posts you can see here now; but if you can't be bothered to bring your own padlock, there's a website – ⓦlucchettipontemilvio.com – where you can attach a virtual padlock as a symbol of your undying love.

Like the bridge, the area on the northern side of the river, around Piazzale di Ponte Milvio, attracts a youthful crowd these days, who increasingly flock here for the cool bars and restaurants that have sprung up in the neighbourhood. There's a cheap and cheerful **market** and a number of good places to eat and drink (see p.254).

The Auditorium

Viale Pietro de Coubertin 30 · Daily 10am–8pm · Free · Guided tours (in Italian) Sat & Sun hourly 11.30am–4.30pm; €9; bookable on ⓣ 06 8024 1281, ⓕ 06 80242, ⓦ www.auditorium.com · Bus #M from Termini, or tram #2 from Piazzale Flaminio

In the heart of the Flaminio district, Rome's **Auditorium** is in fact three auditoriums built in one complex, their large bulbous shapes making them look like three giant, lead-skinned armadillos crouched together. Designed by everyone's favourite Italian architect, **Renzo Piano**, and opened in spring 2006, it's a clever building: the foyers all join up and, above, the three buildings make a large amphitheatre, used for outdoor performances given in the piazza below. It's clever, too, in the way it has incorporated the remains of a Republican-era villa between two of the concert halls, which was discovered when building began, and actually halted the project for two years while it was excavated.

Each concert hall is conceived and designed for a different kind of musical performance: the smallest, the Sala Petrassi on the right side, accommodates 700 people and is designed for chamber concerts; the middle Sala Sinopoli holds 1200; while the largest of the three, the eastern Sala Santa Cecilia, can seat 2700 listening to big symphonic works, and is now home to Rome's flagship orchestra, the Academy of Santa Cecilia. You can walk right around the building outside, exploring the Parco della Musica, as it's known. The main entrance is on Via Pietro de Coubertin, home to a great book and CD shop and decent café (*ReD;* see p.254) or you can cut through to the park from Viale Maresciallo Pilsudski, where there's a children's playground.

Parioli

The area immediately to the east of the Auditorium, and north of Villa Borghese, is the **Parioli** district, which extends roughly over as far as the massive Villa Ada park (see below), and whose quiet, winding streets, large villas and lush, leafy gardens make up one of Rome's wealthier neighbourhoods. Its main drag, Viale dei Parioli, is home to some decent restaurants, and the Villa Glori park provides a splash of green on its northern edge, but the main reason you might find yourself here is before or after attending a concert at the Auditorium, or maybe after a trip to Villa Ada.

Villa Ada

Immediately east of Parioli, the enormous expanse of **Villa Ada** is Rome's largest public park, flanked on the far side by Via Salaria – the old trading route between the Romans and Sabines, so called because the main product transported along here was salt. The Villa Ada was once the estate of King Vittorio Emanuele III and is a nice enough place in which to while away an afternoon, with a bucolic atmosphere that is a world away from the busy streets of the city centre; the lake on the Via Salaria side is full of turtles, and you can rent bicycles, canoes or ponies from the southerly reaches of the park, where there is also a children's playground. The original royal villa is now the site of the Egyptian embassy, but you can also visit the catacombs of Priscilla just outside the park walls (see below), and the "Roma Incontra il Mondo" world music festival has been held here every June since 1994, at which you may get to hear the rap-reggae sounds of local band Villa Ada Posse.

Catacombe di Priscilla

Via Salaria 430 · Tues–Sun 8.30am–noon & 2.30–5pm · €8 · ☎ 06 8620 6272, ⓦ catacombepriscilla.com · Bus #63 from Piazza Venezia or #92 from Termini

Just outside Villa Ada, the **Catacombe di Priscilla** are among Rome's most extensive, a frescoed labyrinth of tunnels on three levels that can be visited on regular (obligatory) guided tours. No one quite knows why these catacombs are here, or whether they are Christian or pagan in origin, but some of the city's most recognized martyrs ended up here, a roll-call of names that echoes from some of the city centre's most prominent churches – Praxedes and Pudenziana, among others. Tours last half an hour and take in a number of locations, best of which is the so-called Greek Chapel whose frescoes, painted between the second and fourth centuries AD, are probably more impressive than you'll see in any of Rome's other catacombs, showing the Adoration of the Magi, Daniel in the lions' den, the resurrection of Lazarus, Noah, the sacrifice of Isaac and other biblical events. There is also the earliest known depiction of the Virgin and Child, though this could simply be a picture of a mother and child, both of whom were probably buried here.

Salario and Quartiere Coppedè

Forming an elongated rhomboid between the city walls, Viale Regina Magherita and Via Nomentana to the south, the **Salario** neighbourhood is a mainly residential district, but one not entirely devoid of interest. Just north of Piazza Buenos Aires, Via Dora signals the edge of the so-called Quartiere Coppedè, a series of Art Nouveau buildings designed by the Florentine architect Gino Coppedè at the end of the nineteenth century. Its centre, **Piazza Mincio** (accessible through the arch on Via Dora), is less a collection of buildings and more the backdrop for a Ruritanian opera, with turrets, grotesque faces, creatures and columns all jumbled together in a riot of eclectic design. The centrepiece is the fountain in the centre, topped by frogs, and with more frogs underneath spewing water into scallop shells held by straining men. Perhaps not surprisingly, the area is regarded as quite a desirable place to live.

MACRO

11

Via Nizza 138 · Tues–Fri & Sun 11am–7pm, Sat 11am–8pm · €11 · ☎ 06 6710 70400, Ⓦ macro.roma.museum · Bus #80 from Piazza Venezia, or bus #38 from Termini

The Museum of Contemporary Art in Rome, or **MACRO**, is housed in the old Peroni brewery stables, just beyond Piazza Alessandria, whose complex of buildings opened in 1999 as an arts and culture centre. There is a permanent collection of contemporary works here, mainly focusing on Italian artists since the 1960s, but its six large exhibition halls are mostly used to host temporary exhibitions, plus there's a library, bookshop and café.

Via Nomentana

From the Porta Pia and busy Corso d'Italia – in effect part of the central ring road that girdles the city centre – the wide boulevard of **Via Nomentana** is an ancient Roman route that leads northeast through a plush neighbourhood of large nineteenth-century villas and apartment blocks. It's a useful rather than a picturesque route, but the neighbourhood it gives its name to is home to a number of attractions.

Villa Torlonia

Via Nomentana 70 · **Gardens** April, May & Sept 7am–7.30pm; June–Aug 7am–8.30pm; Oct & March 7am–6pm; Nov–Feb 7.30am–5pm · **Museums** Tues–Sun 9am–7pm · Casino Nobile €8, Casino delle Civette €5, €10 for all buildings · ☎ 06 0608, Ⓦ museivillatorlonia.it · Access also possible from Via Siracusa and Via Spallanzani · Bus #62 from Piazza Venezia/San Silvestro

A few hundred metres down Via Nomentana from the Porta Pia is the large nineteenth-century estate of **Villa Torlonia,** which in the 1930s was given by the banker **Prince Giovanni Torlonia** to Mussolini to use for as long as he needed it.

Casino Nobile

Mussolini lived in the Villa Torlonia from 1925 to 1943, occupying the central **Casino Nobile**, all for the nominal rent of one lira a year. Designed by Valadier in the early nineteenth century, the house was a sumptuous place to live. Various rooms are decorated with cycles of frescoes whose unifying theme is frolicking and nakedness, alongside a general deference to bygone ages, with ancient Roman tableaux, including Antony and Cleopatra, hieroglyphics and portraits of great artists and thinkers. The Mussolinis didn't alter the house much, just installing a couple of en-suite bathrooms between their bedrooms on the first floor (since removed) and strengthening the basement to withstand an air raid; the gardens became a bit of a playground, with tennis courts and a riding track for Il Duce to show off – as evidenced by the photos on display here.

Casino dei Principi
Close to the Casino Nobile, the smaller **Casino dei Principi** is now used for temporary exhibitions but was originally a farm building that was remodelled and used as an annexe to the main villa, to which it's connected by a tunnel. Its most impressive permanent feature is the room at the end, decorated in the mid-nineteenth century with views of the Bay of Naples.

Casina delle Civette
Finally, don't miss the **Casina delle Civette** in the southeastern corner, the "small house of the owls". This is something unusual in Rome – a Liberty-style dwelling full of Art Nouveau features, such as stained glass, wood panelling and inlays, that contribute to the kind of complete design vision that was common at the end of the nineteenth century. Though originally designed in 1840, it was transformed in 1917 by one Vincenzo Fasoli into a comfortable residence for a Roman aristocrat – in this case Prince Torlonia – in the fashionable style of the time. The house's name derives from the prince's love of owls and their dominance in the decoration of the building (although much of this hasn't survived). Indeed, the prince was keen on all things of the night, as his upstairs bedroom shows, decorated as it is with a night sky and a bat-encrusted chandelier. The bird scheme continues in the **Room of the Swallows** (with its stucco birds in each corner, and swallow-themed stained glass), and there are owls in the stained-glass windows at the front of the house and the relief above the back door. The rest of the park remains in restoration, and there are plans to return its other features, including an outdoor theatre, to their original splendour too.

Casino Medievale
The latest part of the Villa Torlonia to have been renovated is the so-called **Casino Medievale**, which has been turned into the comfortable *La Limonaia* café-restaurant where you can sit outside in a lime-tree-filled garden, and a kids' attraction known as Technotown (in Italian only). But whether they will ever get around to restoring the third-century AD Jewish catacombs, which are said to extend under the gardens for some 10km, remains to be seen.

Casa di Pirandello
Via Antonio Bosio 13b · Mon & Tues 9am–2pm, Wed, Thurs & Fri 9am–6pm · Free · ☎ 06 4429 1853, ⓦ studiodiluigipirandello.it · Metro B to Bologna

Five minutes' walk from Via Nomentana, and about the same from Piazza Bologna's metro station, the building known as the **Casa di Pirandello** was the home of the Italian writer for twenty years, and he spent the last three years of his life, until his death in 1936, in the second-floor apartment here. This was more or less outside the city centre at that time, and he would have had a clear view of the Villa Torlonia from his bedroom balcony. The apartment is untouched from that time, with his desk in the corner of the main sitting room left as if he had just got up to make a cup of coffee; the engraved cigar box was given to him by the Italian writer and politician Gabriele d'Annunzio, and the landscapes that hang behind were painted by Pirandello himself, and complement the portraits done by his son Fausto, who lived downstairs with his family.

Sant'Agnese fuori le Mura
Villa Nomentana 364 · Mon 9am–noon, Tues–Sat 9am–noon & 4–6pm, Sun 4–6pm · Catacombs tours take 30min and cost €5 · ⓦ santagnese.org · Bus #84 from Piazza Venezia or Termini, #60 from Piazza Venezia or Repubblica, or #36 or #90 from Termini

About a mile up Via Nomentana from the Porta Pia, the church of **Sant'Agnese fuori le Mura** is dedicated to the 13-year-old saint who was martyred in Domitian's Stadium in 303 AD (see p.44). It's part of a small complex of early Christian monuments that also includes the catacombs underneath and the neighbouring church of Santa Costanza, and in fact is the modern-day survivor of an enormous basilica complex that was built here by Constantine at the same time as the other patriarchal basilicas – the remains of which you can see in the grounds.

Sant'Agnese

Apart from some very out-of-place later fixtures, the church of **Sant'Agnese** is much as it was when it was built by Pope Honorius I in the seventh century, when he reworked Constantine's original structure – which had in turn been built over St Agnes's grave. Entrance is either through the outside courtyard or down a long staircase plastered with fragments of Roman reliefs and inscriptions. Inside has been updated in Baroque style, but the apse mosaic is contemporary with Honorius's building, showing Agnes next to the pope, who holds a model of his church, in typical Byzantine fashion. And if you don't want to bother with the catacombs tours, you can see St Agnes's tomb in the crypt (see below); take the stairs to the right of the apse.

The catacombs

The **catacombs** that sprawl below the church are among the best preserved and most crowd-free in Rome – indeed if you have time for only one set of catacombs during your stay in Rome (and they really are all very much alike), you could make it these. Originally dating back to the late second century, the growing cult of St Agnes meant they became much expanded over subsequent years, and at their peak there were around 55,000 bodies buried here. Tours take you through the choicest passages, picking out often touching inscriptions to beloved wives, husbands and children, into a vaulted family chapel, and conclude with the tomb of Agnes herself beneath the altar, moved here by Paul V from its original burial place nearby; Agnes lies inside a sarcophagus alongside her sister but minus her head, which remains in the church dedicated to her on Piazza Navona (see p.44).

Santa Costanza

After the catacombs, the guide will show you the church of **Santa Costanza**, whose decorative and architectural features illustrate the transition from the pagan to Christian city better than almost any other building in Rome. Built in 350 AD as a mausoleum for Constantia and Helena, the daughters of the Emperor Constantine, it's the only intact part of Constantine's original basilica, a round structure which follows the traditional shape of the great pagan tombs (consider those of Hadrian and Augustus elsewhere in the city); indeed the mosaics on the vaulting of its circular ambulatory – fourth-century depictions of vines, leaves and birds – would have been as at home on the floor of a Roman domus as they were in a Christian church. Unfortunately, the porphyry sarcophagus of St Constantia herself has been moved to the Vatican (see p.199), and what you see in the church is a plaster copy.

The Vatican

On the west bank of the Tiber, directly across from Rome's historic centre, the Vatican City was established as an independent sovereign state in 1929. It's a tiny territory, with a population of around a thousand, surrounded by high walls on its western side, while its eastern side opens its doors to the rest of the city in the form of St Peter's and its colonnaded piazza. The Latin name Mons Vaticanus (Vatican Hill) is a corruption of an Etruscan term, indicating a good place for observing the flights of birds and lightning on the horizon – believed to prophesy the future. It's thought that St Peter himself was buried in a pagan cemetery nearby, giving rise to the building of a basilica to venerate his name and the later location of the headquarters of the Roman Catholic Church.

Apart from entering St Peter's or the museums, you wouldn't know at any point that you had left Rome and entered the Vatican; indeed the area around it, known as the Borgo, holds one or two sights that are technically part of the Vatican (like **Castel Sant'Angelo**), but is also one of the most cosmopolitan districts of Rome, full of hotels, restaurants and scurrying tourists and pilgrims – as it has been since the King of Wessex founded the first hotel for pilgrims here in the eighth century. There are many mid-range **hotels** here and in the neighbouring nineteenth-century district of Prati (named after the pastures that used to lie here), just to the north, although unless you're a pilgrim you might prefer to base yourself in the more atmospheric historic centre and travel back and forth on the useful **#64 bus** or by taking **metro line A** to Ottaviano, from where it's a 5min walk to the Vatican, and 10min to St Peter's. However much you try, one visit is never anywhere near enough. The **Vatican Museums** (see p.195) and **St Peter's** (see p.190) are both open to visitors (knees and shoulders must be covered for St Peter's). For opening times and prices, see the individual attractions that follow.

Vatican Gardens It's possible to visit the Vatican Gardens, which offer great views of St Peter's. You can only visit on a guided tour (daily except Wed & Sun; 2hr; book in advance on ☏ 06 6988 3145 or ☏ 06 6988 4676, ⊕ vatican .va; €32 per person, payable on the day). Tickets include entry to the Vatican Museums so you'll probably want to make a day of it; the dress code is as for St Peter's.

Papal audiences You can, if you wish, attend a papal audience: these happen once a week, on Wed in the Audiences Hall of Paul VI on the south side of St Peter's, and are by no means one-to-one affairs – you'll be with hundreds of others. During the summer months they are sometimes held in the square or at the pope's country residence in Castel Gandolfo (see p.220). They're free, you don't have to be a Catholic to attend, and it's often possible to get a place if you apply in advance, by sending a letter or fax with your name, your home address, your Rome address and your preferred date of audience to the office of the Prefettura della Casa Pontificia, 00120 Città del Vaticano (☏ 06 6988 5863), on the right-hand side of St Peter's Square. Bear in mind that the pope also appears each Sunday at noon to bless the crowds on St Peter's Square – or, in late July and throughout August, in Castel Gandolfo.

Vatican Necropolis You need to book tours (€12), usually several months in advance, through the Scavi office, either in person – it's through the arch to the left of St Peter's (Mon–Sat 9am–5pm), by phone, fax or email – ☏ 06 6988 5318, ☏ 06 6987 3017, ✉ scavi@fsp.va.

Post To send a postcard with a Vatican postmark, there are Vatican post offices close to the basilica on both sides of Piazza San Pietro, and inside the Vatican Museums.

Castel Sant'Angelo

Lungotevere Castello 50 • Tues–Sun 9am–7.30pm • €10.50 • ☏ 06 681 9111, ⊕ castelsantangelo.com

The best route to the Vatican and St Peter's is across **Ponte Sant'Angelo**, flanked by angels carved to designs by Bernini and known as his "breezy maniacs". On the far side is the great circular hulk of **Castel Sant'Angelo**, designed and built by the Emperor Hadrian as his own mausoleum (his ashes were interred here until a twelfth-century pope appropriated the sarcophagus, which was later destroyed in a fire). The original building was a grand monument, faced with white marble, surrounded by statues and topped with cypresses, similar in style to Augustus's mausoleum across the river. It was renamed in the sixth century, when Pope Gregory the Great witnessed a vision of St Michael here that ended a terrible plague. The mausoleum's position near the Vatican was not lost on the papal authorities, who converted the building for use as a fortress and built a passageway to link it with the Vatican as a refuge in times of siege or invasion – a route utilized on a number of occasions, most notably when the Medici pope,

THE WORLD'S SMALLEST COUNTRY

The **Vatican** ruled Rome until 1870, when Italian Unification led to an impasse, and a period of over fifty years when the pope didn't leave the Vatican. After reaching an uneasy agreement with Mussolini, the Vatican became a sovereign state in 1929, and nowadays has its own radio station, daily newspaper (*L'Osservatore Romano*), its own version of the euro complete with the pope's head (collector's items, incidentally, should you be given one), postal service and security service in the colourfully dressed Swiss Guards. Its relationship with the Italian state nowadays is, not surprisingly, anything but straightforward.

Clement VII, sheltered here for several months during the Sack of Rome in 1527. Incidentally the **café** upstairs offers one of the best views of Rome and excellent coffee.

Inside, a spiral ramp leads from the monumental **entrance hall** up into the centre of the mausoleum itself, passing through the chamber where the emperor was entombed and over a drawbridge, one of the defensive modifications made by the Borgia pope, Alexander VI, in the late fifteenth century. It continues to the main level at the top, where a small palace was built to house the papal residents in appropriate splendour.

After the Sack of Rome, Pope Paul III had some especially fine renovations made, including the beautiful **Sala Paolina**, which features frescoes by Pierno del Vaga, among others. The gilded ceiling here displays the Farnese family arms, and on the wall is a trompe-l'oeil fresco of one of the family's old retainers coming through a door from a darkened room. You'll also notice Paul III's personal motto, *Festina lente* ("make haste slowly"), scattered throughout the ceilings and in various corners of all his rooms. Elsewhere, some rooms hold swords, armour, guns and the like, while others are lavishly decorated with grotesques and paintings (don't miss the bathroom of Clement VII on the second floor, with its prototype hot and cold water taps and mildly erotic frescoes). Below are **dungeons** and storerooms (not visitable), which can be glimpsed from the spiralling ramp, testament to the castle's grisly past as the city's most notorious Renaissance prison – Benvenuto Cellini and Cesare Borgia are just two of its more famous detainees.

Ospedale di Santo Spirito

Lungotevere in Sassia 1/Borgo Santo Spirito 2 · Currently closed for restoration · ⓦ asl-rme.it/Percorso_Monumentale/HOME.htm

12

One of the cornerstones of the Borgo neighbourhood is the **Ospedale di Santo Spirito**, the oldest hospital in Rome, founded in the eighth century by Pope Innocent III, who, as legend has it, was moved after dreaming of dead and unwanted babies being tossed into the Tiber. It was later developed by Sixtus IV as a hospital for pilgrims; the oldest buildings date from this time. These two giant halls, each 60m long and joined by an octagonal hall that used to serve as the main entrance, served as wards until 2000. **Frescoes** illustrating the lives and deeds of Innocent III and Sixtus IV, twelve of whose building projects around Rome are illustrated, line the main walls, while outside the main door a window contains a barrel in which *proietti* or abandoned babies were left anonymously – alongside a slot for donations. Behind the two wards the hospital still functions, and tours take in two cloisters, one originally designated for nuns, the other for monks, and the main courtyard of the later Palazzo del Commendatore. You can in fact peek into the latter – an elegant courtyard that's now used as a car park by the hospital officials – without going on a tour.

Museo Storico dell'Arte Sanitaria

Lungotevere in Sassia 3 · Mon, Wed, Fri 10am–noon, Sat & Sun by appointment · Free · ☎ 06 683 3262, ⓦ museiscientificiroma.eu /artesanitaria

If you're in the mood for more hospital history, walk around the corner to the river side of the complex, where, just before the modern entrance to the hospital, the **Museo Storico dell'Arte Sanitaria**, housed behind an old medical lecture theatre, hosts a rather macabre jumble of ancient medical artefacts. There's a model of the original hospital, anatomical models of body parts and casts, horrible pickled babies in jars, vile-looking scalpels, forceps and syringes as well as the inevitable old-style pharmacy – not for the squeamish.

Piazza San Pietro

The approach to St Peter's from Castel Sant'Angelo is disappointing, and has been so since Mussolini created the approach of Via della Conciliazione, when he realized the earlier plan of Pope Nicholas V and swept away the houses of the previously narrow

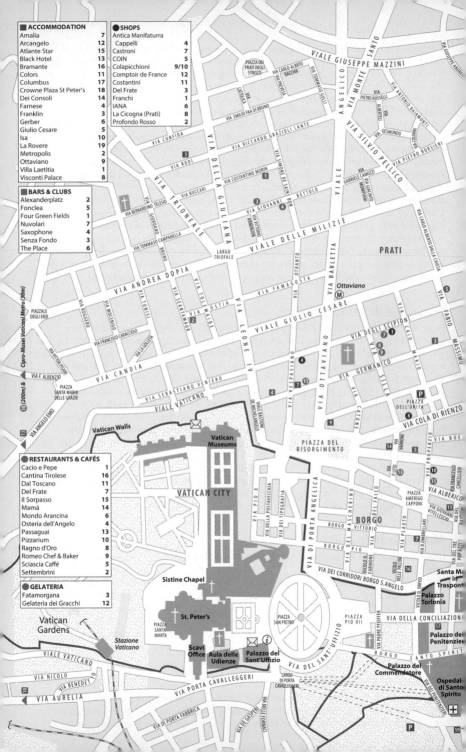

ACCOMMODATION

Amalia	7
Arcangelo	12
Atlante Star	15
Black Hotel	13
Bramante	16
Colors	11
Columbus	17
Crowne Plaza St Peter's	18
Dei Consoli	14
Farnese	4
Franklin	3
Gerber	6
Giulio Cesare	5
Isa	10
La Rovere	19
Metropolis	2
Ottaviano	9
Villa Laetitia	1
Visconti Palace	8

SHOPS

Antica Manifattura Cappelli	4
Castroni	7
COIN	5
Colapicchioni	9/10
Comptoir de France	12
Costantini	11
Del Frate	3
Franchi	1
IANA	6
La Cicogna (Prati)	8
Profondo Rosso	2

BARS & CLUBS

Alexanderplatz	2
Fonclea	5
Four Green Fields	1
Nuvolari	7
Saxophone	4
Senza Fondo	3
The Place	6

RESTAURANTS & CAFÉS

Cacio e Pepe	1
Cantina Tirolese	16
Dal Toscano	11
Del Frate	7
Il Sorpasso	15
Mamá	14
Mondo Arancina	6
Osteria dell'Angelo	4
Passaguai	13
Pizzarium	10
Ragno d'Oro	8
Romeo Chef & Baker	5
Sciascia Caffè	5
Settembrini	2

GELATERIA

Fatamorgana	3
Gelateria dei Gracchi	12

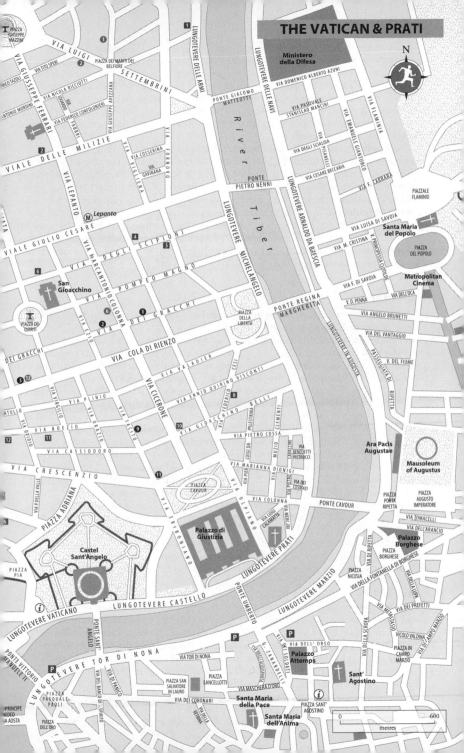

THE VATICAN & PRATI

PIAZZA GIUSEPPE MAZZINI

VIA LUIGI SETTEMBRINI

PIAZZA DEI MARITI DEL BELFIORE

Ministero della Difesa

VIA DOMENICO ALBERTO AZUNI

VIA PASQUALE STANISLAO MANCINI

VIA FLAMINIA

VIA GIUSEPPE FERRARI

VIA NICOLA RICCIOTTI

VIA FEDERICO CONFALONIERI

VIALE DELLE MILIZIE

PONTE GIACOMO MATTEOTTI

VIA EMANUELE GIANTURCO

PIAZZALE FLAMINIO

VIA COSSERIA

VIA GAVINANA

FORNOVO

PONTE PIETRO NENNI

VIA CESARE BECCARIA

VIA F. CARRARA

VIA LEPANTO

River Tiber

VIA LUISA DI SAVOIA

Santa Maria del Popolo

Lepanto

VIALE GIULIO CESARE

VIA DEGLI SCIPIONI

VIA MARCANTONIO COLONNA

POMPEO MAGNO

VIA DEI GRACCHI

VIA M. CRISTINA

V. PRINCIPESSA CLOTILDE

PIAZZA DEL POPOLO

San Gioacchino

PONTE REGINA MARGHERITA

VIA F. DI SAVOIA

VIA DELL'OCA

Metropolitan Cinema

PIAZZA DEI QUIRITI

PIAZZA DELLA LIBERTÀ

VIA ANGELO BRUNETTI

V. D. PENNA

DEI GRACCHI

VIA COLA DI RIENZO

VIA VALADIER

VIA DEL VANTAGGIO

VIA PLINIO

VIA VIRGILIO

VIA ORAZIO

VIA TACITO

VIA CICERONE

VIA ENNIO QUIRINO VISCONTI

VIA FEDERICO CESI

V. DEL FIUME

VIA BOEZIO

VIA GIOACCHINO BELLI

PALESTRINA

VIA CLEMENTI

VIA PIETRO COSSA

VIA CASSIODORO

LUNGOTEVERE IN AUGUSTA

PASSEGGIATA DI RIPETTA

VIA CRESCENZIO

VIA LUIGI RE

VIA MARIANNA DIONIGI

VIA DEI COSMATI

VIA BENEDETTO PISTRUCCI

Ara Pacis Augustae

Mausoleum of Augustus

PIAZZA ADRIANA

VIA COLONNA

PONTE CAVOUR

PIAZZA PORTA RIPETTA

PIAZZA AUGUSTO IMPERATORE

PIAZZA CAVOUR

VIA ULPIANO

VIA LUIGI CICLAMATTA

VIA TOMACELLI

VIA DELL'ARANCIO

Palazzo di Giustizia

Palazzo Borghese

Castel Sant'Angelo

VIA DELLA VALLE

VIA TRIBUNIANO

LUNGOTEVERE PRATI

PIAZZA BORGHESE

VIA DELLA FONTANELLA DI BORGHESE

VIA DELLA LUPA

PIAZZA PIA

PONTE UMBERTO

LUNGOTEVERE MARZIO

PIAZZA NICOSIA

VIA MONTE BRIANZO

VIA DEI PREFETTI

LUNGOTEVERE CASTELLO

LUNGOTEVERE VATICANO

PONTE SANT'ANGELO

VICOLO VALDINA

PIAZZA IN CAMPO MARZIO

PONTE VITTORIO EMANUELE II

LUNGOTEVERE TOR DI NONA

VIA TOR DI NONA

VIA DELL'ORSO

G. ZANARDELLI

VIA DEI SOLDATI

Palazzo Attemps

VIA DELLA SCROFA

PIAZZA PRINCIPE AMEDEO DI AOSTA

VIA DEL BANCO DI SANTO SPIRITO

VIA DI PANICO

PIAZZA SAN SALVATORE IN LAURO

PIAZZA LANCELLOTTI

VIA MASCHERA D'ORO

VIA DEI CORONARI

Sant' Agostino

PIAZZA PASQUALE PAOLI

Santa Maria della Pace

PIAZZA SANT'AGOSTINO

PIAZZA DELL'ORO

Santa Maria dell'Anima

0   600
metres

streets and replaced them with this wide, sweeping avenue. Nowadays St Peter's somehow looms too near as you get closer, and the vastness of Bernini's **Piazza San Pietro** is not really apparent until you're right on top of it. In fact, in tune with the spirit of the Baroque, the church was supposed to be even better hidden than it is now: Bernini planned to complete its colonnade with a triumphal arch linking the two arms, so obscuring the view until you were well inside the square, but this was never carried out and the arms of the piazza remain open, symbolically welcoming the world into the lap of the Catholic Church.

The **obelisk** in the centre was brought to Rome by Caligula in 36 AD, and it stood for many years in the centre of Nero's Circus on the Vatican Hill (to the left of the church); according to legend, it marked the site of St Peter's martyrdom. It was moved here in 1586, when Sixtus V ordered that it be erected in front of the basilica, a task that took four months and was apparently carried out in silence, on pain of death. The matching **fountains** on either side are the work of Carlo Maderno (on the right) and Bernini (on the left). In between the obelisk and the two fountains, a circular stone set into the pavement marks the focal points of an ellipse, from which the four rows of columns on the perimeter of the piazza line up perfectly, so that the colonnade appears to be supported by a single line of columns.

St Peter's

Daily: April–Sept 7am–7pm; Oct–March 7am–6pm • Free • Free guided tours in English Tues & Thurs at 9.45am from the Vatican info office on the left-hand side of the square • Ⓦ saintpetersbasilica.org

12

The piazza is so grand that you can't help but feel a little let down by the sight of **St Peter's**, or to give it its full name, the Basilica di San Pietro. From here, its facade – by no means the church's best feature – obscures the dome that signals the building from just about everywhere else in the city. Amid a controversy similar to that surrounding the restoration of the Sistine Chapel a few years ago, the facade has also recently been restored, leaving the previously sober travertine facade a decidedly yellowish grey.

The experience of **visiting St Peter's** has changed quite a bit over recent years. Not so long ago you could freely stroll around the piazza and wander into the basilica when you felt like it. Now much of the square is fenced off, and you can only enter St Peter's from the right-hand side (exiting to the left); you also have to go through security first, and the queues can be long unless you get here early in the morning. Once you get close to the basilica, you're channelled through various entrances depending on what you want to see first, all of which is strictly enforced by the unsmiling suited functionaries that appear at every turn. A carefree experience it is not. One of the channels funnels you into the basilica, with the other two leading to the underground grottoes (see p.194) and the ascent to the dome (see p.195) – both of the latter have exits into the main church, allowing you to visit the three sights in an order of your choice. Bear in mind that whichever you opt for first, you need to observe the **dress code** to enter, which means no bare knees or shoulders – a rule that is very strictly enforced.

Brief history

Built to a plan initially conceived at the beginning of the sixteenth century by **Bramante** and finished off, heavily modified, over a century later by **Carlo Maderno**, St Peter's is a strange hotchpotch of styles, bridging the gap between the Renaissance and Baroque eras with varying levels of success. It is, however, the principal shrine of the **Catholic Church**, built as a replacement for the run-down structure erected here by Constantine in the early fourth century on the site of St Peter's tomb. As such it cannot fail to impress: worked on by the greatest Italian architects of the sixteenth and seventeenth centuries, it occupies a site rich with historical significance. In size, meanwhile, St Peter's beats most other churches hands down (although it's not officially the largest in terms of area – that honour belongs to the Basilica of Our Lady of Peace, Côte d'Ivoire).

Bramante had originally conceived a Greek cross plan rising to a high central dome, but this design was altered after his death and revived only with the elderly **Michelangelo**'s accession as chief architect. Michelangelo was largely responsible for the dome, but he too died before its completion (in 1564). He was succeeded by Vignola, and the dome was eventually finished in 1590 by Giacomo della Porta. Carlo Maderno, under orders from the Borghese Pope Paul V, took over in 1605, and stretched the church into a Latin cross plan, which had the practical advantage of accommodating more people and followed more directly the plan of Constantine's original basilica. But in so doing he completely unbalanced all the previous designs, not least by obscuring the dome (which he also modified) from view in the piazza. The inside, too, is very much of the Baroque era, largely the work of Bernini, who created many of the most important fixtures. The church was finally completed and reconsecrated on November 18, 1626, exactly 1300 years to the day after the original basilica was first consecrated. At least the inscription on the façade – "Paul V, Roman, Pontiff, in the year 1612, the seventh in his pontificate, in honour of the Apostles" – leaves no doubt as to who was responsible for getting the job finished: as Pasquino commented at the time, "I thought it was dedicated to St Peter!"

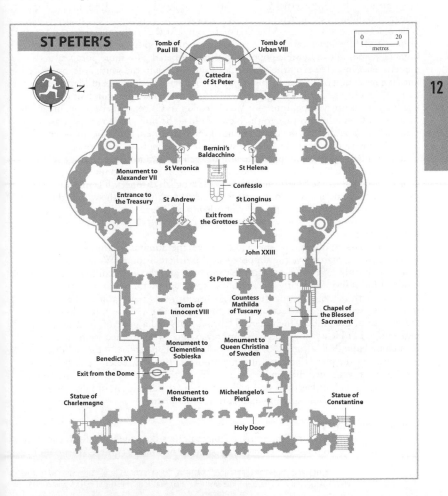

Michelangelo's Pietà

Entering the basilica, to the left of the Holy Door, which is only opened every fifty years and was last kept open during the jubilee year 2000 by John Paul II, the first thing you see on the right is **Michelangelo's Pietà**, completed when he was just 24. Following an attack by a vandal a few years back, it sits behind glass, strangely remote from the life of the rest of the building. When you look at the piece, its fame comes as no surprise: it's a sensitive and individual work, and an adept one too, draping the limp body of a grown man across the legs of a woman with grace and ease. Though you're much too far away to read it, etched into the strap across Mary's chest are words proclaiming the work as Michelangelo's – the only piece ever signed by the sculptor and apparently done after he heard that his work, which had been placed in Constantine's basilica, had been misattributed by onlookers. You can see the inscription properly on the plaster cast of the statue in the Pinacoteca of the Vatican Museums.

The nave

Women dominate the north aisle of the **nave**. Just after the *Pietà*, on a pillar, is a monument to the controversial Queen Christina of Sweden (see p.159), in the shape of a huge medallion (she's buried in the grottoes downstairs), while on the next pier along is Bernini's statue of Countess Mathilda of Tuscany. At the end of the aisle, the remains of John XXIII lie under a wax effigy, and get a lot of attention from pilgrims, a suitably humble memorial to a humble pope. John is remembered with more pomp by a modern relief in a chapel on the other side of the basilica in the south aisle, opposite a kneeling rendering of an equally pious pope, Benedict XV, the work of Pietro Canonica (see p.175). On a pillar to the right of here is Antonio Pollaiuolo's tomb of the late-fifteenth-century pope, Innocent VIII – banker to Queen Isabella of Spain and the financier of Columbus's voyage to the New World – the only tomb to survive from the Constantinian basilica. In the upper statue of the monument the pope holds what looks like a mason's trowel – in fact the spearpoint of Longinus, given to him by the Ottoman sultan Bajazet II to persuade him to keep the sultan's brother and rival in exile in Rome. On the last pillar of the south aisle is an austere monument by Canova depicting the last of the Stuart pretenders to the English throne, while opposite, over the exit from the dome, is a monument to Clementina Sobieska, the wife of the Stuart James III – the third of the three women buried in St Peter's.

The crossing

Under the **crossing** of the transepts and the nave, the dome is breathtakingly imposing, rising high above the supposed site of St Peter's tomb. With a diameter of 44m, it is only 1.5m smaller than the Pantheon, and the letters of the inscription inside its lower level are nearly 2m high. It's supported by four enormous piers, decorated with reliefs depicting the basilica's "major relics": St Veronica's handkerchief, which was used to wipe the face of Christ and is adorned with his miraculous image; the lance of St Longinus, which pierced Christ's side; and a piece of the True Cross, in the pier of St Helen (the head of St Andrew, which was returned to the Eastern Church by Pope Paul VI in 1966, was also formerly kept here). On the right side of the nave, near the pier of St Longinus, the bronze statue of St Peter is another of the basilica's most venerated monuments, carved in the thirteenth century by Arnolfo di Cambio; its right foot has been polished smooth by the attentions of pilgrims. On holy days the statue is dressed in papal tiara and vestments.

The baldacchino

Bernini's **baldacchino** is the centrepiece of the sculptor's Baroque embellishment of the interior, a massive 26m high (the height, apparently, of Palazzo Farnese), cast out of

CLOCKWISE FROM TOP LEFT SCHOOL OF ATHENS, RAPHAEL ROOMS (P.202); THE SWISS GUARD (P.186); PIAZZA SAN PIETRO FROM THE TOP OF THE BASILICA (P.195); STATUE OF ST PETER, ST PETER'S SQUARE (P.187) >

12

927 tonnes of metal removed from the Pantheon roof in 1633. To modern eyes, it's an almost grotesque piece of work, with its wild spiralling columns copied from columns in the Constantine basilica. But it has the odd personal touch, with female faces expressing the agony of childbirth on each corner except the front right one, where there's a beaming baby – said to have been commissioned by a niece of Bernini's patron (Urban VIII), who gave birth at the same time as the sculptor was finishing the piece. You'll also notice the bees that adorn just about anything to do with the Barberini family – in this case Bernini's patron Urban VIII.

The apse

Bernini's feverish sculpture decorates the **apse**, too, his bronze *Cattedra* enclosing the supposed chair of St Peter in a curvy marble and stucco throne, surrounded by the doctors of the Church (the two with bishops' mitres are St Augustine of Hippo and St Ambrose, representing the Western Church; the two to the rear are portraits of St John Chrysostom and St Athanasius of the Eastern Church). Puffs of cloud surrounding the alabaster window displaying the dove of the Holy Spirit (whose wingspan, incidentally, is 2m) burst through brilliant gilded sunbeams. On the right, the **tomb of Urban VIII**, also by Bernini, is less grand but more dignified, while on the left, the tomb of **Paul III**, by Giacomo della Porta, was moved up and down the nave of the church before it was finally placed here to balance that of Urban.

The transepts

Off the north transept, the wonderful gilded Baroque **Chapel of the Blessed Sacrament** was designed by Borromini, with work by Pietro da Cortona, Domenichino and Bernini. It's not open to the casual sightseer, but it is worthy of a visit, which can be managed if you go there to pray along with the clergy, who maintain a vigil there during the time the basilica is open. On the opposite side of the church, in the south transept, Bernini's monument to **Alexander VII** is perhaps the most dramatic papal monument of them all, its winged skeleton struggling underneath the heavy marble drapes, upon which the Chigi pope is kneeling in prayer. The Grim Reaper clutches an hourglass: the Baroque at its most melodramatic and symbolic. On the left sits Charity, on the right, Truth Revealed in Time; to the rear are Hope and Faith.

The treasury

Daily: April–Sept daily 9am–6.15pm; Oct–March daily 9am–5.15pm • €5

An entrance off the south aisle, under a giant monument to Pius VIII, leads to the rather steeply priced **treasury**, where a wall tablet records the names of all the popes buried in St Peter's. Along with more recent additions, it holds artefacts from the earlier church: a spiral marble column (the other survivors form part of the colonnade around the interior of the dome), once thought to be from the old temple of Jerusalem; a wall-mounted tabernacle by Donatello showing the dead Christ being revealed by angels (the latter carved by Michelozzo); a rich blue-and-gold dalmatic that is said once to have belonged to Charlemagne (though this has since been called into question); the vestments and tiara for the bronze statue of St Peter in the nave of the basilica; and the massive though fairly ghastly late-fifteenth-century bronze tomb of Sixtus IV by Pollaiuolo, viewable from above – said to be a very accurate portrait.

The grottoes

Daily: summer 8am–6pm; winter 7am–5pm

The middle channel outside leads to the **Vatican grottoes**, which extend right under the main footprint of the main church and hold some column bases from Constantine's original basilica, as well as a number of beautiful mosaics. The majority of the popes are buried here, with the more significant honoured by monuments. Canova's statue of Pius VI hogs the central aisle, while the tombs in the south aisle include a plain slab

12

commemorating Paul VI, John Paul I, who reigned for just 33 days and whose death has been clouded by numerous (mostly disproved) conspiracy theories, and a little further down on the left, John Paul II – whose plain tomb perhaps unsurprisingly receives by far the most attention. The last pope specifically requested that he should rest down here, and perhaps not entirely accidentally he lies in the space previously occupied by the revered John XXIII. Leaving, you emerge in the main basilica, by Bernini's statue of St Longinus.

Ascending to the roof and dome

Daily: April–Sept 8am–6pm; Oct–March 8am–4.45pm • €7 via lift, €5 using the stairs

You can make the ascent to the **roof** and **dome** by taking the furthest right of the three entrances to the basilica complex, through the northern courtyard between the church and the Vatican Palace. You'll probably need to queue when you get here, and, even with the lift (which takes care of 200 steps), there's a long climb via a slender stairway that spirals up the dome – another three hundred or so steps that grow increasingly narrow as you get higher. The views from the gallery around the interior of the dome give you a fantastic sense of the vast size of the church, and the roof has views all around, though sadly you can't get right up behind the statues of the Apostles any longer. There's a small café serving coffee and soft drinks, along with a souvenir shop, and from here you make the final ascent to the lantern at the top of the dome, from which the views over the city are as glorious as you'd expect – pretty much the best in the city. Remember, though, that it is a fairly claustrophobic climb through the double shell of the dome to reach the lantern; you should give it a miss if you're either in ill health or uneasy with heights or confined spaces. The exit leads you back into the south aisle of the church itself.

Vatican necropolis

The baldacchino and *confessio* are supposed to mark the exact spot of the **tomb of St Peter**, and excavations in the 1940s under Pius XII did indeed turn up – directly beneath the baldachino and the remains of Constantine's basilica – a row of Roman family tombs with inscriptions confirming that the Vatican Hill was a well-known burial ground in classical times. It is possible to take an **tour** of the **Vatican necropolis** in English, but you need to book well in advance with the Scavi office (see p.186). The tombs are decorated with frescoes, mosaic floors and stucco figures, and surround an ancient tomb that is believed to be that of the apostle. You can see what's left of the canopy that used to cover it, a graffitied wall and behind it a transparent plastic box – one of nineteen such boxes – that may contain his remains, or at least those of an elderly man who died in the first century AD.

Vatican Museums

Viale Vaticano 13 • Mon–Sat 9am–6pm, last entrance at 4pm, last Sun of each month 9am–2pm, last entrance at 12.30pm; closed public and religious holidays; May–July & Sept & Oct also open Fri 7–11pm • €16, under-18s and under-26s with student ID €8; all tickets pre-booked online €4 extra; last Sun of the month free; audioguides €6 • Ⓦ vatican.va; book tickets online at Ⓦ biglietteriamusei.vatican.va • Tours in groups no larger than 6 are available through Context Travel • 4hr • €60 per person • ☎ 06 9762 5204, Ⓦ contexttravel.com

A fifteen-minute walk out of the northern side of the piazza takes you up to the only part of the Vatican Palace you can visit independently, the **Vatican Museums** – quite simply, the largest, richest, most compelling and perhaps most exhausting museum complex in the world. If you have found any of Rome's other museums disappointing, the Vatican is probably the reason why: so much booty from the city's history has ended up here, and so many of the Renaissance's finest artists were in the employ of the pope, that the result is a set of museums so stuffed with antiquities as to put most other European collections to shame.

As its name suggests, the complex actually holds a collection of museums on very diverse subjects, with displays of classical statuary, Renaissance painting, Etruscan relics and Egyptian artefacts, not to mention the furnishings and decoration of the palace itself. There's no point in trying to see everything in one visit. Once inside, you have a choice of routes, but the only features you really shouldn't miss are the **Raphael Rooms** and the **Sistine Chapel** – and there are plenty of signs to make sure you don't. Above all, decide how long you want to spend here, and what you want to see, before you start; you could spend anything from an hour to the better part of a day inside, and it's easy to collapse from museum fatigue before you've even got to your most important

12

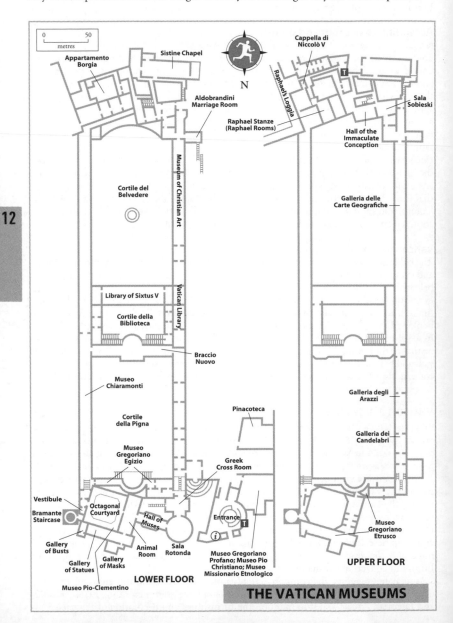

THE VATICAN MUSEUMS

THE VATICAN PALACE AND THE MUSEUMS' LAYOUT

The **Vatican Palace** complex was built piecemeal over the years, and in fact the two long corridors that make up most of the "museum" space were built to join the original palace next to St Peter's, constructed around 1450, with a newer building, the Belvedere, built on the higher ground to the north by Innocent VIII in 1490 as a summer casino. Bramante oversaw the connection of the two buildings in the 1500s, creating a vast courtyard that during the early sixteenth century was used for festivals and banquets, until Sixtus V divided it into separate quadrangles. It was divided again by the construction of the nineteenth-century Braccio Nuovo, resulting in its current form.

The museums occupy four principal structures: the **original Palace** at the end nearest St Peter's; the **Belvedere Palace** to the north, and the two long **galleries**. In the middle of all are the three **courtyards**: the **Cortile del Belvedere** at the southern end, the small **Cortile della Biblioteca** in the middle, created by the construction of the Vatican Library and Braccio Nuovo, and, the northernmost of the three, the **Cortile della Pigna** – named after the huge bronze pine cone mounted in the niche at the end, an ancient Roman artefact that was found close to the Pantheon. In classical times this was a fountain with water pouring out of each of its points. Also in this courtyard is a large modern bronze sculpture of a sphere within a sphere, which occasionally rotates – though to an erratic schedule. If you're on a guided tour, you'll stop here to be talked through the Sistine Chapel paintings before going in, as it's forbidden to speak inside. Even if you're not, it can be worth listening in if there's one being given in English, but be discreet.

The old main entrance to the museums was created by Pope Pius XI, in 1932, and its huge bronze spiral staircase, the work of one Giuseppe Momo, provides a dignified exit to the museums. On it are displayed the heraldic arms of all the popes from 1447 (Nicholas II) to Pius XI's predecessor (Benedict XV), while the staircase is in the form of a double helix, one half ascending, the other descending – an idea that Frank Lloyd Wright copied when designing the Guggenheim in New York. The museum entrance has since been modernized, and you now enter through a door in the bastion wall to the left of the monumental entrance, through a large hall and a new monumental marble staircase. An escalator carries you up to the actual museum. Finally, bear in mind that the collections of the Vatican Museums are in a constant state of restoration, and are often closed and shifted around with little or no notice, though the most important departments are usually open; check ⓦvatican.va for up-to-date details.

12

target of interest. Be conservative – the distances between different sections alone can be vast and very tiring.

Finally, bear in mind that in high season at least there may be a queue to get into the museums, and even getting here before opening may mean you have to stand in line for a while. It's always a good idea to **avoid Mondays**, when the rest of the city's museums are closed and everyone flocks to the Vatican and St Peter's, and getting to the museums late morning or after lunch can often mean a shorter wait. But the best thing to do is to pay a little extra and book online and thereby jump the queues altogether. The other thing you may want to do is take a **tour**: Enjoy Rome's are popular (see p.25), but you will be in a large group and tours take in St Peter's as well; Context Travel's tours (see p.25) are excellent, and focus just on the Vatican Museums.

Museo Pio-Clementino

To the left of the Museums' entrance, the **Museo Pio-Clementino** is home to some of the Vatican's best classical statuary, and is perhaps the only must-see apart from the Sistine Chapel and Raphael Rooms.

The Octagonal Courtyard

Its vestibule contains a copy of Lysippos's fourth-century BC statue *Apoxyomenos*, showing an athlete scraping dirt from his body, while the adjoining **Octagonal Courtyard** holds two statues that proved a huge influence on Renaissance artists: the serene *Apollo Belvedere*, in the left corner as you go in, a Roman copy of a fourth-century BC original, and the first-century BC *Laocoön* in the far left corner. The latter was discovered near Nero's Domus Aurea in 1506 by a ploughman who had inadvertently dug through the roof of a buried part of Trajan's Baths, and depicts the prophetic Trojan priest with his sons being crushed by serpents, sent by the gods to punish him for warning his fellow citizens of the danger of the Trojan horse. It is perhaps the most famous classical statue ever, referred to by Pliny who thought it carved from a single piece of marble, and written about by Byron – who described its contorted realism as "dignifying pain". Some scholars theorize that the statue is in fact a sixteenth-century fake by Michelangelo, which isn't as mad is it sounds – Michelangelo did design a substitute arm for the statue, and this was found to be an almost exact match for the "original". Diagonally opposite the *Apollo Belvedere* is a statue of Hermes that Poussin thought the greatest male nude he'd ever seen, while diagonally opposite the *Laocoön* is a group of nineteenth-century classical figures by Canova. In between the two stands a statue of Venus from the second century AD, said to be a portrait of Marcus Aurelius's wife Faustina.

Animal Room and Gallery of Masks

Leave the courtyard between the two howling dogs and you're in the **Animal Room**, named for its animal sculptures, although only a few are of ancient provenance and perhaps the most impressive features are the floor and wall mosaics, all from Hadrian's villa at Tivoli. There are more mosaics from Hadrian's villa through the Gallery of Statues in the small **Gallery of Masks**. This room is often closed but you can still peer in to see the masks, an ancient Roman toilet and the statue of Venus of Cnidos, the first known representation of the goddess, with towel and pitcher, and full of grace and movement.

Gallery of Statues and Gallery of Busts

The **Gallery of Statues** has an impressive array of ancient statuary along its long corridor, including two seated Roman nobles that mark its far end, from the first and third century BC. Beyond, the most interesting part of the **Gallery of Busts** is on your immediate right, where the shelves groan with great emperors, from Julius Caesar and Augustus (as a young man and also as a god, crowned with wheat) right up to Trajan at the other end. On the upper shelves you'll see how in subsequent centuries it became fashionable to sport a beard, starting with Antoninus Pius and Marcus Aurelius right up to the intense gaze of Caracalla.

Hall of the Muses

Back past the Animal Room, the frescoed **Hall of the Muses**, so called for the statues that line its central section, has as its centrepiece the so-called Belvedere Torso, which was found in the Campo de' Fiori during the reign of Julius II. It's signed by Apollonius, a Greek sculptor of the first century BC, and is generally thought to be a near-perfect example of male anatomy. Its portrayal, either of Hercules sitting on his lion skin or Ajax resting, was studied by most key Renaissance artists, including Michelangelo, who incorporated its turning pose into his portrait of *Christ in the Last Judgement* in the Sistine Chapel.

Sala Rotonda

A short corridor leads to the **Sala Rotonda**, centring on a vast bowl from the Domus Aurea and with a floor paved with a second-century AD Roman mosaic from the town of Otricoli, north of Rome, depicting battles between men and sea monsters. There is more classical statuary around the room, notably a huge gilded bronze statue of a rather dim-witted-looking Hercules, also from the second century AD and the only surviving gilded bronze statue on display in the Vatican Museums. On either side of the statue are busts of the Emperor Hadrian and his lover Antinous, who is also depicted in the same room, to the right of the entrance, as a huge statue dressed as Bacchus. Opposite this is a beautiful white marble statue of Claudius, in the guise of Jupiter, with his oak-leaf crown and an eagle at his feet.

Greek Cross Room

Beyond here, the **Greek Cross Room** is decorated in Egyptian style, although the pharaonic statues flanking the entry door are nineteenth-century imitations. Another Roman mosaic, from the second century AD, shows Minerva and the phases of the moon, while the two huge porphyry boxes are the sarcophagi of Helena and Constantia. On Helena's, soldiers vanquish their enemies, a reference to the fact that she was the mother of Constantine, while that of Constantia, the daughter of the emperor, shows putti carrying grapes, loaves of bread and lambs – a reference to the Eucharist, as she was a devout Christian.

Museo Gregoriano Egizio

The **Museo Gregoriano Egizio**, founded in the nineteenth century by Gregory XVI, isn't one of the Vatican's main highlights. But this says more about the rest of the Vatican than the museum, which has a distinguished collection of ancient Egyptian artefacts. It holds some vividly painted mummy cases (and two mummies), along with the alabaster vessels in which the entrails of the deceased were placed. There is also a partial reconstruction of the Temple of Serapis from Hadrian's Villa near Tivoli, along with another statue of his lover Antinous, who drowned close to the original temple in Egypt and so inspired Hadrian to build his replica – dressed here as Osiris. The Egyptian-style statues in shiny black basalt next door are also Roman imitations, as is the reclining figure of the Nile river god, complete with crocodile, next door. Hadrian collected some original Egyptian bits and pieces, too, some of which are housed in the room which curves around the niche containing the pine cone, including various Egyptian deities – look out for the laughing dwarf god Bes. The next rooms contain Egyptian bronzes from the late pharaonic period and early days of the Roman Empire, including a group of items from the cult of Isis, which became popular in Rome itself. Beyond are a couple of rooms with clay tablets inscribed in cuneiform writing from Mesopotamia; Assyrian, Sumerian and Persian bas-reliefs on stone tablets; and, in the last room, a lovely relief of a kneeling winged god from 850 BC.

Museo Gregoriano Etrusco

Past the entrance to the Egyptian Museum, a grand staircase, the Simonetti Stairs, leads up to the **Museo Gregoriano Etrusco**, which holds sculpture, funerary art and applied art from the sites of southern Etruria – a good complement to Rome's specialist Etruscan collection in the Villa Giulia, although you have to be keen on the Etruscans to visit both.

The Regolini-Galassi tomb

The first exhibits on display are finds from the seventh-century BC **Regolini-Galassi tomb**, which was discovered near Cerveteri, and contained the remains of three Etruscan nobles, two men and a woman; the breastplate of the woman and her huge fibula (clasp) are of gold. Take a look at the small ducks and lions with which they are decorated, fashioned in the almost microscopic beadwork for which Etruscan goldsmiths were famous. There's also armour, a bronze bedstead, a funeral chariot and a wagon, as well as several enormous storage jars, in which food, oil and wine were contained for use in the afterlife.

The Mars of Todi and finds from Northern Lazio

Beyond here are **Etruscan bronzes**, including weapons, candelabra, barbecue sets (skewers and braziers); beautiful make-up cases known as *cistae* and, most notably, the

12

so-called *Mars of Todi*, a three-quarter-size votive statue found in the Umbrian town of Todi. On a flap of the figure's armour an inscription gives the name of the donor. Further on, there is a large collection of Etruscan sarcophagi and stone statuary from Vulci, Tarquinia and Tuscania in northern Lazio. Particularly interesting here are the finely carved horses' heads from Vulci and the sarcophagus of a magistrate from Tarquinia which still bears traces of the paint its reliefs were coloured with. There is also Etruscan jewellery, with exquisite goldsmith work, crowns of golden oak and laurel leaves, necklaces, earrings and rings set with semiprecious stones and a fibula complete with the owner's name etched on it in such small writing that a magnifying glass is provided for you to read it.

The Statue of Adonis and Greek krater

Heading up some stairs from this room you come to a series of large rooms which look out from the north side of the Belvedere Palace and offer stunning views of the hill of Monte Mario. Inside, you'll find lots of vases, assorted weapons and items of everyday household use, as well as a magnificent terracotta **statue of Adonis** lying on a lacy couch, found near the town of Tuscania in the 1950s. Finally, don't miss the **Greek krater**, among a lot of Greek pottery found in Etruscan tombs, which shows Menelaus and Ulysses asking the Trojans for the return of Helen. It's housed in a special display case and can be rotated by pressing the electrical switch on the bottom of the case.

Galleria dei Candelabri

Outside the Etruscan Museum, the staircase leads back down to the main – and consequently crowded – Sistine route, taking you first through the **Galleria dei Candelabri**, the niches of which are adorned with huge candelabra taken from imperial Roman villas. This gallery is also stuffed with ancient sculpture, its most memorable piece a copy of the famous statue of Diana of Ephesus, on the right, whose multiple breasts are, according to the Vatican official line, bees' eggs.

Galleria degli Arazzi

Beyond Galleria dei Candelabri, the deliberately darkened **Galleria degli Arazzi** has, on the left, Belgian tapestries (*arazzi*)to designs by the school of Raphael which show scenes from the life of Christ and, on the right, tapestries made in Rome at the Barberini workshops during the 1600s, showing scenes from the life of Maffeo Barberini, who became Pope Urban VIII.

Galleria delle Carte Geografiche

By the Galleria degli Arazzi is the **Galleria delle Carte Geografiche** (Gallery of the Maps), which is as long (175m) as the previous two galleries put together. It was decorated in the late sixteenth century at the behest of Pope Gregory XIII, the reformer of the calendar, to show all of Italy, the major islands in the Mediterranean and the papal possessions in France, as well as large-scale maps of the maritime republics of Venice and Genoa. The maps are fantastic, illustrative yet precise, and this gallery, with its ceiling frescoes showing scenes that took place in the area depicted in each adjacent map, is considered by many to be the most beautiful in the entire museum complex.

Hall of the Immaculate Conception

After the Gallery of the Maps, there is a hall with more tapestries and, to the left, after one more room, the **Hall of the Immaculate Conception**, which sports nineteenth-century frescoes of Pope Pius IX declaring the Doctrine of the Immaculate Conception of the Blessed Virgin Mary on December 8, 1854. From here all visitors are directed to a covered walkway suspended over the palace courtyard of the Belvedere, which leads through to the Raphael Rooms.

Raphael Rooms

The **Raphael Rooms** or Stanze di Raffaello are, apart perhaps from the Sistine Chapel, the Vatican's greatest work of art. This set of rooms formed the private apartments of Pope Julius II, and when he moved in here he commissioned Raphael to redecorate them in a style more in tune with the times. Raphael died before the scheme was complete, but the two rooms that were completed by him, as well as others completed by pupils, are among the highlights of the Renaissance.

Stanza di Costantino

The first of the Raphael Rooms you come to, the **Stanza di Costantino**, was not in fact done by Raphael at all, but painted partly to his designs about five years after he died by his pupils Giulio Romano, Francesco Penni and Raffaello del Colle, between 1525 and 1531. It shows scenes from the life of the Emperor Constantine, who made Christianity the official religion of the Roman Empire. The enormous painting on the wall opposite the entrance is the *Battle of the Milvian Bridge* by Giulio Romano and Francesco Penni – a depiction of the decisive battle in 312 AD between the warring co-emperors of the West, Constantine and Maxentius. With due regard to the laws of propaganda, the victorious emperor is in the centre of the painting mounted on his white horse while the vanquished Maxentius drowns in the river to the right, clinging to his black horse. The painting to your left as you enter, the *Vision of Constantine* by Giulio Romano, shows Constantine telling his troops of his dream-vision of the Holy Cross inscribed with the legend "In this sign you will conquer". Opposite, the *Baptism of Constantine*, by Francesco Penni, is a flight of fancy; Constantine was baptized on his deathbed about thirty years after the battle of the Milvian Bridge.

Sala dei Chiaroscuri, Raphael's Loggia and the Cappella di Niccolò V

Beyond the Stanza di Costantino, the **Sala dei Chiaroscuri** was originally painted by Raphael, but curiously Pope Gregory XIII had his paintings removed and the room repainted in the rather gloomy style you see today – although there is a magnificent gilded and painted ceiling which bears the arms of the Medici. Through the windows you can glimpse a covered balcony known as **Raphael's Loggia**, which was built by Bramante in 1513 and decorated by Raphael and his pupils, but there's usually no entry to it. A small door on the other side of the room leads into the little **Cappella di Niccolò V**, with wonderful frescoes by Fra Angelico painted between 1448 and 1450, showing scenes in the lives of saints Stephen and Lawrence.

Stanza di Eliodoro

The **Stanza di Eliodoro** is really the first of the Raphael rooms proper, with a fresco on the right of the entrance, the *Expulsion of Heliodorus from the Temple*, that tells the story of Heliodorus, the agent of the Hellenistic king Seleucus IV, who was slain by a mysterious rider on a white horse while trying to steal the treasure of Jerusalem's Temple. It's an exciting piece of work, painted in the years 1512–14 for Pope Julius II, and the figures of Heliodorus, the horseman and the fleeing men are adeptly done, the figures almost jumping out of the painting into the room. The group of figures on the left, however, is more interesting – Pope Julius II, in his papal robes, Giulio Romano, the pupil of Raphael, and, to his left, Raphael himself in a self-portrait.

On the left wall as you enter, the *Mass of Bolsena* is a bit of anti-Lutheran propaganda, and relates a miracle that occurred in the town in northern Lazio in the 1260s, when a German priest who doubted the transubstantiation of Christ found the wafer bleeding when he broke it during a service – the napkin onto which it bled can be seen in the cathedral at Orvieto, 90km north of Rome. The pope facing the priest is another portrait of Julius II. The composition is a neat affair, the colouring rich, the onlookers kneeling, turning and gasping as the miracle is realized. On the window wall opposite, the *Deliverance of St Peter* shows the saint being assisted in a jail-break by the Angel of

12

the Lord – a night scene, whose clever chiaroscuro pre-dates Caravaggio by nearly one hundred years. It was painted by order of Pope Leo X, as an allegory of his imprisonment after a battle that took place in Ravenna a few years earlier. Finally, on the large wall opposite the *Expulsion of Heliodorus from the Temple, Leo I Repulsing Attila the Hun* is an allegory of the difficulties the papacy was going through in the early 1500s and shows the chubby cardinal Giovanni de' Medici, who succeeded J ulius II and became Leo X in 1513. Leo later had Raphael's pupils paint a portrait of himself as Leo I, so, confusingly, he appears twice in this fresco, as pope and as the equally portly Medici cardinal just behind.

Stanza della Segnatura

The next room, the **Stanza della Segnatura**, or Pope's Study, is probably the best known – and with good reason. Painted in the years 1508–11, when Raphael first came to Rome, the subjects were again the choice of Julius II, and, composed with careful balance and harmony, it comes close to the peak of the painter's art. The **School of Athens**, on the near wall as you come in, steals the show, a representation of the triumph of scientific truth in which all the great minds of antiquity are represented. Plato and Aristotle discuss philosophy at the centre of the painting: Aristotle, the father of scientific method, motions downwards; Plato, pointing upward, indicating his philosophy of otherworldly spirituality, is believed to be a portrait of Leonardo da Vinci. On the far right, the crowned figure holding a globe was meant to represent the Egyptian geographer, Ptolemy; to his right the young man in the black beret is Raphael, while in front, demonstrating a theorem to his pupils on a slate, the figure of Euclid is a portrait of Bramante.

Spread across the steps is Diogenes, lazily ignorant of all that is happening around him, while to the left Raphael added a solitary, sullen portrait of Michelangelo as Heraclitus writing – a homage to the artist, apparently painted after Raphael saw the first stage of the Sistine Chapel almost next door. Other identifiable figures include the beautiful youth with blonde hair on the left looking out of the painting, Francesco Maria della Rovere, placed here by order of Julius II. Della Rovere, the Duke of Urbino, also appears as the good-looking young man to the left of the seated dignitaries, in the painting opposite, the *Disputation over the Sacrament*, an allegory of the Christian religion and the main element of the Mass, the Blessed Sacrament – which stands at the centre of the painting being discussed by all manner of popes, cardinals, bishops, doctors, even the poet Dante.

Stanza dell'Incendio and Sala Sobieski

The last room, the **Stanza dell'Incendio**, was the last to be decorated, to the orders (and the general glorification) of Pope Leo X, and in a sense it brings together three generations of work. The ceiling was painted by Perugino, Raphael's teacher, and the frescoes completed to Raphael's designs by his pupils (notably Giulio Romano). The most striking of them is the *Fire in the Borgo*, facing the main window – an oblique reference to Leo X restoring peace to Italy after Julius II's reign but in fact describing an event that took place during the reign of Leo IV, when the pope stood in the loggia of the old St Peter's and made the sign of the cross to extinguish a fire. As with so many of these paintings, the chronology is deliberately crazy: Leo IV is in fact a portrait of Leo X, while on the left, Aeneas carries his aged father Anchises out of the burning city of Troy, two thousand years earlier. This last Raphael Room is connected to the **Sala Sobieski**, with its nineteenth-century painting of the Polish king driving Turks out of Europe, by the small Chapel of Urban VI, with frescoes and stuccoes by Pietro da Cortona.

Appartamento Borgia

Outside the Raphael Rooms, you can either proceed direct to the Sistine Chapel, or take the stairs down to the **Appartamento Borgia**, which was inhabited by Julius II's hated predecessor, Alexander VI – a fact which persuaded Julius to move into the new set of rooms he called upon Raphael to decorate. Nowadays host to a large collection of modern religious art, the Borgia rooms were almost exclusively decorated by Pinturicchio in the years 1492–95, on the orders of Alexander VI, though sadly the lighting is poor – more focused on the modern art than it is on the ceilings.

The first room is named after its ceiling decorations of the twelve sibyls, and the next shows Euclid kneeling at Geometry's throne above the fireplace, but it's the frescoes in the third, the **Sala dei Santi**, that are especially worth seeing, typically rich in colour and detail and depicting the legend of Osiris and the Apis bull – a reference to the Borgia family symbol. Among other images is a scene showing St Catherine of Alexandria disputing with the Emperor Maximilian, in which Pinturicchio has placed his self-portrait behind the emperor. The Arch of Constantine is clearly visible in the background. The figure of St Catherine is said to be a portrait of Lucrezia Borgia, and the room was reputedly the scene of a decidedly un-papal party to celebrate the first of Lucrezia's three marriages, which ended up with men tossing sweets down the fronts of the women's dresses.

The religious collection is spread throughout the main apartments and the forty or so rooms include works by some of the most famous names in the **modern art** world: a typically tortured Van Gogh *Pietà*; an exquisite pastel drawing of *Joan of Arc* by Redon; liturgical vestments designed by Matisse; a fascinating *Landscape with Angels* by Salvador Dalí, donated by King Juan Carlos of Spain; and one of Francis Bacon's studies of *Innocent X after Velázquez*.

Sistine Chapel

Steps lead up from the Appartamento Borgia to the **Sistine Chapel** (Cappella Sistina), a huge, barn-like structure built for Pope Sixtus IV between 1473 and 1483. It serves as the pope's official private chapel and the scene of the conclaves of cardinals for the election of each new pontiff. The ceiling paintings here, and the *Last Judgement* on the wall behind the altar, together make up arguably the greatest masterpiece in Western art, and the largest body of painting ever planned and executed by one man – **Michelangelo**. They are also probably the most viewed paintings in the world: it's estimated that on an average day about fifteen thousand people trudge through here to take a look, and during the summer and on special occasions the number of visitors can exceed twenty thousand. It's useful to carry a pair of binoculars with you in order to see the paintings better, but bear in mind that it is strictly forbidden to take pictures of any kind in the chapel, including video, and it is also officially forbidden to speak – although this is something that is rampantly ignored.

The wall paintings

Upon completion of the structure, Sixtus brought in several prominent painters of the Renaissance to decorate the walls. The overall project was under the management of Pinturicchio and comprised a series of paintings showing (on the left as you face the altar) scenes from the life of Moses and, on the right, scenes from the life of Christ. There are paintings by, among others, Perugino, who painted the marvellously composed cityscape of *Jesus Giving St Peter the Keys to Heaven*; Botticelli, with the *Trials of Moses and Cleansing of the Leper*; and Ghirlandaio, whose *Calling of St Peter and St Andrew* shows Christ calling the two fishermen to be disciples, surrounded by onlookers, against a fictitious medieval landscape of boats, birds, turrets and mountains. Some of the paintings were in fact collaborative efforts, and it's known that Ghirlandaio and Botticelli in particular contributed to each other's work. Anywhere else they would be pored over very closely indeed. As it is, they are entirely overshadowed by Michelangelo's more famous work.

The ceiling frescoes

Michelangelo's frescoes depict scenes from the Old Testament, from the *Creation of Light* at the altar end to the *Drunkenness of Noah* over the door. The sides are decorated

12

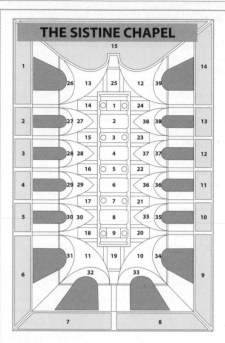

THE SISTINE CHAPEL

CEILING PAINTINGS

1 The Creation of Light

2 The Creation of the Sun and the Moon

3 The Separation of Land and Water

4 The Creation of Adam

5 The Creation of Eve

6 The Temptation and Expulsion from the Garden of Eden

7 The Sacrifice of Noah

8 The Story of the Flood

9 The Drunkenness of Noah

10 David and Goliath

11 Judith and Holofernes

12 The Punishment of Haman

13 The Brazen Serpent

14 The Libyan Sibyl

15 Daniel

16 The Cumaean Sibyl

17 Isaiah

18 The Delphic Sibyl

19 Zachariah

20 Joel

21 The Erythraean Sibyl

22 Ezekiel

23 The Persian Sibyl

24 Jeremiah

25 Jonah and the Whale

26 Aminadab

27 Salmon, Booz, Obed

28 Roboam, Abia

29 Ozias, Joatham, Achaz

30 Zorobabel, Abiud, Elichiam

31 Achim, Eliud

32 Jacob, Joseph

33 Eleazar, Matthan

34 Azor, Sadoch

35 Josias, Jechonias, Salathiel

36 Ezekias, Manasses, Amon

37 Asa, Josophat, Joram

38 Jesse, David, Solomon

39 Naasson

WALL PAINTINGS

1 Perugino
Moses' Journey into Egypt

2 Botticelli
The Trials of Moses

3 Rosselli
Crossing of the Red Sea

4 Rosselli
Moses and the Law

5 Botticelli
Punishment of the Rebels

6 Signorelli
Testament and Death of Moses

7 Matteo da Lecce
Fight over the Body of Moses

8 Arrigo Palludano
Resurrection of Christ

9 Rosselli
Last Supper

10 Perugino
Jesus giving St Peter the Keys of Heaven

11 Rosselli
Sermon on the Mount

12 Ghirlandaio
Calling of St Peter and St Andrew

13 Botticelli
Cleansing of the Leper

14 Perugino
Baptism of Christ

15 Michelangelo
The Last Judgement

with prophets and sibyls and the ancestors of Jesus. Julius II lived only a few months after the Sistine Chapel ceiling was finished, but the fame of the work he had commissioned soon spread far and wide. Certainly, it's staggeringly impressive, all the more so for its recent restoration (financed by a Japanese TV company to the tune of $3 million in return for three years' world TV rights), which has lifted centuries of accumulated soot and candle grime off the ceilings to reveal a much brighter, more vivid painting than anyone thought existed.

The decorative scheme

The restorers have also been able to chart the progress of Michelangelo as he moved across the vault. Images on fresco were completed before the plaster dried, and each day a fresh layer of plaster would have been laid, on which Michelangelo would have had around eight hours or so before having to finish for the day. Comparing the different areas of plaster, it seems the figure of Adam, in the key *Creation of Adam* scene, took four days; God, in the same fresco, took three. You can also see the development of Michelangelo as a painter when you look at the paintings in reverse order. The first painting, over the door, the *Drunkenness of Noah*, is done in a stiff and formal style, and is vastly different from the last painting, the *Creation of Light*, over the altar, which shows the artist at his best, the perfect master of the technique of fresco painting.

Entering from behind the altar, you are supposed, as you look up, to imagine that you are peering into heaven through the arches of the imaginary architecture that springs from the sides of the chapel, supported by little putti caryatids and *ignudi* or nudes, bearing shields and the oak-leaf garlands of the Della Rovere family of Julius II. Look at the pagan sibyls and biblical prophets which Michelangelo also incorporated in his scheme – some of the most dramatic figures in the entire work, and all clearly labelled by the painter, from the sensitive figure of the Delphic Sibyl to the hag-like Cumaean Sibyl, whose biceps would put a Bulgarian shot-putter to shame. Look out, too, for the figure of the prophet Jeremiah – a brooding self-portrait of an exhausted-looking Michelangelo.

The paintings

We've detailed the paintings of the central panels in the chart (see opposite), but, specifically, they start with a large portrait of *Jonah and the Whale* and move on, consecutively, to the *Creation of Light* – God's arms bowed, beard flowing, as he separates light from darkness; the *Creation of the Sun and the Moon*, in which Michelangelo has painted God twice, once with his back to us hurling the moon into existence and simultaneously displaying another moon to the audience; the *Separation of Land and Water*; and, in the fourth panel, probably most famous of all these paintings, the *Creation of Adam*, in which God sparks Adam into life with the touch of his finger. God's cape billows behind him, where a number of figures stand – representatives of all the unborn generations to come after Adam. The startled young woman looking at Adam is either Eve or the Virgin Mary, here as a witness to the first events in human history.

The fifth panel from the altar shows the *Creation of Eve*, in which Adam is knocked out under the stump of a Della Rovere oak tree and God summons Eve from his side as he sleeps. She comes out in a half-crouch position with her hands clasped in a prayer of thanksgiving and awe. The sixth panel is the powerful *Temptation and Expulsion from the Garden of Eden*, with an evil spirit, depicted as a serpent, leaning out from the tree of knowledge and handing the fruit to Adam. On the right of this painting the Angel of the Lord, in swirling red robes, is brandishing his sword of original sin at the nape of Adam's neck as he tries to fend the angel off, motioning with both hands. The eighth panel continues the story, with the *Story of the Flood*, the unrighteous bulk of mankind taking shelter under tents from the rain while Noah and his kin make off for the Ark in the distance. Panel seven shows the *Sacrifice of Noah* as he and his family make a

---

JULIUS II AND THE ORIGINS OF THE SISTINE CHAPEL FRESCOES

When construction was completed in 1483 during the reign of Pope Sixtus IV, the Sistine Chapel ceiling was painted as a blue background with gold stars to resemble the night sky. Over the altar there were two additional paintings by Perugino and a large picture of the Virgin Mary. Sixtus IV was succeeded by Innocent VIII, who was followed by Alexander VI, the Borgia pope who, after the brief reign of Pius III, was succeeded in 1503 by Giuliano della Rovere, who took the name **Julius II**. Though a Franciscan friar, he was a violent man with a short temper; his immediate objective as pope was to try to regain the lands that had been taken away from the papacy during the reigns of Innocent VIII and Alexander VI by the French, Germans and Spanish. For this purpose he started a series of wars and secret alliances.

Julius II was also an avid collector and patron of the arts, and he summoned to Rome the best artists and architects of the day. Among these was **Michelangelo**, who, through a series of political intrigues orchestrated by Bramante and Raphael, was assigned the task of decorating the Sistine Chapel. Work commenced in 1508. Oddly enough, Michelangelo hadn't wanted to do the work at all: he considered himself a sculptor, not a painter, and was more eager to get on with carving Julius II's tomb – now in San Pietro in Vincoli (see p.113) – than the ceiling, which he regarded as a chore. Pope Julius II, however, had other plans, drawing up a design of the twelve Apostles for the vault and hiring Bramante to design a scaffold for the artist to work from. Michelangelo was apparently an awkward, solitary character: he had barely begun painting when he rejected Bramante's scaffold as unusable, fired all his staff and dumped the pope's scheme for the ceiling in favour of his own. But the pope was easily his match, and there are tales of the two men clashing while the work was going on – Michelangelo would lock the doors at crucial points, ignoring the pope's demands to see how it was progressing, and legend has the two men at loggerheads at the top of the scaffold one day, resulting in the pope striking the artist in frustration.

12

---

sacrifice of thanksgiving to the Lord for their safe arrival after the flood; one of Noah's sons kneels to blow on the fire to make it hotter, while his wife brings armloads of wood. Lastly, there's the *Drunkenness of Noah*, in which Noah is shown getting drunk after harvesting the vines and exposing his genitals to his sons – it is strictly prohibited in the Hebrew canon for a father to show his reproductive organs to his children. Oddly enough, Noah's sons are naked too.

The Last Judgement

The Last Judgement, on the altar wall of the chapel, was painted by Michelangelo more than twenty years later, between 1535 and 1541. Michelangelo wasn't especially keen to work on this either – he was still engaged on Julius II's tomb, under threat of legal action from the late pope's family – but Pope Paul III, an old acquaintance of the artist, was keen to complete the decoration of the chapel. Michelangelo tried to delay by making demands that were likely to cause the pope to give up entirely, insisting on the removal of two paintings by Perugino and the closing of a window that pierced the end of the chapel. Furthermore, he insisted that the wall be replastered, with the top 15cm out of the perpendicular to prevent the accumulation of soot and dust. Surprisingly, the pope agreed.

The painting took **five years**, again single-handed, and is probably the most inspired and most homogeneous large-scale painting you'll ever see, Michelangelo's technical virtuosity taking a back seat to the sheer exuberance of the work. The human body is fashioned into a finely captured set of exquisite poses, in which even the damned can be seen as a celebration of the human form. Perhaps unsurprisingly, the painting offended some, and even before it was complete **Rome was divided** as to its merits, especially regarding the etiquette of introducing a display of nudity into the pope's private chapel. But Michelangelo's response to this was unequivocal, lampooning one of his fiercer critics, the pope's master of ceremonies at the time, Biagio di Cesena, as Minos, the doorkeeper of hell, with ass's ears and an entwined serpent in the bottom right-hand corner of the picture. Later the pope's zealous successor, **Pius IV**, objected to the painting and would have had it removed entirely had not Michelangelo's pupil, **Daniele da Volterra**, appeased him by carefully – and selectively – adding coverings to some of the more obviously naked figures, forever earning himself the nickname of the "breeches-maker". During the recent work, most of the remaining breeches have been discreetly removed, restoring the painting to its former glory.

Briefly, the painting shows the last day of existence, when the bodily resurrection of the dead takes place and the human race is brought before **Christ** to be either sent to eternity in Paradise or condemned to suffer in Hell. The centre is occupied by Christ, turning angrily as he gestures the condemned to the underworld. **St Peter**, carrying his gold and silver keys, looks on in astonishment at his Lord filled with rage, while **Mary** averts her eyes from the scene. Below Christ a group of angels blasts their trumpets to summon the dead from their sleep. Somewhat amusingly, one angel holds a large book, the book of the damned, while another carries a much smaller one, the book of the saved. On the left, the dead awaken from their graves, tombs and sarcophagi (one apparently has the likeness of Martin Luther) and levitate into the heavens or are pulled by ropes and the napes of their necks by angels who take them before Christ. At the bottom right, **Charon**, keeper of the underworld, swings his oar at the damned souls as they fall off the boat into the waiting gates of Hell. Among other characters portrayed are many martyred saints, **the Apostles**, Adam and, peeking out between the legs of the saint on the left of Christ, **Julius II**, with a look of fear and astonishment.

Museum of Christian Art

After the Sistine Chapel, you're channelled all the way to the exit by way of the **Museum of Christian Art**, which is not of great interest in itself, but does give access to a small room off to the left that contains a number of ancient Roman frescoes and mosaics, among them the celebrated *Aldobrandini Wedding*, a first-century BC Roman fresco that shows the preparations for a wedding in touching detail. Other items in a room that is extremely rich in interest include frescoes showing scenes from the *Odyssey*, and another, later piece from Ostia depicting a ship being loaded with grain, as well as some fantastic mosaics of wild beasts.

12

Vatican Library

The Museum of Christian Art corridor turns into the **Vatican Library**, home to around a million books and manuscripts (you can't touch any of them) and decorated with scenes of Rome and the Vatican as it used to look. Over one of the doors of the corridor you can see the facade of St Peter's as it was in the late 1500s, before Maderno's extension of the nave; over the facing door you can see the erection of the obelisk outside in the Piazza San Pietro, showing the men, ropes, animals and a primitive derrick, with the obelisk being drawn forward on a sled. Beyond, the corridor opens out into the dramatic **Library of Sixtus V** on the right, a vast hall built across the courtyard in the late sixteenth century to glorify literature – and of course Sixtus V himself.

Braccio Nuovo

Off the Cortile della Pigna, the **Braccio Nuovo** and Museo Chiaramonti (see below) both hold classical sculpture, although be warned that they are the Vatican at its most overwhelming – close on a thousand statues crammed into two long galleries – and you need a keen eye and much perseverance to make any sense of it all. The Braccio Nuovo was built in the early 1800s to display **classical statuary** that was particularly prized, and it contains, among other things, probably the most famous extant image of Augustus addressing the army, hand outstretched, found on the Via Flaminia, near the Villa di Livia (the cupid riding the dolphin is a reference to the imperial family's descent from Venus and her son Aeneas). There's also a nice statue of Silenus clutching an infant Dionysus nearby, and a bizarre-looking statue depicting the Nile, whose yearly flooding was essential to the fertility of the Egyptian soil. It is this aspect of the river that is represented here: crawling over the hefty river god are sixteen babies, thought to allude to the number of cubits the river needed to rise to fertilize the land.

Museo Chiaramonti

The 300-metre-long **Chiaramonti gallery** is especially unnerving, lined with the chill marble busts of hundreds of nameless, blank-eyed ancient Romans, along with the odd deity (such as a colossal head of Neptune from Hadrian's villa). It pays to have a leisurely wander, for there are some real characters here: sour, thin-lipped matrons with their hair tortured into pleats, curls and spirals; kids, caught in a sulk or mid-chortle; and ancient men with flesh sagging and wrinkling to reveal the skull beneath. Many of these heads are ancestral portraits, kept by the Romans in special shrines in their houses to venerate their familial predecessors, and in some cases family resemblances can be picked out. The fine head of Athena, on the right, has kept her glass eyes, a reminder that most of these statues were originally painted to resemble life, with eyeballs where now a blank space stares out.

Pinacoteca

The **Pinacoteca**, housed in a separate building on the far side of the Vatican's main spine, ranks possibly as Rome's best picture gallery, with works from the early primitives right up to the nineteenth century.

The Gothic period to the Umbrian School

The display is chronological, and starts with a beautiful collection of works from the **Gothic period**, among them an amazing, almost mosaic-like *Last Judgement* by Nicolò and Giovanni from the second half of the twelfth century in the first room, and the stunning Simoneschi triptych by Giotto in the next room, depicting the *Martyrdom of Sts Peter and Paul* and painted in the early 1300s for the old St Peter's, where it remained until 1506 when it was removed for the rebuilding of the new church. In the rooms that follow are lovely pieces by Masolino, Fra Angelico and Filippo Lippi, while the next room has the **naturalistic works** of Marco Palmezzano and Melozzo da Forlí's musical angels – fragments of a fresco commissioned for the family church of Santi Apostoli by Giuliano della Rovere, the future Pope Julius II. Another part of the same fresco resides in the Palazzo Quirinale (see p.109). Julius II also makes an appearance in da Forlí's *Sixtus IV Opening the Vatican Library* in the same room – he's the large figure in red, and the painting is as much a family scene as anything, also showing the pope's brother Raffaele Riario (Giuliano's father) behind him (in blue), another nephew, Girolamo, also in blue, and on the far left Giuliano's brother Giovanni, then the prefect of Rome. The next room holds Carlo Crivelli's magnificently angst-ridden *Pietà*, while beyond here lie the rich backdrops and elegantly clad figures of the **Umbrian School** painters, Perugino and Pinturicchio.

Raphael and Leonardo

Raphael has a room to himself, with three very important oil paintings, and, in climate-controlled glass cases, the tapestries that were made to his designs to be hung in the Sistine Chapel during conclave. The cartoons from which these tapestries were made are now in the Victoria and Albert Museum in London. Of the three paintings, the *Coronation of the Virgin*, on the right, was done when he was only 19 years old; the *Transfiguration*, in the middle, was interrupted by his death in 1520 and finished by his pupils; and the *Madonna of Foligno*, on the left, shows saints John the Baptist, Francis of Assisi and Jerome, and was painted as an offering after a cannonball (in the centre of the painting) struck his house. Leonardo's **St Jerome**, in the next room, is unfinished, too, but it's a remarkable piece of work, with Jerome a rake-like ascetic torn between suffering and a good meal. Look closely at this painting and you can see that a 25-centimetre square, the saint's head, has been reglued to the canvas after

12

the painting was used as upholstery for a stool in a cobbler's shop in Rome for a number of years.

Caravaggio and beyond

Caravaggio's *Descent from the Cross*, two rooms on, however, gets more attention, a warts 'n' all canvas that unusually shows the Virgin Mary as a middle-aged mother grieving over her dead son, while the men placing Christ's body on the bier are models that the artist recruited from the city streets – a realism that is imitated successfully in Reni's *Crucifixion of St Peter* in the same room: the Baroque at full throttle. Take a look, too, at the most gruesome painting in the collection, Poussin's *Martyrdom of St Erasmus*, which shows the saint stretched out on a table with his hands bound above his head in the process of having his small intestine wound onto a drum – basically being "drawn" prior to "quartering". The views over the Vatican Gardens nearby, with the dome of St Peter's in the background, provide a suitable antidote if you need it.

Museo Gregoriano Profano

Outside the Pinacoteca, you're well placed for the further grouping of museums in the modern building next door – and their lack of popularity can be something of a relief from the crowds in the rest of the museum. The **Museo Gregoriano Profano** holds more classical sculpture, mounted on scaffolds for all-round viewing, including mosaics of athletes from the Baths of Caracalla and Roman funerary work, notably the Haterii tomb friezes, which show backdrops of ancient Rome and realistic portrayals of contemporary life. It's thought the Haterii were a family of construction workers and that they grabbed the opportunity to advertise their services by incorporating reliefs of the buildings they had worked on (including the Colosseum), along with a natty little crane, on the funeral monument of one of their female members.

12

Museo Pio Cristiano

The **Museo Pio Cristiano**, adjacent to the Museo Gregoriano Profano, has intricate early Christian sarcophagi and, most famously, an expressive late-third-century AD statue of the Good Shepherd – a subject you'll see on many of the other fourth-century sarcophagi nearby. One of the best is the "Two Brothers" sarcophagus from 325 AD, swathed in biblical scenes and meditations on the deceased.

Museo Filatelico e Numismatico

The **Museo Filatelico e Numismatico**, below, is unsurprisingly quiet, displaying stamps and coins from the Vatican through the ages, while below that the **Museo Missionario Etnologico** has art and artefacts from China, Japan and the rest of the Far East collected by Catholic missionaries. It's quite enlightened in its way, at pains to explain the principles of Taoism, Buddhism, Shintoism and the rest, and keen to point out that missionary work is not about conquest, but there's no getting away from the fact that this is the darkest and most neglected part of the entire museum complex.

Day-trips from Rome

You may find there's quite enough of interest in Rome to keep you occupied during your stay. But it can be a hot, oppressive city, and if you're around long enough you really shouldn't feel any guilt about seeing something of the countryside. Two of the most popular day-trip attractions are admittedly ancient Roman sites (Ostia Antica and Hadrian's Villa at Tivoli), but just the process of getting to them can be energizing. North of the city, the Etruscan sites of Cerveteri and Tarquinia are atmospheric alternatives, and Bracciano has an airy lakeside location. To the south, the Castelli Romani provide the most appealing stretch of countryside close to Rome, and the coastal towns of Anzio one of its most accessible beaches, although there are many choices if all you want to do is flop (see p.222).

Tivoli and around

Perched high on a hill and looking back over the plain, **Tivoli** has always been something of a retreat from the city, due to its fresh mountain air and pleasant position on the Aniene River. In classical days it was a retirement town for wealthy Romans; later, during the Renaissance, it again became the playground of the moneyed classes, attracting some of the city's most well-to-do families out here to build villas. Nowadays the leisured classes have mostly gone, but Tivoli does very nicely on the fruits of its still-thriving travertine business, exporting the precious stone worldwide (the quarries line the main road into town from Rome), and supports a small airy centre that preserves a number of relics from its ritzier days. To do justice to its celebrated villas, Villa d'Este, Villa Gregoriana and Villa Adriana – especially if the latter is on your list – you'll need most of the day; set out early, and try to be in Tivoli by mid-morning at the latest.

Villa d'Este

Piazza Trento 5 • Tues–Sun: May–Aug 8.30am–6.45pm; Sept 8.30am–6.15pm, Oct 8.30am–5.30pm, Jan, Nov & Dec 8.30am–4pm, Feb 8.30am–5.15pm, April 8.30am–6.30pm • €8 • ☎ 199 766 166, ⓦ www.villadestetivoli.info • The Villa d'Este is a 2min walk from Tivoli's Piazza Garibaldi

Tivoli's major sight is the **Villa d'Este**, across the main square of Largo Garibaldi. Once a convent, it was transformed into a country villa by Pirro Ligorio in 1550 for Cardinal Ippolito d'Este, and is now often thronged with visitors even outside peak season. The villa itself is worth a visit: it has been recently restored to its original state, with beautiful Mannerist frescoes in its seven ground-floor rooms showing scenes from the history of the d'Este family in Tivoli.

But most people come here to see the **gardens**, which peel away down the hill in a succession of terraces. It's probably the most contrived garden in Italy, but also the most ingenious, almost completely symmetrical, its carefully tended lawns, shrubs and hedges interrupted at decent intervals by one playful fountain after another. Newly restored and once again fully open to the public, the **fountains** are collectively unique and a must-see if you're in Tivoli; just make sure that you don't touch or drink the water in the fountains – it comes directly from the operating sewers of Tivoli.

Among the highlights, the central, almost Gaudí-like **Fontana del Bicchierone**, by Bernini, is one of the simplest and most elegant. On the right lies the Fontana dell'Ovato, topped with statues on a curved terrace around artificial mountains, behind which is a rather dank – and accessible – arcade; beyond are the dark, gushing Grottoes of the Sibyls. Behind this the Fontana dell'Organo is a giant and very elaborate water organ, whose air pipes are forced by water valves, and play every couple of hours. Right in front, the similarly large Fontana del Nettuno ejects a massive torrent down into a set of central fish ponds, while at the far end the many pendulous breasts of the somewhat denuded fountain of Diana of Ephesus gush yet more water. Finish up on the far side of the garden, where the Rometta or "Little Rome" has reproductions of the city's major buildings and a boat holding an obelisk.

Villa Gregoriana

Piazza Tempio di Vesta • March, Nov & Dec Tues–Sat 10am–4pm; April–Oct Tues–Sun 10am–6.30pm • €6 • ☎ 0774 332650, ⓦ villagregoriana.it • To get to the Villa Gregoriana, turn right off Piazza Garibaldi in Tivoli to Piazza Santa Croce and follow Via del Trivio through the pedestrianized old town to Piazza del Plebiscito, where Via Palatina continues down to the bridge over the gorge. Cross over, and the back entrance is just around the corner on the left – a 10min walk in all

Tivoli's other main attraction, the **Villa Gregoriana** isn't actually a villa at all, but an impressively wild set of landscaped gardens, created when Pope Gregory XVI diverted the flow of the river here to ease the periodic flooding of the town in 1831. At least as interesting and beautiful as the d'Este estate, it remains less well known and less visited, and has none of the latter's conceits – its vegetation is lush and overgrown, descending into a gorge over 60m deep. It's harder work than the Villa d'Este – if you blithely

13

saunter down to the bottom of the gorge, you'll find that it's a long way back up the other side – but it is in many ways more rewarding.

There are two main **waterfalls** – the larger Grande Cascata on the far side, and a small Bernini-designed one at the neck of the gorge. The best thing to do is walk the main path in reverse, starting at the back entrance, over the river, and winding down to the bottom of the canyon. The ruins of a Republican-era villa cling to the far side of the gorge, and you can peek into them and then catch your breath down by the so-called

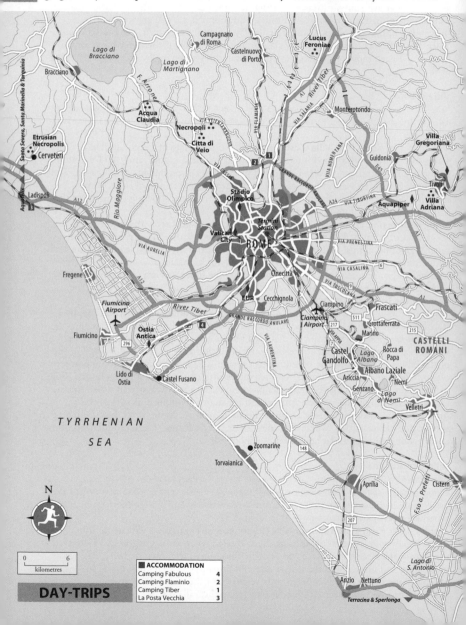

DAY-TRIPS

■ ACCOMMODATION
Camping Fabulous	4
Camping Flaminio	2
Camping Tiber	1
La Posta Vecchia	3

13

Grotto of the Mermaid, before scaling the other side to the Grotto of Neptune, reached by a tunnelled-out passage through the rock, where you can sit right by the roaring falls, the dark, torn shapes of the rock glowering overhead. The path leads up from here to an exit and the substantial remains of an ancient **Temple of Vesta**, which you'll have seen perched on the side of the hill, and which marks the main entrance to the villa. You can take a breather at the small **café** here, and the view is probably Tivoli's best – down into the chasm and across to the high green hills that ring the town.

Villa Adriana

Via Imperatore Adriano • Daily 9am–1hr before sunset • €12 • ⓦ villaadriana.beniculturali.it • The Auditorium in Rome organizes a series of open-air music and dance events here from mid-June to mid-July; see ⓦ auditorium.com/villaadriana for details • ☎ 06 3996 7900 •
Ask the Rome–Tivoli bus to drop you off, or take the CAT #4 bus from Tivoli's Piazza Garibaldi; it's a 10min walk from the main road

Once you've seen the two villas in town you've really seen Tivoli – the rest of the town is nice enough but there's not much to it. But just outside, at the bottom of the hill, the **Villa Adriana** puts the achievements of the Tivoli popes and cardinals very much into the shade. This was probably the largest and most sumptuous villa in the Roman Empire, the retirement home of the Emperor Hadrian between 135 AD and his death three years later, and it occupies an enormous site. You need time to see it all; there's no point in doing it at a gallop and, taken with the rest of Tivoli, it makes for a long day's sightseeing.

The site

The site is one of the most soothing spots around Rome, its stones almost the epitome of romantic, civilized ruins. The imperial palace buildings proper are in fact one of the least well-preserved parts of the complex, but much else is clearly recognizable. Hadrian was a great traveller and a keen architect, and parts of the villa were inspired by buildings he had seen around the world. The massive **Pecile**, for instance, through which you enter, is a reproduction of a building in Athens. The **Canopus**, on the opposite side of the site, is a liberal copy of the sanctuary of Serapis near Alexandria, its long, elegant channel of water fringed by sporadic columns and statues leading up to a temple of Serapis at the far end. Near the Canopus a **museum** displays the latest finds from the ongoing excavations, though most of the extensive original discoveries have found their way back to Rome and many museums in Europe. Walking back towards the entrance, make your way across the upper storey of the so-called Pretorio, a former warehouse, and down to the remains of two **bath complexes**. Beyond is a fish pond with a **cryptoporticus** (underground passageway) winding around underneath. It's enjoyable to walk through the cryptoporticus and look up at its ceiling, picking out the names of the seventeenth- and eighteenth-century artists (Bernini, for one) who visited and wrote their signatures here using a smoking candle. Behind this are the relics of the emperor's imperial apartments. The **Teatro Marittimo**, adjacent, with its island in the middle of a circular pond, is the place to which it's believed Hadrian would retire at siesta time to be sure of being alone.

ARRIVAL AND DEPARTURE · TIVOLI

By bus Buses for Tivoli leave every 10min from outside Ponte Mammolo metro station in Rome (line B), dropping off on Tivoli's main square, Piazza Garibaldi (journey time 30–45min).

EATING AND DRINKING

Ai Portici Piazza Garibaldi 5. Right in the centre of town, this is a good place to get a piece of *baccalà* or slice of pizza, and has tables outside. It's just two minutes from the Villa d'Este, so handy for a break between sights. Daily 8am–8pm.

Sibilla Via Sibilla 50 ☎ 0774 335 281, ⓦ ristorantesibilla .com. Overlooking the Villa Gregoriana park, this is the most scenically situated restaurant in Tivoli, and also serves some of its best food, with great pasta in particular, and a fantastic setting if you can bag an outside table. Daily except Mon noon–3pm & 7.30–11.30pm.

13 Ostia Antica

Viale dei Romagnoli 717 • Nov to mid–Feb Tues–Sun 8.30am–4.30pm; mid–Feb to mid–March Tues–Sun 8.30am–5pm; late March Tues–Sun 8.30am–5.30pm; April–Sept Tues–Sun 8.30am–7pm; Oct Tues–Sun 8.30am–6.30pm • last admission 1hr before closing • Museo Ostiense same hours, but opens at 10.30am • €10; parking €2.50 • ☎ 06 5635 0215, ⓦ ostiaantica.beniculturali.it

There are two Ostias. One is the over-visited seaside resort of Lido di Ostia (see p.222), while the other is one of the finest ancient Roman sites you'll find, comprising the excavated remains of the port of **Ostia Antica**. These ruins are on a par with anything you'll see in Rome itself and easily merit a half-day out.

The site of Ostia Antica marked the coastline in classical times, and the town which grew up here was the port of ancient Rome, a thriving place whose commercial activities were vital to the city further upstream – until the Emperor Constantine developed a new port nearby (of which nothing survives). Until the 1970s, the site was only open one day a week and few people realized how well the port had been preserved by the Tiber's mud, but in recent decades more and more of the port has been unearthed and nowadays it's much easier to conjure the look and feel of a Roman town from this than from any amount of pottering around the Forum – or even Pompeii. It's an evocative site too, in part at least because it's relatively unvisited, but it is also very spread out, so be prepared for a fair amount of walking. Carry some **water** and maybe even bring a picnic – there's a **café-restaurant** on the site, but it's nothing special. Also be aware that signage on the site is poor.

The site

From the entrance, the **Via Ostiense** leads west, passing an ancient burial ground on the left (the Romans always buried their dead outside the city walls), before reaching the scant remains of the **Porta Romana**, once a main gate. Beyond, the **Decumanus Maximus**, main street of Ostia, passes the tumbledown **Baths of the Cisiarii** on the right before reaching, also on the right, a pavement **mosaic** inscribed with a cup that marks what would have been a bar, the **Caupona di Fortunato**. Then **Via della Fontana** that leads off here is a wonderfully preserved street, which gives a good idea of a typical Roman urban layout, with its ground-floor shops and upper-floor apartments. The fountain that gives the street its name is on the right, a long coffin-shaped thing that would have been a source of fresh water for the homes and businesses nearby. About halfway along, turn right down Via della Palestra and on the left is the **Caserma dei Vigili**, the barracks of the nightwatch, where the courtyard includes a shrine devoted to the cult of the Emperor.

Piazzale delle Corporazioni

Back on Decumanus Maximus, it's just a few metres to the town's commercial centre, **Piazzale delle Corporazioni**, where the remains of shops and trading offices still fringe the central square. These represented commercial enterprises from all over the ancient world and each was once fronted by a mosaic of boats, fish and suchlike to denote their trade as well as their origin (Carthage, for example). Flanking the southern side of the square, the **theatre** has been much restored but is nonetheless impressive, enlarged by Septimius Severus in the second century AD to hold up to four thousand people; it sometimes hosts performances of classical drama during the summer. On the left-hand side of the square, mosaic floors and a dark-aisled **mithraeum** (a shrine devoted to the cult of Mithras) were unearthed in the **House of Apuleius**, but these are currently kept under wraps.

Casa Diana and Thermopolium

Returning to the main street, Decumanus Maximus runs past the substantial remains of one of Ostia's largest *horrea* (warehouses), buildings that once stood all over the city. Then you turn right up **Via dei Molini** to reach the **Casa Diana**, probably the best-preserved private house in Ostia, with a dark series of rooms set around a central courtyard, and again with a mithraeum at the back. Just along the street is the

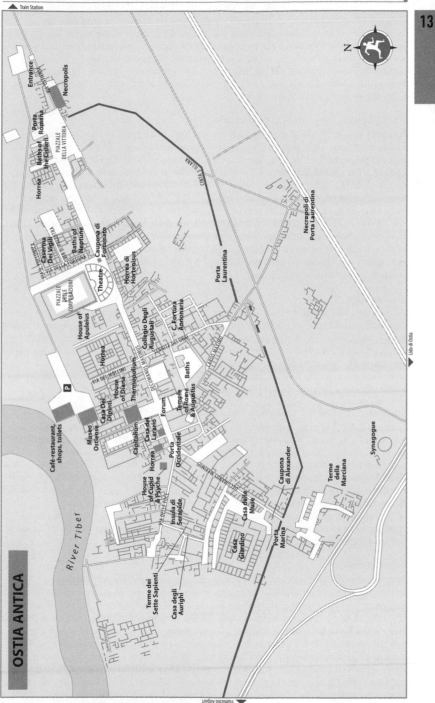

OSTIA ANTICA

Train Station

N

River Tiber

Café-restaurant, shops, toilets

Entrance

Necropolis

Porta Romana

Baths of the Cisiarii

PIAZZALE DELLA VITTORIA

Horrea

Caserma Dei Vigili

Baths of Neptune

Caupona di Fortunato

VIA DELLA FORTUNA

VIA DELLA CASA DI DIANA

Theatre

Horrea di Hortensius

House of Apuleius

PIAZZALE DELLE CORPORAZIONI

Collegio Degli Augustali

C. Fortuna Annonaria

Porta Laurentina

Horrea

VIA DEI MOLLINI

Thermopolium

House of Diana

DECUMANUS MAXIMUS

Baths

SEMITA DEI CIPPI

VIA DELLA FOCE

CARDO MAXIMUS

Museo Ostiense

P

Casa Dei Dipinti

Casa del Larario

Forum

Temple of Rome & Augustus

Capitolium

Horrea

Porta Occidentale

House of Cupid & Psyche

DECUMANUS MAXIMUS

Insula di Serapide

Caupona di Alexander

Terme della Marciana

Synagogue

Terme dei Sette Sapienti

Casa degli Aurighi

Casa Giardino

Casa delle Muse

Porta Marina

CINTA DI SILLANA

Necropoli di Porta Laurentina

Lido di Ostia

Fiumicino Airport

13

delightful **Thermopolium**, an ancient Roman café, complete with seats outside, a high counter, display shelves and even wall paintings of parts of the menu. At the back is a marble wall slab which once held hooks for hanging coats, beyond which is what would have been a small courtyard with a fountain. Opposite the Thermopolium, steps lead to the top of the **Casa dei Dipinti**, giving a fine view over the site. The house itself is sometimes locked but if you can get in you'll be rewarded with a wonderful mosaic fragment showing birds and people.

The Capitolium, Forum and Casa del Larario

Just beyond the Thermopolium, you'll spy the high brick walls of the **Capitolium**, Ostia's most important temple dating from the second century AD, fronted by a wide flight of steps and overlooking the shattered columns of both the **Forum** and the **Temple of Rome and Augustus**. Continuing on down the main street, there are more *horrea* off to the right, superbly preserved and complete with pediment over the entrance and names inscribed on the marble; although you can't enter, you can peer into the courtyard. A few yards further on, the Porta Occidentale or western gate, at the junction of the Decumanus Maximus and Via delle Foce, is marked by what may have been a **fish shop**, judging by its floor mosaics, still with its shelves and marble table. Continuing on down Decumanus Maximus, next up is the **Casa del Larario**, on the right, a well–preserved courtyard complex that served as a combined market and religious centre with several shrines.

Via delle Foce

At the Porta Occidentale, veer right along Via delle Foce to visit one of the most sacred parts of Roman Ostia, where three Republican temples cluster together, possibly dating back to the time of Sulla. The ruins are a little hard to decipher, but immediately behind them is the third–century **House of Cupid and Psyche**, which has a courtyard you can walk into and holds a copy of the statue of Cupid and Psyche that you can see in the museum; its rooms are clearly discernible on one side, a colourful marbled floor at the top and a columned nymphaeum, with marble niches, on the right.

Terme dei Sette Sapienti, Casa degli Aurighi and the Porta Marina

Keep on down Via delle Foce and you soon reach the **Terme dei Sette Sapienti** on the left, with its round arcaded courtyard and wonderfully intact floor mosaic. Steps lead up to the roof for good views over this part of the site and the fragments of wall paintings below. The atmospheric arcaded passageways of the complex lead to the **Casa degli Aurighi**, which you can ascend for more excellent views, beyond which Via degli Aurighi takes you back to the main Decumanus Maximus. A right turn takes you down to the **Porta Marina**, or sea gate, marked by the **Caupona di Alexander** on the left, a wine shop with flower mosaics identifying the owner and showing various forms of combat. Beyond here the road continues on for a little way to what was once the sea – but is now just the main road.

Museo Ostiense

Next door to the visitor centre, the half-dozen rooms of the **Museo Ostiense** are full of sculptural finds from the site which are well worth seeing. In a room to the left as you enter is a wall painting of *Mithras Slaying the Bull* from one of Ostia's mithraeums. The central room has a fine headless male figure in repose, his foot resting on a column base, and a figure of Trajan in full battle-dress, between two busts of him and another of Hadrian, along with a likeness of Commodus as a young boy. The room beyond has a statue of Septimius Severus next to his wife, Julia Domna, as the goddess Ceres, while, opposite, a beautifully preserved figure of Maxentius and his sister Fausta look on. In a room off here are various carved sarcophagi found on Via Ostiense, all amazingly well preserved, including one of a young boy, decorated with cupids, while

off to the other side are various representations of Venus and a wall painting of the
Three Graces from the second century AD.

13

Cerveteri

Cerveteri provides the most accessible Etruscan taster from Rome. The settlement here
dates back to the tenth century BC and was once a trading heavyweight, one of the
Mediterranean's largest centres. Cerveteri, also known as Caere, ranked among the top
three cities in the twelve-strong Etruscan federation, its wealth derived largely from
the mineral-rich Tolfa hills to the northeast – a gentle range that gives the plain a
much-needed touch of scenic colour. In its heyday, the town spread over 8km
(something like thirty times its present size), controlling territory 50km up the coast.
Rot set in from 351 BC, when the Romans assumed control without granting full
citizenship rights.

The Etruscan necropolis
Piazzale Mario Moretti • Tues–Sun: May–Sept 8.30am–6.30pm; Oct–April 8.30am–4pm • €6, €8 including the Museo Nazionale Cerite

The present town is a thirteenth-century creation, dismissed by D.H. Lawrence –
and you really can't blame him – as "forlorn beyond words", and on arrival you
should make straight for the **Etruscan Necropolis** or the Necropoli di Banditaccia,
the largest extant Etruscan burial site: from the seventh to first century BC, the
Etruscans constructed a literal city of the dead here, weird and fantastically well
preserved, with complete streets and homes. Some tombs are strange round pillboxes
carved from cliffs; others are covered in earth to create the barrows that ripple the
surrounding plateau. Archaeologists speculate that women were buried in separate
small chambers within each "house" – easy to distinguish – while the men were laid
on deathbeds (occasionally in sarcophagi) hewn directly from the stone. Indeed
archaeological evidence suggests that the position of women in Etruscan society was
roughly on a par with that of men. Cremated slaves lie in urns alongside their
masters – civilized by comparison with the Romans, who simply threw them into
mass burial pits. The twelve or so show-tombs, lying between the two main roads,
open and close in random rotation. If possible, don't miss the **Tomba Bella** (Tomb of
the Bas-Reliefs), **Tomba dei Letti Funebri** (Tomb of the Funeral Beds) and the **Tomb
of the Capitals**.

Museo Nazionale Cerite
Piazza Santa Maria • Tues–Sun 8.30am–7.30pm • €6, €8 including the necropolis

Housed in the sixteenth-century Castello Ruspoli, at the top of Cerveteri's old quarter,
the **Museo Nazionale Cerite** is well worth a visit. Most of the best Etruscan stuff from
here was whisked away long ago to the Villa Giulia in Rome (see p.176), but the
museum has two large rooms containing a decent fraction of the huge wealth that was
buried with the Etruscan dead – vases, terracottas and a run of miscellaneous day-to-
day objects.

ARRIVAL AND DEPARTURE — CERVETERI

By bus You can get to Cerveteri from Rome's Cornelia
station on metro line A by COTRAL bus (every 30min; 1hr);
buses drop off in Piazza Aldo Moro. The same Rome–
Cerveteri bus also links to the train station 7km away at
Ladispoli, which you can reach from Termini station in about
45min (every 30min). The site is just over 1km away in
Banditaccia and is well signposted from the town; you can
take bus D from the town centrre but it's a fairly simple walk.

EATING AND DRINKING

Tuchulcha Via della Necropoli Etrusche 28 ☏ 338 203
5860. Named after an Etruscan demon, this little trattoria on
the necropolis road serves hearty country-style food and
crisp Cerveteri white wines. No credit cards. Daily except
Mon 1–3pm & 8–10pm.

13

Tarquinia

Second only to Cerveteri among northern Lazio's Etruscan sites, **Tarquinia** is a pleasant town, its partial walls and crop of medieval towers making it a good place to pass an afternoon after seeing the ruins. Its museum is also the region's finest outside Rome.

Necropolis of Monterozzi

Via Monterozzi Marina • Tues–Sun: summer 8.30am–1hr before sunset; winter 8.30am–2pm • €6, €8 including museum • Take one of the regular buses from the central Barriera San Giusto, or it's a 20min walk: follow Via Umberto I from Piazza Cavour, pass through the Porta Romana, cross Piazza Europa, follow Via IV Novembre/Via delle Croci up the hill, and the site is on the left

Once the artistic, cultural and probably political capital of Etruria, the wooden city has now all but vanished and all that is left is the **Necropolis of Monterozzi**. Founded in the tenth century BC, the city's population peaked around 100,000, but the Roman juggernaut triggered its decline six hundred years later and only a warren of graves remains. Since the eighteenth century, six thousand tombs have been uncovered (nine hundred in 1958 alone), with many more to go. Grave-robbing is common (thieves are known as *tombaroli*).

Fresh air and humidity have also damaged the wall paintings and attempts at conservation mean tombs are open on a rotating basis. Some **frescoes** depict the inhabitants' expectations of the afterlife: scenes of banqueting, hunting and even a *ménage à trois*. The famed **Tomba dei Caronti** makes a darker prediction with demons greeting the deceased. The earliest paintings emphasize mythical and ritualistic scenes, but the sixth- to fourth-century works – in the dell'Orco, degli Auguri and della Caccia e Pesca tombs – show greater social realism. This style is a mixture of Greek, indigenous Etruscan and eastern influences: the ease and fluidity point to a civilization at its peak. Later efforts grow increasingly morbid with purely necromantic drawings – enough to discourage picnic lunches on the pleasant, grassy site.

Museo Nazionale Tarquiniense

Piazza Cavour 2 • Tues–Sun 8.30am–7.30pm • €6, €8 including necropolis

In the centre of Tarquinia, the **Museo Nazionale Tarquiniense** has a choice collection of Etruscan finds, sensitively housed in the attractive Gothic-Renaissance Palazzo Vitelleschi. The ground floor exhibits superb sculpted sarcophagi, many decorated with warm and human portraits of the deceased. Upstairs are displays of exquisite Etruscan gold jewellery, painted ceramics, bronzes, candlesticks, heads and figures. The impressive top floor houses the collection's finest piece – the renowned **winged horses** (fourth century BC), probably from a temple frieze. The **Sala delle Armi** boasts panoramic views of the countryside and sea.

Tarquinia Lido

Reachable by bus from the train station, or the Barriera San Giusto, **Tarquinia Lido** is a fairly developed stretch of coast, with lots of bars, restaurants and hotels lining its sandy beaches, some of which are free. It might just hit the spot after a dose of the Etruscans – as might the adjacent nature reserve and bird sanctuary, adapted from the nearby salt marshes.

ARRIVAL AND DEPARTURE
TARQUINIA

By train Trains run roughly hourly to Tarquinia from Rome's Termini and Ostiense stations; journey time is around 1hr 20min from Termini, just under 1hr from Ostiense. The train station is 2km below the town centre, connected with the central Barriera San Giusto by regular local shuttles.

By bus There are around 8 buses a day from Rome's Lepanto station on Metro line A (2hr).

EATING AND DRINKING

La Cantina dell'Etrusco Via Menotti Garibaldi 13 ☎ 0766 858 418. Rustic local fare in a converted fourteenth-century *cantina*, with great pasta, a short menu of meat dishes and plates of cheese with honey and other usual wine-bar goodies. Daily except Thurs 1–3pm & 8–10.30pm.

Bracciano and around

Around 30km north of Rome, and easily accessible by train, **Bracciano** is a small town that enjoyed fifteen minutes of fame when Tom Cruise and Katie Holmes got married here in 2006. It's an unassuming place, dominated by the castle where Cruise and his wife celebrated their nuptials, and enjoying a great position on the western shore of the lake it gives its name to, which is a wonderful place to swim, do watersports or just eat in one of the shoreline restaurants.

Castello Odescalchi

Piazza Mazzini 14 • April to mid-Oct Tues–Sat 10am–noon & 3–6pm, Sun 9am–12.30pm & 3–6.30pm; mid-Oct to March Tues–Sat 10am–noon & 2 4pm, Sun 10am–12.30pm & 2.30–5pm; tours every 30min, last 1hr • €7.50 • ☎ 06 9980 4348, ⓦ odescalchi.it

Tom Cruise and Katie Holmes tied the knot at the imposing Castello Odescalchi which dominates Bracciano, a late-fifteenth-century structure privately owned by the Odescalchi family. The outer walls, now mostly disappeared, contained the rectangular piazza of the medieval town; nowadays the castle is a little run-down, its interior home to rusting suits of armour and faded frescoes, but the view from the ramparts, over the broad blue oval of the lake, is worth the admission price alone.

Lago di Bracciano

The closest of northern Lazio's lakes to Rome, the smooth, roughly circular expanse of **Lago di Bracciano** fills an enormous volcanic crater. It's nothing spectacular, with few real sights and a landscape of rather plain, rolling countryside, but is popular with Romans escaping the heat of the city. The lake's shores are fairly peaceful even on summer Sundays, and you can eat excellent lake fish in its restaurants. The best place to swim in the lake is from the beach at Lungolago Argenti, below Bracciano town, where you can rent a boat and enjoy a picnic. The shore between Trevignano and Anguillara also boasts fine swimming spots, as well as some good restaurants.

ARRIVAL AND DEPARTURE   BRACCIANO AND AROUND

By train Trains run to Bracciano from Roma Ostiense every 30min (direction Viterbo), and take just over 1hr (less from Trastevere and San Pietro, where they also stop).

By bus There are hourly buses from Saxa Rubra station on the Roma Nord line, which also take around 1hr. Bracciano's train station is reasonably central, just a 10min walk from the castle and centre of town. Trains run on from Bracciano to Anguillara, from where there are regular buses to Trevignano.

EATING AND DRINKING

AREA BRACCIANO

Da Tonino Lungolago Argenti 18 ☎ 06 9980 5580. Decent, long-established restaurant that serves good pasta and fish dishes right on the water's edge. Not expensive either. Daily except Thurs noon–3pm & 7–11pm.

Trattoria del Castello Piazza Mazzini 1 ☎ 06 9980 4339, ⓦ trattoriadelcastello.net. Perhaps the town's best restaurant, with lovely pasta, an upscale place with prices to match; try their *tonnarelli cacio e pepe*, along with great mussels and fish. Daily except Wed 12.30–2.30pm & 7.30–10.30pm.

Vino e Camino Piazza Mazzini 11 ☎ 06 9980 3463, ⓦ vinoecamino.it. Great local restaurant in an unbeatable location right by the castle. It's been run by an enterprising brother-and-sister team since the mid-1990s, and has a lovely short menu based on hearty local ingredients, mostly meat but always with a few vegetarian dishes too. Tues–Sat 12.30–2.30pm & 7.30–10.30pm, Sun 12.30–2.30pm.

AREA TREVIGNANO

Casina Bianca Via della Rena 78 ☎ 06 999 7231. A popular place that serves fresh fish on a terrace overlooking the lake. Daily except Mon 12.30–2.30pm & 7.30–10.30pm.

13 # The Castelli Romani

Just free of the sprawling southern suburbs of Rome, the sixteen towns that make up the **Castelli Romani** date back to pre-Roman times. These hills – the **Colli Albani** – have long cooled rich and powerful urbanites, who also treasure the area's extraordinary white **wines**, inspired by the rich volcanic soil, and the spectacular views of Lago Albano. The region is now pretty heavily built up, with most of the historic centres ringed by unprepossessing suburbs, and summer weekends see traffic jams of Romans trooping out to local trattorias. But off-peak, it's worth the journey, either as an excursion from Rome or a stop on the way south.

Frascati

At just 20km from Rome, **FRASCATI** is the nearest of the Castelli towns and also the most striking, with a nice old centre and some great places to eat and drink. Its main square, **Piazza Marconi**, is dominated by the majestic **Villa Aldobrandini**, designed by Giacomo della Porta at the start of the seventeenth century. The Baroque *palazzo* is off-limits, but the **gardens** are open (Mon–Fri: summer 9am–1pm & 3–6pm; winter 9am–1pm & 3–5pm; free). Sadly the elaborate water theatre, where statues once played flutes, is not in top form, but the view from the front terrace is superb, with Rome visible on a clear day. You can also visit the rough-hewn **Scuderie Aldobrandini** or stables of the Villa, at Piazza Marconi 6 (Tues–Fri 10am–6pm, Sat & Sun 10am–7pm; €5.50; ❶06 941 7195), where they've assembled a collection of Roman finds from the nearby site of Tusculum and added an extra floor for local art exhibitions.

Just beyond here is the pedestrianized old centre, which revolves around the two squares of **Piazza San Pietro** and **Piazza del Mercato**. Frascati is also about the most famous of the Colli Albani **wine** towns: ask at the tourist office for details of winery tours and tastings.

Abbazia San Nilo, Grottaferrata

Corso del Popolo 128 • Church daily 9am–12.30pm & 3.30pm–1hr before sunset • Monastery Sat & Sun: May–Sept tours at 5pm; Oct–April tours at 4pm • Free

Some 3km south of Frascati, **GROTTAFERRATA** is also known for its wine and for its eleventh-century **Abbazia San Nilo**, at the bottom of the main Corso del Popolo – a Greek Orthodox monastery surrounded by high defensive walls and a now-empty moat. The monastery itself is only open briefly at weekends, but you can visit the little **church of Santa Maria** any time, which has a very ancient and atmospheric Byzantine-style interior decorated with thirteenth-century mosaics above the high altar, and, in the chapel of St Nilo off to the right, some big, busy frescoes by Domenichino. Look in also on the so-called **Cripta Ferrata**, a first-century AD edifice where Mary appeared to saints Bartholomew and Nilo and they resolved to build a church here.

Castel Gandolfo

To the southwest of Grottaferrata, the road joins up with the ancient Roman Via Appia, which travels straight as an arrow down the west side of Lago Albano. **CASTEL GANDOLFO** is the first significant stop, best known as the **Pope's summer retreat** – between July and September he gives sporadic midday addresses on Sundays. Four hundred metres above Lago Albano, it's a pleasantly airy place, and enjoys great views over the lake from its terraces close by the main **Piazza della Libertà**, a pleasant oblong of cafés and papal souvenir shops, at the end of which is the imposing bulk of the Papal Palace itself. Below the town, there's a pleasant lido along the lakeshore with lots of restaurants and pizzerias and a small stretch of grey **beach** from where you could stroll the whole shoreline in about two hours. The road leads down from the main highway, just north of Castel Gandolfo's old centre.

13

Ariccia

ARICCIA enjoys a dramatic location on the ancient Via Appia, poised between two gorges, and with spectacular views on all sides. The main road crosses the town's central piazza, a well-proportioned square that owes its appearance to Baroque master Bernini. His Pantheon-inspired church of Santa Maria dell'Assunzione sits across the Piazza della Repubblica from the massive **Palazzo Chigi** he built for Pope Alexander VII (guided tours April–Sept Tues–Fri at 11am, 4pm, 5.30pm, Sat & Sun hourly from 10.30am–12.30pm & 4–7pm; Oct–May Tues–Fri at 11am, 4pm & 5.30pm, Sat & Sun hourly from 10.30am–12.30pm & 3–6pm; €7; ⓦpalazzochigiariccia.it). The palace is a mightily impressive example of a Baroque provincial palace of the seventeenth century, and its *piano nobile* is home to the Chigi collections of paintings, sculpture and objects of applied art, which includes works by Salvator Rosa and Il Baciccio – the artist who painted the ceiling of the Gesù church in Rome. His work here also includes a striking self-portrait in the palace's so-called Baroque Museum, which features pieces by more Rome ceiling painters – Pietro da Cortona and Andrea Pozzo, among others.

Museo delle Navi, Nemi

Via Tempio di Diana 13 • Mon–Sat 9am–6.30pm, Sun 9am–2pm • €3 • ❶ 06 939 8040, ⓦ www.museonaviromane.it

The town of **NEMI**, built high above a tiny crater lake, isn't much to write home about, but it's famous for its strawberries and the local **Museo delle Navi** below the town on the lake's northern shore. This vast hangar-like building was purpose-built by Mussolini in the 1930s and contains two ancient Roman pleasure boats, floating villas built by Caligula. In the last days of the German occupation in 1944 they were set on fire, so apart from a few plans and wooden shutters that survived the fire, what you see today are modern reconstructions of the imperial ships. The building itself is worth the trip, and also displays finds from the ships (though the best are in the Palazzo Massimo in Rome) as well as stretches of a Roman road that passes right through the site.

ARRIVAL & INFORMATION   THE CASTELLI ROMANI

By bus and train COTRAL buses serve most of the major towns in the area from Rome's Anagnina metro station (line A), with services every 30min to Frascati (30min) and Grottaferrata (45min), and less frequently to Castel Gandolfo. Regular trains depart from Termini station for Frascati, Albano, Marino and Velletri, from where regular buses connect to Ariccia and Nemi.

Tourist office Frascati's tourist office is the best for the region and very convenient at Piazza Marconi 5 (daily 10am–8pm; ❶ 06 942 0331).

EATING AND DRINKING

FRASCATI

Grappolo d'Oro Piazza Filzi ❶ 06 942 2014, ⓦ ilgrappolodorofrascati.it. One of many *enoteche* in town, with tables outside or long tables inside under stone arches, and with a nice, easy-going vibe and really good pasta for €6 – *all a gricia, cacio e pepe, carbonara* – along with *porchetta coppiette* and lovely plates of prosciutto and buffalo mozzarella. Daily noon–midnight; closed Tues in winter.

Osteria al 25 Via Regina Margherita 25 ❶ 338 420 1421. One of several *osterie* that make the most of the wide-ranging views across the countryside south of Rome from this street on the far edge of the old town, and serving a well-priced menu featuring lots of local specialities – all the Roman classic pasta dishes for €7–8, plus mains like *tripe alla Romana, abbachio* (baked lamb) and *coda alla vaccinara*

(oxtail stew) for €8–10. Daily 12.30–2.30pm & 7.30–10.30pm.

Pinocchio Piazza del Mercato 21 ❶ 06 941 6694, ⓦ hotelpinocchio.it. A much more extensive menu than most of the other more basic Frascati offerings, with lots of *bruschette*, good, ultra-thin Roman pizzas from €6.50, a large array of pasta dishes from €7.50, both traditional and a bit more inventive, and meat and fish mains for around €16. Daily noon–3pm & 7–11pm.

ARICCIA

L'Aricciarola Via Borgo S. Rocco 9 ❶ 06 933 4103, ⓦ www.osterialariccarola.it. One of a number of restaurants on this street, just outside Ariccia's old centre, with tables outside and a traditional and affordable menu featuring *primi* for €5–7 and main courses for €10. They do

13

WHERE TO FLOP: THE BEST BEACHES NEAR ROME

There are plenty of places to head to near Rome if you fancy a day at the **beach** – and on a hot summer's day in the city there's sometimes nothing else for it but to get out of town. Some of the best seaside spots are listed below, starting with closest ones to Rome then heading south, followed by the closest ones to Rome then heading north.

LIDO DI OSTIA

Lido di Ostia has for years been the number one, or at any rate the closest and most accessible, seaside resort for Romans. The beaches are fine, and much cleaner than they used to be, but you have to pay to use them and the town doesn't have a great deal to recommend it apart from its thumping nightlife in summer. Ostia is, however, easy to get to, just 30min by train from Porta San Paolo station, next door to Piramide metro on line B; get off at Lido Centro or the last stop, Cristoforo Colombo, where the crowds might be thinner. A €1.50 ATAC ticket is sufficient.

TORVAIANICA

South of Ostia, towards **Torvaianica**, the water is cleaner and the crowds not so thick, plus there are gay and nudist sections of the beach, and not a lot of development. Buses run from Cristoforo Colombo station in Ostia; take #07 or #061. The beaches along this stretch are known as the **cancelli**, after the numbered gates to the beach; the higher the number, the better the beach so it's worth staying on the bus for a bit.

ANZIO

About 40km south of Rome, and fairly free of the pull of the capital, **Anzio** is worth visiting both for its beaches and its history – much of the town was damaged during a difficult Allied landing here on January 22, 1944, to which two military cemeteries (one British, another, at nearby Nettuno, American), as well as a small museum, bear testimony. It was also a favoured spot of the Roman Emperor Nero, the ruins of whose villa spread along the cliffs above and even down onto the beach. Anzio is a good place to eat lunch: it hosts a thriving fishing fleet and some great restaurants down on the harbour: *La Cicala*, right by the water at Riviera Zanardelli 11 (☎06 984 6747; closed Wed), is as good as any, with outside seating and decent food and service; or try *Fiaschetta del Mare* on the harbour, where they will bring you an endless supply of fishy specialities depending on the day's catch, for a fixed price of €16 a head. The town is easy to get to, with trains every hour from Termini; the journey takes an hour and it's just a 10min walk from the station down to the main square and harbour, with the beaches stretching out north of the centre.

TERRACINA AND SPERLONGA

The resorts of **Terracina** and **Sperlonga** are a bit of a schlep; they are doable as a day-trip, though you might want to consider staying overnight. **Terracina** boasts lovely sandy beaches and a welcoming small-town feel, as well as a couple of good restaurants. A little further south, little **Sperlonga** is a more chichi resort, with equally good beaches and an attractive old quarter piled up on the headland just beyond. The ruins of the so-called **Grotto of Tiberius**

great *amatriciana* and *cacio e pepe*, or you could try the excellent *pappardelle allo sugo cinghiale* (with wild boar sauce) for €7 following it with grilled steak or local pork, all washed down with a litre of local wine for €4. Or just order cheese and cold cuts from the amazing spread at the counter. Tues–Sun noon–2.30pm & 7.30–10pm.

Palestrina

About 30km south of Rome, **PALESTRINA** was built on the site of the ancient Praeneste, originally an Etruscan settlement and later a favoured resort for patrician Romans. "Cool Praeneste", as Horace called it, was the site of an enormous Temple of Fortune whose foundations more or less determine the modern centre, which steps up the hillside in a series of terraces.

lie just to the south of the town, a sea cave once filled with sculptures that have found their way into a purpose-built museum nearby.

You can get to both Terracina and Sperlonga by train from Termini to Fondi (hourly), which takes just over an hour, and a local bus from there. There are direct trains to Terracina, which take around 1hr 30min, but the first doesn't leave till after lunch so they're not much use unless you're staying the night.

FREGENE

A little way north of Ostia, **Fregene** is one of the busier resorts in the Rome area; it's posher and more family-orientated than its neighbour, though its beaches are equally crowded and expensive. Take a train from Termini or Ostiense to Maccarese (around 30min), from where it's a short local bus ride to Fregene.

LADISPOLI

Ladispoli is one of the best of the resorts to the north of the capital. There are swimming spots about a 10min walk from the town's station, although the nicest are further north, a 20min walk away around the **Torre Flavia**. This medieval construction was restored in 1565 by an Orsini cardinal, and is now collapsing elegantly into the water in four equal parts. Trains run twice an hour from Termini to Ladispoli-Cerveteri station and take about 40min.

SANTA SEVERA

There's not much to sleepy **Santa Severa**, but it has everything you need for a day at the beach, with long stretches of sand – some free, the rest given over to the usual *letti* and *ombrelloni* – and a decent *tavola calda* right on the seafront; there's also a **castle** at the southern end of the beach, home to a small municipal museum. The only drawback is the fact that the train station is a 20min walk from the town and beach, with erratic connecting buses and no alternative transport. But trains are regular and quick: hourly from Termini station, and the journey takes just under an hour.

SANTA MARINELLA

One train stop beyond Santa Severa, and much livelier, **Santa Marinella** is one of the most popular spots north of the capital, and rightly so. It has a lovely crescent of beach, 5min walk from the train station, and although most is pay-only, the sand is fine and clean and the water shallow – perfect for kids. Trains are hourly from Termini, and they take an hour. There are also one or two good places to eat: *La Piazzaetta*, five minutes' walk from the beach at Piazza Trieste 13/14, which does great fish, and *La Mucca e Il Faro*, down in the Porto Turistico, which does equally good fish and seafood pasta dishes, and pizzas too.

CAPALBIO

Far to the north of Rome and almost in Tuscany, **Capalbio** feels a long way from the capital and its satellite towns; it's a comparatively upscale resort, with fine beaches, clean water and good restaurants. It's not too hard to reach either: about five trains a day run from Termini station and journey time is roughly 1hr 40min. The beaches are about 2km from the station; if you don't fancy the walk, there are infrequent buses.

Palazzo Barberini and the Museo Nazionale Archeologico Prenestino

Piazza della Cortina • Daily 9am–1hr before sunset • €5, tickets also give access to the sanctuary in front of the site • ☎ 06 953 8100

The stepped streets of Palestrina encourage casual strolling, but you need to save your energy for Palestrina's real attraction, the **Palazzo Barberini**, right on top of the hill, which houses the **Museo Nazionale Archeologico Prenestino**, originally built in the eleventh century and greatly modified in 1640. The palace and the terraces below were carved out of a Republican temple which previously stood on this site, and the views are magnificent from the top, surveying the countryside around as far as the eye can see. Among the collection's highlights are a number of ancient Roman pieces found locally: a torso of *Fortune* in slate grey marble; the *Triade Capitolina*, showing Juno, Jupiter and Minerva, illegally excavated in the early 1990s and narrowly apprehended in the Stelvio Pass on its way out of the country; Etruscan funerary *cistae*; and, the

13

museum's prize possession, a marvellous first-century-BC *Mosaic of the Nile* housed at the very top of the building, which traces the flooding river from source to delta, chronicling everyday Egyptian life in amazing detail.

ARRIVAL AND INFORMATION PALESTRINA

By bus The bus trip from Rome takes 65min (frequent departures from Ponte Mammolo on metro B), terminating at Via degli Arcioni, from where the trudge up to the town is a steep one.

Tourist office Piazza S. Maria degli Angeli 2 (Mon–Sat 8am–7pm; ☎ 06 957 3176).

ACCOMMODATION AND EATING

A Modo Via Anicia 11 ☎ 06 9531 0035. This inviting restaurant is tucked away down an alley off the old town's main artery – head here for fresh fish and grilled meat. Daily except Wed noon–3pm & 6–11pm.

Bottiglieria del Gallo Via Anicia 6 ☎ 06 9531 2012. Just off the main square, this *enoteca* is a nice place for a glass of wine and also does food, with lots of salads, pasta and grills. A wide choice of wine by the glass for €3, and a good selection of artisanal Italian beers. Excellent value and very friendly too. Tues–Sun 10am–2pm & 5–9.30pm.

Stella Piazzale della Liberazione 3 ☎ 06 953 8172, ⓦ www.hotelstella.it. Just past the cathedral, this hotel is central and good enough for a night or two, with 30 sparsely but quite tastefully furnished en-suite rooms with satellite TV. It also has a lovely big and airy traditional restaurant serving wonderful Roman pasta classics (€7–9) and various grilled meat and fish mains for €9. Restaurant open daily 1–3pm & 8–10pm. **€70**

ROME CAVALIERI HOTEL

Accommodation

As you might expect, there is no shortage of accommodation in Rome, and, for much of the year, you can usually find something without too much trouble. In recent years, the amount of lodging has increased significantly at all levels, especially among boutique options, with sumptuous *palazzi* all over the city centre being given designer makeovers in the hope of attracting a better-heeled clientele. There has always been a decent range of budget hotels, and some of them enjoy great locations in the historic centre, as well as a sprinkling of hostels that includes low-priced choices with religious orders. It's always worth booking in advance if you want to snag a bargain, especially in high season: from Easter to July and September to the end of October, and during Christmas and New Year.

14

You'll enjoy Rome most if you stay right in the heart of things – in the **Centro Storico**, such as around Piazza Navona or near the **Campo de' Fiori**. There are plenty of hotels in these areas, and several that aren't all that expensive, but they fill quickly, so you need to book well in advance, if you can. The **Tridente** and the area east of Via del Corso, towards **Via Veneto** and around the **Spanish Steps**, is a prime hunting ground for more upscale accommodation, but there are more affordable options here too, and it is a good and equally central place to base yourself. Consider also staying across the river: in **Prati**, the pleasant nineteenth-century neighbourhood close to the **Vatican** and nicely distanced from the hubbub of the city centre, or in lively **Trastevere** which boasts a number of budget options and is within easy walking distance of the centre of the city and the major sights. Otherwise, many of the city's hostels and cheaper hotels are located close to **Termini** – convenient if you have to catch an early train or flight, but not the city's most atmospheric quarter, and a bus ride away from the Centro Storico. For those on a tight budget, however, this is where you'll find the widest choice of accommodation: the streets both sides of the station are stacked full of bargain hotels and hostels, and some buildings have several pensions to choose from. The area has also become somewhat more interesting – and for the most part less seedy – in recent years, particularly north of the station and across Via XX Settembre, as well as in the more upscale Quirinale neighbourhood; the recently gentrified area of Monti, in particular, is a vibrant and convenient part of the city to stay.

ESSENTIALS

RATES

Apart from taxes (see box, p.227), hotel prices are fairly transparent. The rates given in our listings are for the cheapest double room in high season excluding this tax. As always, they're only a guide, and can change from day to day (or even hour to hour); there's really no substitute for getting online or even on the phone and checking out the best deals at the time you want to go. In general, hotel rates in Rome have crept up over recent years, but tourist numbers are fragile and there are often deals to be had, as hotels try to fill their rooms. Rates vary hugely, but as a very rough guide, you'll pay around €100 for a basic en-suite room, though don't expect much in the way of decor; €120–180 will get you a few homely touches and perhaps a more central location; for more comfort and a bit of elegance, plan for €200–300, with the price rising the closer you are to the centre; €300–500 (and occasionally beyond) is the price of grand, five-star luxury or the most exclusive of the boutique hotels. Hostel beds tend to go for around €20 a night, and private rooms in hostels for €60–90.

Last-minute booking The Italian hotel booking site ⓦvenere.com based in London is a good last-minute option (you can also call them on ☎+44 020 3027 7153; Mon–Sat 10am–8pm), as are the usual international hotel booking sites (such as ⓦbooking.com, ⓦlaterooms.com, ⓦlastminute.com and ⓦexpedia.com), but bear in mind that out of season you can sometimes get better rates by booking directly with the hotel. Indeed, in more upmarket hotels, out of season or at weekends, there are often excellent last-minute, non-refundable offers that can make some of the city's better hotels accessible to those on more modest budgets. You're most likely to pick up a bargain in low season,

particularly during the heat of August, when many places, especially the higher-grade hotels, drop their prices steeply.

FACILITIES

Breakfast A simple continental breakfast is usually included (although it's always a good idea to confirm this), except in high-end places, where you can expect to pay upwards of €30 per person for a sumptuous buffet breakfast.

Internet and TV Most hotels now have wi-fi, although unfortunately the more upmarket and old-fashioned places still tend to charge for this; the majority also offer satellite TV with English-language news stations.

Apartments / kitchen facilities A new trend is a hybrid of apartment and hotel, which often has rooms larger than the standard hotel room and occasionally rudimentary kitchen facilities.

Parking Very few hotels in the Centro Storico have their own parking, but they may have a contract with local garages, which charge €25–35 a day.

Swimming pools Unsurprisingly, swimming pools and spas are confined mostly to the five-star hotels, but they are normally open to all – at a price (see p.300).

Bars and restaurants Some of the top hotels have great on-site bars and renowned restaurants that are venues in their own right, with fantastic food, great patios or terraces or stupendous views – and sometimes all three (see box, p.261).

CENTRO STORICO

Albergo del Senato Piazza della Rotonda 73 ☎06 678 4343, ⓦalbergodelsenato.it; map p.38. A classy choice with friendly service and magnificent views of the

ACCOMMODATION TAX

The Rome city authorities now levy a **hotel tax** which ranges from €1 per night in campsites to €2–3 per night in hotels; it is applied to each occupant for each night, in all overnight accommodation inside Rome's boundaries – except hostels, which are exempt – and is always charged separately in cash. Children under the age of 10 are exempt, and you pay nothing after ten days (five for camping).

14

Pantheon (which is next door) from some rooms; also has great views of the city from the roof. Big discounts in low season. **€365**

Cesàri Via di Pietra 89a ☎ 06 674 9701, ⓦ albergocesari .it; map p.38. In a perfect position close to the Pantheon, this has been a hotel since 1787, as they will be sure to tell you – the Stendhal room was named for their most famous former guest. The quiet, comfortable rooms are elegant and modern, and you can enjoy the hotel's roof terrace at breakfast and for drinks on summer evenings. **€260**

Due Torri Vicolo del Leonetto 23 ☎ 06 6880 6956, ⓦ hotelduetorriroma.com; map p.38. Tucked away down a quiet side street just north of Piazza Navona, this little hotel was once a residence for cardinals, after which it served as a brothel. It's been completely remodelled since then but remains cosy, and some rooms have small terraces with rooftop views. They also have a second hotel *Fontanella Borghese*, a few streets away at Largo Fontanella Borghese 84 (☎ 06 688 0954, ⓦ fontanellaborghese.com), which has slightly higher rates. **€200**

Genio Via G. Zanardelli 28 ☎ 06 683 3781, ⓦ hotelgenioroma.it; map p.38. Perfectly located for Piazza Navona and the rest of the Centro Storico, this comfortable, recently refurbished hotel draws tour groups as well as individual travellers. The view from the rooftop terrace is superb; a few rooms also have the same view, and each comes with a desk. **€450**

Locanda Navona Via di Tor Millina 35 ☎ 06 6830 8281, ⓦ locandanavona.com; map p.38. This new venture by the affable owner of the *Navona* (see below) has six bright rooms overlooking this busy intersection of streets just off Piazza Navona. Free breakfast either in your room or at the bar downstairs. **€150**

Mimosa Via Santa Chiara 61 ☎ 06 6880 1753, ⓦ hotelmimosa.net; map p.38. You get what you pay for at this cheap one-star place in the city centre, but its updated rooms now have their own bathrooms and a/c, and the hotel enjoys a great position on a quiet street close to Santa Maria sopra Minerva and the Pantheon. Nice family rooms, too. Free wi-fi, though it's on the second floor and there's no elevator. **€135**

Navona Via dei Sediari 8 ☎ 06 686 4203, ⓦ hotelnavona.com; map p.38. Completely renovated *pensione*-turned-hotel in a building that dates back to the first century AD, built on the ancient Roman baths of Agrippa. A great location, very close to Piazza Navona, and

rooms and service are excellent. It also has sister hotels, the *Zanardelli* (see p.228) and *Argentina Residenza* (see p.228). The lobby and breakfast areas have free wi-fi, and there's a laptop at reception for brief (free) internet use. Some stairs, and no lift. Breakfast €10. **€250**

Nazionale Piazza Montecitorio 131 ☎ 06 695 001, ⓦ hotelnazionale.it; map p.38. This sixteenth-century *palazzo* in peaceful Piazza Montecitorio, perfectly located halfway between Piazza Navona and Piazza di Spagna, is next door to the Italian parliament and popular with visiting politicians and dignitaries. Rooms are pretty old fashioned but well fitted out with every modern convenience. **€360**

Pantheon Via Pastini 131 ☎ 06 678 7746, ⓦ hotelpantheon.com; map p.38. This comfortable four-star hotel is, as you might expect, a stone's throw from the Pantheon. The well-equipped rooms range from the functional, with beamed wooden ceilings, to deluxe suites on two levels with sky-lit sitting rooms. **€315**

Portoghesi Via dei Portoghesi 1 ☎ 06 686 4231, ⓦ hotelportoghesiroma.com; map p.38. Decent, modern rooms and a very handy location, just off Via della Scrofa and 5min from the heart of the Centro Storico. Breakfast is served on the roof terrace. **€260**

Raphaël Largo Febo 2 ☎ 06 682 831, ⓦ www .raphaelhotel.com; map p.38. Set on a quiet, picturesque piazza just off Piazza Navona, the *Raphaël* is a mix of plush traditional style – antiques and rich colours – and sleek contemporary furnishings by American architect Richard Meier (of Ara Pacis fame; see p.99) on the second and third floors. It's part of the ecologically friendly Bio-Hotels group, and you can dine on the lovely rooftop organic restaurant (book ahead), so close to the church dome that you can see its rivets. There's also a bar, a library, free wi-fi in all rooms and two free internet points, an exercise room and free street parking (limited). **€480**

★ **Relais Orso** Via del Orso 88 ☎ 06 9357 9573, ⓦ relaisorso.com; map p.38. This small hotel enjoys one of the best locations in the Centro Storico and is one of a new breed of small boutiquey places in the city centre, with just sixteen rooms and a contrived yet effective contemporary-meets-distressed antique style. Rooms aren't large, but the bathrooms are a good size, with walk-in showers; wi-fi is reliable and rooms have flatscreen TVs and Nespresso machines. There's a rooftop bar, too, that's good for early evening drinks. **€289**

14

Residenza Canali Via dei Tre Archi 13 ☎ 06 6830 9451, ⓦ residenzacanali.com; map p.38. On a side street close to Piazza Navona, this family-run hotel enjoys a great location and has the rooms and service to go with it. The bright rooms with wood-beamed ceilings all have modern bathrooms and are great value, especially rooms 1 and 2, each of which has a terrace. There are several flights of stairs and no lift. Free internet terminal in the lobby. **€210**

Residenze Art & Breakfast Chiostro del Bramante Arco della Pace 5 ☎06 6880 9035, ⓦwww .chiostrodelbramante.it; map p.38. Just off the lovely Chiostro del Bramante right in the heart of the Centro Storico, close by Piazza Navona, this place has three beautifully furnished apartments, one two-bedroom, a one-bedroom and a large studio. One – La Torretta – has a rooftop terrace and all have cooking facilities, though the only one with an oven is the one-bed. Breakfast is served in the cloister's cafeteria on the upstairs portico. **€450**

Santa Chiara Via Santa Chiara 21 ☎ 06 687 2979, ⓦ albergosantachiara.com; map p.38. A friendly, family-run hotel in a great location, on a quiet street behind the Pantheon. Tastefully furnished rooms, too, some of which overlook the church of Santa Maria sopra Minerva, and wi-fi is free. **€260**

★ **Teatro Pace** Via del Teatro Pace 33 ☎ 06 687 9075, ⓦ hotelteatropace.com; map p.38. This beautifully restored *palazzo*, a few paces from Piazza Navona, was once home to one of the Vatican's most prominent cardinals. Leading off an impressive Baroque spiral staircase (no lift) are four floors of elegant, mostly spacious rooms with original wood beams, floor-sweeping drapes and luxurious bathrooms. **€210**

★ **Zanardelli** Via G. Zanardelli 7 ☎06 6821 1392, ⓦ hotelnavona.com; map p.38. Just north of Piazza Navona, this is the sister hotel of the *Navona* (see p.227), and ever so slightly more lavish, housed in a former papal residence that retains many original fixtures. Rooms are elegant, with antique iron beds, silk-lined walls and modern amenities. The lobby and breakfast areas have free wi-fi, and there's a laptop for brief free internet use. **€250**

CAMPO DE' FIORI AND THE GHETTO
Argentina Residenza Via di Torre Argentina 47 ☎06 6813 5794, ⓦ argentinaresidenza.com; map pp.54–55.

TOP 5 HOTELS WITH VIEWS
Eden see p.232
Forty Seven see p.230
Hassler see p.231
Palazzo Manfredi see p.234
Roma Cavalieri see p.235

This former noble carriage house has been converted to a six-room hotel by the *Navona* folk (see p.227), and it's an elegant affair, antique ceilings combining effectively with the well-chosen modern furnishings and amenities. It's in a perfect location, too, in the core of the Centro Storico but also close to the major transport hub of Largo Argentina. **€175**

Campo de' Fiori Via del Biscione 6 ☎ 06 6880 6865, ⓦ hotelcampodefiori.com; map pp.54–55. A friendly hotel with rooms that have been recently renovated in a deliberately plush, boutique style, and a large roof terrace affording great views. The hotel also owns two simple small apartments in the piazza (€189 a night for 2 people, although it can cost a lot more in peak season). **€400**

★ **Lunetta** Piazza del Paradiso 68 ☎ 06 6839 5056, ⓦ hotellunetta.com; map pp.54–55. This place has recently reopened after a lengthy renovation and now has 30 boutique-style rooms of various shapes and sizes and a small spa. Breakfast is free (and includes an "English" option upon request), plus there's free wi-fi and access to the spa. **€430**

Pomezia Via dei Chiavari 13 ☎06 686 1371, ⓦ hotelpomezia.it; map pp.54–55. Always slightly more upscale than its budget neighbours, this city-centre budget hotel is still a bit of a dying breed, family run and with a 24hr reception and small bar. **€150**

Relais Giulia Via Giulia 93 ☎06 9558 1300, ⓦ relaisgiulia.com; map pp.54–55. This hotel, opened in 2012, has minimalist-style rooms in neutral colours that face an interior courtyard, though one of the suites has a balcony overlooking Via Giulia itself. Some of the rooms are a bit small, but the breakfasts are great, and it's brilliantly situated for visiting Centro Storico, the Ghetto, Trastevere and the Vatican. **€270**

Relais Teatro Argentina Via del Sudario 35 ☎06 9893 1617, ⓦ relaisteatroargentina.com; map pp.54–55. Situated on a side street right by the Teatro Argentina, this newish B&B doesn't only have a good location but also exhibits great flair in the colours and textiles chosen for the guest rooms. They don't, however, always have staff present, so be sure to coordinate your arrival time. Free breakfast, served in your room, plus a decent DVD collection. **€210**

Residenza Farnese Via del Mascherone 59 ☎06 6821 0980, ⓦ residenzafarneseroma.it; map pp.54–55. On a quiet side street right by Palazzo Farnese, rooms here are large and mostly tastefully appointed, while some overlook the French embassy gardens. The staff are very helpful, and the location is handy for both the Centro Storico and Trastevere, just across the bridge. Parking in the courtyard, but only by advance request. Considerable discounts often available. **€270**

St George Via Giulia 62 ☎06 686 611, ⓦ stgeorgehotel .it; map pp.54–55. Situated on one of Rome's most beautiful streets, this is a stylish and contemporary five-star done out in minimalist style with touches of neo-Baroque

14

whimsy. There's a spa and fitness centre, as well as chic restaurant, *I Sofà di Via Giulia*, and an inviting bar. **€390**

Sole Via del Biscione 76 ☎ 06 6880 6873, ⌨ www .solealbiscione.it; map pp.54–55. Enjoys one of the best locations in the centre and has reasonable rooms with TVs and phones, plus several roof terraces with spectacular views of the nearby domes. No breakfast; cash only. **€145**, shared bathroom **€110**

Teatro di Pompeo Largo del Pallaro 8 ☎ 06 687 2812, ⌨ www.hotelteatrodipompeo.it; map pp.54–55. Built above the remains of Pompey's ancient Roman theatre, the rooms here are comfortable, with high-beamed wooden ceilings, marble-topped furniture and (in some) sweeping views. **€220**

PIAZZA VENEZIA AND THE CAPITOLINE HILL

Forty Seven 47 Via Petroselli 47 ☎ 06 678 7816, ⌨ fortysevenhotel.com; map p.64. Contemporary boutique hotel with Art Deco-inspired decor and crisply furnished rooms that boast minibars, free wi-fi and full satellite TV. Some also have great views of the ancient temples opposite and the Circus Maximus beyond, as does the hotel's rooftop *Circus* restaurant. **€270**

Kolbe Via di San Teodoro 48 ☎ 06 679 8866, ⌨ kolbehotelrome.com; map p.64. This former convent, near the Circus Maximus on the south side of the Palatine, has been upgraded from a long-standing budget hotel to a more serious place altogether, and is a tranquil oasis to be sure, with a spruce modern lobby, good buffet breakfast and a lovely secluded garden. Rooms are on the bland side of contemporary, and the overall feel is one of affordable rather than boutique luxury, but the location is good, especially if you can snag a room overlooking the Forum. Wi-fi free but erratic. **€330**

Palazzo al Velabro Via del Velabro 16 ☎ 06 679 2758 or ☎ 06 679 7879, ⌨ velabro.it; map p.64. Discreet apartment hotel near Bocca della Verità; some rooms have views of the Arch of Janus and temple of Hercules, while others look towards the Palatine Hill (some with a small terrace). There's a breakfast café, fitness facilities and 24hr concierge service. **€250**

Torre Colonna Via delle Tre Cannelle 18 ☎ 06 6228 9543, ⌨ torrecolonna.com; map p.64. A 1247 defensive tower built by the noble Colonna family is now a five-room guesthouse decorated in contemporary style with modern art and a rooftop jacuzzi with panoramic views over the Forum and neighbouring Piazza Venezia. **€290**

THE TRIDENTE AND TREVI

Babuino 181 Via del Babuino 181 ☎ 06 3229 5295, ⌨ romeluxurysuites.com; map p.93. Rome Luxury Suites operates this and two other locations at Margutta 54 and Mario de' Fiori 37 (see p.231). Decorated with contemporary

Italian flair, the accommodation is stylishly comfortable and includes breakfast and concierge service. **€360**

★ **Casa Howard** Via Capo le Case 18 & Via Sistina 149 ☎ 06 6992 4555, ⌨ casahoward.com; map p.93. This boutique hotel offers a series of themed rooms in two locations, one close to Piazza di Spagna, the other just off Piazza Barberini (map p.105). Rooms are on the small side, but elegantly and stylishly furnished; service is very personal and welcoming and there's free wi-fi throughout. Breakfast is served in your room. **€210**

Condotti Via Mario de' Fiori 37 ☎ 06 679 4661, ⌨ hotelcondotti.com; map p.93. The *Condotti* is cosy and inviting, with rooms that are comfortable, if a little lacking in personality. The staff are cheerful and welcoming though, and there's a free internet point in the lobby and wi-fi in the rooms. Not a bad price for the location, and there are often big discounts on the official rates. **€295**

★ **Crossing Condotti** Via Mario de' Fiori 28 ☎ 06 6992 0633, ⌨ crossingcondotti.com; map p.93. Classy modern suites and apartments, all with rudimentary kitchen facilities in a great location close to Piazza di Spagna, furnished with antiques and painted in elegant, neutral tones. Hotel services too, including daytime staff and a daily linen change. Free wi-fi and snacks. **€260**

★ **De Russie** Via del Babuino 9 ☎ 06 328 881, ⌨ hotelderussie.it; map p.93. The abode of choice for visiting movie stars and well-heeled trendsetters, with stylishly understated doubles, quirkily furnished with plentiful references to the city's ancient heritage. If you're not staying here, you can still experience the buzz downstairs in the courtyard *Stravinski Bar* (see p.268), or stop by to enjoy the patio and excellent weekday lunch buffet. **€850**

Dei Borgognoni Via del Bufalo 126 ☎ 06 6994 1505, ⌨ hotelborgognoni.it; map p.93. A surprisingly big hotel considering its location down a quietish street not far from Piazza di Spagna, this four-star has pleasant, nicely renovated large rooms. You pay for wi-fi in your room but not in the public areas, and the lobby also has a free internet terminal. The bar serves light meals, and there's a cosy library with fireplace. **€310**

D'Inghilterra Via Bocca di Leone 14 ☎ 06 699 811, ⌨ royaldemeure.com; map p.93. This old favourite, formerly the apartments of the princes of Torlonia, is pretty good value compared to the cost of hotels of similar quality in this location. Intimacy, opulence, exquisite antiques, frescoed rooms and all the delights of the ancient city centre. A nice, old-fashioned bar too, and the hotel's *Romana* restaurant is lovely inside or out. **€450**

Erdarelli Via dei Due Macelli 28 ☎ 06 679 1265, ⌨ erdarelliromehotel.com; map p.93. A rather plain, no-frills place, with no internet access, TV only in the lobby and a/c only in some rooms, but it's welcoming enough, and for the location, just around the corner from the Spanish Steps, it's a bargain. **€139**, shared bathroom **€109**

★ **Grand Hotel Plaza** Via del Corso 126 ☎ 06 6992 1111, ⊛ grandhotelplaza.com; map p.93. One of Rome's most sumptuous hotels and sometime backdrop to films like *Angels and Demons* and *Ocean's Twelve*. The fantastic lobby, with plush velvets, sumptuous brocades, chandeliers and stained-glass ceiling, gives you some idea of what to expect in the rooms, and they don't disappoint: huge, pleasantly renovated and well-appointed, all with wi-fi. One of the city's better places for a treat. €400

Hassler Trinità dei Monti 6 ☎ 06 699 340, ⊛ hotelhasslerroma.com; map p.93. Location, location, location – at the top of the Spanish Steps, you can't get a much more commanding position above Rome. A luxury hotel with simple, elegant rooms and every convenience a guest could possibly require, including a spa, but what you're paying for is the reputation and – of course – the view. €790

Homs Via della Vite 71–72 ☎ 06 679 2976, ⊛ hotelhoms.it; map p.93. In the heart of the Spanish Steps neighbourhood, this small four-star hotel has a very friendly atmosphere – not always a sure thing in this area. The rooms have been recently refurbished, and there's a two-bedroom rooftop apartment. Double €230, apartment €250

Hotel Art Via Margutta 56 ☎ 06 328 711, ⊛ hotelart.it; map p.93. Ingeniously converted from a convent and with an impressive bar and lobby fashioned out of a vaulted chapel, the *Art Hotel* ticks most of the right boxes: it's in a great location, tucked away on Via Margutta, and its design theme is for the most part well-realized and luxurious. The rooms are excellent too, although, oddly for a strivingly cutting-edge hotel, they don't have wi-fi or satellite TV. €340

★ **Locarno** Via della Penna 22 ☎ 06 361 0841, ⊛ hotellocarno.com; map p.93. Arguably the most characterful and inviting hotel in central Rome: a quirky, engaging old place whose courtyard bar between its two wings draws a crowd every evening. The rooms aren't the most luxurious or facility-laden, but they're comfy and individually furnished, and a big hit with the hotel's media and arty clientele. Considering the location, it's well priced too, and there's a fleet of bikes for guests if you want to explore further afield. €250

Manfredi Via Margutta 61 ☎ 06 320 7676, ⊛ hotelmanfredi.it; map p.93. This sixteenth-century building once housed a theatre, renamed Teatro delle Dame because it was the first place in the city where women were allowed to perform. On picturesque Via Margutta, the hotel is moments from the Spanish Steps. Rooms have been given a makeover and are fairly fancy for the price. The wine bar, with its triple-domed ceiling, makes a pleasant spot for a drink. €295

Mario de Fiori 37 Via Mario de' Fiori 37 ☎ 06 6992 1907, ⊛ romeluxurysuites.com; map p.93. This small hotel is one of three properties of Rome Luxury Suites, and

its elegantly stylish rooms are situated in a great location close to the Spanish Steps. Bathrooms are a good size and rooms well equipped and decently furnished. The only downside is for breakfast: you have to walk to one of their other properties at Via del Babuino 181 (see p.230), but that's no great hardship. €210

Piazza di Spagna Via Mario de Fiori 61 ☎ 06 679 3061, ⊛ www.hotelpiazzadispagna.it; map p.93. This small hotel, just a few minutes' walk from the Spanish Steps, is a good alternative to the sumptuous palaces that characterize this area. Family-owned and run, its rooms are comfortable, all have a/c and TV, and some have jacuzzis. Friendly staff, too. €250

★ **Portrait Suites** Via di Bocca di Leone 23 ☎ 06 6938 0742, ⊛ lungarnohotels.com; map p.93. A relative newcomer to the boutique hotel circuit, this converted townhouse with fourteen suites, owned and designed by fashion designer Salvatore Ferragamo, is a bastion of luxury and comfort. Prices are high, but the suites are superbly appointed, and there's a lovely rooftop bar. Wi-fi or the loan of a laptop is free, and service is second to none. €480

Residenza Napoleone III Largo Goldoni 56 ☎ 06 6880 8083, ⊛ residenzanapoleone.com; map p.93. In the opulent setting of the sixteenth-century Palazzo Ruspoli, two rooms are sumptuously furnished with priceless antiques and vast oil paintings – a level of luxury of which the famous one-time resident obviously approved. €730

THE QUIRINALE AND VIA VENETO

Aleph Via di San Basilio 15 ☎ 06 422 901, ⊛ boscolohotels.com; map p.105. A slick hotel with ultra-cool, contemporary rooms (4 with terraces) and every facility, including a health club housed in a former bank vault and a quirky lobby with a Las Vegas take on Egyptian–Roman history. Dining options now include a sixth-floor roof-terrace restaurant. €320

Daphne Via di San Basilio 55 & Via degli Avigonesi 20 ☎ 06 8745 0086, ⊛ daphne-rome.com; map p.105. A welcoming place in two locations either side of Piazza Barberini, run by an American woman and her Roman husband. Most of the rooms are bright, modern and spacious (though a few are not), and you can choose between shared bathrooms and en suite. €230

TOP 5 LUXURY CHOICES

De Russie see p.230
Grand Hotel Plaza see above
Palazzo Manfredi see p.234
Roma Cavalieri see p.235
Villa Spalletti Trivelli see p.232

14

14

TOP 5 BUDGET CHOICES
The Beehive see p.272
Cervia see below
Locanda Navona see p.227
Mimosa see p.227
Romae see p.233

★ **Eden** Via Ludovisi 49 ☎ 06 478 121, ⓦ edenroma .com; map p.105. Just off Via Veneto, this former private residence is one of Rome's most enchanting hotels, with an inviting lobby and a fireplace that blazes in winter. Rooms on the fifth floor are very special, with balconies offering spectacular views of the city. Or take in the views in the excellent rooftop restaurant, *La Terrazza dell'Eden* (see p.252), where Fellini had a regular table and conducted most of his interviews. Good rates out of season. **€450**

La Residenza Via Emilia 22 ☎ 06 488 789, ⓦ hotel-la -residenza.com; map p.105. Combining the luxury and atmosphere of a grand hotel with the easy-going comforts and intimacy of a private home, this is a great option in the pricey Via Veneto area. Very tranquil too, set well away from the main drag. **€250**

Majestic Via Veneto 50 ☎ 06 421 441, ⓦ hotelmajestic .com; map p.105. Via Veneto's oldest hotel (1889) has ceiling frescoes, silk hangings and big, elaborate antiques that are reminders of its nineteenth-century origins, but colours that have been brightened for a more contemporary feel. Rooms are elegant and spacious, with huge marble bathrooms, free wi-fi and internet points, and the upstairs terrace is devoted to *Filippo La Mantia*, a great Sicilian restaurant, bright with antique mirrors and natural light. **€480**

Modigliani Via della Purificazione 42 ☎ 06 4281 5226, ⓦ hotelmodigliani.com; map p.105. A young artist couple run this tastefully modern hotel with a small garden courtyard on a quiet street just off Piazza Barberini. Splash out on a superior room with a view of St Peter's. Free wi-fi in common rooms. **€230**

Splendide Royal Via di Porta Pinciana 14 ☎ 06 421 689, ⓦ splendideroyal.com; map p.105. This old Veneto area favourite exudes neo-Baroque charm with spacious, light bedrooms decorated in rich gold, cream and red; those that face the Aurelian Wall have magical views of the umbrella pines below. Film buffs should check out the lobby chandelier, which once glittered above Burt Lancaster and Claudia Cardinale in *The Leopard*. Don't miss the rooftop bar, where the views are enhanced by mirrors. **€650**

Victoria Via Campania 41 ☎ 06 473 701, ⓦ hotelvictoriaroma.com; map p.105. Newly remodelled in imperial Roman style, this Swiss-managed hotel is situated between the super-deluxe grandeur of Via Veneto and the verdant freedom of Villa Borghese. Many rooms enjoy views of the ancient walls and beyond **€250**

★ **Villa Spalletti Trivelli** Via Piacenza 4 ☎ 06 4890 7934, ⓦ villaspalletti.it; map p.105. Count Giangiacomo Spalletti Trivelli's family home makes for an elegant yet pleasantly intimate stay, nestled between Via Nazionale and the Quirinale. Its twelve rooms feature family antiques, and there's a lovely garden, spa, fireplace and restaurant, making for a special stay. **€480**

Westin Excelsior Via Veneto 125 ☎ 06 47 081, ⓦ starwoodhotels.com; map p.105. This grand ivory palace on Via Veneto was renovated to its original turn-of-the-century Empire style, adding an indoor pool and spa to keep it the choice of visiting royalty – though the rooms, crammed with antiques, crystal chandeliers and tapestries, are beginning to show signs of wear. The extravagant Villa La Cupola suite is contender for the priciest night in town. **€550**

THE ESQUILINE, MONTI AND TERMINI

★ **Alpi** Via Castelfidardo 84 ☎ 06 444 1235, ⓦ hotelalpi.com; map pp.114–115. One of the more peaceful yet convenient options close to Termini, recently renovated, with spruce and contemporary (if sometimes somewhat small) en-suite doubles – better than you would expect in a hotel of this category. An excellent choice given its proximity to Termini. **€195**

Artorius Via del Boschetto 13 ☎ 06 482 1196, ⓦ hotelartoriusrome.com; map pp.114–115. On a cobbled Monti street and with just ten rooms, decorated in classic style, this family-run hotel is an appealing mid-range option. The attractive courtyard makes a pleasant spot for breakfast in fine weather and for drinks after dark. No wi-fi, but rooms have free internet access via cable. **€250**

Astoria Garden Via Bachelet 8 ☎ 06 446 9908, ⓦ hotelastoriagarden.it; map pp.114–115. In a peaceful area east of Termini near Piazza Indipendenza, this renovated 1904 *palazzo* was once the home of an Italian count. Rooms are lovely and quiet and some have balconies that look onto the Mediterranean plants and orange trees in the large garden. Guests are entitled to an hour's free wi-fi. There's a bar in the lobby too. **€150**

★ **The Beehive** Via Marghera 8 ☎ 06 4470 4553, ⓦ the-beehive.com; pp.114–115. This cheery and friendly ecological – and economical – hotel is run by an American couple and has fairly basic but very well-decorated doubles (a few with private bathrooms) and a more spartan dorm, plus they have some rooms in shared apartments west of Termini. Wi-fi and internet are free, and there are some games in the lounge area, plus they have a peaceful grden that feels like a real haven so close to Termini. Dorm beds **€35**, double **€90**

Cervia Via Palestro 55 ☎ 06 491 057, ⓦ hotel cerviaroma.com; map pp.114–115. Basic but clean rooms in a lively and very friendly small hotel; *Rough Guide* readers can request a 5 percent discount on Basic (no a/c) rooms. They also now have two dorms, one for women, one for men. Free cribs and wi-fi in lobby. Great value. Dorm **€20**, double **€90**

Crosti Via Castelfidardo 54 ☎06 446 8597, ⍟crostihotel.it; map pp.114–115. Not boutique, but designed with the Italian business traveller in mind, this relative newcomer is modern and comfortable. Close to Termini, in the quieter district near the British embassy. **€180**

De Monti Via Panisperna 95 ☎06 481 4763, ⍟hoteldemonti.com; map pp.114–115. Situated on the third floor (no lift) of a sixteenth-century *palazzo* in the heart of trendy Monti, this small hotel has spacious, simply but stylishly furnished rooms with nice bathrooms. Very friendly and hospitable, if not especially cheap, with good breakfasts served in guest rooms. **€360**

Des Artistes Via Villafranca 20 ☎06 445 4365, ⍟hoteldesartistes.com; map pp.114–115. One of the better hotels in the Termini area – exceptionally good value, spotlessly clean and with a wide range of rooms, including dorms. En-suite rooms have wi-fi, and you can eat breakfast or recover from a long day of sightseeing on the breezy roof terrace. Dorm **€30**, double **€160**

Duca d'Alba Via Leonina 14 ☎06 484 471, ⍟hotelducadalba.com; map pp.114–115. A reliable three-star in the heart of Monti, just steps from the district's best restaurants and nightlife, with stylish, recently renovated rooms with free wi-fi and a/c; some also have balconies. Heavy discounts are common. **€250**

Elide Via Firenze 50 ☎06 488 3977, ⍟hotelelide.com; map pp.114–115. A *pensione* for over fifty years, this has clean, simple rooms and friendly staff. Many of the rooms are right on a busy street, though; if noise bothers you, ask for one at the back. Free wi-fi in rooms and the lobby. **€225**

Exedra Piazza della Repubblica 47 ☎06 489 381, ⍟boscolohotels.com; map pp.114–115. Opened in 2003 in a Neoclassical *palazzo* that curves around part of the piazza, the *Exedra* breathed new life into the Termini area, with large, elegantly furnished rooms, a champagne bar and a lovely spa, which includes a small outdoor roof pool (see p.300). **€400**

Giuliana Via A. Depretis 70 ☎06 488 0795, ⍟hotelgiuliana.com; map pp.114–115. This fairly newly renovated Termini area hotel has a loyal following and a friendly and helpful owner. Very simple rooms, but well maintained. **€180**

IQ Hotel Via Firenze 8 ☎06 488 0465, ⍟www.iqhotelroma.it; map pp.114–115. It's not the most characterful hotel in the city but very convenient for Termini and the opera house and has a large roof terrace for relaxing. There is a free gym and sauna, and a nearby garage has pay parking. Good breakfasts, too. For do-it-yourselfers, there is a coin-operated laundry. **€250**

★ **Leon's Place** Via XX Settembre 90/94 ☎06 890 871, ⍟leonsplacehotel.it; map pp.114–115. This Termini area boutique hotel is on the edge of an upscale residential area with good shops and dining, and has a spacious lobby with a bar at the far end that serves light meals and a small courtyard garden. Though on the small side, the rooms are sleekly modern, all black and white with splashes of colour and deft design touches. Free wi-fi and a decent buffet breakfast. **€260**

Nicolas Inn Via Cavour 295 ☎06 9761 8483, ⍟nicolasinn.com; map pp.114–115. A brief stroll from the Colosseum, this B&B is run by a friendly American–Italian couple keen to make guests feel at home. The rooms are a good size, spotless and elegant, and have free wi-fi. Breakfast is included but is served in a nearby bar. **€200**

Perugia Via del Colosseo 7 ☎06 679 7200, ⍟hperugia.it; map pp.114–115. Tucked away in Monti, on a narrow street off Via Cavour, close to the Forum and Colosseum, and under the same ownership since 1984. Rooms here are small but bright and clean, with white tiled floors and crisp modern furniture. Five floors, no elevator. **€160**

Quirinale Via Nazionale 7 ☎06 470 7804 or ☎06 4707, ⍟hotelquirinale.it; map pp.114–115. Giuseppe Verdi greeted the Teatro dell'Opera crowds here after the 1893 Rome premiere of *Falstaff*, and it's still a pleasantly old-fashioned place with a fireplace in its lobby. A secret passageway leads directly to the opera house without going onto the street (open to hotel or dinner guests with a performance ticket). Rooms are large and antique-filled with spacious marble bathrooms and wi-fi (for a fee). There's a free internet point in the lobby, and parking is relatively cheap at €15 a night. **€270**

Radisson Blu Es Via F. Turati 171 ☎06 444 841, ⍟radissonblu.com/eshotel-rome; map pp.114–115. One of the first hotels to spark the renaissance of the Termini area, with starkly aesthetic rooms and a state-of-the-art rooftop bar and pool. The rooms are great, the hotel is very comfortable, wi-fi is free and the location is very convenient for Termini – if not in the most upmarket part of town, given the rates. **€450**

Residenza Cellini Via Modena 5 ☎06 4782 5204, ⍟residenzacellini.it; map pp.114–115. The rooms here are pleasant and large with a slightly old-fashioned feel. Staff are extremely friendly and wi-fi is free, as is the lobby's internet point. **€250**

★ **Romae** Via Palestro 49 ☎06 446 3554, ⍟hotelromae.com; map pp.114–115. Extremely comfortable, with thirty contemporary rooms that offer some of the best value in the Termini area, or indeed the city, all presided over by Australian–Italian owners. Free wi-fi and iPads for rent. Great value. **€120**

Rosetta Via Cavour 295 ☎06 4782 3069, ⍟rosettahotel.com; map pp.114–115. Family-run *pensione* in a nice location very close to the Colosseum. The

14

14

small rooms are a bit shabby and lacking in frills, but they're comfortable enough and have private baths. Wi-fi in the lobby only. No breakfast. €95

Suite Dreams Via Modena 5 ☎06 4891 3907, ⓦsuitedreams.it; map pp.114–115. Simple but stylish rooms, quite spacious with generous bathrooms, free wi-fi and a DVD library for guests' use. The location is a good one – well distanced from but still easy walking from Termini. €180

Yes Via Magenta 15 ☎06 4436 3836, ⓦyeshotel.it; map pp.114–115. About 5min from Termini (and even closer to the airport bus stop), this is not only extremely convenient for the station but also a huge step up from some of the grotty options in the area – and you'll pay far less here than for a similar room in the centre. Tailored to the needs of Termini's business travellers rather than its backpackers, the rooms are comfortable if a little bland. €170

THE CELIAN HILL AND SAN GIOVANNI

Capo d'Africa Via Capo d'Africa 54 ☎06 772 801, ⓦhotelcapodafrica.com; map pp.130–131. A former nineteenth-century convent, this sleek hotel has a brightly modern interior with contemporary art and furniture, and, although the TVs have no English-language channels, the rooms are spacious and very comfortable. Good, welcoming service too. Enjoy the lively lobby with bar downstairs and the roof-terrace breakfast room, which has a good view of Colle Oppio and the Colosseum. €420

★ **Lancelot** Via Capo d'Africa 47 ☎06 7045 0615, ⓦlancelothotel.com; map pp.130–131. Just 2min from the Colosseum, this friendly family-run hotel has rooms with oriental carpets on wood or terrazzo floors, and an attractive bar. Dinner is good too, served at intimate round tables with other guests for €25 a head. The terrace and some rooms have a view of the Colosseum and the staff are well informed and helpful. Wi-fi is free, as is the lobby internet point. Limited parking for €10. €170

★ **Palazzo Manfredi** Via Labicana 125 ☎06 775 91380, ⓦhotelpalazzomanfredi.com; map pp.130–131. This hotel couldn't help but be a haven, given the traffic and tourist mayhem outside, but its lobby, rooms and fabulous top-floor restaurant are truly an oasis of peace and tranquillity in one of Rome's busiest tourist hotspots. Its fourteen rooms and suites are thoughtfully and very stylishly furnished and equipped, with big beds, beautiful bathrooms, Nespresso machines, iPads and more, and the views of the Colosseum from some of them are arguably Rome's best. It's a genuinely luxurious boutique hotel experience, and one that's all too rare in Rome – hence the high prices. €520

THE AVENTINE HILL AND SOUTH

Abitart Via P. Matteucci 10–20 ☎06 454 3191, ⓦabitarthotel.com; map pp.140–141. Eight quirky art-themed suites – Metaphysical, Pop Art, Deconstructionist and so on – just off Via Ostiense, a 5min walk from Piramide

metro station (line B), and very handy for going out in Testaccio. Free wi-fi and internet, generous breakfasts and garage parking (€18). Often lower rates at weekends. €170

★ **Sant'Anselmo** Piazza Sant'Anselmo 2 ☎06 570 057, ⓦaventinohotels.com; map pp.140–141. One of the most peaceful places you could stay in arguably central Rome's most upscale residential neighbourhood, the *Sant'Anselmo* has beautifully furnished rooms (each with a different theme) that have been fairly recently renovated. Breakfast is good, there's a nice lounge and garden, and parking is free. Deals available outside high season. €260

TRASTEVERE AND THE JANICULUM HILL

Antico Borgo di Trastevere Vicolo del Buco 7 ☎06 588 3774, ⓦtrasteverehouse.it; map pp.160–161. This small, seventeenth-century palace has been neatly done up. Some rooms are a bit cramped and TVs have no English-language channels, but this quiet corner in a bustling district is just seconds away from all the action – and guests can use free wi-fi at the sister *Domus Tiberina* (see below). €170

Carmel Via G. Mameli 11 ☎06 580 9921, ⓦhotelcarmel.it; map pp.160–161. Pleasant, simply furnished en-suite rooms, two with their own terrace, on the western side of Trastevere. There's also a leafy roof terrace for all guests, free wi-fi in the lobby and a kosher kitchen, although no English-language TV. €140

Cisterna Via della Cisterna 7–9 ☎06 581 7212, ⓦcisternahotel.it; map pp.160–161. Friendly two-star with a homely feel, bang in the middle of Trastevere. Twenty rooms, some with colourful tiled floors and wood-beamed ceilings; all have private bathrooms. The peaceful terrace garden out the back is a treat. Free internet point and wi-fi. €95

Domus Tiberina Via in Piscinula 37 ☎06 580 3033, ⓦhoteldomustiberina.it; map pp.160–161. Located on the quieter side of Trastevere, this small hotel nevertheless lies within a few minutes' walk of everything. Rooms are small, but newly refurbished. Free wi-fi in the lobby, though TVs have no English-language channels. €170

Gran Meliá Rome Via del Gianicolo 3, ☎06 925 901, ⓦgranmeliarome.com; map pp.160–161. Once the site of the villa of Nero's mother, Agrippina, and in 2012 transformed into an urban resort hotel, with pools and gardens, spa, a library, lovely sitting areas, stylish bars and a gourmet restaurant – *Vivavoce* – under the guidance of award-winning chef, Alfonso Iaccarino. Just above the Tiber, it's an easy walk to the centre and the Vatican. Some of the posher rooms have private terraces with panoramic views. €725

Grand Hotel del Gianicolo Viale delle Mura Gianicolensi 107 ☎06 5833 3405, ⓦgrandhotelgianicolo.it; map pp.160–161. Commanding the heights of the Janiculum Hill, close to the Doria Pamphilj Park and with views over the

TOP 5 BOUTIQUE CHOICES

Leon's Place see p.233
Lunetta see p.228
Portrait Suites see p.231
Relais Orso see p.227
Sant' Anselmo see opposite

entire city, this former convent has elegant and understated rooms and a large, mosaic-tiled swimming pool set in subtropical gardens. Easy bus connection to the centre of town (20min). On-site parking. **€230**

Residenza Arco de' Tolomei Via Arco de' Tolomei 27 ☎06 5832 0819, ⓦbbarcodeitolomei.com; map pp.160–161. In an attractively crumbling *palazzo* on Trastevere's quieter, eastern side, this old-world B&B is full of family antiques, but remains decidedly unstuffy. A generous breakfast is served in the conservatory. **€205**

Residenza Santa Maria Via dell'Arco di San Calisto 20 ☎06 5833 5103, ⓦhotelsantamaria.net; map pp.160–161. Run by the same owners as the *Santa Maria* (see below), but a bit better for families or groups, in that four of the six rooms are triples or quads. There's wi-fi, an internet point in the lobby and bikes for guests' use – all free; parking is reasonable. **€250**

Santa Maria Vicolo del Piede 2 ☎06 589 4626, ⓦhotelsantamaria.net; map pp.160–161. Near Piazza Santa Maria, in the heart of Trastevere, the rooms of this small three-star surround an orange-tree-filled garden, making it feel far removed from the city. The hotel has free bikes for guests to use, free wi-fi and internet and serves *aperitivi* in the afternoon. Parking €15–25. **€260**

Trastevere Via Luciano Manara 24–25 ☎06 581 4713, ⓦhoteltrastevere.net; map pp.160–161. A good place to stay if you want to be in the heart of Trastevere, with nicely renovated doubles, and apartments for up to five people. Simply furnished, yet homely. Ground-floor windows are double-glazed and wi-fi is free. **€120**

Villa della Fonte Via della Fonte d'Olio 8 ☎06 580 3797, ⓦvillafonte.com; map pp.160–161. This attractive, hidden-away place feels almost secret, yet is just a few steps from Piazza Santa Maria in Trastevere. Rooms are cosy and old-fashioned but have free wi-fi. **€190**

VILLA BORGHESE AND NORTH

Aldrovandi Palace Via Ulisse Aldrovandi 15 ☎06 322 3993, ⓦaldrovandi.com; map pp.170–171. Just north of Villa Borghese, this luxurious hotel has a bright interior looking out over a lovely landscaped garden with swimming pool, and crisp, contemporary and spacious rooms. It's also home to the fabulous *Oliver Glöwig* restaurant (see p.254). It's a bit of a way from the city centre, but their free car service will whisk you to the Via Veneto and the Spanish Steps in no time. Parking is free. **€660**

Casa Montani Piazzale Flaminio 9 ☎06 3260 0421, ⓦcasamontani.com; map pp.170–171. Just outside the Porta del Popolo, this self-styled "luxury town house" has only five rooms, all designed by the friendly French–Italian owners and decked out in a chic palette of neutral colours with touches of luxury, including designer bathrooms and breakfast served in your room on fine porcelain. Free internet point and wi-fi. Book well ahead. **€260**

Fenix Viale Gorizia 5–7 ☎06 854 0741, ⓦfenixhotel.it; map pp.170–171. Just off Via Nomentana, the rather drab exterior of this hotel belies the bright silks, carpets and antique furniture within. It's very comfortable, with magazines everywhere, an eclectic library, free internet terminal and wi-fi. Its cheery little restaurant, *Nini*, is reasonably priced, and much favoured by business travellers. Relax in the small garden with an *aperitivo*, on comfy divans under a gauzy gazebo. **€180**

★ **Giorni Felici** Viale Ippocrate 116 ☎335 838 4927, ⓦbbgiornifelici.it; map pp.170–171. Feel like a proper Roman in this beautifully furnished apartment with two lovely, excellent-value double rooms, each with its own bathroom. You're not far from Termini and in any case the Bologna neighbourhood is great, as are the couple who run the place. **€80**

★ **Rome Cavalieri** Via A. Cadlolo 101 ☎06 350 91, ⓦromecavalieri.com; map pp.170–171. Rome's best hotel is quite a way out of the city centre, but if you can afford it it is worth staying here once, not only to check out Heinz Beck's legendary three-Michelin-star rooftop restaurant (see p.254) but also to enjoy its curious mix of 1960s glamour and old-fashioned style. The rooms are large and comfortable, with balconies that enjoy perhaps the best and most all-encompassing view of Rome; there are three lovely pools (two outdoor, one indoor) and service which is impeccably gracious and professional. So good is it in fact, you may not care to venture into the city at all; if you do, it's good to know that the hotel runs regular free shuttle buses to Piazza Barberini. **€550**

THE VATICAN AND PRATI

Amalia Via Germanico 66 ☎06 3972 2356, ⓦhotelamalia.com; map pp.188–189. Located on an attractive corner of a busy shopping area near the Vatican, like its second hotel, the more upmarket *Dei Consoli* (see p.236), this place provides four-star amenities at three-star prices, including quiet (double-glazing on all windows) and nicely renovated double rooms. **€170**

Arcangelo Via Boezio 15 ☎06 687 4143, ⓦhotelarcangeloroma.com; map pp.188–189. This clean and reliable hotel on a quiet street near the Vatican was renovated relatively recently and emphasizes comfort and elegance in its rooms and public spaces, which have a warm, clubby feel. Free wi-fi. Parking free but space is limited. **€180**

14

14

Atlante Star Via Vitelleschi 34 ☏ 06 687 3233, ⌨ atlantehotels.com; map pp.188–189. Just a 5min walk from the Vatican, this is perhaps Prati's most luxurious option; it offers lovely, antique-filled rooms with marble floors and pleasant retro touches, or more modern, minimalist options, usually preferred by its business clientele. Some rooms (like 406) have lovely views of St Peter's dome, and the impressive rooftop terrace restaurant offers a 360-degree view of the city. There are free airport pick-ups (3 days' notice required). **€285**

Black Hotel Via Raffaello Sardiello 18 ☏ 06 6641 0148, ⌨ blackhotel.it; map pp.188–189. Although quite a way out (7km southwest of the Vatican), this is a good budget option with an outdoor pool for summer swims. Rooms are cheerfully bright despite the black exterior and corridors. Free parking. Metro A to Cornelia, then bus #246. **€145**

Bramante Vicolo delle Palline 24 ☏ 06 6880 6426, ⌨ hotelbramante.com; map pp.188–189. Small and welcoming hotel that has a great location on this peaceful Borgo street and nicely furnished en-suite rooms with large bathrooms. **€245**

Colors Via Boezio 31 ☏ 06 687 4030, ⌨ colorshotel .com; map pp.188–189. This hostel/hotel in a quiet neighbourhood near the Vatican renovated all its rooms a few years ago and they are still prim and well-kept, plus they have the bonus of kitchen facilities, free wi-fi in the lobby, in-room TV and small terrace. En-suite rooms go for around €30 more than those with shared bath, and they also rent self-catering apartments. Dorm **€30**, double **€90**, 2-person apartment **€80**

★ **Columbus** Via della Conciliazione 33 ☏ 06 686 5435, ⌨ hotelcolumbus.net; map pp.188–189. On the main route to St Peter's, discreetly set in Palazzo della Penitenzieri, this cardinal's palace now belongs to the Order of the Holy Sepulchre. Rooms are plainly furnished with simple antiques, and the public areas are comfortable and feature the spartanly elegant *Colonne* bar. The *Veranda* restaurant has a fifteenth-century frescoed ceiling, lovely by candlelight, or you can dine on the patio in warm weather. Free parking, and Ipads for the use of guests. **€190**

Crowne Plaza St Peter's Via Aurelia Antica 415 ☏ 06 66420, ⌨ crowneplaza.com; map pp.188–189. A bit of a bus ride west of the Vatican, but the comforts here include a spa, swimming pools indoors and out, garden and tennis courts – pretty good considering the price. Decor is a bit utilitarian, but rooms are spacious with modern conveniences. Free parking. Metro A to Cornelia, then bus #889 (Sun bus #98). **€180**

★ **Dei Consoli** Via Varrone 2d ☏ 06 6889 2972, ⌨ hoteldeiconsoli.com; map pp.188–189. Right in the heart of Prati, this is one of the best choices in the Vatican area, with thoughtfully designed rooms, a lovely roof terrace and excellent, friendly service. Parking available for €20 a night. **€300**

TOP 5 CHOICES UNDER €250

Alpi see p.232
Lancelot see p.234
Locarno see p.231
Teatro Pace see p.228
Zanardelli see p.228

Domus Mazzini Via Monte Zebio 9 ☏ 06 4542 1592, ⌨ domushotel.it; map pp.170–171. Small *pensione* with just four nicely decorated double rooms. A bit of a hike from the Vatican and St Peter's, but the neighbourhood is pleasant, and the place has the feel of staying in someone's home. Free wi-fi. **€130**

Farnese Via Alessandro Farnese 30 ☏ 06 321 1953, ⌨ farnese.hotelinroma.com; map pp.188–189. Another grand aristocratic residence that has been turned into an upscale hotel. The rooms have handmade walnut furniture, marble bathrooms and soundproof windows and doors. Some feature private balconies, and the rooftop terrace breakfast room offers a great view of the Vatican. Free wi-fi. Limited free parking (first-come, first-served). **€260**

Franklin Via Rodi 29 ☏ 06 3903 0165, ⌨ franklinhotel .info; map pp.188–189. The central theme here is music – everywhere: don't be surprised to find a snare drum for a night table or a disco ball in the bathroom. Rooms have Bang & Olufsen stereos and the reception loans from its library of hundreds of CDs. Free wi-fi. Now a Best Western hotel. **€195**

Gerber Via degli Scipioni 241 ☏ 06 321 9986, ⌨ hotelgerber.it; map pp.188–189. Great value for its convenient location on a quiet street not far from the Vatican, with elegant, comfortable rooms and free in-room wi-fi. Ten percent discount for *Rough Guide* readers. **€175**

Giulio Cesare Via degli Scipioni 287 ☏ 06 321 0751, ⌨ hotelgiuliocesare.com; map pp.188–189. No longer the Villa Patricia, home of an Italian countess, but you may feel charmed like royalty as you enter the foyer, with its glistening golden ceiling. Attentive staff lead you down mirror-lined hallways to elegant rooms with marble bathrooms – all very handsome. **€240**

Isa Via Cicerone 39 ☏ 06 321 2610, ⌨ hotelisa.net; map pp.188–189. A 10min walk from the Vatican, this Prati hotel has moderately large rooms, some with balconies, and is furnished in neutral tones with shiny marble fittings in the bathrooms. Free wi-fi and internet in the lobby, and a great roof-garden bar. Excellent value. **€230**

La Rovere Vicolo Sant'Onofrio 4–5 ☏ 06 6880 6739, ⌨ hotellarovere.biz; map pp.188–189. Just round the corner from St Peter's and across the bridge from Piazza Navona, this attractive small hotel is tucked away from all the bustle. The terrace garden and antique-filled common areas are perfect for relaxing. Rooms are simply furnished but nice enough. Free internet point and wi-fi. **€190**

Metropolis Via delle Milizie 26 ☎06 375 12539, ⓦhotelmetropolisrome.com; map pp.188–189. The Deco origins of the *Metropolis* are played up with modern furnishings inspired by the Twenties and Thirties. It's popular with business travellers and has free wi-fi and a busy bar that lays on periodic wine tastings. **€290**

Villa Laetitia Lungotevere delle Armi 22 ☎06 322 6776, ⓦvillalaetitia.com; map pp.188–189. The Fendi fashion family restored this fourteen-room Art Nouveau villa along the Tiber, filling it with antiques from all over the world to complement the marble pillars and ornate ceilings perfectly. Just the thing if you're after a gracious, old-world feel. **€200**

Visconti Palace Via Federico Cesi 37 ☎06 3684, ⓦviscontipalace.com; map pp.188–189. Near Piazza Cavour and the Justice Palace, this modern hotel has 242 spacious rooms and does a lovely buffet breakfast, light lunch at the bar and a rooftop barbecue dinner (May-Oct). Free (30min) wi-fi in lobby and a small 24hr gym. **€360**

AROUND ROME

La Posta Vecchia Palo Laziale Ladispoli ☎06 994 9501, ⓦlapostavecchia.com; map p.212. Situated by the sea about 40km northwest of Rome, just outside Ladispoli, oil baron John Paul Getty's former villa is a luxurious and romantic hotel choice, with a beautiful garden, tennis court, a spa and small pool overlooking the water. Trains run regularly from Termini to Ladispoli station, from where it's a short taxi ride. **€440**

HOSTELS

Rome has plenty of **hostels**, although they can get pretty crowded during peak season. Some places separate guests by gender, and most have private rooms as well as dorms. In addition to the options below, *Cervia* (see p.232), *Colors* (see p.236), *Des Artistes* (see p.233) and *The Beehive* (see p.232) have dorm accommodation. These and the hostels below offer breakfast (usually extra) and, with the exception of the *YWCA*, none of them has a curfew. However, some places impose age restrictions for dorms.

Alessandro Palace Via Vicenza 42 ☎06 446 1958, ⓦhostelalessandro.com; map pp.114–115. This has been voted one of the top hostels in Europe, and it sparkles with creative style. Pluses include no lock-out or curfew, a good bar with free pizza every night, internet access and satellite TV. You can stay in dorm beds or private rooms, with shared bath about €20 cheaper than en suite. They have another branch close by but on the city-centre side of

---

SHORT-RENTAL APARTMENTS

Renting an **apartment** in Rome has many advantages: for families with children or small groups, it can be a cheaper option than a hotel and much more flexible. Short-term rentals are becoming very popular, however, so book well in advance. All of the agencies listed below have accommodation ranging from small city-centre apartments to grand villas outside the city. Several **hotels** also rent apartments, among them the *Campo de' Fiori* (see p.228), *The Beehive* (p.232), *Colors* (p.236) and the apartment-hotel *Palazzo al Velabro* (see p.230). If you really want to do things in style, you can rent the apartment in the Keats-Shelley House on Piazza di Spagna, through the UK's Landmark Trust (see p.94), or stay on the coast at J. Paul Getty's former villa, *La Posta Vecchia* (see p.237). Finally, sites like ⓦairbnb.com, ⓦhouse-trip .com and others have excellent choices in Rome.

APARTMENT AGENCIES

At Home Via Margutta 13 ☎06 3212 0102, ⓦat -home-italy.com. One of the city's best choices of short-let apartments, for anything from a week to six months. They also have two lovely bed-and-breakfasts not far from Termini (see ⓦathometownhouse.com).

City Apartments Viale Opita Oppio 78 ☎06 7698 3140, ⓦroma.cityapartments.it. A great selection of apartments all over the city, from around €140 a night, and very flexible on length of stay, especially out of season.

Cross-Pollinate ☎06 9936 9799, ⓦcross-pollinate .com. The guys at *The Beehive* (p.232) also run this fab apartment-booking service with properties in the major cities of Italy and around Europe. Not surprisingly, they're big on Rome, and have a wide variety of different-sized places all over the city, at a range of prices. Above all, they're nice people, with a strong focus on customer service and satisfaction.

GowithOh ☎ +44 203 499 5148, ⓦgowithoh.co.uk. Great UK holiday apartment site that focuses on European cities and has a good range of properties in the centre of Rome – mostly at excellent rates.

Welcome in Rome Via Ottaviano 73 ☎06 3975 1474, ⓦhomesinrome.com. Fairly upscale apartments in the city centre, with prices starting at around €150 a night for a one-bedroom to several times that for three to four bedrooms. Has a good selection of larger options.

14

14

Termini, *Alessandro Downtown*, at Via C. Cattaneo 23 (☎06 4434 0147; dorm €25, double €95). Dorm €26, double €110

Ottaviano Via Ottaviano 6 ☎06 3973 8138, ⓦpensioneottaviano.com; map pp.188–189. This simple hostel near the Vatican is very popular with backpackers; book well in advance. Facilities are a bit sparse: no wi-fi, one internet connection and no TV in the rooms, though the communal TV does play DVDs. Dorm €28, twin €50

Sandy Via Cavour 136 ☎06 488 4585, ⓦsandyhostel .com; map pp.114–115. Run by the same management as the *Ottaviano*, but arguably with better facilities which include free internet, bed linen and hot showers. Dorm €19, double €90

Yellow Via Palestro 44 ☎06 4938 2682, ⓦthe-yellow .com; map pp.114–115. Friendly, youthful hostel that's self-consciously cool, and encourages a lively scene in the downstairs bar, so if you're over 39 or after somewhere quiet, you might want to enquire about a private room. Free wi-fi, no curfew. Dorm €26, en-suite double €60

YWCA Via C. Balbo 4 ☎06 488 0460, ⓦywca-ucdg.it; map pp.114–115. Opera, ballet and music fans on a budget can stay right by the Teatro dell'Opera. Open to women and men, with single rooms available for €30 less than doubles, and just a 10min walk from Termini, although the market outside may wake you up earlier than you might want. Midnight curfew. Common room with TV, no wi-fi, but there is an internet point. Double €80, triple/quad €28 per person

CONVENTS

Rome has lots of accommodation run by **religious organizations**. Many are no longer as cheap as they used to be, and hotel websites often have the better bargains, but they can often be found in central locations (see ⓦmonasterystays.com for more). Bear in mind that most have strict rules about curfews and often a single-gender policy.

Casa di Santa Brigida Piazza Farnese 96 ☎06 6889 2596, ⓦbrigidine.org; map pp.54–55. In a hard-to-beat location, and with clean and comfortable rooms with private bathroom and no curfew, this is perhaps the best convent in town. It's not cheap, although breakfast is included. They also have a sister residence that costs less,

north of the centre at Via delle Isole 34 (☎06 814 393), near Via Nomentana and Santa Costanza. €190

Suore Mantellate Serve di Maria Via S. Giuseppe Calasanzio ☎06 6880 3344; map p.38. Bang in the centre near Piazza Navona, this place has clean and decent double rooms. €80

CAMPING

For those determined to sleep outdoors, there are a few **campsites** – unsurprisingly, some way out of the city. However, they are easy enough to get to and also offer bungalows. Bear in mind they are only open from spring to early autumn.

Camping Fabulous Via di Malafede 205, Acilia ☎06 525 9354, ⓦcamping.it/lazio/fabulous; map p.212. Set just off Via Cristoforo Colombo, the main road down to the sea, this can be a bit noisy, but the setting is great – shaded by majestic umbrella pines and with a pool, tennis courts, minigolf and other facilities. If you arrive by bus, come during the day, as the bus stop is a bit isolated and might be tricky in the dark. Wi-fi points and breakfast cost extra. Take the train from Roma San Paolo to Acilia, or metro line B to EUR Fermi and then bus #709. Bungalow €40, camping €11 per person plus €12 per pitch.

Camping Flaminio Via Flaminia Nuova 821 ☎06 333 2604, ⓦvillageflaminio.it; map p.212. The closest site to the city, 8km north of the centre, offering tent camping or bungalows for up to five people. Also has a swimming pool

and restaurant. Take the Roma-Nord train from Piazzale Flaminio to Due Ponti, or bus #910 to Piazza Mancini and then bus #200 (ask the driver to drop you at the "fermata più vicino al campeggio". March–Oct. Tent pitch €6 plus €10 per person, 2-person bungalow €52, 5-person €155

Camping Tiber Via Tiberina Km1400 ☎06 3361 0733, ⓦcampingtiber.com; map p.212. This campsite, right beside the Tiber, is quiet, spacious and friendly, with a supermarket, bar/pizzeria, swimming pool and really hot showers. It has some 100 bungalows, as well as three camping areas. March–Oct. The Roma-Nord train from Piazzale Flaminio (about 20min), then a free shuttle bus (8am–11pm every 30min) from the nearby Prima Porta station. Tent pitch €5 plus €11 per person, double bungalow with bath €42

Eating

Rome is undeniably a major-league city, but it doesn't compare to London or Paris for cutting-edge trendiness, which can be bad news for nightlife but it's great news for food. The city is changing, to be sure – that wonderful, cheap, traditional trattoria serving high-quality authentic Roman cuisine has become a bit harder to find in the last decade or so, and eating out as a whole has become pricier. But food remains one of the highlights of any trip to the city, and, as long as you choose carefully, you're unlikely to be disappointed with either the quality on offer or the choice.

Most city-centre restaurants offer standard Italian dishes, and many specialize purely in **Roman cuisine** (see box, pp.242–243), but there have been a few more adventurous places cropping up of late. At the geographical centre of the country, the capital also has numerous establishments dedicated to a variety of **regional cuisines** (see box, p.249) and a reasonable number of **ethnic restaurants** (see box, p.251). The city is also blessed with an abundance of good, honest **pizzerias** (see box, p.254), churning out thin, crispy-baked pizza from wood-fired ovens, loads of good **bars and cafés**, where you can get a sandwich and sometimes a full meal, and a **gelateria** on every corner selling top-quality ice cream and fruit shakes (see box, p.244). Consider also eating at a **wine bar** (p.265) – Rome has some fabulous ones, serving cold cuts and cheeses and often hot food, too. If you want to cut costs and hang out with the cool people, Rome has a host of places offering a "free" *aperitivo* buffet with a drink on weekday evenings – we've detailed a few (see p.266), but they're listed throughout the text.

Most Italians start their day in a bar, their **breakfast** consisting of a cappuccino and a *cornetto* – a glazed or jam-, custard- or chocolate-filled croissant, sweeter than the French variety. **Sandwiches** (panini) can be pretty substantial and are served throughout the day for €2–3; bars also offer *tramezzini*, ready-made sliced white bread with mixed fillings – generally less appetizing than panini but still popular and slightly cheaper at around €2 a time. Don't forget that **bakeries** and **delis** are also great places to pick up a spot of lunch (see p.289). We also have information on **food markets** (see p.295) and city-centre **supermarkets** (see p.290).

If you want hot **takeaway food**, **pizza** by the slice (*pizza al taglio*) is sold pretty much everywhere. Expect to pay €2–3 for a decent-sized slice. A *rosticceria* (literally a "roaster", specializing in roasted meat, particular chickens), or **tavola calda** (literally "hot table", an informal, usually self-service restaurant or café that serves affordable hot food at lunchtime) is a reliable bet for Roman specialities – *supplì* or *arancini* (deep-fried rice balls), *filetti di baccalà* (pieces of battered cod) and other deep-fried delights, as well as roast potatoes and rotisserie chickens. A complete meal for two at one of these places can cost less than €20, and although they're usually standing-only, some have a counter and a few chairs. Otherwise **prices** in all but the really swanky places remain pretty uniform throughout the city, as do menus, especially in traditional Roman-cuisine restaurants. In an average trattoria, a substantial meal – an antipasto or a pasta dish, plus main course, dessert and house wine, will set you back €30–40 a head, and of course you can spend much less.

CAFÉS AND BARS

There isn't a big difference between **cafés** and **bars** in Rome. Italian bars are typically open from 7am for breakfast and remain open for coffee, tea and snacks throughout the day, closing between 8pm and midnight. Bars do serve alcohol (see p.264) but are rarely places to linger over a drink. We've listed those places where you might like to spend an evening in the following chapter (see pp.263–270). An establishment calling itself a café is more likely to have seating and be a little less functional than the standard Roman bar, the sort of place you might want to have lunch but probably not dinner. Note that many cafés and bars are closed during part or all of **August**.

BAR ETIQUETTE

It's important to be aware of the procedure when you enter an Italian bar. It's cheapest to drink standing at the counter (there's often nowhere to sit anyway), in which case you pay first at the cash desk (*cassa*), present your receipt (*scontrino*) to the barperson and give your order.

RIP-OFF FOOD

In the past decade, truly bad food and rip-off prices have become more commonplace in Rome. With this in mind, it may be wise to **avoid places** that are adjacent to some major monuments such as the Pantheon, Piazza Navona or the Vatican. The food in these places can be poor, and the prices outlandish, sometimes as much as three times the going rate.

It's customary to leave an extra 10c coin on the counter as a tip for each beverage, although no one will object if you don't. If there's waiter service, just sit where you like, though bear in mind that this will cost perhaps twice as much – and often quite a bit more – especially if you sit outside (*fuori*). The difference is usually shown on the price list as a *tavola* (table).

DRINKS

Coffee and tea is generally very good, drunk small and black (espresso, or just *caffè*) and costing €0.80–1 a cup, or as a cappuccino, which costs €1.20–1.50. If you want your espresso watered down, ask for a *caffè americano* or *caffè lungo*. Coffee with a shot of alcohol is *caffè corretto*; with a drop of milk, it's *caffè macchiato*; a full small cup of the same is *caffè macchiato lungo*. Many places also now sell decaffeinated coffee (ask for the brand "Café Hag", even when it isn't), while in summer you might want to have your coffee cold (*caffè freddo*). For a real treat, ask for

granita di caffè – cold coffee with crushed ice, usually topped with cream. In summer, you can drink iced tea (*tè freddo*) – excellent for taking the heat off; hot tea (*tè caldo*) comes with lemon (*con limone*), unless you ask for milk (*con latte*). Milk itself is rarely drunk on its own; you can get warm milk with a dash of coffee (*latte macchiato* or *caffè latte*) and sometimes as milk shakes – *frappe* or *frullati*.

Soft drinks A *spremuta* is a fresh fruit juice, squeezed at the bar, usually orange, but sometimes lemon or grapefruit. There are also crushed-ice *granitas*, offered in several flavours, and available with or without whipped cream (*panna*) on top. Otherwise, there's the usual range of fizzy drinks and concentrated juices; the home-grown Italian version of Coca-Cola, Chinotto, is less sweet and works well with a slice of lemon. Tap water (*acqua del rubinetto*) is quite drinkable, and you won't pay for it in a bar. Mineral water (*acqua minerale*) is a more common choice, either still (*liscia* or *naturale*) or sparkling (*con gas* or *frizzante*) – about €1.50 for a small bottle.

15

RESTAURANTS AND PIZZERIAS

There are numerous good restaurants in the **Centro Storico**, and it's still surprisingly easy to find places that are not tourist traps. The **Tridente** and around **Campo de' Fiori** are similarly well served, and the neighbouring **Ghetto** is full of appealing restaurants (kosher and non) serving traditional Roman-Jewish cuisine. The area around **Termini** is packed with cheap places to eat, although some of them are of dubious reliability, and you might do better heading up to the nearby student area of **San Lorenzo**, where you can often eat far better for the same money. South of the centre, **Testaccio** is well endowed with decent, moderately priced trattorias, a few serving the best of Rome's offal specialities, while across the river, **Trastevere** is Rome's traditional restaurant enclave and is accordingly thronged with eating options – and people. The result is that the number of authentic trattorias in the area has declined over recent years, but you'll still easily find good – and often great – meals here, at all price levels.

As for cafés and bars, many restaurants are closed during part or all of **August** – we have specified after each listing where that's the case.

THE MENU

Antipasto and starters/pasta An Italian meal traditionally starts with the antipasto (literally "before the meal"), consisting of various cold cuts of meat, cheeses or vegetable dishes. A plateful of antipasti from a self-service buffet will set you back €8–10 a head, an item chosen from the menu around the same. Bear in mind that, if you're moving on to pasta, let alone a main course, you may need quite an appetite to tackle this. The next course, *il primo*, consists of a soup or pasta dish, and it's fine to eat just this and nothing else; pasta dishes go for around €8–12 (though pricey places will charge more).

Main courses *Il secondo* – the meat or fish course – is usually served alone, except for perhaps a wedge of lemon, a garnish of salad or a potato or two. Watch out when ordering fish, which will either be served whole or by weight: 250g is usually plenty for one person, or ask to have a look at the fish before it's cooked. Main fish or meat courses will normally be €12–20 (more only in the most upscale restaurants). Vegetarians will find plenty of options: many pasta dishes and pizzas, of course, are made

entirely without meat; lentils and other beans and pulses are a part of traditional cookery; and wonderful fresh vegetables and cheeses are always available. Side dishes – *contorni* – are ordered and served separately, and sometimes there won't be much choice: potatoes will often come roasted (*patate arroste*) or chips (*patatine fritte*); salads are either green (*verde*) or mixed (*mista*).

Desserts After *il secondo*, you nearly always get a choice of *frutta* (fresh fruit) and a selection of *dolci* (desserts) – sometimes just ice cream, but often more elaborate items such as *zuppa inglese* (sponge cake or trifle). Many Italians wouldn't dream of going out to eat and not ordering a full five-course meal, plus wine, mineral water, coffee and a *digestivo* such as an *amaro* (home-made herb liqueur) – but don't feel you have to follow suit; you can order as little or as much as you want, and no one will raise an eyebrow. There are tips on what to drink later in the guide (see p.263).

OPENING HOURS AND THE BILL

Opening hours Roman restaurants keep pretty rigid opening hours, generally from 12.30pm to 2.30pm or 3pm

15

CUCINA ROMANA

Rome is rightly proud of its own cuisine (*cucina Romana*), and has numerous restaurants serving **local specialities** to a clientele that would be satisfied with nothing less. Roman cooking is dominated by the earthy preferences of the working classes, with a little influence from the city's millennia-old Jewish population thrown in. Pasta is a staple, and sauces are hearty and satisfying, while meat dishes famously lean towards various unspeakable parts of cows and lambs. You can eat Roman cuisine all over the city centre, but there are some restaurants that do the **classics** better than anywhere else: **Roman-Jewish specialities** like *carciofi alla giudia* ("Jewish-style artichokes"), or the **meat and offal** dishes typical of Testaccio such as *coda alla vaccinara* (oxtail stew) and *pajata* (calf's intestine). And some places excel at all three. A glossary of **food and drink terms** is given later in the guide (see p.340).

PASTA

The most popular varieties of pasta are **tonnarelli** or **bucatini** – thick, hollow spaghetti, basically – which stand up well to the coarse, gutsy sauces the Romans prefer: *cacio e pepe* (pecorino and ground black pepper); *alla carbonara* (with beaten eggs, cubes of pan-fried *guanciale* – cured pork jowl – or pancetta, and pecorino cheese); *alla gricia* (with pecorino and *guanciale*); and *all'amatriciana* (with tomato and *guanciale*). Spaghetti *alle vongole* (with baby clams) is also common, best when a little *peperoncino* is added to give it an extra kick, and *maccheroni alla ciociara*, with slices of sausage, prosciutto and tomato is another favourite. Pasta *al la pajata* (with calf's intestines) is an old Roman standard, as are gnocchi, in Rome usually served with a meat sauce and traditionally eaten on Thursdays.

MAIN COURSES

The classic Roman meat dish is *abbacchio*, milk-fed **lamb** roasted to melting tenderness with rosemary, sage and garlic; you'll also find it *allo scottadito* – grilled and eaten with the fingers. *Saltimbocca alla romana*, thin slices of **veal** cooked with a slice of prosciutto and sage on top, is ever popular. Otherwise, Roman meat dishes are defined by the so-called *quinto quarto* (fifth quarter) of the animal: basically **offal**, which you'll still find on the menus of traditional places, especially those in the old slaughterhouse district of Testaccio. One of the most palatable dishes is *coda alla vaccinara*, oxtail stewed in a rich sauce of tomato and celery. You'll also come across *pajata*, as well as *lingua* (tongue), *rognone* (kidney), *milza* (spleen – delicious as a pâté on toasted bread) and *trippa* (tripe). Look out too for *testerelle d'abbacchio* (lamb's head baked in an oven with herbs and oil) and *coratella* (lamb's heart, liver, lungs and spleen cooked in olive oil with lots of black pepper and onions). More conventionally, **fish** also features, usually as cod (*baccalà*), and best eaten Jewish-style, deep-fried in batter: like British fish and chips, without the chips, sometimes eaten as a starter or snack.

and from 7.30pm to 10.30pm, although some stay open later, especially in summer, and bear in mind that last orders are likely to be a little bit earlier. Many places are closed for two or more weeks in August, sometimes the entire month. It's always an idea to book a table, particularly towards the weekend.

The bill Getting the bill (*il conto*) can sometimes be a struggle – nothing moves fast in Rome when it comes to mealtimes – but when you do service of 10–15 percent will occasionally be included, and if so it must be clearly indicated on the menu and itemized bill. Otherwise, a small tip is fine, rounding the bill up €2–3 or so, as waiters in Italy are paid well. Keep in mind though that despite being made illegal in Lazio years ago, almost everywhere adds a cover charge of around €2 a head; on your bill it will either be labelled as "*coperto*" or "*pane*". There's not much you can do about this except pay it.

CENTRO STORICO

CAFÉS AND BARS

★ **Caffè Sant'Eustachio** Piazza Sant'Eustachio 82 ☎ 06 6880 2048, ⓦ santeustachioilcaffe.it; map p.38. Just behind the Pantheon you'll find what many believe is Rome's best coffee, usually served Neapolitan style – that is, very, very sweet. You can ask for it without sugar, but they'll think you're weird. They also do a good line in coffee-based sweets and cakes. Daily 8.30am–1am, Fri till 1.30am, Sat till 2am.

Boulangerie MP Corso del Rinascimento 34 ⓦ www .boulangeriemp.com; map p.38. Within days of opening in 2013, Roman baker Matteo Piras' flair for French baking quickly had diplomats from the nearby embassy beating a path to his door for fantastic baguettes and croissants, while savvy politicians wander over from Parliament to seek his creative panini or grab a slice of pizza. Most of the

PIZZA, SNACKS AND FRITTI

Rome is surpassed only by Naples in the quality of its **pizzas**, and even this is arguable if you prefer the thin and crispy Roman variety, best when baked in a wood-burning oven (*forno a legna*). Other Roman street food includes various deep-fried specialities, or **fritti**, like *supplì* (fried rice balls with mozzarella), *arancini* (*supplì* with added tomato), as well as **spit-roast** chicken and *porchetta* – pork stuffed with herbs and roasted on a spit; you'll find the latter most commonly in the Castelli Romani, where it's munched between thick hunks of rustic bread.

VEGETABLES

Artichokes (*carciofi*) are the quintessential Roman **vegetable**, best in late winter and early spring, either served *alla romana* (stuffed with garlic and roman mint and stewed) or *alla giudia*, flattened and deep fried in olive oil. Another not-to-be-missed side dish is **fiori di zucca** (batter-fried courgette blossoms stuffed with mozzarella and a sliver of anchovy). Among **other vegetables**, you can find heavenly roast potatoes cooked with rosemary and served with lamb or chicken; great fresh asparagus in spring; *puntarelle* (chicory salad) and various broccoli-like greens in winter; and haricot and borlotti bean dishes year-round.

CHEESE AND DESSERTS

The king of Roman cheeses is **pecorino romano**, sharp, salty and crumbly and used in cooking instead of parmesan. The very best **buffalo mozzarella** from Campania has also become more common in Rome, which is close enough to Naples for it to be rushed up here and eaten fresh.

As for desserts, you may want to try a **tartufo** – chocolate ice cream covered in chocolate, basically – or just have an ice cream on its own: the city centre's **gelaterie** are among the country's best, and there's nothing like enjoying your dessert Italian-style, strolling through the streets after the sun has gone down; we've listed our pick of the best (see box, p.244).

CASTELLI WINES

Much of the wine served in Rome comes from the Castelli Romani, just south of the city. The best known is **Frascati**, a light, easy-drinking white made from a blend of Malvasia and Trebbiano grapes – like many Italian wines, it's much better than the exported varieties would have you believe. The small town of Marino has a great wine **festival** on the first Sunday of October, at which you can sample Castelli Romani wines to your heart's content. Elsewhere in Lazio, the big wine is called **Est! Est! Est!**, another drinkable white that hails from Montefiascone. The story goes that in the twelfth century a bishop's servant was sent to find the best wines of the region and to indicate the ones he liked by daubing the word "Est" on the door of the producer. He liked the wines of Montefiascone so much he daubed the word three times for emphasis. Hopefully, you'll feel the same.

food and ingredients are organic, and there are always tasty vegan options, as well as traditional Italian and wholegrain breads. Mostly standing-room only, but there are a few seats. Mon–Thurs 8.30am–8pm, Fri & Sat 8am–2am, Sun 11am–10pm.

Chiostro di Bramante Via Arco della Pace 5 ☎06 688 090 36, ⓦchiostrodelbramante.it; map p.38. This caffetteria-bistro is an atmospheric and rather stylish hideaway located on the first-floor loggia of this historic fifteenth-century palace (the Raphael fresco here dates to about 1515; see p.47). A great venue for breakfast, lunch, snacks and *aperitivi*, and it's open even when there are no exhibitions on. Good salads, risottos and burgers at reasonable prices. Mon–Fri 10am–8pm Sat & Sun 10am–9pm; lunch served 11.30am–3pm.

La Caffetteria Piazza di Pietra 65 ☎06 679 8147, ⓦgrancaffelacaffettiera.com; map p.38. Bureaucrats flock to this Neapolitan café from the nearby Parliament: the pastries are imported from Naples daily, and the espresso is among Rome's best. Good for lunch, too, with pasta dishes, quiches and suchlike for around €12 and up. Tues–Sun 8.30am–midnight.

Lo Zozzone Via del Teatro Pace 32 ☎06 6880 8575; map p.38. This Roman legend, just around the corner from Piazza Navona and with outside seating, serves *pizza bianca* filled with whatever you want, as well as lots of delicious *pizza al taglio* choices. Daily 10am–9pm, Sat & Sun till 11pm, closed Sun in Oct–March.

Pascucci Via di Torre Argentina 20 ☎06 686 4816, ⓦpascuccifrullati.it; map p.38. This small, stand-up bar is *frullati* central: your choice of fresh fruit whipped up with ice and milk – the ultimate Roman refreshment on a hot day – although it does coffee and all the usual bar stuff, too. Mon–Sat 6am–midnight.

Tazza d'Oro Via degli Orfani 84 ☎06 678 9792, ⓦtazzadorocoffeeshop.com; map p.38. Just a few paces

15

ICE CREAM

Italian **ice cream** (*gelato*) is justifiably famous. However, there is a big difference between the artisanal kind made in the traditional way with wholesome natural ingredients and the highly coloured, industrial pap that is increasingly available across the city centre, so be sure to choose carefully and when in doubt look for the words "*proprio artigianale*" or "*gelato artigianale*". You should reckon on paying around €2 for a cone (*un cono*) with one or two flavours (*gusti*), with the price rising with each flavour you add. Most bars have a fairly mediocre selection, so for real choice go to a proper *gelateria*, where the range is a tribute to the Italian imagination and flair for display; our favourites are below.

Alberto Pica Via della Seggiola 12, Ghetto ☎ 06 686 8405; map pp.54–55. Long-running and award-winning Ghetto-area favourite with lots of unusual flavours. The place to try rice-pudding ice cream, if you've ever fancied it. Mon–Sat 8.30am–2am, July–Sept & Dec also Sun 4.30pm–2am.

Alla Scala Piazza della Scala 51, Trastevere ☎ 06 581 3174; map pp.160–161. This Sicilian-owned joint in Trastevere has some of the very best ice cream in town. Sublime consistency and unusual flavours such as cinnamon and cassata. The cherry and coconut are also great. Daily 1pm–midnight, Sat & Sun till 1am.

Cremeria Monteforte Via della Rotonda 22, Centro Storico ☎ 06 686 7720; map p.38. There's no better place to eat ice cream than sitting on one of the walls that surround the Pantheon, and this award-winning *gelateria* has lots of flavours, including *cremolato di mandorla*, a sweet almond slush, or the intriguing rose petal – like cold Turkish Delight. Tues–Sun 11am–11pm.

Fatamorgana Via G. Bettolo 7, Prati ☎ 06 3751 9093, ⓦ gelateriafatamorgana.it; map pp.188–189. Undoubtedly one of the top *gelaterie* in Rome, *Fatamorgana* serves up scoops of creative and seasonal flavours. Look out for the one-of-a-kind "Kentucky": chocolate with tobacco. There are other branches in Salario (Via Largo di Lesina 9/11), Monti (Piazza degli Zingari 5) and Trastevere (Piazza San Cosimato).

★ **Gelateria Corona** Largo Arenula 27 Campo de' Fiori ☎ 06 6880 8054; map pp.54–55. This family *gelateria* offers some delicious artisanal *sorbetti* (sorbets) and ice cream. Look for classic or creative combinations, like ricotta-saffron or, in season, zesty celery-lime, fresh *melograno* (pomegranate) or *gelsi* (mulberries). Sept brings a chocolate frenzy, when more than a dozen varieties appear, from classic to eccentric (but delicious) pairings. Daily noon–9pm.

Gelateria dei Gracchi Via dei Gracchi 272, Prati ☎ 06 321 6668; map pp.188–189. This unassuming place is the most popular *gelateria* in Prati, with a small but perfectly realized range of flavours, such as nutty alternatives like hazelnut or pistachio or fruity ones like melon. Daily 11am–1am.

Gelateria del Teatro Via dei Coronari 65/66, Centro Storico ☎ 06 4547 4880; map p.38. Superb ice cream, with traditional options as well as innovative combinations like raspberry and sage. There's a pleasant sitting area inside, or perch outside and watch the frantic bridge traffic.

Giolitti Via degli Uffici del Vicario 40, Centro Storico ☎ 06 699 1243, ⓦ giolitti.it; map p.38. Italian institution that once had a reputation – now lost – for the country's best ice cream. Still pretty good, however, and always very busy, with a choice of seventy flavours. Daily 7am–2am.

Grom Via della Maddalena 30a, Centro Storico ☎ 06 6821 0447, ⓦ grom.it; map p.38. The top-quality Turin ice-cream maker now has a home in Rome, and its ice cream undeniably delicious, with lots of seasonal flavours, though the stark white interior of the shop feels a bit chain-like and unwelcoming. Other locations at Via dei Giubbonari 53 (Campo) and on Piazza Navona at Via Agonale 3. Daily 11am–midnight.

★ **Il Gelato di Claudio Torcè** Viale Aventino 59, Aventine ⓦ web.tiscali.it/ilgelatodiclaudiotor; map pp.140–141. One of seven outlets serving the outstanding ice cream of Claudio Torcè, founder of the city's natural *gelato* movement. Flavours range from classic hazelnut and chocolate to the more obscure habanero pepper and black sesame. The other central branch is located on Piazza Monte d'Oro, near the Ara Pacis. Daily 11.30am–11.30pm.

★ **Palazzo del Freddo di Giovanni Fassi** Via Principe Eugenio 65/67a, Esquiline ☎ 06 446 4740, ⓦ palazzodelfreddo.it; map pp.114–115. Known as "Fassi", believe it or not this was Rome's first-ever ice cream parlour; it's a wonderful, huge and airy place that has been doing brilliant fruit ice creams and milk shakes since 1880. Always good. Tues–Sat noon–midnight, Sun 10am–midnight.

★ **San Crispino** Via della Panetteria 42, Trevi ☎ 06 679 3924, ⓦ ilgelatodisancrispino.it; map p.93. Near the Trevi Fountain, this place was once considered by many to make the best ice cream in Rome. They've slipped in recent years, but still do interesting flavours like ginger and cinnamon, and their meringue is stellar. Other branches at Piazza Maddalena 3, right by the Pantheon, at Via Acaia 56 in San Giovanni and in Terminal A at Fiumicino airport. Daily noon–12.30am, Fri & Sat till 1.30am.

from the Pantheon, *Tazza d'Oro* ("Golden Cup") is well named, since it is by common consent the home of one of Rome's best cups of coffee, and also serves decent iced coffee and sinfully rich *granita di caffè*, with double dollops of whipped cream. Also does tasty pastries and sandwiches. Daily 7.30am–1am.

Vitti Piazza San Lorenzo in Lucina 33 ☎06 687 6304, ⓦcaffetteriavittiroma.it; map p.38. A Roman institution, serving a wide selection of pastries and sandwiches, along with delicious coffee; there are a few tables inside and lots on the square. A short lunch menu, is served from 12.30pm – pasta dishes and suchlike – though it's not always the best value. Daily 8am–midnight.

RESTAURANTS

Armando al Pantheon Salita de' Crescenzi 31 ☎06 6880 3034, ⓦarmandoalpantheon.it; map p.38. Surprisingly unpretentious surroundings and moderately priced hearty food in this long-standing staple close by the Pantheon (open since 1961). Great Roman classic pasta dishes and main courses, from *cacio e pepe* to *saltimbocca*, *trippa alla Romana* (tripe, Roman-style, with lots of tomato sauce) and *abbachio scottadito* (lamb chops). Mon–Fri 12.30–3pm & 7–11pm; also Sat 12.30–3pm.

Beere Vicole della Cancellaria 13 ☎06 6821 6986, ⓦpalazzo-olivia.it; map p.38. The newish city-centre location of a long-standing favourite on the edge of Prati (Carlo Passaglia 1), and a good place to go if you can't decide what to eat, with all sorts of cheese and salami plates (one served with honey from the restaurant's own organic farm) for €6–8, classic Roman pasta dishes for €8–10 and mostly grilled meat mains – steaks, burgers and spicy chicken – for €12–18. Drink a delicious artisanal Italian beer, on tap or in the bottle, at one of the outside tables or in the cosy interior. Daily 11am–2am, Sat & Sun from 6pm.

Bocondivino Piazza in Campo Marzio 6 ☎06 6830 8626, ⓦboccondivino.it; map p.38. A short walk from the Pantheon, in a nice setting with outdoor seating, *Bocondivino* aspires to be a chicer brand of diner. Don't let the slightly higher prices put you off, though, as the food – fairly traditional choices from admirably short menus of pasta dishes and mains – is invariably excellent: good *tonnarelli cacio e pepe*, *pasta amatriciana* and simple but well-presented chicken and beef dishes for around €15. Mon–Sat 12.30–3pm & 7.30–11pm.

⭐ **Casa Bleve** Via del Teatro Valle 48 ☎06 686 5970, ⓦcasableve.it; map p.38. This atmospheric, echoing hall, in the heart of the Centro Storico, is where Rome's beautiful folk come to enjoy great wine and the food to go with it. There's a huge wine list and a menu of assorted cured meats and cheeses, pastas, fish and meat courses. It's not cheap – most mains go for €18–22, and there are no wines under €25 – but the food is great and the service attentive and knowledgeable. There's also a wine shop out front. Tues–Sat 12.30–3pm & 7.30–11.30pm.

Da Alfredo e Ada Via dei Banchi Nuovi 14 ☎06 687 8842; map p.38. Tiny, long-established restaurant that used to be the domain of the formidable Ada and continues her tradition of serving good home-cooked food just like your Italian granny used to make. There's no menu, just three or four pasta dishes which may include a *carbonara* or lasagne, followed by three or four hearty dishes like veal stew with peas or chicken *cacciatore* (with lots of tomatoes and herbs). The joy is, you won't know what you're going to get till you sit down. Reckon on spending around €25 for two courses including wine. Mon–Fri 12.30–3.30pm & 6–10pm, closed Aug.

Da Baffetto Via del Governo Vecchio 114 ☎06 686 1617, ⓦpizzeriabaffetto.it; map p.38. A tiny, highly authentic pizzeria that has long been a Rome institution, though it now tends to be swamped by tourists. Amazingly, it's still good value, and has tables outside in summer, although you will always have to queue. The *bruschette* are especially delicious. Pizzas from €5. Another branch – *Baffetto 2* – is on Piazza del Teatro del Pompeo near Campo de' Fiori. Daily except Tues 6.30pm–12.30am, Sat & Sun also 12.30–3.30pm.

Da Francesco Piazza del Fico 29 ☎06 686 4009; map p.38. Not just delectable pizzas in this full-on pizzeria in the heart of the Centro Storico, but good antipasti, *primi* and *secondi* too. The service can be slapdash, but the food is decent and the atmosphere second to none. Two-course dinner with wine around €25 a head. Daily 12.30–3.30pm & 7pm–midnight.

⭐ **Da Tonino** Via del Governo Vecchio 18/19 ☎06 687 7002; map p.38. Basic Roman food, always freshly cooked, and always delicious, is the order of the day at this unmarked Centro Storico favourite. It's a little more upmarket than it once was, but still serves the same simple Roman pasta dishes for around €6–8 and main courses for €8–10. The few tables fill up quickly, so come early or be prepared to queue. No credit cards. Mon–Sat 12.30–3.30pm & 7–11pm.

⭐ **Dal Cavalier Gino** Vicolo Rosini 4 ☎06 687 3434; map p.38. Down a small alley right by the Parliament building, Gino presides over his constantly bustling restaurant with unhurried authority, serving a determinedly traditional Roman menu at keen prices – pasta dishes €8, mains €9–10. Try the house speciality – *tonnarelli ciociara*, with peas, mushrooms and ham – and top it off with the excellent *saltimbocca alla romana*. It's been very much discovered by tourists, but at heart it remains a locals' joint. No credit cards. Mon–Sat 1–2.45pm & 8–10.30pm.

Dal Paino Via di Parione 34/35 ☎06 6813 5140; map p.38. In a great location, a few blocks from Piazza Navona, this dependable pizzeria, run by the son of the owner of *Da Baffetto* (see above), is a good Centro Storico standby, serving well-above-average pasta dishes and mains, although its tasty, well-priced Roman-style pizzas, ultra-crisp and light, are the highlight here. Tables outside in summer – as good a place to eat as you'll find in this part of town. Mon–Sat 12.30–3pm & 7.30–11pm.

15

TEN TRADITIONAL ROMAN RESTAURANTS

Agustarello See p.259
Checchino dal 1887 See p.259
Da Oio a Casa Mia See p.259
Da Paris See p.260
Dal Cavalier Gino See p.245
Matricianella See opposite
Nonna Betta See p.249
Piperno See p.249
Pommidoro See p.256
Trattoria Lilli See below

15

Enoteca Corsi Via del Gesù 87/88 ☎06 679 0821, ⌨enotecacorsi.com; map p.38. Tucked away between Piazza Venezia and the Pantheon, this is an old-fashioned Roman trattoria and wine shop where you eat what they happen to have cooked that morning. The menu changes each day, and it gets very busy at lunchtimes; you may have to wait for a table if you haven't booked. The food is reliable and pretty cheap – €7 for a pasta dish, €9 or so for a main course. Mon–Sat noon–3pm, closed Aug.

Il Bacaro Via degli Spagnoli 27 ☎06 687 2554, ⌨ilbacaro.com; map p.38. This tiny restaurant tucked away down a small side street has a small, focused menu featuring an interesting selection of antipasti and pasta dishes (€14–18) and mostly meaty mains, particularly beef (€22–24). The feel of the place is quite romantic, but it's really too cramped for a truly private liaison. Daily 6.30pm–midnight, Sat & Sun also noon–3pm.

La Montecarlo Vicolo Savelli 12 ☎06 686 1877, ⌨lamontecarlo.it; map p.38. This busy pizzeria not far from Piazza Navona is owned by the daughter of the owner of *Da Baffetto* (see p.245) and serves similar crisp, blistered pizza from €5.50, along with heaped dishes of pasta (from €7) and decent Roman *fritti*. Good, simple food, and tables outside in summer; it will always be crowded but is pretty big so you don't usually have to wait for a table. Tues–Sun noon–3pm & 7pm–1am.

La Terrazza Bramante Hotel Raphael, Largo Febo 2 ☎06 682 831 ⌨raphaelhotel.com; map p.38. The picturesque secluded piazza and ivy-covered facade of the hotel *Raphaël* (see p.227) is home to *La Terrazza Bramante*, where the flower-filled roof terrace exudes romance; chef Jean Luc Bruneau's menu emphasizes organic products, and refreshingly for a high end hotel restaurant the focus is on vegetables and fish – saffron risotto, vegetable *carbonara* and a good aubergine *parmigiana*. Primi €16–18, *secondi* €18–24 – not bad for food and surroundings of this quality. Daily 12.30–2.30pm & 7–10pm.

Maccheroni Piazza delle Coppelle 44 ☎06 6830 7895, ⌨ristorantemaccheroni.com; map p.38. This friendly restaurant enjoys a wonderful location right in the heart of the Centro Storico. Inside, it's plainly decorated yet comfortable, with basic furniture, marble-topped counters and the kitchen in view, while the outside tables make the most of the pretty square. The food is basic Italian fare and they do a nice *pasta alla gricia*, nice steaks and chicken dishes, and it's affordably priced and cheerfully served. Daily 1–3pm & 7.30–11.30pm.

★ **Matricianella** Via del Leone 4 ☎06 683 2100, ⌨matricianella.it; map p.38. Handily placed just off Via del Corso, this old favourite is perhaps the best place to try real Roman food in the city centre, with classic deep-fried dishes like *filetti di baccalà* and various vegetable *fritti*; traditional Roman pasta dishes, such as *cacio e pepe*, and a great wine list. You can eat in the bustling main dining room or on the outside terrace. Pasta dishes around €11, main courses €16. Mon–Sat 12.30–3pm & 7.30–11pm.

Osteria dell'Ingegno Piazza di Pietra 45 ☎06 678 0662; map p.38. A relaxed bistro on a happening square, with tables outside and plenty of room within. There's an inventive menu that breaks free from the Roman specialities you'll find elsewhere, with dishes inspired by most of the country's regions. There are variations on traditional classics like pumpkin gnocchi and *cacio e pepe* with "square" pasta, and buffalo steaks and seafood with couscous – all to a background of cool jazz. A wide choice of wine, too. Main courses from around €12. Daily 12.30–3pm & 7.30pm–midnight.

Osteria del Pegno Vicolo Montevecchio 8 ☎06 6880 7025, ⌨osteriadelpegno.it; map p.38. Set on the ground floor of a fifteenth-century *palazzo*, tucked away and hard to find, this small restaurant (just 8–10 tables) serves Roman classics – *carbonara*, *abbacchio al forno* – alongside earthier food from the countryside like fettuccini with porcini mushrooms and Ischian-style rabbit (stewed in wine, tomatoes and herbs) as well as a few fish dishes such as delectable *gnochetti* with clams. They also serve pizzas cooked in a wood-burning oven. Good service and prices – *primi* €8–12, *secondi* €10–13 – and a lovely location. Daily except Wed 12.30–3pm & 7.30–10.30pm.

The Perfect Bun Largo del Teatro Valle 4 ☎06 4547 6337, ⌨theperfectbun.it; map p.38. Sometimes you just have to have a burger, and this, by Rome standards, is burger heaven: a big, vaulted room with a long, high table down the middle and tables round the side and upstairs, that serves burgers, steaks, grilled chicken and other Tex-Mexish delights. Burgers are excellent and come with every kind of accessory for €13–17, although this doesn't include the stupidly priced options – one comes topped with 3 fried eggs, 6 rashers of bacon, cheese and, er, cheesy fries. Daily 12.45pm–3pm & 6pm–2am, Sun brunch 11.45am–3pm.

★ **Trattoria Lilli** Via di Tor di Nona 23 ☎06 686 1916, ⌨trattorialilli.it; map p.38. One of the city centre's most

authentic and untouristy trattorias, tucked away below the riverbank, on the northern edge of the Centro Storico. Serves a good selection of classic Roman staples, including a broad range of earthy pasta specials, well prepared and served with gritty Roman directness – *primi* and *secondi* for €10–12. There's outside seating, too. Tues–Sat 12.30–3pm & 7.30–11pm, also Sun 12.30–3pm.

CAMPO DE' FIORI AND THE GHETTO

CAFÉS AND BARS

★ **Antico Forno Roscioli** Via dei Chiavari 34 ☎ 06 686 4045, ⊛ salumeriaroscioli.com; map pp.54–55. Old bakery that's associated with the pricey restaurant and deli round the corner; does great bread, lots of different kinds of pizza and other savoury and sweet delights to take out. Mon–Sat 7am–8pm, closed Sat eve in summer.

Barnum Café Via del Pellegrino 87 ☎ 06 6476 0483, ⊛ barnumcafe.com; map pp.54–55. This friendly circus-themed café with free wi-fi is handy for breakfast, coffee and cake or a light lunch. After dark, it's a relaxing bar with great cocktails, and there's a popular nightly *aperitivo* buffet. Daily 8.30am–midnight, Sat & Sun till 2am.

Caffè Camerino Largo Arenula 30 ☎ 06 687 5970; map pp.54–55. Conveniently located near Largo Argentina, this bar has excellent coffee and mouthwatering pastries but also serves inexpensive cafeteria-style lunches and sandwiches. Daily 7.30am–8pm.

Caffè Farnese Via dei Baullari 106 ☎ 06 6880 2125; map pp.54–55. Popular with business types and beautiful young things, but actually not expensive, this café, right on Piazza Farnese, is an enjoyable place to come for breakfast or lunch, as well as evening drinks. Excellent cappuccino, *cornetti*, pizza and sandwiches. There's free seating at the window bar, but you might want to pay to sit outside on a warm evening for the view of Palazzo Farnese. Daily 7am–2am.

Caffè Peru Via Giulia 84 ☎ 06 686 1310; map pp.54–55. When the friendly young owner took over the helm of this family bar in 2012, he remodelled it slightly, keeping it casual and still serving great coffee (some say, it's the best in Rome) but adding home-made, hot lunch specials and an *aperitivi* hour in the evening, when a small hot dish and a glass from the good selection of wines will set you back about €8. A mixed clientele, from local families to priests and nuns and the odd diplomat, while late evening brings young revellers spilling onto the street. Daily 7.30am–9.30pm.

Il Forno di Campo de' Fiori Campo de' Fiori 22 ☎ 06 6880 6662, ⊛ fornocampodefiori.com; map pp.54–55. Great Campo bakery that's always busy with devotees. The *pizza rossa* here (with a smear of tomato sauce) and *pizza bianca* (just drizzled with olive oil on top) are Roman legends, while porcini mushrooms or mozzarella with anchovies and courgette blossoms are especially good. Mon–Sat 7.30am–2.30pm & 5–8pm, closed Sat eve in summer.

Vino e Camino Piazza d'Oro 6 ☎ 06 6830 1332, ⊛ vinoecamino.it; map p.38. Open since 2010, this friendly restaurant has its origins in northern Lazio – the original branch is in Bracciano (see p.219) – and its menu is mainly meat based, with fine-quality steaks and other grilled meats, although there are plenty of vegetarian options, such as pasta with walnut pesto. Mon–Sat 7.30–10.30pm.

RESTAURANTS

Al Bric Via del Pellegrino 51/52 ☎ 06 687 9533, ⊛ albric .it; map pp.54–55. A rather refined option that takes its wine and food very seriously – as evidenced by the hushed atmosphere, gigantic wine list and highish prices. The food influences come from all over Italy, with some interesting starters and pasta dishes, from classics like *cacio e pepe* and *amatriciana* to pappardelle with wild boar ragu, and a good array of meat *secondi* – excellent steaks, lamb shoulder with pecorino and veal in tomato sauce. The wine list has quite a few options at good prices, too. Pastas €13–17, mains €20–25. Daily 7.30–midnight.

Al Pompiere Via Santa Maria dei Calderari 38 ☎ 06 686 8377, ⊛ alpompiereroma.com; map pp.54–55. Housed in a frescoed old *palazzo*, in the heart of the Ghetto, this old-fashioned restaurant exudes tradition and serves up some of the best Roman-Jewish food you'll find (especially good *fiori di zucca*) and at decent prices, too, in its busy warren of high-ceilinged rooms. The owner's delightfully eclectic wine list features her favourites, many from small wineries. Mon–Sat 12.30–3pm & 7.30pm–midnight.

Ar Galletto Piazza Farnese 102 ☎ 06 686 1714, ⊛ ristoranteargallettoroma.com; map pp.54–55. This place is situated on one of Rome's stateliest piazzas and just off one of its trendiest, too. Recently it moved into an adjacent space and upscaled both its decor and prices, but it still offers traditional Roman cookery with a homely touch (*coda alla vaccinara* and all the pasta classics), along with other more mainstream Italian dishes. In warmer months, you can sit outside and enjoy the magnificent Renaissance square. Primi €10–12, *secondi* €16–22. Mon–Sat 12.30–3pm & 7.30–11.30pm.

Ba' Ghetto Via Portico d'Ottavia 57 ☎ 06 6889 2868, ⊛ baghetto.it; map pp.54–55. This moderately priced meat-kosher restaurant in the middle of the Ghetto serves Roman, North African – the owners are Libyan Jews – and Middle Eastern Jewish specialities. The *börek* (cheese pie) and *shacsuca* (eggs served in a piquant tomato sauce) are particularly good, and there is another branch serving dairy-kosher food, couscous and pizzas diagonally across the street at Via Portico d'Ottavia 2a. Mon–Thurs & Sun 12.30–3pm & 7.30–10pm, Fri 12.30–3pm, Sat 7.30–10.30pm.

Baires Corso Rinascimento 1 ☎ 06 686 1293, ⊛ www .baires.it; map pp.54–55. The 2013 arrival of a new pope shone a new spotlight on Argentina, and this long-running

Roman mini chain of Argentinian steakhouses, which has been a convivial fixture on the city's dining scene for a decade or more. The steaks are excellent – mostly Argentine with some Tuscan Chianina beef too – and they serve some good Argentine wines that aren't so easy to find elsewhere. Other menu options reflect their Italian location, with mainly pasta *primi*. The lunch specials are generous and popular, attracting both local families and Senate staff to the flagship city-centre location. Daily 12.30–3.30pm & 7pm–12.30am.

Da Sergio Via delle Grotte 27 ☎06 686 4293; map pp.54–55. Towards the river from Campo de' Fiori, this is an out-of-the-way, cosy trattoria with a traditional, limited menu and the deeply authentic feel of old Rome – a decent *carbonara*, *spaghetti alle vongole* and lamb, and all for around €25 a head including wine. Limited outdoor seating in summer. Mon–Sat 12.30am–3.30pm & 7pm–midnight.

Ditirambo Piazza della Cancelleria 74 ☎06 687 1626, ⊛ristoranteditirambo.it; map pp.54–55. In a fantastic location around the corner from the Campo de' Fiori, this restaurant offers much more than your typical tourist haven. With a few tables outside, and lots of room within, its food is an inventive take on traditional Italian dishes and ingredients. Service is breezy and bright, and, if you don't want to sample their more complex offerings, you can always go for their *tonnarelli cacio e pepe* (€9.50) which is as tasty as anywhere in the city centre. Daily 1–3pm & 7.30–11.30pm; closed Mon evening & Aug.

Grappolo d'Oro Zampanó Piazza della Cancelleria 80 ☎06 689 7080, ⊛hosteriagrappolodoro.it; map pp.54–55. Owned and run by the same team as nearby *Ditirambo* (see above), this place is a long-running Campo favourite but remains relatively unscathed by the tourist hordes and serves Roman cuisine in a traditional trattoria atmosphere. Excellent value, with pasta dishes costing €9–10 and mainly meat main courses at €15–17; try the pasta with bacon and artichokes followed by roast pork; lots of *fritti* and *baccalà* too. Daily 7.30–11.30pm, also 1–3pm Mon & Fri–Sun; closed Aug.

TEN REGIONAL RESTAURANTS

Baia Chia (Sardinia) See p.255
Cantina Cantarini (Le Marche) See p.253
Colline Emiliane (Emilia-Romagna) See p.251
Dal Bolognese (Emilia-Romagna) See p.251
Dal Toscano (Tuscany) See p.262
Palatium (Lazio) See p.252
Piccolo Abruzzo (Abruzzo) See p.253
Tajut (Friuli) See p.258
Tram Tram (Puglia) See p.256
Trattoria Monti (Le Marche) See p.256

Il Sanlorenzo Via dei Chiavari 4/5 ☎06 686 5097, ⊛ilsanlorenzo.it; map pp.54–55. Between Largo Argentina and Campo de' Fiori, this fine fish restaurant serves the freshest and most creatively prepared catch in the city centre. The sleek dining rooms – including a rare ventilated smoking hall – attract a rather pretentious clientele, but if you can tolerate the slightly snooty atmosphere and service you will be treated to quite exceptional food such as spaghetti with sea urchin roe and tilapia with braised fennel and saffron. Pasta *primi* €20–22, *secondi* from around €30. Daily 7.30–11.45pm, also 12.45–2.45pm Tues–Fri.

Nonna Betta Via del Portico d'Ottavia 16 ☎06 6880 6263, ⊛nonnabetta.it; map pp.54–55. The best kosher restaurant in the Ghetto serves all the classics of the *cucina Romana*: ebraica *carciofi alla giudia* (deep-fried artichokes; €5), *aliciotti con indivia* (a sort of tart of anchovies with curly endive; €10) – as well as a selection of Middle Eastern dishes like falafel (€5) and couscous (€10–15). Daily 12.30–3pm & 7.30–10pm, closed Fri eve and Sat lunch.

★ **Piperno** Monte de' Cenci 9 ☎06 6880 6629, ⊛ristorantepiperno.com; map pp.54–55. There's perhaps no more atmospheric place to sample Roman food than at *Piperno*, tucked away on a tiny piazza. It's not cheap, and the service can be a bit snooty, but it's a lovely space and the food is great, plus there's outside seating on the secluded hill square in the summer. All the traditional Roman starters – *carciofi alla giudia*, fried *baccalà*, *fiori di zucca* – for around €15, pasta dishes for about the same, and mains for €25. A good wine list, too, with lots of decent choices from €18 a bottle. Tues–Sat 12.45–2.20pm & 7.45–10.20pm, Sun 12.45–2.20pm.

Roscioli Via dei Giubbonari 21 ☎06 687 5287, ⊛salumeriaroscioli.com; map pp.54–55. Is it a deli, a wine bar or fully fledged restaurant? Actually, it's all three, and you can either just have a glass of wine (good selection) and some cheese or go for the full menu, which has great antipasti and pasta dishes. Nothing is cheap here, and the service can be a bit high-handed, but the food is good – stand-outs include the buffalo mozzarella, *burrata* (*mozzarella with cream*) and the *carbonara*, which is one of the best in Rome. Basic pasta dishes start at €12, main courses can be anything from €15 to €30. Deli 9am–midnight, restaurant 12.30–3pm & 7.30pm–midnight (cold plates and wine till 4pm and from 6pm).

Taverna degli Amici Piazza Margana 37 ☎06 6992 0637, ⊛tavernamici.it; map pp.54–55. The outside tables at this long-established restaurant, on a quiet, lovely square, offer a decent place for lunch after the rigours of the Forum or Ghetto, and an atmospheric spot for dinner too. The menu is relatively unadventurous, but there are lots of Roman classics, as well as less obvious options. Prices are moderate and the food decent – pasta dishes €12, mains €15–20 – but really, it's the location you pay for here. Tues–Sun 12.30–3pm & 7.30–11pm.

15

SUMMER DINING AND ENTERTAINMENT BY THE TIBER

Summer brings all manner of **taverns** out along the **Tiber River**, pop-up places that set up on the embankment between early June and early September, and are generally good quality and value; look out for the pointy tent tops that line the riverbanks. Also, **L'Isola del Cinema** on **Isola Tiberina** (Ⓦ isoladelcinema.com; see p.280) shows open-air movies (at least two nightly), and, sometimes, a region of Italy or an embassy will set up a booth for a night or two to promote travel and culture, or a free jazz concert will pop up. Isola Tiberina is a splendid location – cool and refreshing by the river rapids, even on a hot, sticky night – and is also the summer location of the gourmet restaurant *Giuda Ballerino* (see p.257), which has a friendly atmosphere and serves everything from economical street food to elegantly presented high-end dishes, with service and wines to match.

15

Vecchia Roma Piazza Campitelli 18 ☎ 06 686 4604, Ⓦ ristorantevecchiaroma.com; map pp.54–55. Located on a peaceful square on the fringe of the Ghetto, but a much slicker experience than the earthy Jewish restaurants of that neighbourhood, this traditional Roman restaurant has a lovely terrace and frescoed interior that are made for a special night out. It can be quite pricey, but the antipasto table is usually loaded, and it's a tremendous bargain for lunch at €16 a head. Great fish and seafood too, and top pasta dishes all-round. *Primi* €13–18, *secondi* €20–22. Daily 1–3.30pm & 8–11pm; closed Wed.

Zoc Via delle Zoccolette 22 ☎ 06 681 92515, Ⓦ zoc22.it; map pp.54–55. Hidden on a back street near a parking garage, this sister restaurant to *Urbana 47* (see p.256) is a delightfully eclectic place. The menu is unlike anything else you'll find in Rome, with an emphasis on exotic Eastern ingredients and methods blended with traditional Roman dishes (fried mozzarella with Thai sauce, or gnocchi with green curry); they also serve a tapas menu. It's a cosy place, with a feel more like someone's living room, plus it has a courtyard patio. Come for breakfast, lunch, snacks or dinner; prices are slightly higher than a moderately priced trattoria (starters and first courses €11–15, mains €17–19), but the atmosphere, service and the unusual and changing menu more than make up for it. Free wi-fi. Open for breakfast daily 9am–noon, lunch 12.30–3.30pm, dinner 7pm–midnight.

PIAZZA VENEZIA AND THE CAPITOLINE HILL

RESTAURANT

Enoteca Provincia Romana Largo di Foro di Traiano 84 ☎ 06 6766 2424; map p.64. This popular wine bar and restaurant beside Trajan's Column does a brisk lunch business serving government bureaucrats from the surrounding office buildings. There are sandwiches, salads, pasta, meat and fish courses, all of which are made with quality ingredients from in and around Rome. The wine list is similarly local. It's traditional food, but often with a twist, *carbonara* with zucchini, pork saltimbocca and suchlike. Prices are moderate. Mon–Sat 1–3.30pm & 6–11pm.

THE TRIDENTE AND TREVI

CAFÉS AND BARS

Antico Caffè Greco Via Condotti 86 ☎ 06 679 1700, Ⓦ anticocaffegreco.eu; map p.93. Founded in 1760, and patronized by among others Casanova, Byron, Goethe and Stendhal, this is nowadays a bit of tourist joint, but Romans still use the stand-up area in the front. For curiosity value only, although the *granita di caffè* (iced coffee) is a hit on a hot summer's day. Mon–Sat 7.30am–11.30pm.

Babington's Tea Rooms Piazza di Spagna 23 ☎ 06 678 6027 Ⓦ babingtons.com; map p.93. In business for over a hundred years, *Babington's* serves light lunches and English tea-time delicacies such as scones with jam. It is extremely expensive – from €10 for a pot of tea for one, €22 for a burger, €29 for a full English breakfast – but very handy, has a great selection of teas and serves Sunday brunch, too. Daily 10am–9pm.

Buccone Via di Ripetta 19/20 ☎ 06 361 2154, Ⓦ www .enotecabuccone.com; map p.93. One of the best places for lunch in the Tridente/Piazza del Popolo area, with lots of tables laid out amid its bottle-lined shelves (see p.290), a separate room out the back and a menu that changes daily. You can eat as much or little as you like – a salad or cold-cut platter (€8–10), a simple slice of *torta rustica* (savoury tart) or *aubergine parmigiana,* or one of the hot daily specials of pasta and meat courses (€7–10) – plus the wine list is very wide-ranging, with lots of choices by the glass. Mon–Sat 12.30–3pm, Fri & Sat also 7.30–10.30pm.

Herbier Nature Via San Claudio 87 ☎ 06 678 5847; map p.93. Well-located bar, just off Piazza San Silvestro, in a small arcade, and thus a real oasis of calm away from the hectic and fumy traffic. Offers snacks or even a full lunch, usually typical *tavola calda* fare – pasta, chicken, roast potatoes, a variety of vegetable dishes, etc, all very cheap. Mon–Sat 8am–8pm.

Museo-Atelier Canova-Tadolini Via del Babuino 150a ☎ 06 3211 0702, Ⓦ canovatadolini.com; map p.93. It's a bit odd eating among the grand sculptures of this café-cum-museum (see p.97), and it's certainly not cheap. But it's very handy and provides one of the few places to sit down along this busy street, plus it serves decent sandwiches, salads and simple pasta dishes, as well as a few hot mains – *cacio e pepe*, *spaghetti alle vongole* and other more adventurous pasta dishes for €13–14, and a variety of beef and chicken main courses for around €20. There are a few outside tables, too, from which you can watch the designer bags bustle by. Daily: bar 8am–midnight, food noon–11pm.

RESTAURANTS

All'Oro Restaurant Hotel First, Via del Vantaggio 14 ☏06 9799 6907, ⓦristorantealloro.it; map p.93. The award-winning chefs Ricardo di Giacinto and Ramona Anello recently moved their restaurant from Parioli here, where they also run the ground floor bar *Miscellamo* and, during summer months, a delightful roof terrace restaurant. The one-Michelin-starred menu has tasting menus for €75 or €95 a head, while à la carte *primi* go for €25–30 and *secondi* for €30–35. It's a lovely, short menu, and often surprisingly simple, with typical pasta dishes such as pasta stuffed with cheese and anchovies and tagliolini with speck, prawns and asparagus, and main courses that include suckling pig, lamb and quail. Mon–Sat 12.30–2.30pm & 7–10.30pm.

Alla Rampa Piazza Mignanelli 18 ☏06 678 2621, ⓦallarampa.it; map p.93. An unashamedly touristy joint, but has one of the best antipasti buffets in town, decent service and pretty good food, with a great selection of pasta dishes and a short menu of steaks and chicken, along with a lot of bog standard but perfectly decent mainstream Italian fare. The outside terrace, just off Piazza di Spagna, is large and undeniably appealing. Moderately priced; no credit cards. Mon–Sat noon–2pm & 8–11pm.

Antica Birreria Peroni Via di San Marcello 19 ☏06 679 5310 ⓦanticabirreriaperoni.net; map p.93. Big, bustling *birreria* with an excellent and cheap Italian-German fusion menu of simple food that's meant to soak up the beer. There are the usual starters and pasta dishes, plus a good selection of meat dishes, *scamorza* (grilled cheese) and various sausage dishes. Its walls are decorated with photos of old Rome and a frieze adorned by cherubs and slogans urging you to drink more beer – something that's very hard to resist in this lovely old wood-panelled space. Pasta dishes go for around €7, as do the *scamorza* and sausages; steaks and suchlike are around €15. Mon–Sat noon–midnight.

Babette Via Margutta 1/3 ☏06 321 1559, ⓦbabetteristorante.it; map p.93. Yes, the name is derived from the Danish foodie film, *Babette's Feast*, but the food here is Italian with a few twists, rather than Danish – try *paccheri* with tomatoes, aubergine and ricotta, followed by rabbit or beef fillet onion compote and gratin dauphinoise, from what is a thoughtful and regularly changing à la carte menu or an all-you-can-eat buffet

lunch on weekends (€28 a head) – plus there's a lovely courtyard to eat it in. Tues–Sun 1–3pm & 8–11.15pm.

Buca di Ripetta Via Ripetta 36 ☏06 321 9391, ⓦlabucadiripetta.it; map p.93. Smallish restaurant not far from Piazza del Popolo. The service is friendly and attentive and though it certainly caters to tourists it does the Roman classics very well, with beautifully executed pasta dishes and classics like *saltimbocca* and *coda alla vaccinara* as flavoursome as you'll get anywhere in the city. Lots of straightforward grilled fish dishes, too, and regular daily specials. Starters €7–12, mains €12–20. Daily 12.30–3pm & 7–11pm.

Ciampini Piazza Trinità dei Monti ☏06 678 5678, ⓦcaffeciampini.com; map p.93. Across the road from the French Academy, and part of a well-known local chain, *Ciampini* is handy for coffee and snacks in the morning and at lunchtime, but it is a restaurant above all, with a great setting in an enclosed garden overlooking the roofs and domes below. Prices are pretty good, considering the location, with a selection of pasta dishes and salads for €10–12, and fish, steaks and chicken from the grill for €16–20. A good place for kids, too, who can watch the turtles playing in the fountain between courses. Daily 8am–midnight.

★ **Colline Emiliane** Via degli Avignonesi 22 ☏06 481 7538; map pp.114–115. Many Italians consider the cuisine of the Emilia Romagna region to be the country's best. Try it for yourself, lovingly prepared at reasonable prices by a family, oddly enough, from the Marche region. Try the *bollito* (boiled) leg of pork or the veal, both cooked in milk. Located just down from Piazza Barberini, on a quiet backstreet parallel to Via del Tritone. Tues–Sun 12.45–2.45pm & 7.30–10.45pm; closed Sun eve.

Dal Bolognese Piazza del Popolo 1 ☏06 361 1426, ⓦdalbolognese.it; map p.93. This elegant – and expensive – restaurant is the place to go to treat yourself to Emilian cuisine; their *tortellini in brodo* is a must, if you like chicken soup. Reservations are recommended, especially if you'd

TEN ETHNIC RESTAURANTS

Chinese restaurants – most of them pretty average – abound in Rome, and there's a slowly growing list of other **international options** in and around the centre. Here is our pick of the best.

Akropolis (Greek) See p.260
Baires (Argentinian) See p.248
Charley's Sauciere (French) See p.257
Doozo (Japanese) See p.255
Hamasei (Japanese) See p.252
Hang Zhou (Chinese) See p.255
Maharajah (Indian) See p.256
Mesob (Ethiopian) See p.258
Take Sushi (Japanese) See p.261
The Perfect Bun (American) See p.246

15

rather eat outside and watch the passers-by in the piazza, but be prepared for some unbelievably sniffy service. Food is great though, and prices moderate: great pasta, including lovely home-made ravioli, *bollito misto* (boiled beef) and veal and pork dishes. Tues–Sun 12.45–3.30pm & 8–11.30pm.

Fiaschetteria Beltramme Via della Croce 39 ☎06 6979 7200, ⓦfiaschetteriabeltramme.info; map p.93. Originally, this place sold only wine, but it's been a full-blown restaurant for some time; now under new management and just a few blocks from the Spanish Steps, it is thriving and just about always packed. Service can be a bit slow, but if you want authentic Roman food, such as *spaghetti pomodoro e basilica* and *Saltimbocca alla romana* in a good atmosphere at affordable prices, then it's a pretty good option in this area. Two courses with wine €40; no credit cards. Daily 12.15–3pm & 7–10.45pm.

'Gusto Piazza Augusto Imperatore 9 ☎06 322 6273, ⓦgusto.it; map p.93. The flagship restaurant of the 'Gusto empire often gets a bad rap these days, and some claim it's resting on its laurels, but we have to say we've always had good food here, and the service is usually acceptable. It's not as chic as it once was, but the atmosphere of the upstairs restaurant remains amiable, and you can still get unusual, well-executed food accompanied by excellent wine. The downstairs pizzeria serves grilled steaks and chicken, as well as great pizzas. They also own the *Osteria della Frezza* on the next street (see below) and the 'Gusto shop next door, among others (see p.292). Daily 12.45–3pm & 7.45pm–1am.

Hamasei Via della Mercede 35/36 ☎06 679 2134, ⓦroma-hamasei.com; map p.93. This elegant Japanese restaurant right in the centre of town has a tranquil, refined atmosphere and a full range of very authentic dishes, including a sushi bar. Moderately priced too: main courses are around €15, while various sushi and sashimi mixes go for €13–40, and the lunch specials are super value at €15 a head. Tues–Sun noon–3pm & 7.15pm–11pm.

Jardin de Russie Hotel de Russie, Via del Babuino 9 ☎06 3288 8870, ⓦhotelderussie.it; map p.93. The *Jardin de Russie* restaurant at the *de Russie* hotel has a secret feel enhanced by its enclosed terraced garden (the buffet at lunch attracts a well-heeled business crowd). It's a great place to eat, no question, and the prices reflect that, but the beautifully presented food has a heartiness not usually associated with fine dining, with dishes like *cacio e pepe* ravioli, *paccheri* with fish sauce and a lovely frittata of calamari, prawns and veg. Weekend brunch is a treat, too, at €48 a head every Sat & Sun (12.30–3pm). Daily 12.30–3pm & 7.30–11pm.

Il Chianti Via del Lavatore 81 ☎06 678 7550, ⓦvineriailchianti.com; map p.93. Just metres from the Trevi Fountain, this Tuscan specialist, both in wine and food, is a find in a part of town not generally known for its value food and drink. There are spreads of cheese and cold meats (€15), a good selection of beef and other meat dishes, and all the usual pastas and decent pizzas at reasonable prices; however, if you don't fancy a full meal you can just stop by for a drink. Sit outside in summer if you can bear the travelling musicians who congregate to entertain the tourists. Mon–Sat 10am–1am.

Il Leoncino Via del Leoncino 28 ☎06 687 6306; map p.93. Cheap, hectic and genuine pizzeria, little known to out-of-towners, and one of the best for lovers of crispy Roman-style pizza baked in a wood oven. Just off Via del Corso, so it's quite a boon, in a neighbourhood where decent pizza is thin on the ground. No credit cards. Mon–Fri 1–2.30pm & 7pm–midnight, Sat 7pm–midnight only; closed Aug.

Imàgo Hassler, Trinità dei Monti 6 ☎06 699 340, ⓦhotelhasslerroma.com; map p.93. See p.231. The *Hassler*, at the top of the Spanish Steps, opens its formal restaurant *Imàgo* only at dinner, but its famous view is always matched by its flawless service and refined Italian cuisine, which includes such signature dishes as terrine of foie gras with morello cherries, saddle of deer with wild mushrooms and sake-glazed black cod; tasting menus go for €110–140 a head. Daily 7pm–10.30pm.

La Terrazza dell'Eden Hotel Eden, Via Ludovisi 49 ☎06 4781 2752, ⓦlaterrazzadelleden.com; map p.93. *La Dolce Vita* might not be much in evidence on Via Veneto anymore, but some of the hotels here still serve up great food in lovely surroundings, in particular *La Terrazza dell'Eden*, which won its first Michelin star in 2012 and consistently offers high-quality creative Roman cuisine (and fabulous views) in its lovely dove-grey-and-cream rooftop perch. The food is pretty wonderful, presented and served with all the ceremonial aplomb you would expect, but it's extremely expensive so it's worth knowing you can still enjoy the view with a drink in the bar. Daily 12.30–2.30pm & 7.30–10.30pm.

★ **Osteria della Frezza** Via della Frezza 16 ☎06 3211 1482, ⓦgusto.it; map p.93. Part of the 'Gusto empire (see above), this place is good for snacks, such as cheese or salami plates, or for full meals – the pasta is top notch and service good, and prices moderate. There's a large wine list, and the whole thing is carried off with panache. Daily noon–3.30pm & 7pm–12.30am.

Otello alla Concordia Via della Croce 81 ☎06 679 1178, ⓦotello-alla-concordia.it; map p.93. This used to be one of the film director Fellini's favourites – he lived just a few blocks away on Via Margutta – and it remains a blessing in a neighbourhood not stacked with great choices. It's an unapologetically traditional place, with an emphasis on classic Roman dishes, all at very affordable prices considering the location (pasta around €12, mains around €15); try their *spaghetti Otello* – just fresh tomatoes and basil with garlic. Mon–Sat 12.30–3pm & 7.30–11pm.

★ **Palatium** Via Frattina 94 ☎06 6920 2132; map p.93. Cool and sleek, this wine bar-cum-restaurant celebrates the produce of the Lazio region and Rome, with a short, regularly changing menu of sparky, inventive takes on traditional dishes using local, seasonal ingredients and a long list of Lazio wines. You can settle for just a plate of salami and cheese, but that would be to miss out on classics like *tonnarelli cacio e pepe*, Viterbese vegetable soup or mains such as sausages or rabbit from the hills to the north and south of the city. A great location, near Piazza di Spagna, and very good value for money, with most *primi* and *secondi* between €12 and €16. Mon–Sat 11am–11pm.

Pizza Ciro Via della Mercede 43/45 ☎06 678 6015, ⓦ www.pizzaciro.it; map p.93. Just up from Piazza San Silvestro, this is a big, friendly pizza place (part of a chain) that also serves *primi* and *secondi*. The pizzas are great (€7–13), but you should also try the *linguine al Ciro*, which comes with seafood. Daily noon–3pm & 7pm–midnight.

Pizza Re Via di Ripetta 14 ☎06 321 1468, ⓦ pizzare.it; map p.93. A short walk from Piazza del Popolo, this place serves up authentic Neapolitan pizza (thicker than Roman) made in a wood-stoked oven for €9 including a drink. There's a larger branch in the Centro Storico, at Largo dei Chiavari 83 (☎06 6880 8074), just east of Campo de' Fiori, and the same people own the posher and more expensive *Recafé* (see below). Daily 12.30–3pm & 7pm–midnight, closed Sun eve.

Recafé Piazza Augusto Imperatore 36 ☎06 6813 4730, ⓦ pizzare.it; map p.93. The entrance on Via del Corso is a Neapolitan café, while, on the Piazza Augusta Imperatore side, you can enjoy proper Neapolitan pizzas (€10 with a drink), pasta and salad dishes and excellent grilled *secondi* for moderate prices: €11–14 or so for a *primo*, €13–22 for a *secondo*. There are Neapolitan desserts and *fritti* too. The ambience is deliberately chic, and the large outside terrace always has a buzz about it. Daily 12.45–3pm & 7.30–11pm.

15

THE QUIRINALE AND VIA VENETO

CAFÉS AND BARS

Gianfornaio Largo Maresciallo Diaz 16 ☎06 333 3472, ⓦ ilgianfornaio.com; map p.105. A great bakery with pizza and other goodies and lots of seating inside and out. There are a couple of other branches, too, in posh residential neighbourhoods around the city, notably on Largo Apollinaire in EUR and at Viale dei Parioli 95 in Parioli. Mon–Sat 7.30am–9pm, Sun 9am–3pm.

Strabbioni Via Servio Tullio 8/10 ☎06 487 2027, ⓦ strabbioni.it; map p.105. Tucked away in the neighbourhood near Piazza Sallustio, this bar dates back to 1888 and has a great atmosphere, as well as Neapolitan pastries, sandwiches, and a restaurant attached serving Italian staples – pasta, cotoletta alla Milanese (veal breaded cutlet), and suchlike – for reasonable prices. Mon–Sat 8am–8pm.

RESTAURANTS

Al Forno della Soffitta Via Piave 62 ☎06 4201 1164, ⓦ alfornodellasoffitta.it; map p.105. Popular restaurant and pizzeria that does excellent *fritti* and thick-crusted Neapolitan-style pizzas, as well as pasta and grilled meat dishes, all very affordable. Really good Neapolitan cakes and desserts too. Always busy. Daily noon–midnight, Sat & Sun from 7pm.

Cantina Cantarini Piazza Sallustio 12 ☎06 485 528; map p.105. This old-style trattoria just off Via XX Settembre serves a very simple menu of food from the Marche region. There's rabbit on the menu, they always serve fish and seafood at the end of the week, and the place has a reassuringly unprepossessing interior, though there are tables outside for much of the year. Good prices too – pasta dishes from €7, main courses €10–12. Mon–Sat 12.30–3.30pm & 7.30–11pm.

Mirabelle Splendide Royal, Via di Porta Pinciana 14 ☎06 4216 8838, ⓦ splendideroyal.com; map p.105. The old-fashioned *Mirabelle* at the *Splendide Royal* continues to excel and has stunning views over the umbrella pines of Villa Borghese that is reflected in its gilt mirrors. If you're looking for a special night out, you could do worse, especially as the food is both unusual and beautifully cooked and presented – choose from things like goose liver terrine and truffles; crispy rolls of corn with ricotta cheese; asparagus and egg yolk; or suckling pig with pumpkin and liquorice. They do a decent children's menu too. You can reckon on spending at least €200 for a meal for two though – and probably more. Daily 12.30–3pm & 7.30–11pm.

★ **Piccolo Abruzzo** Via Sicilia 237 ☎06 4282 0176, ⓦ piccoloabruzzo.it; map p.105. A 5min stroll up unprepossessing Via Sicilia from Via Veneto, and a great alternative to the glitzy, mob-run places on the *Dolce Vita* street, with no menu, just a seemingly endless parade of goodies plonked on your table at regular intervals. What you get depends on what they have that day, but there's a fair chance it will include mozzarella and/or ricotta, a vegetable course, a couple of pasta dishes, a meat course and a dessert – plus as much wine as you can manage from the barrel. All for around €35 a head. Daily 1–3pm & 7pm–midnight.

VILLA BORGHESE AND NORTH

CAFÉS AND BARS

Casina dell'Orologio Pincio Gardens, Viale dei Bambini I ☎06 679 8515, ⓦ lacasinadellorologio .net; map p.173. This is a handy bar in the Pincio Gardens with sandwiches and cakes, a shady garden to eat them in, as well as a full-service restaurant with pasta dishes for €10 or so. A much better place for a snack or even a meal than the far pricier and rather full-of-itself *Casina Valadier* across the way. Daily except Wed 8am–8.30pm.

Sesto Piazza Buenos Aires 3 ☎06 855 9652; map pp.170–171. *Sesto* is a modern *tavola calda*-style café and restaurant, where you can order at the counter from a range of salads, pasta dishes and hot meat and fish options, and then eat from your tray in the cool, functional interior. Perfect for lunch, and there's a €7 *aperitivo* buffet from 6pm. Daily 8am–2am.

RESTAURANTS

Arancia Blu Via Cesare Beccaria 3 ☎06 361 0801, ⓦristorantearanciabluroma.com; map pp.170–171. This long-standing vegetarian restaurant has moved all over town but is now settled in a Flaminio location. It still reckons itself a cut above the rest – and with some justification, although, in a city with very few vegetarians, it doesn't have to try too hard. *Arancia Blu* prides itself on serving good food using fresh ingredients in an imaginative fashion, and decent salads – red pesto spaghetti, asparagus and cheese risotto, courgette parmigiana. *Primi* and *secondi* are both around the €10–12 mark. Daily noon–3pm & 7pm–midnight.

Da Emilio Via Alessandria 189 ☎06 855 8977; map pp.170–171. A real regular's joint, that bills itself as specializing in "*cucina casareccia*" or rustic cuisine. It is indeed very simple, serving classic Roman dishes with the odd seasonal variation – asparagus in spring for example, plus the usual pasta specialities and *secondi* such as *vitello al forno*, meatballs with mash and *coda alla vaccinara* or oxtail stew. *Primi* and *secondi* €9–12. Mon–Fri 12.30–2.30pm & 7.30–9.30pm.

Dulcamara Via Flaminia Vecchia 449 ☎06 333 2108, ⓦdulcamararoma.it; map pp.170–171. This busy bar-restaurant, up in the increasingly hip neighbourhood across the Ponte Milvio, serves a varied menu of good pasta dishes, soups and salads – everything from *cacio e pepe* to Indonesian rice dishes. The food is surprisingly good; there's usually a couple of daily specials on offer, and they also have a good range of artisanal Italian beers, on tap or in the bottle. Tues–Sat 12.15pm–2am.

Giggetto Via Alessandria 43/49 ☎06 841 2527; map pp.170–171. Namesake of the more famous Jewish Ghetto restaurant, this big and bustling pizzeria proclaims itself "king of pizza". Great, crispy-thin Roman pizzas, for just €6–8, lots of *fritti* and main dishes too. Daily 12.30–3pm & 7pm–1am.

La Pergola Rome Cavalieri, Via Alberto Cadiolo 101 ☎06 3509 2152, ⓦromecavalieri.com/lapergola; map pp.170–171. The undisputed pioneer of Rome's creative fine-restaurant dining is Heinz Beck, the chef at *La Pergola*, situated atop the spectacular *Rome Cavalieri* hotel. Frequently voted Italy's best restaurant here Beck has put hotel dining front and centre for quality and creativity, with dishes like *fagotelli carbonara* (his signature dish), John Dory with liquorice and soya poached beef fillet with garlic

---

TEN PLACES FOR PIZZA

There's nothing like thin, crispy Roman **pizza**, baked in a wood-fired oven, and naturally there are loads of places to try it. Here are our ten favourites, most of them sit-down places (*Pizzarium* is the only takeaway but is so good, we had to include it):

Ai Marmi See p.259
Al Grottino See p.257
Alle Carrette See p.255
Da Baffetto See p.245
Da Francesco See p.245
Dal Paino See p.245
Da Remo See p.259
Formula 1 See p.255
Giggetto See below
Pizzarium See p.261

---

dandelion and wasabi. It is probably Rome's most expensive restaurant: their 9-course tasting menu costs €210, and à la carte prices start at €44 for antipasti, about the same for pasta dishes and €54 for mains. Dress code – jackets for gentlemen! Tues–Sat 7.30–11pm.

La Scala Via dei Parioli 79d, Parioli ☎06 808 4463, ⓦwww.lascalavialeparioli.it; map pp.170–171. One of Parioli's posh choices, but sedate rather than pretentious, and always busy. Serves excellent, moderately priced food in the cosy inside rooms and on the outdoor terrace, with great fish and seafood pasta and risotto, good Roman pasta dishes and tasty grilled meat dishes. Daily 12.30–3pm & 7.30pm–midnight.

Oliver Glöwig Aldrovandi Villa Borghese, Via Ulisse Aldrovandi 15 ☎06 321 6126 ⓦoliverglowig.com; map p.173. *La Pergola* chef Heinz Beck's mission to bring fine dining to Rome has been continued by another German chef, Oliver Glöwig, at the *Aldrovandi Palace* (see p.254), whose restaurant has a tasteful, tranquil atmosphere and – like his *L'Olivo* restaurant on Capri – is starting to rack up awards and recently won its second Michelin star. His style is stripped down to an extreme, with a concentration on pure flavour and elegant presentation. Reckon on spending a couple of hundred euros a head, with wine. Mon–Sat 1–3pm & 8–11pm.

ReD Via Pietro de Coubertin 12/16 ☎06 8069 1630, ⓦredrestaurant.roma.it; map pp.170–171. Part of the Auditorium complex (see p.180), this sleek designer bar-restaurant is good for a drink or something to eat before or after a performance, with a short menu that is more traditionally Roman (mains such as swordfish with aubergine and basil for €16) and not as pricey as you might expect, given the surroundings; they also do €30 and €40 set menus. Daily 9am–2am.

THE ESQUILINE, MONTI AND TERMINI

CAFÉS AND BARS

Antico Caffè del Brasile Via dei Serpenti 23 ☎ 06 488 2319; map pp.114–115. Reliable old Monti café that has been selling great coffee, snacks and cakes for around a century; there are a handful of seats and tables at the back. Mon–Sat 6am–8.30pm, Sun 7am–2pm.

Caffè Fagi Piazza dei Cinquecento 39 ☎ 06 488 3885; map pp.114–115. In the piazza just to the left as you come out of Termini, this is the flagship café of the *Paranà* coffee group and serves excellent coffee made with their own blend of fair trade organic beans, along with an assortment of sweet and savoury snacks – a blessing, in what is a relative wasteland for palatable food and drink. Daily 7am–10pm.

★ **Dagnino** Galleria Esedra, Via E. Orlando 75, Termini ☎ 06 481 8660, ⓦ pasticceriadagnino.com; map pp.114–115. Good for both a coffee and snack or light lunch, this long-established Sicilian bakery, *gelateria* and café-restaurant is a peaceful retreat in the Termini area, with tables outside in a small shopping arcade. Great pastries and sandwiches, and a full menu of pasta and other hot dishes, too. Daily 7.30am–10.30pm.

La Bottega del Caffè Piazza Madonna dei Monti 5 ☎ 06 474 1578; map pp.114–115. Bang in the heart of the best bit of Monti, just a short walk from the Colosseum, this is a good place for a lunchtime snack and an early-evening drink, with tables outside on the square. Excellent value and service, and, later on, when the square becomes crowded with drinkers, it's an excellent place to take in the action. Daily 8am–2am.

RESTAURANTS

Agata e Romeo Via Carlo Alberto 45 ☎ 06 446 6115, ⓦ agataeromeo.it; map pp.114–115. Much-lauded chef Agata Parisella takes traditional Roman cuisine to more refined heights in this slightly old-fashioned restaurant, with dishes such as *baccalà* cooked five ways. Unusually pricey for this part of town, but a great place for a blow-the-budget feast – antipasti, *primi* and desserts €30, mains €40, or menus €110–130. Go for the more exotic stuff though – the *cacio e pepe* here is excellent, but it's hardly worth €30 for a dish so simple. Booking essential. Mon–Sat 7.30–10pm, Tues–Fri also 12.30–2.30pm.

Alle Carrette Via Madonna dei Monti 95 ☎ 06 679 2770; map pp.114–115. Inexpensive and large pizzeria just up Via Cavour from the Imperial Forums. It's always crowded – expect to wait for the exceptional pizza here. There are great home-made desserts too. Daily 8pm–midnight.

Baia Chia Via Machiavelli 5 ☎ 06 7045 3452, ⓦ www .ristorantebaiachia.it; map pp.114–115. This moderately priced Sardinian restaurant – pasta €9–12, mains €14–16 – has lots of good fish starters and tasty first courses, and the fish baked in salt is spectacular. For dessert, try the *sebadas*

(hot pastries stuffed with cheese and topped with Sardinian honey). Mon–Sat 12.30–3.30pm & 7.30–11.30pm.

Da Danilo Via Petrarca 13 ☎ 06 7720 0111, ⓦ trattoriadadanilo.it; map pp.114–115. This determinedly traditional restaurant sticks to what it knows best, and that's what makes it more of a locals' than a tourist joint. A short menu zeroes in on classics like *cacio e pepe* and simple rigatoni with tomato sauce, along with an *abbachio scottadito* that is as good as it gets. Homely trattoria food, though at perhaps slightly more than trattoria prices, due to its long-standing fame – something evidenced by the photos of the proprietor with all manner of celebs that plaster the walls; pasta dishes go for around €10, mains for Mon–Sat 7.30–11.30pm, Tues–Sat also 12.30–3pm.

Doozo Via Palermo 51/53 ☎ 06 481 5655, ⓦ doozo.it; map pp.114–115. Arguably the best Japanese restaurant in Monti, a zone known for its ethnic eateries. Part restaurant, part art gallery and bookshop, *Doozo* serves affordable lunch menus (€15–20) – dinner is a bit pricier (€35–40). There are bento boxes at lunchtime, great sushi and sashimi, tempura and soba noodles, among other things. In the summertime the outdoor seating is in a leafy courtyard with an ancient wall. Tues–Sun 7.30–11pm, Tues–Sat also 12.30–3pm.

Enoteca Cavour 313 Via Cavour 313 ☎ 06 678 5496, ⓦ cavour313.it; map pp.114–115. This lovely, wood-panelled old wine bar has long stood out amongst the pizza joints at this end of Via Cavour, just a stone's throw from the Forum. You can enjoy mixed plates of salami and cheese on wooden benches for around €10 or a daily selection of different hot dishes, from couscous to lasagne, as well as a selection of veggie alternatives. Excellent and enthusiastic service, too, and a great choice of wine. Mon–Sat 12.30–2.45pm & 7.30pm–12.30am, Sun 7.30pm–12.30am, closed Sun in summer.

Formula 1 Via degli Equi 13 ☎ 06 445 38661; map pp.114–115. Cheap and justifiably popular San Lorenzo pizzeria, with tables outside in summer. Try their delicious *pizza all'ortolana* (with courgettes, aubergines and peppers), and courgette-flower fritters. Pizzas cost around €7. Mon–Sat 6.30pm–12.30am.

Hang Zhou Via Principe Eugenio 82 ☎ 06 487 2732; map pp.114–115. Rome isn't the best place to find good, authentic Chinese food, but this old favourite, plastered with photos of the sociable owner, is the most popular place in the city centre to do so, and cheaply, too. Lunch buffets cost €15 a head, dinner buffet €20. Daily noon–3pm & 7pm–midnight.

Il Tempio di Mecanate Largo Leopardi 14/18 ☎ 06 487 2653; map pp.114–115. A top location right by the Maecenas temple, with lots of outside seating. You'll find this place is popular with tourists of all stripes, but the service is friendly and there's an excellently executed array

15

15

of Roman staples – a decent *carbonara, sauté di cozze e vongole* (mussels and clams), *saltimbocca* – okay pizzas and moderate prices: €8–10 for a *primo*, €12–14 for a *secondo*. Daily noon–2pm & 7.30–10.30pm.

L'Asino d'Oro Via del Boschetto 73 ☎ 06 4891 3832; map pp.114–115. The Rome location of legendary Orvieto chef Lucio Sforza, who blends traditional Roman ingredients in both complex and simple combinations that you won't find anywhere else in the city. His bacon with sage and vinegar starter is to die for; follow it with lamb with artichokes or rabbit with vinegar and tomato. Desserts are great too, using unexpected ingredients such as sage and rosemary, and it's not that expensive, especially considering the cool Monti vibe and bustling outside terrace – *primi* from €10, *secondi* from €13. It's a good idea to book ahead. Daily 12.30–3pm & 7.30–10.30pm.

La Barrique Via del Boschetto 41b ☎ 06 4782 5953; map pp.114–115. Formerly more of a wine bar and always a good place to stop off for an early evening glass of wine and a snack, this place has had a makeover and is now a proper restaurant. It's managed to lose none of its edge in the transition, as far as the wine list goes, and now complements it with a regularly changing seasonal menu that always hits the spot – think simple, well-cooked pasta dishes, meat courses like rabbit confit and steaks – all of which you can enjoy inside or at the few tables out on the street. Mon–Fri 6pm–2am, Sat also 1–3.30pm

La Carbonara Via Panisperna 214 ☎ 06 485 5176, ⊛ lacarbonara.it; map pp.114–115. Always crowded, this staple of the Monti eating scene maintains a refreshingly basic distance from the more rarefied offerings of the neighbourhood, with a very seasonal menu in a bustling wood-panelled dining room. You can expect to wait for a table, but it's no hardship to sit at the small bar and take in the activity before tucking into a selection of low to moderately priced Roman pasta staples – good *alla gricia* and *carbonara* – and mainly meat-orientated *secondi* – *straccetti* (slices) or fillet of beef, *saltimbocca, coda alla vaccinara*, fish on Fri and tripe on Sat. There's a pretty decent wine list too. Mon–Sat 12.30–2.30pm & 7.30–10.30pm

Maharajah Via dei Serpenti 124 ☎ 06 474 7144 ⊛ maharajah-roma.com; map pp.114–115. This long-established neighbourhood favourite serves Indian classics at reasonable prices on Monti's main street. Always busy, and one of the best bets for a decent curry in town. The popular lunch specials start at around €12. Daily 12.30–3pm & 7.30–11pm.

Monti DOC Via Giovanni Lanza 93 ☎ 06 487 2696; map pp.114–115. Comfortable Santa Maria Maggiore neighbourhood wine bar, with an excellent wine list and decent food – cold cuts and cheese, soups, quiches, salads and pastas (including some good veggie dishes) – all chalked on the blackboard daily. Most things go for €10–15. Tues–Sun 7pm–1am, Tues–Fri also 1–3.30pm.

Open Colonna Palazzo delle Esposizioni, Via Milano 9a ☎ 06 4782 2641, ⊛ opencolonna.it; map pp.114–115. The top floor of the newly refurbished Palazzo delle Esposizioni (see p.123) is the domain of big-shot Italian chef Antonello Colonna, who presides over this impressively light-drenched modern space given over to eating, drinking – and looking cool. The food is great, if rather expensive – €26 for a *primo*, €38 for a *secondo* – but its weekday €16 lunch buffet is an institution, as is the €30 weekend brunch. A modern Rome experience. Tues–Sun 12.30–3.30pm & 8–10.30pm.

★ **Pastificio San Lorenzo** Via Tiburtina 196 ☎ 06 9727 3519, ⊛ pastificiocerere.com; map pp.114–115. The big interior space and windows give a contemporary feel to the old Cerere pasta factory, where the ground-floor restaurant, with its elegant long bar and generously spaced tables, is the perfect environment to enjoy the modern twists on classic Roman food they specialize in here. Mains go for €15–19, pasta dishes €10–12, and might include a *carbonara* or *cacio e pepe*, a lamb dish or their house burger. The rest of the building houses an art foundation that hosts regular exhibitions. Mon–Sat 8–11.30pm (bar 7pm–2am).

★ **Pommidoro** Piazza dei Sanniti 44 ☎ 06 445 2692; map pp.114–115. Family-run Roman trattoria that's been around forever and serves great Roman home-cooking: it's very seasonal, with an emphasis on grilled lamb and game cooked on a big open grill. All the pasta classics, too, with a great *carbonara* among other things, all at good prices. Once the favourite haunt of film-director Pasolini, it has a breezy open veranda outside on the square in summer. Mon–Sat 12.30–3pm & 7.30–11pm.

★ **Tram Tram** Via dei Reti 44/46 ☎ 06 490 416, ⊛ tramtram.it; map pp.114–115. A grungy location but a cosy spot, this trendy, animated San Lorenzo restaurant serves Pugliese pasta dishes, fish and seafood and unusual salads, with mains at €15–18. Reservations recommended. There's also a bar if you want to carry on drinking after dinner. Tues–Sun noon–3pm & 7.30pm–midnight, closed Sun in July & Aug.

★ **Trattoria Monti** Via di San Vito 13a ☎ 06 446 6573; map pp.114–115. Small, family-run and moderately priced restaurant that specializes in the cuisine of the Marche region, which means hearty food from a short menu – great pasta and interesting cabbage-wrapped *torte* as starters, and mainly meaty *secondi*, with beef, lamb and rabbit predominating. Close enough to Termini to be convenient, but this is as homely and friendly a restaurant as you could want – something places in this neighbourhood often aren't. Tues–Sun 12.30–3pm, Tues–Sat also 7.30–11pm.

Urbana 47 Via Urbana 47 ☎ 06 4788 4006, ⊛ urbana47.it; map pp.114–115. This Monti stalwart takes itself pretty seriously, with its "zero food kilometres" and post-industrial decor, not to mention a slight attitudinal approach to service. But, when it comes down to the food, it's a thoroughly agreeable restaurant with its heart in the right place, serving a variety of intriguing takes on traditional Roman cuisine. Pasta dishes go for around €14 and mains for €16–18, and the menu changes every month – if you can't decide, just settle for a wine-bar-style plate of cheese and salami. They also run a summer cinema club next door. Daily 7pm–midnight, Sat & Sun also 12.30–3.30pm.

Valentino Via del Boschetto 37 ☎06 488 0643; map pp.114–115. Easy to miss, with only a faded Peroni sign above the door, but well placed at the top of one of Monti's most atmospheric streets, this is both trattoria and *birreria*, and as cheap as that implies. Inside, it's always buzzing, with waiters zipping between the closely packed tables. You'll find lots of grilled meat options, a *scamorza* (grilled cheese) menu, and as such it's great for vegetarians, too. Mon–Sat 12.45–2.45pm & 7.30–11.30pm.

> ### FIVE PLACES FOR VEGGIES
>
> It's relatively easy for **vegetarians** to survive and even eat extremely well all over Italy, even in Rome, whose core traditional cuisine consists of the unmentionable and rarely eaten parts of animals – though to be honest there are plenty of non-meat dishes besides. You certainly don't need to go to a specifically vegetarian restaurant, which is just as well, as well as there aren't many in Rome. Here are some of our favourite places to eat top-notch, meat-free meals across the capital.
>
> **Agustafello** See p.259
> **Arancia Blu** See p.254
> **Ditirambo** See p.249
> **Mesob** See p.258
> **Valentino** See opposite

15

THE CELIAN HILL AND SAN GIOVANNI

CAFÉS AND BARS

Conter Piazza di San Giovanni in Laterano 64, no phone; map pp.130–131. Right across from the basilica of San Giovanni, this bar is a handy place for a bite between sights, with snacks, an assortment of craft beers and a few tables. Daily 8am–8pm.

Valentini Piazza Tuscolo 2 ☎06 7720 7427; map pp.130–131. Café, pastry shop and *tavola calda*, just 5min from San Giovanni and a great spot for lunch, with outside seating, too. Daily 8am–6pm.

RESTAURANTS

Al Grottino Via Orvieto 6 ☎06 702 4440, ⓦ algrottino .com; map pp.130–131. You can always tell a decent Roman pizzeria by the crowd of people hanging about outside waiting for takeaways, and this one fits that bill perfectly, a 10min walk from San Giovanni metro station. There's a huge choice of pizzas, though as ever the classics are best not overloaded so you can appreciate the crispy charred bases, cooked to perfection, which are slightly less thin than the usual Roman style. There's a good choice of antipasti too, with *fritti* and suchlike. They also have an amazingly complete selection of Belgian beers. Expect to wait for a table, especially if you want to sit outside – it's always busy. Pizzas from €5. Daily 7.30–11.30pm.

Aroma Palazzo Manfredi, Via Labicana 125 ☎06 7759 1380, ⓦ palazzomanfredi.com; map pp.130–131. You could be forgiven for just going to *Aroma*, at the beautifully revamped *Palazzo Manfredi* hotel, for its unsurpassed views of the Colosseum. But the food is so good that we'd recommend it if it were in a windowless basement – Italian, somewhat Roman, but with a lot of twists. It's not at all cheap – *primi* around €30, *secondi* around €40 – but

its tasting menu (7 courses for €125) is worth the splurge if you throw in the excellent, understated service. Daily 12.30–2.30pm & 7.30–10.30pm.

Caffè Propaganda Via Claudia 15 ☎06 9453 4255, ⓦ caffepropaganda.it; map pp.130–131. Relatively new Celio bar-restaurant that's unashamedly not of the traditional trattoria school: this is more the kind of place that offers bread in a paper bag and where the menu is a faux-newspaper. Those affectations aside, it's a bright, well-realized space, very handily placed for the Colosseum and the food ain't at all bad – a simple if unadventurous menu of pasta dishes – *carbonara, amatriciana, alle vongole* – and a short list of main courses that includes a decent if overpriced burger, along with salads and *frittate*. Always a few specials, too, and service is brisk and friendly. *Primi* €10–13, *secondi* €18–22. Daily noon–1am, Sun till 4pm.

Charley's Sauciere Via di San Giovanni in Laterano 270 ☎06 7049 5666, ⓦ cucinafrancesearoma.com; map pp.130–131. If the background *chansons* don't make you think you're in France – albeit a mythical one from the 1930s – the menu certainly will, with lots of French classics – *coq au vin*, onion soup and excellent steaks. This French–Swiss old-timer does fondues, too. Moderate prices – soups and starters €8–10, mains €18, and it's just a 5min walk from the Colosseum. Mon–Sat 12.30–3pm & 7.30–11pm.

Giuda Ballerino Largo Appio Claudio 346 ☎06 715 84807, ⓦ giudaballerino.it; map pp.130–131. One of Rome's best places to eat is way down in the south of the city, on the doorstep of the Cinecittà studios (p.153). *Giuda Ballerino* is run by Romolo Di Francesco and chef Andrea Fusco, who share their mutual passion for comic books, great food and wine. You can choose between the more casual (and economical) *osteria*, where all *primi* are €16 and *secondi* €19, and the pricier, Michelin-starred restaurant, or just enjoy cocktails and great wines by the glass with bar food that is well above average. There's collection of comic memorabilia to look at, too. Despite their lavish lifestyles on and off the set, it's hard to imagine that Taylor and Burton would have dined so well in 1960s Rome. *Osteria* daily 1–3pm & 7.30–11.30pm, *ristorante* daily except Wed 7.30–11pm.

Il Bocconcino Via Ostilia 23 ☎06 7707 9175, ⊛ilbocconcino.com; map pp.130–131. Not the greatest service, but a cut above most of the other places within sight of the Colosseum, with high-quality Roman food served in an old-fashioned environment. Their *tonnarelli cacio e pepe* is great bargain for €6.50, while most main courses – meatballs, roast lamb, stewed rabbit – go for €8.50–10.50. Daily except Wed 12.30–3pm & 7.30–11pm.

Luzzi Via di San Giovanni in Laterano 88 ☎06 709 6332; map pp.130–131. Midway between San Giovanni in Laterano and the Colosseum, this bustling restaurant is a dependable choice amid the tourist joints of the neighbourhood. The food is hearty and simple (if unspectacular), there's outside seating, and it's extremely cheap – *secondi* go for €6–9. There's pizza, too, but only in the evening. Daily except Wed noon–3pm & 7pm–midnight.

Mesob Via Prenestina 118 ☎338 251 1621, ⊛mesob .it; map pp.130–131. Arguably the city's most interesting ethnic food – Ethiopian – reaches its zenith at *Mesob*, located in a renovated garage on the cusp of Pigneto. The vegetarian options, including rich lentil and vegetable stews, are the highlight, and the home-made *injera* (flatbread) is the best in town. Mains are very reasonable, starting at around €8. Tues–Sun 7.30–10pm.

Primo al Pigneto Via del Pigneto 46 ☎06 701 3827, ⊛primoalpigneto.it; map pp.130–131. *Primo al Pigneto* epitomizes the cool vibe of modern-day Pigneto, with its clean, contemporary interior and short menu of well-chosen dishes (such as roasted duck with roast potatoes and *cacciatore* sauce), most of which are examples of simple yet modern cooking, and usually delicious. *Primi* go for around €12, *secondi* €15–28. Reservations are recommended for dinner. Tues–Sun 7pm–1am, Sun also 12.30–3pm.

Tajut Via San Giovanni in Laterano 244 ☎349 641 8088, ⊛iltajut.it; map pp.130–131. This cosy restaurant claims to be the only Friulian restaurant in Rome, which seems a crime, because the food here is excellent: sort of Italian with a Central European twist – good pasta and duck dishes – and with its relaxed wine-bar vibe you can eat as much or as little of it as you like. It's not a million miles from the Colosseum, but definitely more of a neighbourhood than a tourist restaurant. There's no outside seating – the pavement's not wide enough – but good either for a quick lunchtime bite or more leisurely evening dinner. Tues–Sun 7–11.30pm.

★ **Taverna dei Quaranta** Via Claudia 24 ☎06 700 0550, ⊛tavernadeiquaranta.com; map pp.130–131. This very relaxed locals' joint with chequered tablecloths offers good, very reasonably priced home cooking. The dishes are Roman with a twist: classics such as roast lamb and courgette flowers, but polenta, too, and some interesting pasta dishes, on a menu that changes regularly. *Primi* €7–8, *secondi* €8–10. Only in Rome could this sort of place exist, 5min from the tourist scrum at the Colosseum. Daily 12.15–3pm & 7.15pm–midnight.

THE AVENTINE AND SOUTH

CAFÉS AND BARS

Caffè del Seme e la Foglia Via Galvani 18 ☎06 574 3008; map pp.140–141. This is a pleasantly low-key café popular with Testaccio trendies and students from the nearby music school. During the day it's good for sandwiches and big salad lunches, and in the evenings it's a mellow place to relax before visiting the area's more energetic offerings. Mon–Sat 8am–1.30am, Sun 6pm–1.30am.

Palombini Piazzale Adenauer 12, EUR ☎06 591 1700, ⊛www.palombini.it; map pp.140–141. This is a great EUR café where the outside terrace and large interior are a haven amid the brutal boulevards. Appropriately housed on the ground floor of EUR's official "restaurant building", it's a café, *tabacchi* and wine shop all rolled into one, and serves excellent cakes and sandwiches. Mon–Thurs 7am–10pm, Fri & Sat 7am–1am, Sun 8am–10pm.

Volpetti Più Via Alessandro Volta 8 ☎06 574 2352, ⊛volpetti.com; map pp.140–141. *Tavola calda* that's attached to the famous deli a few doors down (see p.292).

CITTÀ DEL GUSTO

This industrial building by the river in the southern reaches of Trastevere is a five-floor testimony to the success of the **Gambero Rosso** food empire, which has grown from a food and wine supplement in the Communist newspaper *Il Manifesto* to Italy's most successful gourmet publisher, with a bestselling magazine, TV programmes, cooking schools and a series of restaurant guides. At their headquarters they run **food and wine tastings**, host a wine bar and *osteria* (see p.260), a shop selling cookbooks and kitchen equipment (Mon–Fri 9am–2.30pm), and a theatre and TV studio.

Great pizza, *supplì*, chicken, deep-fried veg and much more. Mon–Sat 10.30am–3.30pm & 5.30–9.30pm.

RESTAURANTS

Agustarello Via G. Branca 98 ☎ 06 574 6585; map pp.140–141. *Agustarello* is a moderately priced Testaccio standard serving genuine Roman cuisine in a simple, old-fashioned atmosphere. It's resolutely traditional, serving a deliberately seasonal menu (no artichokes outside autumn/winter for example) that includes all the Roman offal classics: *coda alla vaccinara*, *pajata*, *coratelle* as well as great steaks, pork chops and tripe – and, as with most Italian restaurants, even vegetarians can find good choices. *Primi* go for €10, mains €12–18. Mon–Sat 12.30–3pm & 7.30–11.30pm.

Checchino dal 1887 Via di Monte Testaccio 30 ☎ 06 574 6318, ⓦ checchino-dal-1887.com; map pp.140–141. Right in the heart of Monte Testaccio's bars and clubs, *Checchino dal 1887* is a historic (and expensive) symbol of Testaccio cookery, and one of the best places to sample the stalwarts of Rome's offal-based cuisine – appropriate, as it's right opposite the old slaughterhouse. It has an excellent wine cellar, too. Tues–Sat 12.30–3pm & 8–11.30pm.

Da Felice Via Mastro Giorgio 29 ☎ 06 574 6800, ⓦ feliceatestaccio.it; map pp.140–141. Always crowded, this joint isn't quite the rough-and-ready establishment it used to be when Felice used to choose his customers from a line outside, and there are those who feel it has lost some of its charm. But it still serves honest, seasonal Roman cooking – *bucatini cacio e pepe*, lamb, and in winter, artichokes: all the classics, well cooked and served. Listen for the daily specials, usually just half a

dozen *primi* (€8–10) and *secondi* (€12–15). Daily 12.30–2.45pm & 8–11.30pm.

★ **Da Remo** Piazza Santa Maria Liberatrice 44 ☎ 06 574 6270; map pp.140–141. *Da Remo* is the best kind of pizzeria: usually crowded with locals, very basic and serving the thinnest, crispiest Roman pizza you'll find. Try also the heavenly *bruschette* and other snacks like *supplì* and *fiori di zucca*. Almost worth travelling out to Testaccio for – and very cheap. Mon–Sat 7.30pm–1am.

Di Oio di Casa Mia Via Galvani 43/45 ☎ 06 578 2680; map pp.140–141. No-nonsense trattoria that does both the full range of Roman pasta favourites: *cacio e pepe*, *alla gricia* and much more – but also all the offal classics that the Testaccio district is renowned for. Pasta dishes go for around €8, mains €12–18 – and you can just have roast lamb or chicken if you're too squeamish for the tripe or *coratelle* (heart, liver, spleen and lung). Mon–Sat noon–2pm & 8–11pm.

Flavio al Velavevodetto Via di Monte Testaccio 97 ☎ 06 574 4194, ⓦ flavioalvelavevodetto.it; map pp.140–141. This very reasonable Testaccio restaurant serves traditional dishes among ancient pottery shards. All the standard Roman classics are on offer, as well as some fish dishes, and its outdoor patios are a delightful venue for summer meals. Tues–Sun 12.30–3pm & 8pm–midnight.

Tuttifrutti Via Luca della Robbia 3a ☎ 06 575 7902, ⓦ ristorantetuttifrutti.it; map pp.140–141. This is a Testaccio favourite, and pretty much the perfect restaurant – family-run, with good food and decent prices. The menu changes daily, and offers interesting variations on traditional Roman dishes, with *primi* around €12, *secondi* €15. Tues–Sun 7.30–11.30pm.

TRASTEVERE AND THE JANICULUM HILL

CAFÉS AND BARS

Café Di Marzio Piazza di Santa Maria in Trastevere 15 ☎ 06 581 6095, ⓦ caffedimarzio.it; map pp.160–161. This bar isn't much on the inside, but it's a friendly place, and the terrace right on Piazza Santa Maria makes it one of the best people-watching spots in Trastevere. Not much in the way of food though you can get a toasted sandwich or panino. Daily 7am–1am.

Gianicolo Piazzale Aurelia 5 ☎ 06 580 6275; map pp.160–161. This is a pleasant, wood-panelled café and bar with a long, shady terrace facing the Porta San Pancrazio (see p.166). Something of a hangout for Italian media stars, writers and academics from the nearby Spanish and American academies. Most customers come here for a drink, but they also serve tasty sandwiches and snacks. Tues–Sat 7am–1am, Sun 7am–9pm.

La Renella Via del Moro 15 ☎ 06 581 7265; map pp.160–161. A long-standing bakery, right in the heart of Trastevere, with focaccia and *pizza al taglio*. Take a number

and be prepared to wait at busy times. You can take away or eat on the premises at its long counter. Daily 9am–9pm.

Sisini Via San Francesco a Ripa 137 ☎ 06 589 7110; map pp.160–161. Just half a block from Viale Trastevere, there's no sign outside this *pizza al taglio* hole-in-the-wall, which is odd as it may well have the best pizza by the slice in Rome. Also roast chicken and potatoes, *supplì* and all the usual *rosticceria* stuff. Try their unique chopped spicy green olive pizza. Mon–Fri 10am–10.30pm.

RESTAURANTS

Ai Marmi Viale Trastevere 53/59 ☎ 06 580 0919; map pp.160–161. Nicknamed "the mortuary" because of its stark interior and marble tables, this place – which confusingly also goes by the name *Panattoni* – serves unique *supplì al telefono* (so named because of the string of mozzarella it forms when you take a bite), fantastic fresh *baccalà* and the best pizza in Trastevere. It has good house red wine, too, and service is quick, despite the crowds, if not always especially

15

friendly. A couple of pizzas and a carafe of house wine will set you back about €30. Daily except Wed 6pm–1am.

Akropolis Via San Francesco a Ripa 103 ☎ 06 5833 2600, ⓦ akropolistavernagreca.com; map pp.160–161. This small Greek restaurant and takeaway has delicious *souvlaki* and all the usual snacks and honeyed sweets. Good prices, too – bank on around €20 per head for more food than you can eat. No bookings. Tues–Sat 7.30–11.30pm.

Antico Arco Piazzale Aurelio 7 ☎ 06 581 5274, ⓦ anticoarco.it; map pp.160–161. Located above Trastevere, next to the Janiculum Hill, this is one of Rome's finest restaurants, serving superb, exquisitely presented dishes, and also has an enormous fine wine list. It's always good, and reservations are definitely required. Daily 7.30pm–midnight.

Bir and Fud Via Benedetta 23 ☎ 06 589 4016, ⓦ birandfud.it; map pp.160–161. This fashionable little place, in one of Trastevere's busiest squares, does great wood-fired pizzas which can be washed down with what is an exemplary range of beers. It gets very busy, so come early or reserve. Mon–Wed 5.30pm–2am, Thurs–Sun 11.30am–2am.

Da Augusto Piazza de' Renzi 15 ☎ 06 580 3798; map pp.160–161. This is a reliable diner-style joint serving Roman basics in an unpretentious, bustling atmosphere. Fine pasta and soup starters, and daily meat and fish specials – not haute cuisine, but decent, hearty Roman cooking. Mon–Sat 12.30–3pm & 8–11pm.

Da Enzo Via dei Vascellari 29 ☎ 06 581 2260, ⓦ daenzoal29.com; map pp.160–161. A tiny restaurant close to the river in Trastevere that does tasty basic Roman food at decent prices – a million miles away from some of the glitzy new places that have opened up over in the district's busier quarter. Mon–Sat 12.30–3pm & 7.30–11pm.

Da Ivo Via di San Francesco a Ripa 158 ☎ 06 581 7082; map pp.160–161. *The* Trastevere pizzeria, almost in danger of becoming a caricature, but still good and with quite reasonably priced pizzas (€7–9), and cheap wine too (from €8 a bottle). A tasty assortment of desserts as well – try the *monte bianco* for the ultimate chestnut cream and meringue confection. Arrive early to avoid a chaotic queue. Daily except Tues 6pm–midnight.

Da Lucia Vicolo del Mattonato 2b ☎ 06 580 3601, ⓦ trattoriadalucia.com; map pp.160–161. Outdoor Trastevere dining in summer is at its best at this wonderful old trattoria, which serves great Roman food at decent prices (€20–25 a head for two courses with wine). Spaghetti *cacio e pepe* is the speciality here – arrive early to nab a table outside. Tues–Sun 12.30–3pm & 7.30–11.30pm.

Da Olindo Vicolo della Scala 8 ☎ 06 581 8835; map pp.160–161. This is a great, family-run Trastevere trattoria in smart and cosy premises that offers traditional Roman food. There's a small menu of staples, and prices are very

competitive: *primi* cost around €7, *secondi* around €9. Mon–Sat 12.30–3pm & 8–11pm.

★ **Da Paris** Piazza San Calisto 7a ☎ 06 581 5378, ⓦ ristoranteparis.it; map pp.160–161. This old-fashioned place still serves good Roman–Jewish food on one of Trastevere's most atmospheric piazzas, with tables outside in summer and a whole host of excellent traditional dishes. It's fairly expensive – reckon on €50 a head, without wine – but offers good cooking in a firmly traditional environment. Tues–Sun 12.30–3pm & 7.30–11pm, closed Aug.

Dar Poeta Vicolo del Bologna 45/46 ☎ 06 588 0516, ⓦ darpoeta.com; map pp.160–161. Don't expect the typical crusty Roman pizza here; the margherita (ask for it *con basilico* – with basil) comes out of the wood-smoked oven soft and with plenty of mozzarella on top. They have good imported darker beers and ales – a rarity outside a pub – as well as a handful of outside tables, though these can sometimes be a bit cramped and crowded. Daily noon–midnight.

Il Ciak Vicolo del Cinque 21 ☎ 06 589 4774, ⓦ ristoranteilciak.com; map pp.160–161. This honest, no-frills Tuscan grill serves up chops, chicken and of course steaks, as well as more arcane meats and game alongside pasta dishes with interesting sauces, such as wild boar. It's a tastefully turned-out trattoria which is refreshingly authentic. *Secondi* are around the €20 mark. Daily 6.30–10.30pm.

Il Winebar Città del Gusto, Via Enrico Fermi 161 ☎ 06 5511 2264, ⓦ ilwinebar.it; map pp.160–161. On the top floor of the modern Città del Gusto (see box, p.258), this is a good place to try good wines or indulge in delicious food while taking in great city views. You can taste a wide variety of wines by the glass in the bar while sampling plates of cheese and salami. Full meals are served in the *osteria* or out on the terrace in summer, with smaller dishes such as grilled octopus with leek and potato sauce (€17) and mains such as steamed salmon with courgette pie (€24). Wine bar Tues–Sat 6.30pm–midnight, *osteria* Mon 9am–4pm, Tues–Fri 9am–12.30am.

★ **Le Mani in Pasta** Via dei Genovesi 37 ☎ 06 581 6017, ⓦ www.lemaniinpasta.com; map pp.160–161. This small and cosy restaurant cooks up great pasta and fish dishes for €10–12 (*primi*) and €16 or so (*secondi*). Often very crowded, and it's worth reserving to be sure of getting in. It has excellent service and fantastic food. Tues–Sun 12.30–3pm & 7.30–11pm.

Pizzeria San Calisto Piazza di San Calisto 9a ☎ 06 581 8256; map pp.160–161. Come here for large pizzas at small prices (€4.50–9). You'll get friendly, fast service and a vibrant, welcoming atmosphere, whether you sit inside or out on the piazza. Tues–Sun 7.30pm–1am.

Sette Oche Via dei Salumi 36 ☎ 06 580 9753, ⓦ setteoche.ea23.com; pp.160–161. Based in a cellar, this

---

THE REVOLVING DOOR: CUTTING-EDGE CUISINE IN ROME'S HOTEL RESTAURANTS

In the past decade or so, some of the **best chefs** working in Italy (both Italian and foreign) have exited and entered the revolving doors of Rome's major **hotels**, and it's the cuisine of these establishments that is often at the cutting edge of Italy's food trends, with fresh local ingredients, some exotic touches and fantastic presentation. It's not surprisingly **expensive** to eat at any of these places, but bear in mind that the food and service are extra special and invariably accompanied by breathtaking views. You should also be aware that a lot of hotel restaurants offer a more economical, pared-down **lunch menu** (or even buffet) to attract business diners, but do check, because some chefs are active only at dinner, with lunch under a separate team that may produce an entirely different style of food. Here's our current top ten:

All'Oro Restaurant at the *The First* (see p.251)
Aroma at the *Palazzo Manfredi* (see p.257)
Imàgo at the *Hassler* (see p.252)
Jardin de Russie at *De Russie* (see p.252)
La Pergola at the *Cavalieri Hilton* (see p.254)
La Terrazza Bramante at the *Raphaël* (see p.246)
La Terrazza dell'Eden at *Hotel Eden* (see p.252)
Mirabelle at the *Splendide Royal* (see p.253)
Oliver Glöwig at *Aldrovandi Palace* (see p.254)
Vivavoce at the *Gran Meliá Rome Villa Agrippina* (see below)

15

---

restaurant, pizzeria and wine bar also has outside seating on a quiet street in the more tranquil part of Trastevere. The menu is short and not ambitious, but they do the basic Roman *primi* and *secondi* well, and prices are decent (€8 *primi*, €11 *secondi*), plus they also do a selection of *focaccie* and *bruschette*. Tues–Sun noon–3.30pm & 7pm–midnight.

★ **Take Sushi** Viale di Trastevere 4 ☎06 581 0075, ✉takesushi.it; map pp.160–161. Located on Trastevere's main avenue, this cosy place comes as a real – and affordable – surprise, serving delicious sushi and sashimi, as well as light, crispy tempura. The sashimi salad is very

special, too. Start off with a flawless *miso* soup and finish with home-made green-tea ice cream. A 16-pieces sushi set costs €24. Tues–Sun 12.30–3pm & 7.30pm–11pm.
Vivavoce Gran Meliá Rome Villa Agrippina ☎06 925 901, ✉ristorantevivavoce.com; map pp.160–161. Up on the Janiculum Hill, the *Vivavoce* in the *Gran Meliá Rome Villa Agrippina*, under the helm of master chef Alfonso Laccarino, is perhaps the newest hotel sensation in town, and brings his famous take on fresh Mediterranean cuisine from Campania to Rome. They do a tasting menu for €110. Mon–Sat 8–11pm.

THE VATICAN AND PRATI

CAFÉS AND BARS
Mondo Arancina Via Marcantonio Colonna 38 ☎06 9761 9214, ✉mondoarancina.it; map pp.188–189. There are great savoury Sicilian classics at this takeaway place, but the real treats are the *arancini*, of which there are any number of varieties – tomato and mozzarella, ham and cheese, bolognese – all delicious and just €2 a throw. There are several locations, including a second branch at Via Flaminia 42–44, just north of Piazza del Popolo. Daily 10am–midnight.

★ **Pizzarium** Via della Meloria 43 ☎06 3974 5416; map pp.188–189. Undoubtedly Rome's best pizza-by-the-slice joint where celebrity baker Gabriele Bonci uses top-notch ingredients to create creatively topped pies like rabbit and raisin or *trippa alla romana*. There is also an assortment of *fritti – suppli, filetti di baccalà and crocchette*. Standing room only inside, and there are only a few benches for dining outside. Mon–Sat 11am–10pm, Sun 1–10pm.

Sciascia Caffè Via Fabio Massimo 80a ☎06 321 1580; map pp.188–189. One of Prati's best coffee joints, with not only excellent coffee but pastries and, hey, places to sit inside! Free wi-fi, too, so not a bad place for a quick pick-me-up between Vatican sights. Mon–Sat 7.30am–6.30pm.

RESTAURANTS
Cacio e Pepe Via Avezzana 11 ☎06 321 7268, ✉www .trattoriacacioepepeprati.com; map pp.188–189. Rough-and-ready Prati cheapie with a menu taped to the wall and great pasta staples like *cacio e pepe, carbonara* and one of the best *pasta alla gricia* in town for around €7; mains go for €9–10 and are equally flavoursome. With mostly outside tables and a small inside space, it's always busy, though it's a bit of a hike from the main sights. No credit cards. Mon–Sat 12.30–3.30pm, & 7.30–11.30pm, closed Sat eve.

15

Cantina Tirolese Via G. Vitelleschi 23 ☎ 06 6813 5297, ⓦ cantinatirolese.it; map pp.188–189. This rustic Prati restaurant was reputedly the last pope's favourite lunch spot when he was still a cardinal, and no wonder – the hearty and wholesome Austrian and German cuisine served here is excellent, and there's lots of it. Choose from dumplings and goulash soup to start (for around €8) and various meaty middle-European meat specialities for your main course; fondue for around €26 for two is about the only vegetarian option you'll find. The lunchtime buffet (noon–3pm) is excellent value at €9.50 a head. Tues–Fri & Sun noon–3pm & 7.30pm–midnight.

★ **Dal Toscano** Via Germanico 58/60 ☎ 06 3972 5717, ⓦ ristorantedaltoscano.it; map pp.188–189. Don't come here for a salad. This restaurant specializes in *fiorentine* (the famous thick Tuscan T-bone steaks), perfectly grilled on charcoal, delicious *pici* (thick home-made spaghetti) and *ribollita* (veg and bread soup) – all at honest prices: *primi* around €10, mains for €12–15. Not far from the Vatican, it's tremendously popular with Roman families, so reservations are recommended for dinner. Tues–Sun 12.30–3pm & 8–11.15pm.

Del Frate Via degli Scipioni 118/122 ☎ 06 323 6437; map pp.188–189. This large wine and spirits shop is a wine bar too, with a great selection of cheeses and cold meats as well as regular pasta dishes – and a good choice of artisanal Italian beers as well as wines by the glass. Very handy for the Vatican, for lunch or at the end of the day. Large mixed cheese and salami plates go for €16–18. Mon–Sat 12.30–3pm & 6.30pm–1am.

Il Sorpasso Via Properzio 31/33 ☎ 06 8902 4554, ⓦ sorpasso.info; map pp.188–189. Wine bar and restaurant with a great choice of wines by the glass – either enjoy the full menu in the comfier back room, or just snack at the table outside or by the marble-topped bar. Lovely prosciutto, cheese and cold cuts, risotto and pasta dishes that change daily, along with steaks and other mains. Try a *trapizzino* – Roman goodies stuffed into a wrap of pizza, sort of like an Italian kebab. Mon–Sat 7.30am–1am (Sat from 9am).

Mamá Via Sforza Pallavicini 19 ☎ 06 6813 9095; map 188–189. Open from breakfast right through to dinner, this contemporary yet homely little restaurant serves an inexpensive menu of hot breakfasts and sandwiches, pasta dishes for €9–12, including Roman favourites and others which change daily, salads and short menus of fish and meat dishes for €12–18. They serve a good-value three-course lunch too, for €15 including water and coffee, and a

good range of artisanal Italian beers. Daily 8am–10pm.

★ **Osteria dell'Angelo** Via G. Bettolo 24 ☎ 06 372 9470; map pp.188–189. Above-average traditional Roman food at extremely reasonable prices, in a highly popular restaurant run by an ex-rugby player. There is an obligatory tasting menu priced at €25 a head, and booking is advisable, as it's often heaving with locals. Mon–Sat 8–11.15pm, Tues & Fri also 12.45–2.30pm.

Passaguai Via Pomponio Leto 1 ☎ 06 874 1358, ⓦ passaguai.it; map pp.188–189. Basement wine bar with seating outside on the street that serves great platters of cheese, cold cuts, salads and various other snacks to go with its excellent choice of wine. A lot of the food is home-produced, and it's always busy, with a great vibe and an emphasis on freshness, quality and seasonality. Unusually, there's no cover or bread charge, and as an added bonus the bread is from Roscioli deli (see p.249); wines start at €13 per bottle. Daily 10am–2am, Sat & Sun from 6pm.

Ragno d'Oro Via Silla 26 ☎ 06 321 2362, ⓦ ragnodoro.org; map pp.188–189. As likely to be full of locals as tourists, this bustling place is a family-run restaurant that despite the picture menu has decent Roman cooking and good (if brusque) service – plus it's also just a 5min walk from the Vatican. Moderate prices too. Daily 12.30–2.30pm & 7.30–11.30pm.

Romeo Chef & Baker Villa Silla 26 ☎ 06 3211 0120, ⓦ romeo.roma.it; map pp.188–189. Very much an example of the recent trend for eating venues that do a bit of everything, *Romeo Chef & Baker* is a collaboration between some of the great and good of the Rome food scene. It is not only a wine bar, baker's and grocer's, but a restaurant too, so you have no excuse not to try it, either for a quick glass of wine and a plate of cheese or salami, or (at lunch or dinner) a full meal, enjoyed in its relentlessly futuristic interior. Not especially cheap – *primi* €11–18, *secondi* €13–20 – but the food is pretty good, and you can have as much or as little as you like. Daily 9am–midnight.

Settembrini Via Luigi Settembrini 27 ☎ 06 323 2617, ⓦ viasettembrini.it; map pp.188–189. A bit out of the way, about fifteen minutes' walk from the Vatican, but the food at this restaurant-café-bookshop is consistently good, whether you tuck into one of their wonderful seafood pasta dishes, a risotto, or just make do with a spectacular plate of cheeses and salami. *Primi* go for €14–16, *secondi* €16–22 – and it's good simple food, from a short regularly changing menu, served in a light contemporary space. Daily 7am–1am, Sun from 8am.

MA CHE SIETE VENUTI A FÀ, TRASTEVERE

Drinking

Drinking is not something Romans do a lot of, at least almost never to drunken excess. Despite that, you'll find plenty of bars in Rome – although, as with the rest of Italy, many are functional daytime haunts and not at all the kinds of places you'd want to spend an evening (see Chapter 15). However, partly due to the considerable presence of Brits and Americans in Rome, partly to a growing craft beer trend, there are plenty of bars and pubs conducive to an evening's drinking, from spit-and-sawdust wine bars to sleek cocktail lounges to laidback pubs. There are also loads of good wine bars, most of which serve food, so it's worth scanning these listings for places to eat, too. Our listings are divided into neighbourhoods: Campo de' Fiori and the Centro Storico, Monti, Trastevere and Testaccio are the densest and most happening areas.

ESSENTIALS

Aperitivi One phenomenon worth noting: a lot of bars lay out an early-evening buffet to tempt drinkers in for a pre-dinner *aperitivo*, with a choice of food free with the price of a drink, or for a set price, and it's become a popular way to kick off an evening. We've noted where places offer free buffets in the reviews, and there's a list of our favourites on p.266.

Bars There can be considerable crossover between Rome's bars, restaurants and clubs: for the most part, the places listed in this chapter are drinking spots, but you can eat, sometimes quite substantially, at many of them. Several could also be classed just as easily as clubs, with loud music and occasionally even an entrance charge; places that are more restaurant than bar are listed in chapter 15; places that are more club than bar are listed in chapter 17.

Opening hours Many bars are slick and expensive excuses for people to sit and pose, but most have the advantage of late hours, sometimes until 3 or 4am in summer, and almost always until 1am – though note that many places are closed at least during part of Aug.

WHAT TO DRINK

Beer *Birra* was once always a lager-type brew, but the trend in craft beer production in Italy means you'll have more to chose from these days than just the industrial Moretti, Peroni and Nastro Azzuro, all of which usually come in one-third or two-third litre bottles, or on draught (*alla spina*). A small beer is a *piccola* (20cl or 25cl), a larger one (usually 40cl) a *media* (pronounced "maydia"). If you want lager, ask for *birra chiara*. You may also come across darker beers (*birra scura* or *birra ambrata*). Prices start at €4–5 for a *media*, but anywhere remotely fancy won't charge less than €6–7.

Spirits All the usual spirits are on sale and known mostly by their generic names. There are also Italian brands of the main varieties: the best Italian brandies are Stock and Vecchia Romagna. A generous shot of these costs about €3, imported stuff much more. The home-grown Italian firewater is *grappa*, available just about everywhere. It's made from the leftovers from the winemaking process (skins, stalks and the like) and is something of an acquired taste; should you acquire it, it's probably the cheapest way of getting plastered. You'll also find fortified wines such as Campari; ask for a Campari-soda and you'll get a ready-mixed version from a bottle; a slice of lemon is a *spicchio di limone*; ice is *ghiaccio*. You might also try Cynar – believe it or not, an artichoke-based sherry often drunk as an aperitif.

Liqueurs There's also a daunting selection of liqueurs. Amaro is a bitter after-dinner drink: it has a base of pure alcohol in which different herbs are steeped, according to various family traditions. It's highly regarded as a digestive aid to cap a substantial meal. Amaretto is much sweeter with a strong taste of almond; Sambuca is a sticky-sweet aniseed concoction; while Strega – yellow, herb-and-saffron-based stuff in tall, elongated bottles – is about as sweet as it looks but not unpleasant.

CENTRO STORICO

Abbey Theatre Via del Governo Vecchio 51 ☎ 06 686 1341, ⓦ www.abbey-rome.com; map p.38. The most central and perhaps most convivial Irish pub in the city, with a good mix of Italians and ex-pats, regular sport on TV and live music, as well as basic pub food. Daily noon–2am.

Bar del Fico Piazza del Fico 26 ☎ 06 889 2321; map p.38. Reopened after a major refit – and with a vast restaurant at the back – this is once again one of the nicest places for an outside drink in the Centro Storico, on its own peaceful square but right at the heart of Rome's urban buzz. Mon–Sat 9am–2am, Sun noon–2am.

★ **Caffe della Pace** Via della Pace 3/7 ☎ 06 686 1216, ⓦ caffedellapace.it; map p.38. Just off Piazza Navona, this is *the* summer bar, with outside tables full of Rome's self-consciously beautiful people. It's at its quietest during the day, when you can enjoy the nineteenth-century interior – marble, mirrors, mahogany and plants – in peace. Daily 10am–2am.

Cul de Sac Piazza Pasquino 73 ☎ 06 6880 1094, ⓦ enstocaculdesac.com; map p.38. Busy, long-running wine bar with an excellent wine list, a great city-centre location with outside seating and decent wine-bar food – cold meats, cheeses, salads and soups. One of the best Centro Storico locations for a snack. Daily noon–4pm & 7pm–12.30am.

Enoteca Achilli Via dei Prefetti 15 ☎ 06 6877 3446; map p.38. A magnet for politicians and the well-heeled, this wine shop and bar has an expensive menu, but at the table the bottles are priced the same as in the shop. They specialize in champagne, great if you're in a celebratory mood, but there is also a decent selection of regular wines. Mon–Sat 9.30am–11.30pm.

Etabli Vicolo delle Vacche 9a ☎ 06 9761 6694, ⓦ etabli .it; map p.38. Lounge-style bar and restaurant in the heart of the Centro Storico's drinking triangle. Comfy sofas, free wi-fi, and a pleasant, not-too-cool vibe. Daily 12.30–3pm & 6pm–2am.

Il Piccolo Via del Governo Vecchio 74/75 ☎ 06 6880 1746; map p.38. As its name suggests, the place is tiny, but the wine selection isn't bad. A friendly happy hour and a few outdoor tables make this a nice, cosy, casual choice near Piazza Navona. Mon–Sat 10.30am–2am, Sun 4pm–2am.

16

TEN WONDERFUL WINE BARS

One of Rome's more traditional types of drinking establishment is the **wine bar**, known as an *enoteca* or *vineria*. The old ones have gained new cachet in recent years, and newer ones, with wine lists the size of unabridged dictionaries, are weighing in too, often with gourmet menus to go with the superb wines they offer: we have reviewed these that feature great food as well as concentrating on the fruit of the vine in Chapter 15 (either under "Cafés" or "Restaurants"). There's also been a recent proliferation of wine-tastings (*degustazioni*), which offer a chance to sample some interesting vintages, often at no cost. Here are our ten favourite places.

Antica Enoteca See p.266
Cavour 313 See p.268
Cul de Sac See p.264
Il Goccetto See below
Il Piccolo See p.264

L'Angolo Divino See p.266
Monti DOC See p.256
Passaguai See p.262
Trimani See p.269
Vinaietto See p.266

Jonathan's Angels Via della Fossa 16 ☎ 06 689 3426; map p.38. This quirky bar, just behind Piazza Navona, certainly wins the "most decorated" award. Every inch (even the toilet, which is worth a visit in its own right) is plastered, painted or tricked out in outlandish style by the former artist/proprietor. Daily 1pm–2am.

Le Coppelle Piazza delle Coppelle 52 ☎ 349 740 4620; map p.38. Snazzy bar decked out in glowing red decor that very much functions outdoors during the warm months, when there's a nice array of sofas and chairs on the usually heaving small piazza to hang out on. Daily 6pm–2am.

Les Affiches Via di Santa Maria dell'Anima 52 ☎ 06 686 8986; map p.38. Cool, slightly scruffy bar bang in the centre of the town that trades on boho chic rather than the vogueish posery more common in these parts. There's sometimes live music later on, and a laidback vibe early evening, with a rudimentary happy-hour buffet too. Does good filled baguettes at lunchtime, along with salads and cold cuts. Mon–Sat 10am–2am.

Livrerie Gourmet Via del Arco dei Banchi 3 ☎ 06 6476 0087; map p.38. A fig tree marks this bookstore/wine bar and café, which in late 2013 changed its focus

from a speciality in travel books to cookbooks. It serves platters of salami and cheeses, a good choice of wines and artisanal Italian beers; its bread comes from *Boulangerie MP* (see p.290), while Matteo's new lunch menu has brought in neighbourhood diners, from stylish office workers to local families with tots. Inexpensive, and a handy stop-off for both the Centro Storico and Prati and the Vatican. Mon & Tues 9am–8pm, Wed–Fri 9am–11pm, Sat & Sun closed.

Salotto 42 Piazza di Pietra 42 ☎ 06 678 5804, ⓦ www .salotto42.it; map p.38. This chic bar facing the ruins of Hadrian's temple does an excellent early-evening buffet and cocktails for around €10 a pop. Tues–Sat 10am–2am, Sun 11am–midnight.

Trinity College Via del Collegio Romano 6 ☎ 06 678 6472, ⓦ trinity-rome.com; map p.38. A warm and inviting establishment offering international beers and food, though its two levels can get quite loud and crowded. Food includes a bit of everything – pasta, burgers, salads, Tex-Mex – and is served until 1am, plus there's a brunch menu on Sat and Sun for €15. Daily noon–3am.

CAMPO DE' FIORI AND THE GHETTO

0.75 Via dei Cerchi 65 ☎ 06 687 5706, ⓦ www.075roma .com; see map pp.54–55. Right by the Circo Massimo, around the corner from the church Santa Maria in Cosmedin, this isn't really in the Ghetto, but it's a convivial bar that does food and has a reasonable *aperitivo* hour buffet every evening, as well as several screens showing live sport. With two largeish rooms and plenty of room to spill out onto the pavement outside, it's a handy place for a drink and a quick bite in a neighbourhood that had few options. Daily 11.30am–2am.

Bartaruga Piazza Mattei 9 ☎ 06 689 2299, ⓦ bartaruga.com; map pp.54–55. This very theatrical bar attracts members of the city's entertainment demi-monde, and even provides costumes for clients who feel like a change of persona. The setting is wonderfully camp, eclectically furnished with all sorts of eighteenth-century

bits and pieces: nothing really matches and the feel is sumptuously comfortable. Tues–Sun 6pm–2am.

Camponeschi Piazza Farnese 52 ☎ 06 687 4927, ⓦ www.ristorantecamponeschi.it; map pp.54–55. Actually this is a posh and, in our view, somewhat overpriced restaurant that doesn't always hit the mark, but its wine bar not only has a great selection of wines but also decently priced pasta dishes and seating on the square. Winemakers sometimes hold tastings here. Mon–Sat 8pm–2am.

★ **Il Goccetto** Via dei Banchi Vecchi 14 ☎ 06 686 4268, ⓦ ilgoccetto.com; map pp.54–55. A short walk from Campo de' Fiori, this is one of the city centre's nicest wine bars, with lots of options by the glass and good plates of cheese and salami to go with it. Mon–Sat 12.30–3pm & 6.30pm–midnight.

16

L'Angolo Divino Via dei Balestrari 12 ☎ 06 686 4413; map pp.54–55. Quite a peaceful haven after the furore of Campo de' Fiori, this wine bar has a large selection of wine, and simple, typical wine-bar fare – bread, cheese, cold cuts and the like, as well as a selection of hot meals. Daily 11am–3pm & 5.30pm–1am; closed Sun & Mon May–Aug.

La Vineria Campo de' Fiori 15 ☎ 06 6880 3268; map pp.54–55. This long-established bar/wine shop right on the Campo, patronized by devoted regulars, has more recently started making concessions to comfort, and offering light meals. Much cheaper if you sit or stand inside. Mon–Sat 9am–2am.

★ **Open Baladin** Via degli Specchi ☎ 06 683 8989; map pp.54–55. Central Rome's ultimate *birreria*, founded by the Baladin brewing company in 2009, and with a stark, modern interior and literally hundreds of mainly artisanal Italian beers to choose from, forty of them on tap. You can eat too – salads, sandwiches, and finger food, most of it pretty good (the burgers are decent enough, although the Caesar salads could so with some more zing instead of an overdose of creamy dressing) – but beer is the main thing here. Daily noon–2am.

> ## FIVE APERITIVO SPOTS
> **Baccano** See below
> **Freni e Frizoni** See p.270
> **Panella** See p.291
> **Sesto** See p.254
> **Rgb46** See p.269

Scholars' Lounge Via del Plebiscito 101b ☎ 06 6920 2208, ⓦ scholarsloungerome.com; map pp.54–55. One of the better city-centre Irish pubs, with regular live music and giant screens showing premier league football and other sports. Monday's quiz night can be fun, as can the karaoke nights on Sun and Tues. Daily 11am–3am.

Vinaietto Via del Monte della Farina 38 ☎ 06 6880 6989; map pp.54–55. This hole-in-the-wall *enoteca* has just a handful of tables, so most of its regulars drink their wine outside on the cobbles. Though it's mainly a wine shop, the enthusiastic owners offer a range of wines to drink by the glass – and it's far less expensive than nearby Campo de' Fiori. Mon–Sat 10.30am–3pm & 6.30–10pm.

THE TRIDENTE AND TREVI

★ **Antica Enoteca** Via della Croce 76b ☎ 06 679 0896, ⓦ anticaenoteca.com; map p.93. Lots of wines by the glass in this friendly wine bar that is in fact one of Rome's oldest, with a lively, casual feel despite the high rent district. It's always open, even on major Italian holidays, and serves a selection of hot and cold dishes, including great platters of cheese and cold cuts, soups and salads and attractive desserts. Intriguing trompe-l'oeil decorations inside, majolica-topped tables outside. Daily 11am–1am.

Baccano Via della Muratte 23 ☎ 06 6994 1166, ⓦ baccanoroma.com; map p.93. They spent a fortune to turn this Trevi bar and restaurant into an Italian version of New York's trendy *Balthazar* and the jury's out on whether it worked or not. The food and service are variable, but it's undeniably a haven in what is a bit of a desert for good places to eat and drink. Do what we do and treat it is as an early evening drink-and-snack stop-off rather than a full dining experience. Daily 10am–2am.

Canova Piazza del Popolo 16 ☎ 06 361 2231, ⓦ canovapiazzadelpopolo.it; map p.93. Once the haunt of the monied classes, *Canova* is not really the place it was. Still, it does all sorts of cocktails and reasonable food, and is a fine place to sit and take the air and watch the world go by on Piazza del Popolo. Politically, *Canova*'s clientele was traditionally a right-wing one, while dyed-in-the-wool lefties patronized *Rosati* across the square (see below). Daily 8am–midnight.

Do Bar Via delle Carrozze 61 ☎ 06 6979 7096; map p.93. A café for breakfast, coffee or a quick snack by day, but the narrow modern interior and its adjacent patio make a fine place for a drink before or after dinner. Daily 8am–midnight.

'Gusto Wine Bar Via della Frezza 23 ☎ 06 322 6273, ⓦ gusto.it; map p.93. This stylish modern bar is part of the *'Gusto* foodie empire that occupies this corner (see also p.252) and serves drinks, sandwiches and Catalan one-bite tapas to Rome's chattering classes. Entrance to the bar is around the corner from the main entrance. Daily 10am–2am.

La Vi Via Tomacelli 23 ☎ 06 4542 7760, ⓦ www.la-vi.it; map p.93. Short for 'Latteria Vineria', this trendy self-consciously minimalist bar-restaurant lures in young Romans with its excellent rooftop terrace. Service and food can be a bit uneven but it's unquestionably a nice place for a drink. Always open too. Daily 7am–2am.

Lowenhaus Via della Fontanella 16b ☎ 06 323 0410; map p.93. Just off Piazza del Popolo, this Bavarian-style drinking establishment serves beer and snacks – and full meals too. A handy place to get a beer in this location. Daily noon–2am.

Rosati Piazza del Popolo 5 ☎ 06 322 5859, ⓦ rosatibar .it; map p.93. This was the bar that hosted left-wingers, bohemians and writers in years gone by, though now it's cocktails and food that draw the crowds to its outside terrace. Daily 8am–midnight.

16

THE QUIRINALE, VENETO, VILLA BORGHESE AND NORTH

Annibale Vini & Spiriti Piazza dei Carracci 4 ☎06 322 3835; map pp.170–171. Right around the corner from the MAXXI, and not far from the Auditorium, this wine bar looks set to benefit from the resurgence of the area, and deservedly so. Its cool white interior is a nice place to sip a glass of wine, and there's an outdoor terrace in summer. Food too, and regular live music and DJs. Mon–Sat noon–2am.

ReRe Bar Via Flaminia Vecchia 475 ☎06 334 0483, ⓦrere.it; map pp.170–171. Just off Piazzale Ponte Milvio, this bar is all dressed up in a kitschy bordello style that draws folk from far and wide. It also serves food and has resident DJs. Daily 6pm–2am.

THE ESQUILINE, MONTI AND TERMINI

★ **Ai Tre Scalini** Via Panisperna 251 ☎06 4890 7495, ⓦaitrescalini.org; map pp.114–115. Great, easy-to-miss little Monti bar, cosy and comfortable with a good wine list, beer on tap and decent food – cheese and salami plates plus *porchetta, lasagne, parmigiana melanzane* and other simple staples. Gets very crowded later on. Mon–Fri noon–3pm & 6pm–midnight, Sat & Sun 6pm–midnight.

Al Vino al Vino Via dei Serpenti 19 ☎06 485 803; map pp.114–115. The Monti district's most happening street offers this seriously good wine bar with a choice of over five hundred labels, many by the glass. Snacks are generally Sicilian specialities. Daily 11.30am–2.30pm & 5.30pm–12.30am.

Bar à Book Via dei Piceni 23 ☎06 9604 3014; map pp.114–115. A welcome addition to studenty San Lorenzo, this friendly bookshop and wine bar makes a very laidback place for a drink. They also organize events, from poetry readings to DJ sets. Tues–Sun 7pm–2am.

★ **Cavour 313** Via Cavour 313 ☎06 678 5496, ⓦcavour313; map pp.114–115. One of the oldest wine

---

16 TEN GREAT HOTEL BARS

Many of Rome's best bars are in **hotels**, and not just the most expensive ones either: some have fantastic or historic spaces, courtyards or gardens, an unusual and alluring clientele or just great views over the city. Here are some of our favourites:

Aleph Via di San Basilio 15 ☎06 422 901; map p.105. The *Aleph*'s cosy *Angelo* bar is the perfect place to sink a cocktail or aperitif, before proceeding upstairs to its *Sin* restaurant.

De la Minerve Piazza della Minerva 69 ☎06 695 201; map p.38. Right behind the Pantheon, the outdoor roof garden bar here gives about the best view you can get over the rooftops and domes of the old centre – an ideal spot to wind up after you've been trudging around at street level all day.

De Russie Via del Babuino 9 ☎06 328 881; map p.93. A haven for chic drinkers, plus the odd celebrity, the *De Russie*'s *Stravinskij* bar always has a buzz about it. It's a minimalist neutral space, with a generous selection of champagnes and wines by the glass, as well as cocktails, and opens out to the lovely courtyard and tiered "secret" garden.

D'Inghilterra Via Bocca di Leone 14 ☎06 699 811; map p.93. The folk at Gambero Rosso (see box, p.258) reckon this to be one of the best bars in Italy, and its clubby interior a perfect place to enjoy an excellent cocktail.

Eden Via Ludovisi 49 ☎06 478 121; map p.105. Expansive views of Rome across the Spanish Steps, the umbrella pines of Villa Borghese and more rooftops and domes than you could count, made this terrace perch a favourite spot for film director Federico Fellini.

Forum Via Tor de' Conti 25–30 ☎06 679 2446; map pp.114–115. The American bar at this Monti four-star commands magical views over the Forum and Colosseum – great for a drink just as the sun is setting.

Hotel First Via del Vantaggio 14 ☎06 9799 6907; map p.93. For a chic upscale drinking experience that has Ruinart champagne as a partner, *Misceliamo* is a lovely find near Piazza del Popolo, where even the snacks are overseen by a prize-winning chef.

★ **Locarno** Via della Penna 22 ☎06 361 0841; map p.93. The slightly decadent atmosphere graced with hip, modern cocktail-sippers and a clubby back room with cosy fireplace make the *Locarno* Rome's most egalitarian hotel bar. It's frequented by literati, artists, princes, paupers, poseurs, fashionistas and just ordinary folk, and the warm weather adds a roof terrace to the mix.

Radisson Blu Es Via Turati 171 ☎06 444 841; map pp.114–115. Rome's sleek *Radisson Blu Es* hotel also sports one of the city's most elegant cocktail bars in *Zest*. Poolside drinks give top-floor views over Termini's train tracks below.

St George Via Giulia 62 ☎06 686 611; map pp.54–55. The open-air rooftop bar here is only open during the summer (Tues–Sat), but its views are great, over the river and the domes and towers of the Centro Storico – you can eat dinner up here too.

bars in Rome, which opened in 1979, *Cavour 313* serves hundreds of labels, mainly Italian, in a wood-clad interior. The food menu includes daily specials with a Middle Eastern flair, as well as the standard cheese, cured meat, salad and carpaccio one expects in a Roman wine bar. Daily 12.30–3pm & 7.30pm–12.30am; closed Sun in summer.

Club Machiavelli Via Machiavelli 49 ☎ 06 700 1757, ⊚ clubmachiavelli.it; map pp.114–115. Located in a historic palace, which accounts for the beautiful vaulted ceilings, off up-and-coming Piazza Vittorio, this place serves wines and cocktails, plus home-made desserts and other treats. There are piano-bar-style evenings too, with occasional live jazz combos and other cultural events. Thurs–Sat 8pm–1am.

Druid's Den Via San Martino ai Monti 28 ☎ 06 4890 4781, ⊚ druidsdenrome.com; map pp.114–115. Appealing Irish pub near Santa Maria Maggiore with a genuine Celtic feel (and owners). It has a mixed expat/Italian clientele, and is not just for the homesick. Cheap and lively, with occasional impromptu Celtic music. Their sister pub, *Druid's Rock*, is located nearby at Piazza Esquilino 1 (open daily noon–2am). Daily 5pm–2am.

Fiddler's Elbow Via dell'Olmata 43 ☎ 06 487 2110, ⊚ thefiddlerselbow.com; map pp.114–115. One of the

two original Irish bars in Rome, one block closer to Santa Maria Maggiore than its rival, the *Druid's Den*. It's a bit roomier, with a decidedly more Latin feel. Mon–Fri 5pm–2am, Sat–Sun 3pm–2am.

Finnegan Via Leonina 66 ☎ 06 474 7026, ⊚ finneganpub.com; map pp.114–115. Another of the area's crop of Irish pubs, with live football on TV, pool and a friendly ex-pat crowd. There's seating outside, too, on this bustling Monti street. Mon–Fri 5pm–2am, Sat–Sun 3pm–2am.

Ice Club Via della Madonna dei Monti 18/19 ⊚ iceclubroma.it; map pp.114–115. This bar constructed of ice, where in summer patrons are given coats to wear inside the freezing atmosphere, has amazingly been open for several years now. Maybe it's the heat of a Roman summer that drives people here? Whatever, you can be sure that your drink will be well-chilled. Daily 6pm–2am.

★ **Trimani** Via Cernaia 37b ☎ 06 446 9630, ⊚ trimani.com; map pp.114–115. This classy wine bar (with Rome's biggest selection of regional Italian vintages) is nice for either a lunchtime or evening tipple and an indulgent snack. You'll spend around €15 to sample a range of good-quality cheeses and cured pork meat, or a soup and salad, including a glass of wine. It also has a wine shop around the corner (see p.292). Mon–Sat 11.30am–3pm & 5.30pm–midnight.

16

THE CELIAN HILL AND SAN GIOVANNI

Pentagrappolo Via Celimontana 21b ☎ 06 709 6301, ⊚ ilpentagrappolo.com; map pp.130–131. Celio wine bar with lots of good wines by the glass, cheese plates and the usual cold cuts, and live piano music several nights a week. Tues–Fri noon–3pm & 6pm–1am, Sat & Sun 6pm–1am.

Tree Folks Via Capo d'Africa 29; map pp.130–131. Lots of Belgian and German brews, as well as food – plates of cold cuts, burgers and chips, salads – and their other speciality is whisky, with a selection of single malts that must be one of the city's best. Daily 6pm–2am.

THE AVENTINE HILL AND SOUTH

Ketumbar Via Galvani 24 ☎ 06 5730 5338, ⊚ ketumbar.it; map pp.140–141. Convenient for all the district's clubs, this ultra-hip Testaccio venue plays laidback world music, and has very attitude-free service, despite its chic clientele. Daily 8–11.30pm; bar open till 2am; closed Aug.

Oasi della Birra Piazza Testaccio 41 ☎ 06 574 6122; map pp.140–141. Unassumingly situated beneath an *enoteca* on Piazza Testaccio, the cosy basement rooms here house an international selection of beers that rivals anywhere in the world – five hundred in all, and plenty of wine to choose from as well. On the menu are generous

plates of cheese and salami and a great selection of *bruschetta* and polenta dishes. It's not particularly Roman, but it's a very alluring place to get inebriated and eat good food nonetheless. Mon–Sat 8am–2.30pm & 4.30pm–1am, Sun 7.30pm–1am.

Rgb46 Via Santa Maria Liberatrice 46 ☎ 06 4542 1608, ⊚ rgb46.it; map pp.140–141. On the main square in Testaccio this café and bookstore specializing in art and design has *aperitivo* Thurs, Fri, and Sat nights and hosts frequent art shows. Mon 4pm–1am, Tues–Sat 10am–1pm & 4pm–1am.

PIGNETO

Il Tiaso Via Ascoli Piceno 20 ☎ 333 284 5283, ⊚ iltiaso.com; map pp.140–141. This relaxed wine bar with free wi-fi has book-lined shelves and lots of wines to try by the glass, accompanied by cheese and salami platters, as well as some more substantial meals. There are often live acoustic sets, too – a great place to kick off an evening out. Daily 6pm–2am.

Necci dal 1924 Via Fanfulla da Lodi 68 ☎ 06 9760 1552,

⊚ necci1924.com; map pp.140–141. Pasolini shot some of his films in the Pigneto district, and this bar-restaurant was one of his favourite places, though it's been considerably upgraded since then. Five minutes' walk from the busy stretch of Via del Pigneto, it has a lovely shady garden where you can have a drink, sandwich or a full meal from its short menu, chalked afresh on the blackboard each day, cooked for you by London-born chef Ben Hirst. Daily 8am–1am.

TRASTEVERE

Artù Largo F. Biondi 5 ☎06 588 0398; map pp.160–161. Bar and pub on one of the district's busiest corners, with a terrace that is great for watching the world go by, plus there's a full, early evening menu if you're peckish. Tues–Sun 6pm–2am.

Enoteca Ferrara Via del Moro 1a ☎06 5833 3920, ⓦenotecaferrara.it; map pp.160–161. Just off Piazza Trilussa, this wine bar has a more restrained atmosphere than the baccanalia at some of the nearby alternatives, and has a good selection of wines by the glass. There's a pricey restaurant next door that's not at all bad, but in recent years a more casual section has opened with lower-priced traditional fare, too. Daily 7.30pm–1am.

Freni and Frezioni Via del Politeama 4/6 ☎06 4549 7499, ⓦfrenifrizioni.com; map pp.160–161. Just off Piazza Trilussa, this former auto workshop – the name means "brakes and clutches" – is now home to a bustling bar with good cocktails. There's a long table piled high with buffet fare between 7 and 10pm, after which everyone gathers on the terrace by the river and DJs take over. Daily 7pm–2am.

Ma Che Siete Venuti A Fà Via Benedetta 25 ☎06 645 2046, ⓦwww.football-pub.com; map pp.160–161. There's an amazing choice of artisanal beers from all over the world in this tiny Trastevere bar. Some of them can't be found anywhere else in the city, or even Italy, and this is a busy place to work your way through them. Daily 3pm–2am.

★ **Ombre Rosse** Piazza di Sant'Egidio 12/13 ☎06 588 4155, ⓦombrerossecaffe.it; map pp.160–161. Pubby yet very Italian café with a shady outside terrace and clubby interior that hosts live jazz and blues. Something of a Trastevere institution, and serving decent wine-bar-style snacks and light meals. Perhaps the neighbourhood's nicest bar. Daily 8am–2am.

San Calisto Piazza San Calisto 3 ☎06 583 5869; map pp.160–161. An old-guard Trastevere bar which attracts a huge crowd of just about everybody on late summer nights; the booze is cheap, and you can sit at outside tables too. Things are slightly less demi-monde-ish during the day, when it's simply a great spot to sip a cappuccino, read and enjoy the sun. Mon–Sat 6am–2am.

16 THE VATICAN AND PRATI

Fonclea Via Crescenzio 82a ☎06 689 6302, ⓦwww.fonclea.it; map pp.188–189. This historic basement joint is loaded with devoted regulars and those who have happily discovered that there is life in the Vatican's sometimes somnolent Borgo and Prati areas. Often high-quality live music adds to the fun (see p.272). Daily 7pm–2am; Happy Hour till 8.30pm.

Four Green Fields Via C. Morin 38–42 ☎06 372 5091, ⓦfourgreenfields.it; map pp.188–189. This large Irish pub, decked out in wood and terracotta, stretches over two floors. Draught Guinness and Kilkenny complement the scene, along with decent pub grub and sport on TV. Mon–Fri noon–2am, Sat 6pm–2am, Sun 6pm–1.30am.

Nuvolari Via degli Ombrellari 10 ☎06 6880 3018; map pp.188–189. A welcoming Borgo bar that serves a full menu next door but also has a free buffet 6.30–8.30pm every night during the week. A good choice of wines, and a pleasant local vibe – not at all what you expect in this part of town. Mon–Sat 6.30pm–2am.

Saxophone Via Germanico 26 ☎06 3972 3039, ⓦsaxophonelivepub.it; map pp.188–189. A welcoming pub in the shadow of the Vatican walls that does a good line in international beers and has Italian football on TV, plus occasional live music. Sun–Thurs 5.30pm–2am, Fri & Sat 5.30pm–3am, Mon 6pm–2am.

Senza Fondo Via Germanico 168 ☎06 321 1415; map pp.188–189. Convivial Prati basement pub with a good choice of beers and decent food. There's sometimes live music too. Sun–Thurs 8pm–2am, Fri & Sat 8pm–3am.

MICCA CLUB

Clubs and live music

As you would expect in a major European capital, there's plenty to do in Rome after dark. Entrance prices tend to be high, and the club scene retains some of the glamorous ethos satirized in Fellini's *La Dolce Vita*, with designer-dressing-up still the order of the day in some places, particular in the city centre, although the hippest venues are increasingly found in grungier neighbourhoods further out. If you're after live music, there are regular summer festivals (see box, p.273), with venues all over town, including free events in Circo Massimo and Piazza del Popolo, although the chances of catching big names are low, partly because promoters tend to favour other Italian cities. Capital city or not, Rome is still a little bit sleepy compared to northern hubs like Milan.

17

ESSENTIALS

Centri sociali To get around the licensing laws, some of Rome's night haunts are run as private clubs – usually known as *centri sociali* or *associazioni culturali*, a device that means you may be stung for a membership fee, particularly where there's music, but entry will be free – although as a one-off visitor some places will let you in without formalities, and others charge no fee at all to be a member. In recent decades these sorts of places have sprung up all over the city, particularly in the suburbs, and are becoming the focus of political activity and the more avant-garde elements of the music and arts scene.

Where to go In the centre the best areas tend to be Ostiense and Testaccio (especially in summer), Trastevere, and the Centro Storico from the Jewish Ghetto to the Pantheon. For what's-on information, check *Wanted in Rome* magazine and their website (Ⓦwantedinrome.com); the newspaper *Il Messaggero* lists major musical events, while *TrovaRoma* in Thurs edition of *La Repubblica* is another handy guide to current offerings.

LIVE MUSIC

Rome's **rock and pop** scene is a relatively limp affair, especially compared to the cities of the north, focusing mainly on foreign bands and the big venues like the Stadio Olimpico. Summer sees local bands giving occasional free concerts in the piazzas – for example on Piazzale del Verano – while the "Rock in Roma" festival takes place at the Ippodromo Capannelle (see below), but the city is much more in its element with jazz, with lots of venues and a healthy array of local talent.

BIG VENUES

For information about events at any of these three venues – really the city's only options for big, internationally renowned visiting bands and solo acts – call the Orbis agency (see p.277).

Atlantico Live Viale dell'Oceano Atlantico 271d ☎06 591 5727, Ⓦatlanticoroma.it; metro B EUR Fermi or bus #714 from Termini; map pp.140–141. A giant tent-like structure 400m from PalaLottomatica, this is one of two arenas where major acts tend to end up. The venue holds about 1500 people and hosts everything from sporting events to club nights, as well as June's "Roma Live" festival.

Ippodromo Capannelle Via Appia Nuova 1255 ☎06 716 771, Ⓦwww.capannelleippodromo.it. Horseracing circuit on the southern fringes of the city that hosts large-scale music events, including the annual "Rock in Roma" summer festival (Ⓦrockinroma.com).

PalaLottomatica Piazzale dello Sport ☎06 540 901, ☎02 488 571, Ⓦpalalottomatica.it; metro B EUR Palasport or bus #714 from Termini; map pp.140–141. This circular hall has upgraded acoustics, and hosts major Italian and foreign acts, sporting events and entertainment spectaculars.

Stadio Olimpico Piazzale del Foro Italico ☎06 36851, Ⓦwww.stadiodi.it/olimpico-roma; bus #32 or tram #2 from metro A Flaminio; map pp.170–171. When huge acts such as U2 and Madonna perform in Rome, they play in this massive, 82,000-spectator stadium in the northern part of the city between Monte Mario and the Tiber.

ROCK AND POP VENUES

Circolo degli Artisti Via Casilina Vecchia 42 ☎06 7030 5684, Ⓦilcircolodegliartisti.it; metro A San Giovanni, or bus #105 from Termini, or #810 from Piazza Venezia or tram #5 or #14 from Termini; map pp.114–115. This very large venue with several bars, dancefloors and exhibition spaces is located beyond Porta Maggiore. A good range of bands, with frequent discos and theme nights – hip-hop, electronica, house, ska and revival. On Fri it hosts "Omogenic" – gay night. In summer its pool is open to the public. Tues–Thurs & Sun 9pm–2am, Fri & Sat 9pm–3am.

★ **Fonclea** Via Crescenzio 82a ☎06 689 6302, Ⓦfonclea.it; metro A Ottaviano or bus #81 from Piazza Venezia, #492 from Largo Argentina or #590 from Termini; map pp.188–189. Busy and happening basement bar in the Vatican area that hosts regular live music – usually jazz, soul and funk – from about 9.30pm. Free except Fri & Sat €7. Happy hour 7–8pm. Daily 7pm–2am.

Forte Prenestino Via F. Delpino 100 ☎06 2180 7855, Ⓦforteprenestino.net; tram #5 from Termini or bus #542 or #544 from metro B Monti Tiburtini; map pp.114–115. Just south of Via Prenestina, this early-twentieth-century fortress, and giant squat since 1986, is home to one of Rome's most active *centri sociali*, with regular live music, film screenings and other events held both inside and out in the castle courtyards. It also boasts a bookshop, various studios and a very inexpensive restaurant (Mon–Fri). Its May Day "non-lavoro" events, held to celebrate the anniversary of the occupation of the building, are popular. Opening hours vary according to the event. Live acts €15–18, otherwise €5.

Planet Roma Via del Commercio 36 ☎06 574 7826, Ⓦwww.planetroma.com; metro B Piramide or bus #30 or #60 from Piazza Venezia, bus #75 from Termini, #95 from metro A Barberini, or #280 from metro A Lepanto; map pp.140–141. Housed in an ex-factory off Via Ostiense, a little way beyond Testaccio, the old Alpheus clubs has space for three simultaneous events – usually a disco, concert and exhibition or piece of theatre. Sat is "Gorgeous" – gay night. Daily 10pm–4am.

Sotto Casa di Andrea Via dei Volsci 126 ☎347 814 6544, Ⓦsottocasa.org; bus #71 from Via del Tritone,

LIVE MUSIC FESTIVALS

Rome hosts a variety of **music festivals**, especially during the summer. There's the annual 'Rock in Roma' festival (🌐 rockinroma.com), basically a series of gigs throughout the summer staged at the Ippodromo Capannelle on the southern edge of the city (see above). There are regular jazz concerts in the **Villa Celimontana** park, with evening performances between early July and the end of August (📞 06 3972 8167, 🌐 villacelimontanajazz.com) – it's a great venue, with some big names, and tickets cost €5–30. Later in the year, the **Rome Jazz Festival** (🌐 romajazz.it) is held at the end of October/early November at the Auditorium. The other main cultural focus of the summer is the **Estate Romana** (📞 06 0608, 🌐 www .estateromana.comune.roma.it), a series of mainly outdoor events that last all summer, including theatrical and musical performances, film projections, art exhibits and events for children staged in venues throughout the city, such as the cloister of San Pietro in Vincoli, the MACRO and the Isola Tiberina.

#492 from Largo Argentina or tram #3 from the Colosseum; map pp.114–115. Multi-room multi-venue in the San Lorenzo district, featuring live rock, reggae and jazz, plus performance art, theatre and cabaret in the main hall. Elsewhere you can dine and chat. Tues–Sun 9pm–3am.

The Place Via Alberico II 27–29 📞 06 6830 7137, 🌐 theplace.it; metro A Ottaviano or bus #40 from Termini, #62 from Largo Argentina, or #87 from Piazza Venezia; map pp.188–189. Singer-songwriters, jazz, Latin and r'n'b and – later – DJs at this Prati live music club. The restaurant serves up interesting fusion cuisine, and admission is free with a drink. Wed–Sun & some Mon & Tues 8pm–2am.

Villaggio Globale Lungotevere Testaccio 1 📞 347 413 1205, 🌐 vglobale.biz; metro B Piramide or bus #95 from metro A Barberini, #170 from Termini; map pp.140–141. Situated in the old slaughterhouse along the river, the "global village" has something on almost every night, whether it's world music, indie rock or avant-garde performance art, in its Spazio Boario. Opening hours depend on events.

JAZZ, LATIN AND BLUES VENUES

Alexanderplatz Via Ostia 9 📞 06 3972 1867 or 📞 06 3974 2171, 🌐 alexanderplatz.it; Metro A Ottaviano or tram #19 from Viale Regina Margherita; map pp.188–189. Rome's top live jazz club/restaurant with reasonable membership (€15 a month) and free entry, except when there's star-billing. Reservations recommended. Doors open at 8pm, concerts at 9.45pm Sun–Thurs, 10.30pm Fri & Sat.

Beba Do Samba Via dei Messapi 8 📞 393 2857 50390, 🌐 bebadosamba.it; tram #3 from the Colosseum or #14 from Termini; map pp.114–115. Brazil Central in Rome, and each night they highlight a new group, with the focus on Latin sounds, while the chill-out room is replete with comfortable cushions and divans. Daily 9pm–2.30am.

⭐ **Big Mama** Vicolo San Francesco a Ripa 18 📞 06 581 2551, 🌐 bigmama.it; bus #75 or #170 from Termini, or

tram #8 from Largo Argentina; map pp.160–161. Trastevere jazz/blues club of long standing, hosting acts five nights a week. Membership €14, and free entry except for star attractions (when it's important to book ahead). Daily 9pm–1.30am; doors open at 9pm, concerts begin at 10.30pm.

Caruso Café de Oriente Via di Monte Testaccio 36 📞 06 574 5019, 🌐 www.carusocafe.com; metro B Piramide or bus #30 from Piazza Venezia, #75 or #170 from Termini, #95 from metro A Barberini, or #280 from metro A Lepanto; map pp.140–141. Three rooms – and a roof terrace in the warm months – host Latin music most of the week, with soul, r'n'b and occasional live cover groups. Tues–Sun 11.30pm–4.30am.

⭐ **Casa del Jazz** Viale di Porta Ardeatina 55 📞 06 704 731, 🌐 casajazz.it; metro B Piramide, or bus #714 from Termini; map pp.140–141. Sponsored by the city, and very much the project of Rome's former mayor, jazz-loving Walter Veltroni, this converted villa in leafy surroundings is the ultimate jazz-lovers' complex, with a book and CD shop and restaurant, recording studios and a 150-seat auditorium that hosts jazz names most nights of the week. Admission €10–15. Most acts start at either 7pm or 9pm, and there are Sun lunchtime concerts at noon; the restaurant is open every night until midnight. Closed Tues & Sun evening.

Escopazzo Via d'Aracoeli 41 📞 389 683 5618, 🌐 escopazzo.it; bus #40, #64 or #H from Termini, #280 from metro A Lepanto, #492 or #630 from metro A Barberini; map pp.54–55. Halfway between Piazza Venezia and Largo Argentina, this friendly bar attracts a crowd of thirty-somethings and offers food and wine along with live concerts or jam sessions most nights. Tues–Sun 10pm–5am.

Gregory's Via Gregoriana 54a 📞 06 679 6386, 🌐 gregorysjazz.com; metro A Spagna or bus #117 from Via Nazionale; map p.93. Just up the Spanish Steps and to the right, this elegant nightspot pulls in the crowds with its live jazz, improvised by Roman and international musicians. Tues–Sun 8pm–3am.

17

CLUBS

Rome's **clubs** run the gamut. There are vast glitter palaces with stunning lights and sound systems, predictable dance music and an over-dressed, over-made-up clientele – good if you can afford it and just want to dance (and observe a good proportion of Romans in their natural Sat-night element). But there are also places that are not much more than ritzy bars with music, and other, more down-to-earth venues to dance, playing a more interesting selection of music to a younger, more cautious-spending crowd (we've listed some of these in chapter 16 as well). There is also a small number of clubs catering specifically to gays and lesbians (see p.282). All clubs tend to open and close late, and **entrance fees** vary from €10 to €30, though they often include a drink and there is the occasional free admission for women. During the hot summer months, many clubs close down or move to outdoor locations like EUR's parks or the beaches of Ostia and Fregene.

CLUB VENUES

Akab Via di Monte Testaccio 69 ☎ 06 5725 0585, ⓦ akabclub.com; metro B Piramide or bus #30 or #60 from Piazza Venezia, #75 from Termini, #95 from metro A Barberini, or #280 from metro A Lepanto; map pp.140–141. One of the longest-running clubs on the Testaccio nightlife scene, *Akab* provides a big, impressive space for dancing and posing, to house and techno mainly but with the odd live act. Admission around €20. Tues–Sat 10pm–4am.

Art Café Via del Galoppatoio 33 ☎ 06 3600 6578, ⓦ art-cafe.it; metro A Spagna; map p.173. Housed in the underground car park at Villa Borghese, this is one of Rome's trendiest clubs. Expect to queue, and dress up – otherwise you might not get in. Tues–Sat 9pm–6am.

Black Out Via Casilina 713 ☎ 06 241 5047, ⓦ blackoutrockclub.com; metro A San Giovanni or Re di Roma or bus #85 from metro B Colosseo or #105 from Termini; map pp.130–131. Murky industrial San Giovanni club that plays punk, heavy metal and Goth music, with occasional gigs by US and UK bands. Thurs–Sat 11pm–4am; closed in summer.

Boeme Via Velletri 13 ☎ 06 841 2212, ⓦ boeme.it; bus #38 from Termini, or #63 from metro A Barberini; map p.105. The two halls here feature baroque splendour and modernistic monochrome. Music ranges from Latin to techno. Tues–Sun 11pm–4am.

Brancaleone Via Levanna 13 ☎ 06 8200 4382, ⓦ brancaleone.it; bus #60 from Piazza Venezia or #84 from Termini; map pp.170–171. Featuring minimalist spaces with the feel of a Berlin squat, this *centro sociale* off the Via Nomentana hosts live acts and DJ sets. Thurs nights see reggae, while Fri is given over to techno and Sat to drum'n'bass. Tues–Sat 11pm–5am.

Gilda Via Mario de' Fiori 97 ☎ 06 678 4838, ⓦ gildabar .it; metro A Spagna or bus #85 or #850 from metro B Colosseo, #95 or #116 from metro A Barberini, or #119 from Piazza Venezia; map p.93. Just a few blocks from the Spanish Steps, this slick, stylish and expensive club is the focus for the city's minor celebs and wannabes. You'll need to dress smart to get in. €20–30. Thurs–Sun 11pm–5am.

Goa Via Libetta 13 ☎ 06 574 8277, ⓦ goaclub.com; metro B Garbatella; map pp.140–141. This long-running Ostiense club near the Basilica di San Paolo was opened by famous local DJ Giancarlino and is still playing techno, house and jungle on its superb sound system. *Goa* has an ethnic feel – a shop sells handmade crafts; there's incense burning, and sofas to help you recover after high-energy dancing. It's where all the biggest DJs that come to Rome spin. Tues–Sat 11pm–4am.

Jackie O' Via Boncompagni 11 ☎ 06 4288 5457, ⓦ jackieoroma.com; bus #52, #53, #61 or #116 from metro A Barberini, #492 from Largo Argentina, #95 or #119 from Piazza Venezia, or #175 from Termini; map p.105. Amazingly, this 1960s Via Veneto jet-set glitter palace is still going strong, even attracting its share of celebs from time to time. It can actually be fun if you enjoy its rather retro notion of a night out, including a preponderance of mainstream Italian pop. Daily 8pm–4.30am; closed Mon in winter.

La Maison Vicolo dei Granari 3 ☎ 06 683 3312; Bus #40, #64 or #175 from Termini; map p.38. Ritzy club whose chandeliers and glossy decor attract Rome's gilded youth for some hardcore dancing to house, hip-hop and R&B. Nov–May Wed, Thurs & Sun 11pm–3am, Fri & Sat 11pm–5am.

Lanificio 159 Via di Pietralata 159 ☎ 06 372 5091, ⓦ lanificio.com; bus #60 from Piazza Venezia or #84 from Termini; map p.105. Set in the restored remains of an industrial textile complex, *Lanificio* is a big, garage-style cub hosting DJs, concerts and art installations. Admission €10. Thurs–Sun 10pm–4am.

★ Micca Club Via Pietro Micca 7a ☎ 06 8744 0079, ⓦ miccaclub.com; bus #105 from Termini, tram #5 or #14 from Termini, or #19 from metro A Ottaviano; map pp.114–115. This cavernous underground club, with brick walls and plenty of cosy booths, has a hugely varied programme, with popular themed nights – from swing and burlesque to funk. Admission €10, €15 after 10pm. Mon, Tues & Thurs–Sat 10pm–4am, Sun 6pm–2am; closed late May to mid-Sept.

Qube Via di Portonaccio 212 ☎ 06 438 5445, ⓦ qubedisco.com; metro B Tiburtina, or tram #5 or #14 from Termini, or #19 from metro A Ottaviano; map pp.130–131. Big Tiburtina club hosting a variety of different nights each week, including live music. Not the most original for music but its well-established Fri gay and drag night – Muccassassina ("Killer Cow"; W muccassassina .com) – draws a big crowd. Thurs 11pm–4am.

Rashomon Via degli Argonauti 16, W rashomonclub .com; metro B Garbatella; map pp.140–141. A live music, performance space and electronic music venue which walks the line between underground club and trendy point of reference for Roman indie musicians, artists and DJs. Fri nights draw the biggest crowds. Wed & Thurs 10pm–2am, Fri & Sat 11pm–4am.

Rising Love Via delle Conce 14 T 06 8952 0643, W risinglove.net; metro Piramide, or bus #30 or #60 from Piazza Venezia, #75 from Termini, #95 from metro A Barberini, or #280 from metro A Lepanto; map pp.140–141. Ostiense club specializing in indie, rock and particularly reggae DJs and live music. Thurs–Sun 10am–3am.

Sinister Noise Via dei Magazzini Generali 4b T 347 331 0648, W sinisternoise.com; metro B Piramide; map pp.140–141. This venue has a more intimate feel than the mega-clubs along this stretch, with a lively bar on the ground floor and a small dancefloor upstairs, where the music tends to be garage, alternative and experimental rock. Admission €5–10. Tues–Sun 7pm–4am.

Vicious Via Achille Grandi 7, W viciousclub.com; map pp.114–115. Low-rent Termini area club that's more about underground vibes than dressing up, playing everything from indie and grunge to house and electronica. They also host a monthly gay night, enticingly entitled 'Butter'. Thurs–Sun 10pm–4am.

Zoobar Via Bencivenga 1 T 339 27 27 995, W zoobar .roma.it; bus #84 or #90 from Termini, or #60 from metro B Colosseo; map pp.170–171. Out near Nomentana station, this club plays a wide range of different music – oldies, ska, funk, r'n'b and much more. Thurs–Sat 11pm–3.30am.

Culture and entertainment

Northern Italy is where creativity in music, dance and, of course, opera flourishes, and even locals would admit that Rome is a bit of a backwater for the performing arts. Relatively few international-class performers put in an appearance here. Nevertheless, the city does have a cultural life, and what the arts scene may lack in quantity or quality is made up for by the charm of the city's settings. Also, various foreign academies, especially Villa Medici, put on a stimulating array of cultural events, from retrospectives to cutting-edge openings. Rome's summer festival ensures a good range of classical music, opera, theatre and cinema throughout the warmer months, often in picturesque locations, and the summer opera performances at the Baths of Caracalla are resounding occasions – worth prolonging a stay for if you can.

ESSENTIALS

Information For current listings information see *Wanted in Rome* magazine, or their website (ⓦ wantedinrome.com) – or the "TrovaRoma" booklet in *La Repubblica*'s Thursday edition. It's worth looking out, too, for old-fashioned street posters and playbills posted on church doors or construction site walls.

What's on where During the winter, you'll find a regular programme of classical music mounted by the city's principal orchestra, the Accademia Nazionale di Santa Cecilia, and other sporadic musical offerings of mixed quality, sometimes in beautiful churches or palatial halls, and on occasions free. Opera is well established in Rome and now and again approaches world-class levels, though perhaps not often enough.

High-quality dance performances are a rarity in Rome, although international companies do show up from time to time, usually at the Teatro Olimpico, Teatro dell'Opera, Auditorium (see p.278) and the Teatro Argentina (see p.279). Unfortunately, cinema-lovers will find few films in the original language, as Italy clings as strongly as ever to its historic dubbing tradition, but we've listed a few places where you might be able to find films in their unadulterated forms.

Ticket agencies HelloTicket ☏ 800 907 080, ⓦ helloticket.it; La Feltrinelli, Largo Argentina 11 ☏ 06 6866 3001, Piazza Colonna 31/35 ☏ 06 697 5051 & Viale Giulio Cesare 88 (Prati) ☏ 06 377 2411; Orbis, Piazza Esquilino 37 (Santa Maria Maggiore) ☏ 06 474 4776.

CLASSICAL MUSIC AND OPERA

Under new directors, Rome's own **orchestras** are approaching international standards, and although the city attracts far fewer prestigious artists than you might expect of a capital, it is becoming more and more a magnet for contemporary works – a sea-change that has been inspired by the completion of Renzo Piano's **Auditorium/Parco della Musica** a few years ago (see p.180). Some critics have said that beauty has been sacrificed for acoustics here, but the three halls definitely deliver on sound quality, while the outdoor space can be used for anything from rock to opera, and even as a skating rink in the winter. Listings magazines (see p.27) and posters around town advertise little-known concerts – a wide range of choral, chamber and organ recitals – in churches like Sant'Agnese in Agone and Sant'Ignazio or other spectacular venues, including the private halls and courtyards of Renaissance or Baroque palaces. Otherwise, the many national academies and cultural institutes – Belgian, Austrian, Hungarian, British, American, French, German, et al. – frequently host concerts. In the summer, concerts are staged in cloisters, in the Teatro di Marcello, just off Piazza Venezia, and in the ancient Roman theatre at Ostia Antica and at Villa Adriana. It may be that you'll just stumble across a concert-in-progress while out on an evening stroll, passing by some ancient church with all its lights on: Rome is a city where such magical musical moments can still happen. The city's opera scene has long been overshadowed by that of Milan, Venice, Parma and Naples, grand opera's acknowledged birthplace, but it is improving. In summer, opera moves outdoors and ticket prices come down. Summer performances are held in the stunning setting of the ancient **Baths of Caracalla**, as well as at several churches and venues all around Rome, as part of the various summer music festivals which have multiplied in recent years.

CLASSICAL MUSIC AND OPERA VENUES

Accademia d'Opera Italiana All Saints' Church, Via del Babuino 153 ☏ 06 784 2702, ⓦ accademiadoperaitaliana.it; metro A Spagna or bus #117 from Via Nazionale or #119 from Piazza Venezia. Performances generally include popular standards such as *La Traviata*, *Tosca* and *The Barber of Seville*, as well as Mozart's *Requiem* and *Carmina Burana*. Tickets €30.

CULTURAL FESTIVALS

Festival delle Letterature ☏ 06 0608, ⓦ festivaldelleletterature.it; metro B Colosseo or bus #75 from Termini, #81 from Largo Argentina, or #87 from Piazza Venezia. A summertime international literature festival set in the spectacular ruins of the Basilica of Maxentius in the Roman Forum. Celebrated authors, mainly English-speaking, lecture or read their works, collaborating with actors and musicians.

Festival Internazionale del Film di Roma Via P. de Coubertin 30 and venues throughout the city ☏ 06 4040 1900, ⓦ romacinemafest.it; bus #53 from Piazza San Silvestro, #217, #910 or line "M"

from Termini station, or tram #2 from Piazzale Flaminio. This film festival is held over nine days in late October at the Auditorium and a variety of other venues around town. Tickets cost €3–23 and can be purchased from the Auditorium box office (see above) or from Lottomatica Italia Servizi (ⓦ listicket.it).

Roma Europa Festival ☏ 06 4555 3050, ⓦ romaeuropa.net. A cultural festival which has gathered pace in recent years, and is now a pretty big deal, with dance, drama and highbrow music events at the Auditorium, MAXXI and other venues around town from October until late November. Tickets cost €15–40.

18

Auditorium/Parco della Musica Via P. de Coubertin 30 ☎ 06 8024 1281, box office ☎ 892 982, ⓦ auditorium .com; bus #53 from Piazza San Silvestro, #217, #910 or line "M" from Termini station, or tram #2 from Piazzale Flaminio. This landmark musical complex is Rome's most prestigious venue. It is home to the city's premier orchestra, the Accademia Nazionale di Santa Cecilia, who are resident part of the year in its largest hall, while two smaller venues host smaller chamber, choral, recital and experimental works. The complex also hosts major rock and jazz names when they come to town, as well as Rome's international film festival in October. Daily 11am–8pm to visit; guided tours €9. Box office daily 11am–8pm.

Aula Magna dell'Università La Sapienza Piazzale Aldo Moro 5 ☎ 06 361 0051, ⓦ www.concertiiuc.it; metro B Policlinico or bus #61 from Piazza San Silvestro, #490 or #495 from Piazzale Flaminio, or tram #19 from Viale Regina Margherita. La Sapienza University's Istituzione Universitaria dei Concerti is deliberately experimental and eclectic, with musical offerings ranging from Bach to Miles Davis, and from Chopin to Kurt Weill. The season runs from October to June, and performances are usually held Tues evenings and Sat afternoons. Tickets €18.50–35.

Oratorio del Gonfalone Via del Gonfalone 32a ☎ 06 8530 1758, ⓦ oratoriogonfalone.com; bus #64 or #40 from Termini, or #116 from Piazza Barberini. This lovely frescoed theatre stages performances of chamber music, with an emphasis on the Baroque every Thurs at 9pm, with the season running from Nov to early June. Tickets cost €15; telephone reservations are strongly recommended. You can visit the Oratorio, or pick up tickets in advance, by appointment only (Mon–Fri 10am–4pm); the entrance is at Vicolo della Scimmia 1b.

Teatro dell'Opera di Roma Piazza Beniamino Gigli 7 ☎ 06 481 601, ⓦ operaroma.it; metro A Repubblica or bus #40, #64 or #70 from Corso Vittorio Emanuele, or #170 from Piazza Venezia. Nobody compares it to La Scala, but cheap tickets are a lot easier to come by at Rome's opera and ballet venue – they start at €24 for opera, less for ballet – and important artists do sometimes perform here. If you buy the very cheapest tickets, bring some high-powered binoculars, as you'll need them in order to see anything at all. Don't miss the summer opera season, set in the Baths of Caracalla. Box office Tues–Sat 9am–5pm, Sun 9am–1.30pm.

Teatro Ghione Via delle Fornaci 37 ☎ 06 637 2294, ⓦ teatroghione.it; bus #46, #64 or #916 from Corso Vittorio Emanuele. This traditional little theatre offers chamber music and recitals, often by well-known musical lights. Tickets €20–25. Box office daily 10am–1pm & 4–7pm.

Teatro Olimpico Piazza Gentile da Fabriano 17 ☎ 06 326 5991, ⓦ teatroolimpico.it; bus #53 from Piazza Barberini, #910 from Termini, tram #2 from metro A Flaminio. Classical standards, chamber music and ballet are performed here, by resident orchestra Accademia Filarmonica Romana (ⓦ filarmonicaromana.org), as well as other companies. The theatre also hosts the occasional contemporary work. Performances run from Sept to early May on Tues & Thurs–Sun. Tickets (€15–38.50) are relatively easy to come by.

THEATRE AND DANCE

There is a great deal of **theatre** in Rome, but it's virtually all in Italian, or even Roman dialect. Very occasional English-language musicals, usually put together by some travelling American company, come to town during the winter season. The venue for such rare events is almost always either the Teatro Olimpico or the Teatro Sistina, sometimes Teatro Argentina. Check the listings magazines (see p.27) for current programmes; incidentally, virtually all Roman theatres close on Mondays. As for **dance**, apart from the very occasional international company, it's generally home-grown troupes doing their thing on the city's stages, rarely an inspiring sight. Though the origins of ballet can be traced back to eighteenth-century Italy, there are at present few Italian companies that rise above amateurish levels. See also Teatro dell'Opera (above) for ballet.

THEATRES
Arciliuto Piazza Montevecchio 5 ☎ 06 687 9419 ⓦ arciliuto.it. A small theatre, sometimes with dinner served, that hosts occasional productions in English or French.

English Theatre of Rome Teatro L'Arciliuto, Piazza Montevecchio 5 ☎ 06 444 1375, ⓦ rometheatre.com; bus #40 or #64 from Termini, or #87 from Piazza Venezia. Rome's longest-established English-language

---

TEATRO VALLE OCCUPATO

There's always something interesting going on at the **Teatro Valle** (ⓦ teatrovalleoccupato.it), a lovely eighteenth-century building right in the heart of the Centro Storico, which was occupied in mid-2011 by a group of actors, directors and technicians after rumours spread that it was going to be shut down. It's the oldest active theatre in Rome and the protest achieved widespread recognition, culminating with its rebirth as an artistic foundation in September 2013.

theatre group performs a few plays each season between Nov and June in this tiny theatre off Piazza Navona. Tickets €15.

Miracle Players ⓦ miracleplayers.org. One of Rome's two English-language theatre companies, performing light-hearted renderings of the classics and lots of material with an ancient Rome theme, often in authentic venues – for example the Forum of Julius Caesar in summer. Tickets are usually free, though donations are welcomed.

Palazzo Santa Chiara Teatro Piazza Santa Chiara 14 ⓣ 06 687 5579, ⓦ palazzosantachiara.it; bus #40 or #64 from Termini, #46, #70 or #916 from Corso Vittorio Emanuele, #62 or #492 from Piazza Barberini, #87 or #628 from Piazza Venezia. Traditional Roman-dialect productions are one of the main focuses in this atmospheric old theatre that runs a handful of productions annually.

Salone Margherita Via Due Macelli 75 ⓣ 06 679 1439, ⓦ salonemargherita.com; metro A Spagna or Barberini or bus #52 or #116 from Villa Borghese, #71 from Via Giolitti (Termini), #95, #119, #160 or #630 from Piazza Venezia. Traditional Roman political satire and cabaret – worth it for the atmosphere, even if you don't understand the admittedly difficult verbal sallies.

Teatro Argentina Largo di Torre Argentina 52 ⓣ 06 684 0001, ⓦ teatrodiroma.net; bus #40 or #64 from Termini, #62 or #492 from Piazza Barberini, #87 or #628 from Piazza Venezia, or tram #8 from Viale Trastevere. One of the city's most important theatres for dramatic works in Italian, as well as the occasional production in English, and for dance. Tickets €12 30. Box office Tues–Sun 10am–2pm & 3–7pm.

Teatro Eliseo Via Nazionale 183 ⓣ 06 488 721, ⓦ teatroeliseo.it; metro A Repubblica, or bus #40, #64 or #70 from Corso Vittorio Emanuele, or #170 from Piazza Venezia. One of Rome's main theatres, hosting plays by Italian playwrights, and adaptations into Italian of foreign works, and featuring some of the top dramatic talent the country has to offer. Tickets start at €11.

Teatro Greco Via R. Leoncavallo 10–16 ⓣ 06 860 7513, ⓦ teatrogreco.it; bus #63 or #630 from Piazza Barberini, or #342 from Via Nomentana. Located well out of the centre, on the far side of Villa Ada, this theatre generally offers some of the best Italian dance and even has its own company, with tickets starting at €15. Box office Tues–Sun 10am–1pm & 4–7pm.

Teatro Prati Via degli Scipione 98 ⓣ 06 3974 0503, ⓦ teatroprati.it; metro A Ottaviano or bus #81 from Largo Argentina, #492 from Piazza Barberini, #590 from Termini. A few blocks away from St Peter's, this is another small space that often features Italian comic classics. Tickets start at €18.

Teatro Romano di Ostia Antica Ostia Antica ⓣ 338 676 7183; Lido train from metro B Piramide to Ostia Antica. In July and August specially scheduled performances of all kinds are offered in the restored ancient Roman theatre – a spectacular, unforgettable setting, even if you don't speak Italian. Performances begin at 9.30pm, but go early for a chance to visit the ruins. It's a 30min train ride to Ostia Antica, then a short walk over the footbridge into the ruins. A great Roman summer experience. Box office daily 10am–2pm & 3–6pm.

Teatro Sistina Via Sistina 129 ⓣ 06 420 0711, ⓦ ilsistina.com; metro A Spagna or Barberini or bus #52 or #116 from Villa Borghese, #71 from Via Giolitti (Termini), #95, #119, #160 or #630 from Piazza Venezia. Every now and then an English-language (American, very off-Broadway) musical revue blows into town and it generally ends up here, just up from Piazza di Spagna. Gershwin seems to be a perennial favourite, along with other jazzy-bluesy musical confections.

Teatro Vittoria Piazza Santa Maria Liberatrice 8–11 ⓣ 06 574 0170, ⓦ teatrovittoria.it; metro B Piramide, Bus #30 from Piazza Venezia, #95 from Metro A Barberini, or #75 or #170 from Termini. In Testaccio's main square, this large theatre sometimes books cabaret-like acts or dance-theatre companies that need no translation.

FILM

There tends to be limited **English-language cinema** in Rome, partly due to lack of foreign demand, partly to the Italian penchant for dubbing. Look out for the words *versione originale* (abbreviated "VO" in listings) to be sure a film isn't dubbed. If your Italian is up to it, you'll naturally find current productions, as well as programmes for movie buffs, from silent films with live music to experimental cinema. You'll find **listings** in all newspapers and **tickets** cost €6–10, though some cinemas offer bargain early shows. Watch out for a myriad of **film festivals** across the year (that generally show films in the original language) from one to five days, some of which show excellent films, especially from France, Spain, and Northern Europe, but plenty from further afield as well. Also, a week or so after the major festivals in Cannes, Locarno and Venice, a selection of those films presented comes to Rome.

CINEMAS

Alcazar Via Merry del Val 14 ⓣ 06 588 0099; bus #75 from metro B Colosseo, #780 from Piazza Venezia, H from Termini or tram #8 from Largo Argentina. This is a Trastevere cinema featuring mainstream films, with V.O. on Mon.

Barberini Piazza Barberini 24/26 ⓣ 06 8639 1361, ⓦ cinemabarberini.it. In 2013 this cinema modified its programming to offer first-run English-language films; now often two or three films weekly occupy its five theatres. Also sells popcorn, sodas, and other snacks.

18

SUMMER FILM VENUES

Summer film offerings tend to be lightweight fare and "popolare" geared to a mainstream local audience, therefore the selection, even though it may lean heavily toward Hollywood fare, nevertheless is mainly dubbed. Here are a few of the outdoor venues that offer alternatives, all in magical settings.

Casa del Cinema Largo Marcello Mastroianni 1 ☏06 0608, ⓦcasadelcinema.it (see p.280). The director here puts together interesting programmes with themes based on studios, actors, directors, and subjects that range from Shakespeare to futuristic Science Fiction, almost all in original language. Set amongst umbrella pines, with a handy café.
L'Isola del Cinema Tiber Island ⓦisoladelcinema .com. Although few films are shown in their original language, there are the occasional special events that bring in directors or actors for V.O. films. Either way, the

setting by the river is magical and there are plenty of good taverns around offering everything from cocktails to creative gourmet food (see p.61).
Villa Medici Viale della Trinità dei Monti ☏06 676 11 ⓦvillamedici.it (see p.97). In summer the French Academy's film programme moves outdoors into the glorious sculptural formal garden and always explores interesting themes; films are shown in the original language, the international selection often includes English and there's always something interesting to see.

Casa del Cinema Largo Marcello Mastroianni 1 ☏06 0608, ⓦcasadelcinema.it; bus #116 from metro A Barberini. Right by the Porta Pinciana entrance to the Villa Borghese, this cinema hosts film premieres, festivals, re-runs and retrospectives, generally in the original language. In summer it moves outside (see box above).
Dei Piccoli Viale della Pineta 15 ☏06 855 3485, ⓦcinemadeipiccoli.it. Near the Casa del Cinema, this charming, tiny cinema in a little green house in the Villa Borghese hosts children's films in the daytime, and in the evenings shows original-language films for adults.
Farnese Campo de' Fiori 56, ☏06 686 4395 ⓦwww .cinemafarnese.eu. Although their general programming includes few V.O. films, the special events and festivals are the time to catch movies in their original language.
Filmstudio Via degli Orti d'Alibert 1c ☏334 178 0632, ⓦfilmstudioroma.com; bus #23 from Via Arenula, or #40 or #64 from Termini. Arty films and themed retrospectives in this renovated old cinema with tiny screens in Trastevere near the Tiber. Check first that the film is V.O. Closed July–Sept.
MAXXI Via Guido Reni 4a ☏06 3996 7350, ⓦfondazionemaxxi.it (see p.179). In 2013, this cultural centre adapted its theatre for films and announced Wed night films in the original language.
Nuovo Olimpia Via in Lucina 16 ☏06 686 1068; metro A Spagna, or bus #63 from Via Veneto, #117 from Via Nazionale or #492 from Largo Argentina. Very central, just off Via del Corso, with two screens, and regularly featuring foreign films in the original language.
Nuovo Sacher Largo Ascianghi 1 ☏06 581 8116, ⓦsacherfilm.eu; bus #75 from metro B Colosseo, #780 from Piazza Venezia, H from Termini or tram #8 from Largo Argentina. Nanni Moretti's Trastevere film theatre, housed in the old Fascist youth HQ, shows current films in their original version on Mon, tending toward independent,

left-leaning works.
Quattro Fontane Via Quattro Fontane 23 ☏06 474 1515; metro A Barberini or bus #64 from Termini, #70 from Corso Vittorio Emanuele, or #170 from Piazza Venezia. Lots of mainstream films and the occasional art-house choice, with an undubbed version now and again.
Politecnico Fandango Via Tiepolo 13/a ☏06 3600 4230, ⓦfandango.com. In the Flaminio area, this small cinema is carved out of what looks like an old garage. Run by a left-leaning film production and distribution company, it often shows feature films in the original language, usually with a social message. Its enchanting little courtyard also houses *Bistrot*, a cosy café and trattoria.
The Space Moderno Piazza della Repubblica 45 ☏892 111, ⓦthespacecinema.it; metro A Repubblica or bus #40 or #64 from Corso Vittorio Emanuele, #170 from Piazza Venezia. This American-style multiplex sometimes shows a Hollywood blockbuster in the original undubbed version on one of its five screens.
Trevi Vicolo del Puttarello ☏06 722 4301, ⓦwww .fondazionecsc.it. This is a treasure trove for buffs seeking films from the Cineteca Nazionale archives, some recently restored or featured in intriguing themes, although you have to check for V.O. otherwise films are dubbed.
Urbana 47 Via Urbana 47 ☏06 4788 4006. This friendly Monti restaurant offers an original language film, a glass of wine and a snack during the summer for €8.
Villa Medici Académie de France à Rome Viale della Trinità dei Monti ☏06 676 11 ⓦvillamedici.it. Of all the foreign academies in Rome, the French is arguably the most international in its approach and most active in its cultural programmes, often showing English-language films and sometimes hosting a surprising line-up of guests. The small cinema is lovely, as is the garden, where films are shown in summer, plus there's a fab bar.

Gay and lesbian Rome

Italy has never had any laws prohibiting same-sex couplings, but it still has quite a bit of catching up to do before it is quite as laidback about gay sex as much of the rest of Europe. Nonetheless Rome has made huge progress over the past decade and the city nowadays has a number of generic gay clubs, as well as devoted bars, restaurants and hotels and all sorts of hetero clubs organizing gay nights to cater for the growing scene. There's also the tremendously successful Gay Village (ⓦgayvillage.it), which holds events throughout the summer at an open-air venue between Ostiense and EUR, and the ever-popular Gay Pride in June (ⓦromapride.it).

WHERE TO GO

The scene is well spread out: apart from a short stretch of **Via di San Giovanni in Laterano**, optimistically dubbed "Gay Street" for its nightlife scene, there's no specifically gay area. Choices exclusively for women remain very few, although most places welcome both gay men and lesbians. Bear in mind that while great strides have been made, Rome remains a city where eyebrows may still be raised at men holding hands in the street and the city is certainly not quite ready for kissing in public. Check out the following **websites** aimed at gay visitors for more details – Ⓦ gayrome4u.com, Ⓦ patroc.com/rome and Ⓦ gayrome.com.

CONTACTS, SHOPS AND SERVICES

ARCI-Gay Ora Via Zabaglia 14 ☎ 06 6450 1102, Ⓦ arcigayroma.it. Rome branch of the Italian gay organization that has gatherings for those new to the city on Tuesdays (7–9pm). Annual membership costs €15 and can be useful for getting into clubs and bars (there's also a cheaper monthly version available). It also runs a gay helpline on ☎ 800 713 713 (Mon, Wed, Thurs & Sat 4–8pm). Office open Mon–Sat 4–8pm.

Casa Internazionale delle Donne Via della Lungara 19 ☎ 06 6840 1720, Ⓦ casainternazionaledelledonne .org. Not a gay organization but rather a group of facilities for women only, including a bookshop, library, restaurant and café, housed, appropriately enough, in an old convent. It also has accommodation in its *Orsa Maggiore* hostel.

(☎ 06 689 3753, Ⓦ foresteriaorsa.altervista.org).

Circolo di Cultura Omosessuale Mario Mieli di Cultura Via Efeso 2a ☎ 06 541 3985, Ⓦ mariomieli.org. Rome's most important gay activist organization offers a broad range of social and health services, including counselling and a helpline – ☎ 800 110 611. Weekly welcome group, political group and volunteer group meetings; call for details. Their magazine, *Aut*, features interesting articles, as well as listings, and is free at many gay spots.

Zipper Via dei Gracchi 17 ☎ 06 4436 2244, Ⓦ zippertravel.it. This Prati-based gay travel agent brokers round-the-world or round-Italy travel for gay and lesbian groups and individuals. Mon–Sat 9.30am–1pm & 2–6.30pm.

BARS AND CLUBS

Coming Out Via di San Giovanni in Laterano 8 ☎ 06 700 9871, Ⓦ comingout.it; map pp.130–131. If any area has developed as Rome's gay zone, it is the stretch between the Colosseum and San Clemente. This little pub is the epicentre of the scene, frequented mostly by a younger clientele. Daily 10am–2am.

Garbo Vicolo di Santa Margherita 1a ☎ 06 5832 0782, Ⓦ garbobar.it; map pp.160–161. Friendly Trastevere bar, just behind Piazza di Santa Maria in Trastevere, with a relaxed atmosphere and a nice setting. Tues–Sun 10pm–3am.

Hangar Via in Selci 69 ☎ 06 488 1397, Ⓦ hangaronline .it; map pp.114–115. About halfway between Termini and the Roman Forum, just off Via Cavour, this is one of Rome's oldest and least expensive gay spots. Older gay men come here, mainly. There's no charge if you show your ARCI-Gay card; without a card, you have to pay for at least one drink. Mon & Wed–Sun 10.30pm–2.30am; closed 3 weeks in Aug.

Il Giardino dei Ciliegi Via dei Fienaroli 4 ☎ 06 580 3423, Ⓦ ilgiardinodeiciliegi.net; map pp.140–141. A gay-friendly café, bar and tea house in lively Trastevere. Mon–Sat 5pm–2am & Sun 1pm–2am.

L'Alibi Via Monte Testaccio 44 ☎ 06 574 3448, Ⓦ lalibi .it; map pp.140–141. This predominantly, but by no means exclusively, male venue is one of Rome's oldest gay clubs, situated in the heart of the city's alternative night scene in Testaccio. It's no longer quite cutting edge, but is a good all-round hangout, with a multi-room cellar disco, an upstairs open-air bar and a big terrace to enjoy in the warm months. Thurs–Sun midnight–5am.

Skyline Via Pontremoli 36 ☎ 06 700 9431, Ⓦ skylineclub.it; map pp.130–131. Gay male strippers, dark zones and a decidedly macho decor make this San Giovanni club a magnet for various creatures of the night, possibly drawn by the heavy cruising along the balcony. Various regular theme nights, including "Naked Party" Mondays. Daily 10.30pm–4am.

RESTAURANTS

Asinocotto Via dei Vascellari 48 ☎ 06 589 8985; map pp.160–161. One of the first restaurants to hang the rainbow flag above its door, this Trastevere joint is run by a gay couple and has a great, Proust-inspired menu of moderately priced pasta, meat and fish dishes. This place is worth a visit whatever your non-culinary preferences. Mon–Fri noon–2.30pm & 7.30–11pm, Sat & Sun 7.30–11pm.

La Taverna di Edoardo II Vicolo Margana 14 ☎ 06 6994 2419; map pp.54–55. Centrally situated in the Jewish Ghetto, just off Piazza Venezia, *La Taverna di Edoardo II* used to be a medieval torture chamber theme bar, and was named after the gay English king. It's now a gay restaurant and still attracts the same young and cruisy crowd. Membership is required, but it's free. Daily except Tues 7pm–12.30am.

19

Luna e l'Altra Via Francesco di Sales ☎ 06 6889 2465 or ☎ 327 082 0721; map pp.160–161. This Trastevere bar and restaurant is housed in the Casa Internazionale di Donna and as such is the only exclusively women's restaurant in town

serving mainly vegetarian food at a lunchtime buffet (when men are also welcome), and from a regular menu including more meat dishes in the evening (when it is strictly women-only). Mon–Sat 12.30–2.30pm & 8.30–11pm.

SAUNAS

Europa Multiclub Via Aureliana 40 ☎ 06 482 3650, ⓦ europamulticlub.com. Near Termini, this sauna has pleasantly stylish, clean facilities and a snack bar. €15 per visit, €12 after 11pm. Mon–Thurs 1pm–midnight, Fri 1pm non-stop until Sun at midnight.

Mediterraneo Via Pasquale Villari 3 ☎ 06 7720 5934, ⓦ saunamediterraneo.it. Close to Piazza Vittorio Emanuele, this is a sauna on three levels, with all the usual choices, including a snack bar. Notably clean and attracts all ages. ARCi-Gay membership required. €15. Daily 1pm–midnight.

ACCOMMODATION

58 Le Real De Luxe Via Cavour 58 ☎ 06 482 3566, ⓦ bed-and-breakfast-rome.com; map pp.114–115. Double rooms in a small gay-friendly Via Cavour *pensione*. €85

Ares Rooms Via Domenichino 7 ☎ 06 474 4525, ⓦ aresrooms.com; map pp.114–115. This is a gay-friendly bed and breakfast near Termini station. Not all

rooms are en suite. €50–70

Gaspare B&B Via Balilla 16 ☎ 06 6482 1660; map pp.114–115. This bed and breakfast is situated just off Via Giolitti by Termini, a 5min walk from the Fiumicino platforms, and is gay friendly with three simply furnished double rooms. €70

19

Shops and markets

At first glance, you may wonder where to start when it comes to shopping in a big, chaotic city like Rome. In fact the city promises a more appealing shopping experience than you might think, abounding with pleasant, frequently car-free shopping streets and markets, many of them in the city centre. What's more, Rome hasn't yet been entirely overrun by the international chain stores that characterize most European city centres. One-stop shopping opportunities are rare, but you will find corners of the city that have been colonized by stores selling the same sort of merchandise – fashion, antiques, food – making it easy for you to check out the competition's products and prices. You will also still find true artisans in central Rome, some of whom sell their products direct to the public.

ESSENTIALS

Opening hours These days quite a few shops in the centre of Rome stay open all day and are open on Sun too. However, many still observe the city's traditional opening hours – roughly Mon 3.30–7.30pm, Tues–Sat 9.30am–1.30pm & 3.30–7.30pm, and are closed on Sun. Food shops are also often closed on Thurs afternoon in winter and Sat afternoon during the summer. Most places accept all major credit cards, but a few stalwarts remain cash-only. Markets tend to open early – around 7am – and close up by 2pm. Supermarkets are generally open all day from 8am until 8pm. Bear in mind that a lot of stores close down during Aug for their annual holiday.

Tax-free shopping It's worth knowing that non-EU residents can save up to 14.5 percent of the purchase price, on a minimum purchase of €154.95. To do this you need to request a Tax Refund Cheque at the time of purchase. Then, before leaving Italy go to the customs desk at the airport with your purchases, receipt, refund cheque and passport, and afterwards go to the designated Tax Free service desk for your credit, either on a card or as a cash refund.

Where to shop The best of Italy is available in Rome. Fashion straight from the catwalk is well represented on the stylish streets close to the Spanish Steps – Via dei Condotti, Via Borgognona, Via Frattina and Via del Babuino – where you'll find all the major A-list designers (see box, p.286) as well as lots of alluring one-off boutiques. You can find more mainstream fashions and all the chains on Via Cola di Rienzo, near the Vatican, and also along Via Nazionale (also good for luggage), near to which the streets of the Monti district are home to an increasing number of stylish independent stores. Bang in the centre

of town, Via del Corso is the home of mainstream young fashion stores and various downscale chains (aside from a new Fendi and a mammoth Zara). Via dei Giubbonari, near Campo de' Fiori, is a good place to shop for affordably priced yet stylish clothes and shoes, and Via del Governo Vecchio is probably the city centre's best stretch of funky, stylish independent fashion boutiques and vintage stores. For more traditional and very stylish shops, especially for men, try the stretch between the Pantheon and Piazza San Lorenzo in Lucina. Among other specialities, antique shops line Via dei Coronari and neighbouring Via dell'Orso and Via dei Soldati, just north of Piazza Navona. Via Giulia, southwest of Campo de Fiori, as well as Via del Babuino and Via Margutta, between Piazza del Popolo and the Spanish Steps, are also good sources of art and antiques; other good haunts are southwest of Campo de' Fiori, along Via Giulia, Monserrato and Banchi Vecchi. For food, we've listed a number of the city's best delis should you want to take home a bottle of extra virgin olive oil or some vacuum-packed porcini mushrooms – or if you just want to put together a DIY lunch. Finally, the city's many markets offer a change of pace from Rome's busy shopping streets. Many of these are bustling local food markets and, even in the centre, are still very much part of Roman life, especially in the mornings. The market in Campo de' Fiori is probably the most central, and certainly the best-known, but we've listed others (see p.295). Otherwise, dedicated bargain-hunters still prowl Trastevere's Porta Portese flea market, selling heaps of antiques, clothing, books and indeed virtually anything else, every Sun morning (see p.165).

20

ANTIQUES

Antichità Archeologia Largo della Fontanella di Borghese 76 ☎ 06 686 4054; map p.38. If you want to take home your own piece of ancient Rome, this is the place for you. Certified genuine Greek, Etruscan and Roman antiquities, such as terracotta oil lamps, figurines and incised jewels, start at about €100. Mon 3.30–7pm, Tues–Sat 10am–1pm & 3.30–7pm.

Arabesco Via dei Coronari 143 ☎ 06 686 9659; map p.38. One of a couple of such stores on this street, this has old Turkish carpets and kilims, oriental glassware and other bits and pieces from the East. Tues–Sat 11am–8pm but call first as times can be erratic.

Oasi Antiquariato Via del Babuino 83 ☎ 06 320 7585; map p.93. One of several fine antiques stores in the area, with a large collection of stunning Italian furnishings from the 1700s. There is also an entrance on Via Margutta. Mon–Sat 9.30am–7.30pm.

Valerio Turchi Via Margutta, 91a ☎ 06 323 5047; map p.93. A bit different from the other antiques shops on Via Margutta, with exquisite pieces from Rome's past – various pieces of Roman statues and sarcophagi dating from as early as 300 AD. Mon 3.30–7pm, Tues–Sat 10am–7pm.

BOOKS

★ **The Almost Corner Bookshop** Via del Moro 45 ☎ 06 583 6942; map pp.160–161. Of all Rome's English bookshops, this stalwart Trastevere store is the best bet for having the very latest titles on your list of must-reads. Mon–Sat 10am–1.30pm & 3.30–8pm, Sun 11am–1.30pm & 3.30–8pm; closed Sun in Aug.

★ **Anglo-American Bookshop** Via della Vite 102 ☎ 06 679 5222; map p.93. Excellent city-centre English-language bookshop, with one of the best selections of new English books in Rome. Especially good on history and academic books, but lots of fiction too. Mon 3.30–7.30pm, Tues–Sat 10.30am–7.30pm; closed 18 days in Aug.

Feltrinelli International Via Vittorio Emanuele Orlando 84 ☎ 06 482 7878; map pp.114–115. Just off Piazza della Repubblica, this international branch of the nationwide chain has a great stock of books in English, as well as French, German, Spanish and Portuguese. The large store at Largo Argentina also has a coffee bar upstairs. Mon–Sat 9am–8pm, Sun 10.30am–1.30pm & 4–8pm.

Giunti al Punto Piazza dei Santi Apostoli 59/62 ☎ 06 6994 1045, ⊗ giuntialpunto.it; map p.93. A great kids' bookshop (see p.306).

Libreria del Cinema Via dei Fienaroli 31d ☎ 06 581 7724, ⊗ libreriadelcinema.roma.it; map pp.160–161. Books, DVDs, magazines on film and everything related to it – some in English. There's a small café too, where you can sip wine or coffee with other film buffs. Mon–Fri 2–10pm,

Sat & Sun 6pm–midnight.

Libreria del Viaggiatore Via del Pellegrino 78 ☎ 06 6880 1048; map pp.54–55. A small store, but with central Rome's best stock of old guides, maps and travel books, many of which are in English. Mon 4–8pm, Tues–Sat 10am–2pm & 4–8pm.

Open Door Bookshop Via della Lungaretta 23 ☎ 06 589 6478, ⊗ books-in-italy.com; map pp.160–161. Although they do have some new titles, especially on Rome and Roman history, used books dominate the shelves at this friendly Trastevere bookshop, where you never know what treasures you might turn up. They also have a selection of books in Italian, German, French and Spanish. Mon–Sat 10.30am–8.30pm.

CLOTHES

Alberta Ferreti Philosophy 34a Via dei Condotti ☎ 06 699 1160; map p.93. Almost every season this designer incorporates a few dresses that hark back to the fluid, soft lines of ancient Rome, as well as some very contemporary styles. Mon 4–7pm, Tues–Sat 10am–7pm.

Angelo di Nepi Via dei Giubbonari 28 ☎ 06 689 3006; Via Frattina 2 ☎ 06 786 568 map pp.54–55; Via Cola di Rienzo 267/a. Fashions under the chili pepper logo range from ethnic to elegant, with flashy touches using bright taffeta, velvet or embroidery. Other branches around town. Mon–Sat 10am–8pm.

Anteprima Roma Via delle Quattro Fontane 38–40 ☎ 06 484 8445, ⊗ anteprimadimoda.com; map pp.114–115. High-spirited elegant fashion with a dose of tongue-in-cheek style. Labels include Florence-based 'Save the Queen'. A definite cut above the nearby Via Nazionale shops. Mon–Sat 9.30am–8pm, Sun 11am–2pm & 3–8pm.

Antichi Kimono Via di Monserrato 43b–44 ☎ 06 6813 5876; map pp.54–55. Vintage kimonos paired with Italian separates. Also check out their reasonably priced jewellery

and accessories. Mon 3.30–7.30pm, Tues–Sat 10am–7.30pm.

Atipika Via di Monserrato 103 ☎ 331 944 9140 (mobile); map pp.54–55. The former Eckletika shop has enlarged its collection, adding some antique furniture, lamps and accessories to its sensual textiles of Venice, shown off to full effect in dresses of brocade, cashmere, silk and wool. Look for flirty capes, fashion jewellery from 1930s-inspired to modern, and smart Parisian bags; prices from €15–300. Mon 3.30–8pm, Tues–Sat 10.30am–2pm & 3.30–8pm.

★ **Arsenale** Via del Governo Vecchio 64 ☎ 06 686 1380; map p.38. This large store is one of the main boutiques along this funky stretch, with great dresses by the owner Patrizia Pieroni and lots of other stuff by small independent designers. Mon 3.30–7.30pm, Tues–Sat 10am–7.30pm.

Aspesi Via del Babuino 144 ☎ 06 323 0376; map p.93. Flagship Rome store of the contemporary Italian designer, with cool designs for both men and women as well as

---

THE BIG DESIGNERS

Blumarine Via Borgognona 81
Bulgari Via dei Condotti 10 ☎ 06 679 3876
Dolce & Gabbana Via Belseana 66 and Piazza di Spagna ☎ 06 6992 4999
Fendi Largo Goldoni ☎ 06 334 501
Ferre Piazza di Spagna 70 ☎ 06 678 6797
Giorgio Armani Via dei Condotti 77 and Via Borgognona 70 ☎ 06 699 1460
Gucci Via dei Condotti 8 ☎ 06 679 0405
Krizia Piazza di Spagna 87 ☎ 06 679 3772
MaxMara Via dei Condotti 17/19; Via Frattina 28; Via delle Vite 59; Via Nazionale; ☎ 06 6992 2104

Missoni Piazza di Spagna 78 ☎ 06 679 2555
Moschino Via Borgognona 32/A ☎ 06 678 1144
Patrizia Pepe Via Frattina 44
Prada Via dei Condotti 88/95 ☎ 06 679 0897
Roberto Cavalli Via Borgognona 25 ☎ 06 6992 5469
Salvatore Ferragamo Via dei Condotti 65 & 73/74 ☎ 06 678 1130/679 1565
Valentino Via dei Condotti 15 ☎ 06 679 0479
Versace Via Bocca di Leone 23 & 26/2 ☎ 06 678 0521

MUSEUM SHOPS

Once almost entirely absent, **museum shops** have flourished in Rome in recent years. Most specialize in books, but those that feature modern exhibitions, like the Palazzo delle Esposizioni, often have designer items too, from jewellery and sculpture to desktop accessories. Hours will generally be the same as the museum's hours – you should never have to pay admission to gain entry.

Galleria Borghese Piazzale del Museo Borghese ☎ 06 32810. Great for titles on the major artistic periods, from the Renaissance to the Baroque.

Linearia Museum Store Corso Vittorio Emanuele 5 ☎ 06 6920 0722. Stocks accessories, books and design trinkets from a selection of Rome's – and indeed Italy's – best museums.

MAXXI Via Guido Reni 4a ☎ 06 3996 7350. Good art bookshop, as you would expect, with the emphasis on contemporary art, architecture and design.

Musei Capitolini Piazza del Campidoglio 1 ☎ 06 0608. Good book selection on Ancient Rome as well as art through the Renaissance and Baroque periods.

Palazzo delle Esposizioni Via Nazionale 194 ☎ 06 3996 7500. Great all-round art and design shop situated in the basement of the building.

Scuderie del Quirinale Via XXIV Maggio 16 ☎ 06 3996 7200. Excellent art bookshop, covering all the major periods and artists.

Trajan's Markets Via IV Novembre 94 ☎ 06 0608. Particularly good for books about Rome, especially on ancient sites and archaeology.

---

textiles in this very sleek store in the heart of the Piazza di Spagna area. Mon–Sat 10am–7pm.

Brighenti Via Frattina 7–10 ☎ 06 679 1484; Via Borgognona 27 ☎ 06 678 3898, ⓦ brighentiboutique.it; map p.93. Full of classy French and Italian lingerie, both of these stores are worthy of a 1950s movies set, from the furnishings to the top-notch fitters and saleswomen. Mon 11am–7.30pm, Tues–Sat 10.30am–7.30pm.

Cinzia Via del Governo Vecchio 45 ☎ 06 686 1791; map p.38. The best of several used clothing shops along this street, where you can find anything from an elegant raincoat to black leather biker jeans, and much more. Mon 10am–7pm, Tues–Sat 10am–2pm & 3.30–7.30pm.

Davide Cenci Via di Campo Marzio 1–7 ☎ 06 699 0681; map p.38. Flagship store of this long-established purveyor of elegant and refined clothing for the past 75 years, offering conservative high-quality fashion, decidedly more interesting for men than women; also threads for pampered children. Always seems to be expanding down the block. Mon 4–8pm, Tues–Sat 10am–2pm & 4–8pm.

Degli Effetti Piazza Capranica 75, 79 & 93 ☎ 06 679 0202; map p.38. Since 1987, these fashion forecasters have been choosing a stylish core collection featuring top Japanese houses Miyake, Comme des Garçons and Yohji Yamamoto. The shop prides itself on fashion quality, research, and its stylish feel for market niches. Mon 10am–7pm, Tues–Sat 10am–2pm & 3.30–7.30pm.

Diesel Via del Corso 186 ☎ 06 678 3933; map p.38. The largest and most central branch of this Italian manufacturer of trendy styles for studiously disaffected youth. Other branches at Via del Babuino 94–95 (☎ 06 6938 0053) and Via Cola di Rienzo 245–249 (☎ 06 324 1895). Mon–Sat 10.30am–7.30pm.

Dress Agency Donna Via del Vantaggio 1b ☎ 06 321 0898; map p.93. Used women's clothing and accessories from Versace, Armani and all the big-name Italian designers. Not as cheap as you might expect, but still worth a rummage. Mon 4–7.30pm, Tues–Sat 10am–1pm & 4–7.30pm.

Emporio Armani Via del Babuino 140 ☎ 06 3600 2197; map p.93. The city-centre branch of the designer's chain of more affordable yet still very stylish stores. Daily 10am–7pm; Sun closes 1hr for lunch.

Energie Via del Corso 179 & 486 ☎ 06 322 7046; map p.93. One of Rome's most popular clothing stores, mainly aimed at teenagers, with trendy gear, loud music and an omnipresent group of kids hanging out. Definitely the place to be seen if you're loaded and under 21. Another branch at Via Cola di Rienzo 143–147. Mon–Sun 10am–8pm.

Ermanno Scervino Via del Babuino 97 ☎ 06 679 3173, ⓦ ermannoscervino.it; map p.93. Actress Asia Argento recently came here to launch this Florence-based designer's new flagship Rome fashion outlet. Sporty, contemporary styles mainly for women, and beautiful lingerie. Mon 4–7pm, Tues–Sat 10am–7pm.

Ermenegildo Zegna Via Borgognona 7e ☎ 06 678 9143; map p.93. This is a leading contender for the ultimate suit maker. At least one Zegna suit hangs in every Italian CEO's wardrobe. There's another store at Via dei Condotti 58. Mon 4–7pm, Tues–Sat 10am–7pm.

Kolby Via Nazionale 203–203a ☎ 06 482 4532; map pp.114–115. Casual styles for men at reasonable prices. There's also a shop on the more picturesque Via del Governo Vecchio 64, near Piazza Navona. Mon–Sat 10am–7pm.

Le Gallinelle Via del Boschetto 76 ☎ 06 488 1017; map pp.114–115. Choose your own fabric from among their own stylish designs, and have a garment made up on the

20

spot at this cool Monti store. Mon 3.30–7.30pm, Tues–Sat Mon–Sat 10am–1pm & 3.30–7.30pm, Sun noon–4pm.

La Perla Via Bocca di Leone 28 ☎ 06 6994 1934; map p.93. The Bologna-based international chain stocks some of Rome's prettiest and most coveted lingerie. Tues–Sat 10am–8pm.

Loro Piana Via dei Condotti 24 ☎ 06 6992 4906, ⓦ loropiana.com; map p.93. Luxurious cashmere is woven and knitted into fine mostly classic styles by this Piemonte-based company. Mon–Sat 10.30am–7.30pm, Sun 11am–2pm & 3–7pm.

Luna & L'Altra Piazza Pasquino 76 ☎ 06 6880 4995; map p.38. Contemporary but not faddish store that stocks designs by Yohji Yamamoto, Issey Miyake, Martin Margiela, Dries Van Noten, Limi feu, + Noir, Rick Owens, Haat, Final Home and others. Mon 3.30–7.30pm, Tues–Sat 10am–2pm & 3.30–7.30pm.

Maga Morgana Via del Governo Vecchio 27 & 98 ☎ 06 687 9995; map p.38. Two shops selling attractive, original women's tops, skirts and knitwear, and great dresses. Mon–Sat 10am–8pm.

Malo Via Belsiana 68 ☎ 06 679 1331, ⓦ malo.it; map p.93. Designer that's famous for luxury cashmere, and

based near Florence. Stocks everything from ultra-classic to some very trendy lines. Mon 4.30–7.30pm, Tues–Sat 10.30am–7.30pm.

Max & Co Via Condotti 46 ☎ 06 678 7946; map p.93. Central Rome branch of MaxMara's more accessible and more youthful chain. Mon–Sat 10am–8pm, Sun 11am–7.30pm.

Miu Miu Via dei Condotti 24 ☎ 06 8881 1280, ⓦ miumiu .com; map p.93. Miuccia Prada used her nickname to launch this spunky Prada spinoff, often sporting some of the more fun if pricey fashions on this full-of-itself street. Mon–Sat 10am–7.30pm, Sun 10am–7pm.

Poems Via del Governo Vecchio 10 ☎ 06 6880 8005; map p.38. This funky shop has its own line of casual clothes and fun cocktail dresses in synthetic fabrics, some inspired by flappers of the 1920s and the mods of the 1960s at prices that hover just above €100. Mon 4–7.30pm, Tues–Sat 11am–7.30pm.

Stella McCartney Via Borgognona 6 ☎ 06 6919 0779; map p.93. Eco-luxury flagship store opened in July 2011 by the Beatle daughter who uses no fur or leather and designs women's clothes which are sexy, sassy and modern. Also lingerie, dresses, sunglasses and children's wear. Mon–Sat 10am–7pm.

SHOES AND ACCESSORIES

Antica Manifattura Cappelli Via degli Scipioni 46 ☎ 06 397 2569, ⓦ antica-cappelleria.it; map pp.188–189. When Patrizia Fari took over this historic hatshop, she kept its aura but added her own elegant and quirky styles for theatre, movies, ceremonies, and just plain glamour. She designs and makes the hats right here and buys vintage pieces, too. Mon–Sat 9am–7pm.

Borsalino Piazza del Popolo 26 ☎ 06 3265 0838; map p.93. Home of the classic fedora as sported by Jean-Paul Belmondo, Johnny Depp and others, as well as a whole host of other kinds of hats. Mon 3–7.30pm, Tues–Sat 9.30am–1.30pm & 3–7.30pm.

Bottega Veneta Piazza San Lorenzo in Lucina 7–12 ☎ 06 6821 0024; map p.38. Probably the best place to look for top-quality leather bags and purses – especially good for intricate braiding. Some of that supple leather also is transformed into jackets and dresses. Mon 4–8pm, Tues–Sat 9.30am–8pm.

Bozart Via Bocca di Leone 4 ☎ 06 6929 2163; map p.93. These fakes are truly fabulous, just the spot to pick up crowns, diadems and body jewellery. Semi-precious stones, as well as Swarovski crystal pieces and resin and wooden elements are freely used to create dazzling costume jewellery, ranging in price from €25 to €300. Mon 4–8pm, Tues–Sat 9.30am–8pm.

Bric's Piazza San Silvestro 25/26 ☎ 06 679 0129, ⓦ brics roma.com; map p.93. Founded in 1952 by Mario Briccola near Lake Como and now run by his sons, this company sells reasonably priced, handsome hand-crafted travel bags,

purses and accessories. Mon–Sat 10am–7.30pm.

Fabio Piccioni Via del Boschetto 148 ☎ 06 474 1697; map pp.114–115. Vintage jewellery store with some original Art Nouveau and Art Deco pieces, though most are 1920s–1970s-inspired reproductions and one-of-a-kind adornments made in the workshop. Mon–Sat 10am–1pm & 3–8pm; closed Sat in summer.

Giorgio Sermoneta Piazza di Spagna 61 ☎ 06 679 1960; map p.93. This long-standing glove specialist has a large collection of Italian gloves in every price range, and has catered to celebrities, politicians and tourists for 35 years. Mon–Sat 9.30am–8pm, Sun 10.30am–7pm.

★ **Ibiz** Via dei Chiavari 39 ☎ 06 6830 7297; map pp.54–55. Great leather bags, purses and rucksacks in exciting contemporary designs made on the premises. Mon–Sat 10am–7.30pm.

Il Gancio Via del Seminario 82–83 ☎ 06 679 6646; map p.38. High-quality leather bags, purses and shoes, all made in the workshop on site. Mon 3.30–7.30pm, Tues–Sat 10am–1pm & 3.30–7.30pm.

La Cravatta su Misura Via di Santa Cecilia 12 ☎ 06 8901 6941; map pp.160–161. This shop sells only one thing – ties. Choose from among the hundreds of ties on display, or from the hundreds of rolls of material and have your own made up. Tues–Sat 10am–2pm & 3.30–7.30pm, June & July closed Sat afternoon.

Lefevre Via del Pellegrino 99 ☎ 06 688 01881; map pp.54–55. Exclusive designs here include seed-pearl ropes hung with cut crystals of ruby, emerald and sapphire matrix,

TERMINI: A SHOPPING CENTRE WITH TRAIN STATION ATTACHED?

Time was when the Mussolini-era masterwork was looking way past its best, but **Termini station** has been updated massively over the past decade and is now almost as much a place to shop as take a train, with one of the city's best bookshops in Borri Books, a branch of the department store COIN and two supermarkets, plus the Sephora perfumery, a wine shop and branches of several of the big Italian chains including Benetton. It's still not a place for a relaxing shopping experience, though – watch out for pickpockets.

for under €100. There are silver frames too, as well as fine porcelains. Mon 4–8pm, Tues–Sat 10am–1pm & 4–8pm.

★ **Loco** Via dei Baullari 22 ☎ 06 6880 8216; map pp.54–55. Very cool shoe store just off Campo de' Fiori with plenty of styles for men and women. Mon 3.30–8pm, Tues–Sat 10.30am–8pm.

Mandarina Duck Via dei Due Macelli 59 ☎ 06 678 6414; map p.93. The main branch of the trendy Bologna bag company is a homage to how to be both practical and stylish. Mon 3.30–7.30pm, Tues–Sat 10am–7.30pm.

Migian Via dei Banchi Nuovi 13 ☎ 06 688 05560; map p.38. Tucked away behind the Chiesa Nuova, these working goldsmiths sell jewellery at a wide range of prices. Mon–4–7pm, Tues–Sat 10am–7pm.

Natural Shoes Via della Lungaretta 94 ☎ 06 581 1190, ⓦ naturalshoes.it; map pp.160–161. This Trastevere shop's comfortable shoes come to the rescue of those who can't navigate Rome's cobblestones in spike heels- or simply need a break from them. Also has styles for wider feet, a rarity in Italy. Mon–Thurs 10am–9pm, Fri & Sat 10am–10pm, Sun 11am–9pm.

Novità Via Sora 17a ☎ 06 686 8685; map p.38. Heaven for do-it-yourselfers who flock here to find glass, plastic,

wood, stone and crystal beads. They also have a wide stock of one-off pieces to repair vintage jewellery. Mon 3.30–7pm, Tues–Sat 9.30am–1pm & 3.30–7pm.

NuYorica Piazza Pollarola 36/37 ☎ 06 6889 1243; map pp.54–55. Just a few steps from Campo de' Fiori, this stylish shop specializes in shoes and bags by contemporary designers – though nothing here comes cheap. Mon–Sat 10.30am–7.30pm.

Pineider Via dei Due Macelli 68 ☎ 06 239 344; map p.93. This exclusive store has been crafting beautiful stationery items and handmade bags and wallets for Roman society since 1774. There's another branch at Via della Fontanella di Borghese 22 (☎ 06 687 8369). Mon 3.30–7.30pm, Tues–Sat 10am–1.30pm & 3.30–7.30pm.

Sciú Sciá Calzature Via di Torre Argentina 8–9 ☎ 06 6880 6777; map pp.54–55. If you can't swing Bottega Veneta prices, try the working gal's alternative – lower-priced leather crochet bags (€165), made in Tuscany near Arezzo. Mon–Sat 10.10am–7.30pm.

Zannetti Via Monte d'Oro 18–23 ☎ 06 6819 2566; map p.38. Flagship store of the distinctive Italian handmade watch specialist and jeweller. Mon–Fri 9am–1pm & 4–7pm.

DEPARTMENT STORES AND MALLS

COIN Via Cola di Rienzo 173 ☎ 06 3600 4298; map pp.188–189. Also at Termini and at Piazzale Appio 7, by San Giovanni metro station (☎ 06 708 0020; Mon–Fri 9.30am–8pm, Sat 9.30am–8pm, Sun 10.30am–8.30pm). Nationwide chain that's good for high-street fashion, kids' clothes, beauty products and so on. Mon–Sat 10am–8pm, Sun 10.30am–8pm.

La Rinascente Galleria Alberto Sordi, Piazza Colonna ☎ 06 678 4209; map p.38. A larger branch is at Piazza Fiume (☎ 06 884 1231; Mon–Sat 9.30am–9.30pm, Sun 10am–9pm). Rome's first department store, and Italy's oldest chain. Still a good place to browse handbags, accessories and mainstream fashion. Daily 10am–9pm.

M.A.S. Piazza Vittorio Emanuele 138 ☎ 06 446 8078; map pp.114–115. It doesn't get any cheaper than this. Situated among the arcades of Piazza Vittorio, the

"Magazzini allo Statuto" (Statutory Warehouses) is like one vast, multi-level rummage sale, but take your time and you might find something you want. There's everything from clothing to housewares. Mon–Sat 9am–1pm & 3.45–7.45pm.

Oviesse Industry Via del Tritone 172 ☎ 06 678 3336; map p.93. Nationwide chain that specializes in well-priced, sometimes stylish men's, women's and children's clothes and accessories. There's another branch on Piazza Santa Maggiore. Mon 3.30–7.30pm, Tues–Sat 10am–7.30pm.

Zara Via del Corso 189; map p.93. Palazzo Bocconi once hosted the Rinascente flagship store, but was given a makeover that transformed it from drab to luminous and it's now occupied by the Spanish retail giant's flagship Rome store. Its fashion savvy at budget prices attracts Romans as well as tourists. Mon–Sun 10am–8pm.

FOOD AND WINE

Antica Caciara Trasteverina Via San Francesco a Ripa 140a/b ☎ 06 5811 2815; map pp.160–161. Athough the

cheeses and wines they sell here come from various parts of Italy and also abroad, the chances are it's the aged

20

pecorino cheeses that you can smell from down the street. This Trastevere institution dates from about 1900 and has a loyal following spanning generations. Mon–Sat 8am–8pm.

Beppe e I Suoi Formaggi Via Santa Maria del Pianto 9a/11 ☎06 6819 2210; map pp.54–55. This newcomer to the Ghetto features Alpine cheeses and cured meats. Their butter outclasses its counterparts from most of central and southern Italy. Mon 4–7pm, Tues–Sat 10am–7pm.

Biblio Tèa Via dei Banchi Vecchi 124 ☎06 454 33114; map p.38. A decent cup of tea is a rarity in Rome, so most likely you'll want to make your own. Here you can find black, green and white teas, some coffee and chocolate, plus pots and accessories. Mon 3.30–7.30pm, Tues–Sat 10am–1.30pm & 3.30–7.30pm.

★ **Boulangerie MP** Corso del Rinascimento 34; map pp.54–55. Bread is the star in this bakery, but they also sell a small selection of well-chosen treats from caviar to old-timey sodas from Le Marche and biscuits. Mon–Thurs 8.30am–8pm, Fri & Sat 8.30am–midnight, Sun11am–8pm.

★ **Buccone** Via di Ripetta 19 ☎06 361 2154; map p.93. Every alcoholic beverage you could dream of, with a large selection of wines from all over the world, plus spirits, and even ten-litre bottles of *grappa*. A good place to grab lunch too (see p.250). Mon–Thurs 9am–8.30pm, Fri & Sat 9am–11.30pm.

Castroni Via Cola di Rienzo 196 ☎06 687 4383, ⓦ castroni.it; map pp.188–189. Huge, labyrinthine food store selling a large selection of Italian treats, including chocolates, pastas, sauces, olive oils, and hard-to-find international favourites such as plum pudding, Vegemite, peanut butter and Mexican specialities. As renowned for its good coffee blend (also served at the bar) as for its rude service. Their other branches at Via Ottaviano 55, Via Frattina 79 and Via Nazionale 71 are a bit friendlier and also have coffee bars. Mon–Sat 7.30am–8pm.

Centro Macrobiotico Italiano Via della Vite 14 ☎06 679 2509; map p.93. The most central shop for natural foods, with wholegrain pastas and other such products from Italy's rich countryside. Mon–Fri noon–4pm & 7–11pm, Sat 7–11pm.

Colapicchioni Via Tacito 76–78 ☎06 321 5405; Via Properzio 23–25 ☎06 6880 1310; map pp.188–189. Long-running Prati food store with two branches, the former mainly a baker's, the later incorporating a deli, but both selling the family's excellent *pangiallo* and other foodie goodies. Mon–Sat 9am–8pm.

Comptoir de France Via Vitelleschi 20–24 ☎06 6830 1516; map pp.188–189. This slick and well-stocked store near Castel Sant'Angelo specializes in over a thousand French wines (including many from small, independent and biodynamic wineries), exceptional cheeses, ciders, mustards and other Gallic goodies. Mon 4–8pm, Tues–Sat 9.30am–8pm.

Costantini Piazza Cavour 16 ☎06 321 3210; map pp.188–189. Prati claims one of the city's best wine stores, with a fantastic selection in its basement *enoteca*, with *grappas*, spirits and liqueurs upstairs. Next door is their elegant and expensive restaurant. Mon 4.30–8pm, Tues–Sat 9am–1pm & 4.30–8pm.

Cristalli di Zucchero Via San Teodoro 88 ☎06 6992 0945, ⓦ cristallidizucchero.it; map p.64. Down at the far end of Via San Teodoro, just off the Circus Maximus, this place has refined tarts, cakes and pastries – delicate works of art that melt in your mouth, and make the perfect accompaniment to the queue for the "Mouth of Truth" just around the corner. Coffee and more down-to-earth pastries too, if all you want is a cornetto. There's another branch across the river in Monteverde at Via di Val Tellina 114 (☎06 5823 0323). Daily except Tues 7.30am–8.30pm.

De Bellis Pasticceria Piazza del Paradiso 56/57 ☎06 6880 5072; map pp.54–55. Cakes to swoon over, made with fine quality butter, flour and other ingredients. A French pastry chef comes in to make macaroons, and

CITY-CENTRE SUPERMARKETS

Rome's food stores and delis are so good that you shouldn't need to use a **supermarket** too often, but for pasta and other basics the supermarkets in the city centre can be useful, especially if you're self-catering or just want somewhere easy to pick up a picnic. Some of the more conveniently located ones are below. The French chain Carrefour has taken over some, which for the most part has improved efficiency.

Carrefour Express/Dì per Dì Villa Borghese Parcheggio; Via del Gesù 58; Via Vittoria 22; Via del Governo Vecchio 119; Via dei Coronari 187; Corso Vittorio Emanuele 290; Via Monterone 5; Via Poli 47; Via dei SS. Quattro Coronati 53.

De Spar Corso V. Emanuele 42; Corso Rinascimento 7; Vicolo di Moretta 10 (off Via Giulia); Via del Pozzetto

123; Via San Bartolomeo de' Vaccinari 78 (Ghetto); Via Nazionale 212–213; Via Alberico II 3 (Prati); Termini station; Via Guicciardini 2.

Elite Via Cavour 230–234.

Sma Via della Frezza 8; Piazza Santa Maria Maggiore.

Standa Via Cola di Rienzo 173; Viale Trastevere 60.

there are elegant tarts, biscuits, and a millefeuille bar where you can choose the creamy filling that you want. Late hours accommodate the Campo crowd and there's a small seating area. Daily noon–midnight.

★ **Del Frate** Via degli Scipioni 118, 122 ❶ 06 321 1612; map pp.188–189. This large wine and spirits shop is located on a quiet street near the Vatican, and has all the Barolos and Chiantis you could want, alongside shelves full of *grappa* and some 2500 labels of liqueurs. See also its *enoteca* (p.262). Mon–Sat 8am–1.30pm, 4–8pm.

★ **Eataly** Piazzale XII Ottobre ❶ 06 9027 9201, ◍ roma .eataly.it; map pp.140–141. A prime example of the resurgence of the Ostiense district, housed in the former air terminal right by Ostiense station (to which it's linked by subway). It's a giant, high-quality artisanal supermarket, more or less, though so much better than that makes it sound, with four floors of food, wine, beer, books, kitchenware and more. The last word in just about every Italian foodstuff and edible product you could think of, and each section has its own eatery, so salivating non-residents can sate their appetites right away. Daily 10am–midnight.

Franchi Via Cola di Rienzo 200 ❶ 06 686 4576; map pp.188–189. One of the best and priciest delis in Rome – a triumph of cheeses, sausages and an ample choice of cold or hot food to go, including delicious *torta rustica* and roast chicken. They'll make up customized lunches for you, and they also have the wines to go with it. Mon–Sat 8.30am–8.30pm.

Gay-Odin Via Stoppani 9 ❶ 06 8069 3023, ◍ gay-odin .it; map pp.170–171. The best Italian chocolate shop in Rome gets its chocolates from its Naples base, changing the recipe slightly to suit the Roman sweet tooth. Mon–Sat 10am–1pm & 4–8pm.

Il Boccione Via del Portico d'Ottavia 1 ❶ 06 687 8637; map pp.54–55. This marvellous tiny kosher Jewish bakery, unmarked but in the heart of the Ghetto, has unforgettable ricotta pies, cornetti, cinnamon biscotti and *pizza giudia* (a hard cake, crammed with dried and candied fruit) that draw quite a crowd. Famously indifferent service. Sun–Thurs 7.30am–7.30pm, Fri 7.30am–3.30pm.

I Dolci di Nonna Vincenza Via Arco del Monte 98/a/b ❶ 06 9259 4322, ◍ dolcinonnavincenza.it; map pp.54–55. Excellent Sicilian pastries from Catania and ice cream too. A superb way to begin the day is with a brioche smeared with pistachio *granita*. There's another location at Piazza Montecitorio 116, but the baking is done here. Friendly staff and a few tables as well. Daily 9am–9pm.

Innocenti Via della Luce 21 ❶ 06 580 3926; map pp.160–161. Trastevere's best *biscottificio*, a family operation for 100 years. Wonderful, chewy *croccantini* – half chocolate, half vanilla, plus *amaretti, brutti ma buoni* (hazelnut biscuits), *straccetti* (almond and hazelnut biscuits) and dozens more varieties. Mon–Sat 9am–1pm & 4–7.30pm, Sun 9am–1pm; closed Aug 15–Sept 15.

Innocenzi Piazza San Cosimato 66 ❶ 06 581 2725; map pp.160–161. Not to be confused with the famed Trastevere *biscotteria*, this is a great dry-goods grocer, with all the usual rice and pasta and Italian goodies but also a large selection of stuff from around the world – tomato ketchup, teas, peanut butter, the works. A good option for homesick expats and foodies alike. Mon–Wed, Fri & Sat 7.30am–1.30pm & 4.30–8pm, Thurs 7.30am–1.30pm.

Ladure Via Borgognona 4 ❶ 06 6994 1625, ◍ laduree .com; map p.93. This French chocolatier set up shop recently in Rome, and is a strong contender for the very best chocolate in the city – though it's maybe better known for its renowned macaroons. Daily 10am–7.30pm.

Moriondo & Gariglio Via del Pie' di Marmo 21–22 ❶ 06 699 0856; map p.38. Just a short walk from the Pantheon, this refined handmade chocolate shop is great for exquisitely wrapped gifts. Mon–Sat 9.30am–1pm & 3.30–7.30pm.

★ **Panella** Via Merulana 54 ❶ 06 487 2435; map pp.114–115. Probably the city's priciest bakery, with fantastic bread and pastries, delicious pizza and a small grocery section. They also do pasta (for example colourful, hat-shaped *sombrerini*, packaged to take home), and have recently added a café, with tables indoors and out, that does a good *aperitivo* hour buffet. Mon–Fri 8am–midnight, Sun 8.30am–1.30pm.

Panificio Arnese Via del Politeama 27; map pp.160–161. This Trastevere *forno* still shovels out authentic Roman everyday bread, *pane casareccia*, crunchy outside and delightfully spongy inside. If you don't need a whole loaf, they'll slice off what you wish. Mon–Sat 9am–8pm.

Peperita Via della Reginella 30 ❶ 347 367 6352; map pp.54–55. Right near the turtle fountain in the Ghetto, this tiny shop opened in 2013 and specializes in hot chili peppers – fresh, in sauces, powdered and in other forms. The owner's Tuscan olive oil is pretty good, too, and priced well. Daily 10.30am–8pm.

Punturi Via Flavia 48 ❶ 06 481 8225; map p.105. One of Rome's many great delis, with a bakery, cheese and cold meat counter, and superb pizza by the slice. Mon–Fri 7.30am–8.15pm, Sat 8.30am–8.15pm.

Regoli Pasticceria Via dello Statuto 60 ❶ 06 487 2812, ◍ pasticceriaregoli.com; map pp.114–115. Generations of Roman families have come to this pastry shop, which still turns out great sweets and pastries and usually is packed. Mon–Sat 9am–7pm.

Roscioli Via dei Giubbonari 21–23 ❶ 06 687 5287; map pp.54–55. First-rate and extremely pricey cheeses and salamis are joined by a surprisingly well-priced and good selection of wine. Their café serves food at lunch and early evening. See also the *Antico Forno Roscioli* bakery nearby at Via dei Chiavari 34 (❶ 06 686 4045). Daily 8.30am–8pm.

Tè e Teiere Tea Shop Via del Pellegrino 85 ❶ 06 686 8824; map pp.54–55. Just steps from Campo de' Fiori, this

20

shop hosts periodic tastings and sells over a hundred varieties of tea, including white, green, black and naturally perfumed. Also stocks teapots, cups and accessories from the Orient and Europe. Mon–Fri 11am–2pm & 4.30–7.30pm.

Totò Via Portico d'Ottavia 2; map pp.54–55. A coffee bar in the Ghetto since 1890, they sell a great coffee blend (Teichner). Ask for a can of ground coffee from the shelf behind the barman. Sun–Fri 7am–9pm.

Trimani Via Goito 20–22 ☎06 446 9661; map pp.114–115. One of the city's largest, best and most historic (since 1821) wine shops, and handily close to Termini if you want to stock up before heading off to the airport. They have a wine bar around the corner, too, with seats for tastings and light fare (see p.269). Mon–Sat 9am–8.30pm.

Un Punto Macrobiotico Via dei Volsci 119/B–121 ☎06 4938 2278; map pp.114–115. This macrobiotic food shop near San Lorenzo (other locations at Cinecittà and Valle Aurelia) also sells soaps and natural cotton T-shirts. Try the self-service café for an economical macrobiotic lunch or early dinner. Mon–Sat 10.30am–7.30pm.

Valzani Via del Moro 37 ☎06 580 3792; map pp.160–161. One of the oldest of the city's confectioners, still keeping up tradition with marvellous *mostaccioli* and *pangiallo* (both are traditional dried fruit and nut honey bars, the former chocolate-covered), *torrone*, *sachertorte* and, at Easter, huge, gift-filled chocolate eggs which you can have your name etched on. Wed–Sun 10am–8.30pm; closed June–Sept 15; extended hours at Christmas & Easter.

★ **Volpetti** Via Marmorata 47 ☎06 574 2352; map pp.140–141. It's worth seeking out this Testaccio deli, which is one of Rome's very best. If you're lucky, one of the staff will give you samples of their truly incredible *mozzarella di bufala*. Volpetti also has its own *tavola calda* round the corner (see p.258). Mon–Sat 8am–2pm & 5–8pm.

HOME AND DESIGN

Arcon Via della Scrofa 104 ☎06 683 3728; map p.38. This sleek, contemporary store is a visual feast for lovers of Italian contemporary furniture design, with lots of easy-to-carry accessories as well as larger pieces. Mon 3.30–7.30pm, Tues–Sat 9am–1pm & 3.30–7.30pm.

Art'e Piazza Rondanini 32 ☎06 683 3907; map p.38. Ultra-modern kitchenware and home furnishings, including lamps, clocks and kitchen utensils and appliances in flashy neon colours and shiny stainless steel. The perfect stylish gift to yourself from Italy. Mon 1–7.30pm, Tues–Sat 9.30am–7.30pm.

Azi Via Manara 7 ☎06 581 8699; map pp.160–161. Anything curiously or cunningly designed for the home is likely to be found here. The owners comb the world for trendy, generally high-tech treasures, and the result is a truly unique shop – in two locations, around the corner from each other in Trastevere. Mon 3.30–7.30pm, Tues–Sat 9.30am–1.30pm & 3.30–7.30pm.

C.U.C.I.N.A. Via Mario de' Fiori 65 ☎06 679 1275; map p.93. A shop filled with modern kitchen appliances, including a large selection of Italian cafetieres. Mon 3.30–7.30pm, Tues–Sat 10am–7.30pm.

De Sanctis Piazza di Pietra 24 ☎06 6880 6850; map p.38. This shop has been selling ceramics since 1890 and their city-centre store offers a slightly classier souvenir than you'll find anywhere else around here. Mon–Sat 10am–1.30pm & 3–7.30pm.

Frette Piazza di Spagna 11 ☎06 679 0673; map p.93. This famous luxury linen shop is happy to fill custom orders and will ship their products anywhere. Mon 3.30–7.30pm, Tues–Sat 9.30am–1.30pm & 3.30–7.30pm.

'Gusto Piazza Augusto Imperatore 7 ☎06 323 6363; map p.93. Everything for the aspiring gourmet: wines, decanters, glasses and kitchen gadgets keep company with a large selection of cookbooks in English. Daily 10.30am–2am.

Il Giardino di Domenico Persiani Via Torino 92 ☎06 488 3886; map pp.114–115. An experience not to be missed – a quiet garden filled to the brim with all sorts of creations in ceramic: everything from glazed tiles to full-sized copies of famous statuary. Pieces made to order. Mon 3.30–7.30pm, Daily 9am–1pm & 3–6pm.

Passamanerie Crocianelli Via dei Prefetti 40 ☎06 687 3592; map p.38. One of Rome's most beautiful selections of ornaments for home furnishings. Don't forget to bring a fabric swatch from home to select the perfect colour cords, tassels, trims or pom-poms to embellish your chair, sofa or curtains. Tues–Sat 9.30am–1pm & 3.30–7.30pm.

Saint Leger Via di Parione 16 ☎06 683 3858; map p.38. Ignore the lacklustre street windows and head inside to this textile shop which has expert service and sensational Italian fabrics for home decorating. Recently they've added a small selection of clothes and accessories too. Mon–Fri 11am–1pm, 4–7pm.

Spazio Sette Via dei Barbieri 7 ☎06 686 9747; map pp.54–55. Designer housewares of all sorts are the speciality here; for decades it's been the shop of choice for Romans who want something chic and stylish for their home or as a gift. Mon 3.30–7pm, Tues–Sat 9.30am–1pm & 3.30–7.30pm.

Le Tele di Carlotta Via dei Coronari 228 ☎06 689 2585; map p.38. Simona hand-embroiders lace finishes on lingerie and linens in this small shop situated among Rome's antique dealers. Mon–Fri 10.30am–1pm & 3.30–7pm.

Yaky Via Santa Maria del Pianto 55 ☎06 6880 7724; map pp.54–55. Quality contemporary and antique Asian crafts and furniture from Japan, Tibet, Mongolia and China.

MUSIC AND VIDEO

Feltrinelli Largo Torre Argentina 18 ☎06 689 3121; map pp.54–55. One of central Rome's largest branches of the nationwide chain, and really more of a bookshop than a music shop, but still with a good selection of CDs and DVDs, and a café upstairs to browse your latest purchases. It has a good English book section, too. There's another branch in the Galleria Alberto Sordi (Mon–Fri 10am–9pm, Sat 10am–10pm, Sun 9am–9pm). Mon–Fri 9am–9pm, Sat 9am–10pm, Sun 10am–9pm.

★ **Soul Food** Via di San Giovanni in Laterano 192–194 ☎06 7045 2025; map pp.130–131. This vinyl junkie's paradise is the city centre's only CD-free zone when it comes to music. Lots of stuff from the 1960s and 1970s, and genuinely enthusiastic staff too. Tues–Sat 10.30am–1.30pm & 3.30–8pm.

PERFUMERIES

Campo Marzio70 Via Vittoria 52 ☎06 979 7739, ⓦcampomarzio70.it; map p.93. Although the original perfume shop is at Piazza della Rotonda 70, this is their new flagship store, where some of the best "noses" arrive from France and far-flung parts of the world. They reckon they can tell the perfect scent for a man or woman as soon as they walk through the door. There's a private room upstairs for the high-rollers. Mon 3–7.30pm, Tues–Sat 10.30am–7.30pm.

Roma-Store Via della Lungaretta 63 ☎06 581 8789; map pp.160–161. Not a football merchandise store but in fact a shop selling classic perfumes – Acqua di Parma, Penhaligons and suchlike – scented soaps, lotions and candles. Only the very finest from Italy, France and England. Mon 4–8pm, Tues–Sat 9.30am–1.30pm & 4–8pm.

20

STATIONERY

Antica Cartotecnica Piazza dei Caprettari 61 ☎06 687 5671; map p.38. Long-running and beautiful pen store near the Pantheon, with lots of new as well as antique models. Mon–Sat 10am–1.30pm & 3–7.30pm.

Campo Marzio Via di Campo Marzio 41 ☎06 6880 7877; map p.38. Part of a chain that has now spread to the UK, this is dedicated to cool, brightly coloured pens and writing accessories, briefcases and pencil cases. Daily 10am–1pm & 2–7pm.

Ditta G. Poggi Via del Gesù 74–75 ☎06 678 4477; map p.38. Fantastic, long-established art materials shop, selling a huge range of specialist paints and accessories, as well as pens, pencils and stationery. Mon–Sat 10am–1pm & 4–7.30pm.

Fabriano Via del Babuino 173 ☎06 3260 0361; map p.93. Fabriano paper from the Marche has been around for hundreds of years and is of the highest quality. This central Rome branch sells bright and contemporary stationery, wallets and briefcases. Mon–Sat 10am–7.30pm.

Il Papiro Via del Pantheon 50 ☎06 679 5597; map p.38. The most central branch of this originally Tuscan chain stocks fine paper and notebooks, as well as the fancy pens to go with them. Daily 10am–8pm.

Stilo Fetti Via degli Orfani 82 ☎06 678 9662; map p.38. Great city-centre pen shop, a tradition since 1893, with lots to choose from and all the major brands – and elegant leather briefcases too. Mon 3.30–7.30pm, Tues–Sat 9am–1pm & 3.30–7.30pm.

MISCELLANEOUS AND GIFTS

Ai Monasteri Corso del Rinascimento 72 ☎06 6880 2783; map p.38. Intriguing cures, jams, spirits, perfumes, honey and even cosmetics among other items made by monks. Mon–Sat 10am–1pm & 3.30–7.30pm, closed Thurs afternoon.

Arkeos Shop Via Quattro Novembre 99 ☎06 6919 0513; map p.64. Archeological reproductions from kitsch to museum quality in this shop, recently take over by a retired police officer with a passion for history and his tour-guide wife. Good reproduction coins make economical "ancient" souvenirs. Daily: April–Oct 9am–7pm; Nov–March 10am–2pm & 3–7pm.

AS Roma Store Piazza Colonna 360 ☎06 6920 0642; map p.93. The best-stocked and most central location for AS Roma merchandise, with the usual shirts, leisurewear and baby-gros. Mon–Sat 10am–6pm.

Becker & Musico Via San Vincenzo 29 ☎06 678 5435; map p.93. This long-established store sells beautiful pipes, inlaid wooden boxes and other lovely handcrafted objects. If you smoke a pipe, hours of fun can be had just lounging around chatting to the guys here about their favourite subject. Tues–Fri 10am–2pm, Sat 10am–7pm.

Carmignani Via della Colonna Antonina 42–43 ☎06 679 5449; map p.38. Even if you don't smoke, you will appreciate the beauty of the handmade pipes, shiny silver cigar holders and cutters and poker sets, in this small shop a few minutes from the Pantheon. Tues–Sat 10am–2pm & 3–7.30pm.

Cesare Diomedi Via E. Orlando 96–97 ☎ 06 488 4822; map pp.114–115. A few minutes' walk from Piazza della Repubblica, two floors filled with luxury leather goods, Versace clocks, Cartier wallets and all sorts of other fancy gifts. Mon–Sat 9am–7.30pm.

Collalti Via del Pellegrino 80a/82 ☎ 06 6880 1084; map pp.54–55. Bicycle-sellers since the nineteenth century. You can purchase new bikes and accessories, get your bike repaired or rent one by the hour or day. Mon–Sat 9am–1pm & 3.30–7pm.

Ferrari Store Via Tomacelli 147–152 ☎ 06 689 2979; map p.93. What better souvenir to take back than an accessory from this Italian motor racing icon? Expensive, but you'll have the latest in both design and technology from pens to desk chairs, as well as the more predictable key rings, T-shirts and cuff links – or test drive a remote-control car. Daily 10am–7.30pm.

★ **Fratelli Alinari** Via Alibert 16a ☎ 06 679 2923, ⓦ alinari.it; map p.93. If you want to know what Rome's piazzas looked like before *McDonald's* came to town, check out the fine selection here of black-and-white photographs of Rome from over 100 years ago. Prices start at around €40. Mon–Sat 3.30–7.30pm.

La Bottega del Marmoraro Via Margutta 53b ☎ 06 320 7660; map p.93. Enrico and Sandro Fiorentini, a father-and-son team, are skilled artisans, creating personalized marble plaques for every occasion, as well as statuary, both ancient and modern reproductions. Mon–Sat 8.30am–7.30pm.

Le Artigiane Via di Torre Argentina 72 ☎ 06 6830 9347; map pp.54–55. Italian artisans – who are often present themselves – sell everything from cashmere to leather and ceramics in this shared space between Largo Argentina and the Pantheon. Also fashion accessories and home design. Daily 10am–7pm.

★ **Old Soccer** Via di Ripetta 30 ☎ 06 321 9448; map p.93. This great shop revels in the past, selling old-fashioned Italian and international football shirts and other nostalgic soccer paraphernalia. Shirts from around €70 – most of which, ironically enough, are made in England. Daily 10am–8pm.

Percossi Papi Atelier Via San Eustachio 16 ☎ 06 6880 1466; map p.38. Housed in an ivy-covered building near the Pantheon, this venerable goldsmith designs his work to flatter the skin tones of the wearer. His necklaces and other pieces have graced stars in major feature films, including Cate Blanchett as Queen Elizabeth I. Tues–Sat 10am–1pm & 4–7pm.

Petrochi Via Margutta 1B ☎ 06 321 5143; map p.93. Long-established jewellers who have counted Audrey Hepburn and Ingrid Bergman among their customers over the years. Visitors today are often intrigued by their small mosaic pieces with Rome scenes, a classy Grand Tour souvenir. Mon 4–7pm, Tues–Sat 10am–1pm & 4–7pm.

Polvere di Tempo Via del Moro 59 ☎ 06 5880 0704; map pp.160–161. For that astrolabe you've always dreamed of, as well as a huge array of ancient and medieval devices for telling the time, stop by this arcane little shop. They also have alchemists' rings that double as sundials and loads more oddities and curiosities. Mon 3.30–8pm, Tues–Sat 10am–1pm & 4–8pm.

Profondo Rosso Store Via dei Gracchi 260 ☎ 06 321 1395, ⓦ profondorossostore.com; map pp.188–189. Horror-film fans flock to director Dario Argento's store, which is dedicated to his own films as well as the genre, with costumes, masks, videos, books (some in English) and various paraphernalia including a stuffed raven. Argento himself makes an appearance every October 31. The basement – or is it dungeon? – has a small museum (€3 admission). Mon–Sat 11am–1pm & 4–7.30pm.

Tempi Moderni Via del Governo Vecchio 108 ☎ 06 687 7007; map p.38. Inexpensive jewellery inspired by Art Deco and other retro styles, along with a few vintage pieces. Daily 10am–7.30pm.

20

MARKETS

Borghetto Flaminio Piazza della Marina 32; map pp.170–171. A partly covered flea market with plenty of knick-knacks, designer clothing and antiques. Rummage alongside Rome's well-heeled shoppers and celebrities.

Sept–July Sun 10am–8pm; entrance €2.

Fontanella Borghese Largo della Fontanella di Borghese; map p.38. A small print and book market off Via del Corso, where you can find expensive antique prints and

---

FOOD MARKETS

Rome's **food markets** are a perfect place to pick up a snack or picnic provisions. The one on Campo de' Fiori is the city's most famous and picturesque, and has been around for the last 400 years. Other central options include: the market between the Termini rail tracks and Piazza Vittorio Emanuele, off Via Lamarmora; Piazza San Cosimato in Trastevere; Piazza dell'Unità in Prati; Piazza Alessandria, east of Villa Borghese; Via Magnagrecia in San Giovanni; and Piazza Testaccio in Testaccio. Most are **open** Mon–Sat 7am–2pm. Check out also Rome's newest covered market, Campagna Amica, on Via San Teodoro, which sells only food produced by local Lazio farmers and is open only Saturday and Sunday.

etchings along with inexpensive reproductions. Mon–Sat 9am–7pm.

Galleria delle Stimmate Largo delle Stimmate 1; map p.38. Mostly household goods, and some jewellery, with some great finds like antique lace, silver serving dishes and old cutlery. Sept–May last Sun of the month 10am–7pm.

La Soffitta Sotto I Portici Piazza Augusto Imperatore ☎ 06 3600 5345; map p.93. Flea market selling a diverse mix of bric-a-brac, jewellery and old records. Sept–July first & third Sun of the month 10am–7pm.

Piazzale Ankara map pp.170–171. Antiques, books and bric-a-brac on this unprepossessing square next door to the Stadio Flaminio. Last Sun of the month 8am–8pm.

Piazza Vittorio Emanuele Between Via Lamarmora and Via Ricasoli; map pp.114–115. The market that used to take place in this square is now over by the Termini railway tracks. One building houses cheap clothes and household goods, the other fresh fruit and veg and other food stalls. Good prices too. Mon–Sat 7am–1pm.

Porta Portese map pp.160–161. Rome's most famous and largest market by far, stretching from Piazza di Porta Portese a mile or so down Via Portuense and into the streets around, with hundreds of stalls selling myriad goods, including antiques, Eastern imports, clothing, carpets, art, tools, appliances, underwear, linens and even puppies. And the brand is expanding: nowadays there's a second Porta Portese market every Sun morning, in Pigneto between Via Togliatti and Via Prenestina (same times). Sun 5am–2pm.

Underground Via Francesco Crispi 96; map p.93. Located in an underground parking garage near Piazza di Spagna, and selling all the usual flea market finds, but with a special section for children's goods. Oct–June first Sun of the month 10.30am–7.30pm.

Via Sannio map pp.130–131. Near San Giovanni metro station, this market sells mostly cheap clothing, bags and trashy jewellery, plus there's an extensive secondhand section at the back. Mon–Fri 9am–1.30pm, Sat 9am–6pm.

20

VILLA BORGHESE BY RISCIO

Sports and outdoor activities

Spectator sports are popular in Italy; the hallowed *calcio*, or football, is far and away the most avidly followed, and tends to overshadow everything else. Rome, with two clubs in the top division (Serie A), is no exception, and football is at the heart of so much of what goes on in the city – just look at the number of people reading sports papers. As for participation in sport, there isn't quite the same compulsion to hit the hell out of a squash ball or sweat your way through an aerobics class after work as there is, say, in Britain or the US. However, the notion of keeping fit is becoming as fashionable here as it is in most European countries, especially when it offers the opportunity to wear the latest designer gear.

21

SPECTATOR SPORTS

Italians are as mad about **sport** as most other European nations, and watching sport, especially **football**, is as valid a part of your holiday in Rome as seeing the sights, whether you catch Roma-Lazio at the Stadio Olimpico or just drop in to a bar to watch a game. And don't forget **rugby**, which galvanises the city when an international match is on almost as much as the football.

FOOTBALL

Teams Rome's two big football teams, AS Roma (Ⓦ asroma.it) and SS Lazio (Ⓦ www.sslazio.it), play on alternate weekends between Sept and May at the Stadio Olimpico, northwest of the city centre. Unsurprisingly, feelings run extremely high between the two teams, and derby games are big – and sometimes violent – occasions. Roma, still captained by the talismanic veteran (and local boy) Francesco Totti, are traditionally the team of the inner-city urban working class, and historically the better of the two sides, while traditionally right-wing Lazio – the team of the outer suburbs – have trailed somewhat over the years. However, after a lot of investment in the team Lazio won the championship in 2000, only to have Roma bounce back in 2001 to take their third *scudetto*. Since then, neither team has been champions but Roma has finished runner-up on several occasions, and it's a breathless rivalry that can go either way when the two sides meet.

Matches Serie A is the top Italian division and the majority of matches take place on Sun afternoons at the Stadio Olimpico (Ⓦ stadiodi.it/olimpico-roma) although games are nowadays staggered across the weekend, between Fri and Mon; Roma and Lazio take turns to play at the Stadio Olimpico so will never both be playing at home the same weekend. Midweek games are rare, although both clubs are often involved in European competitions, which are played on weekday evenings. The Stadio Olimpico is enormous, with a capacity of close to 80,000, and at most games, except perhaps Roma–Lazio clashes, you should be able to get a ticket for all but the cheapest seats. Lazio supporters, who wear blue and white with the eagle symbol, traditionally occupy the Curva Nord end of the ground, where you can sometimes get seats for €15–25 (but the atmosphere can be intimidating and not altogether pleasant); seats in the *distinti* (corners of the ground) or the *tribuna* (along the sides) are more expensive. *Distinti* tickets go for about €25–35, and you

should reckon on paying around €60–150 for a reasonable *tribuna* ticket. Fans of Roma, who wear red and yellow with the symbol of a wolf, occupy the Curva Sud, which is usually completely sold out to season-ticket holders, making a visit to a Roma game a slightly more expensive business, since the cheapest seat you'll find will be in the *distinti*.

Purchasing tickets You can buy tickets through booking agencies on websites such as Ⓦ www.listicket.it, Ⓦ ticket one.it or Ⓦ viagogo.co.uk (who also have a deal with Ⓦ football-italia.net); if the tickets are unavailable to buy online, the agencies will point you to a recognized sales outlet at the stadium or at the AS Roma store in the city centre (see p.294). Bear in mind though that due to crowd trouble you must carry photo ID when you purchase a ticket and when you go to the game.

Getting to the stadium The stadium is located at Piazzale del Foro Italico. On public transport, you can take tram #2 from Piazzale Flaminio to Piazza Mancini or bus #910 from Termini and then walk across the river; alternatively, take bus #32 from Piazza Risorgimento or #271 from Piazza Venezia direct.

RUGBY

For info on Italian rugby current fixtures and tickets, go to Ⓦ federugby.it.

International rugby Since Italy joined the Five Nations (since renamed the Six Nations) tournament over a decade ago, rugby union has grown in popularity, and the national team is followed enthusiastically by a small but committed group of supporters. International matches used to be held at the Stadio Flaminio, Via delle Stadio Flaminio 196, north of the city centre, close to the Auditorium (tram #2 from Piazzale Flaminio runs nearby), although in the last couple of years they have been moved to the much larger Stadio Olimpico – proof, if needed, that interest in Italian rugby is on the rise.

CALCIO IN INGLESE

If you want more information about the **Italian football season** in general, take a look at Ⓦ football-italia.net, which is one of the best and most up-to-date of several English-language websites, with **calcio** fixtures, club details and lots of news, including a summary of the main stories in the Italian sports papers. Others include Ⓦ forzaitalianfootball.com and Ⓦ football italiano.co.uk. If your Italian is good enough, get hold of one of the Italian sports newspapers. They are published daily and inevitably focus heavily on football. The Rome-based *Corriere dello Sport* (Ⓦ corrieredellosport.it) will have details of any upcoming games, as will the other two papers: *Tuttosport* (Ⓦ tuttosport.com) and the pink *Gazzeta dello Sport*, which has an English version of the website (Ⓦ english.gazzetta.it).

National rugby Domestic rugby is mainly confined to the north and central regions of Italy, where teams compete in the National Championship of Excellence. Rome's teams are SS Lazio Rugby 1927 (a sister side to the Lazio football team), who play in Serie A and Fiamme Oro, who play in Serie B.

TENNIS

Rome Masters The massive Foro Italico sports complex (see p.179) by the Stadio Olimpico hosts the Italian Open, or Rome Masters as it's now known, one of the city's biggest annual sporting events, held during the first two weeks of May. Tickets for the final matches sell out several months before the event, but you can get seats for other matches nearer the time from ⓦ internazionalibnlditalia .com or the Foro Italico box office itself (☎ 06 3685 8218).

For more information contact the Federazione Italiana Tennis, Via Eustachio 9 (☎ 06 855 894, ⓦ www .federtennis.it).

RUNNING

The Rome Marathon Rome has one of the most scenic marathon routes in the world. It starts by the Colosseum and heads south to the basilica of San Paolo before going back up the Tiber and skirting the city centre, passing through Prati as far north as Ponte Milvio. It then returns south, heading straight through the heart of the city to end where it began, at the Colosseum. The start/finish is probably the best place to view the race, but there are loads of vantage points and none gets too offputtingly crowded. You can, of course, also take part (see p.301).

PARTICIPATING SPORTS AND ACTIVITIES

There are lots of opportunities to spend time on your favourite **sport** or **hobby** while you're in Rome, whether it's **tennis**, **golf** or just going to the **gym**, and of course there are few more visual places to go for a jog. Time your visit around the Rome Marathon, and you can join a 40km-city sightseeing tour of the city and keep fit at the same time.

GOLF

If you simply can't go a week or two without hitting a ball, it's worth knowing that golf is becoming a popular sport in Italy, aided recently by the success of the country's most famous pro players, the Molinari brothers. Most clubs welcome non-members, but you must be able to produce a membership card from your hometown club. For more information, get in touch with the Federazione Italiana Golf, Viale Tiziano 74 (☎ 06 323 1825, ⓦ federgolf.it).

Circolo del Golf di Roma Aquasanta Via Appia Nuova 716a ☎ 06 780 3407, ⓦ golfroma.it. This year-round, 18-hole golf course is just south of the centre of Rome, not far from the catacombs and Cinecittà. In addition to the par-71 course, there's also a bar, table tennis and an outdoor pool, so plenty to keep non-golfing friends occupied. Green fees range from €80 to €120. Tues–Sun.

Country Club Castel Gandolfo Via Santo Spirito 13, Castel Gandolfo ☎ 06 931 2301, ⓦ countryclub castelgandolfo.it. Situated in Castel Gandolfo, down in the Castelli Romani (see p.220), this is the pope's local course – open year-round, 18 holes, par 72 – and it has excellent facilities, including a restaurant, outdoor pool and bar. Green fees are €65–90. Take the train or bus to Castel Gandolfo. Daily.

GYMS

Farnese Fitness Vicolo delle Grotte 35, near Campo de' Fiori ☎ 06 687 6931, ⓦ farnesefitness.net. This is a decent gym right in the centre of town, with good equipment and lots of regular fitness classes. Entry is €10 per day. Mon–Fri 7am–11pm, Sat 9am–11pm, Sun 9am–2pm.

Fitnext Piazza Mignanelli 23, Piazza di Spagna ☎ 06 679 6003. Very centrally located gym, and one class is included in the fee (€20 per day), including yoga and Pilates. Mon–Fri 8am–10pm, Sat 11am–7pm; closed Aug.

Hard Candy Fitness Via Capo d'Africa 5, Celio ☎ 06 7049 0452, ⓦ hardcandyfitnessroma.it. Madonna's fitness club franchise has opened a couple of locations in the centre of Rome; this one is very near the Colosseum, and there is another in the residential district of Parioli (Viale Romania 4; ☎ 06 807 5577). Daily 7am–11pm.

Roman Sport Center Viale del Galoppatoio 33, Villa Borghese ☎ 06 320 1667, ⓦ romansportcenter.com. Rome's largest, oldest and most prestigious fitness centre, in Villa Borghese, has a host of offerings, including Olympic-sized pools, squash courts and hydromassage and saunas. Entry is €26 per day. Mon–Fri 7am–10.30pm, Sat 7am–8.30pm, Sun 9am–3pm.

HORSERIDING

Il Galoppatoio Viale del Galoppatoio 23 ☎ 06 322 6797. This riding club offers expensive lessons in an idyllic atmosphere in the heart of Villa Borghese – take the metro to Spagna and follow the signs to Villa Borghese. Lessons last an hour but you have to sign up for ten (around €150). Tues–Sat 9am–7pm, Sun till 1pm.

Maneggio Cavalieri dell'Appia Antica, Via dei Cerceni 15 ☎ 06 780 1214, ⓦ cavalieriappia.altervista.org. Only group bookings are taken at Maneggio, where you'll pay around €25 each for a gentle 1hr trot. Tues–Sun: summer 9am–1pm & 4–7pm; winter 9am–1pm & 3–6pm.

SPLASHING OUT: ROME'S HOTEL POOLS

Hotel swimming pools are relatively rare in Rome, especially in the centre, and not surprisingly the hotels that have them are generally five star. However if you're not willing – or able – to splash out on a fancy room, you can still cool off in one of the hotel pools listed below, though facilities may only be available in restricted hours, and **entrance fees** to non-guests are fairly hefty. You should reckon on paying €20–25 for a half-day, €40–50 for a full day, and more if you opt for one of the spa treatments that are often available.

One of Rome's prettiest, most secluded pools is at the **Aldrovandi Palace** (see p.235) on the northern edge of Villa Borghese. Surrounded by lush foliage, it's large enough for a good swim. Nearby is the **Parco dei Principi**, Via Frescobaldi 5 (📞06 854 421, 🌐parcodeiprincipi.com), whose 25m pool, set in a garden edged by umbrella pines, is close enough to the zoo that you can hear the lions roar at late-afternoon feeding time. More centrally, the **Radisson Blu Es** (see p.233) has a lovely rooftop pool that's open from noon until 8pm, and the **Exedra** (see p.233) nearby stays true to the area's ancient function as the Baths of Diocletian, with an outdoor pool that's close to the bar and restaurant and has a view over the rooftops beyond the square, though it's really designed for a cooling soak rather than a vigorous swim; there's also a spa.

On Via Veneto, the **Westin Excelsior** (see p.232) has a small indoor pool, set among Neoclassical columns intended to suggest the baths of ancient Rome; spa treatments are available, as well as a jacuzzi, steam bath, sauna and gym. Near the Colosseum, the functional **Mercure Roma Delta Colosseo**, Via Labicana 144 (📞06 770 021, 🌐mercure.com), has uninspired decor and caters to tour groups, but its rooftop pool features a bar and has good views of the ancient arena. Across the Tiber, the **Roma Cavalieri** (see p.235) has lovely gardens and three swimming pools – two of them outdoor – which are about as good as they get in Rome. West of the Vatican, along Via Aurelia Antica, the **Crowne Plaza St Peter's** (see p.236) has a 25m outdoor pool and spa with a small indoor pool and gym, and is open fairly late in the evening. Deep enough for a good swim, the black-tiled pool at **Black Hotel** (see p.236), has free morning shuttles to and from metro Ottaviano. North towards Trastevere, the newcomer to Rome's pool scene is the **Gran Meliá Rome** (see p.234), which has a secluded outdoors pool by a lovely garden while, further up the Janiculum Hill, the **Grand Hotel del Gianicolo** (see p.234) features a curvaceous mosaic-tiled outdoor swimming pool to keep visitors from plunging into the nearby seventeenth-century fountain.

SWIMMING

If you feel like cooling off on a hot summer's day, a dip in a swimming pool may be the perfect cure. Unfortunately, most of Rome's pools are privately run and can be quite expensive, especially in hotels (see box above), though there are a couple of affordable public pools, and you can also use the pools in some gyms (see p.299). If you fancy a spot of real pampering it's worth booking a day at a hotel spa.

Centro Sportivo Jolly Via Concesio Prima Porta 📞06 3361 3375, 🌐jollysportingclub.it. Sports club in the north of the city that has both indoor and outdoor pools. Open all year and sessions cost €10–12 per person. Indoor pool Mon–Fri 8.30am–9.45pm, Sat 8.30am–5.15pm, Sun 9am–1.45pm; outdoor pool June–Aug 9.30am–7pm.

Oasi di Pace Via degli Eugenii 2, Appia 📞06 718 4550, 🌐ct-oasidipace.it. The "Oasis of Peace" sports club is just off the Via Appia and has an open-air pool that makes for a wonderfully atmospheric place to take a dip, as well as spa treatments. Cost is a flat fee of €10 per day. June–Sept daily 9.30am–6pm.

OS Pool Via delle Terme di Traiano 4a, Monti 📞06 4891 9876, 🌐osclub.it. This upscale Monti-based restaurant/café/private club sets up a lovely temporary open-air swimming pool right by the Colosseum during the summer months. Obligatory temporary membership costs €25; entry is €20 a day on weekdays, €25 a day on weekends (half days €15 and €20 respectively). Late July to Sept daily 10am–7pm.

Piscina delle Rose Viale America 20, EUR 📞06 5422 0333, 🌐piscinadellerose.it. Down in EUR, and easily reachable on metro line B, this is Rome's largest public pool, accessible at a rate of €14 per half-day, €16 per day. Mid-May to Sept Mon–Fri 10am–10pm. Sat & Sun 9am–7pm.

TENNIS

Centro Sportivo Jolly Via Concesio Prima Porta 📞06 3361 3375, 🌐jollysportingclub.it. A large sports and fitness centre in the north of the city with swimming pools and various gyms, and where you can also hire outdoor tennis courts in spring and summer for €10–12 an hour.

Oasi di Pace Via degli Eugenii 2 ☎06 718 4550, ⓦct-oasidipace.it. South of the centre of Rome, just off the Via Appia and near the Aquasanta golf course (see p.299), this big sports club has courts for €10–12 per hour. Daily 8am–8pm.

RUNNING

Jogging on the roads in Rome when there is no official race on is impossible, and sometimes even dangerous, due to the traffic and congestion, but luckily there are plenty of green spaces to escape the traffic. The most popular is Villa Borghese, where there are plenty of places to jog, including the Piazza di Siena, a grass horse-track in the centre of the park. Other good options include the Villa Ada, a lush and vast green space north of the city centre, which has a running track, and the Villa Doria Pamphilj above Trastevere, which offers nice paths with exercise stations along the way. For more central – and public – jogging, the Circus Maximus is the perfect size and shape, though it does sometimes feel like you're jogging around a vast traffic roundabout.

The Rome Marathon (ⓦwww.maratonadiroma.it) circles around the city's most famous monuments on the third Sun in March, and is a nice opportunity to run through the city centre free of cars and crazy drivers. It starts and finishes on Via dei Fori Imperiali and the course follows the river, going as far north as the Ponte Milvio and as far south as the Basilica di San Paolo. If you're not up for a full marathon, or even anything like it, it's worth knowing that there's also a 4km fun run through the Centro Storico on the same day.

The Rome–Ostia Half Marathon is held every Feb/March (ⓦromaostia.it) and the route goes from EUR in the south of the city to the seafront in the heart of Ostia Lido.

The Roma–Appia 14k takes place at the end of April (ⓦappiarun.it) and takes you past all the sights of the Appian Way.

Kids' Rome

Italians love children. Don't be surprised by how much attention people pay them here: peeking into strangers' buggies and cheek-pinching are quite normal, as is helping lug pushchairs up steps and giving up a seat for parents and their children on public transport. That said, though there have been significant improvements of late, Rome has a surprisingly limited number of activities specifically geared towards children. Luckily, just touring the sights of Rome might be enough – there are plenty of things that will appeal to kids of all ages, from sights specifically targeted at children, such as the Explora museum for children, to the perennially popular sites of ancient Rome.

This city is in many ways a natural one for kids: there are lots of open spaces, squares and pedestrian areas for just dashing about and playing, and some of the sights can really appeal to a younger audience. For ancient sites, it's worth getting hold of one of the *Rome Then and Now* book with overlay transparencies that are available in most tourist shops: they can work wonders to bring piles of weathered stones to life. Hopping on and off one of the many **open-top bus tours** (see p.25) can be a fun introduction to the highlights, and some of the sights in between have a special appeal – **Castel Sant'Angelo** and its dungeons (see p.186), the **Colosseum** (where you'll always find a gladiator or two; see p.87), throwing coins into the **Trevi Fountain** (see p.100) and of course sticking a hand in the **Bocca della Verità** and daring to tell a fib (see p.72). There are also a handful of attractions aimed at children, notably the **Explora museum for children** (see p.305); the **Time Elevator** (see p.306); and the city centre's largest park, the **Villa Borghese** (see p.168), which has rowing boats and bikes. On the park's northeastern side, there's also the Bioparco or **city zoo** (see p.303) – as well as plenty of open space for little ones to let off steam. There are always **shops** if you're desperate, but if it's hot and you're having a hellish time in the city itself, it might just be best to get away for a **day-trip**, perhaps to a beach (see p.222); a quiet town, such as Bracciano (see p.219); the ancient port of Ostia Antica (see p.214); Tivoli (see p.211), with its villa and Roman site; the Renaissance play park of Parco dei Mostri (see p.304); or one of the sites out of Rome listed in this chapter (see p.250).

22

ESSENTIALS

Babysitting If you simply have to have a break from the kids for a day or an evening, English-speaking babysitters are available through Angels, Via dei Fienili 98 (☎06 678 2877 or ☎338 667 9718, ☜web.tiscali.it/angelsstaff).

Food Eating out with kids in Rome is easy – the numerous pasta and pizza options ensure that there's something for even the fussiest of eaters, while relaxed waiting staff go out of their way to charm and amuse the kids. If the menu fails to offer anything suitable, the kitchen is almost always willing to rustle you up a plate of plain spaghetti with butter or parmesan. And if you're on the go, you can always head to the nearest *gelateria*, or grab a slice of juicy pizza to keep them quiet.

Transport Rome is a reasonably kid-friendly city when it comes to getting around: children under 10 travel free on all public transport, and there are lots of streets and squares that enable you to plan a fairly traffic-free route across the city centre. If you've got very small children, a pushchair or buggy isn't much help and can be a positive hindrance, given the number of steps, cobbles, and – most irritatingly – scooter-jammed kerbs and pavements.

Information If you speak Italian, you may find website ☜romaperbambini.it a useful resource for kids' activities in the city.

PARKS AND OUTDOOR ACTIVITIES

CITY CENTRE

Bioparco Via del Giardino Zoologico, Villa Borghese ☎06 360 8211, ☜bioparco.it. Rome's zoo, on the northern edge of Villa Borghese (see p.168), is a large, typical city-centre offering, recently much improved and reinvented as the "Bioparco", focusing on conservation and education yet still providing the usual animals kids are after, including tigers, apes, giraffes, elephants, hippos, a separate reptile house and a new colony of lemurs. The Museo di Zoologia next door (see p.305) has also been revamped. Tram #3 runs around the city centre to the northern side of Villa Borghese via the Bioparco. Adults €12.50, children over 1m tall €10.50, under 1m free. Daily: April–Oct 9.30am–6pm (till 7pm Sat & Sun April–Sept); Nov–March 9.30am–5pm. Bus #910 from Termini or #63 from Piazza Venezia to Museo Borghese and a ten-minute walk; without a walk, tram #3 from Policinico Umberto or tram #19 from Piazzale Flaminio.

Janiculum Hill High up on the Janiculum, this park is a good place to keep kids amused, with pony rides, carousels, balloon-sellers and puppet shows, while adults enjoy a great view of the city below. The puppet shows (see box, p.305), are top-notch and kids can choose to take their favourite character home with them from the colourful selection on sale. You might want to time your visit to coincide with the daily firing of the cannon at noon (see p.166).

Orto Botanico Via Corsini. A peaceful oasis in the heart of Trastevere, the city's botanical gardens have palm-lined paths, fountains, a meandering rose garden, towering bamboo patches and lush greenhouses to keep the kids amused for a while. The benches and paths around the Fountain of Tritons, near the entrance, are a meeting-place for local mothers, nannies and toddlers (see p.162). Adults €4, 6–11yrs €2, under-6s free. Tues–Sat 9.30am–6.30pm.

22

PIAZZAS, PLAYGROUNDS AND PUSSYCATS

Rome's abundant **piazzas,** with their cobbled expanses, fountains and cafés, are often just as much fun for kids to run around in as playgrounds – especially in the early evening when everyone's out for a stroll and the street sellers and buskers liven things up even more. **Piazza Santa Maria** in Trastevere (see p.158) is always an energetic place, as are **Piazza di Spagna** (see p.94) and **Piazza Navona** (see p.42) – which has the added attraction of two toy shops (see p.306). **Villa Borghese** (see p.168), **Villa Sciarra** (see below), **Villa Ada** (see p.181) and **Villa Celimontana** (see p.129) all have **playgrounds**; there are also very good play areas in **Piazza Vittorio Emanuele** (see p.120), **Piazza Santa Maria Liberatrice** in Testaccio (see p.143) and **Piazza San Cosimato** in Trastevere (see p.158).

The city's **cat colonies** are usually a big hit with kids – check out the one at **Largo di Torre Argentina** (see p.157) where cat-spotting among the ancient ruins is a popular pastime. At the cat sanctuary alongside, kids can get up close to some of the inhabitants that are up for adoption. The volunteers who look after the cats here are always happy to show you round, and they also take care of other colonies around the city – ones to visit are those at **Piazza Vittorio Emanuele** (see p.120) and around the **Piramide Cestia** in Testaccio (see p.145). Find out more at ⓦromancats.com.

Villa Borghese This huge park offers plenty of entertainment for young ones. Enter at the northern side, via the Viale delle Belle Arti entrance, to find pony rides, a children's train, swings and paddleboats on the lake – which comes complete with a Greek temple. On the southern side of the park, the Pincio Gardens have a playground and carousels and places to hire bikes or a *risciò*, the latter particularly good fun for families (see p.168).

Villa Celimontana Up on the Celian Hill, these public gardens have nice views over the river, a playground and pony rides (see p.129).

Villa Doria Pamphilj Main entrance on Via di San Pancrazio. A 10min walk east from the Janiculum Hill, Rome's largest park is a great place for kids to let off steam – more like real countryside in parts, it's the perfect walking, cycling or picnic spot and has a pretty lake filled with basking turtles and surrounded by woods (see p.166).

Villa Sciarra Entrances on Via Calandrelli and Viale delle Mura Gianicolensi. A little way to the south of the Janiculum Hill, this small park is a bit out of the way but has a lovely little playground, though the adjacent aviary has seen better days and is now populated largely by pigeons. Tram #8 from Piazza Venezia to Viale Trastevere.

BEYOND ROME

Aquafelix Via Terme di Traiano, Civitavecchia, 80km northwest of Rome ☎0766 32221, ⓦaquafelix.it. Situated on the edge of Civitavecchia, this is one of the most popular waterparks near the capital, and isn't too hard to reach on public transport – there are regular trains to Civitavecchia from Termini, and a bus from the station to the park at 10.10am and 11.10am, returning at 6.10pm. Adults €20, children €17.50. June–Sept daily 10am–6.30pm.

Aquapiper Via Maremmana Inferiore 29.3km, Guidonia, about 30km from Rome ☎0774 326538, ⓦaquapiper.it. This very well-equipped waterpark not far from Tivoli has loads of rides, including the biggest wave machine in Europe, and is perfect for restoring sight-fatigued families. But avoid summer weekends when it can get very busy. Metro B to Ponte Mammolo, then the Roma–Palombara bus (every 50min) to the park, or in summer there are sometimes special buses laid on from Piazza della Repubblica and Piazzale Ostiense (check the website for details). Adults €16 (Sun €20), children 11–15yrs €6, 0–10yrs free. Daily 9am–9pm.

Parco dei Mostri Località Giardino, Bomarzo, 93km north of Rome ☎0761 924 029, ⓦbomarzo.net. "The Park of Monsters" is basically a garden but with crazy sculptures, weird buildings and surreal conceits that make it one of north Lazio's top tourist attractions. You can get to Bomarzo by bus from Viterbo, which in turn is easily reached by train from either Stazione San Pietro or the Laziale platform at Termini. Adults €9, 4–8yrs €7, under-4s free. Daily 8am–sunset.

Villa Ada This is a large, beautiful park just north of the city with plenty to keep youngsters amused, including a roller-skating rink, bike paths, two playgrounds and ponds (see p.181).

Zoomarine Via Zara Torrevaianica ☎06 9153 4001, ⓦzoomarine.it. A marine park with all the usual dolphins, seals, penguins and the rest, along with a handful of waterpark attractions. Morning shuttle buses run from Rome Termini and EUR Palasport metro station, or you can take the train to Lido di Ostia and then a bus. Adults €25, children €18, children under 1m free. Daily: April & Sept, check website for hours; May 10am–5pm, closed Mon; June 10am–6pm; July & Aug 10am–7pm.

MUSEUMS AND ATTRACTIONS

Castel Sant'Angelo Lungotevere Castello 50 ⓦcastelsantangelo.com. Along with the Colosseum, this is one of the most exciting of the city's ancient monuments for kids. Through the centuries, Hadrian's mausoleum has served as a papal escape route in times of trouble and the city's prison; it has all the grisly, dungeon-like spookiness you'd expect from such a history, and a wide, spiral ramp leading to the mausoleum itself adds to the atmosphere. There are also great views over the city from the top (see p.186). Adults €10.50, children free. Tues–Sun 9am–7.30pm.

Colosseum Piazza del Colosseo. Advance tickets at ⓦticketclic.it. Loaded with atmosphere given its setting as the stage for many a grisly end for both humans and beasts, Rome's most famous ancient monument can't fail to capture kids' imaginations (see p.87). Adults €12, under-18 EU citizens free, non-EU €7.50. Daily: Mid-Feb to mid-March 8.30am–4pm; mid- to end March 8.30am–4.30pm; April–Aug 8.30am–6.15pm; Sept 8.30am–6pm; Oct 8.30am–5.30pm; Nov to mid-Feb 8.30am–3.30pm.

Explora – Museo dei Bambini di Roma Via Flaminia 82 ☎06 361 3776, ⓦmdbr.it. Geared towards kids under 12, this learn-as-you-play centre aims to teach children about themselves and the world they live in through hands-on activities. It's all laid out in the form of a small city and there's also plenty of purely fun stuff, such as a puppet theatre and a playground. Tram #2 or a short walk from Piazzale Flaminio. Adults and children over 3 €7, 1–3yrs €3, 0–1yrs free. Timed entry for 1hr 45min slots: Tues–Sun at 10am, noon, 3pm & 5pm (Aug no 10am slot); advance booking recommended.

Museo della Civiltà Romana & Planetario Piazza Agnelli 10 ☎06 0608, ⓦmuseociviltaromana.it. This museum has lots of stuff that will interest ancient Rome-addicted kids, among them replicas of the city's famous statues and buildings as well as more everyday artefacts. But the real favourite is the museum's scale model of Rome in the time of Constantine, which takes up a whole room. On the same site, there's also a planetarium and astronomy exhibition, but it's not as thrilling as you'd expect and audio shows are only in Italian. Metro line B to EUR Fermi. €8.50, or €9.50 including planetarium & astronomy exhibition, children up to age 6 free. Museum Tues–Sun 9am–2pm, Planetarium Mon–Fri 9am–2pm, Sat & Sun 9am–7pm, sometimes during later during July & Aug; call ☎06 06 08 to reserve a seat for the planetarium – advisable at weekends.

Museo di Zoologia Via Aldrovandi 18 ☎06 6710 9270, ⓦwww.museodizoologia.it. Located next to the Bioparco (see p.303), this museum has a permanent exhibit – Animals and their Habitats – in one wing, while a variety of stuffed animals fill the older part of the museum, though sadly labels are in Italian only. Bus #910 from Termini or #63 from Piazza Venezia to Museo Borghese and a 15min walk; without a walk, take tram #3 from Policinico Umberto or tram #19 from Piazzale Flaminio. Adults €6, under-18s free. Tues–Sun 9am–7pm.

22

PUPPETRY AND FILMS

Puppetry has been **delighting Italian children** for hundreds of years, and Rome has a few venues for viewing puppeteers in action. Sometimes you can find a show in English, but the storyline is visually explanatory and kids don't seem to care whether they understand the words or not. Most films will be dubbed into Italian, but occasionally you can find one showing in the original language and there's also the excellent children's cinema in the Villa Borghese.

PUPPET SHOWS

Teatro di Pulcinella Piazza Giuseppe Garibaldi, Trastevere ☎06 582 7767. This is said to be one of only two places left in Rome to view true puppeteers. Usually puts on Punch & Judy shows. Free, although a small donation is expected. Sat & Sun mornings at 10am–1pm & 4–7pm.

Teatro San Carlino Viale dei Bambini, Pincio Villa Borghese ☎06 6992 2117, ⓦsancarlino.it. Newer than the Teatro Verde (see p.168), this theatre puts on regular weekend shows for kids throughout the year. Adults €9, children under 14 €7.

Teatro Verde Circonvallazione Gianicolense 10, Trastevere ☎06 588 2034, ⓦteatroverde.it. Located just by Trastevere station, this children's theatre puts on weekend musicals and marionette shows as well as plays. Train to Trastevere from Termini or Ostiense, or bus #H from Termini or Piazza Venezia. Family tickets €9. Shows Sat & Sun at 5pm.

CINEMA

Cinema dei Piccoli Viale della Pineta 15, on the Via Veneto side of Villa Borghese ☎06 855 3485, ⓦwww.cinemadeipiccoli.it. Almost opposite the Casa del Cinema, this is not only the smallest public cinema in the world, with just 63 seats, but also one of the oldest, in business since 1934. Showings Wed–Fri at 5pm & 6.30pm & weekends at 3.30pm, 5pm & 6.30pm.

LA BEFANA

There are many stories about **La Befana**, always depicted as an ugly old woman who flies along on a broom draped in black. The most recognized version is that she was outside sweeping when three kings walked by; she stopped them and asked where they were going. The kings responded that they were following a star in search of a newborn baby. They invited her to come along, but she declined, saying she had too much sweeping and cleaning to do. When she found out who it was the kings were off to find, her regret for not having joined them was so great that she has spent eternity rewarding good children with presents and sweets and bad children with pieces of coal on the day of Epiphany, **January 6**. Each year, from early December until this day, Piazza Navona sets up the **Befana toy fair**, where endless stalls tempt children with every sort of sticky sweet and even chunks of black sugar made to look like coal. There are also toy stands and manger scenes where children leave letters for La Befana, asking her for specific presents and toys.

Ostia Antica Viale dei Romagnoli, Ostia Antica ☎ 06 563 50215, ⓦ ostia-antica.org. Every bit as atmospheric and mesmerizing as Pompeii, the ruins of Rome's ancient port, Ostia, will give kids a great feel for what a Roman city was like. It's a must-see for any child who's read *The Thieves of Ostia*, the first in the *Roman Mysteries* series by Caroline Lawrence, in which a sea captain's daughter solves a mystery in 79 AD. Metro B to Piramide and then a 25min train from Porta San Paolo on the Lido di Ostia line. €10. Mid-Feb to mid-March Tues–Sun 8.30am–5pm; late March Tues–Sun 8.30am–5.30pm; April–Sept Tues–Sun 8.30am–7pm; Oct Tues–Sun 8.30am–6.30pm; Nov to mid-Feb Tues–Sun 8.30am–4.30pm; last admission 1hr before closing (Museo Ostiense same hours but opens at 10.30am).

Time Elevator Via dei SS. Apostoli 20 ☎ 06 6992 1823, ⓦ time-elevator.it. Flight-simulator seats and headphones (English audio available) set the stage for a virtual tour of three thousand years of Roman history: an excellent way to prime the kids (not to mention their parents) for the sights they will be seeing. Adults €12, children 5–12yrs €9; not suitable for under-5s. Daily 10.30am–7.30pm; shows every hour, lasting 45min.

SHOPS: BOOKS, TOYS AND CLOTHING

Al Sogno Piazza Navona 53, Centro Storico ☎ 06 686 4198, ⓦ alsogno.com; map p.38. Perfectly located at the north end of Piazza Navona, with two floors of cuddly toys, handmade dolls, board games and replicas of Roman soldiers. Mon–Sat 9.30am–1pm & 3.30–7.30pm (closed Mon morning).

Benetton Via Cesare Battisti 129–131, Prati ☎ 06 6992 4010, ⓦ benetton.com; map pp.188–189. Just one of several locations of this famous Italian chain that sells clothes for children and adults. This one conveniently has a children's hairdresser on the second floor. Mon–Sat 9.30am–1pm & 3.30–7.30pm (closed Mon morning).

Bertè Piazza Navona 108, Centro Storico ☎ 06 687 5011, ⓦ bertegiocattoli.it; map p.38. One of Rome's oldest toy stores at the other end of the piazza from Al Sogno (see above), with toys for children of all ages. Mon–Sat 9.30am–1pm & 3.30–7.30pm (closed Mon morning).

Città del Sole Via della Scrofa 66, Centro Storico ☎ 06 6880 3805, ⓦ cittadelsole.it; map p.38. This shop sells toys, games and books for kids in a great central location. Mon 3.30–7.30pm, Tues–Sat 11am–1.30pm.

Giunti al Punto Piazza Santi Apostoli 59/62, Trevi ☎ 06 6994 1045, ⓦ giuntialpunto.it; map p.64. This is a fantastic specialist kids' bookshop, mainly Italian but with a small stock of books in foreign languages, as well as DVDs, puzzles and games. Tues–Sat 9.30am–7.30pm, Sun 10.30am–1pm & 4–7.30pm.

IANA Via Cola di Rienzo 182, Prati ☎ 06 6889 2668; map pp.188–189. Popular Italian chain store offering moderately priced kids' clothes. Really nice selection and quality, from babywear to early teens. Mon–Sat 10am–1.30pm & 3.30–7.30pm (closed Mon morning).

La Cicogna Via Frattina 138, Tridente ☎ 06 679 1912 and Via Cola di Rienzo 268, Prati ☎ 06 689 6557, ⓦ lacicognafrettolosa.com; map p.93. From newborns to adolescents, these outlets of the stylish national chain ("The Stork") carries designer everything for kids and maternity wear as well, though the clothes are not cheap. Mon–Sat 10.30am–7.30pm, Sun 11am–7pm.

Little Big Town Via Cesare Battisti 108, Piazza Venezia ☎ 06 6992 4226, ⓦ littlebigtown.it; map p.64. Just off Piazza Venezia, this is billed as one of the largest toy shops in Italy, but in reality it's relatively modest. However, it's hard to imagine that your little ones won't find something they like. Daily 10am–8pm.

Marina Menasci Via del Lavatore 87, Trevi ☎ 06 678 1981; map p.93. Toy store selling exclusively wooden toys, in a great location a few steps from the Trevi Fountain. Mon–Sat 9.30am–1pm & 3.30–7.30pm (closed Mon morning).

STATUE OF BEARDED DIONYSUS, CENTRALE MONTEMARTINI

Contexts

308 History

319 Architecture

322 Writing on Rome

332 Books and films

338 Language

History

The history of Rome is almost the history of the Western world, and as such is hard to encapsulate in a potted guidebook form. Inevitably the best we can do here is provide the basic framework. However, knowing at least some Roman history is crucial to an understanding of the city – its sights and monuments are often interconnected and will mean much more if you have a basic grasp of the continuum of events and their relationship to each other. We've tried to contextualize as much of the information in the guide as possible, but we recommend you take a look at some of the historical texts we list in "Books and films", pp.332–337.

Beginnings

No one knows precisely when Rome was founded, though excavations on the Palatine Hill have revealed the traces of an **Iron Age** village dating back to the ninth or eighth century BC. The **legends** relating to Rome's earliest history tell it slightly differently. Rhea Silvia, a Vestal Virgin and daughter of a local king, Numitor, had twin sons – the product, she alleged, of a rape by Mars. They were supposed to be sacrificed to the gods but instead the two boys were abandoned and found by a wolf, which nursed them until their adoption by a shepherd, who named them **Romulus and Remus**. Later they laid out the boundaries of the city on the Palatine Hill (after arguing as to its exact location Remus chose the Aventine Hill and Romulus the Palatine Hill, and the latter won), but it soon became apparent that there was only room for one ruler, and, unable to agree on the signs given to them by the gods, they quarrelled, Romulus killing Remus and becoming the city's first ruler, in 753 BC.

Whatever the truth of this, there's no doubt Rome was an obvious spot to build a city: the Palatine and Capitoline hills provided security, and there was, of course, the River Tiber, which could be easily crossed here by way of the Isola Tiberina, making this a key location on the trade routes between the neighbouring regions of Etruria and Campania.

The Etruscans

The **Etruscans** dominated Etruria – the area of Italy from the northern part of the peninsula as far south as Rome. Little of their history is known, but their language was of non-Indo-European origin, the architecture that survives is almost exclusively that of tombs, and their art has a particular and personal quality quite unlike that of the Romans or even the Greeks. Long before other Italic tribes, they took the important steps towards creating central urban nuclei, with twelve city-states, and at the height of their civilization in the sixth century BC one of their greatest cities, Cerveteri (or Caere) had a population of over 25,000. Rome may or may not have been

8th century BC	753 BC	509 BC	509 BC–82 BC
First Iron Age settlement on Palatine Hill	Romulus assumes power in Rome	End of reign of Tarquinius Superbus – and of Rome as a kingdom.	Period of the Roman Republic

an Etruscan town, but the Etruscans' influence on the kingdom of Rome was very strong, and three of its legendary seven kings were Etruscan, the first being **Tarquinius Priscus** (616–579 BC). Under his rule, Rome began to develop as a city: the first buildings of the Forum were raised, the rudiments of the city's sewerage and water system – the Cloaca Maxima – were put in place, and the walls of the Capitoline Hill were built. Rich finds from this period include the contents of the Regolini-Calassi tomb, displayed in the Vatican museum, and there are numerous artefacts from all over northern Lazio in the city's marvellous Villa Giulia. Although the Romans finally overcame the Etruscans and obliterated much of their history, it is likely that the Etruscan influence on Rome continued long into the Republic – indeed it was an Etruscan soothsayer, Spurinna, who warned Julius Caesar about the Ides of March.

The Roman Republic

Rome as a kingdom lasted until about 509 BC, when the people rose up against the last, tyrannical Etruscan monarch, **Tarquinius Superbus**. Tarquinius was a brutal, unpopular ruler, but the crunch came when his son, Sextus, raped a Roman noblewoman, Lucretia. She committed suicide shortly afterwards, and her husband, along with one Lucius Junius Brutus, helped to lead an uprising that led eventually to the establishment of a **Republic** – a reaction, basically, against the autocratic rule of the Etruscan monarchs. The Roman Republic was to last nearly five hundred years, and was a surprisingly modern and democratic form of government, based on the acknowledged fact that the fates of the Roman people and its patrician classes were inextricably bound up together. (The acronym SPQR, which you still see everywhere, stands for "Senatus Populusque Romanus" or "The Roman Senate and People" – or as the French cartoon character Obelix would have it "Sono Pazzi Questi Romani": "These Romans are crazy".) The **Senate** represented the patrician families, and elected two consuls from their number to lead Rome – in itself a forward-thinking act after years of absolute rule – while the people were allowed to elect two tribunes to represent their interests, even vetoing the appointment of senators they disagreed with. The city prospered under the Republic, growing greatly in size and subduing the various tribes of the surrounding areas – the Volsci and Etruscans to the north, the Sabines to the east, the Samnites to the south. The Etruscans were finally beaten in 474 BC, at the battle of Cumae, and the Volsci and Sabines soon afterwards. Rome later drew up its first set of laws, in 451 BC, inscribing them on bronze tablets and displaying them prominently in the Forum – by now the city's most important central space.

The expanding empire

Despite a heavy defeat by the **Gauls** in 390 BC, when they took the entire city except for the Capitoline Hill (a night assault was reputedly foiled by the cackling of sacred geese kept on the hill which woke the besieged soldiers), by the following century Rome had begun to extend its influence beyond the boundaries of what is now mainland Italy, pushing south into Sicily and across the ocean to Africa and Carthage. In the meantime Rome was also trying to subdue the **Samnites**, who occupied most of the land in the southern part of what is now Italy, waging wars on and off between 343 BC and 290 BC that led eventually to the Romans occupying most of the region that is

474 BC	264 BC	146 BC	87–82 BC
Defeat of the Etruscans	First Punic war	Defeat of Carthage	Civil war in Rome

now Campania, south of Rome. Beyond mainland Italy, the next hundred years or so were taken up by the **Punic Wars**, against **Carthage**, the other dominant force in the Mediterranean at the time, and really the only thing standing between Rome and total dominance of the region. The First Punic War, fought over Sicily, began in 264 BC and continued for around twenty years until Carthage surrendered all rights to the island, while the Second Punic War was famously started in 218 BC by Hannibal's march across the Alps by elephant, and ended, after years of skirmishes in southern Italy, in 202 BC. By the time Rome had fought and won the Third Punic War, in 146 BC, it had become the dominant power in the Mediterranean, subsequently taking control of present-day Greece and the Middle East, and expanding north, also, into what is now France, Germany and Britain.

Domestic turmoil

Domestically, the Romans built **roads** – notably the Via Appia, which dates back to 312 BC and was built as a means of moving troops around during the Samnite wars – and developed their civic structure, with new laws and far-sighted political reforms, one of which cannily brought all of the Republic's vanquished enemies into the fold as **Roman citizens**. However, the history of the Republic was also one of internal strife, marked by factional fighting among the patrician ruling classes, as everyone tried to grab a slice of the riches that were pouring into the city from its plundering expeditions abroad – and the ordinary people, or plebeians, enjoying little more justice than they had under the Roman monarchs. In 87 BC, a power struggle between two consuls, Lucius Cornelius Sulla and Gaius Marius, led to a **civil war** in which Sulla, in 82 BC, eventually emerged as the sole leader of Rome. He initiated terrifying revenge against his opponents and introduced laws which greatly reduced the powers of the city's elected and appointed officials.

Gaius Marius's nephew, **Julius Caesar**, later emerged as a powerful military leader and over the course of eight long years conquered Gaul and Britain before returning to fight another civil war against his rival Pompey, which he won. Following this victory, he was proclaimed "dictator of Rome". It was the last straw for those eager to restore some semblance of the republican vision, and Caesar was murdered in the Theatre of Pompey on March 15, 44 BC, by conspirators concerned at the growing concentration of power into one man's hands. However, rather than returning Rome to the glorious days of the Republic, the murder of Caesar in fact threw it back into turmoil.

After his death, Julius Caesar's deputy, **Mark Antony**, briefly took control, joining forces with Lepidus and Caesar's adopted son, Octavian, in a **triumvirate**. Their armies fought against, and defeated those controlled by, Caesar's assassins, Brutus and Cassius, in a famous battle at Philippi, in modern-day Greece, in 42 BC. Their alliance was further cemented by Antony's marriage to Octavian's sister, Octavia, in 40 AD, but in spite of this things did not go well for the triumvirate. Lepidus was imprisoned and Antony, unable to put his political ambitions before his emotional bond with the queen of Egypt, Cleopatra, was defeated by Octavian at the battle of Actium in 31 BC. Antony escaped to Alexandria, where he committed suicide with his lover, the queen, leaving Octavian in command.

44 BC	27 BC	27 BC–337 AD	44 BC–68 AD
Assassination of Julius Caesar	Accession of Octavian Caesar (Augustus)	Period of imperial Rome	Julio-Claudian dynasty

THE RULERS OF ROME

ROMAN KINGS

Romulus (753–716 BC)
Numa Pompilius (715–674 BC)
Tullus Hostilius (673–642 BC)
Ancus Marcius (642–617 BC)
Lucius Tarquinius Priscus (616–579 BC)
Servius Tullius (578–535 BC)
Lucius Tarquinius Superbus (535–509 BC)

ROMAN REPUBLIC

c.509 BC–82 BC (death of Marius)

ROMAN DICTATORS AND TRIUMVIRS

Sulla (82–78 BC)
Triumvirate of Julius Caesar, Pompey and Crassus (60–53 BC)
Pompey (52–47 BC)
Julius Caesar (45–44 BC)
Triumvirate of Antony, Octavian Caesar (Augustus) and **Lepidus** (43–27 BC)

ROMAN EMPERORS

Augustus (27 BC–14 AD)
Tiberius (14–37)
Caligula (37–41)
Claudius (41–54)
Nero (54–68)
Galba (68–69)
Otho (69)
Vitellius (69)
Vespasian (69–79)
Titus (79–81)
Domitian (81–96)
Nerva (96–98)

Trajan (98–117)
Hadrian (117–138)
Antonius Pius (138–161)
Lucius Verus (161–169) co-emperor with **Marcus Aurelius** (161–180) co-emperor with **Commodus** (177–192)
Pertinax (192–193)
Didius Julianus (193)
Septimius Severus (193–211) co-emperor with **Geta** (209–211) co-emperor with **Caracalla** (211–217)
Macrinus (217–218)
Elagabalus (218–222)
Alexander Severus (222–235)
Maximinus Thrax (235–238)
Gordian III (238–244)
Marcus Philippus (244–249)
Decius (249–251)
Trebonianus Gallus (251–253)
Aemilianus (253)
Valerian (253–260) co-emperor with **Gallienus** (253–268)
Claudius II (268–270)
Quintillus (270)
Aurelian (270–275)
Marcus Claudius Tacitus (275–276)
Florianus (276)
Probus (276–282)
Carus (282–283)
Carinus (283–285) in competition with **Diocletian** (284–305)

The imperial era

A triumph for the new democrats over the old guard, **Augustus** (27 BC–14 AD) – as Octavian became known – was the first true Roman emperor, in firm control of Rome and its dominions; indeed "Augustus" became the name by which all future Roman emperors were known. Responsible more than anyone for heaving Rome into the imperial era, Augustus was determined to turn the city – as he claimed – from one of brick to one of marble, building arches, theatres and monuments of a magnificence suited to the capital of an expanding empire. Perhaps the best and certainly the most politically canny of Rome's many emperors, Augustus reigned for forty years.

69–96 AD	193–235 AD	275	590 AD
Flavian dynasty	Severan dynasty	Building of the Aurelian Walls	Accession of Pope Gregory I

Augustus was succeeded by his stepson, **Tiberius** (14–37 AD), who ruled from the island of Capri for the last years of his reign, and he in turn by **Caligula** (37–41 AD), a poor and possibly insane ruler who was assassinated after just four years in power. **Claudius** (41–54 AD), his uncle, followed, at first reluctantly, and proved to be a wise ruler, only to be succeeded by his stepson, **Nero** (54–68 AD), whose reign became more notorious for its excess than its prudence, and led to a brief period of warring and infighting after his murder in 68 AD, with Vitellius, Galba and Vespasian all vying for the position of emperor. **Vespasian** (69–79 AD) was eventually proclaimed emperor, thus starting a dynasty – the **Flavian** – which was to restore some stability to Rome and its empire.

The Flavian and Severan dynasties

Vespasian started as he meant to go on, doing his best to obliterate all traces of Nero, not least with an enormous amphitheatre in the grounds of Nero's palace, later known as the Colosseum. Vespasian was succeeded by his son, **Titus** (79–81 AD), and soon afterwards by his other son – Titus's brother – **Domitian** (81–96 AD), who reverted to imperial type, becoming an ever more paranoid and despotic ruler until his murder in 96 AD, when all his decrees were declared void. **Nerva** was declared emperor (96–98 AD), thus beginning the rule of the "five good emperors", who were known for their moderate policies and for giving Rome much-needed stability under the Pax Romana. He was succeeded by his adopted son (successors being chosen by merit), **Trajan** (98–117 AD), whose enlightened leadership once again allowed Rome and its colonies to settle to some sort of stability. Trajan also expanded the empire greatly, conquering the lands to the east – Turkey and modern-day Romania – and it was under his rule that the empire reached its maximum limits.

Trajan died in 117 AD, giving way to his cousin, **Hadrian** (117–138 AD), who continued the grand and expansionist agenda of his predecessor, and arguably provided the empire's greatest years. The city swelled to a population of a million or more, its people housed in cramped apartment blocks, or *insulae*; crime in the city was rife, and the traffic problem apparently on a par with today's, prompting one contemporary writer to complain that the din on the streets made it impossible to get a good night's sleep.

But it was a time of peace and prosperity, the Roman upper classes living a life of indolent luxury, in sumptuous residences with proper plumbing and central heating such as Hadrian's own villa at Tivoli. Hadrian's successors, **Antoninus Pius** (138–161 AD) and then **Marcus Aurelius** (161–180 AD), ruled over a largely peaceful and economically successful empire, until 180 AD, when Marcus Aurelius's son, **Commodus** (180–192 AD), assumed the throne but wasn't up to the task, and Rome entered a more fragile phase. Predictably, Commodus was murdered, and eventually replaced by **Septimius Severus** (193–211 AD), thus initiating the Severan dynasty – again a time of relative calm, although the political and military skills of Severus unfortunately weren't matched by those of his sons, Geta and Caracalla. **Caracalla** (211–217 AD) murdered his brother before assuming power for himself in 211 AD.

The decline of the city

The decline of Rome is hard to date precisely, but it could be said to have started with the reign of **Diocletian** (284–305 AD), an army officer from present-day Croatia

753 AD	800 AD	1305	1347
Lombard Invasion	Charlemagne is proclaimed Holy Roman Emperor	Transfer of papal court to Avignon	Cola di Rienzo crowned "Tribune of Rome"

who assumed power in 284 AD and, in an attempt to consolidate the empire, divided it into two parts, east and west. Known also for his relentless persecution of Christians, Diocletian abdicated in 305 AD, retiring to the vast palace he had built for himself in what is now Split, on the Dalmatian coast, giving rise to a power struggle that concluded with the battle of the Ponte Milvio in Rome, in which Constantine defeated his rival, Maxentius, at the same time as converting to Christianity due to a vision of a cross in the sky he saw the evening before the battle. The first Christian emperor, **Constantine** (306–337 AD), ended Diocletian's persecution of the faith, and shifted the seat of power to Byzantium in 325 AD, renaming it Constantinople. Rome's heady period as capital of the world was over, and the wealthier members of the population moved east. A series of invasions by Goths in 410 AD and Vandals about forty years later only served to quicken the city's ruin. The imperial buildings decayed and became buried, the Roman Forum

PAPAL REIGNS

Celestine III (1191–1198)	Martin V (1417–1431)	Alexander VII (1655–1667)
Innocent III (1198–1216)	Eugenius IV (1431–1447)	Clement IX (1667–1669)
Honorius III (1216–1227)	Nicholas V (1447–1455)	Clement X (1670–1676)
Gregory IX (1227–1241)	Callixtus III (1455-1458)	Innocent XI (1676–1689)
Celestine IV (1241)	Pius II (1458–1464)	Alexander VIII (1689–1691)
Innocent IV (1243–1254)	Paul II (1464–1467)	Innocent XII (1691–1700)
Alexander IV (1254–1261)	Sixtus IV (1471–1484)	Clement XI (1700–1721)
Urban IV (1261–1264)	Innocent VIII (1484–1492)	Innocent XIII (1721–1724)
Clement IV (1265–1268)	Alexander VI (1492–1503)	Benedict XIII (1724–1730)
Gregory X (1271–1276)	Pius III (1503)	Clement XII (1730–1740)
Innocent V (1276)	Julius II (1503–1513)	Benedict XIV (1740–1758)
Adrian V (1276)	Leo X (1513–1521)	Clement XIII (1758–1769)
John XXI (1276–1277)	Adrian VI (1522–1523)	Clement XIV (1769–1774)
Nicholas III (1277-1280)	Clement VII (1523–1534)	Pius VI (1775–1799)
Martin IV (1281–1285)	Paul III (1534–1549)	Pius VII (1800–1823)
Honorius IV (1285–1287)	Julius III (1550–1555)	Leo XII (1823–1829)
Nicholas IV (1288–1292)	Marcellus II (1555)	Pius VIII (1829–1830)
Celestine V (1294)	Paul IV (1555–1559)	Gregory XVI (1831–1846)
Boniface VIII (1294–1303)	Pius IV (1559–1565)	Pius IX (1846–1878)
Benedict XI (1303–1304)	Pius V (1566–1572)	Leo XIII (1878–1903)
Clement V (1305–1314)	Gregory XIII (1572–1585)	Pius X (1903–1914)
John XXII (1316–1334)	Sixtus V (1585–1590)	Benedict XV (1914–1922)
Benedict XII (1334–1342)	Urban VII (1590)	Pius XI (1922–1939)
Clement VI (1342–1352)	Gregory XIV (1590–1591)	Pius XII (1939–1958)
Innocent VI (1352–1362)	Innocent IX (1591)	John XXIII (1958–1963)
Urban V (1362–1370)	Clement VIII (1592–1605)	Paul VI (1963–1978)
Gregory XI (1370–1378)	Leo XI (1605)	John Paul I (1978)
Urban VI (1378–1389)	Paul V (1605–1621)	John Paul II (1978–2005)
Boniface IX (1389–1404)	Gregory XV (1621–1623)	Benedict XVI (2005–2013)
Innocent VII (1404–1406)	Urban VIII (1623–1644)	Francis I (2013–)
Gregory XII (1406–1415)	Innocent X (1644–1655)	

1376	1503	1527	1585
Return of papal court to Rome from Avignon	Accession of Julius II	Sack of Rome	Accession of Sixtus V

languishing beneath the Campo Vaccino, or "cow pasture", and by the sixth century the city was a devastated and infection-ridden shadow of its former self, with a population of just twenty thousand.

The rise of the papacy

It was the **papacy**, under Pope **Gregory I** ("the Great"; 590–604) in 590, that rescued Rome from its demise. Thomas Hobbes described the papacy as none other than "the Ghost of the deceased Roman Empire, sitting crowned upon the grave there of", and in an eerie echo of the empire, Gregory sent missions all over Europe to spread the word of the Church. The missions publicized its holy relics, so drawing pilgrims, and their money, back to the city, and in time making the papacy the natural authority in Rome. The pope took the name "Pontifex Maximus" after the title of the high priest of classical times (literally "the keeper of the bridges", which were vital to the city's well-being). Four of the city's great basilicas were built during this time, along with a great many other early Christian churches, underlining the city's phoenix-like resurrection under the popes, who as well as building their own new structures converted those Roman buildings that were still standing – for example fortifying the Castel Sant'Angelo to repel invaders and converting the Pantheon into a Christian church. The crowning a couple of centuries later of Charlemagne as **Holy Roman Emperor**, with dominions spread Europe-wide but answerable to the pope, intensified the city's revival, and the pope and city became recognized as head of the Christian world.

Conflict: Pope versus Emperor

There were times over the next few hundred years when the power of Rome and the papacy was weakened. Conflict between the pope and the Holy Roman Emperor raged. While the Holy Roman Emperor could claim absolute power over the secular world, the pope claimed not only spiritual power but also the right to crown and therefore validate the emperor. At times popes excommunicated emperors, at other times emperors imprisoned popes. The Ghibellines (supporters of the emperor) and the Guelphs (supporters of the pope) ravaged many Italian cities and Rome was attacked on several occasions. Robert Guiscard, the Norman king, sacked the city in 1084; a century later, a dispute between the city and the papacy led to a series of popes relocating in Viterbo. Things became so unstable that in 1308 the French-born Pope **Clement V** (1305–14) transferred his court to Avignon. In the mid-fourteenth century, Cola di Rienzo, a self-styled "tribune" of Rome, seized power, setting himself up as the people's saviour from the decadent ways of the city's rulers and forming a new Roman republic. But the increasingly autocratic ways of the new ruler soon lost popularity; Cola di Rienzo was deposed, and in 1376 Pope **Gregory XI** (1370–78) returned to Rome. However, things got distinctly worse shortly after Gregory's death when a dispute over his successor's election led to the Great Schism and the unnerving proposition of two popes – one in Rome and the other in Avignon. This was finally resolved in 1417, with the election of the Colonna family pope, Martin V, but the battling popes had taken their toll on the fabric of Rome.

1623	1798–1815	1849–1870	1870
Accession of Urban VIII	Napoleonic Republic	Italian Wars of Unification	Rome becomes capital of the Kingdom of Italy

The Renaissance

As time went on, power gradually became concentrated in a handful of wealthy Roman **families**, who swapped the top jobs, including the papacy itself, between them. Under the burgeoning power of these popes, the city began to take on a new aspect. The names of the families are etched on the city's buildings – Villa Borghese, Piazza Barberini, Palazzo Farnese. Churches were built, the city's pagan monuments rediscovered and preserved, and artists began to arrive in Rome to work on commissions for the latest pope, who would invariably try to outdo his predecessor's efforts with ever more glorious self-aggrandizing buildings and works of art.

This process reached a head during the **Renaissance**; Bramante, Raphael and Michelangelo all worked in the city, on and off, throughout their careers. The reigns of Pope **Julius II** (1503–13) and his successor, the Medici pope **Leo X** (1513–21), were something of a golden age: the city was at the centre of Italian cultural and artistic life and site of the creation of great works of art like Michelangelo's frescoes in the Sistine Chapel, the Raphael Rooms in the Vatican Palace and fine buildings like the Villa Farnesina, Palazzo Farnese and Palazzo Spada, not to mention the commissioning of a new St Peter's as well as any number of other churches. Many of the capital's national art collections began life under these patrons of the arts. The city was once again at the centre of things, and its population had increased to a hundred thousand. However, in 1527 all this was brought abruptly to an end, when the armies of the Habsburg monarch and Holy Roman Emperor, **Charles V**, swept into the city determined to avenge himself after having been excommunicated by Pope Clement VII (1523–34). He occupied the city and wreaked havoc for a year while the pope cowered in the Castel Sant'Angelo, witnessing the end of the splendours of Renaissance Rome.

The Counter-Reformation

The ensuing years were ones of yet more restoration, and perhaps because of this it's the **seventeenth century** that has left the most tangible impression on Rome today, the vigour of the **Counter-Reformation** throwing up huge, sensational monuments like the Gesù church that were designed to confound the scepticism of the new Protestant thinking, and again using pagan artefacts (like obelisks), not to mention the ready supply of building materials provided by the city's ruins, in ever more extravagant displays of wealth. The Farnese pope **Paul III** (1534–49), was perhaps the most efficient at quashing anti-Catholic feeling; later, Pope **Sixtus V** (1585–90) was perhaps the most determined to mould the city in his own image, ploughing roads through the centre and laying out bold new squares at their intersections. This period also saw the completion of St Peter's under **Paul V** (1605–21), and the ascendancy of Gian Lorenzo Bernini as the city's principal architect and sculptor under the Barberini pope **Urban VIII** (1623–44) – a patronage that was extended under the Pamphilj pope, **Innocent X** (1644–55).

The eighteenth and nineteenth centuries

The **eighteenth century** saw the decline of the papacy as a political force, a phenomenon marked by the occupation of the city in 1798 by Napoleon's forces; **Pius VI** (1775–99) was unceremoniously sent off to France as a prisoner, and **Napoleon**

1922	1929	1943	1944
Mussolini leads the March on Rome	Lateran Pact guarantees independence for The Vatican	Rome is declared an "open city"	Liberation of Rome

declared another Roman republic, with himself at its head, which lasted until 1815, when papal rule was restored under **Pius VII** (1800–23). The years that followed were fairly quiet in Rome, if not in the rest of Italy, where the relatively despotic rules of the various city-states and fiefdoms that made up what we now know as Italy were at odds with the new ideas of centralization and modernization espoused by the **reunification movement**, led by Giuseppe Mazzini. The revolutionary year of 1848, when popular revolts were sparked all over Europe, led to widespread unrest in Italy. In 1849 a pro-Unification caucus under **Mazzini** declared the city a republic and forced Pope Pius IX to leave Rome in disguise. However, Mazzini was chased out after a short four months by Emperor Napoleon III of France, who restored the papacy. There was further fighting all over Italy in 1859 and 1860 as forces for the Risorgimento or Unification of Italy gathered strength. Victor Emmanuel of Savoy and his prime minister, Camillo Benso, Conte di Cavour, managed to bring the French on board against the Austrians who had control of the Lombardy–Venetia region. But, despite winning the second war of independence, they were betrayed by the French, who made a private settlement with the Austrians whereby the Austrians would hold on to Venetia while giving up Lombardy.

Garibaldi and reunification

This came to nothing, but growing anger at this outrage galvanized the movement still further and forces under Giuseppe **Garibaldi**, who had defended Rome with Mazzini in 1849, waged an effective guerrilla campaign in Sicily and southern Italy, which ceded the territories to King Victor Emmanuel. Eventually Florence became the capital of the new kingdom in 1864. Garibaldi made repeated attempts to capture Rome – occupied by Pope Pius IX and protected by the French – but he was arrested and sidelined by the new regime, embarrassed by his growing power and charisma. In 1870 French troops were withdrawn from Rome to fight the Franco–Prussian war, allowing Italian forces to storm the walls at Porta Pia and retake the city. Rome was declared the capital of the new Italy under Victor Emmanuel II (who moved into the Quirinale Palace), and the by now powerless pontiff, **Pius IX** (1846–78), was confined in the Vatican until agreement was reached on a way to coexist. The initial **Law of Guarantees** drawn up by the new government defined the relationship between the state and the papacy, and acknowledged the pope as sovereign within the Vatican but no further; it was rejected by the pope, leaving the status of the Vatican in limbo for years to come. In the meantime **Agostino Depretis** became the first prime minister of the new Italian state, and one of its greatest politicians, remaining in power until 1887, and seeing the new country through the difficult early years.

Modern times

As capital of a modern European country, Rome was (some would say still is) totally ill-equipped. The **Piemontese rulers**, from the region in northwest Italy, set about building a city fit to govern from, cutting new streets through Rome's central core (Via Nazionale and Via del Tritone) and constructing grandiose buildings like the Altar of the Nation. **Mussolini** took up residence in Rome in 1922, and in 1929 signed the **Lateran Pact** with Pope **Pius XI** (1922–39), a compromise which finally forced the

1970s	1978	1992	1994
The "Years of Lead"	Assassination of Aldo Moro	Mani Pulite scandal	Silvio Berlusconi becomes prime minister of Italy for the first time

Vatican to accept the new Italian state and in return recognized the Vatican City as sovereign territory, together with the key basilicas and papal palaces in Rome, which remain technically independent of Italy to this day. Mussolini had typically bombastic visions for the city, and not only constructed new buildings and neighbourhoods such as Foro Italico, the University, EUR and Cinecittà, but also new thoroughfares and views within the historic centre itself. He created grand avenues, the better to march his troops along, including Via della Conciliazione, which connected St Peter's to the river, a scheme going back to the times of Pope Nicholas V (1447–55). Mussolini also "liberated" the monuments of imperial Rome from the surrounding mess of buildings – the Arch of Janus, the Temple of Vesta, the Theatre of Marcellus. But he also bulldozed his way through ancient sites such as the Roman Forum and medieval *borghi* of the city to achieve this, behaving not unlike the popes and families of old.

Rome was declared an "open city" during **World War II**, and as such emerged from the war relatively unscathed. However, after Mussolini's death, and the end of the war, the Italian king, Victor Emmanuel III, was forced to abdicate and Italy was declared a republic – still, however, with its capital in Rome. **After the war** Italy became known as a country which changes its government, if not its politicians, every few months, and for the rest of Italy Rome came to symbolize the inertia of their nation's government – at odds with both the slick, efficient north and the poor, corrupt south. Despite this, the city's growth was phenomenal in the postwar years, its population soaring to close on four million and its centre becoming ever more choked by traffic. Rome was in the spotlight for fifteen minutes during the **Sixties**, when it was the (cinematic) home of Fellini's Dolce Vita and Italy's bright young things. However, in the **Seventies**, when the so-called Anni Piombi, or "years of lead", arrived, Rome became a focus for the polarization and terrorism that was going on nationwide in Italian politics – a period when there were troops on the streets and the country often seemed on the brink of civil disruption. Since then, beginning with the "Mani Pulite", or "clean hands", investigations of the **early 1990s**, the landscape of Italian politics has changed massively, and Rome in particular saw a period of stable government under mayor **Francesco Rutelli**, and a clean-up of the city for the **Millennium**, when buildings and monuments that had been closed for decades were restored and reopened.

The twenty-first century

This process continued under the popular and urbane mayor, **Walter Veltroni**, who worked hard to improve cultural life and public services, launching Rome's first annual film festival, opening the Casa del Jazz and Casa del Cinema and building the new Auditorium on the north side of the city centre, which opened to great fanfare in 2006. Veltroni stepped down in 2008 to become leader of the new Italian Democratic Party, and the city's ambitions have stalled a little bit since. Indeed Veltroni's successor as mayor, **Gianni Alemanno**, a former neo-fascist and the city's first right-wing mayor for sixty years, reversed many of his predecessor's initiatives, criticizing Veltroni's focus on the arts and picking up on popular concerns about immigration and public services. He was replaced in 2012 by the centre-left **Ignazio Marino**, who has pledged to run Rome in a more inclusive way. Whether he makes the city a better place to live, or to visit, remains to be seen, but hopefully the new metro line C will open during his tenure; and indeed there is even talk now of an additional metro line D. But for now,

1993–2001	2001–2008	2011	2012
Francesco Rutelli is mayor of Rome	Walter Veltroni is mayor of Rome	Silvio Berlusconi stands down	Mario Monti stands down as prime minister of Italy

perhaps uniquely among European capitals, Rome retains a feel in its central districts that is still peculiarly local – and defiantly Roman.

Finally, the **abdication of Pope Benedict XVI**, successor to the popular Pope **John Paul II** (due to be canonized, **along with John XXIII,** in April 2014), was an unexpected event at the beginning of 2013. Benedict was the first pope to resign in over seven hundred years, and the subsequent election of the Argentinian Jorge Mario Bergoglio as the 266th pope in March 2013 took even insiders by surprise. They were further taken aback when he became the first pontiff to take the name of Pope **Francis**. In contrast to his predecessor, Benedict XVI, Francis has won plaudits for the friendly, informal approach he has adopted and his apparent indifference to the material baubles of the Vatican. Whether he manages to sort out the web of vested interests and mini-empires that make up much of the Vatican's administration is another matter.

2012	2013	2013
Ignazio Marino becomes mayor of Rome	Enrico Letta becomes prime minister of Italy	Benedict XVI becomes the first pope to abdicate in more than 700 years – he is succeeded by Francis I.

Architecture

Rome is an open-air museum, with its architecture as the main exhibit. The city's organic growth is often plain to see, with periods and styles crowded together and sometimes even built one on top of the other. It's this sense of the city as a living organism, the notion that each generation has made use of what has gone before and then left its own mark, that makes Rome so endlessly fascinating. What is perhaps missing is a contemporary sense: the last big building boom was over a hundred years ago and apart from Mussolini's EUR experiment and a few notable recent examples, you sometimes long to see a distinguished twentieth-century building sprouting in its pristinely preserved centre.

The classical era

Just as much of ancient Rome's architecture was based on Greek models, the buildings of the imperial city formed the blueprint for more or less everything that has followed, right up to the present day. The Romans were keen and innovative architects, and their legacy is everywhere you look: they invented concrete, brickwork, the dome and of course the column-and-pediment designs of ancient Roman temples that have been recycled countless times over the years.

Most of ancient Rome lies in ruins, but the **Forum** and **Palatine Hill** still manage to conjure up a sense of its grandeur, as do the **Baths of Caracalla** just to the south. Among more intact structures, the dome of the **Pantheon** is still the second largest in the city; the design of the **Colosseum** is as impressive today as it ever was; the recently restored **Trajan's Markets** are a model for modern shopping centres; and the ruins of **Ostia Antica** give us a glimpse of ancient urban life. But perhaps the most enduring structure of ancient Rome is the imposing **Aurelian Wall**, built by the eponymous emperor in the late third century AD to keep the barbarians at bay.

The Middle Ages

The Aurelian Wall may continue to stand but it was breached many times, and the city was more pillaged than developed in the centuries that followed the collapse of Roman power. Despite this, in the early seventh century Pope Gregory I reinvigorated the city as the headquarters of the Catholic faith, building many of its great holy shrines and churches, the earliest of which adopted the Roman basilica as their model (and indeed used old Roman columns and other recycled building materials) and were erected on

---

TOP TEN FOUNTAINS

A perfect blend of form and function, the numerous fountains of Rome both decorate the city's many piazzas and traditionally provide water – and sometimes advice! – to the city's inhabitants.

Fontana dell'Acqua Paola p.165
Fontana delle Api p.104
Fontana del Babuino p.97
Fontana della Barcaccia p.94
Fontana del Mascherone p.56

Fontana delle Naiadi p.123
Fontana dei Quattro Fiumi p.44
Fontana delle Tartarughe p.60
Quattro Fontane p.108
Trevi Fountain p.100

the site of saints' martyrdoms, for example the first basilica of St Peter's on the Vatican Hill. A great many of these early basilicas still stand, and they are among the most beautiful churches in the city. Examples are **Santa Sabina** on the Aventine Hill, **San Clemente** in the Celio district, **Santa Croce in Gerusalemme** and venerable Santa Maria Maggiore on the Esquiline, although this last is encased within a cocoon of later buildings. Gregory I also presciently preserved Hadrian's tomb as the **Castel Sant'Angelo** to withstand invaders – a purpose that was much needed in the centuries that followed; indeed it's significant that many of the medieval structures that remain in Rome are military buildings and watchtowers.

The Renaissance and the Baroque

Rome flourished during the Renaissance, drawing Italy's best artists and architects, who contributed to its transformation from a papal city to a more worldly one. Michelangelo was active in the city, not just in the **Sistine Chapel**, but laying out the **Piazza del Campidoglio**, finishing off the **Palazzo Farnese** and overseeing the rebuilding of **St Peter's**, though this would continue well into the **Baroque period** – an era of flamboyance in art and architecture that grew out of the Catholic Church's bid to reassert itself following the Reformation. More than anything, Rome is a Baroque city: the facade of the **Gesù** (1575), designed by Giacomo della Porta, became a model for Roman churches for the next century, and the curvy and playful buildings, fountains and sculptures of the style's main protagonists – Maderno, Bernini and Borromini – are everywhere you look in Rome today. The most famous of these is perhaps St Peter's itself, which was largely the work of Carlo Maderno in the end, and proved a fitting centrepiece to the embrace of Bernini's piazza, but there are many other examples of the Baroque period in the city: the enormous **Palazzo Barberini**, built by Bernini's main patron, Pope Urban VIII, Borromini's small and clever **San Carlo alle Quattro Fontane**, the grand ceiling and dome of **Sant'Ignazio** and its theatrical square, and of course the studied histrionics of Piazza Navona itself, to name only the most obvious examples.

The nineteenth century

Rome changed hugely during the nineteenth century, particularly after becoming capital of Italy in 1870, when the Italian royals were desperate to turn the city into a worthy showpiece. The city expanded outwards into the new suburbs of Prati, Nomentana and Salaria, among others, with their stately apartment blocks and rigid grid plans, and new thoroughfares were ploughed through the city centre – **Via Cavour**, **Via Nazionale** and **Piazza Vittorio Emanuele** – while plodding Neoclassical palaces were built to house the newly formed departments of state, although their most memorable legacy to Rome's skyline is without doubt the still hideously inappropriate **Vittoriano** in Piazza Venezia.

The modern era

Rome is dominated by its past, and that's nowhere more true than in its architecture, which in the city centre at least, is relentlessly pre-twentieth century, apart from a number of buildings from the Fascist era. Mussolini's preferred architect was **Marcello Piacentini**, who was responsible for some of the most celebrated of the Duce's architecture – the Stadio dei Marmi, the housing complex of Garbatella and the southern suburb of **EUR**, which was planned as a futuristic city extension in the 1930s and still feels quite contemporary today. Piacentini worked on EUR's Palazzo dello Sport with **Pier Luigi Nervi**, a celebrated Italian architect who specialized in buildings based around prefabricated and reinforced concrete and who later built the city's

Olympic Stadium and the Papal Audience Chamber next to St Peter's. More recently still, the revitalization of the city at the beginning of this century has led to some prestige architectural projects overseen by internationally renowned architects – most notably Richard Meier's controversial structure to house the **Ara Pacis** and the **Auditorium** on the northern edge of the city centre, by perhaps the best-known Italian architect of the current era, **Renzo Piano**. There's also Zaha Hadid's celebrated new **MAXXI** arts complex nearby, which is a bold and futuristic statement if ever there was one. Finally, it seems, Rome is joining the modern world, and doing so with some degree of style and success.

Writing on Rome

There has been so much written about Rome over the years that picking out something that encapsulates the city in a few words is a hard if not impossible task. There's nothing, however, quite like the reaction that Rome induces in first-time visitors. However much they may have read, and no matter how well travelled they are, no one is ever quite prepared for the exuberant confusion of the city. The three pieces we have chosen are all about coming to Rome for the first or second time; all were written in the modern era, and as such are still highly relevant to what you see today, but they were written long enough ago to be also enjoyed as history.

Elizabeth Bowen

A novelist and travel writer, Elizabeth Bowen was born in Dublin in 1899. Her book, *A Time in Rome*, from which the following extract was taken, was first published in 1960.

The Confusion

Too much time in too little space, I thought, sitting on the edge of my bed at the end of the train journey from Paris. Never have I heard Rome so quiet before or since. I had asked for a quiet room, this was it. It was on the fourth floor, at the back. The bed was low, the window was set high up, one half of it framing neutral sky, the other a shabby projection of the building. Colour seemed, like sound, to be drained away. The hour was half-past four, the day Tuesday, the month February. I knew myself to be not far from the Spanish Steps, which had flashed past the taxi like a postcard. These anti-climactic first minutes became eternal. My bedroom's old-fashioned double room, with key in the lock and the tab dangling, had been shut behind him by the outgoing porter; stacked on trestles at the foot of the bed here was my luggage for three months. Through a smaller doorway showed the tiles of a bathroom wanly reflecting electric light. I was alone with my tired senses.

The hotel, from what I had seen of it, was estimable and dignified, nothing gimcrack. The corridor, dark and extremely long, had been lined with noble old-fashioned furniture, and in here was more of it, on top of me. Close to my pillows was the telephone, sharing the marble top of a commode with a lamp with the Campidoglio on its shade. After my one thought I felt unequal to any others and lay down flat. The bedhead was in a corner, so I switched on the lamp and tipped up the shade, to continue my reading of a detective story – interrupted just at the crucial point by my train's arrival at Rome station.

When I emerged from the story, darkness had fallen and I was hungry. Taking with me the *Walks of Rome of Augustus Hare*, I left the hotel to look for dinner. In these surrounding little streets, lit up like aquariums and tonight anonymous, saunterers passed me in vague shoals. Restaurant after restaurant was empty; blue-white electricity, hatless hatstands, as chalky and void as the tables' napery. Here and there a waiter posed like a waxwork. Spying through glass doors or over blinds, I began to fear something had gone wrong – actually all that had happened was, I was ahead of the Roman dinner-hour. So I ended in yellow-brocaded *Ranieri's*, where they showed a polished lack of surprise, among foreigners other than myself. Great gilt candelabra were on the chimney-piece, and for each of us a little vase of anemones. But here I was afflicted by something else: it seemed uncouth to read while dinner was served. Stealing a glance now and then at *Augustus Hare*, I never succeeded in getting further than Dr Arnold's 1840 letter to his wife: "Again this date of Rome; the most solemn and interesting that my hand can write, and even now more interesting than when I saw it last." This was not my first visit to Rome either.

Next day, I changed my room for an outside corner one, a floor higher. This, with the freshness following on what seemed more absolute than a mere night's sleep, altered the feeling of everything like magic. I found myself up in a universe, my own, of sun-coloured tiled floor, sunny starchy curtains. Noise, like the morning, rushed in at the open windows, to be contained by the room in its gay tranquillity. Roses, bleached by seasons of light, rambled over the cretonne coverings of the two beds. The idea of Rome, yesterday so like lead, this noonday lay on me lighter than a feather. Life at this level had a society of its own: windows across the way, their shutters clamped back, looked pensively, speakingly at mine. The quarter in which the *Hotel Inghilterra* stands is early nineteenth century. It fills the slight declivity, shallow as the hollow of a hand, between the Pincio and the Corso, and is bisected by the de luxe Via Condotti, apart from which the quarter is unassuming. It has acoustics of its own, echoes and refractions of steps and voices, now and then of the throb of a car in low gear nosing its way among the pedestrians. Every narrow street in this network is one-way; the system is dementing to motorists, who do not embroil themselves in it willingly. Radio jazz, a fervent young singer at her exercises, a sewing-machine tearing along, and the frenetic song of a small-caged bird, hooked to my sill, were my sound-neighbours. From top-but-one storey windows I beheld one crinkled continuous tawny roofline: all the buildings fitted into this quarter, like segments of a finally solved jigsaw, are one in height as they are in age. They are ochre, which was giving off a kind of August glow on to the mild spring-winter morning: on throughout the chilliest time of year smoulders the afterglow of Rome's summers. And my streets, on a grid plan, sunken deep between buildings, also are all alike: sunless, down there, for the greater part of the day, they stretch so far that they fade away at the ends. Small shops, workshops, bars and restaurants line them, with apartments or offices above. Banal, affable, ripe to become familiar, this was the ideal Rome to be installed in: everything seemed to brim with associations, if not (so far) any of my own. I began to attach myself by so much as looking. Here I was, centred. I dared to hope that all else might prove as simple. It did not.

One trouble is that Rome's north-south axis, Via del Corso, does not run due north, due south. It slants, thereby throwing one's sense of direction, insofar as one has one, out of the true. The Piazza Venezia, at one end, is east of Piazza del Popolo at the other.

Then, there are the exaggerated S-curvings of the Tiber; one minute the river is at one's elbow, the next lost. A stroll along the embankment is one of the least enjoyable in Rome; the dustiest, baldest, most unrewarding. (To stand on a bridge is another thing.) The Tiber is not intended to be followed; only trams do so, and those in very great numbers. They grind by unceasingly, and one does well to take one. Then again, there are far more than seven hills: how is one to be clear which the seven are? This seems to be one of the primal facts which guidebooks are obstinate in withholding. Viewed from above, from the Janiculum lighthouse or a terrace of the Pincio gardens, Rome as a whole appears absolutely flat, or, if anything, sunken in the middle like a golden-brown pudding or cake which has failed to rise. Down again in the city, you register gradients in aching foot muscles – this does establish that Rome is hilly. Knowledge of Rome must be physical, sweated into the system, worked up into the brain through the thinning shoe-leather. Substantiality comes through touch and smell, and taste, the tastes of different dusts. When it comes to knowing, the senses are more honest than the intelligence. Nothing is more real than the first wall you lean up against sobbing with exhaustion. Rome no more than beheld (that is, taken in through the eyes only) could still be a masterpiece in cardboard – the eye I suppose being of all the organs the most easily infatuated and then jaded and so tricked. Seeing is pleasure, but not knowledge.

In shape the Capitoline and the Palatine are hills unmistakably; so is the Aventine, at the other side of the trough of the Circo Massimo. But the Caelian, Esquiline, Viminal and Quirinal are ambiguously webbed together by ridges. On the whole I have come to suppose that these are the Seven – but if so, what of the Pincian, "hill of gardens" and Janiculum, bastion across the river? I asked a number of friends, but no two gave me the same answer; some did not want to be pinned down, others put forward their own candidates. That I should be set on compiling a definitive list of the Seven Hills, eager to check on all, to locate each, was, I can see, disillusioning to people who had hoped I might show more advanced tastes. So, given the equal unwillingness of guidebooks to disgorge anything like a list, I left Rome, when the end of my time came, no more certain as to the Seven Hills.

An excerpt from A Time in Rome, *reprinted with the kind permission of Curtis Brown Group Ltd on behalf of the estate of Elizabeth Bowen. ©Elizabeth Bowen 1960*

William Weaver

William Weaver served as an ambulance driver during World War II and first visited Rome a few years later. He became the most sought-after translator of Italian literature of the second half of the twentieth century, translating most of the modern Italian literary greats at one time or another. The following extract, part of his introduction to Steerforth Press's anthology of modern Roman literature, details his first impressions of the city, and his relationships with some of the writers he later came to work with.

Open City

It was raining when we arrived, and the rickety bus finally emptied us – me and my Neapolitan friend Raffaele – into a small, dark square near the Borsa. This was Rome? True, there were some scarred ancient columns along a street-front, but they were grimy with soot. I had imagined a city of snowy white, elegant classical forms, resembling perhaps the columned Citizens National Bank in Front Royal, Virginia, my childhood paragon of fine architecture. Rome, I saw, in shock, was different from the black-and-white Alinari photographs of art history courses; it was orange, yellow; rust-color; there were even a few neon signs blinking on baroque facades in the early winter dusk.

From the Piazza di Pietra we went to our pensione. Again, with reminiscences of E.M. Forster in my head, I imagined a place of relaxed conversation and, of course, a room with a view. The *Pensione Sieben* had once been a solid, spacious, middle-class apartment. Now the Siebens (he was an elderly German, a retired translator) lived in the kitchen and in a crammed bedroom next to it. An old lady, Herr Sieben's mother, occupied the next bedroom. In the front of the apartment, my friends Peppino and Mario shared the former salon, a once-splendid room now almost empty save for two cots, a desk, and a wood-burning stove, jutting from what was a formerly decorative fireplace.

Across the vestibule was a much smaller room, where I was to sleep. It also contained two cots, but the few square meters could not accommodate even a small desk. The cot farther from the door was occupied by Achille, another Neapolitan friend, an actor just getting his first small roles in a repertory company specializing in new Italian plays (they were not usually very good, so the bill changed often; Achille was building a large, useless repertory). Until the previous week, my cot had been occupied by yet another Neapolitan, Francesco Rosi, an aspiring film-maker; now he had landed an enviable job, as assistant to Luchino Visconti, and had just gone off to Sicily to join the director in working on what was to prove an enduring masterpiece, *La terra trema*. The room's single window gave on an air-shaft and a blank wall.

Achille was a trying roommate. Unless he had a rehearsal, he slept until midday (so I had to dress in the dark). Afternoons, he received his lovely and long-suffering girl-friend, and I was expected to go out for an extended walk – it was a rainy winter

– and stay out until dark. He was a hypochondriac, and when he discovered my super-giant family-size bottle of aspirin – calculated to last me for my whole Italian stay – he began happily popping pills; the aspirin level in the big jar descended at an alarming rate. He was also fascinated by my clothes, ordinary as they were, and constantly borrowed them, with or without asking me first. He particularly liked to wear them on stage; so I became used to seeing my Princeton sweatshirt or my favorite striped pyjamas turn up on a set representing an Italian living room.

After a few days in Rome, I dutifully made my way to the University, planning to enrol in some courses, to justify and, presumably, enrich my Italian stay. My first real tangle with Italian bureaucracy ensued: a nightmare of waiting in the wrong line, lacking this or that document, failing to understand angry, shouted directions from the grouchy staff behind the windows or the confusing attempts at help from equally beleaguered Italian students.

I gave up (two years later, thanks to a Fulbright, I actually enrolled at the University and attended a few classes), and determined to dedicate myself to my other Roman project: the novel I expected to write. Having published two stories in national magazines (*Harper's Bazaar* and *Mademoiselle*, which had published stories of Truman Capote and other rising stars), I – and my friends – assumed that a novel was the next step. There was just one difficulty: I had nothing I particularly wanted to write about. But I didn't let that stop me. Mornings, when Peppino had gone off to his job at the Rai, the Italian State Radio, and Mario to his classes at the Accademia di Arte Drammatica, I moved into the former salon, sat at their desk, opened my copious notebooks (a Gide fan, I could not contemplate writing a novel without keeping journals, *cahiers*), and tried to work. I had never been successfully self-critical. But even permissive me soon had to concede that the novel was a dud.

If the rain let up, I soon found an excuse to go out. The excuse was always the same: my determination to get to know Rome. It was not a matter of visiting churches, studying frescoes, deciphering inscriptions. I wanted to gulp down real Roman coffee in the morning, eat real Roman pasta at lunch, drink all the real Roman wine I could afford. I wanted to read the newspapers, see the movies and the plays, hear the music.

I was perfectly situated. Dreary as the *Pensione Sieben* looked at first, it turned out to be a hive of cultural, and social activity; a center of fun. The big salon of Peppino and Mario served as a gathering-place for a host of young people from the Accademia, writers from the Rai, and other newly-arrived Neapolitans aiming to break into film or journalism.

And I had a trump-card of my own. I was an American, and to the Italians – whatever their ages or degree of fame – that nationality inspired endless curiosity. For many I was the first American they had encountered, except perhaps for a stray GI a few years earlier. And so I was consulted as the expert on everything American: my opinion on William Wyler was seriously pondered. I was asked whether I would place Gershwin in the mainstream of white jazz or in the area of classical music (the question, for me, was unanswerable, as I knew far more about Puccini than about my popular compatriot). I was invited to contribute to nascent literary magazines, some of them born only to die after the first issue, which perhaps included my little piece on Karl Shapiro or John O'Hara.

Through a visiting American I met the Italian painter and writer Dario Cecchi, a few years my senior, scion of an Italian literary/artistic family with ramifications extending into every area of Italy's cultural life. Dario's father was the eminent and powerful critic Emilio Cecchi; his sister was Suso Cecchi d'Amico, the script-writer of Visconti and others, and her husband, Fedele d'Amico, was a brilliant, polemical music critic and polymath, eventually to become a treasured friend and colleague.

The chain of acquaintances grew, link by link, creating degrees not of separation but of connection. And some of these connections soon became hubs, branching off in one direction after another. It was Dario who took me first to meet Princess Marguerite Caetani. He told me little about her beyond the fact that she was American-born (a Chapin from Connecticut), a patron of the arts who had lived for many years in France, but had returned to Italy with her musician husband before the second world war and had remained in Rome. In Palazzo Caetani she edited an international literary review, *Botteghe Oscure*, after the name of the street where the Palazzo had stood for many centuries. The fact that Communist Party Headquarters now stood in that same street, making its name a synonym for the pci, was a minor nuisance that the Principessa airily dismissed.

We stepped into the dark courtyard of the great, grim palace, took an elevator to the piano nobile, and were shown into a huge, high-ceilinged hall, hung with dusty portraits (I looked around for Boniface VIII, the Caetani pope pilloried by Dante, but I couldn't identify him): then Dario, who knew his way around the palace, led me to a modern corkscrew staircase in a corner of the room. We climbed it and, passing through a plain little door at its top, stepped into a large, but cozy, New England living room: sofas covered in beige monkscloth, low tables, a fire in the fireplace, French windows revealing a broad terrace beyond. A large tea-pot stood on one table, and plates of sandwiches circulated.

The Principessa, in heather tweeds, only a few wisps of her gray hair out of place (to hint at her artistic side?), welcomed me warmly. And the welcome was equally warm from other guests, all clearly frequenters of the house. They were not many, and I remember almost all of them, as they all became friends of mine very soon: Elena Croce, the daughter of the philosopher but with a lively mind of her own; Umberto Morra, an aristocratic anti-Fascist and old friend of Bernard Berenson; Ignazio Silone – whose works I had read in translation – with his beautiful, ebullient Irish wife Darina, whom I had already met for a fleeting moment. And Giorgio Bassani, titular editor of *Botteghe Oscure*, though Marguerite clearly made all the operative decisions, while encouraging Bassani to propose new writers, especially for the Italian section of the magazine. At that time, Bassani was known, if he was known at all, as a poet; he had just published the first of what were to become the now classic *Five Stories of Ferrara*.

After that first visit, I returned to Palazzo Caetani countless times, and each visit was memorable, especially those when I was alone with Marguerite, who soon discovered – and exploited – my boarding-school experience as a proofreader. The Italian printers, excellent artisans, inevitably made gibberish of some of the magazine's English and French texts, and complaining authors drove Marguerite to despair ("Alfred Chester called me this morning from Paris, he cried all last night because of the mistakes in his story.") My work was unpaid – and I put in long hours – but I had ample occasion to appreciate Marguerite's real generosity. Not only did she soon publish my work: she also invited me to any number of meals. Food at the Caetani table was plain, but as I lived from day to day, a steak gained was a steak earned.

And the company! For foreign literary visitors of a certain level, Palazzo Caetani was an obligatory stop. One week there would be a tea-party for "Cousin Tom" (known to me as T.S. Eliot), in Rome to give a reading at the British Council, but also to enjoy a honeymoon with his new wife Valerie. The great poet's radiant happiness was evident, irrepressible. For much of the party he and his wife sat side-by-side on one of Marguerite's comfortable low sofas, and he could not refrain from touching her, patting her hand, pressing her arm, like an enamored schoolboy. Standing not far away, I pointed out Eliot's enraptured behavior to Alberto Moravia. "Senile sexuality," the novelist commented tartly. I remembered this remark some decades later when Moravia himself, by then close to eighty, married Carmen Llera, forty-odd years his junior.

Between the world wars, Marguerite had lived much of the time in Paris, where her house just outside the city was also an intellectual gathering place (Berenson's letters tell of visits there from the Armistice meetings, which he was attending). So the Palazzo in Rome welcomed many French visitors, among them René Char, Francis Ponge, Henri Sauguet. And there were also musicians, partly because of Prince Roffredo's background as a composer (he was Liszt's godson and had known the Wagners); in the Caetani salon I first heard Gian Carlo Menotti and Tommy Schippers discuss a festival they were beginning to think about, a place for young artists in some Umbrian town, perhaps Todi, or perhaps Spoleto.

Umberto Morra, a Piedmontese count, whose family had been close to the royal family (Umberto's father, a general, had served as the Savoys' ambassador to the court of the Czar), lived in a single room in Rome, in the apartment of some old friends. But he led an intense social life, and he particularly enjoyed entertaining new arrivals to Rome, arranging introductions. Often he would invite a new acquaintance, with perhaps one or at most two old friends, to tea at *Babington's* tea rooms in Piazza di Spagna. The atmosphere at *Babington's* certainly belonged to another world, but what world was it? I suppose the unpretentious setting was meant to evoke pre-war England (pre-first war, that is), and the motherly old ladies with their starched frilly caps who brought the tea and scones and cake looked like Margaret Rutherford stand-ins, imported directly from some Staffordshire village. But then you realized they spoke little English, and that smattering came out with a thick Italian accent.

In any case, the tea was authentic and delicious, the scones came with homemade jams; and the company was always stimulating. Whether at *Babington* or, for grander luncheons, at the *Stanze dell'Eliseo*, a quirkish private club, with Morra you were always sure to meet someone who was not just interesting but was actually a person you were eager to know: Jimmy Merrill was a Morra gift to me, and so – in Florence – was Bernard Berenson. Later, when Morra headed the Italian Institute in London, he introduced me to the great Maurice Bowra, to the equally legendary Judge Learned Hand. His was a mobile salon. When you came to know him really well, he would invite you for a weekend at his comfortable, slightly shabby villa in Tuscany (Moravia "stole" the villa to use as his setting of his novel *Conjugal Love*). Again the house party was always varied, relaxed, unexpected. Even the occasional bore – the garrulous widow of a distinguished anti-Fascist friend, for example – was, somehow, a bore you were glad to meet.

An excerpt from Open City: Seven Writers in Postwar Rome, *edited by William Weaver, published by Steerforth Press of Hanover, NH. ©William Weaver 1999*

William Murray

William Murray wrote regularly on Italy for the *New Yorker*. The following piece – one of many from his now out-of-print collection of Italian writings, *Italy: The Fatal Gift*, records his early years living in the city at the start of the 1950s, in particular a Campo de' Fiori that perhaps no longer exists but is still eminently recognizable today.

Voices

I don't think I began to understand Rome, and my own involvement in Italian life, until I moved to the apartment on the fourth floor of a run-down Renaissance palazzo at one end of a piazza called the Campo de' Fiori. The piazza is in the middle of the old papal city, surrounded by narrow, twisting little streets that thread their way among blocks of ancient houses dating back, many of them, to the fourteenth century. The rooms of my apartment were huge, with beamed and frescoed ceilings, thick walls, and tiled floors, and there was a terrace, awash in flowers and trellised ivy. I slept, or tried to, in a front room with a large window looking out over the piazza. At first, I was startled by the noise. There were lulls, but never long periods of uninterrupted silence. In the very early morning hours, I would sometimes be wakened by the explosive buzzing of a motor scooter, the rumbling of cart wheels over the cobblestones, the crash of some unbelievably heavy objects onto the pavement. Mostly, however, even at night, the sounds consisted of voices, individual and concerted, blending into and succeeding each other in a never ending choral composition of pure cacophony. It was astonishing.

Actually the sheer volume of sound at certain periods of the day didn't surprise me. I had known all along that the Campo de' Fiori was the site, six days a week, of a large open-air market. I would get up in the morning and open my shutters to look down over a sea of gray canvas umbrellas sheltering perhaps as many as two hundred stands. A great crowd of shoppers ambled and pushed down narrow aisles between rows of heaped edibles of all kinds. Directly beneath my window alone, at the northwestern end, of the piazza, I counted thirteen vendors of vegetables and several selling preserves, cheeses, and sausages. On my way across the piazza to a café where I often had breakfast and read the morning paper, I would pass pushcarts of fresh vegetables piled into great green mounds, tables buried under soft white and brown mushrooms, pyramids of cherries, apples, oranges sliced to reveal their dripping interiors, pears, apricots, bunches of white and green asparagus, enormous beets and onions, tiny round potatoes, huge heads of fresh lettuce, green and red peppers, artichokes, tomatoes, carrots and wild strawberries. Along one whole side of the piazza stretched a seemingly endless line of butcher stands, behind which the butchers themselves, in soiled white smocks, wielded their cleavers and large flat knives under the plucked bodies of chickens and the bloody carcasses of lambs and kids hanging in rows from steel hooks. There were also bunches of pigs' feet, chunks of tripe, chains of plump sausages. At the far end of the piazza, the fishmongers presided over damp boxes and baskets of the day's catch – fish of all shapes, flaming red, blue, and silver, soft masses of squid and small octopuses, mountains of white-and-gray minnows with tiny, dead bright-button eyes, dozens of small, dark-red clawless Mediterranean lobsters.

And scattered along the periphery of these crowded rows of comestibles were still other stands, selling pots and pans, dishes, glassware, cheap toys, shoes, and clothing. The stone face of the piazza, roughly rectangular and roughly the same size as a football field, disappeared every morning of the week but Sundays and holidays under umbrellas, the tons of merchandise, the shuffling feet of thousands of shoppers.

Many other voices besides those of the market invaded my room. The most insistent and violent one belonged, I guessed, to a woman in her thirties. She lived in one of the apartments near the corner of Via dei Cappellari, somewhere behind the lines of laundry that hung, dripping relentlessly, across the street. Her voice was shrill and hard and piercing: it would come soaring across the piazza from behind the wall of laundry like a battle cry from the ranks of an army advancing behind flapping pennants. "Ah Massimo-o-o" it would scream. "Massimo-o-o, where the hell are you, you dirty monkey? Get the hell up here right this minute! Massimo-o-o! If you aren't home in two minutes, you little bastard, I'll break your head! Massimo-o-o imbecile! You hear me? Get right up here now before I come down and break your arm! Ah Massimo-o-o! Massimo-o-o! Cretino! Imbecille! A' vie' qua-a-a!" These tirades often became so vituperative, menacing and foul-mouthed that I'd find myself wondering how the woman could keep it up. I'd go to the window and gaze down into the piazza, hoping to spot Massimo among the hordes of children swarming through the market or, on Sunday, around the base of Bruno's statue. The voice would scream on, threatening mayhem and the vengeance of heaven on the object of its wrath, but no little boy would separate himself from his fellows and go running across the cobblestones. At least, I never noticed him.

Massimo apparently did hear, however, and eventually he would come home. The voice would cease its screaming imprecations and remain silent for some time. After a while, though, I'd hear it again – usually around two o'clock in the afternoon, when the market had closed up and the commercial uproar had abated somewhat. The intensity and depth of emotion would still be evident in the voice, but the tone had altered dramatically. "Massimo! Massimo!" I would hear it shout. "Treasure of my heart, flower of my life, why don't you eat? Eat, eat! You want to die of hunger? You want your mother to perish of grief? You want your papa to die of shame, to tell me I don't cook like I used to? My love, my sweet, my angel, have another tomato, eat your bread, drink your milk. Eat, eat, love of my life! Here, Mama will give you a big hug and a kiss! You eat now! Massimo-o-o! Tesoro! Amore! Mangia, che ti fa bene! Cocco! Angelo!"

I tried often to imagine what Massimo looked like. I saw a small boy of seven or eight with dirty knees and scuffed shoes, black hair and red eyes, red cheeks, and sturdy shoulders, but too fat for his age. I'd see him climb the stairs to the sounds of threats and fury, bursting in to be met by a hug and a light cuff and a mound of steaming spaghetti. Who, anywhere around the Campo, would not have heard of him? At the newsstand, I once idly enquired about him, but the young man who sold me my newspaper couldn't identify him, either. "Ah, Signore, it could be any one of them," he said, indicating with a flick of his hand a crowd of urchins then engaged in kicking a soccer ball around the piazza. "Massimo? A common enough name. And here everyone shouts from the windows all the time. Do you not notice?"

This young man's name was Remo. He and his family had been tending their stand, on the corner of Via dei Baullari, for thirty-five years. They would take turns sitting like benevolent gnomes inside a very small wooden booth festooned with magazines and newspapers. Nothing escaped their vigilant attention. Remo rarely smiled, and he thought that life in the piazza had deteriorated a good deal since he first began to observe its goings-on. "Ah Signore," he said to me one day, "you like this market? It is not what it was. No indeed it isn't. On Saturdays you had to fight your way into the piazza, that's what I remember. Now – ". He shrugged. "Now, it's nothing. People are moving out. The ones who were brought up in this quarter, they do not like the old palazzi. When they have money, they move away. The rich and the foreigners are moving into the buildings now, but they don't buy in the market. They go to the supermarkets in the Parioli – drive all the way out there rather than buy in the piazza. No, it's not what it was." He was unhappy, too, about the crime in the area. "Dirty people," he said. "Gentaccia, that's what they are. The quarter is full of them. Every thief in town lives here. Do you have a car?" I told him I didn't.

"That's lucky for you," he said. "It would be stolen. Don't trust anyone you meet in the piazza. Anyone can see you're an American." At the time, I had seen no evidence of crime in the piazza, and I paid no attention to Remo's advice.

One night at about 2am I was awakened by the sound of loud masculine laughter and conversation outside my window. I looked down and saw a group of men directly below. They were talking and joking, making no effort to keep from disturbing the neighbourhood. I shouted down at them to keep quiet. One of them looked up briefly, but otherwise paid no attention. Their hoarse, merry voices continued to resound in the night air. After about ten minutes more of this, I went to the kitchen and came back with a large pot full of water. I asked them one more time to keep quiet, but I was ignored. I then leaned out of the window and poured cold water on their heads. Bellowing and cursing, they quickly scattered out and regrouped beyond the fountain, out in the piazza and well out of range. Through the slats in my shutters I saw them conferring angrily and occasionally pointing up toward my window. Slightly uneasy, I went back to bed.

The next morning, when I stepped out into the piazza, I was greeted by a young tough in wrinkled slacks and a torn jersey. He was unshaven, with close-set eyes and a snarl of oily-looking curls, and he had evidently been lounging against the wall of my building, waiting for me. "Hey you," he said hoarsely. "Hey, are you the one who threw water on us last night?"

The market was in full swing and the piazza crowded with people. I made up my mind not to be intimidated. "Yes," I said. "You woke me up." The youth shook his head gravely.

"That was a very stupid thing to do." "Listen," I said. "I have some rights. I asked you twice to keep quiet and you paid no attention. You have no right to wake everybody up." "And you have no right to throw water on people."

This seemed a rather weak rejoinder to me, so I pressed my luck a little. "I could have called the police, you know."

The tough smiled, revealing a bright row of gold teeth. "No, no," he said, shaking his head. "You would not do that. No one in this quarter would do such a stupid thing. You have to live here – no?"

"I don't live here all the time," I said. "Besides, I don't like to be threatened."

The tough smiled again and spread his hands out wide. "Threatening you? Who is threatening you, Signore? I? I merely wish to protest against being doused with water in the middle of the night, that's all. That's not unreasonable, is it?"

"Mario, introduce me to the gentleman," I heard someone say.

I turned, and was confronted by a short, stocky, bald Roman in a rumpled but well-tailored brown suit. He had a round, affable face with large brown eyes and a strong, prominent, straight nose. He was smiling broadly. "Mario does not know my name," I said, and I introduced myself.

"Of course he does," the new arrival declared. "You are the American who lives on the fourth floor. Everyone knows who you are. I myself have often seen you in the piazza. Pleased to meet you. My name is Domenico. My friends call me Memmo."

"Were you also in the piazza last night?" I asked.

Memmo laughed. "Alas, yes," he admitted, "Luckily, you missed me. Mario, here, was soaked. That probably accounts for his sour face." He turned to Mario and clapped him roughly on the shoulder. "Hey Mario, cheer up! The bath did you good, eh? The first one you've had in weeks."

Mario made an effort to smile, but it did not seem entirely genuine. I concentrated on Memmo. "I'm sorry about it," I said. "But I was tired and wanted to get some sleep. You were directly under my window, and I asked you all several times to be quiet."

"Right," said Memmo. "Quite right. I think we will not chat there again. However, caro Signore" – he took my arm confidentially and pulled me a few feet off to one side – "don't do such a thing again. For your own good, Signore. No one would harm you, of course – Dio Mio, an American! But Mario and his friends can play such tricks, Signore! The apartment is so full of beautiful things. I have not seen it, but I know that it is. Apartments can be broken into, Signore, and even the most beautiful object can be made to disappear. What is the sense in playing tricks on people like Mario, eh?"

I looked back at Mario, who was still standing by the entrance to the building and regarding me sourly. "And you?" I asked. "What about you?"

"I?" he said. "Oh, I'm a friend of Mario's. He runs little errands for me. I have a shop here, just around the corner. You've passed it many times. Electrical equipment – radios, iceboxes, toasters, things like that. You've seen my shop, haven't you?"

I said that I had passed it often.

"Well, of course you have," Memmo said. "It's a very well-known store. Everyone in the neighbourhood knows me. Ask anyone."

"It's very kind of you to warn me," I said. Memmo looked astonished. "Warn you?" he said. "Signore, I would not think of presuming to warn you. Still, it is important that you know how things are here on the piazza, eh?"

"Yes, I understand," I said. "Thanks very much."

"Forget it," Memmo said. "Forget the whole thing. And don't worry about Mario. Nothing will happen. Come and see me in the shop. Drop in any time – right there, just around the corner." He shook my hand and departed in the direction of his store. As he went, I saw him nod almost imperceptibly to Mario, who went off with him, not casting so much as a backward glance in my direction.

A couple of days later, I did drop in on Memmo. From the outside, the store looked like any other small shop dealing in electrical housewares, but since my encounter with Mario and Memmo and our oblique conversation, I had become curious about it. When I stepped inside the door, I discovered that the place was all but empty of merchandise. The window display featured a cheap washing machine and a secondhand refrigerator, but except for a couple of toasters and a small radio or two the store looked cleaned out. Mario and a couple of other shady-looking men lounged against the walls, smoking American cigarettes, while Memmo sat behind a small wooden desk. He had been talking into the telephone, but he hung up immediately when I came in. "Ah, buon giorno, buon giorno," he said, coming out from behind his desk and rubbing his hands briskly together. "How nice to see you! Thanks for dropping in."

"Business seems to be a little slow," I said.

"On the contrary," Memmo answered, smiling broadly. "Business could not be better."

"You've sold everything in the shop, then?"

"Well, not quite," Memmo said. "Come back here."

Memmo led me back to his desk, opened a top drawer, and pulled out a large, flat box full of Swiss wristwatches. "Look at this," he said, holding one up by the strap. "Fifty thousand lire, this watch costs. I sell it for thirty. Would you like it? "I told Memmo that I already had a watch. He put the watch back in the drawer and closed it. "Well, then, how about this?" he opened another drawer and showed me a pile of cigarette lighters. "Or these?" He produced boxes of cufflinks, tie clasps, studs, men's and women's bracelets, earrings, electric razors, razor blades, small bottles of cheap cologne, key rings, charms. Finally, with an elaborate little flourish of one hand, he opened srill another drawer and took out a long, thin, expensive-looking case. "Perhaps there is a lady in your life?" He opened the box to reveal a handsome pearly necklace. "For you," he said, "for my friend the American, only a hundred thousand lire, eh?"

"No, thanks," I said. "I can't afford it."

Memmo sighed, cheerfully stuffed the box back into the drawer, and closed it.

"You seem to be selling everything here," I said.

Memmo smiled and shrugged. "Well, Signore, I believe in floating with the traffic, eh?" What you Americans call, I believe, the laws of supply and demand."

"How can you afford to sell these things so cheaply?" I asked.

"Signore, we have our own direct sources of supply," Memmo said. "We eliminate the middleman, as you would say. We import everything directly. You understand?"

"I think so," I said.

After that, I became increasingly aware of Memmo and his boys. Mario and half a dozen other young toughs strolled in and out of the shop, and several times I noticed them peddling objects through the marketplace. Once, I found Mario and a friend presiding at the corner of Via dei Baullari over a large stack of shoeboxes. They were selling sandals for five hundred lire a pair – a ridiculously low price. Occasionally, they would operate out of the back of a panel truck, selling everything from shirts to hardware. I never saw Memmo anywhere except inside his store, usually on the phone or in deep conversation with one of his young men.

One day, at the newsstand, I asked Remo about Memmo and his friends. Remo glanced sharply at me, then looked around to see if we were alone. "Stay away from them, Signore," he said in an undertone. "They are no good, that bunch. I let everything I hear go in one ear and out the other. It is better that way. But I tell you this Signore – the police drop in there from time to time, and it is not to pass the hours chatting, Memmo wasn't around for a long time last year, and that Mario – you know him?"

I said that I did.

"A bad one," Remo said. "He was a carpenter. Then he killed a man one day just because the fellow clapped him too hard on the back, or something. He did three and a half years. A hood, un vero teppista. Don't have anything to do with them."

"But who are they? Are they from around here?"

"All from this quarter, Signore, every one of them," Remo said sadly. "They give it a bad name. All over Rome, people say the Campo de' Fiori is a den of thieves. Memmo and his crowd – they're responsible for that. It's really too bad."

An excerpt from Italy: The Fatal Gift, *reprinted with the kind permission of the author.* ©William Murray

Books and films

There have been an enormous number of books published about Rome sover the years, both in English, and of course in Italian, and the list below is inevitably extremely selective, concentrating on entertaining travelogues, key texts on history and art and on works of fiction that might be instructive – or fun – to read while you're in the city. Rome has been a focus for moviemakers over the years too, whether it's trying to recreate the drama of ancient times, portray the modern city's dark side or just revelling in its ready-made grand settings. We've included a rundown of our favourite Roman movies – and movie locations – on pp.334–335.

ANCIENT HISTORY

Juvenal *The Sixteen Satires*. Savage attacks on the follies and excesses of Rome at the end of the first century and start of the second.

Livy *The Early History of Rome*. Lively chronicle of the city's evolution from the days of Romulus and Remus.

Marcus Aurelius *Meditations*. The classic text of Stoic thought, written by one of the few Roman emperors it's easy to admire.

Petronius *Satyricon*. A fragmentary, spicy narrative written by one of Nero's inner circle; Fellini's film of the same name gives a pretty accurate idea of the tone.

Suetonius *The Twelve Caesars*. The inside story of Caligula,

Nero, Domitian and others, elegantly written and very enjoyable, by the private secretary to Hadrian, who made the most of his unique access to the annals of recent imperial history.

Tacitus *Annals of Imperial Rome*. Covers much of the terrain dealt with by Suetonius, but from the stance of the diligent historian and serious moralist.

Virgil *The Aeneid*. The central work of Latin literature, this epic book depicts the adventures of Aeneas after the fall of Troy, and in doing so it celebrates Rome's heroic lineage.

ANCIENT ROME IN FICTION

Robert Graves *I Claudius; Claudius the God*. Having translated Suetonius's *Twelve Caesars*, Graves used the madness and corruption of the Imperial Age to create a gripping, if not necessarily historically accurate, tale. The classic book on the imperial Caesars.

Robert Harris *Imperium; Lustrum*. No one brings to life the Roman Republic quite as vividly as Harris, viewing the power struggles and intrigues of the main protagonists through the eyes of Cicero's faithful secretary, the freed slave Tiro. There are several to choose from, but this is perhaps the best dramatization of the period you can read.

Conn Iggulden *The Gates of Rome; The Death of Kings; The Field of Swords; The Gods of War*. Iggulden's engaging four-book series, *Emperor*, is a historical romp documenting the rise and fall of Julius Caesar, from the rites of passage of the young man during the turmoil of the last decades of the Republic to his eventual murder in Pompey's theatre.

Allan Massie *Augustus; Tiberius; Caesar; Caligula*. Massie's series of novels aspires to recreate the Roman Empire at its height through the imagined memoirs of its key figures, and does so with great success, in a series of novels that offers a well-researched but palatable way into the minutiae of the era.

Stephen Saylor *Roma; Empire*. Saylor is better known for his Giordanius detective yarns set in the days of the Roman Republic, but this epic novelization of the city's history up to the growth of the empire – two volumes so far – is perhaps more appealing to the general reader.

Thornton Wilder *The Ides of March*. A suppositional reconstruction of the last year of the life of Julius Caesar through his letters, writings and reports.

ROMAN CRIME

Lindsey Davis *Venus in Copper; The Jupiter Myth;* and others. These crime novels set in the age of the Emperor Vespasian follow super-sleuth Marcus Didius Falco as he unpicks mysteries and dastardly doings.

Michael Dibdin *Cabal; Ratking;* and others. Not all of the late Michael Dibdin's novels are set in Rome, but the author was as interested in Italy as in his characters, with the result that his Aurelio Zen novels tell us plenty about the way Italian society operates – and they're well-plotted whodunits to boot, with Zen as the classically eccentric loner detective.

Conor Fitzgerald *The Dogs of Rome; The Fatal Touch;* and others. Fitzgerald's complex thrillers, set in the capital, are crammed full of intrigue and local colour, and keep you reading until the last page.

David Hewson *A Season for the Dead; The Villa of Mysteries; The Sacred Cut;* and others. Hewson's popular series of thrillers, starring detective Nic Costa, are mostly set in Rome, and are good yarns, well told, and full of local Roman colour and locations.

Tobias Jones *The Salati Affair* The latest lover of Italy to set tales of murder and intrigue in the country, Jones (author of *The Dark Heart of Italy;* see p.336) understands the country better than most, and as such is eminently suited to assume the mantle of the late Michael Dibdin. His detective, Castagnetti, is a classic gumshoe – he doesn't do things by the book and has a chaotic personal life. This book, and the subsequent Castagnetti novels, *Death of a Showgirl,* and his latest, *Blood on the Altar,* are not all set in Rome but are great accompaniments to any trip to the city.

Iain Pears *The Raphael Affair; The Bernini Bust; The Titian Committee; Death and Restoration;* and others. Recently reissued, and rightly so, Pears's successful series of thrillers with an art-historical theme are all set in Rome and make great holiday reading. There are plenty of local settings and descriptions, not to mention fast-paced art-world intrigue, with robbery, forgery and general skulduggery.

HISTORY

Jonathan Boardman *Cities of the Imagination: Rome.* Like other books in the series, this is both a history of Rome and a celebration of the city and how it has featured in literature through the years.

Jerome Carcopino *Daily Life in Ancient Rome.* Originally published in 1941, and consistently in print since, Carcopino's book is a classic, bringing to life the beliefs, social life and customs of ordinary Romans at the height of the empire.

Edward Gibbon *The History of the Decline and Fall of the Roman Empire.* This abridged version is your best chance to read this classic text, conceived amid the ruins of the Roman Forum in the latter part of the eighteenth century and covering the period from the second century AD to the fall of Constantinople in 1453. Continuum also publishes a handy single volume, but if you want the whole thing, Everyman publishes the full works in three volumes.

Christopher Hibbert *Rome: The Biography of a City.* Simply put, the most entertaining and accessible introduction to the city that you can buy – no less than you would expect from this most prolific of popular historians.

Tom Holland *Rubicon.* This readable book pinpoints a specific but crucial period of Roman history, beginning with the Roman Republic at the height of its greatness and charting its decline up to the death of Augustus in AD 14. Good narrative history, documenting a fascinating era.

Robert Knapp *Invisible Romans.* Knapp's book concentrates on the "Romans that history forgot" – the prostitutes, slaves, freedmen, criminals and other members of the Roman underclass who made the empire, and city, tick. It's not just about Roman lowlife, however, and is especially compelling on the everyday existences of ordinary Roman men and women.

Philip Matyszak *Ancient Rome on Five Denarii a Day.* A mock guide to the city for the imperial-era visitor, with lots of entertaining advice along the lines of "there's no need to pack a toga", but in fact provides a very detailed – and digestible – insight into the life, monuments and customs of the time.

★ **Anthony Majanlahti** *The Families Who Made Rome.* Part history and part on-the-ground itinerary, this book brings the buildings to life with "strange but true" histories of families such as the Borghese, Chigi and Farnese, whose stamp is all over Rome.

Paul Vallely *Untying the Knots.* All is not quite what it seems with the new, more inclusive and socially liberal Pope Francis I, argues Paul Vallely, who has spent time researching the pope's past in Argentina. He discovers that it's true that the new pope took the part of the Argentine poor, albeit from a socially conservative position, but this same man was also badly compromised in his dealings with the military junta that ran the country for so many years. Well-written and well-researched, this is the best book to read for background on the new pope.

ROME IN THE MOVIES

Accatone (1961). Pasolini's eponymous petty thief and pimp is perhaps one of cinema's least likeable creations, but the movie, relentlessly bleak in black-and-white, is most memorable for its no-holds-barred depiction of the hopelessness and amorality of life in Rome's poorest neighbourhoods in the 1960s.

Angels and Demons (2009). Ok, it's not the greatest Rome-based film ever made, but it's better than the other Dan Brown Vatican thriller (*The Da Vinci Code*), and does include a lot of Rome colour and locations; indeed it could have been subsidized by the tourist board, with Tom Hanks and his beautiful sidekick dashing dramatically from one classic location to another.

Belly of an Architect (1987). One of the best movies set in Rome made in (relatively) recent times, Peter Greenaway's film follows the (mis)fortunes of Brian Dennehey's middle-aged architect who arrives in the city to supervise an exhibition of the work of a French rival. A film about creativity, sickness, curvaceous forms (including bellies), but most of all about Rome.

The Bicycle Thieves (1948). A young boy is the witness to his father's humiliation in De Sica's classic movie, set in the poorer quarters of Rome, when he sees him steal a bicycle out of desperation (to get his job back) and immediately get caught. The child's illusions are dashed, and society is held to account, although the masses are also hostile and the only hope seems to lie in the family unit, which the hero falls thankfully back on at the end.

Caesar Must Die (2013). Filmed entirely on location in Rome's Rebibbia prison, this is the Taviani brothers' (*Padre Padrone* is their most famous film) first film for six years, a version of Shakepeare's *Julius Caesar* performed by the hardest-of-the-hard prison inmates. Harshly realistic, and shot in grainy black and white for enhanced realism.

The Conformist (1970). Bertolucci's bold and disturbing film of Moravia's novel follows the career of fascist functionary and assassin Marcello up to the fall of Mussolini. It features some of Rome's more cinematic corners – among them Ponte Sant'Angelo and the Colosseum – among its locations.

Dear Diary (1993). Director, actor and screenwriter Nanni Moretti is seen by some as Rome's Woody Allen, chronicling the lives and neuroses of the city's inhabitants with a series of gentle, well-acted and sophisticated human comedies. Moretti achieved great acclaim with this film in three parts. A gently idiosyncratic and comic work, it covers a range of the director's personal obsessions – apartment blocks, children, telephones, Pasolini's unsolved murder, as well as his own fight against cancer. Very entertaining.

Eat Pray Love (2010). Naturally the "Eat" part of this film takes place in Italy, specifically Rome, where Julia Roberts "finds herself" by discovering the true meaning of food, buying meat from a real butcher's shop just south of Campo de' Fiori and being served by a real butcher!

The Eclipse (1962). Antonioni used the impersonal environs of EUR as the background to this slow-moving tale of doomed love. Short on plot, but with a memorable visual subtlety.

Good Morning Night (2003). This powerful film tells the story of the kidnapping and eventual murder of the Italian prime minister Aldo Moro, from the point of view of one of the participants, who becomes increasingly uncomfortable with events as they unfold.

The Great Beauty (2013). Paolo Sorrentino's latest film has achieved the rare distinction of being feted by arthouse movie critics and notching up commercial success at the same time. It's a Fellini-ish look at the lives of the city's beautiful people – visually ravishing, with gorgeous scenes of Rome, and extremely gripping in its way.

La Dolce Vita (1960). Marcello Mastrioanni is the now-iconic paparazzo in Fellini's stylish 1960s movie about celebrity, style – and ultimately emptiness. Lots of scenes shot on the Via Veneto, in the days when it was considered the city's most fashionable street.

Light of My Eyes (2001). Set in Rome, this is a haunting exploration of the alienation that many feel in their lives and their romantic relationships. The story is particularly strong thanks to the character of Maria, the female lead, free of the usual stereotypes and beautifully acted. Directed by Giuseppe Piccioni.

Mamma Roma (1962). Sort of *Rome Open City* part two – or at least two decades later – with Anna Magnani playing a Roman prostitute who tries to give up life on the street but is forced into petty crime and ends up in prison. One of Pasolini's earliest movies, and one of his most accessible, although it's no barrel of laughs by any means, deliberately showing a stark contrast between Rome the eternal city and the lives of the lowest strata of its underclass.

Massacre in Rome (1973). Based on the book by Robert Katz, this gritty black-and-white drama depicts the true story of an attack on a German SS brigade in Via Rasella and the merciless Nazi backlash that follows, resulting in the Via Ardeatine massacre. Tightly directed, it has a great cast too, starring an excellent Richard Burton as the Gestapo chief who orders the reprisal and Marcello Mastroianni as a conscience-wrangling priest.

Mid-August Lunch (2008). This was the directorial debut of *Gomorrah* scriptwriter Gianni di Gregorio, and it couldn't be more different to his other movie. This is a gentle comedy about a hapless middle-aged man who cares for his mother in a rundown but respectable Trastevere flat. For once, a movie that celebrates being old.

A Perfect Day (2008). Daily life for a number of characters in Rome, but a series of events leads to a tragedy. A fast-moving story of the contemporary city, well told and well acted.

Quiet Chaos (2008). Nanni Moretti is pitch-perfect in this tale of a successful Roman executive dealing with the sudden death of his wife. There are only glimpses of any bits of Rome you might recognize, and for the most part its focus is on the well-heeled suburbs of the city and the nearby beaches. But it's brilliantly acted, with the odd flash of humour, and rather gripping, despite the fact that nothing much happens.

Quo Vadis (1951). Imperial Rome gets the full Hollywood treatment in this epic movie, featuring Robert Taylor and Deborah Kerr in an all-star cast that includes Peter Ustinov as Nero and Sophia Loren as an uncredited extra. The focus in on the decadence and corruption of the empire under Nero, and – and in true Hollywood style – the emergence of Christianity as the only viable alternative. Grand and compelling, but not really a history lesson.

Roma (1972). Fellini's collection of disconnected Roman scenes is completely compelling, switching between wartime and the present-day and including some unforgettable sequences, from a hyper-realistic brothel scene to a grotesque clerical fashion parade.

Roman Holiday (1953). Gregory Peck and Audrey Hepburn (in her first major role) are at their sparkling best in this popular and successful romantic comedy, which uses the city, in particular Piazza di Spagna and around, as a backdrop, with flair and invention. Indeed it gave the city an enormous boost in tourism after its 1953 release. Prize for the least obvious location is the scene in the "embassy", which is actually Palazzo Barberini.

Rome Open City (1945). As the tanks were rolling out of Rome in 1945, Roberto Rossellini cobbled together the bare minimum of finances, crew and equipment and started shooting this movie, using real locations, documentary footage and low-grade film, and coming up with a grainy, idiosyncratic style that influenced not only his Italian contemporaries, but also the American film noir of the late 1940s.

To Rome with Love (2012). Woody Allen's homage to the city is laden with romantic clichés and feels a bit thrown together, but as a visual portrait of the city, it's very watchable indeed. Recognizable spots include Cinema Farnese, *Sabatino* in Trastevere, the *Caffe della Pace*, and the *Vecchia Pineta* restaurant, overlooking the sea in Ostia Lido.

Sacro GRA (2013). This survey of the lives of the people who inhabit the areas around Rome's ringroad, the Grande Raccordo Annulare, was the first documentary to win the Golden Lion award at the Venice film festival, and you can see why – its portraits of the various characters are penetrating, insightful and entertaining. A compelling view of contemporary life in Italy, in the capital's nether regions.

The Talented Mr Ripley (1999). Matt Damon plays the cool and charismatic Ripley in this slick thriller, which is mostly set in the Naples area but has a few choice scenes set in Rome, including Piazza Mattei and the Ghetto (where Ripley bases himself while in the city), Piazza Navona and *Caffé Latino* in Testaccio.

Three Coins in a Fountain (1954). Having chucked their coins into the Trevi Fountain, three American girls search for romance in Rome, and of course succeed big-time, with a variety of handsome suitors.

We Have a Pope (2011). Nanni Moretti's latest film follows a man elected against his will as the new pope, and how he deals with the panic that ensues. Sadly, filming isn't allowed inside the Vatican, so Villa Medici and Palazzo Farnese substituted for the real Vatican interiors.

Yesterday, Today, Tomorrow (1965). This Vittorio die Sica comedy tells the stories of three Italian women: a cigarette-seller in Naples, a prostitute in Rome and the wife of an industrialist in Milan. Marcello Mastroianni is superb, as is Sophia Loren, who also gets her kit off (well, almost).

ART AND ARCHITECTURE

Amanda Claridge *Oxford Archaeological Guides: Rome*. Newly updated and expanded, this is an excellently written concise guide to the archaeology of the ancient city – a good investment if this is your particular area of interest.

Christopher Duggan *A Concise History of Italy*. The best all-round history of the Italian nation that you can buy – this is concise and well written, covering everything from the fall of the Roman Empire to Unification and beyond.

Andrew Graham-Dixon *Michelangelo and the Sistine Chapel*. This is the story of the most brilliant creation of the Renaissance, beautifully retold as a warts-and-all tale of gritty endeavour, political wilfulness and pure genius.

★ **Andrew Graham-Dixon** *Caravaggio: A Life Sacred and Profane*. A page-turner in the best sense, charting the painter's dangerous life at the heart of the Rome art scene in racy yet informed prose that brilliantly analyses his most famous paintings but also grippingly conjures up the man and the period. So much more than a book about painting.

Keith Hopkins and Mary Beard *The Colosseum*. An extremely readable history of the famous monument, full of architectural, literary and often very funny anecdotes. Not only does it give you the background to its construction, demise and resurrection but also advice on site visits.

Robert Hughes *Rome*. The Australian art historian's stab at writing a definitive, chronological guide to the city's art and architecture, and not a bad effort – a big book, but an engagingly written one, with lots of cultural and historical background, anecdote and opinion.

Keith Miller *St Peter's*. Part of Profile's excellent series focusing on great monuments, this is the last word on St Peter's, covering both its long development and construction and its far-reaching influence.

Giorgio Vasari *The Lives of the Artists*. There is no better background work on the artists of the Renaissance, written by a contemporary and correspondent of his subjects, who include Raphael, Michelangelo and others less relevant to Rome. Available in a very readable English translation.

Margaret Visser *The Geometry of Love*. Basically an extended tour of the church of Sant'Agnese fuori le Mura, and an absorbing study not just of the building and its history but also of the iconography and architecture of all Christian churches. Currently out of print.

David Watkin *The Roman Forum*. Another in Profile's "Wonders of the World" series, Watkin's book brings to life the stones and rubble of the Forum better than anyone else has yet managed.

TRAVEL, IMPRESSIONS AND FOOD

Elizabeth Bowen *A Time in Rome* (see p.332). Though written in the 1950s, Bowen's book endures because it is so engaging, and because it summarizes so well the longevity and continuity of Rome.

Anthony Doerr *Four Seasons in Rome*. The American novelist Anthony Doerr's recent memoir captures the modern city with clarity and imagination, describing both domestic issues like bringing up two tiny babies in a foreign city and earth-shattering events such as the funeral of Pope John Paul II with the same degree of wit and perspicacity. One of the more relevant and evocative recent travelogues you could read.

David Downie & Alison Harris *Food Wine Rome*. Part of the *"Terroir Guides"* series, this beautiful book tells you everything you need to know about the food and wine of Rome and its region, with some fascinating background on local produce and ingredients, beautiful photos and great recommendations for authentic local restaurants and shops.

Tobias Jones *The Dark Heart of Italy*. Not specifically about Rome, indeed it barely touches on the city at all, but Jones's book is a refreshingly contemporary take on Italy, and as such is a good book to take with you on any trip to the capital – assuming, that is, you want to read about the sleaze, corruption and dysfunctionality that make up the contemporary nation.

Carlo Levi *Fleeting Rome*. Posthumously published in 2002, this collection of 33 essays, written over a decade spent in Rome in the Sixties and Seventies by the great twentieth-century writer and politician, skilfully and evocatively encapsulate a city that no longer exists.

Diane Seed *Love Food Love Rome*. A comprehensive illustrated guide to the best of the city's cuisine, with listings of shops, restaurants, wine bars and markets – and recipes for all the Roman classics – by a long-time Roman expat and foodie.

H.V. Morton *A Traveller in Rome*. Like all Morton's books, this is a marvellously personal stroll around the sights, reflecting on history, architecture and culture.

William Murray *Italy: The Fatal Gift*. Out of print, but worth trying to get hold of for its perceptive essays on history and modern Italian life and culture, especially with regard to Rome, where Murray lived for many years, filing regular pieces for the *New Yorker*. Try also the in-print *City of the Soul*, Murray's latest slim volume of essays, walks and musings on the city. See also p.327.

David Winner *Al Dente: Madness, Beauty and the Food of Rome*. Winner is clearly fascinated by every aspect of Rome past and present, and hops from one subject to another like any passionate devotee. Much more than a book about food, this is great to read on any trip to Rome, full of the sort of profound and trivial detail that enhances any visit.

LITERATURE

Niccolo Ammaniti *Let the Games Begin*. Ammaniti is one of Italy's most popular and successful literary novelists writing today. His latest book, set in a dysfunctional vision of Rome, is both a dystopian fantasy and a critique of a corrupt society that has become obsessed by money, celebrity and public image.

Carlo Emilio Gadda *That Awful Mess on Via Merulana*. Superficially a detective story, this celebrated modernist novel is so dense a weave of physical reality and literary diversions that the reader is led away from a solution rather than towards it; it enjoys the sort of status in Italian fiction that *Ulysses* has in English.

Nathaniel Hawthorne *The Marble Faun*. A nineteenth-century take on the lives of Anglo-American expats in the Eternal City: sculptors, passionate lovers – the usual mad mix and excessive goings-on that you'll still find today.

Margaret Mazzantini *Don't Move*. Intense psychological novel of midlife crisis, sex and obsession in Rome that was a massive bestseller in Italy and made into a movie directed by the author's husband. The city and its outskirts form a bleak, rain-soaked backdrop.

Elsa Morante *History*. Capturing daily Roman life during the last war, this is probably the most vivid fictional picture of the conflict as seen from the city.

★ **Alberto Moravia** *The Conformist*. A psychological novel about a man sucked into the abyss of Fascism by his desperation to conform. In *The Woman of Rome*, Moravia uses the Rome of the Mussolini era as a delicate backdrop for this detached yet compassionate tale of a Roman model and prostitute. Also worth a read is *Roman Tales*, a collection of short stories that has the lives of ordinary Romans as its thread.

★ **Glyn Pursglove (ed)** *Rome: a Collection of the Poetry of Place*. A wonderful little book, made up of a well-chosen selection of poems and extracts relating to all aspects and all eras of the city.

Tom Rachman *The Imperfectionists*. A collection of interwoven stories about the various people who work on a long-running but declining English-language newspaper in Rome. Very much a novel of the city, with an, at times, forensic scrutiny of the often sad, random and occasionally hilarious lives of a well-realised and credible set of characters. Literate and intelligent, but also very readable.

Matt Rees *A Name in Blood*. Crime writer Rees gets to grips with the story of Caravaggio's time in Rome and his flight to Malta following the murder of a rival, with bold storytelling and well-crafted, page-turning prose that brings the era to life in what is a high-quality historical thriller.

Leonard Sciascia *The Moro Affair*. Sciascia is one of Italy's – and in particular Sicily's – greatest postwar writers, and this is one of his least-known works, a non-fiction account of the events that led up to the murder of the Italian prime Minister in 1978 (see p.58). Grippingly written, with good background on the political landscape of the time, including many of Moro's own letters.

Irving Stone *The Agony and the Ecstasy*. Stone's dramatized life of Michelangelo, popular "faction" that is entertaining even if it doesn't exactly get to the root of the artist's work and times.

William Weaver (ed) *Open City: Seven Writers in Postwar Rome* (see p.324). An anthology of pieces by some of the best modern Italian novelists – Bassani, Silone, Moravia, Ginzburg, among others – selected and with an introduction by one of the most eminent postwar Italian translators.

Marguerite Yourcenar *Memoirs of Hadrian*. Yourcenar's reflective narrative details the main events of the Emperor Hadrian's rule, most of it in the form of letters to his nephew, Marcus Aurelius, documenting at once the Roman Empire at its height and the very human anxieties of perhaps its wisest and most accomplished leader. See also Yourcenar's conceptual Roman novel, now out of print, *A Coin in Nine Hands*.

Language

The ability to speak English confers prestige in Italy, and there's often no shortage of people willing to show off their knowledge, especially in Rome. But using at least some Italian, however tentatively, can mark you out from the masses in a city used to hordes of tourists, and having a little more can open up the city no end. The words and phrases below should help you master the basics. If you want a decent phrasebook, look no further than the *Rough Guide Italian Phrasebook*, which packs a huge amount of phrases and vocabulary into a handy dictionary format. There are lots of good pocket dictionaries – the Collins range represents probably the best all-round choice, with their Gem or Pocket formats perfect for travelling purposes.

When speaking to strangers, the third person is the polite form (ie: *lei* instead of *tu* for "you"); using the second person is a mark of disrespect or stupidity. It's also worth remembering that Italians don't use "please" and "thank you" half as much as we do: it's all implied in the tone, but if in doubt, err on the polite side.

PRONUNCIATION

Italian is one of the easiest European languages of which to learn the basics, especially if you already have a smattering of French or Spanish. Easiest of all is the pronunciation, since every word is spoken exactly as it's written, and usually enunciated with exaggerated, open-mouthed clarity. All Italian words are stressed on the penultimate syllable unless an accent (´ or `) denotes otherwise. The only difficulties you're likely to encounter are the few consonants that are different from English:

c before e or i is pronounced as in **ch**urch, while ch before the same vowels is hard, as in **c**at.

sci or **sce** are pronounced as in **sh**eet and **sh**elter respectively. The same goes with **g** – soft before e or i, as in **g**eranium; hard before a, o, u and h, as in **g**arlic.

gn has the ni sound of onion.

gl in Italian is softened to something like li in English, as in stallion.

h is not aspirated, as in **h**onour.

WORDS AND PHRASES

BASICS

Good morning	Buongiorno	I'm fine	Bene
Good afternoon/evening	Buonasera	Do you speak English?	Parla inglese?
Good night	Buonanotte	I don't understand	Non ho capito
Hello/goodbye	Ciao (informal; to strangers use phrases above)	I don't know	Non lo so
		Excuse me	Mi scusi
		Excuse me (in a crowd)	Permesso
		I'm sorry	Mi dispiace
Goodbye	Arrivederci	I'm here on holiday	Sono qui in vacanza
Yes	Sì	I'm English	Sono inglese
No	No	Scottish	scozzese
Please	Per favore	Welsh	gallese
Thank you (very much)	Grazie (molte/Grazie mille)	Irish	irlandese
You're welcome	Prego	American (masculine/ feminine)	americano/a
All right/that's OK	Va bene		
How are you? (informal/ formal)	Come stai/sta?	Australian (masculine/ feminine)	australiano/a

a New Zealander	neozelandese
Today	Oggi
Tomorrow	Domani
Day after tomorrow	Dopodomani
Yesterday	Ieri
Now	Adesso
Later	Più tardi
Wait a minute!	Aspetta!
Let's go!	Andiamo!
In the morning	Di mattina
In the afternoon	Nel pomeriggio
In the evening	Di sera
Here/There	Qui/Là
Good/Bad	Buono/Cattivo
Big/Small	Grande/Piccolo
Cheap/Expensive	Economico/Caro
Early/Late	Presto/Tardi
Hot/Cold	Caldo/Freddo
Near/Far	Vicino/Lontano
Quickly/Slowly	Velocemente/Lentamente
With/Without	Con/Senza
More/Less	Più/Meno
Enough, no more	Basta

SIGNS

Entrance/Exit	Entrata/Uscita
Free entrance	Ingresso libero
Gentlemen/Ladies	Signori/Signore
No smoking	Vietato fumare
WC/Bathroom	Gabinetto/Bagno
Open/Closed	Aperto/Chiuso
Closed for restoration	Chiuso per restauro
Closed for holidays	Chiuso per ferie
Pull/Push	Tirare/Spingere
Cash desk	Cassa
Go, walk	Avanti
Stop, halt	Alt

ACCOMMODATION

Hotel	Albergo
Is there a hotel nearby?	C'è un albergo qui vicino?
Do you have a room…	Ha una cámera…
for one/two/three person/people	per una/due/tre persona/e
for one/two/three night/s	per una/due/tre notte/i
for one/two week/s	per una/due settimana/e
with a double bed	con un letto matrimoniale
with a shower/bath	con una doccia/un bagno
with a balcony	con balcone
hot/cold water	acqua calda/fredda
How much is it?	Quanto costa?

It's expensive	È caro
Is breakfast included?	È compresa la prima colazione?
Do you have anything cheaper?	Ha qualcosa che costa di meno?
Full/half board	Pensione completa/ mezza pensione
Can I see the room?	Posso vedere la camera?
I'll take it	La prendo
I'd like to book a room	Vorrei prenotare una camera
I have a booking	Ho una prenotazione

QUESTIONS AND DIRECTIONS

Where? (Where is/ where are…?)	Dove? (Dov'è/Dove sono…?)
When?	Quando?
What? (What is it?)	Cosa? (Cos'è?)
How much/many?	Quanto/Quanti?
Why?	Perché?
It is/there is	C'e…? (Is it/is there…?)
What time is it?	Che ore sono?
How do I get to…?	Per arrivare a…?
How far is it to…?	Quant'è lontano…?
Can you tell me when to get off?	Mi può dire dove scendere?
What time does it open/close?	A che ora apre/chiude?
How much does it/ do they cost?	Quanto costa/costano?
What's it called in Italian?	Come si chiama in italiano?

DAYS OF THE WEEK

Monday	Lunedì
Tuesday	Martedì
Wednesday	Mercoledì
Thursday	Giovedì
Friday	Venerdì
Saturday	Sabato
Sunday	Domenica

MONTHS OF THE YEAR

January	gennaio
February	februario
March	marzo
April	aprile
May	maggio
June	giugno
July	luglio
August	agosto
September	settembre
October	ottobre
November	novembre
December	dicembre

NUMBERS

1	uno	20	venti
2	due	21	ventuno
3	tre	22	ventidue
4	quattro	30	trenta
5	cinque	40	quaranta
6	sei	50	cinquanta
7	sette	60	sessanta
8	otto	70	settanta
9	nove	80	ottanta
10	dieci	90	novanta
11	undici	100	cento
12	dodici	101	centuno
13	tredici	110	centodieci
14	quattordici	200	duecento
15	quindici	500	cinquecento
16	sedici	1000	mille
17	diciassette	5000	cinquemila
18	diciotto	10,000	diecimila
19	diciannove	50,000	cinquantamila

MENU READER

BASICS AND SNACKS

Aceto	Vinegar
Aglio	Garlic
Arancini	Stuffed rice-balls
Biscotti	Biscuits
Burro	Butter
Caramelle	Sweets
Cioccolato	Chocolate
Formaggio	Cheese
Frittata	Omelette
Marmellata	Jam
Olio	Oil
Olive	Olives
Pane	Bread
Pepe	Pepper
Riso	Rice
Sale	Salt
Uova	Eggs
Yogurt	Yoghurt
Zucchero	Sugar
Zuppa	Soup

Minestrina	Clear broth with small pasta shapes
Minestrone	Thick vegetable soup
Paccheri	Big hollow pasta tubes
Pasta al forno	Pasta baked with minced meat, eggs, tomato and cheese
Pasta e fagioli	Pasta with beans
Pastina in brodo	Pasta pieces in clear broth
Penne	Smaller version of rigatoni
Rigatoni	Large, grooved tubular pasta
Stracciatella	Broth with egg
Tagliatelle	Pasta ribbons, another word for fettuccine
Tonnarelli	The same as bucatini, see above
Tortellini	Rings of pasta, stuffed with meat or cheese
Vermicelli	Thin spaghetti ("little worms")

THE FIRST COURSE (IL PRIMO)

Bucatini	Thick, hollow spaghetti – classically Roman
Brodo	Clear broth
Farfalle	Butterfly-shaped pasta
Fettuccine	Narrow pasta ribbons
Gnocchi	Small potato and dough dumplings
Maccheroni	Macaroni pasta

PASTA SAUCES (SALSA)

Amatriciana	Tomato sauce with diced guanciale or bacon (literally pig's cheek)
Arrabbiata	Spicy tomato, with chillies ("angry")
Carbonara	Bacon, pecorino cheese and beaten egg
Cacio e pepe	Pecorino cheese and freshly ground pepper

Alla gricia	Pecorino cheese and chunks of guanciale or bacon
Alla pajata	With calves' intestines
Peperoncino	With olive oil, garlic and fresh chillies
Pomodoro	Tomato
Puttanesca	Tomato, anchovy, olive oil and oregano ("whorish")
Al ragù	With meat sauce
Alle vongole	With baby clams

THE SECOND COURSE (IL SECONDO)
MEAT (CARNE)

Abbacchio	Young, roast lamb
Agnello	Lamb
Bistecca	Steak
Carpaccio	Slices of raw beef
Cervello	Brain, usually calves'
Cinghiale	Wild boar
Coda alla vaccinara	Stewed oxtail
Coniglio	Rabbit
Coratella	Sweetmeats
Costoletta	Cutlet, chop
Fegato	Liver
Lingua	Tongue
Maiale	Pork
Manzo	Beef
Milza	Spleen
Ossobuco	Shin of veal
Pancetta	Bacon
Pollo	Chicken
Polpette	Meatballs
Porchetta	Roast suckling pig
Rognoni	Kidneys
Salsiccia	Sausage
Saltimbocca	Veal with ham and sage
Spezzatino	Stew
Trippa	Tripe
Vitello	Veal

FISH (PESCE) AND SHELLFISH (CROSTACEI)

Acciughe	Anchovies
Anguilla	Eel
Aragosta	Lobster
Baccalà	Dried salted cod, usually served fried in batter
Calamari	Squid
Cefalo	Grey mullet
Cozze	Mussels
Dentice	Sea bream
Gamberetti	Shrimps
Gamberi	Prawns
Granchio	Crab
Merluzzo	Cod
Ostriche	Oysters
Pesce spada	Swordfish
Polpo	Octopus
Rospo	Monkfish
Sampiero	John Dory
Sarde	Sardines
Sogliola	Sole
Tonno	Tuna
Trota	Trout
Vongole	Clams

VEGETABLES (CONTORNI), HERBS (ERBE AROMATICHE) AND SALAD (INSALATA)

Asparagi	Asparagus
Carciofi	Artichokes
Carciofini	Artichoke hearts
Cavolfiore	Cauliflower
Cavolo	Cabbage
Cipolla	Onion
Fagioli	Beans
Fagiolini	Green beans
Fiori di zucca	Courgette flowers, sometimes stuffed with anchovies
Finocchio	Fennel
Funghi	Mushrooms
Insalata verde/mista	Green/mixed salad
Lenticchie	Lentils
Melanzane	Aubergine
Patate	Potatoes
Peperoni	Peppers
Piselli	Peas
Pomodori	Tomatoes
Puntarelle	A kind of chicory, very Roman
Radicchio	Red salad leaves
Spinaci	Spinach

USEFUL TERMS

Ai ferri	Grilled without oil
Al dente	Firm, not overcooked
Al forno	Baked
Al sangue	Rare
Alla brace	Barbecued
Alla griglia	Grilled
Alla milanese	Fried in egg and breadcrumbs
Alla pizzaiola	Cooked in tomato sauce
Allo spiedo	On the spit
Arrosto	Roast
Ben cotto	Well done

Bollito/lesso	Boiled
Cotto	Cooked (not raw)
Crudo	Raw
Fritto	Fried
In umido	Stewed
Ripieno	Stuffed
Stracotto	Braised, stewed

CHEESE (FORMAGGI)

Dolcelatte	Creamy blue cheese
Fontina	Northern Italian cheese, often used in cooking
Gorgonzola	Soft, strong, blue-veined cheese, available in "dolce" (creamy) or "piccante" (strong) varieties
Pecorino	Strong, hard sheep's cheese, used in Rome instead of parmesan
Provola/Provolone	Smooth, round mild cheese, made from buffalo or sheep's milk; sometimes smoked
Ricotta	Soft, white sheep's cheese

SWEETS (DOLCI), FRUIT (FRUTTA) AND NUTS (NOCI)

Amaretti	Macaroons
Ananas	Pineapple
Anguria/Coccomero	Watermelon
Arance	Oranges
Banane	Bananas
Cacchi	Persimmons
Ciliegie	Cherries
Crostata	Pastry tart with a jam, chocolate or ricotta topping
Fichi	Figs
Fichi d'India	Prickly pears
Fragole	Strawberries
Gelato	Ice cream
Limone	Lemon

Macedonia	Fruit salad
Mandorle	Almonds
Mele	Apples
Melone	Melon
Pangiallo	A heavy cake of fruit and nuts
Pere	Pears
Pesche	Peaches
Pinoli	Pine nuts
Pistacchio	Pistachio nut
Torta	Cake, tart
Uva	Grapes
Zabaglione	Dessert made with eggs, sugar and marsala wine
Zuppa Inglese	Trifle

DRINKS

Acqua minerale	Mineral water
Aranciata	Orangeade
Bicchiere	Glass
Birra	Beer
Bottiglia	Bottle
Caffè	Coffee
Cioccolato caldo	Hot chocolate
Ghiaccio	Ice
Granita	Crushed ice with coffee or fruit
Latte	Milk
Limonata	Lemonade
Spremuta	Fresh fruit juice
Spumante	Sparkling wine
Succo	Concentrated fruit juice with sugar
Tè	Tea
Tonica	Tonic water
Vino	Wine
rosso/bianco/rosato secco/dolce	red/white/rosé/dry/ sweet
Litro	Litre
Mezzo	Half
Quarto	Quarter
Caraffa	Carafe
Salute!	Cheers!

Small print and index

344 Small print

345 About the author

346 Index

357 Map symbols

A ROUGH GUIDE TO ROUGH GUIDES

Published in 1982, the first Rough Guide – to Greece – was a student scheme that became a publishing phenomenon. Mark Ellingham, a recent graduate in English from Bristol University, had been travelling in Greece the previous summer and couldn't find the right guidebook. With a small group of friends he wrote his own guide, combining a highly contemporary, journalistic style with a thoroughly practical approach to travellers' needs.

The immediate success of the book spawned a series that rapidly covered dozens of destinations. And, in addition to impecunious backpackers, Rough Guides soon acquired a much broader readership that relished the guides' wit and inquisitiveness as much as their enthusiastic, critical approach and value-for-money ethos.

These days, Rough Guides include recommendations from budget to luxury and cover more than 120 destinations around the globe, as well as producing an ever-growing range of eBooks.

Visit **roughguides.com** to find all our latest books, read articles, get inspired and share travel tips with the Rough Guides community.

Rough Guide credits

Editors: Helen Abramson, Mandy Tomlin
Layout: Jessica Subramanian
Cartography: Rajesh Chhibber
Picture editors: Michelle Bhatia, Mark Thomas
Proofreader: Stewart Wild
Managing editor: Monica Woods
Assistant editor: Prema Dutta

Production: Charlotte Cade
Cover design: Wilf Matos, Jessica Subramanian
Editorial assistant: Olivia Rawes
Senior pre-press designer: Dan May
Programme manager: Helen Blount
Publisher: Joanna Kirby

Publishing information

This sixth edition published May 2014 by
Rough Guides Ltd,
80 Strand, London WC2R 0RL
11, Community Centre, Panchsheel Park,
New Delhi 110017, India
Distributed by Penguin Random House
Penguin Books Ltd,
80 Strand, London WC2R 0RL
Penguin Group (USA)
345 Hudson Street, NY 10014, USA
Penguin Group (Australia)
250 Camberwell Road, Camberwell,
Victoria 3124, Australia
Penguin Group (NZ)
67 Apollo Drive, Mairangi Bay, Auckland 1310,
New Zealand
Penguin Group (South Africa)
Block D, Rosebank Office Park, 181 Jan Smuts Avenue,
Parktown North, Gauteng, South Africa 2193
Rough Guides is represented in Canada by Tourmaline
Editions Inc. 662 King Street West, Suite 304, Toronto,
Ontario M5V 1M7
Printed in Malaysia by Vivar Printing Sdn.Bhd.

MIX
Paper from
responsible sources
FSC
www.fsc.org
FSC™ C018179

Help us update

We've gone to a lot of effort to ensure that the sixth
edition of **The Rough Guide to Rome** is accurate and up-
to-date. However, things change – places get "discovered",
opening hours are notoriously fickle, restaurants and
rooms raise prices or lower standards. If you feel we've got
it wrong or left something out, we'd like to know, and if
you can remember the address, the price, the hours, the
phone number, so much the better.

Please send your comments with the subject line
"**Rough Guide Rome Update**" to ✉ mail@uk.roughguides
.com. We'll credit all contributions and send a copy of the
next edition (or any other Rough Guide if you prefer) for
the very best emails.

Find more travel information, connect with fellow
travellers and plan your trip on ⓦ roughguides.com

ABOUT THE AUTHOR

Martin Dunford is the author of Rough Guides to Rome, Italy, Amsterdam and New York, among others, and is a freelance writer and editor. He lives in London and Norfolk with his wife and two daughters. Martin fell in love with Rome twenty years ago, when he spent a summer there, and has travelled back every year since, gradually introducing members of his family to the delights of Roman food, Caravaggio's painting and lazing around in the Villa Borghese.

Acknowledgements

Big thanks to Judy Edelhoff and Phil Lee for their invaluable contributions. Thanks also to all those who wrote in with suggestions and comments on the last edition; to Steve Brenner at Cross-Pollinate and the Beehive; to GowithOh apartments; to Helen Abramson for smoothly seeing this one through; and as always to Caroline, Daisy and Lucy for happy days in Rome and many more to come.

Photo credits

All photos © Rough Guides except the following:
(Key: a-above; b-below/bottom; c-centre; f-far; l-left; r-right; t-top)

p.1 4Corners/Sandra Raccanello
p.2 Alamy Images/Adam Eastland
p.7 4Corners/Luigi Vaccarella (br)
p.10 Corbis/MAX ROSSI (c)
p.13 Getty Images/Alex Grimm (b); SuperStock (t)
p.14 Alamy Images/Carlo Bollo (t)
p.36 Alamy Images
p.43 Corbis/Danny Lehman
p.51 Corbis/Guido Cozzi
p.69 Robert Harding Picture Library/Riccardo Sala (t); Gari Williams (b)
p.83 Robert Harding Picture Library/Raimund Kutter (t); John Miller (b)
p.121 Alamy Images/Susan Wright (tr)
p.149 Robert Harding Picture Library/Raimund Kutter (tr)
p.163 Alamy Images/Susan Wright (tl); SuperStock/Jochen Tack (b); Gari Williams (tr)

p.225 4Corners/Bernhart Udo
p.229 SuperStock/Gonzalo Azumendi (tl)
p.239 SuperStock
p.247 SuperStock/Degas Jean-Pierre (tl)
p.267 SuperStock (b)
p.271 Micca Club PR/Ursula Persiani
p.284 Alamy Images/Stephane Gautier

Front cover The Vatican City, view to St Peter's Basilica © JLImages/Alamy Images
Back cover Via dei Baullari looking towards Campo de' Fiori © Robert Harding Picture Library/Mirko Milovanovic (a); Palazzo Massimo © Rough Guides/Roger Mapp (bl); Gelato sign © Rough Guides/Natascha Sturny (br)

Index

Maps are marked in grey

A

Abbazia delle Tre Fontane......156
Abbazia 220
Accademia di San Luca 101
accessories...........................288
accommodation.......... 225–238
Acqua Felice Aqueduct 110
airlines 20
airport enquiries 21
airports 21
Alemanno, Gianni..................317
Alexander VII, Pope...............194
Algardi, Alessandro................ 71
All Saints Church.................... 97
Altemps Chapel...................... 48
ambulance 29
American Academy 33, 166
American Express 28
Ancient Rome...................74–90
Ancient Rome...................... 76
Palatine Hill 86
Roman Forum 80–81
Andreotti, Giulio 58
antiques 285
Anzio 222
apartment rentals 237
aperitivo spots......................266
Appartamento Borgia.............202
Aqua Claudia.........................153
Aquinas, Thomas 40
Ara Pacis............................... 99
Aracoeli Staircase.................. 67
Arch of Constantine............... 89
Arch of Janus........................ 73
Arch of Septimius Severus
.... 84
Arch of Titus 85
Archeobus 25, 148
architecture 319–321
Ariccia 221
arrival 21
ATAC 23
ATM machines 28
Auditorium...........................180
Auditorium of Maecenas........122
Augustus..........................98, 99
Aula Ottagona 124
Aurelian Wall 147
Aventine Hill.........................138
Aventine Hill and south, the
.... 138–156
Aventine Hill and south, the
.... 140–141

B

babysitting services................303
banks 28
Barberini family....................104
bars (by area)............... 264–270
Aventine Hill and south, the........269
Campo de' Fiori and the Ghetto... 265
Celian Hill and San Giovanni, the
.................................269
Centro Storico 264
Esquiline, Monti and Termini, the
.................................268
Pigneto 269
Quirinale, Veneto, Villa Borghese
and north, the 268
Trastevere 270
Tridente and Trevi, the 266
Vatican and Prati, the 270
bars (by name) 264–270
0.75....................................265
Abbey Theatre.....................264
Ai Tre Scalini.......................268
Al Vino al Vino 268
Aleph.................................268
Annibale Vini & Spiriti..........268
Antica Enoteca....................266
Artù 270
Baccano 266
Bar à Book..........................268
Bar del Fico 264
Bartaruga...........................265
Caffe della Pace 264
Camponeschi.......................265
Canova...............................266
Cavour 313 268
Club Machiavelli..................269
Cul de Sac 264
D'Inghilterra........................268
De la Minerve......................268
De Russie............................268
Do Bar 266
Druid's Den.........................269
Eden..................................268
Enoteca Achilli.....................264
Enoteca Ferrara....................270
Etabli.................................264
Fiddler's Elbow....................269
Finnegan 269
Fonclea 270
Forum................................268
Four Green Fields.................270
Freni and Frezioni................270
'Gusto Wine Bar 266
Hotel First...........................269
Ice Club..............................269
Il Goccetto 265
Il Piccolo 264
Il Tiaso 269
Jonathan's Angels 265
Ketumbar............................269

L'Angolo Divino...................266
La Vi..................................266
La Vineria...........................266
Le Coppelle 265
Les Affiches 265
Locarno..............................266
Lowenhaus 266
Ma Che Siete Venuti A Fà 270
Necci dal 1924.....................269
Nuvolari.............................270
Oasi della Birra 269
Ombre Rosse 270
Open Baladin.......................266
Pentagrappolo.....................269
Radisson Blu Es....................268
ReRe Bar 268
Rgb46.................................269
Rosati.................................266
Salotto 42...........................265
San Calisto 270
Saxophone 270
Scholars' Lounge 266
Senza Fondo 270
St George............................268
Trimani 269
Trinity College 265
Vinaietto.............................266
Basilica di San Pietro... 190–195
Basilica Emilia...................... 81
Basilica Julia........................ 82
Basilica of Maxentius............. 84
Basilica Ulpia 77
Baths of Caracalla 143
Baths of Diocletian................124
Baths of Septimius Severus 87
beaches...............................222
bed and breakfast 237
beer....................................264
Befana, La 306
Belvedere Palace...................193
Bembo, Pietro 40
Bernini, Gianlorenzo 37,
40, 44, 50, 98, 104, 122,
169–174, 190, 194, 320
Bernini, Pietro 94
bike rental 25, 26
bike sharing......................... 25
BIRG tickets......................... 26
BNL Building........................107
Bocca della Verità 72
Bonaparte, Carlotta 49
Bonaparte, Letizia................. 49
Bonaparte, Napoleon............. 49
books about Rome...... 332–337
bookshops 285
Borghese, Pauline..................172
Borghese, Scipione Caffarelli
.................................169
Borgo 186

Borromini..........41, 44, 46, 53, 56, 100, 104, 108, 320
Boscolo Hotel Palace...............107
Bowen, Elizabeth ...322–324, 336
Bracciano........................219
Braccio Nuovo 207
Bramante......................47, 165, 190
Brawne, Fanny 94
Brigate Rosse.......................58
British Embassy 111
British School 33
British War Cemetery 145
Brueghel the Elder 37
Bruno, Giordano......................52
Bus #110 25
bus stations 22
buses........................23, 24
buses, around Lazio..................26
Byron......................94

C

cafés (by area) 242–261
Aventine Hill and south, the........258
Campo de' Fiori and the Ghetto ... 248
Celian Hill and San Giovanni, the 257
Centro Storico 242
Esquiline, Monti and Termini.......255
Quirinale and Via Veneto, the......253
Trastevere and the Janiculum Hill 259
Tridente and Trevi, the 250
Vatican and Prati, the 261
Villa Borghese and north 254
cafés (by name)........... 242–261
Antico Caffè del Brasile...............255
Antico Caffè Greco................250
Antico Forno Roscioli 248
Babington's Tea Rooms.............250
Barnum Café........................248
Boulangerie MP.........................242
Buccone........................250
Café Di Marzio........................259
Caffè Camerino.................248
Caffè del Seme e la Foglia 258
Caffè Fagi 255
Caffè Farnese 248
Caffè Peru.........................248
Caffè Sant'Eustachio...............242
Casina dell'Orologio...............254
Chiostro di Bramante 243
Conter........................257
Dagnino..........................255
Gianfornaio..................253
Gianicolo........................259
Herbier Nature 250
Il Forno di Campo de' Fiori............248
La Bottega del Caffè................255
La Caffetteria 243
La Renella........................259
Lo Zozzone........................243
Mondo Arancina 261
Museo-Atelier Canova-Tadolini 250
Palombini........................258
Pascucci.........................243
Pizzarium........................261
Sciascia Caffè...................261
Sesto........................254
Sisini.........................259
Strabbioni......................253
Tazza d'Oro......................243
Valentini......................257
Vitti.........................245
Volpetti Più....................258
calling cards 33
Campo de' Fiori 52
Campo de' Fiori and the Ghetto 51–61
Campo de' Fiori and the Ghetto 54–55
Campo Verano cemetery........127
campsites 238
Camping Fabulous 238
Camping Flaminio 238
Camping Tiber...................238
Capalbio........................223
Capella di Niccolo V................201
Capitoline Hill 66
Capitoline Hill, Piazza Venezia, and the 64
Capitoline Museums 67–70
Capo di Bove...................152
Capuchin Cemetery..............106
car breakdown 26
car rental 26
Carabinieri........................29
Caravaggio..... 37, 41, 70, 98, 162, 170, 174, 209
Carnevale........................26
Carracci, Annibale 37, 52, 70, 98, 102, 159
carta telefonica 33
Casa di Chirico 94
Casa di Dante 158
Casa di Goethe 92
Casa di Pirandello.................183
Casa Moravia 179
Casale Rotondo 152
Case Romane (Celian) 130
cash machines 28
Casina delle Civette.............183
Casino dei Principi 183
Casino dell'Aurora Pallavicini 110
Casino Medievale 179
Casino Nobile..................182
Castel Gandolfo..................220
Castel Sant'Angelo...............186
Castelli Romani 220–222
Castor and Pollux 82, 109
Cat Sanctuary......................57
Catacombe di Priscilla 181
Catacombs of San Callisto......150
Catacombs of San Sebastiano 151
Catacombs of Santa Domitilla 150
Cavallini, Pietro...................71, 164
Celian Hill and San Giovanni, the 128–137
Celian Hill and San Giovanni, the 130–131
Cenci, Beatrice 60
Centrale Montemartini...........145
Centro Storico 36–50
Centro Storico 38
Cerveteri......................217
Cestius, Caius 145
Chapel of the Blessed Sacrament (St Peter's)...................194
Charlemagne......................314
Charles V.......................315
Chiesa Nuova 46
Chigi Chapel.......................98
children, travelling with.........302
childrens' museums.............305
childrens' Rome........... 302–306
childrens' shops................306
Chiostro del Bramante..............47
churches 34, 35
Ciampino 21
cinemas........................279
Circus Maximus 139
Circus of Maxentius 151
Citta del Gusto.................258
Citta della Acqua 101
classical music...................277
Clement VII, Pope 40
Clement XII, Pope 56
clerical fashions..................40
climate........................28
Clivo di Scauro...................130
Cloaca Maxima 73
clothes shops...................286
clubs.............................. 274
Akab........................274
Art Café........................274
Black Out........................274
Boeme........................274
Brancaleone...................274
Gilda........................274
Goa........................274
Jackie O'.......................274
La Maison.......................274
Lanificio 159...................274
Micca Club......................274
Qube........................274
Rashomon......................275
Rising Love....................275
Sinister Noise...................275
Vicious........................275
Zoobar........................275
clubs and live music.... 271–275
coach tours 25
Coenatio Rotunda 87
coffee........................241
Cola di Rienzo 67
Colonna dell' Immacolata.........94

Colosseum..........................86–89
Column of Marcus Aurelius 49
Column of Phocas......................82
Complesso del Vittoriano.........66
Constantine..........85, 180, 312
Convento dei Cappuccini.......106
convents....................................238
   Casa di Santa Brigida....................238
   Suore Mantellate Serve di Maria
  238
cookery courses.......................252
Cordonata...................................67
Corsini Throne.........................159
Corso d'Italia...........................182
Corso Vittorio Emanuele II.......45
Cortile del Belvedere...............197
Cortile della Biblioteca...........197
Cortile della Pigna..................197
COTRAL.......................................26
Counter Reformation...............315
credit cards.................................28
crime..28
Crypta Balbi................................59
Cryptoporticus............................85
cucina Romana.........................242
cultural festivals.......................277
culture and entertainment
.... 276–280
Curia..81

D

da Cortona, Pietro........42, 46, 70,
   71, 104
da Volterra, Daniele....................96
dance...278
day-trips from Rome... 210–224
day-trips 212
de Chirico, Giorgio ...96, 174, 176
debit cards..................................28
dentists..30
department stores...................289
Depretis, Agostino...................316
designer shops.........................286
di Angelo, Nicolo......................147
di Cambio, Arnolfo...................147
dialling codes.............................32
Dioscuri....................................109
disabled travellers.....................34
discounts.....................................34
doctors..30
Dome of St Peter's...................195
Domine Quo Vadis...................150
Domitian..............42, 78, 86, 312
Domus Augustana.....................85
Domus Aurea............................116
Domus Flavia..............................86
Domus Tiberiana........................85
drinking...263–270 see also bars
driving...26

E

Easter..26
eating..... 239–262 see also cafés
   & restaurants
Ekberg, Anita............................100
electricity.....................................29
Elephant Statue...........................40
Elizabeth Bowen.......................322
embassies....................................29
emergencies................................29
Emperors of Rome....................311
English-speaking theatres......278
entry requirements.....................29
Esposizione Universale Roma
   (EUR) 154–156
Esquiline, Monti and Termini,
   the 112–127
Esquiline, Monti and Termini,
   the............................... 114–115
Esquiline Hill............................112
ethnic restaurants...................251
Etruscans 177, 199, 308
EUR 154–156
EUR............................... 155
euros..28
exchange.....................................28
exchange bureaux......................28

F

Farnese Gardens.........................85
Fatebenefratelli..........................60
festa dei noantri.........................27
festivals 26, 273, 277
film festivals...................277, 280
films in Rome............... 334–335
fire service..................................29
Fiumicino....................................21
flights to Rome...........................19
Fontana dei Quattro Fiumi......44
Fontana del Mascherone..........53
Fontana del Moro.......................44
Fontana del Nettuno.................44
Fontana del Tritone.................104
Fontana dell'Acqua Felice......107
Fontana della Barcaccia...........94
Fontana delle Api.....................104
Fontana delle Naiadi...............123
Fontana delle Tartarughe.........59
Fontana delle Tartarughe.........59
Fontana di Acqua Paola..........165
Fontana di Trevi.......................100
food markets............................295
food shops................................289
football.....................................298
Foro Italico...............................179
Forum of Augustus....................77
Forum of Caesar.........................77

Forum of Nerva...........................78
Forum of Trajan..........................77
Fountain of Marforio..................70
Fountain of the Bees................104
Fountains of Rome...................319
Francis I....................................318
Frascati.....................................220
Fregene.....................................223
French Academy..........................97

G

Galileo..97
Galleria Alberto Sordi.............100
Galleria Borghese 168–174
Galleria Colonna......................101
Galleria degli Arazzi................200
Galleria dei Candelabri...........200
Galleria delle Carte Geografiche
....200
Galleria Doria Pamphilj............37
Galleria Nazionale d'Arte
   Moderna..............................175
Galleria Nazionale d'Arte di
   Palazzo Corsini....................159
Galleria Nazionale di Arte
   Antica 104–106, 159
Galleria Nazionale di Arte di
   Palazzo Barberini.................106
Galleria Spada............................53
Gammarelli.................................40
Garbatella.................................146
Garibaldi, Giuseppe.................316
gay accommodation.................283
gay bars....................................282
gay clubs...................................282
gay contacts.............................282
gay restaurants........................282
gay Rome 280–283
gay saunas................................283
gelaterie 244
   Alberto Pica.................................244
   Alla Scala.....................................244
   Cremeria Monteforte..................244
   Fatamorgana...............................244
   Gelateria Corona.........................244
   Gelateria dei Gracchi..................244
   Giolitti...244
   Grom...244
   Il Gelato di Claudio Torcè...........244
   Palazzo del Freddo di Giovanni
      Fassi.......................................244
   San Crispino................................244
Gesù..57
Ghetto, the........................59–61
Ghetto, Campo de' Fiori, and
   the................................. 54–55
gift shops..................................294
Giorgione....................................63
gladiators....................................89
glossary 338–342
golf..299

Gramsci, Antonio 144
Grande Raccordo Anulare 22
grappa 264
Greek Cross Room (Vatican) ... 199
Gregory I, Pope 131, 314
Grottaferrata 220
Grottoes, St Peter's 194
gyms 299

H

Hadrian 213, 312
Hadrian VI, Pope 47
Hall of the Immaculate
  Conception 200
haute cuisine 261
health 29
history 308–318
hospitals 30
hostels 237
  Alessandro Palace 237
  Ottaviano 238
  Sandy 238
  Yellow 238
  YWCA 238
hotel bars 268
hotel pools 300
hotel rates 226
hotel reservations 226
hotels (by area) 226–237
  around Rome 237
  Aventine Hill and south, the 235
  Campo de' Fiori and the Ghetto ... 228
  Celian Hill and San Giovanni, the
    234
  Centro Storico 226
  Esquiline, Monti and Termini, the
    232
  Piazza Venezia and the Capitoline
    Hill 230
  Quirinale and Via Veneto, the 231
  Trastevere and the Janiculum Hill
    234
  Tridente and Trevi, the 230
  Vatican and Prati, the 235
  Villa Borghese and north 235
hotels (by name) 226–237
  Abitart 234
  Albergo del Senato 226
  Aldrovandi Palace 235
  Aleph 231
  Alpi 232
  Amalia 235
  Antico Borgo di Trastevere 234
  Arcangelo 235
  Argentina Residenza 228
  Artorius 232
  Astoria Garden 232
  Atlante Star 236
  Babuino 181 230
  Beehive, The 232
  Black Hotel 236
  Bramante 236
  Campo de' Fiori 228
  Capo d'Africa 234

Carmel 234
Casa Howard 230
Casa Montani 235
Cervia 232
Cesàri 227
Cisterna 234
Colors 236
Columbus 236
Condotti 230
Crossing Condotti 230
Crosti 233
Crowne Plaza St Peter's 236
D'Inghilterra 230
Daphne 231
De Monti 233
De Russie 230
Dei Borgognoni 230
Dei Consoli 236
Des Artistes 233
Domus Mazzini 236
Domus Tiberina 234
Duca d'Alba 233
Due Torri 227
Eden 232
Elide 233
Erdarelli 230
Exedra 233
Farnese 236
Fenix 235
Forty Seven 230
Franklin 236
Genio 227
Gerber 236
Giorni Felici 235
Giuliana 233
Giulio Cesare 236
Gran Meliá Rome 234
Grand Hotel del Gianicolo 234
Grand Hotel Plaza 231
Hassler 231
Homs 231
Hotel Art 231
IQ Hotel 233
Isa 236
Kolbe 230
La Posta Vecchia Palo Laziale ... 237
La Residenza 232
La Rovere 236
Lancelot 234
Leon's Place 233
Locanda Navona 227
Locarno 231
Lunetta 228
Majestic 232
Manfredi 231
Mario de Fiori 231
Metropolis 237
Mimosa 227
Modigliani 232
Navona 227
Nazionale 227
Nicolas Inn 233
Palazzo al Velabro 230
Palazzo Manfredi 234
Pantheon 227
Perugia 233
Piazza di Spagna 231
Pomezia 228
Portoghesi 227

Portrait Suites 231
Quirinale 233
Radisson Blu Es 233
Raphaël 227
Relais Giulia 228
Relais Orso 227
Relais Teatro Argentina 228
Residenza Arco de' Tolomei 235
Residenza Canali 228
Residenza Cellini 233
Residenza Farnese 228
Residenza Napoleone III 231
Residenza Santa Maria 235
Residenze Art & Breakfast 228
Romae 233
Rome Cavalieri 235
Rosetta 233
Sant'Anselmo 234
Santa Chiara 228
Santa Maria 235
Sole 230
Splendide Royal 232
St George 228
Suite Dreams 234
Teatro di Pompeo 230
Teatro Pace 228
Torre Colonna 230
Trastevere 235
Victoria 232
Villa della Fonte 235
Villa Laetitia 237
Villa Spalletti Trivelli 232
Visconti Palace 237
Westin Excelsior 232
Yes 234
Zanardelli 228
House of Augustus 86
House of Livia 85
House of the Vestal Virgins 84

I

ice cream 244
  see also gelaterie
Ignazio Marino 317
Imperial Forums 75
INA Building 107
information kiosks 34
Innocent VIII, Pope 192
Innocent X, Pope 42, 50, 63,
  68, 106
insurance 30
international calls 33
international codes 32
internet cafés 31
Isola Tiberina 61
Italian menu reader 340
Italian Unification 66
Italian words and phrases 338

J

Janiculum Hill 165
Janiculum Hill, Trastevere and
  160–161

jazz venues 273
Jesuits 57
Jewish Rome 59
John Paul II, Pope 47, 126, 195
John XXIII, Pope 192
Julius Caesar..........57, 75, 82, 310
Julius II, Pope 116, 206

K

Keats-Shelley Memorial House
....94
Keats, John............................94, 144
kids' Rome **302–306**
Knights of Malta.........................142

L

La Befana......................................306
La Dolce Vita.............107, 317, 334
Lacus Curtius..................................82
Ladispoli..223
Lago di Bracciano.......................219
Lago di Nemi................................221
Landmark Trust 94
language **338–342**
Lapis Niger......................................82
Largo di Torre Argentina...........56
Largo di Villa Perretti................124
Lateran Baptistry 135
Lateran Palace 134
laundries...31
Lazio travel.....................................26
Leo X, Pope...................40, 56, 202
Leonardo da Vinci International
....21
libraries...33
Lido di Ostia 222
liqueurs...264
literature festivals......................277
live music..272
   see also music venues
lost property 31
Lotto, Lorenzo................................70
Ludus Magnus 90

M

MACRO 182
MACRO Testaccio.........................144
Madam Lucretia 65
Maderno, Carlo.... 45, 56, 60, 111,
   190
Madonna dei Monti.................113
magazines.......................................27
mail...31
Mamertine Prison.........................71
Mani Pulite.....................................58
maps..31
Marcus Aurelius, Column of 50

Marforio 70
Mark Anthony.....................84, 310
markets 295
Martin V, Pope 101
Mattatoio.......................................144
Mausoleo delle Fosse Ardeatine
....151
Mausoleum of Augustus...........98
MAXXI 179
Mazzini, Giuseppe......................315
media...27
Meier, Richard................................99
Memling, Hans 37
menu reader..................................340
menus...241
Meta Sudans 90
metro...23
Michelangelo.....40, 52, 67, 111,
   123, 192, 203–207
minibuses 28
Ministry for Economic
   Development 107
Missionario della Carita..........132
mobiles...32
money...28
Monte Mario.................................180
Monte Testaccio...........................144
Monti.............................. 113–120
Monti, the Esquiline, Termini,
   and 114–115
moped rental 26
Moravia, Alberto 179
Morgan, J.P....................................123
Moro, Aldo 58
Morris, William 123
Mother Theresa of Calcutta ...132
Mouth of Truth 72
Murray, William 327–331, 336
Museo Barracco.............................45
Museo Boncompagni-Ludovisi
....107
Museo Carlo Bilotti 174
Museo Chiaramonti.....................208
Museo Criminologico................56
Museo dell'Alto Medioevo 155
Museo della Civilta Romano
....155
Museo della repubblica romana
   e della Memoria Garibaldina
....166
Museo della Via Ostiense........145
Museo delle Cere.........................102
Museo delle Mura.........................147
Museo delle Navi 221
Museo delle Terme di
   Diocleziano 124
Museo di Risorgimento............66
Museo di Roma 44
Museo di Roma in Trastevere
....159
Museo Ebraica 60

Museo Gregoriano Egizio.......199
Museo Gregoriano Etrusco 199
Museo Gregoriano Profano
....209
Museo Hendrik Christian
   Andersen 178
Museo Mario Praz........................49
Museo Missionario Etnologico
....209
Museo Napoleonico 49
Museo Nazionale delle Arti e
   delle Tradizioni Popolari 154
Museo Nazionale di Arte
   Orientale...................................122
Museo Nazionale Etrusco di
   Villa Giulia.................. 176–178
Museo Nazionale Preistorico ed
   Etnografico Luigi Pigorini
....154
Museo Nazionale Romano
....48, 59, 124
Museo Palatino............................85
Museo Pietro Canonica 175
Museo Pio Cristiano................209
Museo Pio-Clementino 197
Museo Storico dei Bersaglieri
....111
Museo Storico dell'Arte Sanitaria
....187
Museo Storico della Liberazione
....135
Museo Storico Vaticano 134
Museo-Atelier Canova-Tadolini
....95, 250
Museum of Christian Art 207
Museum of Contemporary Art of
   Rome..182
Museum of the Roman Republic
....166
museum shops.............................287
music festivals 273
music shops..................................294
music venues......................... 272
   Alexanderplatz.............................273
   Atlantico Live................................272
   Beba Do Samba.............................273
   Big Mama.......................................273
   Caruso Café de Oriente...............273
   Casa del Jazz.................................273
   Circolo degli Artisti.....................272
   Escopazzo......................................273
   Fonclea...272
   Forte Prenestino...........................272
   Gregory's..273
   Ippodromo Capannelle 272
   PalaLottomatica............................272
   Planet Roma...................................272
   Sotto Casa di Andrea...................272
   Stadio Olimpico............................272
   Place, The.......................................273
   Villaggio Globale..........................273
Mussolini 63, 75, 107, 178,
   316, 320

N

Napoleon.........................49, 315
national holidays 32
National Museum of Musical
  Instruments 136
Nemi.....................................221
Neri, Filippo 46
Nero........................88,116, 312
newspapers............................278
night buses........................23, 24
nightlife 272–275
north, Villa Borghese, and
 170–171
Nymphaeum of Alexander
  Severus...............................122

O

opera....................................277
opera festivals........................277
Oratorio dei Filipini..................46
Orte Botanico.........................160
Ospedale di Santo Spirito.......187
Ostia Antica 214–217
Ostiense 145

P

Palatine Hill......................85–87
Palazzo Altemps......................48
Palazzo Altieri 57
Palazzo Barberini....................106
Palazzo Bonaparte....................65
Palazzo Braschi........................44
Palazzo Cenci 60
Palazzo Chigi...........................50
Palazzo Colonna......................101
Palazzo Corsini.......................159
Palazzo dei Conservatori 68
Palazzo del Quirinale..............108
Palazzo della Cancellaria...........45
Palazzo della Civiltà del Lavoro
 154
Palazzo della Sapienza 41
Palazzo delle Esposizioni 123
Palazzo di Montecitorio 49
Palazzo Doria Pamphilj.............37
Palazzo Falconieri 56
Palazzo Farnese........................52
Palazzo Madama 41
Palazzo Massimo......................122
Palazzo Mattei..........................60
Palazzo Nuovo 70
Palazzo Odelscalchi 102
Palazzo Pallavicini-Rospigliosi
 110
Palazzo Pamphilj......................42
Palazzo Primoli 49

Palazzo Senatorio 67
Palazzo Spada..........................53
Palazzo Valentini......................65
Palazzo Venezia 63
Palazzo Wedekind 50
Palestrina..............................222
Pantheon.................................39
Papal reigns...........................313
Parco degli Acquedotti...........153
Parco di Colle Oppio...............113
Parco Regionale dell'Appia
  Antica.................................150
Parioli....................................181
parking 26
parks.....................................303
Pasquino 44
Passeggiata del Gianicolo 165
patriarchal basilicas 34
Paul II, Pope 64
Paul III, Pope 194, 315
Paul IV, Pope 40
Paul V, Pope 169, 191
Pauline Chapel (Santa Maria
  Maggiore)............................118
perfumeries 294
pharmacies 30
phone cards.............................33
phones 32
Piacentini, Marcello 107, 154
Piazza Barberini......................104
Piazza Belli..............................158
Piazza Bocca della Verità........72
Piazza Campo de' Fiori..............52
Piazza Colonna.........................50
Piazza dei Cinquecento..........126
Piazza del Augusta Imperatore
 98
Piazza del Biscione...................52
Piazza del Gesù 57
Piazza del Orologio...................46
Piazza del Popolo 97
Piazza del Quirinale................109
Piazza della Navicella 129
Piazza della Repubblica 123
Piazza della Rotonda 39
Piazza delle Cinque Scuole.......60
Piazza di Campidoglio..............66
Piazza di Campitelli..................59
Piazza di Montecitorio..............49
Piazza di Pietra 39
Piazza di Sant'Ignazio 37
Piazza di Spagna.......................94
Piazza Esedra..........................123
Piazza Farnese.........................52
Piazza Madonna dei Monti 113
Piazza Marconi........................154
Piazza Navona 42
Piazza Pasquino.......................44
Piazza San Lorenzo in Lucina...50
Piazza San Pietro....................187
Piazza San Silvestro 100

Piazza Sant'Apollinare..............48
Piazza Sant'Egidio 155
Piazza Santa Maria in Trastevere
 158
Piazza Trilussa 159
Piazza Venezia..........................63
Piazza Venezia and the
  Capitoline Hill 62–73
Piazza Venezia and the
  Capitoline Hill 64
Piazza Vittorio Emanuele II.....120
Piazzale Aurelio......................166
Piazzale di Ponte Milvio 180
Piazzale Garibaldi...................166
Piazzale Metronio....................136
Piccola Farnesina 45
Pietà (Michelangelo) 192
Pigneto 137
Pinacoteca (Vatican)...............208
Pincio Gardens 168
Pirandello...............................183
Piranesi..................................142
Pius IX, Pope...........................127
Pius XI, Pope...........................316
pizza places 254
Planetario e Museo Astronomico
 156
playgrounds 304
police 29
Polizia Statale...........................29
Pompey 52
Ponte Fabrico 61
Ponte Milvio 180
Ponte Palatino 73
Ponte Rotto..............................61
Ponte Sant'Angelo 186
Ponte Sisto...............................53
pop music 272
Popes of Rome 313
Porta Asinaria 136
Porta del Popolo 98
Porta Maggiore 137
Porta Magica 122
Porta Pia.................................111
Porta Portese 161
Porta San Pancrazio.................166
Porta San Paolo 145
Porta San Sebastiano 147
Portico d'Ottavia......................59
Poussin, Nicolas........................50
Pozzo, Andrea 39, 58
Prati, the Vatican and
 188–189
Praz, Mario 49
Primoli, Joseph 49
Priorato di Malta.....................142
Priscus, Tarquinius...................309
Prometheus Unbound...............143
pronunciation.........................338
Protestant Cemetery 144
public holidays 26

public telephones 33
Pulsating Lung, The 77
Punic Wars..................................310
puppet theatres.........................305
Pyramid of Caius Cestius 145

Q

Quartiere Coppede..................182
Queen Christina of Sweden
.... 159, 192
Quirinale and Via Veneto, the
.... 103–111
Quirinale and Via Veneto, the
.... 105

R

rail contacts 21
Raphael ..40, 42, 47, 98, 104, 162,
   173, 201, 208
Raphael Rooms 201
Raphael, tomb of........................ 39
Raphael's Loggia.......................201
Red Brigades 58
Regia 80
regional restaurants 249
Reni, Guido ...50, 53, 63, 106, 110
restaurants (by area)... 245–262
   Aventine Hill and south, the........259
   Campo de' Fiori and the Ghetto ... 248
   Celian Hill and San Giovanni, the
  257
   Centro Storico 245
   Esquiline, Monti and Termini, the
  255
   Quirinale and Via Veneto, the......253
   Trastevere and the Janiculum Hill
  259
   Tridente and Trevi, the 251
   Vatican and Prati, the 261
   Villa Borghese and north 254
restaurants (by name) ...245–262
   Agata e Romeo 255
   Agustarello 259
   Ai Marmi..259
   Akropolis..260
   Al Bric 248
   Al Forno della Soffitta 253
   Al Grottino.....................................257
   Al Pompiere 248
   All'Oro Restaurant........................251
   Alla Rampa 251
   Alle Carrette 255
   Antica Birreria Peroni...................251
   Antico Arco 260
   Ar Galletto 248
   Arancia Blu 254
   Armando al Pantheon....................245
   Aroma...257
   Ba' Ghetto 248
   Babette 251
   Baia Chia...255
   Baires...248

Beere..245
Bir and Fud 260
Boccondivino 245
Buca di Ripetta 251
Cacio e Pepe 261
Caffè Propaganda...........................257
Cantina Cantarini 253
Cantina Tirolese 261
Casa Bleve.......................................245
Charley's Sauciere...........................257
Checchino dal 1887 259
Ciampini 251
Colline Emiliane..............................251
Da Alfredo e Ada............................245
Da Augusto 260
Da Baffetto 245
Da Danilo 255
Da Emilio 254
Da Enzo..260
Da Felice 259
Da Francesco 245
Da Ivo 260
Da Lucia 260
Da Olindo 260
Da Paris 260
Da Remo 259
Da Sergio...249
Da Tonino 245
Dal Bolognese 251
Dal Cavalier Gino...........................245
Dal Paino 245
Dal Toscano 262
Dar Poeta 260
Del Frate 260
Di Oio di Casa Mia 259
Ditirambo..249
Doozo...255
Dulcamara 254
Enoteca Cavour 313 255
Enoteca Corsi..................................246
Enoteca Provincia Romana............250
Fiaschetteria Beltramme 252
Flavio al Velavevodetto.................259
Formula 1 255
Giggetto 254
Giuda Ballerino 257
Grappolo d'Oro Zampanó 249
'Gusto 252
Hamasei...252
Hang Zhou 255
Il Bacaro 246
Il Bocconcino 258
Il Chianti 252
Il Ciak 260
Il Leoncino 252
Il Sanlorenzo 249
Il Sorpasso 262
Il Tempio di Mecenate...................255
Il Winebar 260
Imàgo 252
Jardin de Russie 252
L'Asino d'Oro 256
La Barrique 256
La Carbonara 256
La Montecarlo 246
La Pergola 254
La Scala 254
La Terrazza Bramante 246
La Terrazza dell'Eden 252

Le Mani in Pasta.............................260
Luzzi 258
Maccheroni 246
Maharajah 256
Mamá 262
Matricianella 246
Mesob 258
Mirabelle 253
Monti DOC.......................................256
Nonna Betta....................................249
Oliver Glöwig 254
Open Colonna..................................256
Osteria del Pegno 246
Osteria dell'Angelo 262
Osteria dell'Ingegno 246
Osteria della Frezza 252
Otello alla Concordia.....................252
Palatium 252
Passaguai 262
Pastificio San Lorenzo 256
Perfect Bun, The 246
Piccolo Abruzzo 253
Piperno 249
Pizza Ciro 253
Pizza Re..253
Pizzeria San Calisto........................260
Pommidoro 256
Primo al Pigneto.............................258
Ragno d'Oro....................................262
Recafé...253
ReD...253
Romeo Chef & Baker......................262
Roscioli 249
Sette Oche 260
Settembrini 262
Tajut 258
Take Sushi 261
Taverna degli Amici........................249
Taverna dei Quaranta 258
Tram Tram 256
Trattoria Lilli 246
Trattoria Monti 256
Tuttifrutti..259
Urbana 47 256
Valentino 257
Vecchia Roma..................................250
Vino e Camino.................................248
Vivavoce...261
Zoc...250
reunification movement........316
riding..299
rock music..................................272
Roma Cristiana 25
Roma pass 34
Roman cuisine 242
Roman emperors.......................311
Roman Forum....................79–85
Roman Republic.........................309
Roman restaurants...................246
Romulus and Remus 308
Rooms of St Ignatius 58
Rostra 84
Rubens, Peter Paul ...46, 162, 169
rugby...298
running 299, 301
Rutelli, Francesco.....................317

S

Sala Rotonda (Vatican) 198
Salario 182
Salita del Grillo 77
Salvi, Niccolò 100
San Bartolomeo 61
San Bernardo alle Terme 107
San Carlo alle Quattro Fontane
....108
San Clemente 132
San Crisogono 158
San Filippo Neri 46
San Francesco a Ripa 164
San Giorgio in Velabro 73
San Giovanni dei Fiorentini 56
San Giovanni in Laterano
.... **133–135**
San Giovanni, the Celian Hill,
and 130–131
San Gregorio Magno 131
San Lorenzo 126
San Lorenzo fuori le Mura 127
San Lorenzo in Damaso 45
San Lorenzo in Lucina 50
San Lorenzo in Miranda 80
San Luca e Martina 71
San Luigi dei Francesi 41
San Marco 63
San Martino ai Monti 120
San Nicolo in Carcere 71
San Paolo alle Tre Fontane 156
San Paolo fuori le Mura 146
San Pietro in Carcere 71
San Pietro in Montorio 165
San Pietro in Vincoli 113
San Saba 142
San Silvestro in Capite 100
San Teodoro 72
Sancta Sanctorum 135
Sant'Ambrogio e Carlo 92
Sant'Andrea 132
Sant'Andrea al Quirinale 108
Sant'Andrea della Valle 45
Sant'Andrea delle Fratte 100
Sant'Agnese fuori le Mura 183
Sant'Agnese in Agone 44
Sant'Agostino 42
Sant'Alessio 139
Sant'Anselmo 142
Sant'Ignazio 39
Sant'Ivo alla Sapienza 41
Sant'Onofrio 166
Santa Barbara 132
Santa Bibiana 122
Santa Cecilia in Trastevere 164
Santa Costanza 184
Santa Croce in Gerusalemme
....136
Santa Francesca Romana 90

Santa Maria degli Angeli 123
Santa Maria dei Miracoli 98
Santa Maria del Popolo 98
Santa Maria dell'Anima 47
Santa Maria della Concezione
....106
Santa Maria della Consolazione
....71
Santa Maria della Pace 47
Santa Maria della Vittoria 111
Santa Maria in Aracoeli 67
Santa Maria in Cosmedin 72
Santa Maria in Domnica 129
Santa Maria in Montesanto 98
Santa Maria in Portico 59
Santa Maria in Trastevere 158
Santa Maria Maggiore
.... **118–120**
Santa Maria Nuova 90
Santa Maria Scala Coeli 156
Santa Maria sopra Minerva 40
Santa Marinella 223
Santa Prassede 120
Santa Pudenziana 117
Santa Sabina 139
Santa Severa 223
Santa Silvia 132
Santa Susanna 110
Santi Apostoli 102
Santi Cosma e Damiano 78
Santi Giovanni e Paolo 129
Santi Nereo ed Achille 143
Santi Quattro Coronati 132
Santi Vicenzo ed Anastasio 101
Santo Stefano Rotondo 129
Scala Santa 135
scheda telefonica 33
scooter rental 26
Scuderie del Qurinale 107
Senate 41
Septizodium 87
Servian Wall 142
Severus, Septimius 84, 312
Shelley, Mary 92, 94, 144
Shelley, Percy 92, 94, 143, 144
Shelley, William 144
shoe shops 288
shops and markets 284–296
accessories 288
antiques 285
bookshops 285
children's shops 306
clothes 286–288
department stores 289
design 292–294
food 289–292
gifts 294
home 292–294
malls 289
markets 295
miscellaneous 294
museum shops 287

music 294
perfumeries 294
shoes 288
stationery 294
video 294
wine 289–292
shopping malls 289
Silvano Toti Globe Theatre 175
SIM cards 32
Sistine Chapel (Santa Maria
Maggiore) 118
Sistine Chapel 203–207
Sixtus IV, Pope 203
Sixtus V, Pope 99, 118, 119
smoking 33
snacks 240
Sobieska, Clementina 192
south, the Aventine Hill, and
.... **140–141**
Spanish Embassy 94
Spanish Steps 96
Sperlonga 222
sports and outdoor activities
.... **297–301**
St Agnes 44, 183
St Augustine 131
St Francis Xavier 58
St Gregory 131
St Ignatius 58
St Paul's-within-the-Walls 123
St Peter's 190–195
St Stanislaus Kostka 108
Stadio dei Marmi 179
Stadio Olimpico 179
Stadium (Palatine) 85
Stadium of Domitian 42, 47
stamps 31
stationery shops 294
study 33
Superbus, Tarquinius 309
supermarkets 290
swimming 219, 223, 300
swimming pools 226, 300
synagogue 60

T

talking statues 66
Tarpeian Rock 70
Tarquinia 218
Tasso's Oak 166
taxis 23
taxis to and from airports 21
Teatro Argentina 57
Teatro di Marcello 59
telephone cards 33
telephone codes 32
Tempietto 165
Temple of Antoninus and
Faustina 80
Temple of Apollo 85

Temple of Castor and Pollux ... 82
Temple of Concordia Augusta 82
Temple of Hercules Victor 72
Temple of Julius Caesar............. 81
Temple of Minerva Medica 122
Temple of Portunus 72
Temple of Romulus..................... 84
Temple of Saturn 82
Temple of Vespasian and Titus 82
Temple of Vesta............................ 84
tennis 299
Termini...........................22, 126, 81
Termini, the Esquiline, Monti, and 114–115
Terracina 222
Testaccio 143
theatres 278
theme parks 304
Tiberius...312
ticket agencies............................277
tickets and passes 23, 26
time 33
Titus..312
Tivoli.....................................211–213
toilets 33
Tomb of Cecilia Metella...........151
Tomb of St Peter 195
Tomb of the Baker......................137
Tomb of the Scipios...................147
Tomb of the Unknown Soldier 65
Torlonia, Prince Giovanni........182
Torre della Scimmia 42
Torre delle Milizie 78
Torvaianica...................................222
Tosca... 45
tour operators.............................. 21
tourist buses................................. 25
tourist information..............33–34
tourist passes............................... 34
tours 25
toyshops..306
train enquiries 22
train stations 22
trains, to Rome 20
trains, around Lazio 26
Trajan..312
Trajan's Baths..............................113
Trajan's Column...........................77
Trajan's Markets........................... 78
trams 23, 24
Trappists, the...............................156
Trastevere and the Janiculum Hill 157–166
Trastevere and the Janiculum Hill..............................160–161

travel agents.................................. 21
travellers' cheques....................... 28
Tre Fontane..................................156
Treasury, Vatican 194
Trelawny, Edward 144
Trevi Fountain 100
Trevi, Tridente, and the 93
Tridente and Trevi, the ...91–102
Tridente and Trevi, the 93

U

Trinità dei Monti 96
Urban VIII, Pope...........41, 70, 100, 106, 172, 194, 200, 315
US Embassy 107

V

Vatican, the 185–209
Vatican and Prati, the 188–189
St Peter's 191
Vatican Museums, the 196
Vatican Gardens.........................186
Vatican Library...........................207
Vatican Museums 195–209
Vatican Necropolis 195
vegetarian restaurants 257
Velázquez, Diego 37
Venus Cloacina............................. 81
Vespasian......................................88, 312
Vettroni, Walter 317
Via Appia Antica 148–152
Via Biberatica 78
Via Caetani 59
Via Cavour 113
Via Cristoforo Colombo...........154
Via dei Coronari.......................... 47
Via dei Fori Imperiali.................. 75
Via dei Funari 59
Via dei Portoghesi 42
Via del Babuino 97
Via del Corso 37, 92
Via del Governo Vecchio.......... 46
Via del Monte Tarpeio............... 70
Via del Pigneto 137
Via del Plebiscito......................... 57
Via del Tritone 104
Via della Conciliazione.............187
Via della Pilotta..........................101
Via della Scrofa 41
Via delle Botteghe Oscure........ 59
Via delle Quattro Fontane......108
Via di Ripetta............................... 98
Via Giulia....................................... 53
Via Margutta................................. 97

Via Nazionale 123
Via Nomentana 182
Via Ostiense 145
Via Portico d'Ottavia................. 58
Via Rasella....................................107
Via Sacra.. 79
Via San Teodoro 72
Via Sannio....................................132
Via Santa Maria dell'Anima 47
Via Sistina 99
Via Veneto....................................107
Via Veneto, the Quirinale, and 105
Via Vittorio Veneto 107
Via XX Settembre......................110
Via Zanardelli.............................. 49
Viale di Trastevere 158
Vigna Barberini 87
Villa Ada 181
Villa Adriana................................213
Villa Aldobrandini.....................123
Villa and Circus of Maxentius 151
Villa Borghese.............................168
Villa Borghese 173
Villa Borghese and north 167–184
Villa Borghese and north 170–171
Villa Celimontana 129
Villa d'Este 211
Villa dei Quintili.........................152
Villa Doria Pamphilj 166
Villa Farnesina............................162
Villa Giulia...................................172
Villa Gregoriana.........................211
Villa Lante...................................166
Villa Medici..................................97
Villa of Maxentius 151
Villa Torlonia 182
visas.. 29
Vittoriano....................................... 65
Vittorio Emanuele II, King 66, 316
Vittorio Emanuele Monument 65

W

walking tours 25
Weaver, William 324–327
websites.. 31
what's on 27
wine bars......................................265
wine merchants 289
World War II 317
worship 35
writing on Rome 322–331

Go with Oh
Your trusted host in Europe

Handpicked holiday apartments across Europe's hottest destinations.
Where will you GowithOh?

BERLIN · LONDON · BARCELONA · ROME · PARIS · FLORENCE · PRAGUE
VIENNA · MADRID · AMSTERDAM · VENICE · NICE · SEVILLE · PISA and more...

GowithOh.com   f facebook.com/GowithOh   🐦 @GowithOh

Maps

Index

Centro Storico	38	EUR	155
Campo de' Fiori and the Ghetto	54–55	Trastevere and the Janiculum Hill	160–161
Piazza Venezia and the Capitoline Hill	64	Villa Borghese and north	170–171
Ancient Rome	76	Villa Borghese	173
Roman Forum	80–81	The Vatican & Prati	188–189
Palatine Hill	86	St Peter's	191
The Tridente and Trevi	93	The Vatican Museums	196
The Quirinale and Via Veneto	105	The Sistine Chapel	204
Esquiline, Monti and Termini	114–115	Day-trips	212
The Celian Hill and San Giovanni	130–131	Ostia Antica	215
The Aventine Hill and south	140–141		

Listings key

- ■ Accommodation
- ● Restaurant/café
- ■ Bar/club/music venue
- ● Shop

City plan

The **city plan** on the pages that follow is divided as shown:

N

Map symbols

✈	Airport	🅿	Parking	⊙	Statue	
∩	Arch	✉	Post office	◆	Place of interest	
△	Pyramid	@	Internet	▨	Building	
∴	Ruins	ⓘ	Tourist information	⇨	Church	
⊼	Campsite	⊞	Hospital	⬭	Stadium	
Ⓜ	Metro	🅣	Toilets	⊞	Cemetery	
✡	Synagogue	⊼	Fountain	▱	Park/gardens	
🛕	Temple	⊠	Gate			

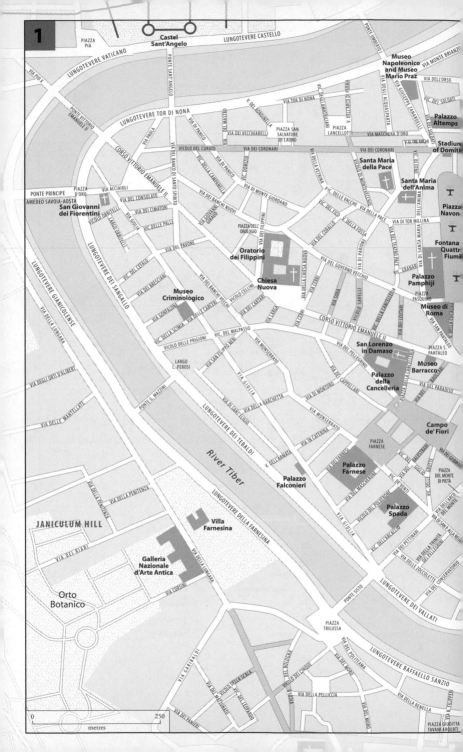

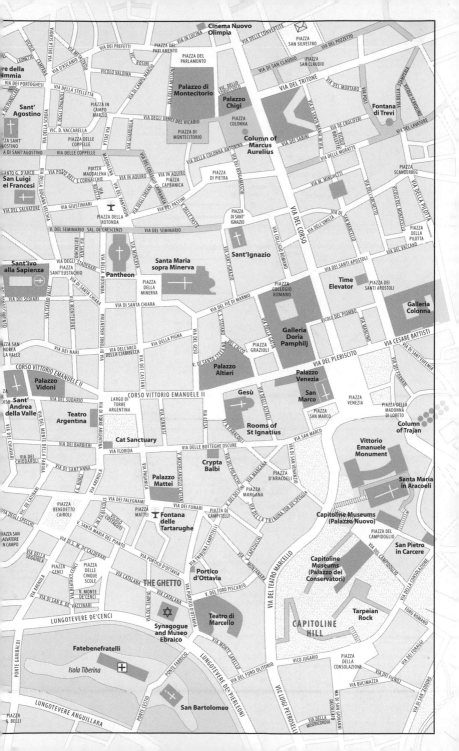

Bioparco

Galleria Nazionale
d'Arte Moderna

VIALE DEL GIARDINO ZOOLOGICO

Bike
Hire

VIALE DEI DAINI

VIALE DELLE TRE MADONNE

VIA SAVERIO MERCADANTE

VIA GIOVANNI B. PERGOLESI

VIA CLAUDIO MONTEVERDI

VIA GAETANO DONIZETTI

VIA LUIGI LUZZATTI

VIA PIETRO RAIMONDI

VIA G. ALENGA

VIA JACOPO PERI

VIALE VILLA GIULIA

VIALE DELL'UCCELLIERA

VIALE DEL GIARDINO ZOOLOGICO

Silvano
Toti
Globe
Theatre

Museo
Pietro
Canonica

VIALE DEI CAVALLI MARINI

Galleria
Borghese

VIA GREGORIO ALLEGRI

VIA PO

VIA SALARIA

PIAZZA
DI SIENA

Villa Borghese

VIALE DEL PUPAZZI

VIA LIVENZA

VIA SALARIA

Museo
Carlo
Bilotti

Casina di
Raffaello

VIALE DEI CAVALLI MARINI

VIA ISONZO

VIA DI SANTA TERESA

VIA SESIA

V. CREMERA

VIA VELLETRI

VIALE DELLA MAGNOLIE

Monument
to Goethe

Cinema
dei Piccoli

Monument to
Umberto I

VIALE DEI PUPAZZI

VIA PINCIANA

VIA ANIENE

VIA ANIENE

VIA VITERBO

VIALE GOETHE

Casa del
Cinema

Bike
Hire

VIA C. PUCCINI

CORSO D'ITALIS

PIAZZA
FIUME

Galoppatoio

VIA CAMPANIA

VIA SARDEGNA

VIA LIGURIA

VIA CALABRIA

VIA PIAVE

Villa
Medici

VIA DI PORTA PINCIANA

VIA EMILIA

VIA TOSCANA

VIA ABRUZZI

VIA SARDEGNA

VIA PIEMONTE

VIA BONCOMPAGNI

VIA SICILIA

VIA BELISARIO

VIA CADORNA

VIA CAMPANIA

VIA LOMBARDIA

VIA SICILIA

VIA VENETO

VIA VITTORIO

VIA BONCOMPAGNI

VIA SALLUSTIANA

PIAZZA
SALLUSTIO

VIA QUINTINO SELLA

VIA SERVIO TULLIO

Spagna

Trinità dei Monti

VIA LUDOVISI

US
Embassy

VIA LUCULLO

VIA PIEMONTE

VIA MARIO CARDUCCI

VIA FLAVIA

Ministry
of
Finance

PIAZZA
DI SPAGNA

Spanish
Steps

VIA LIGURIA

VIA SALLUSTIANA

VIA GIOSUE CARDUCCI

VIA XX SETTEMBRE

Keats-Shelley Memorial House

VIA DEGLI ARTISTI

VIA SAN BASILIO

Santa Maria
della Vittoria

VIA A. SALANDRA

Casa di
Chirico

VIA SISTINA

VIA GREGORIANA

Convento dei
Cappuccini

VIA MOLISE

Ministry of
Agriculture

LARGO DI
SANTA SUSANNA

Fontana
dell'Aqua
Felice

Museo delle
Terme di
Diocleziane

VIA DI CAPO LE CASE

VIA F. CRISPI

VIA SISTINA

Fontana
delle Api

Santa
Susanna
(American
Church)

San Bernardo
Alle Terme

VIA MARIO DEI FIORI

VIA DI PROPAGANDA

VIA DEL CAPPUCCINI

VIA DI SAN NICOLA DA TOLENTINO

PIAZZA DI
S. BERNARDO

Aula
Ottagona

VIA DELLA MERCEDE

Barberini

VIA BARBERINI

Santa Maria
degli Angeli

VIA DEL POZZETTO

PIAZZA
BARBERINI

Fontana
del
Tritone

Galleria Nazionale
d'Arte Antica

VIA TORINO

PIAZZA DELLA
REPUBBLICA

VIALE LUIGI EINAUDI

VIA DEL TRITONE

VIA DEGLI AVIGNONESI

Palazzo
Barberini

VIA DELLE QUATTRO FONTANE

Repubblica

VIA DELLA STAMPERIA

V. DEI MARONITI

VIA RASELLA

VIA DEL GIARDINI

Ministry
of Defence

VIA XX SETTEMBRE

Palazzo
Massimo

Fontana
di Trevi

VIA DEL LAVATORE

VIA IN ARCIONE

San Carlo alle
Quattro Fontane

British
Council

VIA NAZIONALE

VIA NAPOLI

Sant'Andrea
al Quirinale

VIA FIRENZE

VIA MASSIMO D'AZEGLIO

VIA CAVOUR

PIAZZA
SCANDERBEG

VIA DELLA DATARIA

Palazzo del
Quirinale

VIA PIACENZA

Palazzo
delle
Esposizioni

PIAZZA
DEL VIMINALE

Time
Elevator

PIAZZA DEL
QUIRINALE

VIA DELLA CONSULTA

VIA MILANO

VIA PALERMO

Santa
Pudenziana

PIAZZA
DELL'
ESQUILINO

Santa Maria
Maggiore

Galleria
Doria
Pamphilj

PIAZZA DEI
SANTI
APOSTOLI

Galleria
Colonna

Scuderie del
Quirinale

Casino
dell'Aurora
Pallavicini

VIA MAZZARINO

VIA DEL BOSCHETTO

VIA CESARE BALBO

VIA SANTA MARIA MAGGIORE

VIA PAOLINA

V. CESARE BATTISTI

VIA DELLA CORDONATA

LARGO
MAGNANAPOLI

VIA PANISPERNA

VIA CIMARRA

Santa
Prassede

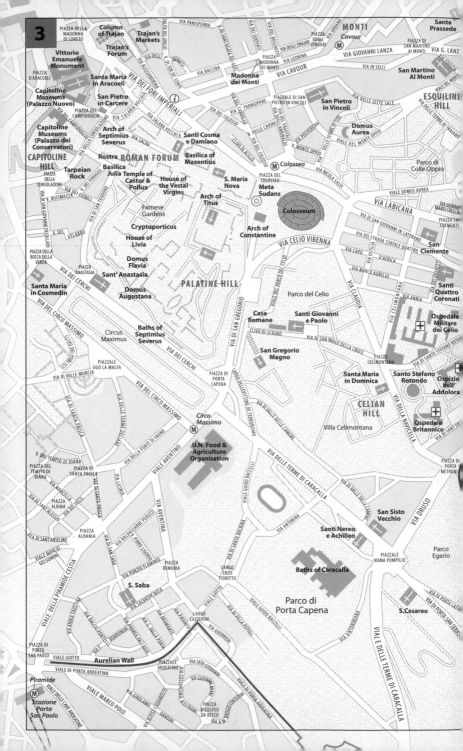

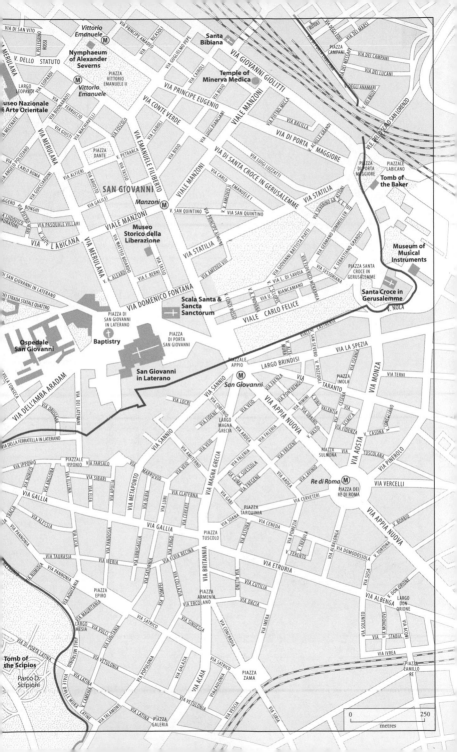

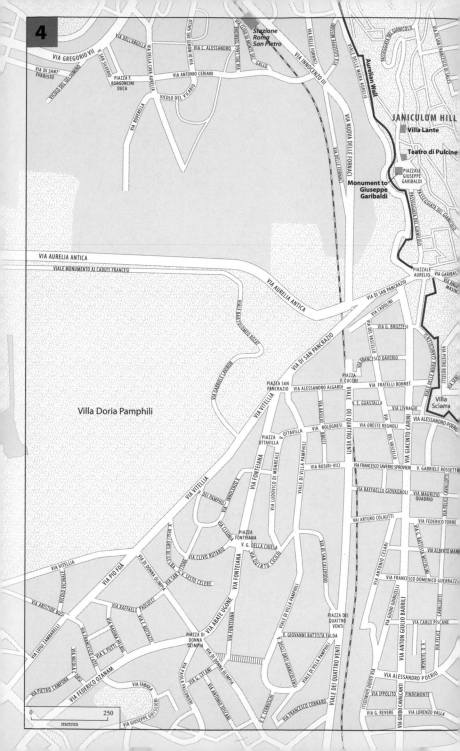

4

VIA GREGORIO VII

VIA DI SANT' EVARISTO

VICOLO DEL GELSOMINO

SAN SEVERO

VIA DELL'ARGILLA

VIA DELLA CAVA AURELIA

VIA DI MONTE DEL GALLO

VIA C. ALESSANDRO

VIA DELL'LAGO TERRIONE

VIA DEL MONTE DEL GALLO

Stazione Roma San Pietro

VIA DELLE FORNACI

VIA INNOCENZO III

PASSEGGIATA DEL GIANICOLO

VIA DI SAN FRANCESCO DI SALES

PIAZZA F. BORGONCINI DUCA

VIA ANTONIO CERIANI

VICOLO DEL VICARIO

VIA ROVERELLA

VIA NUOVA DELLE FORNACI

VIA DELLE FORNACI

Aurelian Wall

VIALE DELLE MURA AURELIE

JANICULUM HILL

Villa Lante

Teatro di Pulcine

PIAZZALE GIUSEPPE GARIBALDI

PASSEGGIATA DEL GIANICOLO

Monument to Giuseppe Garibaldi

PASSEGGIATA DEL GIANICOLO

VIA AURELIA ANTICA

VIALE MONUMENTO AI CADUTI FRANCESI

PIAZZALE AURELIO

VIA GARIBA

VIA AURELIA ANTICA

VIA AURELIA ANTICA

VIA DI SAN PANCRAZIO

VIA ANGE MASIN

VIALE BARTOLOMEO ROZAT

VIA GABRIELE CLAVDIO

VIA CADOLINI

VIA DI SAN PANCRAZIO

VIA G. BRUZZESI

VIA DEL VASCELLO

VIA FRANCESCO DAVERIO

VIA SAVERIO DE' VASCELLO

VIA CARLO BATTISTA NICCOLINI

Villa Doria Pamphili

PIAZZA SAN PANCRAZIO

PIAZZA F. CUCCHI

VIA FRATELLI BONNET

VIA ALESSANDRO ALGARDI

V. E. GUASTALLA

VIA LIVRAGHI

Villa Sciarra

VIA VITELLIA

VIA BASILIO

VIALE DEI QUATTRO VENTI

VIA ORESTE REGNOLI

VIA GIACINTO CARINI

VIA ALESSANDRO POERIO

PIAZZA OTTAVILLA

OTTAVILLA

VIA BOLOGNESI

VIA FONTEIANA

VIA LUDOVICO DI MONREALE

VIALE DI VILLA PAMPHILI

VIA BUSIRI-VICI

VIA FRANCESCO SAVERIO SPROVIERI

V. GABRIELE ROSSETTI

VIA VITELLIA

VIA DEI PAMPHILI

VIA INNOCENZO

VIA RAFFAELLO GIOVAGNOLI

VIA MAURIZIO QUADRIO

VIA FELICE CAVALLOTTI

VIA UGONE

VAI ARTURO COLAUTTI

PIAZZA FONTEIANA

V. G. DELLA CHIESA

VIA DI SAN CALEPODIO

VIA FEDERICO TORRE

VIA DI CLIVI DI CINTA

VIA CLIVO RUTARIO

VIA IN IO CECILIO

VIA ALBERTO MARI

VIA VITELLIA

VIA PIO FOA

VIA DI DONNA OLIMPIA

VIA SAN V. SESTO CELERE

VIA FONTEIANA

VIA DI VILLA PAMPHILI

VIA ANTONIO CESARI

VIA FRANCESCO DOMENICO GUERRAZZ

VIA ARISTIDE BUSI

VICOLO VICENZIA

VIA RAFFAELE PAGLIUCCI

VIA V. PUTTI

VIA ABATE UGONE

PIAZZA DI DONNA OLIMPIA

VIA DI DONNA OLIMPIA

V. GIOVANNI BATTISTA FALDA

VIALE DI VILLA PAMPHILI

PIAZZA DEI QUATTRO VENTI

VIA GUIDO GUINIZELLI

VIA ANTON GIULIO BARRILI

VIA CARLO PISCANE

VIA LUIGI ZAMBARELLI

VIA FRANCESCO CACCINI

VIA MADONNA DEL RIPOSO

VIA F. BATTAZZA

VIA C. CELANI

VIA A. FALCONIERI

VIA DEGLI ORTI DI GIANICOLENSI

VIALE DEI QUATTRO VENTI

VIA ALESSANDRO POERIO

VIA PIETRO CAMPORA

VIA FEDERICO OZANAM

VIA FABIOLA

VIA G. CELANI

VIA ANTONIO TOSCANI

LE CERMUSCHI

VIA FRANCESCO CORNARO

VIA IPPOLITO PINDEMONTE

VIA GUIDO CAVALCANTI

VIA G. REVERE

VIA LORENZO VALLA

VIA PIETRO COSSA

VIA GIUSEPPE GHISLIERI

0   250
metres

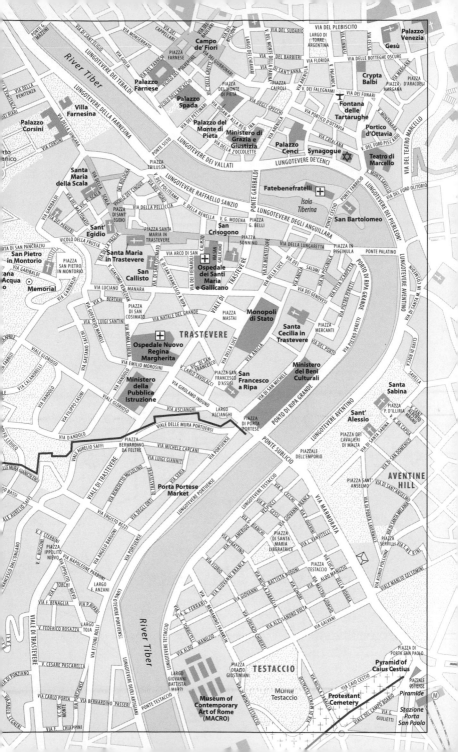

5

VIA DARDANELLI
VIA MONTE NERO
VIA MONTE SANTO
VIALE G. FALCONE E PAOLO BORSELLINO
PIAZZALE CLODIO
VIA BOMA ROMEI
VIA CARLO MIRABELLO
VIALE ANGELICO
VIA FULCIERI PAULUCCI DE CALBOLI
VIA SABOTINO
VIA PLOTINO
VIA TRIONFALE
VIA DELLA GIULIANA
VIALE PLATONE
VIA RAFFAELE ROSSETTI
VIA MARIO AMATO
VIA A. RIBOTY
VIA A. AVOGLI
VIA ANDREA BAFILE
VIALE GIUSEPPE MAZZINI
VIALE GIUSEPPE MAZZINI
PIAZZA GIUSEPPE MAZZINI
PIAZZA DEI PRATI DEGLI STROZZI
CIRCONVALLAZIONE CLODIA
VIA NAZARIO SAURO
VIA GIUSEPPE PALUMBO
VIA TIBERINA
VIA TOMMASO ISORI
VIA G. ANDREOLI
VIA G. POMA
PIAZZA GIOVINE ITALIA
VIA SILVIO PELLICO
VIA PIO
VIA M. BELMONTI
VIA F.F. ROSSELLI ALBERTO
LARGO DELLA GANCIA
VIA DE SANCTIS
VIA PREMUDA
VIA EMILIO FAA DI BRUNO
VIA GESMUNDO
VIA P. BORSIERI
VIA CUNFIDA
VIA RICCARDO GRAZIOLI LANTE
VIALE ANGELICO
VIA GABRIELE CAMOZZI
VIA T.G. MOMPIANI
VIA CARLO ALBERTO DELLA CHIESA
VIA C. POMA
VIA PLATONE
VIA FEDRO
VIA GIOVANNI BOVIO
VIA GIROLAMO
VIA RODI
VIA COSTANTINO MORIN
VIA SIMONE DE SAINT BON
VIA V. GARROCCI
VIA TOMMASO D'AQUINO
PIAZZALE SOCRATE
VIA C. NEPOTE
VIA ANTONIO LABRIOLA
VIA GIORDANO BRUNO
VIA GIOVANNI BETTOLO
VIA VITTORIO AMMINIO
VIA G. BARZELLOTTI
VIA BERNARDINO TELESIO
VIA BUCCARI
PRATI
CIRCONVALLAZIONE TRIONFALE
VIA TOMMASO CAMPANELLA
SAVONAROLA
VIALE DELLE MILIZIE
VIA FAMAGOSTA
VIA BARLETTA
VIA GIANNONE
VIA ANDREA DORIA
LARGO TRIONFALE
VIA OTRANTO
Ottaviano Ⓜ
VIALE DELLE MEDAGLIE D'ORO
LARGO MONTEZEMOLO
VIA FRANCESCO CARACCIOLO
VIA DELLE FORNACI
VIA TUNISI
VIA DI OSTIA
VIALE GIULIO CESARE
VIA DEGLI SCIPIONI
VIA MACHIAVELLI
VIA S. ZIANI
VIA GIULIO VENTICINQUE
PIAZZALE DEGLI EROI
VIA VITTOR PISANI
VIA RUGGERO FIORE
VIA SANTAMAURA
VESPASIANO
VIA OTTAVIANO
VIA CAIO MARIO
VIA GERMANICO
VIA LUIGI RIZZO
VIA FRA ALBENZIO
VIA CANDIA
VIA SEBASTIANO VENIERO
VIA GERMANICO
VIA DEI GRACCHI
PIAZZA DELL'UNITÀ
VIA TIBULLO
VIA MASSIMO
VIA RIALTO
VIA MOLINORI
VIA LUMISI
VIA CRESCENZIO
VIA PROPERZIO
VIA CIPRO
VIALE VATICANO
PIAZZA RISORGIMENTO
VIA VARRONE
VIA DELLA MELORIA
Cipro Ⓜ
PIAZZA DI SANTA MARIA DELLE GRAZIE
PIAZZALE AMERIGO CAPPONI
VIA ALBER
VIA MARCANTONIO SABELLICO
VIA ANGELO EMO
VIA GIOVANNI VITEL
VIA RUGGERO BONGHI
VIA FOGLIANO
BORGO ANGELICO
BORGO
VIA MILLELIRE
VIALE VATICANO
BORGO VITTORIO
VIA DELLE PALLINE
VIA DETRE PUNZII
VIA DEI CORRI
VICOLO DEL FARINONE
BORGO PIO
VIA DEGLI OMBRELLARI
Vatican Walls
Vatican Museums
VATICAN CITY
SALITA AI GIARDINI
VIA DELLA POSTA
VIA DELLA TIPOGRAFIA
VIA DEL PELLEGRINO
BELVEDER
Palazzo Torlonia
VIA DELL'ERBA
VIA OSPEDALE
Vatican Gardens
Sant
Sistine Chapel
Mari
Trasp
PIAZZA PIO XII
VIA DELLA CONCILIAZIONE
Palazzo dei Penitenzieri
VIA DEL FONDAMENTO
St Peters
PIAZZA SAN PIETRO
Ospeda di Sant Spirito
VIA DELLA STAZIONE VATICANA
PIAZZA DI SANTA MARIA
Scavi Office
VIA TUNICA
BORGO SANTO SPIR
VIA PAOLO VI
Stazione Vaticano
Aula delle Udienze
Palazzo del Sant'Uffizio
Palazzo del Commendatore
VIALE VATICANO
PIAZZA DELLA ROVERE
VIA NICOLÒ V
VIA DELLA STAZIONE VATICANA
VIA DI PORTO CAVALLEGGERI
VIALE DELLE MURA AURELIE
VIA BENEDETTO
VIA AURELIA
VIA LEONE IX
VIA S. GREGORIO
VIA DI POSTA FABBRICA
VIA ALESSANDRO III
VIA DI VILLA ALBERICI
VIA AURELIA
VIA DELLE FORNACI
VIA DI SANTA ONOFRIO
SALITA DI SANTA ONOFRIO
VIA CARDINAL AGLIARDI
VIA PAOLO II
VIA DE GASPERI
PIAZZA SANTA MARIA ALLE FORNACI
PIAZZA DI SANTA ONOFRIO
VIA DEL GIANICOLO
VIA DEL CROCIFISSO
VIA NICOLÒ III
VIA DOMENICO SILVERI
VIA MONTE
Stazione Roma San Pietro

0 _____ 250
metres

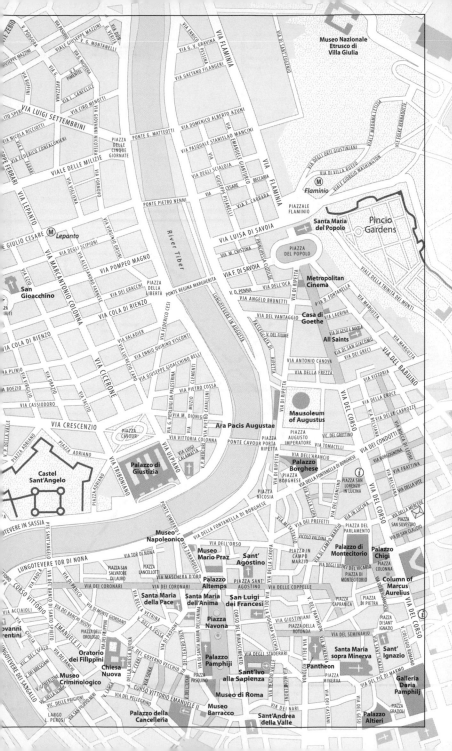